Renewable Energy Arbitration – Quo Vadis?

Nijhoff International Investment Law Series

VOLUME 23

The titles published in this series are listed at *brill.com/iils*

Renewable Energy Arbitration – Quo Vadis?

Implications of the Spanish Saga for International Investment Law

By

Filip Balcerzak

BRILL
NIJHOFF

LEIDEN | BOSTON

The open-access publication of this book was made possible by the National Science Centre, Poland, research project number 2018/28/C/HS5/00087.

Cover illustration: kallerna, CC BY-SA 4.0 https://creativecommons.org/licenses/by-sa/4.0, via Wikimedia Commons

The Library of Congress Cataloging-in-Publication Data is available online at https://catalog.loc.gov
LC record available at https://lccn.loc.gov/2022053414

Typeface for the Latin, Greek, and Cyrillic scripts: "Brill". See and download: brill.com/brill-typeface.

ISSN 2351-9542
ISBN 978-90-04-50933-7 (hardback)
ISBN 978-90-04-50934-4 (e-book)

This book is printed on acid-free paper and produced in a sustainable manner.

Contents

Acknowledgments

The book is part of research project number 2018/28/C/HS5/00087, financed by the National Science Centre, Poland.

The open-access payment was also financed by the National Science Centre, Poland, as part of research project number 2018/28/C/HS5/00087.

Tables

Abbreviations

BCG	– Boston Consulting Group
BIT	– Bilateral Investment Treaty
CAPEX	– Capital Expenditure
CETA	– Comprehensive Economic and Trade Agreement
CIL	– Customary International Law
CJEU	– Court of Justice of the European Union
CNE	– National Energy Commission (as derived from the Spanish name *Comisión Nacional de Energía*)
CPI	– Consumer Price Index
CSP	– Concentrated Solar Power
DCF	– Discounted Cash Flow
EC	– European Commission
ECHR	– European Convention on Human Rights (Convention for the Protection of Human Rights and Fundamental Freedoms)
ECT	– Energy Charter Treaty
ECtHR	– European Court of Human Rights
EEC	– European Economic Community
EU	– European Union
FET	– Fair and Equitable Treatment
FIT	– Feed-In-Tariff
ICC	– International Chamber of Commerce
ICJ	– International Court of Justice
ICSID	– International Centre for Settlement of Investment Disputes
ICSID Convention	– Convention on the Settlement of Investment Disputes between States and Nationals of Other States
IDAE	– Institute for Energy Diversification and Savings (as derived from the Spanish name *Instituto para la Diversificación y Ahorro de la Energía*)
ILC	– International Law Commission
IPC	– Consumer Price Index (as derived from the Spanish name *Índice Nacional de Precios al Consumo*)
IRENA	– International Renewable Energy Agency
IRR	– Internal Rate of Return
ISDS	– Investor-State Dispute Settlement
IVPEE	– Tax on Value of Produced Electricity (as derived from the Spanish name *Impuesto al Valor de la Producción de la Energía Eléctrica*)
LCIA	– London Court of International Arbitration

LSE	–	Spanish Law on the Electric Sector from 1997 (as derived from the Spanish name *Ley del Sector Eléctrico*)
MFN	–	Most-Favored Nation
MIC	–	Multilateral Investment Court
MoU	–	Memorandum of Understanding
NAFTA	–	North American Free Trade Agreement
OPEX	–	Operating Expenditure
PCIJ	–	Permanent Court of International Justice
PPA	–	Power Purchase Agreement
PV	–	Photovoltaic
RAIPRE	–	Administrative Registry of Energy Production Facilities (as derived from the Spanish name *Registro Administrativo de Instalaciones de Producción de Energía Eléctrica*)
RD	–	Royal Decree
RDL	–	Royal Decree-Law
RE	–	Renewable Energy
REIO	–	Regional Economic Integration Organization
RRR	–	Reasonable Rate of Return
SCC	–	Stockholm Chamber of Commerce
SPV	–	Special Purpose Vehicle
TEU	–	Treaty on European Union
TFEU	–	Treaty on the Functioning of the European Union
TMR	–	Average Electricity Tariff (as derived from the Spanish name *Tarifa Media de Referencia*)
UN	–	United Nations
UNCITRAL	–	United Nations Commission on International Trade Law
UNCTAD	–	United Nations Conference on Trade and Development
UNDP	–	United Nations Development Programme
UNEP	–	United Nations Environment Programme
UNFCCC	–	United Nations Framework Convention on Climate Change
USMCA	–	United States-Mexico-Canada Agreement
VCLT	–	Vienna Convention on the Law of Treaties
WACC	–	Weighted Average Cost of Capital

CHAPTER 1

Introduction

Energy is "the backbone of our economies".[1] However, its importance extends beyond the economy and economic growth. It is important for each of us, a crucial element of our daily lives.[2] In this sense, it is no exaggeration to say that energy "makes the world go round".[3]

As part of the overall energy supply, renewable energy is more important than ever. This is true from a purely economic perspective, where a shift away from the "petroleum-centric" character of energy investment is clearly visible.[4] In 2021 alone, worldwide investments in new renewable energy power plants were valued at approximately USD 371 billion.[5]

This would, however, be a limited perspective. From a broader perspective, the development of renewable energy production constitutes a crucial element in the fight against climate change. The 2015 Paris Agreement, which

1 Pascal Lamy, Foreword, in: Yulia Selivanova (ed.), Regulation of Energy in International Trade Law. WTO, NAFTA and Energy Charter (Wolters Kluwer 2011), p. XXIII.

2 Maxi Scherer, Introduction, in: Maxi Scherer (ed.), International Arbitration in the Energy Sector (Oxford University Press 2018), p. 1: "On an individual level, we all depend on energy in our daily lives. No lightbulb burns, no food cooks, and no car runs without energy".

3 Joachim Karl, FDI in the Energy Sector: Recent Trends and Policy Issues, in: Eric De Brabandere, Tarcisio Gazzini (eds.), Foreign Investment in the Energy Sector. Balancing Private and Public Interests (Brill 2014), p. 9. Energy is "the basis for any farther-reaching economic activity, such as production of goods and rendering of services" – Stephan W. Schill, Foreign Investment in the Energy Sector: Lessons for International Investment Law, in: Eric De Brabandere, Tarcisio Gazzini (eds.), Foreign Investment in the Energy Sector. Balancing Private and Public Interests (Brill 2014), p. 262.

4 Peter D. Cameron, Stabilization and the Impact of Changing Patterns of Energy Investment, Journal of World Energy Law & Business, 10:5 (2017), p. 390.

5 International Energy Agency, World Energy Investment 2021 (IEA Publications 2021), available at: https://iea.blob.core.windows.net/assets/5e6b3821-bb8f-4df4-a88b-e891cd8251e3/WorldEnergyInvestment2021.pdf, p. 7: "Renewables dominate investment in new power generation and are expected to account for 70% of 2021's total of USD 530 billion spent on all new generation capacity".

 | DOI:10.1163/9789004509344_002

implements the United Nations Framework Convention on Climate Change ("UNFCCC")[6] and supplements the Kyoto Protocol,[7] recognizes that it:

> aims to strengthen the global response to the threat of climate change, in the context of sustainable development and efforts to eradicate poverty, including by: (a) Holding the increase in the global average temperature to well below 2°C above pre-industrial levels and pursuing efforts to limit the temperature increase to 1.5°C above pre-industrial levels, recognizing that this would significantly reduce the risks and impacts of climate change.[8]

To meet this aim, the contracting parties:

> aim to reach global peaking of greenhouse gas emissions as soon as possible, recognizing that peaking will take longer for developing country Parties, and to undertake rapid reductions thereafter in accordance with best available science, so as to achieve a balance between anthropogenic emissions by sources and removals by sinks of greenhouse gases in the second half of this century, on the basis of equity, and in the context of sustainable development and efforts to eradicate poverty.[9]

Renewable energy is indispensable to meeting these goals, i.e. to help the move away from fossil fuels and achieve the long-term objective of carbon neutrality and related reductions in CO_2 emissions.[10] In short, the fight against climate change is doomed without renewable energy.

The process of moving away from fossil fuels, and particularly decarbonization, is a fact. By way of an example, the EU announced its European Green Deal initiative, which declared that Europe would be a carbon-neutral continent by

---

6 United Nations Framework Convention on Climate Change, done in New York (09.05.1992). This is considered to be an "umbrella agreement" for more specific agreements, such as the Paris Agreement and Kyoto Protocol – see: Andrina Sukma Dwi, Green Technology Disputes in Stockholm (2019), available at: https://sccarbitrationinstitute.se/sites/default/files/2022-11/green-technology-disputes-in-stockholm.pdf, p. 10.

7 Kyoto Protocol to the United Nations Framework Convention on Climate Change, done in Kyoto (11.12.1997).

8 The Paris Agreement, adopted on 12.12.2015 at the twenty-first session of the Conference of the Parties to the United Nations Framework Convention on Climate Change.

9 Ibid, Art. 4.

10 See for example: UNEP, "Emissions Gap Report 2019" (United Nations 2019), p. XXII: "Renewables and energy efficiency, in combination with electrification of end uses, are key to a successful energy transition and to driving down energy-related CO_2 emissions".

2050.[11] This is supported by legal instruments such as the Just Transition Fund.[12] This is a global trend which is not limited to the European context. Worldwide, 51 states have pledged a net-zero emissions target.[13] For example, China has announced that it "will strive to peak carbon dioxide emissions before 2030 and achieve carbon neutrality before 2060".[14]

The growth of renewable energy is also understood as an element of sustainable development.[15] It is relevant in the context of Sustainable Development Goals nos. 7, 12 and 13, envisaged in the United Nations' 2030 Agenda for Sustainable Development.[16] In particular, Sustainable Development Goal

---

11 European Commission, The European Green Deal. Communication from the Commission to the European Parliament, the European Council, the Council, the European Economic and Social Committee and the Committee of the Regions, COM (2019) 640 final (11.12.2019), pp. 2, 4, 6.

12 Regulation (EU) 2021/1056 of the European Parliament and of the Council of 24 June 2021 establishing the Just Transition Fund (OJ L 231, 30.06.2021, pp. 1–20).

13 UNEP, The Heat Is On. A world of climate promises not yet delivered. Emissions Gap Report 2021 (United Nations 2021), available at: https://wedocs.unep.org/bitstream/handle/20.500.11822/36990/EGR21.pdf, p. xx:

> Globally, 51 countries and one party (the EU27 in addition to the net-zero pledges made by its individual member states) have pledged a net-zero emissions target that is stated in national legislation, in a policy document or in a public announcement by the government or a high-level government official. These pledges cover more than half of current global domestic GHG emissions, over half of gross domestic product (GDP) and one third of the global population. Thirteen targets covering 12 per cent of global emissions are enshrined in law.

14 Xi Jinping, Bolstering Confidence and Jointly Overcoming Difficulties To Build a Better World, statement given by the President of China at the general debate of the UN General Assembly's 76th session on 21.09.2021, available at: https://estatements.unmeetings.org/estatements/10.0010/20210921/AT2JoAvm71nq/KaLk3d9ECB53_en.pdf, p. 4. The stated goals are reflected in China's 14th Five-Year Plan for 2021–2025 – see: Outline of the People's Republic of China 14th Five-Year Plan for National Economic and Social Development and Long-Range Objectives for 2035 (unofficial translation of the Center for Security and Emerging Technology), available at: https://cset.georgetown.edu/wp-content/uploads/t0284_14th_Five_Year_Plan_EN.pdf, p. 94, China Energy Transition Status Report 2021. Sino-German Energy Transition Project (2021), p. 12.

15 As envisaged, for example, in Principle 4 of the 1992 Rio Declaration, "[i]n order to achieve sustainable development, environmental protection shall constitute an integral part of the development process and cannot be considered in isolation from it" – Rio Declaration on Environment and Development, UN A/CONF.151/26 (1992). Environmental protection is, in turn, closely linked to renewable energy production.

16 Sustainable Development Goal no. 7 "Ensure access to affordable, reliable, sustainable and modern energy for all". Sustainable Development Goal no. 12: "Ensure sustainable consumption and production patterns". Sustainable Development Goal no. 13: "Take urgent action to combat climate change and its impacts". See: UN General Assembly Resolution

no 7.2. calls to "increase substantially the share of renewable energy in the global energy mix" by 2030.[17] As noted by the UN Secretary General:

> Energy is the golden thread that connects economic growth, increased social equity, and an environment that allows the world to thrive. Development is not possible without energy, and sustainable development is not possible without sustainable energy.[18]

Additionally, the development of renewable energy can help to mitigate the problem of an uneven geographic distribution of fossil fuels deposits – a fact which causes many states to become dependent upon importing oil, gas and/or coal.[19]

In this context, it comes as no surprise that, in the past, states have adopted policies which provide subsidies and other support mechanisms to encourage renewable energy investments. Most likely, they will continue to do so in the future. Such support schemes exist in various forms, such as green certificates, tax exemptions or direct price support, including feed-in-tariffs and feed-in-premiums (or combinations thereof).[20]

Foreign investments are an important element of the renewable energy sector and its development. Even if one agrees that, strictly speaking, they

---

No. 70/1 (25.09.2015), Transforming our world: the 2030 Agenda for Sustainable Development (UN A/RES/70/1), p. 14.

17 Ibid, p. 19. There is also a link between access to energy and public health – Valentina Vadi, Foreign Investment in the Energy Sector and Public Health, in: Eric De Brabandere, Tarcisio Gazzini (eds.), Foreign Investment in the Energy Sector. Balancing Private and Public Interests (Brill 2014), p. 240.

18 UNDP, Delivering Sustainable Energy in a Changing Climate. Strategy Note on Sustainable Energy 2017–2021 (United Nations 2016), p. 5.

19 This may have an impact on global geopolitics. See for example: Global Commission on the Geopolitics of Energy Transformation, A New World: The Geopolitics of the Energy Transformation (International Renewable Energy Agency 2019), available at: https://www.irena.org/-/media/Files/IRENA/Agency/Publication/2019/Jan/Global_commission_geopolitics_new_world_2019.pdf, p. 24.

20 Hans Vedder, Anita Rønne, Martha Roggenkamp, Iñigo del Guayo, EU Energy Law, in: Martha M. Roggenkamp, Catherine Redgwell, Anita Rønne, Iñigo del Guayo (eds.), Energy Law in Europe: National, EU, and International Regulation (Oxford University Press 2016), p. 322, Nikos Lavranos, Cees Verburg, Renewable Energy Investment Disputes: Recent Developments and Implications for Prospective Energy Market Reforms, European Energy Law Report, 12 (2018), pp. 67–68. On more detailed analysis of different forms of renewable energy support see for example: Richard L. Ottinger, Lily Mathews, Nadia Elizabeth Czachor, Renewable Energy in National Legislation: Challenges and Opportunities, in: Don Zillman, Catherine Redgwell, Yinka Omorogbe, Lila K. Barrera-Hernández (eds.), Beyond The Carbon Economy: Energy Law in Transition (Oxford University Press 2008), pp. 192–200.

are not indispensable (i.e. the sector can grow without them), they certainly facilitate and accelerate this growth.

Investments in renewable energy are, by their nature, long-term and capital intensive upfront.[21] This means that invested capital is recouped only over a long period, typically between 20 and 30 years.[22] This is one of the reasons why investments in the renewable energy sector are often funded by banks, financial institutions and other third parties.[23] More importantly, however, the need for a long-term commitment of funds explains why a stable legislative environment is of vital importance from the business perspective.[24] It came as no surprise, as early as 20 years ago, that the "stability of key investment conditions and protection against abuse or excess of regulatory powers is then of essence to the foreign investor" in sectors such as energy, "where investment is long-term, high risk, capital intensive and highly dependent on the exercise of government's regulatory powers".[25] In the absence of stability, investors are more hesitant to deploy their funds to this kind of long-term investments and, even if they do, the expected rate of return must be higher to compensate for the related risk.[26] As rightly described by Cameron,

21 See for example: SolEs v. Spain, ICSID Case No. ARB/15/38, Award (31.07.2019) [415]:

> PV plants cannot compete with conventional forms of energy production without substantial public subsidy or other form of incentive. They are capital-intensive, meaning that most of an investor's costs are incurred prior to operation (90%, according to Claimant's expert). They face a long period for capital recovery. Investments in PV plants are usually heavily leveraged (in the range of 55–80% leverage).

22 See for example, although not limited to renewable energy but with reference to energy in general: André Mernier, Introductory Remarks, in: Graham Coop (ed.), Energy Dispute Resolution: Investment Protection, Transit and the Energy Charter Treaty (JurisNet 2011), p. XLV.

23 Emma Johnson, Lucy McKenzie, Matthew Saunders, International Arbitration of Renewable Energy Disputes (Globe Law and Business 2021), p. 16. It is observed that in "typical" renewable energy projects, the third-party financing "amounts to 60 to 80% of the total investment cost for the facility, thus leaving the equity portion contributed by the shareholders at 20 to 40%" – see: Alexander Reuter, Retroactive Reduction of Support for Renewable Energy and Investment Treaty Protection from the Perspective of Shareholders and Lenders, Transnational Dispute Management, 3 (2015), pp. 4, 49, 76.

24 Johnson, McKenzie, Saunders, ibid, p. 17.

25 Thomas Waelde, Abba Kolo, Environmental Regulation, Investment Protection and Regulatory Taking in International Law, International and Comparative Law Quarterly, 50:4 (2001), p. 819.

26 See for example: Giuseppe Bellantuono, The Misguided Quest for Regulatory Stability in the Renewable Energy Sector, Journal of World Energy Law & Business, 10:4 (2017), p. 275. He notes, however, that the lower cost of capital is linked to a "more credible regulatory framework", rather than to stability *per se*.

> after the bulk of the investment has been made, the allocation of risks shifts rapidly from the capital-hungry host state to the investor. Negotiating leverage shifts during the project life cycle: the investors require a long period to achieve their expected return while, once the investment is made, the host state has what it requires. For a variety of reasons, the host state may then conclude that the original bargain is obsolete and force a revision of its terms.[27]

This has been described as "the hostage effect of sunk investment".[28] From the perspective of states, such imbalance "creates an almost irresistible temptation" to change the rules of the game during the game.[29] If this happens, the new situation puts investors in a situation described as the "prisoner's dilemma" – they have no choice other than to accept the new reality. A decision to exit the host state would produce even greater losses, as it would mean the total loss of the investment and any further return on it.[30]

Despite the need for stability, recent years have witnessed examples of states drastically changing their domestic regulations in the renewable energy sector. These changes have resulted in numerous arbitral proceedings commenced by foreign investors, based mainly on the multilateral Energy Charter Treaty ("ECT").[31] The ECT, in common with most bilateral investment treaties ("BITs"), provides for a dispute resolution system in the form of investor-state arbitration, based on specific dispute resolution provisions. These provisions

27 Peter D. Cameron, International Energy Investment Law: The Pursuit of Stability (Oxford University Press 2010), pp. 4–5.

28 Thomas W. Waelde, George Ndi, Stabilizing International Investment Commitments: International Law Versus Contract Interpretation, Texas International Law Journal, 31:2 (1996), p. 225.

29 N. Stephan Kinsella, Noah D. Rubins, International Investment, Political Risk, and Dispute Resolution: A Practitioner's Guide (Oceana Publications 2005), p. 5:

> Where a project is long-term with heavy capital investment (sunk costs) at the start, and uses assets that are not easily sold or converted to other purposes, the government has a great deal of leverage over the foreign investor, who cannot credibly threaten to abandon his investment plans if conditions deteriorate. This imbalance creates an almost irresistible temptation for local officials to extract short-term political advantage by shifting foreign investment profits to constituents either within the government or the public at large.

30 Scherer, *supra* note 2, p. 16.

31 Based on the number of the contracting parties to the ECT, Gazzini calculated that, if translated into bilateral relations, "this is the equivalent of 1,081 bilateral investment treaties (BITs) between the State parties" – see: Tarcisio Gazzini, Energy Charter Treaty: Achievements, Challenges and Perspectives, in: Eric De Brabandere, Tarcisio Gazzini (eds.), Foreign Investment in the Energy Sector. Balancing Private and Public Interests (Brill 2014), p. 105.

allow foreign investors to commence arbitration against host states which violate investment treaties (in most such cases, without needing to refer the dispute to the local, state courts). This is a powerful tool, as the awards rendered in these arbitral proceedings are final and binding. There are only very limited grounds on which a party to a dispute may seek the revision of an arbitral award. Once the award becomes final, it is executable on the same rules as arbitral awards rendered in traditionally understood, international commercial arbitration. Thus, the award can be executed not only in the territory of the respondent host state, but essentially around the globe, wherever the assets of the respondent host state are located.

Spain is a model example of a state which was sued as the respondent in investor-state arbitrations resulting from changes it made to its regulatory framework governing the renewable energy sector. Based on publicly available information, Spain has faced at least 49 investor-state arbitrations triggered by its reforms of renewable energy regulations.[32] This allows to calculate that the Spanish saga cases represent approximately 80% of all investor-state arbitrations in the renewable energy sector.[33] However, Spain is not alone in this. Other examples include the Czech Republic, Italy, Romania and Poland (although the latter introduced regulatory changes which affected not all renewables, but rather wind energy in particular). These regulatory changes to renewable energy laws are "likely to be the new Black Swan in the investment arbitration world".[34] Recent years have witnessed "a boom in renewable energy arbitration".[35]

---

32 Based on publicly available information as of 15.04.2022 (https://www.energychartertreaty.org/cases/list-of-cases/). The actual number may be higher, given the confidentiality of potential cases based on treaties other than the ECT.

33 According to Viñuales, "between 1972 and 2020, at least 178 foreign investment claims with environmental components were filed. [...] Approximately 80% (143) of these disputes have been brought after 2008, and over half of them (76) concern the energy transition, mostly (61) modern renewable energy projects (solar, wind and geothermal)" – see: Jorge E. Viñuales, Geopolitics of the Energy Transformation, Revue Européenne du Droit (Governing Globalization), 2 (2020), pp. 148–155, available at: https://geopolitique.eu/en/articles/geopolitics-of-the-energy-transformation/.

34 Ivaylo Dimitrov, Legitimate Expectations in the Absence of Specific Commitments According to the Findings in Blusun v. Italy: Is there Inconsistency Among the Tribunals in the Solar Energy Cases? Kluwer Arbitration Blog (18.08.2017), available at: http://arbitrationblog.kluwerarbitration.com/2017/08/18/legitimate-expectations-absence-specific-commitments-according-findings-blusun-v-italy-inconsistency-among-tribunals-solar-energy-cases/.

35 Fernando Dias Simões, Charanne and Construction Investments v. Spain: Legitimate Expectations and Investments in Renewable Energy, Review of European, Comparative & International Environmental Law, 26:2 (2017), p. 174. Hobér describes this increase of number of cases as an "explosion", which is "mainly linked to the legal reforms affecting

Unsurprisingly, investor-state arbitrations triggered by regulatory changes can cause significant criticism amongst the public opinion. States enjoy regulatory freedom, stemming from their very identity as sovereign actors on the international scene. One of the reasons for the growing criticism and alleged lack of legitimacy of international investment law in the eyes of public opinion stems from potentially limiting such regulatory freedom (and the related understanding of state sovereignty itself) as host states, as contracting parties to the ECT and to BITs, are sued in international investment arbitrations because they exercised their right to regulate national law.

Examples exist of the reasons underpinning the backlash against BITs, the ECT and investor-state arbitration in general. There are also voices that renewable energy investor-state arbitrations, and especially the renewable energy cases against Spain are "a prime example of problems that the ISDS regime can present for sustainable development in the energy sector specifically".[36] In a more general context, unrelated to the Spanish cases, there have been calls to ensure "an appropriate balance between protection commitments and regulatory space" for sustainable development in investor-state arbitrations.[37]

The ECT makes the energy sector the only one with a sector-specific, multilateral investment treaty.[38] Since it covers the energy sector as a whole, it comes as no surprise that the ECT is considered as "technology neutral".[39] This means that the same protection is granted to renewable energy investments as

the renewable energy sector in Europe" – see: Kaj Hobér, Overview of Energy Charter Treaty Cases, in: Maxi Scherer (ed.), International Arbitration in the Energy Sector (Oxford University Press 2018), pp. 176–177.

36 Isabella Reynoso, Spain's Renewable Energy Saga: Lessons for international investment law and sustainable development, Investment Treaty News (27.06.2019), available at: https://www.iisd.org/itn/en/2019/06/27/spains-renewable-energy-saga-lessons-for-international-investment-law-and-sustainable-development-isabella-reynoso/. She links the threat to sustainable development with a regulatory chill, which is "deadly for states pursuing sustainable development goals, which requires states to be able to regulate freely".

37 UNCTAD, Investment Policy Framework for Sustainable Development (United Nations 2015), p. 78.

38 Schill, *supra* note 3, p. 262. In addition, it is "the only forum that is open to all countries along the energy chain: producers, consumers and transit states; industrialized, transition and developing economies" – Yulia Selivanova, The Energy Charter and the International Energy Governance, in: Yulia Selivanova (ed.), Regulation of Energy in International Trade Law. WTO, NAFTA and Energy Charter (Wolters Kluwer 2011), p. 375.

39 In the words of the Secretary-General of the ECT: "The ECT is technology neutral: it covers all sorts of energy from biomass all the way to uranium and thorium" – Urban Rusnák, Comment: Quo Vadis Energy Charter Treaty?, Energy Charter Secretariat News (12.04.2021), available at: https://www.energycharter.org/media/news/article/comment-quo-vadis-energy-charter-treaty/.

to non-renewable ones, such as oil, gas and coal.[40] BITs, which have been or will be the legal basis for claims concerning energy disputes, can be similarly considered as "technology neutral" when it comes to energy disputes.

This is one of the reasons behind the initiative to modernize the ECT.[41] As the EU has stated, "the key objectives" of its "proposal for the modernisation of the ECT are to update investment protection standards in order to ensure that the ECT facilitates the EU's climate action and energy transition in line with the European Green Deal and the Paris Agreement".[42] The EU's proposal includes a call for explicit recognition of the states' right to regulate "to achieve legitimate policy objectives, such as the protection of the environment, including combatting climate change […]"[43] and of the "urgent need of pursuing the ultimate objective of the United Nations Framework Convention on Climate Change (UNFCCC) and the purpose and goals of the Paris Agreement in order to effectively combat climate change and its impacts, and committed to enhancing the contribution of trade and investment to climate change mitigation and adaptation […]".[44]

This book discusses the current challenges faced by international investment law in the renewable energy sector. This topic is relevant not only from a theoretical perspective, but primarily from a practical one. Since 2013, claims concerning the renewable energy sector have outnumbered any other claims based on the ECT. This tendency has remained valid and is evidenced by the last available official statistics, published on 01.12.2021.[45]

This issue is approached from the perspective of the "Spanish saga cases" – i.e. a group of cases concerning the same disputed measures, namely legislative

---

40 Nathalie Bernasconi-Osterwalder, Martin Dietrich Brauch, Redesigning the Energy Charter Treaty to Advance the Low-Carbon Transition, Transnational Dispute Management, 1 (2019), p. 4.

41 Ibid, p. 11: "a modernized ECT should abandon its energy-source neutrality and, instead, expressly discriminate between carbon-intensive energy investments, which should receive less favourable treatment and ultimately be eliminated, and low-carbon energy investments, which should be encouraged".

42 European Commission, Energy Charter Treaty: Progress continues in modernisation negotiations, News Archive (05.10.2021), available at: https://trade.ec.europa.eu/doclib/press/index.cfm?id=2307.

43 New article to be added in Part III of the ECT – EU text proposal for the modernisation of the Energy Charter Treaty (ECT), p. 4.

44 New article to be added in Part IV of the ECT – EU text proposal for the modernisation of the Energy Charter Treaty (ECT), p. 11.

45 https://www.energychartertreaty.org/fileadmin/DocumentsMedia/Statistics/All_statistics_-_1_December_2021_Rev.pdf.

reforms to Spain's regulatory framework for renewable energy investments. The following five research questions are posed.

Research Question 1: Which facts led to the unprecedented number of investor-state arbitrations filed against Spain, an EU member state?

The answer to this question can be found in Chapter 2, which describes the factual backdrop to the Spanish saga cases. What is unique in this group of cases is that the disputed measures are almost identical in all of the publicly known cases (despite nuanced differences in the reforms made to the regulatory framework, depending on the type of renewable energy plant involved). For this reason, these cases provide a perfect case study. They can be considered as providing a "laboratory" for lawyers and academics, this term being understood as a space "providing opportunity for experimentation, observation, or practice in a field of study"[46] and "where scientific experiments, analyses, and research are carried out".[47] In the same circumstances (same factual background) one can look at a number of cases and compare the observations, analysis and legal reasoning presented in each of them.

The Chapter is intended to provide a description which is detailed enough to enable the reader to understand the analysis which follows in the later Chapters, but does not immerse the reader in unnecessary details on every issue raised in each case. In other words, this Chapter does not aim to describe every possible nuance of the facts, but merely to provide a balanced level of detail so as to allow the reader to benefit from the analysis provided in the subsequent Chapters.

Research Question 2: Can the arbitral awards rendered against Spain have an impact on proceedings commenced against other states (both EU Member States and non-members) in the future?

It is a truism to say that the doctrine of precedent (or *stare decisis*) does not apply in investor-state arbitrations.[48] However, the persuasive views of one tribunal may inform the reasoning of other tribunals in later disputes.[49] Therefore, it should come as no surprise that the hypothesis underpinning this

46 Definition from Merriam Webster dictionary, available at: https://www.merriam-webster.com/dictionary/laboratory.

47 Definition from Collins dictionary, available at: https://www.collinsdictionary.com/dictionary/english/laboratory.

48 See for example: AES v. Argentina, ICSID Case No. ARB/02/17, Decision on Jurisdiction (26.04.2005) [23.d)], [30]–[32]. Christoph H. Schreuer, Loretta Malintoppi, August Reinisch, Anthony Sinclair, The ICSID Convention. A Commentary (Cambridge University Press 2009), p. 1101.

49 In the words of the *de Nul* tribunal, "it is not bound by earlier decisions, but will certainly carefully consider such decisions whenever appropriate" – de Nul v. Egypt, ICSID Case No. ARB/04/13, Decision on Jurisdiction (16.06.2006) [64].

research question is that the Spanish saga cases can impact on proceedings commenced against other states in the future. If it proves possible to draw general conclusions from all of the Spanish sage cases, this question must be answered positively.

These general conclusions are considered as "lessons learned". In this sense, the lessons apply to the future and to a more general context, not limited to the situation in Spain, nor indeed to the EU or the ECT. Following a detailed analysis of each of the Spanish saga cases, the book zooms out to take a "helicopter view" of the collection of cases as a whole, from the broader perspective of international investment law, to enable general conclusions to be drawn.

The more specific answers to this research question (i.e. exactly which general conclusions can be drawn?) are provided in each of the following Chapters, which separately cover all the stages of arbitral proceedings (jurisdiction being covered in Chapter 3, merits being covered in Chapter 4 and remedies being covered in Chapter 5).

Research Question 3: Which legal grounds in international law serve, or may potentially serve, as the basis for investors' claims in the renewable energy sector?

The answer to this question can be found in Chapter 4, which analyses the merits of the Spanish saga cases. The research and analysis which can be conducted in the "Spanish saga laboratory" concern all of the various standards of protection envisaged in Art. 10(1) and Art. 13 ECT, which are also found in the vast majority of at least 2,646 BITs in force around the world at the end of 2020.[50] This book focuses on the most relevant of these standards, i.e. those at the heart of most of the Spanish saga cases. These are: the Fair and Equitable Treatment ("FET"), expropriation and the umbrella clause. The Chapter distills lessons learned about these selected standards of protection.

Research Question 4: Are the apparently mutually exclusive arbitral awards issued against Spain really contradictory, or can the different outcomes be explained by differences in the facts or the applicable law of those cases?

This question is legitimate in the light of apparent contradictions between three groups of cases: (i) where tribunals dismissed the claims, (ii) where tribunals awarded compensation, having concluded that a "full" violation of the FET had occurred, and (iii) where tribunals awarded limited compensation (when compared to the second group) for a violation of the FET, but limited by the concept of a reasonable rate of return ("RRR").[51]

---

50 UNCTAD, World Investment Report 2021. Investing in Sustainable Recovery (United Nations 2021), p. 122.

51 Some authors consider them to be a "rollercoaster ride" as regards "the fortunes of investors and states" in renewable energy arbitrations against the EU member states. See: Richard

The answer to this question is also found in Chapter 4. The hypothesis is that (i) the cases are not contradictory and in fact present a uniform line of jurisprudence if one takes a broader view of them, and that (ii) the discrepancies are apparent and can be explained by nuanced differences in the facts of each case (concerning differences in the type and time of the investment at the heart of the dispute which, in turn, impacts on assessing legitimate expectations as part of the FET).

Research Question 5: What relevance does EU law have on treaty-based arbitrations based on the ECT?

This question became particularly relevant after the Court of Justice of the European Union ("CJEU") gave judgment in the *Achmea* case on 06.03.2018. The Spanish saga cases enable an analysis of this judgment's impact on cases pending on the day it was handed down (in terms of its impact on ongoing arbitral proceedings) and cases commenced after it was issued.

The answer to this question can be found in Chapter 3, which analyses the jurisdictional stage of arbitral proceedings. The hypothesis is that the *Achmea* judgment left arbitral tribunals unimpressed. This effectively moves the impact of the judgment to issues of enforcement and setting aside proceedings before the state courts.

The analysis contained in the following Chapters is significant for the future. As flagged in the second research question, much can be learned from the Spanish saga cases. An obvious assumption would be that the lessons learned will be useful for parties to treaty-based arbitrations commenced in the future, and for the arbitrators who adjudicate such disputes. With the growing number of investments in the renewable energy sector, it is "very likely that the number of renewable energy arbitrations will significantly rise in the future".[52]

However, this perspective would be too narrow. The lessons learned can become relevant earlier, even before a dispute arises. They can be useful to help policymakers understand where the boundary lies between non-compensable regulatory changes and regulatory changes which result in liability to pay compensation. In other words, to comprehend where lies the "red line" which a state can cross freely, but with encountering certain consequences at the level

---

Power, Novenergia v. Kingdom of Spain, the ECT and the ECJ: Where to now for intra-EU ECT claims?, Kluwer Arbitration Blog (20.03.2018), available at: http://arbitrationblog.kluwerarbitration.com/2018/03/20/novenergia-v-kingdom-of-spain/.

52 Marie-Provence Brue, Shaparak Saleh, 'Paris Arbitration Week Recap: Renewable Energies and Arbitration', Kluwer Arbitration Blog (16.04.2022), available at: http://arbitrationblog.kluwerarbitration.com/2022/04/16/paris-arbitration-week-recap-renewable-energies-and-arbitration/.

of international law. After all, it is human nature to look into history to find similar stories from the past when one faces something new.[53]

The book's conclusions are helpful for the entire renewable energy sector. This is important if one keeps in mind that, although Spain is the EU member state which has encountered the most claims regarding its reforms of its renewable energy regulatory framework, it is not the only one. This book's conclusions are not confined to the European context. Similar patterns of state behavior can also be expected from states outside the EU. Moreover, its conclusions are relevant to the renewable energy sector as a whole. Tourist brochures may suggest that solar energy is the only relevant renewable energy source in Spain, but the analysis covers also other renewable energy sources, including wind and hydro energy projects.

The analysis will be relevant to the future, despite significant decreases in the costs of producing solar and wind energy in recent years. Technologies which in 2010 were "an expensive niche" and more expensive than fossil fuel energy became, by the end of 2020, capable of competing with fossil fuels.[54]

---

53 Andrey A. Konoplyanik, Multiple Investment Regimes for Russian Subsoil Resources: Work in Progress or Utopia?, in: Eric De Brabandere, Tarcisio Gazzini (eds.), Foreign Investment in the Energy Sector. Balancing Private and Public Interests (Brill 2014), p. 32.

54
> The decade 2010 to 2020 represents a remarkable period of cost reduction for solar and wind power technologies. The combination of targeted policy support and industry drive has seen renewable electricity from solar and wind power go from an expensive niche, to head-to-head competition with fossil fuels for new capacity. In the process, it has become clear that renewables will become the backbone of the electricity system and help decarbonise electricity generation, with costs lower than a business-as-usual future

– International Renewable Energy Agency, Renewable Power Generations Costs in 2020 (International Renewable Energy Agency 2021), available at: https://www.irena.org/-/media/Files/IRENA/Agency/Publication/2021/Jun/IRENA_Power_Generation_Costs_2020.pdf, p. 14. Similarly: World Meteorological Organization, United In Science 2020: A Multi-Organization High-Level Compilation of the Latest Climate Science Information (World Meteorological Organization 2020), available at: https://library.wmo.int/doc_num.php?explnum_id=10361, p. 19:

> Renewables are by now the cheapest source of new power generation in most parts of the world, with the global weighted average purchase or auction price for new solar power photovoltaic systems and onshore wind turbines now competitive with the marginal operating cost of existing coal plants by 2020.

See also: International Energy Agency, World Energy Outlook 2020 (IEA Publications 2020), available at: https://iea.blob.core.windows.net/assets/a72d8abf-de08-4385-8711-b8a062d6124a/WEO2020.pdf, p. 18: "With sharp cost reductions over the past decade, solar PV is consistently cheaper than new coal- or gas- fired power plants in most countries, and solar projects now offer some of the lowest cost electricity ever seen". Also: Communication from the Commission to the Council and the European Parliament, Renewable Energy Road Map Renewable energies in the 21st century: building a more sustainable future, Brussels, COM(2006) 848 final (10.01.2007), p. 15: "the cost of renewable energies varies significantly

Renewable energy has matured and reached a stage when it is now considered as "the cheapest source of new power generation in most parts of the world".[55] In the period 2010–2020, the global weighted average production cost of utility scale solar photovoltaic ("PV") electricity for newly commissioned projects fell by 85%. In the same period, the costs of concentrated solar power ("CSP") fell by 68%, of onshore wind projects by 56% and of off-shore wind projects by 48%.[56] It seems that these technologies no longer require state support to be economically viable.[57]

Nonetheless, a "new wave of incentivisation of renewable energy projects" has recently been noted in the industry.[58] This comes as no surprise if one is aware that capital flows are essential to the growth of renewable energy

according to the resource base and the technologies concerned, but generally still exceeds that of conventional energy sources at present".

55 United In Science ..., *supra* note 54, p. 19, Johnson, McKenzie, Saunders, *supra* note 23, p. 8.

56 Renewable Power ..., *supra* note 54, p. 14, using the measure of LCOE – the levelized cost of electricity. The fall in price was a long process, visible long before 2010. In 2007 the European Commission noted:

> As an example, the cost of wind energy per kWh has fallen by 50% over the last 15 years while at the same time the size of the turbines has increased by a factor of 10. Solar photovoltaic systems today are more than 60% cheaper than they were in 1990

– see: Renewable Energy Road Map, *supra* note 54, p. 15.

57 Ibid, p. 16:

> As costs for solar PV and onshore wind have fallen, new renewable capacity is not only increasingly cheaper than new fossil fuel fired capacity, but increasingly undercuts the operating costs alone of existing coal fired power plants. Indeed, in Europe in 2021, coal-fired power plant operating costs are well above the costs of new solar PV and onshore wind (including the cost of CO_2 prices).

See also for example:

> [...] up to a few years ago, renewables were more costly than their alternatives, prompting States to provide support in the form of feed-in-tariffs, which were the main drive in the industry. This has changed fundamentally, and renewables are now becoming competitive in many jurisdictions without the need for State subsidies.

– see: Brue, Saleh, *supra* note 52. Back in time, "subsidies were deemed necessary in most of EU countries to kick-start investment in renewable installation facilities due to the high cost of production" – see: Ernesto Bonafé, Gökçe Mete, Escalated interactions between EU energy law and the Energy Charter Treaty, Journal of World Energy Law & Business, 9:3 (2016), p. 185.

58 Brue, Saleh, *supra* note 52. As noted by Taylor, the energy sector is subsidized by states and will remain so, even if to a lesser extent. However, a rebalancing is expected, i.e. lowering subsidies to fossil fuels and increasing subsidies to renewable energies. See: Michael Taylor, Energy Subsidies: Evolution in the Global Energy Transformation to 2050 (International

production, since "most transition-related energy investment will need to be carried out by private developers, consumers and financiers responding to market signals and policies set by governments".[59] This shows that the form and degree of state support may change, but it will continue to be relevant and states will inevitably continue to support renewable energy projects. First, this new wave of incentivization is expected to become stronger in Europe, with the EU expected to undertake efforts to stop being net buyer of energy after the Russian invasion on Ukraine. Second, comparable energy production cost decreases do not apply to all types of renewable energy technologies. For example hydro, geothermal and biomass energy have not witnessed such spectacular falls in prices.[60] Third, COVID-19 pandemic and war in Ukraine are expected to have a negative impact on the supply side of the market, causing likely increase in prices.

Most importantly, however, the Spanish saga cases offer lessons for the future. One can expect that other technologies which currently are – or will be in future years – an "expensive niche", comparable to solar and wind back in 2010 and earlier, will need to be incentivized by states before they become economically viable. States will incentivize such technologies in the hope of achieving their long-term sustainable development and decarbonization

Renewable Energy Agency 2020), available at: https://www.irena.org/-/media/Files/IRENA/Agency/Publication/2020/Apr/IRENA_Energy_subsidies_2020.pdf, p. 7:

> The world's total, direct energy sector subsidies – including those to fossil fuels, renewables and nuclear power – are estimated to have been at least USD 634 billion in 2017. [...] IRENA's roadmap for more sustainable energy development sees a rebalancing of energy subsidies away from environmentally harmful ones to fossil fuels and towards support for renewables and energy efficiency by 2050.

59 International Energy Agency, World Energy Outlook 2021 (IEA Publications 2021), available at: https://iea.blob.core.windows.net/assets/4ed140c1-c3f3-4fd9-acae-789a4e14a23c/WorldEnergyOutlook2021.pdf, p. 18.

60 Whilst the analyzed Spanish saga cases did not relate to geothermal or biomass renewable energy, the lessons learned for the future are as equally applicable to these technologies as to others. Biomass differs from other renewable energies, since it produces energy not from a constantly replenished source (like sun, wind or water), but from organic matter (such as grasses, woodchips or crop waste products). It falls within the category of renewable energy because the waste feedstock used in energy production is replenishable – see: Johnson, McKenzie, Saunders, *supra* note 23, p. 13.

goals.[61] A "renewable hydrogen" is an illustrative example.[62] It has been described as "the missing link in the energy transition".[63] Without doubt, it is merely one example of numerous technologies that will have a role to play in the coming years.

With the exception of Chapter 2 (which describes the factual background of the analyzed cases), the following Chapters commence with a review of the Spanish saga awards on the particular topic discussed in that Chapter. The review is ordered chronologically. The aim behind this approach is to reflect whether development of the case law over time reveals different analyses and decisions. This is an essential element for identifying patterns and drawing general conclusions.

The analysis in the subsequent Chapters is limited by a cut-off date, which is closely linked with a word count restraints. Accordingly, the analysis offered in this book covers 21 arbitral awards rendered in the Spanish saga – i.e. first 21 awards in chronological order: *Charanne, Isolux, Eiser, Novenergia, Masdar, Antin, Foresight, RREEF, Cube, NextEra, 9REN, SolEs, InfraRed, OperaFund, BayWa, Stadtwerke, RWE, Watkins, PV Investors, Hydro, Cavalum.*[64] It is, of course, tempting to keep updating the text to include the latest publicly

---

61 International Energy Agency identified "a boost to clean energy innovation" as one of four solutions to meet the emission cuts goals, noting that:

> all the technologies needed to achieve deep emissions cuts to 2030 are available. But almost half of the emissions reductions achieved in the NZE [Net Zero Emissions – author's note] in 2050 come from technologies that today are at the demonstration or prototype stage.

– see: World Energy Outlook..., *supra* note 59, p. 18.

62 European Commission, A hydrogen strategy for a climate-neutral Europe. Communication from the Commission to the European Parliament, the European Council, the Council, the European Economic and Social Committee and the Committee of the Regions, COM(2020) 301 final (08.07.2020). On p. 2 it recognizes, among others, that:

> Investment in hydrogen will foster sustainable growth and jobs, which will be critical in the context of recovery from the COVID-19 crisis. [...] However, today renewable and low-carbon hydrogen are not yet cost competitive compared to fossil-based hydrogen. To harness all the opportunities associated with hydrogen, the European Union needs a strategic approach.

63 International Renewable Energy Agency, Hydrogen from Renewable Power: Technology Outlook for the Energy Transition (International Renewable Energy Agency 2018), available at: https://www.irena.org/-/media/Files/IRENA/Agency/Publication/2018/Sep/IRENA_Hydrogen_from_renewable_power_2018.pdf, p. 7: "Hydrogen could therefore be the missing link in the energy transition: renewable electricity can be used to produce hydrogen, which can in turn provide energy to sectors otherwise difficult to decarbonise through electrification".

64 The chronological order adopted is based on the date of the award (final or partial) on liability, regardless of the date of partial awards on jurisdiction and/or damages (if bifurcated).

available arbitral award (or annulment decision in the ICSID context). This is, however, either impossible or would at least have delayed publication of this book for many years. The most recent case was triggered in 2022.[65] This shows that the Spanish saga is far from over.[66]

65 WOC v. Spain, ICSID Case No. ARB/22/12, registered on 05.04.2022.

66 This is not to mention the existence of possible "follow-up" legal battles regarding enforcement. After all, a dispute ends when the arbitral award is settled, not merely issued.

CHAPTER 2

Facts

1 Introduction

The evolution of Spain's policies on renewable energy ("RE") subsidies lies at the heart of the Spanish saga cases. Consequently, these cases concern a multi-layered factual background, involving various levels of a regulatory framework and multiple amendments implemented over many years. The cases also take place against the backdrop of relevant surrounding activities of the state authorities. It is noticeable, however, that all of the analyzed cases involve an almost identical factual background in terms of the disputed measures. Spain's actions which resulted in arbitral proceedings being initiated are the same in all of the cases. Also, Spain's previous activities – i.e. those surrounding the moment at which the investments were made and which were subsequently disputed – overlap significantly.

Obviously, differences exist between the various cases. However, at a general level, the differences are limited to two issues: (i) the moment of making the investment, and (ii) the type of the power plant(s) involved, i.e. whether the energy is produced from the sun (and, if so, by using which solar technology), from the wind or from water (hydro).

This Chapter commences with a brief description of the types of RE technologies which are relevant to understanding the Spanish saga cases. It then describes the European legal context, which is indispensable to have a full picture of Spain's domestic regulations, albeit limited to those EU directives which formed the background to the Spanish domestic legislation. The next section describes the development of the Spanish regulations during 1997–2010, i.e. activities which sought to incentivize investments (both foreign and domestic) in the RE sector. Next, it analyses the regulatory changes introduced by Spain in 2010–2014, which replaced the previous regime with a new one, and which were later disputed by foreign investors in the arbitrations analyzed in the following Chapters. It then presents the Spanish saga cases that are analyzed in the subsequent Chapters, ordered chronologically. The Chapter terminates with brief conclusions.

The following presentation is not intended to be exhaustive. Rather, it seeks to balance the temptation to provide an exhaustive level of detail with the practical need to ensure that this description is readable. Accordingly, it is limited to those issues which are necessary to fully understand the analysis in the following Chapters. A comprehensive description of the factual background would qualify for publication as a separate book. This should not come as a surprise, if one keeps in mind that the facts underpinning the Spanish saga concerned developments in the regulatory framework over a 20-year period.

2 RE Technologies Relevant to the Spanish Saga

This section briefly presents the types of RE technologies that are relevant to the Spanish saga cases. The description is not intended to cover all existing RE technologies. Rather, it focuses on those related to the investments which were at the center of the arbitral proceedings initiated to challenge the Spanish reforms discussed in the following sections.[1]

When thinking about Spain, one's first thought is typically linked to the sun and, in the context of energy law, to solar energy. Indeed, solar energy played a crucial, but not an exclusive, role in the Spanish saga cases. Hydro and on-shore wind energy projects were also involved.

The types of solar energy technologies relevant to the Spanish saga cases can be divided between utility scale solar photovoltaic ("PV") and concentrated solar power ("CSP").

PV plants typically generate electric power by using "solar cells to convert energy from the sun into a flow of electrons".[2] In other words, they convert solar radiation directly into electrical energy by the "photovoltaic effect", i.e. an electrical field which is created across layers of a material (for example silicon) when the layers are illuminated with electromagnetic radiation (here – solar radiation).[3] A typical PV system consists of a number of solar panels, each comprising a number of solar cells.[4] An important feature of utility scale PV facilities is that they require large areas of land.[5]

1 Other renewable technologies, not discussed below, may include biomass or thermal technologies. As noted in the Introduction, biomass differs from other renewable energies, as it produces energy from organic matter (such as grasses, woodchips or crop waste products) rather than from a constantly replenished source (such as the sun, wind or water). Nevertheless, it falls within the category of RE because the waste feedstock used in the energy production is replenishable – see: Emma Johnson, Lucy McKenzie, Matthew Saunders, International Arbitration of Renewable Energy Disputes (Globe Law and Business 2021), p. 13.

2 9REN v. Spain, ICSID Case No. ARB/15/15, Award (31.05.2019) [fn 2].

3 Johnson, McKenzie, Saunders, *supra* note 1, p. 12, https://www.idae.es/en/technologies/renewable-energies/electricity-generation/photovoltaic-solar-energy.

4 9REN v. Spain, *supra* note 2 [fn 2].

5 Johnson, McKenzie, Saunders, *supra* note 1, p. 12.

CSP plants use lenses or mirrors to concentrate solar radiation on a single focal point. This creates high temperatures and heats a thermo-oil heat transfer fluid inside absorber tubes. This fluid then converts water into steam by using a steam generator. The steam then drives a turbine, which is connected to a generator and produces electricity.[6] In this sense, the way of producing technology is comparable to "traditional" power plants, with the significant difference that the heat which moves the turbine is created by solar radiation rather than by burning coal or natural gas.[7] Nevertheless, some CSP power plants use fossil fuels, particularly natural gas, in order to boost their power-generation capacity, increase their solar-to-electric conversion efficiency and increase the reliability of their energy production.[8] CSP facilities are less common than PV facilities due to their relatively higher costs at all stages: construction, operation and maintenance.[9] There are variations of CSP technology, which differ mainly in terms of the manner in which they capture and concentrate solar radiation.[10] Some CSP plants can store electricity, although this is considered as not fully-mature technology.[11]

On-shore wind energy ("Wind energy") plants use the kinetic energy from wind to generate electricity. This is achieved by the rotation of turbine blades (by wind), which turn a generator that produces energy. On-shore wind energy facilities are constructed on land, whereas off-shore installations are constructed in the ocean or other bodies of water.[12]

Hydroelectric ("Hydro energy") power stations use falling or fast-running water. They generate energy using the gravity or kinetic energy of a water source, respectively.

There are at least three relevant, common features of all of the RE technologies briefly presented above.

First, they have a significant, positive impact on the environment.[13] As underlined by the *Antin* tribunal, the main reason for this is that they use a

6 Antin v. Spain, ICSID Case No. ARB/13/31, Award (15.06.2018) [71], Stadtwerke v. Spain, ICSID Case No. ARB/15/1, Award (02.12.2019) [80]. Alternatively, the heat can be transferred into a thermal storage system for later use.

7 Eiser v. Spain, ICSID Case No. ARB/13/36, Award (04.05.2017) [95], Stadtwerke v. Spain, *supra* note 6 [80].

8 Antin v. Spain, *supra* note 6 [72], Stadtwerke v. Spain, *supra* note 6 [81].

9 Ibid.

10 https://www.idae.es/en/technologies/renewable-energies/electricity-generation/solar-thermoelectric-energy.

11 Johnson, McKenzie, Saunders, *supra* note 1, p. 12.

12 Ibid, pp. 11–12.

13 See for example: The PV Investors v. Spain, PCA Case No. 2012-14, Final Award (28.02.2020) [589]: "It is not disputed that renewable energy (including photovoltaic, thermal, solar, wind and certain other technologies) offers significant environmental benefits".

renewable source of energy (instead of consumable fossil fuel) and "introduce little or no pollution into the atmosphere".[14]

Second, investments in such types of RE plants are, by their very nature, long-term and capital intensive up-front. In other words, such investments are "front-end loaded", requiring huge amounts of capital to plan, design and construct the plants before they can commence operations, generate energy and, ultimately, generate income.[15] This means that the costs of such investments are recouped only over a long period, typically between 20 and 30 years.[16]

An example of PV facilities shows that approx. 90% of the total installed costs are upfront capital costs, incurred when the facility is constructed.[17] These costs are "sunk" upon completion and do not decrease later. Operating costs are relatively low and represent approx. 8% of the total installed costs.[18]

The lengthy period between making an investment and the moment at which its costs are recovered (through selling energy and acquiring any applicable subsidies) explains why such investments are often financed with a high proportion of capital from third-party lenders.[19] Such financing is available because the steady long-term cash flows expected from the production and sale of electricity allow a reasonable, low-risk business plan to be created. At the same time, it is the cause of one particular financial vulnerability of RE projects. As the *9REN* tribunal noted, "once money is "sunk" in the PV facilities,

14 Eiser v. Spain, *supra* note 7 [96].

15 RREEF v. Spain, ICSID Case No. ARB/13/30, Decision on Responsibility and on the Principles of Quantum (30.11.2018) [89]: "renewable energy investments are, at the outset capital-intensive, and the ongoing operating costs are relatively low".

16 See for example, although not limited to RE but with reference to energy in general: André Mernier, Introductory Remarks, in: Graham Coop (ed.), Energy Dispute Resolution: Investment Protection, Transit and the Energy Charter Treaty (JurisNet 2011), p. XLV. See also: SolEs v. Spain, ICSID Case No. ARB/15/38, Award (31.07.2019) [102]: "The 2007 CNE Report also noted that the facilities subject to the Special Regime are capital-intensive, with a long period for capital recovery".

17 See for example: SolEs v. Spain, ibid [415]:

> PV plants cannot compete with conventional forms of energy production without substantial public subsidy or other form of incentive. They are capital-intensive, meaning that most of an investor's costs are incurred prior to operation (90%, according to Claimant's expert). They face a long period for capital recovery. Investments in PV plants are usually heavily leveraged (in the range of 55–80% leverage).

18 Foresight v. Spain, SCC Case No. V 2015/150, Final Award (14.11.2018) [273]. Note that this is tribunal's recapitulation of claimants' position.

19 Johnson, McKenzie, Saunders, *supra* note 1, p. 16. It is observed that in "typical" RE projects, the third-party financing "amounts to 60 to 80% of the total investment cost for the facility, thus leaving the equity portion contributed by the shareholders at 20 to 40%" – see: Alexander Reuter, Retroactive Reduction of Support for Renewable Energy and Investment Treaty Protection from the Perspective of Shareholders and Lenders, Transnational Dispute Management, 3 (2015), pp. 4, 49, 76.

the funds of the developer (and its bankers) are locked into the FIT contracts with their investments effectively (as the Claimant put it) long-term hostages".[20]

Third, during the relevant period when the investments at the center of the Spanish saga cases were made, all of the aforementioned RE technologies were "an expensive niche", costing more than fossil fuel energy.[21] Later, significant decreases occurred in the costs of constructing PV, CSP and Wind energy plants.[22] However, given the up-front capital intensity of the investments described above, the decreased costs of constructing new facilities had a limited, if any, impact on the constructed installations.[23] Thus, at the relevant time, state support was needed to make these RE investments economically viable.[24] For example the *SolEs* tribunal noted that PV plants "cannot compete with conventional forms of energy production without substantial public subsidy or other form of incentive" because they are capital-intensive and require a long period to ensure capital recovery.[25] The *Antin* tribunal summarized that "it seems undisputed that due to their high investment costs, CSP power-generation projects require government-backed incentives to be cost-competitive with conventional energy projects".[26] It also correctly noted the causal link between state support and the resulting decrease in the costs of new installations for such technologies, underlying that "the purpose of

---

20 9REN v. Spain, *supra* note 2 [311].

21 International Renewable Energy Agency, Renewable Power Generations Costs in 2020 (International Renewable Energy Agency 2021), available at: https://www.irena.org/-/media/Files/IRENA/Agency/Publication/2021/Jun/IRENA_Power_Generation_Costs_2020.pdf , p. 14.

22 In 2010–2020 period the global weighted average cost of electricity of utility scale PV facility for newly commissioned projects fell by 85%, of CSP facility by 68%, and of onshore wind facility by 56% – see: ibid, p. 14.

23 See at the example of a PV facility:

> A PV plant typically has an operating life of 25 years or more. In the time period relevant to this case, there have been technological advances in the PV sector, leading to significant reductions in the cost of constructing PV plants. However, once a plant is installed using then-existing technologies, it cannot take advantage of these technological advances in order to reduce its operating costs.

– see: SolEs v. Spain, *supra* note 16 [416].

24 RREEF v. Spain, *supra* note 15 [90].

25 SolEs v. Spain, *supra* note 16 [415]. Similarly: The PV Investors v. Spain, *supra* note 13 [589]:

> Nor is it contested that, due to the high capital requirements, renewable energy plants have not been able to compete with conventional forms of power generation utilizing fossil fuels. In other words, the market price of electricity is not sufficient to cover the costs of installing and operating renewable energy plants.

See also: RREEF v. Spain, ibid [89]: "RE projects are not cost-competitive, at either the whole sale or retail level".

26 Antin v. Spain, *supra* note 6 [77].

subsidization in this context is to allow the technologies to be developed in the hope that over time the costs associated therewith will decline, thus making RE technologies more competitive".[27]

3 European Context

Spain is an EU member state. Therefore, the EU law context is relevant to understand the background against which Spain adopted its domestic legislation.[28] This is particularly relevant when it comes to EU directives, which "shall be binding, as to the result to be achieved, upon each Member State to which it is addressed, but shall leave to the national authorities the choice of form and methods".[29] Thus, directives leave space for EU member states to decide how they shall be implemented into their domestic legal orders.

The EU has been active in developing the policy to reduce greenhouse gasses through the development of RE. In 2001, Directive 2001/77/EC (the "2001 Directive") stipulated binding targets for the consumption of RE.[30]

The 2001 Directive fixed Spain's national indicative target for electricity produced from RE sources at 29.4%, compared to 22.1% for the EU as a whole. This was to be achieved by 2010.[31] It also set national indicative targets of 12%

27 Ibid [540], quoted with approval for example by The PV Investors v. Spain, *supra* note 13 [589].

28 This section does not discuss EU state aid law. Whilst this ultimately transpired to be a relevant issue, this became known only after all of the disputed measures had been adopted. As such, EU state aid rules played no role in the development of the Spanish regulatory framework, analyzed below. They became relevant only in 2017, when the EC issued Decision C(2017)7384 regarding the Spanish State Aid Framework for Renewable Sources, dated 10.11.2017 ("2017 EC Decision") – see for example: OperaFund v. Spain, ICSID Case No. ARB/15/36, Award (06.09.2019) [290], BayWa v. Spain, ICSID Case No. ARB/15/16, Decision on Jurisdiction, Liability and Directions on Quantum (02.12.2019) [222], RWE v. Spain, ICSID Case No. ARB/14/34, Decision on Jurisdiction, Liability, and Certain Issues of Quantum (30.12.2019) [233].

29 Art. 288 TFEU.

30 Directive 2001/77/EC of the European Parliament and of the Council of 27 September 2001 on the promotion of electricity produced from renewable energy sources in the internal electricity market (OJ L 283, 27.10.2001, p. 33–40).

31 Art. 3(2) and Annex of the Directive 2001/77/EC, Antin v. Spain, *supra* note 6 [83], Foresight v. Spain, *supra* note 18 [69], NextEra v. Spain, ICSID Case No. ARB/14/11, Decision on Jurisdiction, Liability and Quantum Principles (12.03.2019) [108], Watkins v. Spain, ICSID Case No. ARB/15/44, Award (21.01.2020) [85].

of gross domestic energy consumption from renewable sources by 2010, in a manner consistent with the global indicative target for the EU as a whole.[32]

The 2001 Directive recognized the need to put in place government-backed financial incentives to attract private sector investment, which was indispensable to achieve these goals. These incentives could take the form of mechanisms such as green certificates, investment aid, tax exemptions or reductions, tax refunds and direct price support schemes.[33]

The EU's intention has been to "promote renewable energy sources as a priority measure given that their exploitation contributes to environmental protection and sustainable development" and to adhere to the aims of reducing greenhouse gases at an international level, including but not limited to the UNFCCC and the Kyoto Protocol.[34]

As summarized by the *Foresight* tribunal, the "broader context" of the EU's and Spain's measures are the international efforts to reduce greenhouse gas emissions, "most notably" the Kyoto Protocol.[35] In the words of the *PV Investors* tribunal, the Spanish regulations:

> were passed in the context of global, regional and national efforts to address climate change, aimed at the reduction of emissions of carbon dioxide. Against the background of the 1992 UN Framework Convention on Climate Change (UNFCCC) and the 1997 Kyoto Protocol to the UNFCCC, the European Union had also adopted rules committing Member States, including Spain, to reduce greenhouse gas emissions.[36]

This was undisputed. For example in the *Antin* case, Spain admitted that its renewable energies regulatory framework "must be understood within [...] the policies of the European Union, both in the field of energy and the environment" and that its domestic regulations at the relevant time were "introduced"

---

32 Para. 7 of the preamble, Art. 3(2) of the Directive 2001/77/EC, Antin v. Spain, ibid [83], Foresight v. Spain, ibid [53].

33 Para. 14 of the preamble of the Directive 2001/77/EC, Masdar v. Spain, ICSID Case No. ARB/14/1, Award (16.05.2018) [105], Antin v. Spain, ibid [83], Watkins v. Spain, *supra* note 31 [84].

34 Paras. 3, 4 and 6 of the preamble of the Directive 2001/77/EC. See for example: Masdar v. Spain, ibid [103]–[104], Antin v. Spain, ibid [82], NextEra v. Spain, *supra* note 31 [100], BayWa v. Spain, *supra* note 28 [86], [219], Stadtwerke v. Spain, ibid [50], RWE v. Spain, *supra* note 28 [143], Watkins v. Spain, ibid [72], [84], Hydro v. Spain, ICSID Case No. ARB/15/42, Decision on Jurisdiction, Liability and Directions on Quantum (09.03.2020) [79], [86], Cavalum v. Spain, ICSID Case No. ARB/15/34, Decision on Jurisdiction, Liability and Directions on Quantum (31.08.2020) [486].

35 Foresight v. Spain, *supra* note 18 [53].

36 The PV Investors v. Spain, *supra* note 13 [591].

and "maintained based on" the UNFCCC and the Kyoto Protocol.[37] It even described the 2001 Directive as "a key driver" behind its "actions to encourage investments in RE projects".[38] In this sense, the beginnings of developing Spain's RE sector date back to the UNFCCC.[39]

In 2007, it became clear that Spain, as many other EU Member States, would not meet its renewables goals for 2010. This prompted the European Commission ("EC") "to issue a new package of policy proposals intended to assist in the realisation of those goals".[40] On 10.01.2007 the EC issued a communication entitled "Energy Policy for Europe".[41] In the words of the *Masdar* tribunal, this communication "led to the enactment of new legislation", in the form of Royal Decree No. 661/2007,[42] "which lies at the heart of" the disputes which arose in later years.[43]

In 2009, the EU adopted Directive 2009/28/EC (the "2009 Directive").[44] It reaffirmed the EU's commitment to promoting RE. The 2009 Directive increased the target level for the EU's total energy consumption from renewable sources to 20% (compared to 12% in the 2001 Directive). This was to be achieved by 2020.[45] The same target applied to Spain.[46]

This allows the conclusion that, to use the words of the *Stadtwerke* tribunal, the actions undertaken by Spain, described below, were "efforts [...] both as a sovereign state and as a member of the EU, to increase its generation of energy from renewable sources".[47]

---

37 Antin v. Spain, *supra* note 6 [82], quoting the respondent's counter-memorial filed in the arbitration.

38 Ibid [84], relying on the respondent's rejoinder filed in the arbitration. See also for example: Foresight v. Spain, *supra* note 18 [53], 9REN v. Spain, *supra* note 2 [7].

39 Masdar v. Spain, *supra* note 33 [103], Stadtwerke v. Spain, *supra* note 6 [51], Watkins v. Spain, *supra* note 31 [71], Cavalum v. Spain, *supra* note 34 [479].

40 Masdar v. Spain, ibid [114].

41 Communication from the Commission to the Council and the European Parliament, An Energy Policy for Europe, COM(2007) 1 final (10.01.2007).

42 See below, fn 98.

43 Masdar v. Spain, *supra* note 33 [115].

44 Directive 2009/28/EC of the European Parliament and of the Council of 23 April 2009 on the promotion of the use of energy from renewable sources and amending and subsequently repealing Directives 2001/77/EC and 2003/30/EC (OJ L 140, 05.06.2009, p. 16–62).

45 Art. 3(1) 2009 Directive, Antin v. Spain, *supra* note 6 [97], Foresight v. Spain, *supra* note 18 [53], NextEra v. Spain, *supra* note 31 [127], OperaFund v. Spain, *supra* note 28 [194], Watkins v. Spain, *supra* note 31 [100], Hydro v. Spain, *supra* note 34 [114], Cavalum v. Spain, *supra* note 34 [508].

46 Annex I to the 2009 Directive.

47 Stadtwerke v. Spain, *supra* note 6 [50]. In the words of another tribunal: "From the mid-1990s, Spain has sought to develop its renewable energy ("RE") generation sector" – RWE v. Spain, *supra* note 28 [128].

4 Relevant Domestic Regulatory Framework

The hierarchy of legal norms in the Spanish legal system can be briefly summarized as follows.[48] The Spanish Constitution is the supreme legal act. Below the Constitution, the next in the hierarchy are Laws, i.e. Acts of Parliament.[49] Royal Decree-Laws ("RDL") have the same rank as Laws. However, they are adopted by the government (the executive) and only in situations of extraordinary need or urgency. They must be subsequently approved by the Parliament. Royal Decrees ("RD") are next in the hierarchy. They are adopted by the government and implement matters regulated by Laws or by RDLs. Orders, adopted by one or more ministries, are below RDs in the hierarchy. At the bottom of the hierarchy are Resolutions, adopted by lower administrative bodies.[50]

Law 54/1997 of 27 November, on the Electric Sector ("LSE", as derived from the Spanish name *Ley del Sector Eléctrico*) is the starting point of the relevant regulatory framework.[51] The LSE liberalized the energy supply market in Spain, opening it up to competition.[52] It ended the previous, state-controlled system.[53]

At the time of the LSE's adoption, coal and nuclear energy were the most relevant sources of energy production in Spain.[54] One of its goals was to ensure

---

48 The summary is simplified and intentionally omits the divisions between legal norms adopted by the central authorities, as opposed to the legal norms adopted at the level of Spain's Autonomous Communities. Further details on this are unnecessary for the purposes of the ongoing analysis, since all of the disputed measures were adopted by the central authorities.

49 Laws can be further divided between ordinary (approved by a simple majority) and organic (approved by an absolute majority in certain matters). Organic laws are irrelevant for the analysis conducted in this book.

50 RREEF v. Spain, *supra* note 15 [104], NextEra v. Spain, *supra* note 31 [99], 9REN v. Spain, *supra* note 2 [66], SolEs v. Spain, *supra* note 16 [96], BayWa v. Spain, *supra* note 28 [82], Stadtwerke v. Spain, *supra* note 6 [58], Watkins v. Spain, *supra* note 31 [73], Hydro v. Spain, *supra* note 34 [70]–[71].

51 BOE-A-1997-25340, *«BOE» núm. 285, de 28 de noviembre de 1997, páginas 35097 a 35126.*

52 Novenergia v. Spain, SCC Case No. 2015/063, Final Arbitral Award (15.02.2018) [78], Foresight v. Spain, *supra* note 18 [55], [64], Cube v. Spain, ICSID Case No. ARB/15/20, Decision on Jurisdiction, Liability and Partial Decision on Quantum (19.02.2019) [243], 9REN v. Spain, *supra* note 2 [74], SolEs v. Spain, *supra* note 16 [97], InfraRed v. Spain, ICSID Case No. ARB/14/12, Award (02.08.2019) [18], BayWa v. Spain, *supra* note 28 [86], Stadtwerke v. Spain, *supra* note 6 [54], Hydro v. Spain, *supra* note 34 [75].

53 Antin v. Spain, *supra* note 6 [74], RREEF v. Spain, *supra* note 15 [105], Watkins v. Spain, *supra* note 31 [76]. There were also regulations concerning RE earlier, see for example: Hydro v. Spain, ibid [73].

54 "While in the eighties energy production in Spain was mainly based on coal, in the mid-nineties nuclear energy became the most important domestic source and today renewable energies represent the prime energetic asset of the country" – Thomas Dromgool, Daniel Ybarra Enguix, The Fair and Equitable Treatment Standard and the

that 12% of the energy demand was supplied by RE by 2010. This was increased to a 20% target by 2020 in subsequent amendments made to the LSE, in line with the 2009 Directive.[55]

Among other provisions, the LSE created the Administrative Registry of Energy Production Facilities ("RAIPRE", as derived from the Spanish name *Registro administrativo de instalaciones de producción de energía eléctrica*).[56]

The LSE introduced two regulatory regimes: (i) one for traditional generation plants (the "Ordinary Regime") and (ii) another for electricity generated from renewable energies (the "Special Regime").[57] Under the Ordinary Regime, remuneration depended exclusively upon the wholesale market price of electricity.[58] The Special Regime was different, as it introduced a premium which was paid over the wholesale market price.[59] This premium was to be set out in RDs, in line with the general principle in Art. 30(4) LSE, the relevant part of which reads as follows:

> The payment regime for electricity production facilities under the special regime shall be supplemented by the earning of a premium, under the terms set by regulation, in the following cases:
>
> a) Facilities referred to in letter a) of section 1 of article 27,[60]

Revocation of Feed in Tariffs – Foreign Renewable Energy Investments in Crisis-Struck Spain, in: Voler Mauerhofer (ed.) Legal Aspects of Sustainable Development (Springer 2016), p. 392.

55 Novenergia v. Spain, *supra* note 52 [78], Foresight v. Spain, *supra* note 18 [53], [64].

56 Arts. 21(4) and 31 LSE, RREEF v. Spain, *supra* note 15 [107], NextEra v. Spain, *supra* note 31 [105].

57 Foresight v. Spain, *supra* note 18 [55], NextEra v. Spain, *supra* note 31 [102], SolEs v. Spain, *supra* note 16 [97], InfraRed v. Spain, *supra* note 52 [20], BayWa v. Spain, *supra* note 28 [87], Stadtwerke v. Spain, *supra* note 6 [55], Watkins v. Spain, *supra* note 31 [78]. Art. 27 LSE read as follows:

> 1. Electrical energy production shall be approved for operation under the special regime in the following cases, and when said activity is carried out in power plants with an installed power capacity that does not exceed 50MW: [...] b) When used as a primary energy source, any of the no-consumable renewable energy, biomass or any kind of biofuel, providing the owner does not operate electricity production activities under the ordinary regime. [...] 2. Energy production under the special regime shall be governed by its specific guidelines and, in matters not covered by them, general applicable electrical production rules shall apply.

58 Masdar v. Spain, *supra* note 33 [105], The PV Investors v. Spain, *supra* note 13 [183].

59 The purpose of the Special Regime was to remedy Spain's problems regarding its lack of energy independence and to meet Spain's international obligations – see: Isolux v. Spain, SCC Case No. V 2013/153, Award (12.07.2016) [87].

60 This refers to "power plants with an installed power capacity that does not exceed 50MW [...] when used as a primary energy source, any of the no-consumable renewable energy, biomass or any kind of biofuel" – fn 57.

> b) Hydroelectric power plants with installed capacity less than or equal to 10 MW, and all other facilities referred to in letter b) of section 1 of article 27. For the purposes of this Act, urban solid waste and hazardous waste will not be considered biomass.
>
> c) Hydroelectric plants between 10 and 50 MW, facilities referred to in letter c) of section 1 of article 27, as well as the facilities mentioned in paragraph two of section 1 of article 27.
>
> To determine the premiums, the voltage level of electricity delivered to the network must be considered, along with the actual contribution to improvement of the environment, primary energy savings, and energy efficiency, the economically justifiable production of usable heat, and the investment costs that have been incurred, for the purpose of achieving reasonable rates of return with respect to the cost of money on the capital market.[61]

The meaning and legal consequences of the term "reasonable rate of return", as well as "with respect to the cost of money on the capital market" used in the last sentence of the quoted provision, became important elements in the factual matrix of the Spanish saga cases.

The first of the RDs to implement the premiums envisaged in Art. 30(4) LSE was Royal Decree 2818/1998, which was enacted on 23.12.1998 ("RD 2818/1998").[62] Its preamble explained that it aimed to reduce greenhouse gas emissions, with the goal to supply 12% of Spain's total energy demand from RE sources by 2010.[63] RD 2818/1998 granted energy producers who qualified under the Special Regime a right to be connected to, and to supply electricity to, the national grid.[64] It also enabled them to sell electricity under a regulated tariff or with a premium paid over wholesale market prices.[65] However, the amount

61 As translated in The PV Investors v. Spain, *supra* note 13 [590]. See also: Masdar v. Spain, *supra* note 33 [105], RWE v. Spain, *supra* note 28 [132], Novenergia v. Spain, *supra* note 52 [80]. The quotation reflects wording of the provision as of when RD 661/2007 was adopted (see: fn 98 below), not how the LSE was worded back in 1997.

62 BOE-A-1998-30041, *«BOE» núm. 312, de 30 de diciembre de 1998, páginas 44077 a 44089, Real Decreto 2818/1998, de 23 de diciembre, sobre producción de energía eléctrica por instalaciones abastecidas por recursos o fuentes de energía renovables, residuos y cogeneración* (on electricity production installations supplied by renewable energy, waste incineration or combined heat and electric resources or sources).

63 Novenergia v. Spain, *supra* note 52 [80], [81], Isolux v. Spain, *supra* note 59 [89].

64 Masdar v. Spain, *supra* note 33 [106].

65 Antin v. Spain, *supra* note 6 [81], Foresight v. Spain, *supra* note 18 [67], Stadtwerke v. Spain, *supra* note 6 [59], RWE v. Spain, *supra* note 28 [136], Watkins v. Spain, *supra* note 31 [82].

of the regulated tariff and the premium was to be reviewed annually, which created uncertainty for prospective investors.[66]

In December 1999, the Institute for Energy Diversification and Savings ("IDAE", as derived from the Spanish name *Instituto para la Diversificación y Ahorro de la Energía*), prepared a renewable energies promotion plan for 2000–2010 (the "2000–2010 Plan").[67] According to the 2000–2010 Plan, a remuneration scheme was to be developed to meet the EU's indicative target of 12% of Spain's total energy production coming from renewables by 2010.[68] The Council of Ministers approved the 2000–2010 Plan on 30.12.1999.[69]

RD 2818/1998 did not attract the desired level of investments.[70] By 2004, Spain had achieved only around 56.2% of its 2006 objective for renewable electricity production, and only 28.4% of its 2010 target.[71] This was noted by the Spanish authorities. On 02.04.2003, the National Energy Commission ("CNE", as derived from the Spanish name *Comisión Nacional de Energía*) issued a report which indicated that it was necessary to increase remuneration and to guarantee incentives throughout a facility's operational life in order to attract the desired level of investments in the RE sector.[72]

On 12.03.2004, Royal Decree 436/2004 ("RD 436/2004") was adopted.[73] It repealed RD 2818/1998.[74] Its preamble stated, among others, that its aim was:

> that by the year 2010, close to one third of electricity demand will be covered by high energy efficient technologies and by renewable energies without any increase in the production cost of the electricity system compared to the forecasts used to set the tariff methodology in 2002. With this contribution of the special regime, it will be possible to reach the goal set

66 Art. 28(3) RD 2818/1998, Masdar v. Spain, *supra* note 33 [107], Cube v. Spain, *supra* note 52 [244].

67 The IDAE is an agency of the Spanish government, operating under the auspices of a competent ministry (the Ministry of Industry, Energy and Tourism at that time) – see: Charanne v. Spain, SCC Case No. V 062/2012, Award (21.01.2016) [95].

68 BayWa v. Spain, *supra* note 28 [91], RWE v. Spain, *supra* note 28 [139].

69 Foresight v. Spain, *supra* note 18 [68].

70 Cube v. Spain, *supra* note 52 [245], 9REN v. Spain, *supra* note 2 [75].

71 Foresight v. Spain, *supra* note 18 [70], [71].

72 Ibid [72].

73 BOE-A-2004-5562, *«BOE» núm. 75, de 27 de marzo de 2004, páginas 13217 a 13238, Real Decreto 436/2004, de 12 de marzo, por el que se establece la metodología para la actualización y sistematización del régimen jurídico y económico de la actividad de producción de energía eléctrica en régimen especial* (establishing the methodology for the updating and systematization of the legal and economic regime for electric power production in the special regime).

74 Novenergia v. Spain, *supra* note 52 [88].

> out in the 1997 Electricity Act, i.e. to ensure that by the year 2010 renewable energy sources cover at least 12% of total energy demand in Spain.[75]

It further stated that "whatever the remuneration mechanism selected, the Royal Decree guarantees owners of special regime installations a reasonable return on their investments and for electricity consumers an also reasonable allocation of costs attributable to the electricity system [...]".[76]

RD 436/2004 also provided for remuneration based on regulated tariff or a premium (i.e. payment over and above the wholesale market price per kWh of energy produced).[77] The only condition for obtaining the remuneration under the Special Regime was to register in the RAIPRE.[78] The Special Regime's incentives were linked to the "Average Electricity Tariff" ("TMR", as derived from the Spanish name *Tarifa media de referencia*).[79] The TMR was fixed by the government and tied to a set of variables that affected the costs of the electricity system, including the cost of the renewables support scheme itself.[80] This resulted in a "feedback loop", i.e. growth in RE production resulted in an increased TMR, which in turn resulted in an increase of the regulated tariffs and premiums and so on.[81] Art. 40(3) RD 436/2004 provided that any revisions made to the regulated tariffs or premiums could not affect facilities that had already commenced operations.[82] It read as follows:

> The tariffs, premiums, incentives and supplements resulting from any of the revisions provided for in this section shall apply solely to the plants that commence operating subsequent to the date of the entry into force referred to in the paragraph above and shall not have a backdated effect on any previous tariffs and premiums.[83]

---

75 As translated in Antin v. Spain, *supra* note 6 [85].

76 As translated in The PV Investors v. Spain, *supra* note 13 [592].

77 Art. 22 RD 436/2004, Novenergia v. Spain, *supra* note 52 [91], Masdar v. Spain, *supra* note 33 [110], Antin v. Spain, *supra* note 6 [85], Foresight v. Spain, *supra* note 18 [74], NextEra v. Spain, *supra* note 31 [110], Cube v. Spain, *supra* note 52 [247], BayWa v. Spain, *supra* note 28 [96], Stadtwerke v. Spain, *supra* note 6 [63], RWE v. Spain, *supra* note 28 [144], Watkins v. Spain, *supra* note 31 [86].

78 Arts. 9 and 15 RD 436/2004, Novenergia v. Spain, ibid [94].

79 Cube v. Spain, *supra* note 52 [246], Stadtwerke v. Spain, *supra* note 6 [64], Hydro v. Spain, *supra* note 34 [88].

80 Foresight v. Spain, *supra* note 18 [75], Masdar v. Spain, *supra* note 33 [110].

81 Foresight v. Spain, ibid, Watkins v. Spain, *supra* note 31 [86].

82 Novenergia v. Spain, *supra* note 52 [93], Masdar v. Spain, *supra* note 33 [110], Antin v. Spain, *supra* note 6 [86], Foresight v. Spain, ibid [76], RWE v. Spain, *supra* note 28 [146].

83 As translated in Cavalum v. Spain, *supra* note 34 [492]. See also for example: BayWa v. Spain, *supra* note 28 [98], Watkins v. Spain, *supra* note 31 [87], Hydro v. Spain, *supra* note 34 [93].

On 14.03.2004, Parliamentary elections were held in Spain. The new government considered the development of RE to be one of its priorities.[84]

On 24.05.2005, IDAE published the first of a series of documents under the slogan "The Sun Can Be All Yours".[85] New versions of this publication followed in 2007 and 2008.[86]

On 26.08.2005, the government adopted a renewable energies plan for 2005–2010 (the "2005–2010 Plan").[87] The 2005–2010 Plan acknowledged the insufficient growth of Spain's renewable electricity capability in the light of the EU's targets.[88] It also clarified that supporting RE constitutes an element in the fight against climate change and supports a sustainable development strategy.[89] Whilst the 2005–2010 Plan did not amend the 2000–2010 Plan as regards the goal of 12% of Spain's energy demand being supplied from renewable sources by 2010, it adopted a new goal of 29.4% as regards energy produced from renewable sources by that year.[90] The 2005–2010 Plan set the capacity target for 2010 for PV technology at 400 MW,[91] for Wind energy at 20.155 MW,[92] for Hydro energy at 2.199 MW (for small Hydro installations, i.e. less than 10MW each) and 3.257 MW (for Hydro installations between 10 and 50 MW each).[93] It also estimated an Internal Rate of Return ("IRR") for

84 Masdar v. Spain, *supra* note 33 [109].

85 Novenergia v. Spain, *supra* note 52 [112], InfraRed v. Spain, *supra* note 52 [24], BayWa v. Spain, *supra* note 28 [102], Charanne v. Spain, *supra* note 67 [95].

86 Novenergia v. Spain, ibid [117], OperaFund v. Spain, *supra* note 28 [117], Charanne v. Spain, *supra* note 67 [102].

87 Available at: https://www.idae.es/publicaciones/plan-de-energias-renovables-en-espana-2005-2010.

88 Charanne v. Spain, *supra* note 67 [96], Eiser v. Spain, *supra* note 7 [105], SolEs v. Spain, *supra* note 16 [99].

89 2005–2010 Plan, p. 8: "The fight against climate change is a political priority in environmental matters, both for the European Union and for Spain, and as such forms part of the corresponding Strategies for Sustainable Development". Chapter 2.1. of the 2005–2010 Plan deals with the RE in the EU context as a "tool for energy sustainable development".

90 2005–2010 Plan, p. 7, Isolux v. Spain, *supra* note 59 [92], Novenergia v. Spain, *supra* note 52 [104], NextEra v. Spain, *supra* note 31 [111], Stadtwerke v. Spain, *supra* note 6 [65], Watkins v. Spain, *supra* note 31 [88].

91 It also projected that PV electricity generation alone would require 1.875 billion Euros in total capital investment and recognized that nearly 80% of that amount would be debt financed – see: Foresight v. Spain, *supra* note 18 [77], 9REN v. Spain, *supra* note 2 [97], SolEs v. Spain, *supra* note 16 [100]. Stadtwerke v. Spain, ibid [67] refers to 77%.

92 RWE v. Spain, *supra* note 28 [152]. Watkins v. Spain, *supra* note 31 [89] suggests a slightly lower number, 20.000 MW.

93 Hydro v. Spain, *supra* note 34 [97].

renewable projects at "around 7%, with own resources (prior to funding) and post-tax".[94]

RD 436/2004 also proved to be unsuccessful in attracting investments in the RE sector at the level desired by Spain.[95]

On 14.02.2007, the CNE published a report on new draft regulations which were to replace RD 436/2004.[96] It observed, among others, that economic incentives were necessary to promote the development of renewables and that "[i]n certain cases, differentiated incentives are justified that lead to higher returns, so that the objectives set in the planning can be achieved". The CNE also argued for the new regulations to include "sufficient guarantees to ensure that the economic incentives are stable and predictable throughout the entire life of the facilities …".[97]

---

94 RREEF v. Spain, *supra* note 15 [93]. See also for example: OperaFund v. Spain, *supra* note 28 [136], BayWa v. Spain, *supra* note 28 [104], Stadtwerke v. Spain, *supra* note 6 [69], RWE v. Spain, *supra* note 28 [153], Hydro v. Spain, ibid [99], Cavalum v. Spain, *supra* note 34 [496].

95 Cube v. Spain, *supra* note 52 [251], 9REN v. Spain, *supra* note 2 [81], Hydro v. Spain, ibid [94]–[95]. As a matter of example, as of 2006 there installed PV capacity was 84 MW, compared to the desired capacity of 400 MW by 2010 – see: Foresight v. Spain, *supra* note 18 [78].

96 *Informe 3/2007 de la CNE relativo a la propuesta de real decreto por el que se regula la actividad de producción de energía eléctrica en régimen especial y de determinadas instalaciones de tecnologías asimilables del régimen ordinario* (Report 3/2007 of the CNE regarding the proposal for a royal decree regulating the activity of electricity production under the special regime and certain installations of assimilable technologies under the ordinary regime), https://www.cnmc.es/sites/default/files/1562569_8.pdf.

97 As translated in Foresight v. Spain, *supra* note 18 [79]. Point 5.b) of the report is relevant in this context. It read as follows:

> Minimise regulatory uncertainty. The National Energy Commission understands that transparency and predictability in the future of economic incentives reduce regulatory uncertainty, which in turn, incentivises investment in new capacity and minimises the cost of project financing, thereby reducing the final cost for consumers. Regulation must offer sufficient guarantee, in order to ensure that economic incentives are stable and predictable throughout the entire life of the installation, setting, where appropriate, both transparent mechanisms to be updated annually, linked to the evolution of strong indices (such as the average or baseline fee, the CPI, ten-year bonds, etc.) and periodic revisions, which would take place every four years, for example, and would only affect new installations, in terms of investment costs, whereby the reduction of operating costs might also affect existing installations.

– as translated in Eiser v. Spain, *supra* note 7 [109]. See also for example: NextEra v. Spain, *supra* note 31 [116], 9REN v. Spain, *supra* note 2 [82], SolEs v. Spain, *supra* note 16 [101], RWE v. Spain, *supra* note 28 [159]–[160].

On 25.05.2007, Royal Decree 661/2007 ("RD 661/2007") was adopted.[98] It became the cornerstone of the Special Regime, and repealed RD 436/2004.[99] It also came to be at the heart of the subsequent Spanish saga disputes. It was relied upon by the claimants in those arbitrations as the principal element of the regulatory framework which led them to develop expectations of stability. The preamble to RD 661/2007 stated, among others:

> The creation of the special regime for the generation of electricity meant an important milestone in the energy policy of our country. […] although the growth seen overall in the special regime for electricity generation has been outstanding, in certain technologies the targets posed are still far from being reached. From the point of view of compensation, the business of the production of electrical energy under the special regime is characterised by the possibility that the compensation system can be supplemented by the receipt of a premium under the terms and conditions established in the regulations, in order to determine which such factors as the voltage level of the energy delivered into the grid, the contribution to the improvement in the environment, primary energy saving, energy efficiency, and the investment costs incurred, may all be taken into account. The modification of the economic and legal framework which regulates the special regime existing to date has become necessary for various reasons. […] The present Royal Decree replaces and repeals [RD 436/2004] while maintaining the basic structure of the regulations therein. The economic framework established in the present Royal Decree develops the principles provided in [LSE] guaranteeing the owners of facilities under the special regime a reasonable return on their investments, and the consumers of electricity an assignment of the costs attributable to the electricity system which is also reasonable, […].[100]

RD 661/2007 maintained two types of remuneration for energy producers operating within the Special Regime: payment of a regulated tariff or a premium,

98 BOE-A-2007-10556, *«BOE» núm. 126, de 26 de mayo de 2007, páginas 22846 a 22886, Real Decreto 661/2007, de 25 de mayo, por el que se regula la actividad de producción de energía eléctrica en régimen especial* (regulating the activity of electricity production under the special regime).

99 Sole derogatory provision of RD 661/2007, Foresight v. Spain, *supra* note 18 [80].

100 As translated in Cavalum v. Spain, *supra* note 34 [499]. See also for example: SolEs v. Spain, *supra* note 16 [103], RWE v. Spain, *supra* note 28 [162]–[163], Watkins v. Spain, *supra* note 31 [92], Hydro v. Spain, *supra* note 34 [102].

both subject to certain floors and caps.[101] The first option was to sell electricity to the system in exchange for a regulated, fixed tariff, expressed in Euro cents per kilowatt/hour ("FIT", from "feed-in-tariffs").[102] RD 661/2007 for the first time fixed the FIT as absolute numbers (c€/kWh), based on a facility's total electricity generation capacity, for the entire life of a facility.[103] The second option was to sell electricity on the electric energy market, for the price obtained on the organized market or a price freely negotiated, supplemented by a premium expressed in Euro cents per kilowatt/hour ("Premium").[104] RE producers could choose between the two options, and their choice applied for a minimum period of one year.[105] PV plants were an exception to this, as only the FIT applied to them.[106] Both options, the FIT and the Premium, were envisaged to apply for the entire operating life of the plants, at a higher level for the first 25 years "and thereafter" at a lower level.[107] The FIT and the Premium, as well as having upper and lower limits, were adjusted by reference to fuel price

101 9REN v. Spain, *supra* note 2 [86], BayWa v. Spain, *supra* note 28 [125], Stadtwerke v. Spain, *supra* note 6 [74], RWE v. Spain, ibid [167], The PV Investors v. Spain, *supra* note 13 [190].

102 Some tribunals used this acronym for both: feed-in-tariffs and the Premium option – see for example: RREEF v. Spain, *supra* note 15 [90], SolEs v. Spain, *supra* note 16 [104].

103 Differently than the previous RDs implementing the Special Regime. Moreover, nothing in RD 661/2007 explains the methodology "by which the fixed FiTs are arrived at" – Foresight v. Spain, *supra* note 18 [81]–[83]. See also for example: RREEF v. Spain, ibid [109], NextEra v. Spain, *supra* note 31 [121], InfraRed v. Spain, *supra* note 52 [28].

104 Art. 24(1) RD 661/2007:

> 1. In order to sell the totality or a part of their net production of electric energy, the owners of facilities to which this Royal Decree applies shall elect one of the following options: a) To sell the electricity to the system through the transportation or distribution grid, receiving a feed in tariff, which shall be the same for all scheduling periods, expressed in Euro cents per kilowatt/hour. b) To sell the electricity in the electric energy production market. In this case, the sale price of the electricity shall be either the price obtained on the organised market or the price freely negotiated by the owner or the representative of the facility, supplemented where applicable by a premium, in Euro cents per kilowatt/hour.

See also for example: NextEra v. Spain, ibid [119], Cube v. Spain, *supra* note 52 [256], Hydro v. Spain, *supra* note 34 [103].

105 Art. 24.c) RD 661/2007.

106 Foresight v. Spain, *supra* note 18 [81], Cube v. Spain, *supra* note 52 [259].

107 Art. 36 RD 661/2007, Cube v. Spain, ibid [260], 9REN v. Spain, *supra* note 2 [90], InfraRed v. Spain, *supra* note 52 [28], BayWa v. Spain, *supra* note 28 [125], The PV Investors v. Spain, *supra* note 13 [191], Hydro v. Spain, *supra* note 34 [106].

indexes and the Consumer Price Index ("IPC", as derived from the Spanish name *índice nacional de precios al consumo*).[108]

Moreover, RD 661/2007 granted RE producers priority of access and priority of dispatch to the electric grid (when compared to conventional energy producers).[109] As a result, RE producers could sell and transmit electricity whenever it was produced.[110] RD 661/2007 also allowed RE plants operating within the Special Regime to use fuels to generate electricity, provided that the electricity produced by such fuels did not exceed a specified percentage of the plant's total energy production.[111]

Art. 44(3) RD 661/2007 proved to be particularly relevant to the future disputes. It provided that Spain would review the FIT and Premium rates in 2010 and every four years thereafter, and that such revisions would guarantee "a reasonable rate of return by reference to the cost of money in the capital markets" and would not apply to facilities already enrolled in the support scheme, i.e. it would operate only prospectively.[112] It read as follows:

> During the year 2010, on sight of the results of the monitoring reports on the degree of fulfilment of the Renewable Energies Plan (PER) 2005–2010, and of the Energy Efficiency and Savings Strategy in Spain (E4), together with such new targets as may be included in the subsequent Renewable Energies Plan 2011–2020, there shall be a review of the tariffs, premiums, supplements and lower and upper limits defined in this Royal Decree with regard to the costs associated with each of these technologies, the degree of participation of the special regime in covering the demand and its impact upon the technical and economic management of the system, and a reasonable rate of profitability [or "return" – author's note] shall always be guaranteed with reference to the cost of money in the capital markets. Subsequently a further review shall be performed every four

108 Art. 44(1) RD 661/2007. See also for example: Antin v. Spain, *supra* note 6 [94], Foresight v. Spain, *supra* note 18 [83], Isolux v. Spain, *supra* note 59 [102], Stadtwerke v. Spain, *supra* note 6 [76].

109 Art. 17(e) RD 661/2007. See also for example: Antin v. Spain, ibid, InfraRed v. Spain, *supra* note 52 [28], Stadtwerke v. Spain, ibid [77], RWE v. Spain, *supra* note 28 [166], with full translation of Art. 17 RD 661/2007.

110 Foresight v. Spain, *supra* note 18 [85].

111 12% if the plant sold energy via the FIT option and 15%, if the plant sold energy via the Premium option – Art. 2(1) RD 661/2007, subgroup b.1.2. See also for example: Eiser v. Spain, *supra* note 7 [112], Antin v. Spain, *supra* note 6 [94], RREEF v. Spain, *supra* note 15 [110], NextEra v. Spain, *supra* note 31 [120], InfraRed v. Spain, *supra* note 52 [28], Stadtwerke v. Spain, *supra* note 6 [78].

112 Cube v. Spain, *supra* note 52 [263], BayWa v. Spain, *supra* note 28 [128].

> years, maintaining the same criteria as previously. The revisions to the regulated tariff and the upper and lower limits indicated in this paragraph shall not affect facilities for which the deed of commissioning shall have been granted prior to 1 January of the second year following the year in which the revision shall have been performed.[113]

RD 661/2007 required a definitive registration in the RAIPRE.[114] This was a *sine qua non* for a facility to be capable of benefitting from the Special Regime.[115] Definitive registration was preceded by pre-registration in the RAIPRE.[116]

It also introduced desired "power targets" for each RE type, by reference to the 2005–2010 Plan.[117] The targets were: 371 MW for PV plants,[118] 500 MW for CSP plants,[119] 2.400 MW for small (i.e. less than 10 MW) Hydro energy plants[120] and 20.155 MW for Wind energy plants.[121] It also envisaged a time-limit for each group or subgroup of the energy types produced. Once 85% of the target capacity was reached, a "tariff window" of at least 12 months was to be fixed in order to be registered in the RAIPRE.[122] Thereafter, new installations would be unable to benefit from RD 661/2007.[123]

On the day that RD 661/2007 was adopted, the competent ministry issued a press release entitled "Government grants profitability and stability with new Royal Decree for renewable energy and cogeneration" ("2007 Press release").[124] It stated, among others:

> Future revision of the tariffs will not affect facilities already operating. This guarantee gives legal certainty for the producer, providing stability

113 As translated in SolEs v. Spain, *supra* note 16 [106]. See also for example: RWE v. Spain, *supra* note 28 [169], Watkins v. Spain, *supra* note 31 [98], The PV Investors v. Spain, *supra* note 13 [194], Hydro v. Spain, *supra* note 34 [110], Cavalum v. Spain, *supra* note 34 [504].

114 Art. 9 RD 661/2007. See also for example: Charanne v. Spain, *supra* note 67 [115].

115 Art. 14(1) RD 661/2007. See also for example: Antin v. Spain, *supra* note 6 [94], Foresight v. Spain, *supra* note 18 [88], NextEra v. Spain, *supra* note 31 [124], 9REN v. Spain, *supra* note 2 [92], RWE v. Spain, *supra* note 28 [165].

116 Arts. 11 and 12 RD 661/2007. See also for example: Isolux v. Spain, *supra* note 59 [95], Antin v. Spain, ibid.

117 BayWa v. Spain, *supra* note 28 [129], Cube v. Spain, *supra* note 52 [264].

118 Art. 37 RD 661/2007, Cube v. Spain, ibid.

119 Art. 37 RD 661/2007, NextEra v. Spain, *supra* note 31 [123].

120 Art. 40 RD 661/2007, Cube v. Spain, *supra* note 52 [264].

121 Art. 38 RD 661/2007, Watkins v. Spain, *supra* note 31 [93].

122 Art. 22 RD 661/2007. See also: RREEF v. Spain, *supra* note 15 [113], Cube v. Spain, *supra* note 52 [264], RWE v. Spain, *supra* note 28 [168], Watkins v. Spain, ibid.

123 Masdar v. Spain, *supra* note 33 [116.(VII)].

124 Cube v. Spain, *supra* note 52 [266], RWE v. Spain, *supra* note 28 [174].

> to the sector and promoting its development. The new regulation will not have retroactive effects. Installations commissioned up until 1 January 2008 will remain under the previous regulation in terms of the fixed-tariff option throughout their service life. [...] The government's commitment in favour of these energy technologies has been the reason why the new regulation seeks stability over time that allows entrepreneurs to plan in the medium to long-term, as well as [granting them] an adequate and reasonable return that, along with stability, make the investment and the activity attractive.[125]

Spain and its agencies – CNE and InvestInSpain (state-owned company promoting Spain as the host state for investments) – conducted several "road-shows" for potential investors around the world, promoting the stability and potential profitability of the RD 661/2007 support scheme.[126]

Over a year after the adoption of RD 661/2007, on 30.07.2008, the CNE issued a report which commented, among other issues, on the legal certainty and protection of legitimate expectations as follows:

> Legal certainty and the protection of legitimate expectations. The stability and predictability of economic incentives (tariffs and premiums) reduce regulatory uncertainty, which encourages investments in new capacity to tackle their projects, while minimizing financing cost, and reducing the final cost to the consumer. The current regulation has established annual updates of economic incentives based on robust indicators (such as CPI, ten-year bonds, etc.) and also periodic reviews every four years, which can only affect new facilities [...] Criteria to minimize regulatory uncertainty. The production facilities under the special regime are often capital intensive with long recovery periods. The regulation of production facilities under the special regime, established by Royal Decree 661/2007, has tried to minimize the regulatory risk of this group, providing security and predictability to the economic incentives during the facilities' lifespan, establishing transparent mechanisms for annual updates [...].[127]

---

125 As translated in SolEs v. Spain, *supra* note 16 [347]. See also: OperaFund v. Spain, *supra* note 28 [158], BayWa v. Spain, *supra* note 28 [130], RWE v. Spain, ibid [174]–[175].

126 Foresight v. Spain, *supra* note 18 [89], OperaFund v. Spain, ibid [118], BayWa v. Spain, ibid [141]–[142], RWE v. Spain, ibid [176].

127 As translated in Novenergia v. Spain, *supra* note 52 [110]. See: *Informe 30/2008 de la CNE en relación con la propuesta de real decreto de retribución de la actividad de producción de energía eléctrica mediante tecnología solar fotovoltaica para instalaciones posteriores a la*

As opposed to earlier regulations which had implemented the LSE, RD 661/2007 succeeded in attracting significant investment in renewables. In as short as four months after RD 661/2007 was enacted, Spain's installed PV capacity exceeded 85% of the target.[128] Reaching this threshold triggered the "tariff window", according to which the Special Regime would cease to apply to any PV installations which had not been registered by 29.09.2008.[129]

New Parliamentary elections took place on 09.03.2008. The outcome was similar to that of the 2004 elections, so the same government remained in power. There was no visible shift in Spain's policy on RE production.

On 16.09.2008, Royal Decree 1578/2008 ("RD 1578/2008") was adopted.[130] It applied exclusively to PV installations, excluding other RE technologies. It opened the possibility to benefit from the Special Regime to PV installations that had missed the deadline for registering in the RAIPRE under RD 661/2007.[131] Whilst the FIT rates under RD 1578/2008 were lower than those applicable under RD 661/2007, other essential features of the incentives were maintained.

---

fecha límite de mantenimiento de la retribución del real decreto 661/2007, de 25 de mayo, para dicha tecnología (Report 30/2008 of the CNE in relation to the proposal for a royal decree on the remuneration of the activity of electricity production using photovoltaic solar technology for installations subsequent to the deadline for maintenance of the remuneration of royal decree 661/2007, of 25 of May, for said technology), pp. 9, 20.

128 "As of August 31, 2007, the percentage achieved with respect to the objective of installed power for photovoltaic solar technology is 91 percent, and that 100 percent of the objective will be achieved in the month of October 2007" – BOE-A-2007-17108, *«BOE» núm. 234, de 29 de septiembre de 2007, páginas 39745 a 39745, Resolución de 27 de septiembre de 2007, de la Secretaría General de Energía, por la que se establece el plazo de mantenimiento de la tarifa regulada para la tecnología fotovoltaica, en virtud de lo establecido en el artículo 22 del Real Decreto 661/2007, de 25 de mayo* (Resolution of 27.09.2007, of the General Secretariat of Energy, which establishes the period of maintenance of the regulated rate for photovoltaic technology, by virtue of the provisions of article 22 of Royal Decree 661/2007, of 25 of May). See also for example: Charanne v. Spain, *supra* note 67 [128], Cube v. Spain, *supra* note 52 [269], 9REN v. Spain, *supra* note 2 [95], SolEs v. Spain, *supra* note 16 [107], OperaFund v. Spain, *supra* note 28 [162].

129 Foresight v. Spain, *supra* note 18 [56], [90], Isolux v. Spain, *supra* note 59 [99], 9REN v. Spain, ibid [98], OperaFund v. Spain, ibid [163].

130 BOE-A-2008-15595, *«BOE» núm. 234, de 27 de septiembre de 2008, páginas 39117 a 39125, Real Decreto 1578/2008, de 26 de septiembre, de retribución de la actividad de producción de energía eléctrica mediante tecnología solar fotovoltaica para instalaciones posteriores a la fecha límite de mantenimiento de la retribución del Real Decreto 661/2007, de 25 de mayo, para dicha tecnología* (on the remuneration for the electric energy production activity using photovoltaic solar technology for installations after the deadline for maintenance of the remuneration of Royal Decree 661/2007, of May 25, for said technology).

131 Masdar v. Spain, *supra* note 33 [117], 9REN v. Spain, *supra* note 2 [99].

RD 1578/2008 did not affect incentives applied to PV facilities which had already registered under RD 661/2007.[132]

On 30.04.2009, Spain adopted Royal Decree-Law 6/2009 ("RDL 6/2009").[133] For the first time Spain addressed the "**tariff deficit**", understood as the financial gap between the costs of subsidies paid to RE producers and revenues derived from energy sales to consumers.[134] RDL 6/2009's preamble explained, among others, that:

> The growing tariff deficit, that is to say, the difference between revenue from the regulated tariffs that are set by the Administration and that consumers pay for their regulated supply and from the access tariffs that are set in the liberalised market and the real costs associated with these tariffs, is causing serious problems which, in the current context of international financial crisis, is having a profound effect on the system and placing at risk not only the financial situation of companies that make up the Electricity Industry, but also the very sustainability of the system. This imbalance is unsustainable and has serious consequences, as it undermines the security and the capacity to fund the investments needed for the supply of electricity at the levels of quality and security that Spanish society requires.[135]

---

132 Foresight v. Spain, *supra* note 18 [58], [91], The PV Investors v. Spain, *supra* note 13 [197].

133 BOE-A-2009-7581, *«BOE» núm. 111, de 23 de mayo de 2009, páginas 39404 a 39419, Real Decreto-ley 6/2009, de 30 de abril, por el que se adoptan determinadas medidas en el sector energético y se aprueba el bono social* (which adopts certain measures in the energy sector and enacts the discount tariff).

134 "[...] the difference between revenue from the regulated tariffs that are set by the Administration and that consumers pay for their regulated supply and from the access tariffs that are set in the liberalised market and the real costs associated with these tariffs" – Preamble of RDL 6/2009, as translated in Stadtwerke v. Spain, *supra* note 6 [297]. See also for example: NextEra v. Spain, *supra* note 31 [128], RWE v. Spain, *supra* note 28 [178]–[179], Watkins v. Spain, *supra* note 31 [101].

135 It followed:

> The current regulation of the special regime does not establish sufficient mechanisms to make it possible to plan facilities that use this type of energy, nor indeed the amount and the distribution over time of the remuneration premiums and therefore the impact on costs that are attributed to the tariff system. The measure envisaged in the Royal Decree-Law, by creating the Remuneration Pre-assignment Registry, makes it possible to correct the situation described above from the very moment of its coming into effect. It will make it possible to know within the deadlines envisaged in the Royal Decree-Law, the facilities that are not only currently projected but which meet the conditions for start-up and for accessing the electricity system with all legal and statutory requirements, the volume of power associated with them and the impact on

RDL 6/2009 established maximum tariff deficit limits for 2009–2012, and provided that the tariff deficit should be eliminated by 2013.[136] For this purposes, RDL 6/2009 created a Pre-Assignment Register, which was a "sub-section" of the RAIPRE ("Pre-RAIPRE", as derived from the Spanish name *Registro de Preasignación de Retribución*).[137] This pre-registration was required in order for plants to be eligible to receive benefits under the Special Regime.[138] After the pre-registration in the Pre-RAIPRE, plants had a deadline of 36 months to be definitively registered in the RAIPRE so as to enable them to benefit from the Special Regime.[139]

According to Spain's arguments during the *Antin* case, the tariff deficit had "arisen from the difference between the regulated tariffs set by the Government and paid by consumers and the real costs associated with said tariffs".[140] The tariff deficit actually refers to the regulated electricity access charges (i.e. retail price for a final consumer) and the cost of the whole electricity system, including but not limited to renewable subsidies.[141] In other words, the tariff deficit is the result of an imbalance between costs to the system (such as subsidies to energy producers) and revenue (consumer payments).[142]

The arbitral tribunals were divided on how to assess the starting point of the tariff deficit. On the one hand, the *RWE* tribunal considered that the tariff deficit was caused by electricity consumption decreases following the global economic crisis in 2008.[143] The drop in electricity demand at that time was undisputed.[144] On the other hand, the *Watkins* tribunal considered that the tariff deficit existed "long before" the economic crisis, and even resulted from

> the costs of the electricity tariff and its calendar. In any event, the rights and expectations of the owners of the facilities are respected, with the necessary caution being exercised and the necessary transitional regime for adaption being envisaged

– as translated in Stadtwerke v. Spain, ibid [297], [298]. See also for example: InfraRed v. Spain, *supra* note 52 [34], Cavalum v. Spain, *supra* note 34 [506].

136 Art. 1 RDL 6/2009, Antin v. Spain, *supra* note 6 [100], Cube v. Spain, *supra* note 52 [323], RWE v. Spain, *supra* note 28 [180], Watkins v. Spain, *supra* note 31 [103], Hydro v. Spain, *supra* note 34 [113].

137 Art. 4(1) RDL 6/2009.

138 NextEra v. Spain, *supra* note 31 [130], InfraRed v. Spain, *supra* note 52 [35], RWE v. Spain, *supra* note 28 [180].

139 Art. 4 RDL 6/2009, Antin v. Spain, *supra* note 6 [100], RREEF v. Spain, *supra* note 15 [117], Watkins v. Spain, *supra* note 31 [104].

140 Antin v. Spain, ibid [99].

141 Foresight v. Spain, *supra* note 18 [56], [114].

142 SolEs v. Spain, *supra* note 16 [434].

143 RWE v. Spain, *supra* note 28 [559].

144 RREEF v. Spain, *supra* note 15 [98], Hydro v. Spain, *supra* note 34 [116].

Spain's "own regulatory conduct".[145] For the *Foresight* tribunal, the tariff deficit first materialized in 2000, although it did not become material until 2005.[146]

Regardless of when the tariff deficit is deemed to have first existed, it was commonly agreed that the 2008 financial crisis ("Financial Crisis") had a material impact on the accumulation of the tariff deficit. That crisis has been described as the "Great Recession in Spain" and the "Great Spanish Depression".[147] It produced "severe effects on both the demand for electricity and capital market yields".[148] In the Spanish saga arbitrations, Spain linked its rationale for adopting the disputed measures to the Financial Crisis.[149]

As of 07.05.2009, when RDL 6/2009 entered into force, the total capacity of CSP facilities registered in the RAIPRE was 81 MW, much below the 500 MW target stipulated in RDL 661/2007. Later this year, on 19.11.2009, there were 104 registration requests, representing 4.499 MW from CSP technology seeking to qualify under the Special Regime.[150] If all of these requests had been accepted, it would have resulted in the total installed capacity exceeding the objectives set forth in RD 661/2007. Despite that, the government approved the progressive registration of all such new facilities in the Pre-RAIPRE and in the RAIPRE, as it also approved their progressive entry into operation until 01.01.2014.[151] This resulted in discussions held between the government and the "CSP and wind RE associations". On 02.07.2010, the government issued a press release announcing an agreement which included "short-term measures, which will allow the impact of the price of electricity from these technologies to be reduced, as well as long-term measures, which will guarantee future

145 Watkins v. Spain, *supra* note 31 [599].

146 This subsequently grew to over 6 billion Euros in 2008, before returning to a surplus in 2014 – see: Foresight v. Spain, *supra* note 18 [116]. Similarly, for example: SolEs v. Spain, *supra* note 16 [116], BayWa v. Spain, *supra* note 28 [213]. On an accumulated basis, by 2013 the tariff deficit exceeded 40 billion Euros (approximately 4% of Spain's GDP), an increase of 271% from 2007, when the accumulated deficit was of approximately 10.8 billion Euros – see: Foresight v. Spain, *supra* note 18 [117]. The amounts are inconsistent, and for example *RREEF* tribunal indicated the amount of 20 billion Euros by 2009 and 26 billion Euro by 2013 – RREEF v. Spain, *supra* note 15 [99], [116]. The *InfraRed* tribunal indicated 20 billion Euros by 2013 – InfraRed v. Spain, *supra* note 52 [33]. The BayWa tribunal considered it as "almost" 30 billion Euros by 2013 – BayWa v. Spain, *supra* note 28 [213].

147 https://en.wikipedia.org/wiki/2008–2014_Spanish_financial_crisis.

148 Novenergia v. Spain, *supra* note 52 [348].

149 See for example: Novenergia v. Spain, ibid [332].

150 InfraRed v. Spain, *supra* note 52 [16].

151 Antin v. Spain, *supra* note 6 [101], NextEra v. Spain, *supra* note 31 [132].

stability for both sectors" (the "2010 Agreement").[152] It provided that the CSP plants had waived their entitlement to the Premium during their first year of operations and accepted a delayed date for commencing their operations, and that the number of energy production hours entitled to compensation above market prices will be limited to reflect the 2005–2010 Plan's assumptions.[153]

5 2010 Disputed Measures

In 2010, Spain accounted for half of all solar power installed globally.[154] It far surpassed the PV energy target specified in RD 661/2007 (by 2010, Spain achieved an aggregate installed PV capacity of over 3.960 MW, compared to its target of 371 MW).[155] RE generally accounted for 13.2% of Spain's total energy consumption and 29.2% of the energy it produced.[156] Thus, Spain exceeded the 2005–2010 Plan's goal of providing 12% of its energy demand from renewable sources by 2010, and it was close to meeting the goal of producing 29.4% of its energy from renewable sources.

This was the situation when Spain adopted the first measures to modify the Special Regime. They later became the disputed measures in the Spanish saga arbitrations.

Royal Decree 1565/2010 ("RD 1565/2010"), adopted on 19.11.2010, was the first of them.[157] It limited to 25 years the period during which the FIT set forth in RD 661/2007 was payable.[158]

152 Antin v. Spain, ibid [102], InfraRed v. Spain, *supra* note 52 [41], Watkins v. Spain, *supra* note 31 [106].

153 Antin v. Spain, ibid, InfraRed v. Spain, ibid [46], RWE v. Spain, *supra* note 28 [184].

154 Foresight v. Spain, *supra* note 18 [92], Eiser v. Spain, *supra* note 7 [94], Elisabeth Rosenthal, Solar Industry Learns Lessons in Spanish Sun, The New York Times (03.08.2010), available at: http://www.geni.org/globalenergy/library/technical-articles/generation/solar/nytimes.com/solar-industry-learns-lessons-in-spanish-sun/index.shtml.

155 Between 2006 and 2007, Spain's installed PV capacity increased from approximately 167 MW to 690 MW, and it further increased to over 3.000 MW by 2008 – Foresight v. Spain, ibid [93].

156 Foresight v. Spain, ibid [93].

157 BOE-A-2010-17976, *«BOE» núm. 283, de 23 de noviembre de 2010, páginas 97428 a 97446, Real Decreto 1565/2010, de 19 de noviembre, por el que se regulan y modifican determinados aspectos relativos a la actividad de producción de energía eléctrica en régimen especial* (regulating and modifying specific aspects related to energy production in the special regime). See also: Isolux v. Spain, *supra* note 59 [112].

158 Foresight v. Spain, *supra* note 18 [58], [124], Cube v. Spain, *supra* note 52 [324], 9REN v. Spain, *supra* note 2 [107]. This period was subsequently extended to 28 years in RDL 14/2010 and 30 years in Law 2/2011.

Second, on 07.12.2010 Spain enacted RD 1614/2010 ("RD 1614/2010").[159] It was intended to "resolve certain inefficiencies in the application of… RDL 6/2009" in line with the 2010 Agreement.[160] It limited the number of hours per year during which CSP and Wind energy plants were entitled to receive payments under the Special Regime.[161] It also stipulated that such plants could not sell electricity under the Premium option during their first year (of the plant's operation or after the entry into force of RD 1614/2010, if the plant had already obtained its final commissioning certificate).[162]

Third, on 23.12.2010, Spain adopted Royal Decree-Law 14/2010 ("RDL 14/2010").[163] Among others, RDL 14/2010 introduced limits on the number of hours for which PV facilities could benefit from the remuneration payable under the Special Regime, by capping the annual operating hours. Once a facility reached the cap limit, it could sell the additional electricity at market prices, but it would not be entitled to benefits under the Special Regime.[164] In addition, RDL 14/2010 introduced an access toll for electricity fed into the grid, i.e. a fee for using the grid's transport and distribution networks, imposed on all energy producers (regardless of whether they operated under the Special or Ordinary Regime).[165]

---

159 BOE-A-2010-18915, *«BOE» núm. 298, de 8 de diciembre de 2010, páginas 101853 a 101859, Real Decreto 1614/2010, de 7 de diciembre, por el que se regulan y modifican determinados aspectos relativos a la actividad de producción de energía eléctrica a partir de tecnologías solar termoeléctrica y eólica* (regulating and modifying certain issues related to the production of energy from CSP and wind sources).

160 Antin v. Spain, *supra* note 6 [105], InfraRed v. Spain, *supra* note 52 [51]–[52], BayWa v. Spain, *supra* note 28 [168]–[169].

161 Art. 2 RD 1614/2010, Antin v. Spain, ibid [105], RREEF v. Spain, *supra* note 15 [122], NextEra v. Spain, *supra* note 31 [136], InfraRed v. Spain, ibid [52], BayWa v. Spain, ibid [171], RWE v. Spain, *supra* note 28 [187], Watkins v. Spain, *supra* note 31 [108], The PV Investors v. Spain, *supra* note 13 [201].

162 Art. 3 RD 1614/2010, Antin v. Spain, ibid [105], NextEra v. Spain, ibid [137].

163 BOE-A-2010-19757, *«BOE» núm. 312, de 24 de diciembre de 2010, páginas 106386 a 106394, Real Decreto-ley 14/2010, de 23 de diciembre, por el que se establecen medidas urgentes para la corrección del déficit tarifario del sector eléctrico* (establishing urgent measures for the correction of the tariff deficit of the electric sector). Its preamble referred to the tariff deficit, described as "the difference between the income generated by the tolls on the access to the electric energy transportation and distribution grids and the costs of regulated activities from the electric sector that said tolls are intended to cover". See for example: Hydro v. Spain, *supra* note 34 [120].

164 First Additional Provision to RDL 14/2010, Antin v. Spain, *supra* note 6 [106], Foresight v. Spain, *supra* note 18 [127], Masdar v. Spain, *supra* note 33 [124], 9REN v. Spain, *supra* note 2 [108], SolEs v. Spain, *supra* note 16 [122], InfraRed v. Spain, *supra* note 52 [55].

165 This was an implementation of Commission Regulation (EU) No 838/2010 of 23 September 2010 on laying down guidelines relating to the inter-transmission system operator compensation mechanism and a common regulatory approach to transmission charging

6 2012 Disputed Measures

On 20.11.2011, Spain held elections which resulted in the formation of a new government.[166] At that time, the tariff deficit "became a political issue".[167] The new prime minister referred to the accumulated tariff deficit and called for structural reforms to the energy system in his inaugural speech.[168] Shortly after, the new government took various steps to turn these words into action.[169]

On 27.01.2012, Spain adopted Royal Decree-Law 1/2012 ("RDL 1/2012").[170] It suspended the registration of new plants in the Pre-RAIPRE and prevented the application of the Special Regime to RE plants that had not been registered in the Pre-RAIPRE by the date of entry into force of RDL 1/2012.[171] RDL 1/2012 did not apply to plants which had already registered in the RAIPRE.[172]

On the same day, the government mandated CNE to prepare a report on the adjudicatory adjustment measures. The CNE prepared the report on 07.03.2012. It underlined the need to adopt urgent regulatory solutions and gave examples of such solutions.[173]

On 27.04.2012, the Spanish government approved the "2012 National Reforms Programme", which confirmed its intention to resolve the tariff deficit problem.[174] It set out a broad economic strategy, addressing the economic

---

(OJ L 250, 24.09.2010, p. 5–11) – Masdar v. Spain, ibid [126]. See also: Foresight v. Spain, ibid [58], [128], 9REN v. Spain, ibid [109], BayWa v. Spain, *supra* note 28 [173], RWE v. Spain, *supra* note 28 [189].

166 InfraRed v. Spain, *supra* note 52 [68], Eiser v. Spain, *supra* note 7 [137].

167 Foresight v. Spain, *supra* note 18 [120].

168 NextEra v. Spain, *supra* note 31 [142], InfraRed v. Spain, *supra* note 52 [68], OperaFund v. Spain, *supra* note 28 [228], Eiser v. Spain, *supra* note 7 [137].

169 Isolux v. Spain, *supra* note 59 [117], Eiser v. Spain, ibid [138].

170 BOE-A-2012-1310, *«BOE» núm. 24, de 28 de enero de 2012, páginas 8068 a 8072, Real Decreto-ley 1/2012, de 27 de enero, por el que se procede a la suspensión de los procedimientos de preasignación de retribución y a la supresión de los incentivos económicos para nuevas instalaciones de producción de energía eléctrica a partir de cogeneración, fuentes de energía renovables y residuos* (proceeding to the suspension of the remuneration pre-assignment procedures and the elimination of the economic incentives for new electric energy production plans using cogeneration, renewable energy sources, and waste).

171 Art. 3–4 RDL 1/2012, Antin v. Spain, *supra* note 6 [136], RREEF v. Spain, *supra* note 15 [125], NextEra v. Spain, *supra* note 31 [144], BayWa v. Spain, *supra* note 28 [180], Hydro v. Spain, *supra* note 34 [135].

172 Antin v. Spain, ibid [136].

173 RWE v. Spain, *supra* note 28 [213]–[214], Hydro v. Spain, *supra* note 34 [133], Cavalum v. Spain, *supra* note 34 [570], Eiser v. Spain, *supra* note 7 [138]. The CNE did not propose replacement of the Special Regime.

174 https://www.hacienda.gob.es/CDI/programanacionaldereformas/pnr_2012.pdf, Masdar v. Spain, *supra* note 33 [129], NextEra v. Spain, *supra* note 31 [146].

and financial crisis in Spain and highlighted the growing public debt.[175] It was not limited to RE, but it identified the Special Regime as one of the most significant costs of Spain's electrical system.[176]

On 20.07.2012, Spain signed a Memorandum of Understanding on financial-sector policy conditionality ("MoU") with the EU.[177] The MoU was signed in the context of the financial crisis and included reference to the Spanish tariff deficit in the energy sector.[178]

On 27.12.2012, Spain adopted Law 15/2012 ("Law 15/2012").[179] It imposed a 7% levy on all electricity fed into the national grid ("IVPEE", as derived from the Spanish name *impuesto al valor de la producción de la energía eléctrica*).[180] The IVPEE applied to production revenues (not profits) and extended to electrical energy produced from all sources (both renewable and conventional) within all applicable regimes (Ordinary Regime and Special Regime), regardless of the quantity or quality of the produced electric energy and the category of the producer.[181] Law 15/2012 introduced another 2.2% levy on Hydro energy producers ("Water Levy").[182] Moreover, it abolished the right to

175 Antin v. Spain, *supra* note 6 [138].

176 Ibid.

177 Novenergia v. Spain, *supra* note 52 [352], although with reference to the MoU from 12.07.2012, not 20.07.2020, RREEF v. Spain, *supra* note 15 [102], OperaFund v. Spain, *supra* note 28 [244], RWE v. Spain, *supra* note 28 [215], Hydro v. Spain, *supra* note 34 [134].

178 Memorandum of Understanding on financial-sector policy conditionality (https://ec.europa.eu/economy_finance/eu_borrower/mou/2012-07-20-spain-mou_en.pdf), [31]:

> Regarding structural reforms, the Spanish authorities are committed to implement the country-specific recommendations in the context of the European Semester. These reforms aim at correcting macroeconomic imbalances, as identified in the in-depth review under the Macroeconomic Imbalance Procedure (MIP). In particular, these recommendations invite Spain to: [...] complete the electricity and gas interconnections with neighbouring countries, and address the electricity tariff deficit in a comprehensive way.

179 BOE-A-2012-15649, *«BOE» núm. 312, de 28 de diciembre de 2012, páginas 88081 a 88096, Ley 15/2012, de 27 de diciembre, de medidas fiscales para la sostenibilidad energética* (on tax measures for energy sustainability).

180 Cube v. Spain, *supra* note 52 [361], 9REN v. Spain, *supra* note 2 [110], Stadtwerke v. Spain, *supra* note 6 [90], RWE v. Spain, *supra* note 28 [216].

181 Arts. 6(1) and 8 Law 15/2012, Novenergia v. Spain, *supra* note 52 [129], Antin v. Spain, *supra* note 6 [141], Foresight v. Spain, *supra* note 18 [58], [129], RREEF v. Spain, *supra* note 15 [127], NextEra v. Spain, *supra* note 31 [150], InfraRed v. Spain, *supra* note 52 [73], BayWa v. Spain, *supra* note 28 [188], Watkins v. Spain, *supra* note 31 [114].

182 Hydro v. Spain, *supra* note 34 [140].

use fossil fuels, including natural gas, in any facility which benefitted from the Special Regime.[183]

7 2013–2014 Disputed Measures

On 01.02.2013, Spain adopted Royal Decree-Law 2/2013 ("RDL 2/2013").[184] Its preamble noted the intention to reduce the costs of the Special Regime and avoid further increases in the fees paid by consumers.[185] It reduced to zero the Premium provided for in RD 661/2007, leaving only the FIT option.[186] Plants

---

183 First Final Provision of the Law 15/2012, Masdar v. Spain, *supra* note 33 [130], Antin v. Spain, *supra* note 6 [139]–[140], InfraRed v. Spain, *supra* note 52 [73]. It also eliminated an exemption of the hydrocarbons levy for the supply and import of natural gas to the extent it was used for any purposes other than engine fuel and heating fuel – Masdar v. Spain, *supra* note 33 [130].

184 BOE-A-2013-1117, *«BOE» núm. 29, de 2 de febrero de 2013, páginas 9072 a 9077, Real Decreto-ley 2/2013, de 1 de febrero, de medidas urgentes en el sistema eléctrico y en el sector financiero* (concerning urgent measures in the electric system and financial sector).

185 For example:

> [...] In recent years, the growing evolution of the cost elements of the electricity system has given rise to the appearance of imbalances between said costs and the revenue obtained from regulated prices. In order to correct these imbalances, a series of urgent measures during 2012 were adopted which affected both elements. [...] Data made public by the National Energy Commission in its report 35/2012, of 20 December, concerning the proposal which established access fees as of 1 January 2013 and tariffs and premiums for special regime facilities, made manifest the appearance of new deviations in the cost and revenue estimates caused by different factors, both for the closure of 2012 and for 2013 which, in the current economic context, would make it almost unfeasible to fund such costs with the electricity fees and the elements expected to derive from the General State Budget. To a great extent these deviations are due to a greater increase in the cost of the special regime on account of an increase in operating hours which was greater than expected, to an increase in remuneration values due to their being indexed to the Brent price, and to a decrease in revenue from fees due to a very marked fall in demand which was consolidated during this tax year. The alternative that was raised would be a new increase in the access fees paid by consumers of electricity. This measure would directly affect household economies and company competitiveness, both in a delicate situation given the current economic situation. Faced with this scenario and in order to palliate this problem, the Government has considered adopting certain urgent cost-reduction measures which avoid consumers having to bear a new burden, thereby contributing to their being able to also collaborate in the economic recovery through consumption and investment. [...]

(as translated in Antin v. Spain, *supra* note 6 [142]).

186 Art. 2 RDL 2/2013, Antin v. Spain, ibid [144], RREEF v. Spain, *supra* note 15 [131], NextEra v. Spain, *supra* note 31 [153], Cube v. Spain, *supra* note 52 [364], InfraRed v. Spain,

registered with the Special Regime, which until that moment had opted to sell their energy using the Premium option were deemed to have switched to the FIT option from 02.02.2013, with effect from 01.01.2013.[187] In addition, RDL 2/2013 amended the IPC, by excluding from its scope changes in the prices of food, energy products and certain tax effects.[188]

On 13.07.2013, Spain adopted Royal Decree-Law 9/2013 ("RDL 9/2013").[189] Its preamble again referred to the tariff deficit.[190] It established a new framework for remunerating RE plants (the "New Regime"), which replaced the Special Regime.[191] This required the amendment of Art. 30(4) LSE.[192] The New Regime

---

supra note 52 [75], BayWa v. Spain, *supra* note 28 [190], Stadtwerke v. Spain, *supra* note 6 [91], RWE v. Spain, *supra* note 28 [217], Watkins v. Spain, *supra* note 31 [117].

187 Arts. 2 and 3 RDL 2/2013, Antin v. Spain, ibid. Technically, they could have notified their decision to stay with the Premium option (reduced to zero), and such decision would have been definitive, with no possibility to switch to the FIT subsequently.

188 Art. 1 RDL 2/2013, Masdar v. Spain, *supra* note 33 [131], Antin v. Spain, ibid [143], Foresight v. Spain, *supra* note 18 [58], NextEra v. Spain, *supra* note 31 [152], BayWa v. Spain, *supra* note 28 [191], Watkins v. Spain, *supra* note 31 [118], 9REN v. Spain, *supra* note 2 [111], Stadtwerke v. Spain, *supra* note 6 [91], RWE v. Spain, *supra* note 28 [217], Hydro v. Spain, *supra* note 34 [143]. Initially, the amended IPC was lower than the general IPC, but the situation reversed from late 2014 – Foresight v. Spain, *supra* note 18 [130].

189 BOE-A-2013-7705, *«BOE» núm. 167, de 13 de julio de 2013, páginas 52106 a 52147, Real Decreto-ley 9/2013, de 12 de julio, por el que se adoptan medidas urgentes para garantizar la estabilidad financiera del sistema eléctrico* (adopting urgent measures to ensure the financial stability of the electric system).

190
> Between the years 2004 and 2012, the revenue of the electricity system due to consumer toll fees increased by 122%, while the increase of the regulated costs of the system during this period has been 197%. Among the cost headings that have contributed the most to the increase are the special regime premiums and the annuities of accumulated deficits, headings that have been multiplied by six and nine respectively in that period. According to the latest data available from the [CNE], there is a balance of accumulated debt of 26,062.51 million euros as of 10 May 2013. Complementary to the calculation of the debt of the electricity system, the [CNE] notes that since 2003 and until 10 May, 2013, the amount paid to finance the deficit of the electricity system through annuities incorporated into the consumer access tolls, at current prices for each year, amounts to 11,823 million euros. These figures give testimony of the unsustainable nature of the deficit of the electricity sector and the need to adopt urgent measures of an immediate effect that would put an end to this situation

(as translated in Cavalum v. Spain, *supra* note 34 [580]). See also: Cube v. Spain, *supra* note 52 [365], Hydro v. Spain, *supra* note 34 [146].

191 Novenergia v. Spain, *supra* note 52 [136]–[137], Masdar v. Spain, *supra* note 33 [132], Foresight v. Spain, *supra* note 18 [58], Cube v. Spain, ibid [366], 9REN v. Spain, *supra* note 2 [112], Watkins v. Spain, *supra* note 31 [121].

192 RWE v. Spain, *supra* note 28 [219], Watkins v. Spain, ibid [122], Hydro v. Spain, *supra* note 34 [147]. Art. 1(2) RDL 9/2013 amended Art. 30(4) LSE to the following wording:

> Additionally, and in the terms legally determined by Royal Decree of the Council of Ministers, for the remuneration for the sale of generated energy valued at market

applied to all plants which were already in operation on the date of its entry into force.[193]

In short, RDL 9/2013 eliminated the entire Special Regime consisting of FIT and Premiums, and replaced it by a system which provided for a "specific remuneration" ("Special Payment") based on "standard" (but not actual) costs per unit of installed power, plus standard amounts for operating costs.[194]

The New Regime was based on the investment costs of "model facilities" defined by reference to "an efficient and well-managed company". The Special

---

> price, the facilities may receive specific remuneration that consists in a term for each installed capacity unit, covering, where applicable, the investment costs of a model facility that cannot be recovered by the sale of energy and a term for operation covering, where appropriate, the difference between operation costs and the revenue for the market share of said model facility.
>
> To calculate said specific remuneration for a model facility, during its regulatory lifespan, and in reference to the activity carried out by an efficient and well-managed company, the following shall be considered:
>
> a) The standard revenue from the sale of generated energy valued at the market price of production.
>
> b) The standard operation costs.
>
> c) The standard value of the initial investment.
>
> For this purpose, under no circumstance shall the costs or investments that are determined by regulation or administrative acts that are not applicable throughout the Spanish territory be taken into account. Similarly, only the costs and investments that respond exclusively to electric energy production shall be taken into account.
>
> As a consequence of the unique characteristics of the insular and non-mainland electric systems, facilities may be exceptionally defined as specific model facilities for each one of them.
>
> This remuneration regime shall not exceed the minimum necessary level to cover the costs that allow the facilities to compete on an equal footing with the rest of technologies and to enable obtaining a reasonable return by reference to the model facility applicable in each case. [...]
>
> This reasonable return shall turn, before taxes, on the average yield of ten year Government bonds on the secondary market, applying the adequate differential.
>
> The parameters of the remuneration regime may be revised every six years.

(as translated in Novenergia v. Spain, *supra* note 52 [138]). See the previous wording above, fn 61.

193 Novenergia v. Spain, ibid [140]–[143].

194 RREEF v. Spain, *supra* note 15 [132], InfraRed v. Spain, *supra* note 52 [77], Stadtwerke v. Spain, *supra* note 6 [92]. The New Regime quashed the incentive applicable under the Special Regime to build more expensive, but also more productive plants – RREEF v. Spain, *supra* note 15 [141]:

> The new regime provides revenues which are no longer correlated only to the actual production of the installation. It becomes less profitable for significant installations like the Claimants' CSP plants but can sometimes generate more revenue stream in certain conditions.

Payment was calculated based on (i) standard revenues for the sale of generated energy valued at market price of production; (ii) standard exploitation (operating) costs and (iii) the standard value of the initial investment, as opposed to the actual energy production which was relevant under the Special Regime.[195] The second and third elements were not defined in RDL 9/2013 and were, instead, left to be defined in future regulations.[196] Point (ii) – "operating incentive" was designed to compensate the gap between the OPEX and the wholesale price of electricity, whereas point (iii) – "investment incentive" was designed to compensate the CAPEX.[197] The Special Payment was subject to review every six years.[198]

On 26.12.2013, Spain adopted Law 24/2013 on the Electric Sector ("New LSE").[199] Its preamble again referred to the tariff deficit.[200] The New LSE

---

195 RREEF v. Spain, ibid [132], NextEra v. Spain, *supra* note 31 [158], Watkins v. Spain, *supra* note 31 [123], The PV Investors v. Spain, *supra* note 13 [206], Isolux v. Spain, *supra* note 59 [135].

196 BayWa v. Spain, *supra* note 28 [194], Hydro v. Spain, *supra* note 34 [149].

197 BayWa v. Spain, ibid [193].

198 Antin v. Spain, *supra* note 6 [148].

199 BOE-A-2013-13645, *«BOE» núm. 310, de 27 de diciembre de 2013, páginas 105198 a 105294, Ley 24/2013, de 26 de diciembre, del Sector Eléctrico* (Law on Energy Sector).

200 [...] a decisive element for undertaking this reform was also the accumulation during the last decade of annual imbalances between income and costs of the electrical system which has brought about the appearance of a structural deficit. The causes of this imbalance lie in the excessive growth of certain costs' items owing to energy policy decisions without ensuring their correlative income from the system. This has all been exacerbated by the lack of growth in electrical demand, essentially the consequence of the economic crisis. [...] The imbalance has reached the point where the accumulated debt of the electrical system is currently in excess of twenty six billion Euros, the structural deficit of the system stands at ten billion per annum and the failure to correct the imbalance has introduced the risk of the bankruptcy of the electrical system. [LSE] has proven insufficient to ensure the financial balance of the system, amongst other reasons because the remuneration system for regulated activities has lacked the flexibility required for its adaptation to major changes in the electrical system or in the evolution of the economy. Hence, the experience of the last decade has made it clear that the economic and financial instability of the electrical system, brought about by the tariff deficit, has prevented the assurance of a stable regulatory framework which is necessary for the smooth carrying out of an activity like the electrical business which is very capital intensive. Hence, the economic unsustainability of the electrical system, along with the continuous evolution in the sector during the last sixteen years, has required the legislator to adapt, on numerous occasions, [LSE] often through the approval of urgent measures by Royal Decree and at present there is a normative dispersion which is not desirable in such a relevant economic sector. [...] Essentially, the continuous normative changes have entailed an important distortion to the normal operation of the electrical system and which needs to be corrected through action by

explicitly recognized the "principle of economic sustainability" of the Spanish electrical system.[201] It replaced the LSE and confirmed that it abolished the distinction between the Ordinary Regime and the Special Regime.[202] All power plants became subject to equal conditions, regardless of the source of their energy production, although RE producers were entitled to the Special Payment introduced by RDL 9/2013.[203] The New LSE maintained the priority right over grid access and priority of dispatch that were enjoyed by RE producers.[204]

In the months following the adoption of RDL 9/2013 and Law 24/2013, the New Regime was not yet operational, and the FIT under the Special Regime (but not the Premium, which had been "zeroed" by RDL 9/2013) continued to apply.[205] However, the value of any payments received during this time

> the legislator which lends the regulatory stability that electrical activity requires. This regulatory safety, combined with the need to undertake the reforms needed to ensure the sustainability of system in the long-term and to resolve the existing shortcomings in system operation would recommend the approval of an overall reform of the sector, based on a new income and expenses regime for the electrical system which tries to return to the system the financial sustainability it lost a long time ago and whose eradication has not been achieved to date through the adoption of partial measures. [...] The remuneration regime for renewable energies, cogeneration and waste will be based on the necessary participation in the market of these installations, complemented by market income with specific regulated remuneration which enables these technologies to compete on an equal footing with the other technologies on the market. This specific complementary remuneration will be sufficient to attain the minimum level to cover any costs which, by contrast to conventional technologies, they cannot recover on the market and will allow them to obtain a suitable return with reference to the installation type applicable in each case.

(as translated in Cavalum v. Spain, *supra* note 34 [584]). See also: Cube v. Spain, *supra* note 52 [368]–[369], Hydro v. Spain, *supra* note 34 [150].

201 Foresight v. Spain, *supra* note 18 [58], InfraRed v. Spain, *supra* note 52 [78], BayWa v. Spain, *supra* note 28 [196], Watkins v. Spain, *supra* note 31 [126].

202 Novenergia v. Spain, *supra* note 52 [145], Masdar v. Spain, *supra* note 33 [133], Antin v. Spain, *supra* note 6 [150], Foresight v. Spain, ibid [135], RREEF v. Spain, *supra* note 15 [135], NextEra v. Spain, *supra* note 31 [163], SolEs v. Spain, *supra* note 16 [129], InfraRed v. Spain, ibid [79], Stadtwerke v. Spain, *supra* note 6 [93], Watkins v. Spain, ibid [127].

203 Art. 14(7) New LSE, Antin v. Spain, ibid [150], NextEra v. Spain, ibid [165].

204 Art. 26(2) New LSE, although not considered as a "right" and subject to "the requirements pertaining to the maintenance of system reliability and safety, under the terms determined in the regulations by the Government". See also: RREEF v. Spain, *supra* note 15 [136], The PV Investors v. Spain, *supra* note 13 [211]. Contrary: Antin v. Spain, ibid [150], considering that the right was removed.

205 NextEra v. Spain, *supra* note 31 [160], BayWa v. Spain, *supra* note 28 [195], The PV Investors v. Spain, ibid [207].

were to be deducted from payments under the New Regime once it became operational.[206]

In 2014, Spain took the final steps in the regulatory process to implement the New Regime. On 06.06.2014, it adopted Royal Decree 413/2014 ("RD 413/2014").[207] It specified the model (formulas) based on a hypothetical "efficient" plant, which were necessary elements of the Special Payment.[208] The remuneration payable was capped at a level which would be received by a notional "standard installation" with a standard operational life of 25 years. The FIT and Premium payments received under the Special Regime were credited towards the total (lifetime) remuneration available under the New Regime. If a RE plant surpassed the "reasonable return" threshold of IRR at 7.398% pre-tax under the New Regime, it was not entitled to receive further subsidies, but it was not obliged to return any "excess" amounts.[209]

However, crucial details of the New Regime still remained unclear, pending the adoption of a ministerial order. This happened on 16.06.2014, when Order IET/1045/2014 ("Order IET/1045/2014") was adopted.[210] It marked the definitive end of the Special Regime, being the last step required to implement the New Regime:

> This order finalizes the changes to the remuneration model for renewable energy, co-generation and wastes, granting financial stability to the system in a definitive manner, at the same time as it guarantees a reasonable return on the installations.[211]

206 Antin v. Spain, *supra* note 6 [150], Foresight v. Spain, *supra* note 18 [134].

207 BOE-A-2014-6123, *«BOE» núm. 140, de 10 de junio de 2014, páginas 43876 a 43978, Real Decreto 413/2014, de 6 de junio, por el que se regula la actividad de producción de energía eléctrica a partir de fuentes de energía renovables, cogeneración y residuos* (on the regulation of the electric energy production activity from renewable energy, cogeneration and waste).

208 InfraRed v. Spain, *supra* note 52 [82], Stadtwerke v. Spain, *supra* note 6 [94], Watkins v. Spain, *supra* note 31 [131].

209 Eiser v. Spain, *supra* note 7 [148], RREEF v. Spain, *supra* note 15 [138], 9REN v. Spain, *supra* note 2 [114], although naming it as the "clawback", Hydro v. Spain, *supra* note 34 [157], [162]-[163], Masdar v. Spain, *supra* note 33 [135], BayWa v. Spain, *supra* note 28 [204].

210 BOE-A-2014-6495, *«BOE» núm. 150, de 20 de junio de 2014, páginas 46430 a 48190, Orden IET/1045/2014, de 16 de junio, por la que se aprueban los parámetros retributivos de las instalaciones tipo aplicables a determinadas instalaciones de producción de energía eléctrica a partir de fuentes de energía renovables, cogeneración y residuos* (approving the remuneration parameters for model facilities applicable to certain facilities of electric energy production using renewable energy resources, cogeneration, and waste).

211 Preamble of Order IET/1045/2014, as translated in Masdar v. Spain, *supra* note 33 [136].

Order IET/1045/2014 was 1.761 pages long and set "remuneration parameters" for 1.517 different "standard facilities".[212] Each facility was assigned one of the "standard" facility codes ("IT Codes"), based on a number of factors, such as its technology type, capacity, date of installation and location. Each IT Code determined the parameters of the Special Payment applicable to that standard facility, such as an imputed investment cost, estimated current operating costs, estimated future operating costs, estimated hours of operation, estimated daily and intraday market prices of electricity and net asset value of the facility.[213]

In summary, the remuneration of RE facilities under the New Regime comprised two elements: (i) market remuneration, i.e. the sale of electricity in the wholesale market, and (ii) the Special Payment. The latter was based on "standard", not actual, costs. It consisted of an "operating incentive", intended to compensate facilities for operating expenses not covered by the wholesale price of electricity, and an "investment incentive" intended to cover investment (capital) costs, and a "reasonable rate of return" over a defined operational life.[214] The "reasonable rate of return" was initially the 10-year average of Spanish 10-year treasury bonds, plus 300 basis points, which was 7.398% pre-tax for 2013–2018.[215] The parameters used to set the operating incentive were subject to revision every three years, whilst the parameters for the investment incentive and the level of the "reasonable rate of return" were subject to revision every six years.[216]

On 14.10.2014, Spain adopted Ministerial Order IET/1882/2014 ("Order IET/1882/2014").[217] In line with Law 15/2012, electricity produced by RE plants with the use of fossil fuels was not entitled to receive Special Payments under the New Regime. Thus, Order IET/1882/2014 ordered that any FIT or Premium payments received for such energy produced since 01.01.2013 (i.e. date of entry into force of the Law 15/2012) must be returned.[218]

---

212 Foresight v. Spain, *supra* note 18 [138], Cube v. Spain, *supra* note 52 [376], Hydro v. Spain, *supra* note 34 [158], Cavalum v. Spain, *supra* note 34 [592].

213 Foresight v. Spain, ibid [139], BayWa v. Spain, *supra* note 28 [200].

214 Foresight v. Spain, ibid [137]. The regulatory life was shortened to 20/25 years, depending on the type of the RE technology, whereas the Special Regime envisaged payments also after the regulatory life, even if in lower amounts – RWE v. Spain, *supra* note 28 [225].

215 Foresight v. Spain, ibid [137], NextEra v. Spain, *supra* note 31 [159], Cube v. Spain, *supra* note 52 [378].

216 Foresight v. Spain, ibid [141].

217 BOE-A-2014-10475, *«BOE» núm. 251, de 16 de octubre de 2014, páginas 83700 a 83707, Orden IET/1882/2014, de 14 de octubre, por la que se establece la metodología para el cálculo de la energía eléctrica imputable a la utilización de combustibles en las instalaciones solares termoeléctricas* (for calculating the electricity produced by solar installations attributable to the use of fossil fuels).

218 Antin v. Spain, *supra* note 6 [152], RREEF v. Spain, *supra* note 15 [140].

The New Regime was not based on any studies conducted by external consultants. Whilst Spain ordered that two reports be prepared, neither of them influenced the preparation or implementation of the New Regime.[219] The final version of a report prepared by Roland Berger "was only issued after the completion of the regulatory reform", and the final report of the Boston Consulting Group ("BCG") "was never issued given that BCG's mandate was prematurely terminated".[220] Despite that, the New Regime was successful in eliminating the tariff deficit.[221] It also did not halt investments in Spain's RE sector. The New Regime attracted over 5 billion Euros in investment in the RE sector in 2015 alone.[222]

8 2019 Measures

On 22.11.2019, the Spanish government adopted Royal Decree-Law 17/2019 ("RDL 17/2019").[223] In accordance with the Special Payment's 6-years' periodical review, RDL 17/2019 fixed a new rate of "reasonable rate of return" for RE producers in 2020–2025 period at 7.09% pre-taxes.[224]

For RE producers which were entitled to the FIT or Premium prior to the entry into force of the New Regime, RDL 17/2019 promised an increased reasonable rate of return for the next two remuneration periods (2020–2031), at the previously applicable 7.398% level. However, in order to benefit from the increased rate, foreign investors must agree not to commence arbitral and/or judicial claims related to the 2013–2014 Disputed Measures. Those which had already commenced such proceedings were required to withdraw such claims before 30.09.2020.[225]

219 OperaFund v. Spain, *supra* note 28 [261], [265], [269].

220 InfraRed v. Spain, *supra* note 52 [466]. See also for example: OperaFund v. Spain, ibid [273]-[274], [286]-[287].

221 See for example: Dromgool, Enguix, *supra* note 54, p. 393. See also for example: BayWa v. Spain, *supra* note 28 [215], Eiser v. Spain, *supra* note 7 [150].

222 Watkins v. Spain, *supra* note 31 [461], Cavalum v. Spain, *supra* note 34 [267], Hydro v. Spain, *supra* note 34 [412].

223 BOE-A-2019-16862, *«BOE» núm. 282, de 23 de noviembre de 2019, páginas 129281 a 129288, Real Decreto-ley 17/2019, de 22 de noviembre, por el que se adoptan medidas urgentes para la necesaria adaptación de parámetros retributivos que afectan al sistema eléctrico y por el que se da respuesta al proceso de cese de actividad de centrales térmicas de generación* (which adopts urgent measures for the necessary adaptation of remuneration parameters that affect the electricity system and which responds to the process of cessation of activity of thermal generation plants).

224 Art. 1(1) RDL 17/2019.

225 Point 2 of the second final disposition of RDL 17/2019, which introduced third final disposition bis to the New LSE.

Publicly available information reveals that some foreign investors decided to withdraw from ongoing arbitrations in order to benefit from the increased rate of reasonable return. This is true of the claimants in the *Masdar*, *RREEF* and *Stadtwerke* cases, plus some of the claimants in the *PV Investors* case. This is most probably not an exhaustive list.[226] It is unclear whether the decisive factor was the amount to be received under RDL 17/2019 or, rather, the uncertainties related to enforcing any arbitral award which awarded compensation (in the light of Spain's attempts to annul or set aside such awards and its visible reluctance to admit any obligation to pay any compensation which had been awarded).

9 Spanish Domestic Courts' Judgments

Numerous proceedings were commenced before the Spanish courts regarding the reforms to the Spanish regulatory framework for the RE sector. In general terms, they can be divided into two groups – cases concluded prior to the disputed measures and those concluded after, concerning the disputed measures.

As regards the first group, in 2005 the Spanish Supreme Court dismissed challenges against RD 436/2004. It explained, among others, that:

> there is no legal obstacle [...] to prevent the Government, in the exercise of the regulatory powers and of the broad entitlements it has in a strongly regulated issue such as electricity, from modifying a specific system of remuneration so long as this is done within the framework established by the [LSE].[227]

226 Lisa Bohmer, Masdar v. Spain case is discontinued (IA Reporter, 01.12.2020, available at: https://www.iareporter.com/articles/masdar-v-spain-case-is-discontinued/), Lisa Bohmer, RREEF and Stadtwerke are said to renounce their arbitration claims against Spain (IA Reporter, 22.10.2020, https://www.iareporter.com/articles/rreef-and-stadtwerke-are-said-to-renounce-their-arbitration-claims-against-spain/). With respect to the Masdar case, it was reported that "the ad hoc Committee issues an order taking note of the discontinuance of the proceeding pursuant to ICSID Arbitration Rule 44" - https://icsid.worldbank.org/cases/case-database/case-detail?CaseNo=ARB/14/1. This suggests that one party requested discontinuance of the annulment proceedings, whereas the other party did not oppose to the discontinuance

227 Supreme Court, judgment of 15.12.2005, STS 7633/2005, 73/2004, as translated in NextEra v. Spain, *supra* note 31 [113]. See also for example: NextEra v. Spain, ibid [115], OperaFund v. Spain, *supra* note 28 [145], Cavalum v. Spain, *supra* note 34 [510], BayWa v. Spain, *supra* note 28 [107].

In 2006 the Supreme Court stated, among others, that:

> electricity producers under the special regime do not have an unalterable right to remain in an unchanged economic regime governing the collection of premiums. The scheme is, in fact, to encourage the use of renewable energy through an incentive mechanism, like all of this genre, and cannot be guaranteed to remain unchanged in the future. [...] If the change has not deviated from these legal guidelines and, again, there is no allegation of infringement of Article 30 of the [LSE], it can hardly be considered unlawful.[228]

On 20.03.2007, the Supreme Court confirmed that Spanish law does not recognize the existence of any vested right to receive a particular incentive:

> what article 30 of the LSE allows companies is to aspire that the premiums would include ... reasonable return rates in relation to the cost of money in the capital market; that is, a reasonable return on their investments. Owners of facilities under a Special Regime are not guaranteed the intangibility of a given benefit or income regime in relation to those obtained in previous years, nor are they guaranteed the indefinite permanence of the formulas used to fix premiums. Changes should be made within the legal limits.[229]

It adopted a similar position in another judgment of 09.10.2007.[230]

On 09.12.2009, the Supreme Court noted that its previous judgments had established a line of case law which clarified that, under Spanish law, there was no "unmodifiable right" to expect that the remuneration scheme would remain unchanged, provided that the reforms remained within the scope of the LSE.[231]

228 Supreme Court, judgment of 25.10.2006, STS 6317/2006, 11/2005, as translated in Cavalum v. Spain, ibid [511]. See also: Hydro v. Spain, *supra* note 34 [124], BayWa v. Spain, ibid [112].

229 Supreme Court, judgment of 20.03.2007, STS 1653/2007, 12/2005, as translated in Cavalum v. Spain, ibid [513]. See also: OperaFund v. Spain, *supra* note 28 [153], [166], Hydro v. Spain, ibid [126], BayWa v. Spain, ibid [121].

230 Supreme Court, judgment of 09.10.2007, STS 6315/2007, 13/2006. See also: Cavalum v. Spain, ibid [514], OperaFund v. Spain, ibid [153], [166], Hydro v. Spain, ibid [126], BayWa v. Spain, ibid [134].

231 Supreme Court, judgment of 09.12.2009, STS 7629/2009, 149/2007. In the same line: Supreme Court, judgment of 03.12.2009, STS 7961/2009, 151/2007. See also: OperaFund v. Spain, ibid [204]–[205], Hydro v. Spain, ibid [127]–[131], BayWa v. Spain, ibid [148]–[149].

The Supreme Court confirmed this position in 2012, when it dismissed challenges to the 2010 Disputed Measures. It reaffirmed that the remuneration regime which applied to RE producers could be validly modified, in accordance with the principle of reasonable return envisaged in the LSE. The Supreme Court did not consider that this amounted to "prohibited retroactivity".[232]

Similarly, as regards the disputed measures that were adopted later, the Supreme Court consistently, although not unanimously, dismissed challenges against them.[233]

On 01.06.2016, it rejected challenges to the 2013–2014 Disputed Measures, reaffirming its previous case law on the lack of any "unmodifiable right" in Spanish law.[234] A similar position was adopted shortly after, on 12.07.2016 and on 22.07.2016.[235] The Supreme Court then underlined that its case law:

232 Antin v. Spain, *supra* note 6 [107], OperaFund v. Spain, ibid [237], BayWa v. Spain, ibid [183]. See for example: Supreme Court, judgment of 12.04.2012, STS 2320/2012, 40/2011, Supreme Court, judgment of 12.04.2012, STS 2577/2012, 59/2011, Supreme Court, judgment of 19.06.2012, STS 4253/2012, 62/2011, all of which stipulated as follows:

> the concept of "prohibited retroactivity" is much more limited than that of mere "retroactivity" [...] the remit of prohibited retroactivity does not include provisions which, lacking any ablative or pejorative effects towards the past (they do not require the revision nor removal of past facts, they do not alter the reality already experienced over time and they do not annul the legal effects exhausted), [...] deploy their immediate effectiveness looking towards the future even if this means impacting a relationship or legal situation which are still in progress. Based on this premise, a regulatory measure such as the one challenged in the present litigation, whose effectiveness is not planned "back" in time but rather "forward", once it has been approved, does not fall within the remit of prohibited retroactivity.

Similarly: Supreme Court, judgment of 24.09.2012, STS 6280/2012, 60/2011, Supreme Court, judgment of 25.09.2012, STS 5894/2012, 71/2011.

233 With exception of judgments annulling parts of the Order IET/1882/2014, for example because of finding "illegitimate omissions" in missing IT Codes (Supreme Court, judgment of 11.05.2016, STS 2059/2016, 833/2014) or "assigning values and parameters that do not conform to reality or correspond to the standards of the sector" to selected IT Codes (Supreme Court, judgment of 20.06.2016, STS 2859/2016, 485/2014). See for example: Supreme Court, judgment of 16.03.2015, STS 966/2015, 118/2013, Supreme Court, judgment of 17.03.2015, STS 1114/2015, 115/2013 Supreme Court, judgment of 17.03.2015, STS 1115/2015, 127/2013 (all three judgments with separate votes of Eduardo Calvo Rojas).

234 Supreme Court, judgment of 01.06.2016, STS 2430/2016, 649/2014. See for example: BayWa v. Spain, *supra* note 28 [210].

235 Supreme Court, judgment of 12.07.2016, STS 3421/2016, 456/2014, Supreme Court, judgment of 22.07.2016, STS 3796/2016, 500/2014. See for example: BayWa v. Spain, ibid [211].

> has been constant over the years on indicating that, in the interpretation and application of the rules ordering the legal and economic system for electricity generation based on renewable energy sources, such regulations guarantee reasonable return on their investments to the owners of these facilities, but do not acknowledge an unmodifiable right to them regarding the unalterability of the remuneration framework approved by the owner of the regulatory powers.[236]

It also stated that:

> it is not possible to counter the support through subsidies for renewable energy generation and the defence of the system's financial sustainability, when the latter is a necessary condition for the very survival thereof, since it is senseless to design a support system for these technologies that is financially unsustainable and, accordingly, is not economically viable in the medium and long term.[237]

It reaffirmed this position in other judgments.[238]

However, three of the seven judges issued dissenting opinions to the 2016 judgments, which were supported by a slight majority of 4 against 3 votes. In the words of one dissenter, the New Regime "is applied with full and absolute retroactivity [...] as if it had been in force from the very first moment that each facility commenced its regulatory life". In the opinion of those who dissented, this was unacceptable.[239]

Spain's Constitutional Court also continuously dismissed challenges to the 2012 and 2013–2014 Disputed Measures. On 06.11.2014, it dismissed constitutional challenges against Law 15/2012 and RDL 2/2013,[240] on 19.02.2015 it dis-

---

236 Supreme Court, judgment of 01.06.2016, STS 3421/2016, STS 456/2014, Supreme Court, judgment of 22.07.2016, STS 3796/2016, 500/2014, as translated in RWE v. Spain, *supra* note 28 [235].

237 Supreme Court, judgment of 12.07.2016, STS 3421/2016, 456/2014, as translated in Foresight v. Spain, *supra* note 18 [150]. See also: Supreme Court, judgment of 22.07.2016, STS 3796/2016, 500/2014.

238 Supreme Court, judgment of 18.05.2017, STS 1971/2017, 4953/2017.

239 Separate vote of Eduardo Espín Templado to the Supreme Court judgment of 12.07.2016, STS 3421/2016, 456/2014, Separate vote of Eduardo Espín Templado to the Supreme Court judgment of 12.07.2016, STS 3421/2016, 456/2014. See also: separate votes of Eduardo Calvo Rojas and Isabel Perelló Domenech to the same judgments. See also for example: BayWa v. Spain, *supra* note 28 [212].

240 Constitutional Court, judgment of 06.11.2014, case no 183/2014.

missed such challenges to RDL 2/2013,[241] and on 17.12.2015 and 18.02.2016 it dismissed challenges to RDL 9/2013.[242] The Spanish Constitutional Court ruled that the New Regime was valid. When assessed from the perspective of the Spanish Constitution, and as a matter of Spanish law, the New Regime neither violated investors' legitimate expectations nor had any prohibited retroactive effect.[243] This analysis did not take into account the (in)compatibility of the New Regime with international treaties, such as the ECT.[244]

10 Cases

This section briefly presents the first 21 Spanish saga cases: *Charanne, Isolux, Eiser, Novenergia, Masdar, Antin, Foresight, RREEF, Cube, NextEra, 9REN, SolEs, InfraRed, OperaFund, BayWa, Stadtwerke, RWE, Watkins, PV Investors, Hydro, Cavalum.* The cases are presented in chronological order, based on the issue date of an award (final or partial) or decision on liability, regardless of the date of any possible earlier partial awards/decisions on jurisdiction and/or later awards/decisions on damages (in bifurcated proceedings).

The presentation which follows below, and the analysis in Chapters 3–5, focuses on these first 21 arbitral awards issued in the Spanish saga cases. In this sense, the analysis is limited in time. Whilst it is tempting to constantly update the text to include the latest publicly available arbitral award (or an annulment decision in the ICSID context), this is either impossible or would cause

---

241 Constitutional Court, judgment of 19.02.2015, case no 28/2015, NextEra v. Spain, *supra* note 31 [152].

242 Constitutional Court, judgment of 17.12.2015, case no 270/2015, Constitutional Court, judgment of 04.02.2016, case no 29/2016, Constitutional Court, judgment of 18.02.2016, case no 30/2016, Constitutional Court, judgment of 17.03.2016, case no 61/2016. See also for example: NextEra v. Spain, ibid [161].

243 Foresight v. Spain, *supra* note 18 [149].

244 See for example: Carmen Otero García Castrillón, Spain and Investment Arbitration: the Renewable Energy Explosion, Investor-State Arbitration Series Paper no. 17, Centre for International Governance (2016), available at: https://eprints.ucm.es/id/eprint/40105/1/ISA%20Paper%20No.17.pdf, p. 7:

> However, international norms are not parameters of constitutionality and the Constitutional Court could not evaluate the eventual infringement of those rules by the internal laws – and, therefore, the violation of the normative hierarchy constitutional principle – since the claim did not include any reasoning on the substantive incompatibility between the ECT articles referred to above and the national provisions supposedly infringing them.

excessive delay in publishing the book.[245] This is confirmed by the simple fact that the most recent case was initiated as late as in 2022.[246]

This section's presentation is limited to a few basic parameters that are useful to set the scene for the analysis in the following Chapters. They include: (i) the date of the award, which explains the adopted chronological order, (ii) the arbitrators who decided the case, which indicates that repeat appointments are rare and therefore of limited impact on the analysis in Chapters 3–5,[247] (iii) the home states of the claimants, which is relevant to the analysis in Chapter 3, concerning the intra-EU scope of most of these cases, (iv) the dates of the investments and (v) the type of RE technology concerned in the cases. These last points are relevant to the analysis of liability, as discussed in Chapter 4.

10.1 *Charanne*

The award rendered in *Charanne v. Spain* is chronologically the first award rendered in the Spanish saga. It was issued on 21.01.2016.[248] The tribunal was composed of: Guido Santiago Tawil (claimants' nominee), Claus von Wobeser (respondent's nominee) and Alexis Mourre (president of the tribunal).[249] The claimants were a Dutch company (Charanne B.V.) and a Luxembourg company (Construction Investment S.r.l.).[250] They were minority shareholders in Grupo T-Solar Global S.A. ("T-Solar"). T-Solar owned 34 PV facilities.[251] The claimants acquired their shares in T-Solar in February and December 2009.[252]

This case is distinguishable from the other cases because it concerned only the 2010 Disputed Measures.[253] This was because, on 28.12.2012, the claimants sold their shares in T-Solar to another entity.[254] The new shareholder commenced a separate arbitration, discussed below.

---

245 This is not to mention possible "follow-up" legal battles at the enforcement front. After all, the disputes end when the arbitral awards are settled, not just issued.

246 WOC v. Spain, ICSID Case No. ARB/22/12, registered on 05.04.2022.

247 For ease of reference and unification, academic titles, professional qualifications and awards are omitted. This by no means is intended to underestimate the accomplishments of the arbitrators selected in the cases. Each of them is renowned figure and deserves the utmost respect.

248 Charanne v. Spain, *supra* note 67.

249 Ibid [19].

250 Ibid [1]–[2].

251 Ibid [4]–[6].

252 Ibid [143].

253 Ibid [395].

254 Ibid [8].

10.2 *Isolux*

The award in *Isolux v. Spain* was issued on 12.07.2016.[255] The tribunal was composed of Guido Santiago Tawil (claimant's nominee), Claus von Wobeser (respondent's nominee) and Yves Derains (president of the tribunal).[256] This was a *de facto* extension of the *Charanne* case, as it concerned the same PV plants owned by T-Solar. However, its scope included measures that were adopted after the sale of shares to the new claimant, a Dutch company (Isolux Infrastructure Netherlands, B.V.).[257] It was also broader, since the claimant's investment went beyond the shares involved in the *Charanne* case, and included shares held also in other Spanish companies, T-Solar Global Operating Assets, S.L. and Tuin Zonne Origen, S.L.U.[258] All three local companies owned, in turn, all or most of the shares in 117 other Spanish companies, which in turn owned 34 PV plants.[259] As to the moment of making the investment, the first agreement to acquire the shares in the local companies was concluded on 29.06.2012,[260] whereas the crucial conditions stipulated in this agreement were met in October 2012.[261]

10.3 *Eiser*

The award in *Eiser v. Spain* was issued on 04.05.2017.[262] The tribunal was composed of Stanimir A. Alexandrov (claimants' nominee), Campbell McLachlan (respondent's nominee) and John R. Crook (president of the tribunal).[263] The claimants were a company incorporated under the laws of the United Kingdom (Eiser Infrastructure Limited) and a company incorporated under the laws of Luxembourg (Energia Solar Luxembourg S.à r.I.).[264] The first claimant directly and wholly owned the second claimant which, in turn, owned shares and debt interests in two Spanish companies, which in turn owned and

255 Isolux v. Spain, *supra* note 59.
256 Ibid [10], [12], [15].
257 See for example: Nikos Lavranos, Cees Verburg, Renewable Energy Investment Disputes: Recent Developments and Implications for Prospective Energy Market Reforms, European Energy Law Report, 12 (2018), p. 78.
258 Isolux v. Spain, *supra* note 59 [1].
259 Ibid [161].
260 Ibid [141].
261 Ibid [147]–[156].
262 Eiser v. Spain, *supra* note 7.
263 Ibid [9].
264 Ibid [2]. Although, formally speaking, the first claimant was incorporated under the laws of England and Wales.

operated 3 CSP plants.[265] The claimants' investment commenced in "early summer of 2007", even though the CSP plants in question "did not become operational until 2012".[266]

The *Eiser* award was annulled on 11.06.2020.[267] However, the annulment was not based on the legal reasoning of the award, but on a lack of disclosure of a relationship between one of the arbitrators (claimants' nominee) and the claimants' damages experts.[268] This led the annulment committee to decide that the arbitral tribunal was not properly constituted.[269] The case was resubmitted to a new tribunal, and the new arbitration remains pending.[270]

10.4 *Novenergia*

In the fourth case, *Novenergia v. Spain*, the award was issued on 15.02.2018.[271] The tribunal was composed of Antonio Crivellaro (claimant's nominee), Bernardo Sepúlveda-Amor (respondent's nominee) and Johan Sidklev (president of the tribunal).[272] The claimant was a company incorporated under the laws of Luxembourg (Novenergia II - Energy & Environment SICAR).[273] It made an investment in 8 PV plants through a Spanish company (Novenergia II Energy & Environment España, S.L.), in which it acquired its interest on 03.07.2007.[274] After a number of corporate structure changes, the claimant held between a 71.47% and 30.14% interest in the respective Special Purpose Vehicles ("SPVs") that owned the relevant PV installations.[275]

10.5 *Masdar*

Masdar v. Spain was chronologically the fifth case. It concluded with an award issued on 16.05.2018.[276] The tribunal was composed of Gary Born (claimant's nominee), Brigitte Stern (respondent's nominee) and John Beechey (president

265 Ibid [114]. It was a minority shareholder, owning 36.95% of shares in the first, and 33.83% of the shares in the second Spanish company – [224].
266 Ibid [229].
267 Eiser v. Spain, ICSID Case No. ARB/13/36, Decision on the Kingdom of Spain's Application for Annulment (11.06.2020) [273].
268 Ibid [205], where details of the relationship are explained.
269 Ibid [143].
270 It was registered on 29.07.2021 – see: https://icsid.worldbank.org/cases/case-database/case-detail?CaseNo=ARB/13/36.
271 Novenergia v. Spain, *supra* note 52.
272 Ibid [9], [17], [18].
273 Ibid [1].
274 Ibid [2].
275 Ibid [5].
276 Masdar v. Spain, *supra* note 33.

of the tribunal).[277] The claimant was a company incorporated under the laws of the Netherlands (Masdar Solar & Wind Cooperatief U.A.).[278] The claimant invested in 3 CSP plants, in November 2008 and in July 2009.[279]

On 28.03.2019, Spain filed with the ICSID an application for annulment of the award.[280] However, on 27.11.2020 the annulment proceedings were discontinued.[281] The probable cause of discontinuation was the creation of the incentives foreseen in the 2019 Measures (see above).

10.6 *Antin*

The sixth award was issued on 15.06.2018 in *Antin v. Spain*.[282] The tribunal was composed of Francisco Orrego Vicuña (claimants' nominee), J. Christopher Thomas (respondent's nominee) and Eduardo Zuleta Jaramillo (president of the tribunal).[283] The claimants were companies incorporated under the laws of Luxembourg (Antin Infrastructure Services Luxembourg S.à.r.l.) and under the laws of the Netherlands (Antin Energia Termosolar B.V.), the second being directly and wholly-owned by the first.[284] In 2011, they invested in 2 CSP plants, which had operated since 2009.[285]

Spain's application to annul the award was dismissed by the annulment committee on 30.07.2021.[286]

10.7 *Foresight*

The award in the seventh case, *Foresight v. Spain*, was issued on 14.11.2018.[287] The tribunal was composed of Klaus Sachs (claimants' nominee), Raúl Emilio Vinuesa (respondent's nominee) and Michael Moser (president of the

277 Ibid [9].

278 Ibid [2]. The claimant was owned and controlled by Abu Dhabi Future Energy Company, holding 99% of the claimant's shares, which in turn was wholly controlled by Mubadala Development Company, which, in turn, was owned by the government of Abu Dhabi – ibid [82]–[83].

279 Ibid [5].

280 Masdar v. Spain, ICSID Case No. ARB/14/1, Annulment Proceeding – Procedural Order No. 3, Decision on the Kingdom of Spain's Request for a Continuation of the Stay of Enforcement of the Award (20.05.2020) [3].

281 https://icsid.worldbank.org/cases/case-database/case-detail?CaseNo=ARB/14/1.

282 Antin v. Spain, *supra* note 6 .

283 Ibid [9].

284 Ibid [2]. Both companies were used by Antin Infrastructure Partners FPCI, a French professional private equity investment fund to carry out investments in the RE sector in Spain.

285 Ibid [70], [110].

286 Antin v. Spain, ICSID Case No. ARB/13/31, Decision on Annulment (30.07.2021) [268].

287 Foresight v. Spain, *supra* note 18.

tribunal).[288] The claimants were: (i) companies incorporated under the laws of Luxembourg (Foresight Luxembourg Solar 1 S.à.r.l. and Foresight Luxembourg Solar 2 S.à.r.l.), (ii) companies incorporated under the laws of Italy (GWM Renewable Energy I S.p.A. and GWM Renewable Energy II S.p.A., subsequently changed its legal form to S.r.l.) and (iii) a company incorporated under the laws of Denmark (Greentech Energy Systems A/S).[289] The investment related to the acquisition of a 100% shareholding in 3 Spanish companies that owned PV solar plants (2 projects consisting of single PV plants each, whereas the third project consisted of 18 PV plants). The claimants acquired the relevant shares between 08.05.2009 and 07.05.2010, and all of the PV plants had already been registered under RD 661/2007 at that time.[290] Two of the three projects were sold during the course of the arbitration.[291]

10.8 *RREEF*

RREEF v. Spain is the eighth award rendered in the Spanish saga. Its decision on responsibility and on the principles of quantum was issued on 30.11.2018.[292] This decision was preceded by a decision on jurisdiction, issued on 06.06.2016,[293] and followed by a final award determining the amount of compensation on 11.12.2019.[294] The tribunal was composed of Robert Volterra (claimants' nominee), Pedro Nikken (respondent's nominee) and Alain Pellet (president of the tribunal).[295] The claimants were a company incorporated under the laws of Jersey (RREEF Infrastructure (G.P.) Limited) and a company incorporated under the laws of Luxembourg (RREEF Pan-European Infrastructure Two Lux S.à.r.l.).[296] In February 2011, they invested in 5 Wind energy plants, by indirectly acquiring 49% of the shares in 3 SPVs.[297] The relevant plants had been already registered in the Pre-RAIPRE (on 11.12.2009), and in the RAIPRE (on 28.10.2010).[298] In June 2011, the claimants invested in 2 CSP plants, by indirectly

288 Ibid [11].
289 Ibid [2].
290 Ibid [54], [94]–[96], [97], [102], [107].
291 Ibid [142]-[144].
292 RREEF v. Spain, *supra* note 15.
293 RREEF v. Spain, ICSID Case No. ARB/13/30, Decision on Jurisdiction (06.06.2016).
294 RREEF v. Spain, ICSID Case No. ARB/13/30, Award (11.12.2019).
295 RREEF v. Spain, Jurisdiction …, *supra* note 293 (06.06.2016) [12].
296 RREEF v. Spain, *supra* note 15 [2], [3], [5]. The first claimant was the general partner of RREEF Pan-European Infrastructure Fund L.P., which held full share capital in RREEF Pan-European Infrastructure Lux S.à.r.l., which in turn held 100% equity stake in the second claimant.
297 Ibid [142], [159].
298 Ibid [160].

acquiring a 90% equity stake.[299] The CSP plants were registered in the RAIPRE in December 2009.[300] Finally, in July 2011 the claimants invested in yet another CSP plant, by indirectly acquiring a 49% equity interest in an SPV.[301] This plant was registered in the Pre-RAIPRE on 11.12.2009, and in the RAIPRE on 25.09.2013.[302]

Spain filed to the ICSID an application for annulment of the award, which was registered on 15.04.2020. The proceeding was closed on 11.03.2022, but no decision on annulment has yet been issued (as of 01.05.2022).[303]

10.9 *Cube*

Cube v. Spain is the ninth case, based on the date of the decision on jurisdiction, liability and partial decision on quantum issued on 19.02.2019.[304] The final award, determining the amount of compensation, was issued on 15.07.2019.[305] The tribunal was composed of James Jacob Spigelman (claimants' nominee), Christian Tomuschat (respondent's nominee) and Vaughan Lowe (president of the tribunal).[306] The claimants were 3 companies incorporated under the laws of Luxembourg (Cube Infrastructure Fund SICAV, Cube Energy S.C.A., and Cube Infrastructure Managers S.A.) and 2 companies incorporated under the laws of France (Demeter 2 FPCI and Demeter Partners S.A.).[307] The claimants' investments could be divided in two groups. The first group concerned investments in the PV plants, by acquitting 100% of the shares in a Spanish company, which in turn owned 3 local companies, each of which owned a PV facility.[308] This investment was made in April-June 2008.[309] The second group concerned the acquisition of 100% of the shares in another Spanish company, which in turn owned 4 Spanish companies, which collectively owned 16 Spanish companies, each of which owned a Hydro energy facility.[310] Part of this investment was made in 2011, and part in June 2012.[311]

---

299 Ibid [142], [174].
300 Ibid [142], [175].
301 Ibid [142], [163].
302 Ibid [142], [165], [169].
303 https://icsid.worldbank.org/cases/case-database/case-detail?CaseNo=ARB/13/30.
304 Cube v. Spain, *supra* note 52.
305 Cube v. Spain, ICSID Case No. ARB/15/20, Award (15.07.2019).
306 Cube v. Spain, *supra* note 52 [9]–[11].
307 Ibid [2].
308 Ibid [70]–[72].
309 Ibid [238].
310 Ibid [70]–[72].
311 Ibid [327].

Spain's application to annul this award was registered on 18.11.2019.[312] It was dismissed on 28.03.2022.[313]

10.10 *NextEra*

The decision on jurisdiction, liability and quantum principles was issued in *NextEra v. Spain* on 12.03.2019, which marks this case as chronologically the tenth one.[314] The final award, determining the amount of compensation, was issued on 31.05.2019.[315] The tribunal was composed of Yves Fortier (claimants' nominee), Laurence Boisson de Chazournes (respondent's nominee) and Donald M. McRae (president of the tribunal).[316] The claimants were two companies incorporated under the laws of the Netherlands (NextEra Energy Global Holdings B.V and NextEra Energy Spain Holdings B.V.).[317] The first claimant owned the second claimant, which in turn indirectly owned 2 Spanish SPVs that had developed 2 CSP plants.[318] The claimants commenced development activities to construct the CSP plants in 2008.[319] The relevant CSP plants were registered in the Pre-RAIPRE on 11.12.2009,[320] constructed in 2011 and 2012 and registered in the RAIPRE on 29.05.2013 and 07.07.2013, respectively.[321]

On 26.09.2019 Spain filed an application for annulment of the award.[322] This was dismissed on 18.03.2022.[323]

10.11 *9REN*

The award rendered on 31.05.2019 in *9REN v. Spain* makes this the eleventh case in the saga.[324] The tribunal was composed of David R. Haigh (claimant's nominee), V.V. Veeder (respondent's nominee) and Ian Binnie (president of the tribunal).[325] The claimant was a company incorporated under the laws of

312 Cube v. Spain, ICSID Case No. ARB/15/20, Decision on the Continuation of the Provisional Stay of Enforcement of the Award (17.04.2020) [3].

313 Cube v. Spain, ICSID Case No. ARB/15/20, Decision on Annulment (28.03.2022) [504].

314 NextEra v. Spain, *supra* note 31.

315 NextEra v. Spain, ICSID Case No. ARB/14/11, Award (31.05.2019).

316 NextEra v. Spain, *supra* note 31 [9].

317 Ibid [2].

318 Ibid [93], [95].

319 Ibid [168].

320 Ibid [170].

321 Ibid [177]–[178].

322 NextEra v. Spain, ICSID Case No. ARB/14/11, Decision on Stay of Enforcement of the Award (06.04.2020) [2].

323 NextEra v. Spain, ICSID Case No. ARB/14/11, Decision on Annulment (18.03.2022) [533].

324 9REN v. Spain, *supra* note 2.

325 Ibid [22].

Luxembourg (9REN Holding S.à.r.l.). [326] The investment concerned the acquisition of 96.5% of the shares in a local company which was developing PV facilities.[327] The investment was completed on 23.04.2008.[328] By 29.09.2008, i.e. the closing date of the window under RD 661/2007, seven PV plants were registered in the RAIPRE.[329] The eighth one was registered later, on 23.03.2011.[330]

Spain's application to annul this award was registered on 07.04.2020.[331] As of 01.05.2022, these annulment proceedings remained pending.

10.12 *SolEs*

SolEs v. Spain is chronologically the twelfth award in the Spanish saga, issued on 31.07.2019.[332] On 05.12.2019, a rectification decision was issued, but this remains confidential.[333] The tribunal was composed of David A. R. Williams (claimant's nominee), Giorgio Sacerdoti (respondent's nominee) and Joan E. Donoghue (president of the tribunal).

However, the tribunal was initially composed of different arbitrators: Stanimir A. Alexandrov (claimant's nominee) and Anna Joubin-Bret (respondent's nominee).[334] The respondent filed a motion to disqualify Stanimir A. Alexandrov.[335] Although the exact reasons underpinning the motion remain confidential, apparently there was a link between the arbitrator and the Brattle group, which appeared as the claimant's expert.[336] This challenge was to be decided by the other two arbitrators, who were, however, "equally divided".[337] Before the challenge was decided by the Chairman of the ICSID Administrative Council, ICSID informed on 24.10.2017 that the arbitrator had resigned of his own accord.[338] On the same day, Anna Joubin-Bret also resigned, following her appointment as Director of the International Trade Law Division in the Office of Legal Affairs of the United Nations and *ex officio* Secretary of the United Nations Commission on International Trade Law.[339] The claimant then

---

326 Ibid [3].
327 Ibid [2], [5], [124].
328 Ibid [127]–[128].
329 Ibid [103].
330 Ibid [105].
331 https://icsid.worldbank.org/cases/case-database/case-detail?CaseNo=ARB/15/15.
332 SolEs v. Spain, *supra* note 16.
333 https://icsid.worldbank.org/cases/case-database/case-detail?CaseNo=ARB/15/38.
334 SolEs v. Spain, *supra* note 16 [11], [46]–[48].
335 Ibid [33].
336 Ibid [30]–[31].
337 Ibid [39].
338 Ibid [41].
339 Ibid [42].

appointed Jonathan Schiller, who resigned a mere 5 days later.[340] Only then were the parties able to appoint arbitrators who remained on the panel until the end of the proceedings.[341]

The claimant was a company incorporated under the laws of Germany (SolEs Badajoz GmbH). It was owned by two other German companies, which in turn were owned by a closed-end fund organized as a limited partnership under the laws of Germany, established for the purpose of investing in RE and which managed all of the relevant investments.[342] On 25.03.2010, the claimant acquired a Spanish company which owned 2 PV plants.[343] The plants were registered in the Pre-RAIPRE prior to the acquisition, but their construction was completed after the investment, on 12.07.2010 and 14.01.2011 respectively.[344]

On 01.04.2020 Spain applied to annul this award.[345] On 16.03.2022 the application was dismissed.[346]

10.13 *InfraRed*

The award in the thirteenth case, *InfraRed v. Spain,* was issued on 02.08.2019.[347] On 08.03.2021 the tribunal issued a decision dismissing the respondent's motion for revision of the award.[348] The tribunal was composed of William W. Park (claimant's nominee), Pierre-Marie Dupuy (respondent's nominee) and Stephen L. Drymer (president of the tribunal).[349] The claimants were 5 private limited companies incorporated under the laws of the United Kingdom, all of them acting in their own names. In addition, one of them acted as a general partner in the name and on behalf of 3 limited partnerships registered in England and Wales.[350] "On or around" 28.07.2011 the claimants acquired 2 Spanish companies owning 2 CSP plants.[351] They were registered in RAIPRE in 2012.[352]

340 Ibid [44]–[45].
341 Ibid [46]–[48].
342 Ibid [132].
343 Ibid [138].
344 Ibid [134]–[137].
345 SolEs v. Spain, ICSID Case No. ARB/15/38, Decision on the Continuation of the Stay of Enforcement of the Award (26.08.2020) [2]-[3].
346 SolEs v. Spain, ICSID Case No. ARB/15/38, Decision on Annulment (16.03.2022) [338].
347 InfraRed v. Spain, *supra* note 52.
348 InfraRed v. Spain, ICSID Case No. ARB/14/12, Decision on Claimant's Objection under ICSID Rule 41(5) to Respondent's Application for Revision (08.03.2021) [81].
349 InfraRed v. Spain, *supra* note 52 [98]–[99], [102].
350 Ibid [6].
351 Ibid [7].
352 Ibid [57].

On 05.12.2019 Spain's application to annul the award was registered. The annulment proceedings were closed on 16.03.2022, but as of 01.05.2022 the annulment decision remained pending.[353]

10.14 *OperaFund*

With an award issued on 06.09.2019, *OperaFund v. Spain* is chronologically the fourteenth concluded Spanish saga case.[354] The award was subsequently rectified on 28.10.2019.[355] The tribunal was composed of August Reinisch (claimants' nominee), Philippe Sands (respondent's nominee) and Karl-Heinz Böckstiegel (president of the tribunal).[356] The claimants were 2 companies, one incorporated under the laws of the Malta (OperaFund Eco-Invest SICAV PLC), and the other under the laws of Switzerland (Schwab Holding AG).[357] The claimants invested between July 2008 and July 2009 in 5 PV facilities in Spain. The investment consisted of (i) shares in SPVs which owned PV installations and (ii) participative loans granted to these SPVs.[358] All the relevant PV facilities were registered in the RAIPRE by 29.09.2008.[359]

On 25.02.2020 Spain filed an application to annul the award, which was registered on 03.03.2020.[360] As of 31.05.2022, the annulment proceedings remained pending.[361]

10.15 *BayWa*

BayWa v. Spain, together with the following case, *Stadtwerke v. Spain*, are chronologically the fifteenth and sixteenth cases in the Spanish saga, with awards issued on the same day – 02.12.2019.[362] As regards the *BayWa* case, this was the date of the decision on jurisdiction, liability and directions on quantum, whereas the final award was issued on 25.01.2021.[363] The tribunal was composed of Horacio A. Grigera Naón (claimants' nominee), Loretta Malintoppi (respondent's nominee) and James R. Crawford (president of the tribunal).[364]

353 https://icsid.worldbank.org/cases/case-database/case-detail?CaseNo=ARB/14/12.
354 OperaFund v. Spain, *supra* note 28.
355 OperaFund v. Spain, ICSID Case No. ARB/15/36, Decision on the Request for the Continuation of the Stay of Enforcement of the Award (16.11.2020) [1].
356 OperaFund v. Spain, *supra* note 28 [6]–[9].
357 Ibid [2].
358 Ibid [173]–[174].
359 Ibid [181].
360 OperaFund v. Spain, Decision ..., *supra* note 355 [5]–[6].
361 https://icsid.worldbank.org/cases/case-database/case-detail?CaseNo=ARB/15/36.
362 BayWa v. Spain, *supra* note 28.
363 BayWa v. Spain, ICSID Case No. ARB/15/16, Award (25.01.2021).
364 BayWa v. Spain, *supra* note 28 [9], [12].

The claimants were 2 companies incorporated under the laws of Germany (BayWa r.e. Renewable Energy GmbH, and BayWa r.e. Asset Holding GmbH).[365] They invested in 2 Wind energy facilities in Spain between 2009 and 2012, by acquiring full 100% of the capital of another German company, which in turn (i) owned shares in Spanish SPVs which owned the Wind energy facilities and (ii) granted participative loans to these SPVs.[366] These Wind energy facilities were developed in 1997.[367] They were registered in the RAIPRE with effect as of 25.11.2002, and around the same time they commenced operations.[368]

On 28.05.2021, Spain's application to annul the award was registered. It remained pending as of 01.05.2022.[369]

10.16 *Stadtwerke*

As flagged above, *Stadtwerke v. Spain* was issued on 02.12.2019, on the same day as the *BayWa* decision.[370] The tribunal was composed of Kaj Hobér (claimants' nominee), Zachary Douglas (respondent's nominee) and Jeswald W. Salacuse (president of the tribunal).[371] The claimants were 9 companies: (i) Stadtwerke München GmbH, (ii) RWE Innogy GmbH, (iii) Rheinenergie AG, (iv), AS 3 Beteiligungs GmbH, (v) Ferrostaal Industrial Projects GmbH, (vi) Ferranda GmbH, (vii) Andasol Fonds GmbH & Co. KG, (viii) Andasol 3 Kraftwerks GmbH and (ix) Marquesado Solar S.L. All of them were incorporated under the laws of Germany, except for the last one, which was incorporated under the laws of Spain.[372] The claimants invested in a CSP plant on 28.10.2009, which was owned by the Spanish SPV (the ninth company listed above), directly and indirectly owned by the other claimants.[373] It commenced operations in 2011.[374]

On 06.04.2020, the claimants' application to annul the award was registered. On 29.01.2021 the annulment committee issued an order "taking note of the discontinuance of the proceeding pursuant to ICSID Arbitration Rule 44".[375]

365 Ibid [3].
366 Ibid [62].
367 Ibid [63].
368 Ibid [67].
369 https://icsid.worldbank.org/cases/case-database/case-detail?CaseNo=ARB/15/16.
370 Stadtwerke v. Spain, *supra* note 6.
371 Ibid [9]–[10], [13]–[14].
372 Ibid [2]. The first claimant was wholly owned by the City Council of Munich in Germany – ibid [108], [133]–[134].
373 Ibid [2], [5], [82], [84].
374 Ibid [2], [82], [79].
375 https://icsid.worldbank.org/cases/case-database/case-detail?CaseNo=ARB/15/1.

The probable cause of this discontinuation was the incentives foreseen in the 2019 Measures (see above).

10.17 *RWE*

RWE v. Spain is chronologically the seventeenth of the concluded Spanish saga cases, with its decision on jurisdiction, liability, and certain issues of quantum issued on 30.12.2019.[376] The final award was issued on 18.12.2020.[377] The tribunal was composed of Judd Kessler (claimants' nominee), Anna Joubin-Bret (respondent's nominee) and Samuel Wordsworth (president of the tribunal).[378] The claimants were RWE Innogy GmbH, a company incorporated under the laws of Germany, and RWE Innogy Aersa S.A.U., a company incorporated under the laws of the Kingdom of Spain.[379] The claimants invested in 4 Hydro energy plants and 16 Wind energy plants.[380] The investments were made in 3 tranches: (i) a series of transactions between 2001 and 2004, (ii) a single transaction in 2008, and (iii) a series of transactions between 2008 and 2012.[381]

On 19.04.2021, the respondent's application to annul the award was registered. As of 01.05.2022, the annulment proceedings remained pending.[382]

10.18 *Watkins*

The award issued in *Watkins v. Spain* on 21.01.2020 makes it the eighteenth Spanish saga case.[383] Subsequently, on 13.07.2020, the tribunal issued a decision on a request for rectification of the award.[384] The tribunal was composed of Michael C. Pryles (claimants' nominee), Hélène Ruiz Fabri (respondent's nominee) and Tan Sri Dato' Cecil W. M. Abraham (president of the tribunal).[385] The claimants were 2 companies incorporated under the laws of Luxembourg (Watkins Holdings S.à.r.l. and Redpier, S.L.), a company incorporated under the laws of the Netherlands (Watkins (Ned) B.V.) and 4 companies incorporated under the laws of Spain (Watkins Spain, S.L., Northsea Spain S.L., Parque

376 RWE v. Spain, *supra* note 28.
377 RWE v. Spain, ICSID Case No. ARB/14/34, Award (18.12.2020).
378 RWE v. Spain, *supra* note 28 [9].
379 Ibid [2].
380 Ibid [190].
381 Ibid [191].
382 https://icsid.worldbank.org/cases/case-database/case-detail?CaseNo=ARB/14/34.
383 Watkins v. Spain, *supra* note 31.
384 Watkins v. Spain, ICSID Case No. ARB/15/44, Decision on Spain's Request for Rectification of the Award (13.07.2020).
385 Watkins v. Spain, *supra* note 31 [9].

Eólico Marmellar, S.L. and Parque Eólico La Boga, S.L.).[386] The claimants invested in 7 Wind energy plants.[387] The investment was made on 12.08.2011, through the acquisition of shares in 2 local companies which owned the Wind energy plants, which had been already registered in the RAIPRE by that time.[388]

On 31.07.2020 the respondent's application to annul the award was registered. As of 01.05.2022, the annulment proceedings remained pending.[389]

10.19 *PV Investors*

PV Investors v. Spain is chronologically the nineteenth award issued in the Spanish saga, being issued on 28.02.2020.[390] This is the date of the final award, whereas the preliminary award on jurisdiction was issued as early as 13.10.2014.[391] Thus, even though the date of the final award puts the *PV Investors* case as nineteenth in the Spanish saga, the decision on jurisdiction – and the decision on the intra-EU objection – was chronologically the first one. It was issued approximately 15 months prior to the decision on this issue was reached by the tribunal in *Charanne*.[392] It is also the only of the analyzed arbitrations which was conducted under the UNCITRAL Arbitration Rules, and not as an ICSID or SCC case.[393]

The tribunal was composed of Charles N. Brower (claimants' nominee), Bernardo Sepúlveda-Amor (respondent's nominee) and Gabrielle Kaufmann-Kohler (president of the tribunal).[394] The claimants were in total 87 legal entities and 1 natural person. They were divided in fourteen groups, and were incorporated in Luxembourg, the Netherlands, Germany and Spain.[395] The claimants invested in a number of PV plants. The investments started after RD 661/2007 was adopted, i.e. after 25.05.2007, and all of the relevant PV plants were registered in the RAIPRE prior to 29.08.2008.[396]

---

386 Ibid [1].

387 Ibid [3].

388 Ibid [134], [139].

389 https://icsid.worldbank.org/cases/case-database/case-detail?CaseNo=ARB/15/44.

390 The PV Investors v. Spain, *supra* note 13.

391 The PV Investors v. Spain, PCA Case No. 2012-14, Preliminary Award on Jurisdiction (13.10.2014).

392 Nevertheless, it remained confidential for significant time.

393 The PV Investors v. Spain, Jurisdiction ..., *supra* note 391 [17]. The place of arbitration was Geneva.

394 Ibid [12], The PV Investors v. Spain, *supra* note 13 [6].

395 The PV Investors v. Spain, Jurisdiction ..., *supra* note 391 [2].

396 The PV Investors v. Spain, *supra* note 13 [181], [195], [196].

On 27.04.2020, Spain filed a motion to set aside the arbitral award. On 23.02.2021 the Swiss court dismissed the motion.[397]

10.20 *Hydro*

The decision on jurisdiction, liability and directions on quantum were issued in *Hydro v. Spain* on 09.03.2020, making it chronologically the twentieth concluded case in the Spanish saga.[398] The final award was issued on 05.08.2020.[399] The tribunal was composed of Peter Rees (claimants' nominee), Rolf Knieper (respondent's nominee) and Lawrence Collins (president of the tribunal).[400] The claimants were two companies, one incorporated under the laws of Luxembourg (Hydro Energy 1 S.à.r.l.) and the other incorporated under the laws of Sweden (Hydroxana Sweden AB).[401] In May 2011 the claimants acquired a portfolio consisting of 14 Hydro energy plants, and in December 2011 they further acquired a second portfolio, consisting of 19 Hydro energy plants.[402] The claimants acquired a 100% equity interest in both portfolios.[403]

On 06.10.2020, the respondent's application to annul the award was registered. As of 01.05.2022, the annulment proceedings remained pending.[404]

10.21 *Cavalum*

The decision on jurisdiction, liability and directions on quantum in *Cavalum v. Spain* was issued on 31.08.2020.[405] It makes the *Cavalum* case the twenty-first concluded Spanish saga case. As of 01.05.2022, the final award determining the amount of compensation was still pending.[406] The tribunal was composed of David R. Haigh (claimant's nominee), Daniel Bethlehem (respondent's nominee) and Lawrence Collins (president of the tribunal).[407] The claimant was a company incorporated under the laws of Portugal (Cavalum SGPS S.A.).[408] It invested in 7 PV facilities, through its Spanish subsidiaries and SPVs which

397 Judgment of the Swiss Federal Tribunal, Case No. 4A_187/2020 (23.02.2021).

398 Hydro v. Spain, *supra* note 34.

399 https://www.iareporter.com/articles/spain-applies-for-annulment-of-small-hydro-award/. The final award remains unpublished.

400 Hydro v. Spain, *supra* note 34 [10].

401 Ibid [2].

402 Ibid [62]. The investments concerned "small-hydro" plants, i.e. hydropower installations with an installed capacity of up to 50 MW – [432].

403 Ibid [64], [68].

404 https://icsid.worldbank.org/cases/case-database/case-detail?CaseNo=ARB/15/42.

405 Cavalum v. Spain, *supra* note 34 .

406 https://icsid.worldbank.org/cases/case-database/case-detail?CaseNo=ARB/15/34.

407 Cavalum v. Spain, *supra* note 34 [7]–[9].

408 Ibid [2].

owned between 50% and 100% of each respective facility.[409] The investments were made between 31.07.2007 and 08.05.2009.[410] The claimant also invested in 3 other projects, which were never developed due to the disputed measures.[411]

11 Conclusions

This Chapter has described the evolution of Spain's policies on RE subsidies, which lie at the heart of the Spanish saga cases. The uniqueness of these cases is that they involve almost the same factual background not only in terms of the measures disputed in the arbitral proceedings, but also as regards the circumstances surrounding the disputed investments. Furthermore, even the investments themselves are comparable, as all of them concern RE power plants, which fall within the category of PV, CSP, Wind energy or Hydro energy installations, affected by the 2010 Disputed Measures, the 2012 Disputed Measures and the 2013–2014 Disputed Measures. Whilst there are differences between each of the case, at a general level they are limited to two issues only: (i) the moment of making the investment, and/or (ii) the type of the power plant(s) involved, i.e. whether the disputed investment concerns PV, CSP, Hydro energy and/or Wind energy.

This Chapter also briefly described the types of RE power plants that are relevant to the analysis of the Spanish saga cases which is in the following Chapters.

It then provided a simplified description of the European context, which is again indispensable to properly understand the analyzed cases, which were brought against an EU member state.

The Chapter described the continuing development of the Spanish regulations in the years 1997–2010, which aimed at incentivizing investments (both foreign and domestic) in the RE sector through the FIT and Premium incentives, plus other mechanisms that were available under the Special Regime.

The next sections described the regulatory changes introduced by Spain. Various regulatory changes, categorized as 2010 Disputed Measures, 2012 Disputed Measures and, finally, 2013–2014 Disputed Measures, progressively dismantled the Special Regime and finally replaced it with a New Regime.

The Chapter ended with a short description of all of the Spanish saga cases which are analyzed in the next Chapters. They are presented in chronological

409 Ibid [84].
410 Ibid [452].
411 Ibid [2], [91].

order.[412] The analysis covers 21 arbitral awards rendered in the Spanish saga – i.e. in chronological order: *Charanne, Isolux, Eiser, Novenergia, Masdar, Antin, Foresight, RREEF, NextEra, 9REN, Cube, SolEs, InfraRed, OperaFund, BayWa, Stadtwerke, RWE, Watkins, PV Investors, Hydro, Cavalum.* The following two tables summarize the basic characteristics of each of these cases.

TABLE 1 Cases by type of the relevant RE technology

No	Case name	PV	CSP	Wind	Hydro
1	Charanne	✓			
2	Isolux	✓			
3	Eiser		✓		
4	Novenergia	✓			
5	Masdar		✓		
6	Antin		✓		
7	Foresight	✓			
8	RREEF		✓	✓	
9	Cube	✓			✓
10	NextEra		✓		
11	9REN	✓			
12	SolEs	✓			
13	InfraRed		✓		
14	OperaFund	✓			
15	BayWa			✓	
16	Stadtwerke		✓		
17	RWE			✓	✓
18	Watkins			✓	
19	PV Investors	✓			
20	Hydro				✓
21	Cavalum	✓			

412 Chronological order is based on date of an award (final or partial) on liability, regardless of the date of partial awards on jurisdiction and/or damages (if bifurcated).

TABLE 2 Details of the Spanish saga cases

No	Case name	Award Date	Arbitrators	Home state(s)[a]	Type of RE	Date(s) of investment(s)	Comments
1	**Charanne**	21.01.2016	Guido Santiago Tawil (c), Claus von Wobeser (r), Alexis Mourre (p)	The Netherlands, Luxembourg	PV	02.2009 and 12.2009	Limited scope of disputed measures
2	**Isolux**	12.07.2016	Guido Santiago Tawil (c), Claus von Wobeser (r), Yves Derains (p)	The Netherlands	PV	06.2012 and 10.2012	
3	**Eiser**	04.05.2017	Stanimir A. Alexandrov (c), Campbell McLachlan (r), John R. Crook (p)	United Kingdom, Luxembourg	CSP	2007 (plants became operational in 2012)	Award annulled (for reasons related to non-disclosure of an arbitrator)
4	**Novenergia**	15.02.2018	Antonio Crivellaro (c), Bernardo Sepúlveda-Amor (r), Johan Sidklev (p)	Luxembourg	PV	03.07.2007	
5	**Masdar**	16.05.2018	Gary Born (c), Brigitte Stern (r), John Beechey (p)	The Netherlands	CSP	11.2008 and 07.2009	
6	**Antin**	15.06.2018	Francisco Orrego Vicuña (c), J. Christopher Thomas (r), Eduardo Zuleta Jaramillo (p)	The Netherlands, Luxembourg	CSP	2011 (plants operating since 2009)	

(*Continued*)

TABLE 2 Details of the Spanish saga cases (*Cont.*)

No	Case name	Award Date	Arbitrators	Home state(s)[a]	Type of RE	Date(s) of investment(s)	Comments
7	**Foresight**	14.11.2018	Klaus Sachs (c), Raúl Emilio Vinuesa (r), Michael Moser (p)	Luxembourg, Italy, Denmark	PV	08.05.2009 - 10.05.2010	
8	RREEF	30.11.2018	Robert Volterra (c), Pedro Nikken (r), Alain Pellet (p)	Jersey, Luxembourg	Wind + CSP	02.2011–07.2011	Decision on jurisdiction - 06.06.2016, final award - 11.12.2019
9	**Cube**	19.02.2019	James Jacob Spigelman (c), Christian Tomuschat (r), Vaughan Lowe (p)	Luxembourg, France	PV + Hydro	04.2008–06.2008 (PV), 2011 and 06.2012 (Hydro)	Final award - 15.07.2019
10	**NextEra**	12.03.2019	Yves Fortier (c), Laurence Boisson de Chazournes (r), Donald M. McRae (p)	The Netherlands	CSP	2008–2009 (development), 2011–2012 (construction)	Final award - 31.05.2019
11	9REN	31.05.2019	David R. Haigh (c), V.V. Veeder (r), Ian Binnie (p)	Luxembourg	PV	23.04.2008	

No	Case name	Award Date	Arbitrators	Home state(s)[a]	Type of RE	Date(s) of investment(s)	Comments
12	**SolEs**	31.07.2019	David A. R. Williams (c), Giorgio Sacerdoti (r), Joan E. Donoghue (p)	Germany	PV	25.03.2010	Rectification - 05.12.2019. Initial composition of the arbitral tribunal was different
13	**InfraRed**	02.08.2019	William W. Park (c), Pierre-Marie Dupuy (r), Stephen L. Drymer (p)	United Kingdom	CSP	28.07.2011	Rectification - 25.03.2010
14	**OperaFund**	06.09.2019	August Reinisch (c), Philippe Sands (r), Karl-Heinz Böckstiegel (p)	Malta, Switzerland	PV	July 2008–July 2009	
15	**BayWa**	02.12.2019	Horacio A. Grigera Naón (c), Loretta Malintoppi (r), James R. Crawford (p)	Germany	Wind	2009–2012 (plants operating since 2002/2003)	Final award - 25.01.2021
16	**Stadtwerke**	02.12.2019	Kaj Hobér (c), Zachary Douglas (r), Jeswald W. Salacuse (p)	Germany	CSP	28.10.2009 (plant commenced operations in 2011)	
17	**RWE**	30.12.2019	Jude Kessler (c), Anna Joubin-Bret (r), Samuel Wordsworth (p)	Germany	Hydro + Wind	2001–2004, 2008 and 2008–2012	Final award - 18.12.2020
18	**Watkins**	21.01.2020	Michael C. Pryles (c), Hélène Ruiz Fabri (r), Tan Sri Dato' Cecil W. M. Abraham (p)	Luxembourg, the Netherlands	Wind	12.08.2011	Rectification - 13.07.2020

(*Continued*)

TABLE 2 Details of the Spanish saga cases (*Cont.*)

No	Case name	Award Date	Arbitrators	Home state(s)[a]	Type of RE	Date(s) of investment(s)	Comments
19	PV **Investors**	28.02.2020	Charles N. Brower (c), Bernardo Sepúlveda-Amor (r), Gabrielle Kaufmann-Kohler (p)	Luxembourg, the Netherlands, Germany	PV	25.05.2007–29.08.2008	Decision on jurisdiction - 13.10.2014
20	**Hydro**	09.03.2020	Peter Rees (c), Rolf Knieper (r), Lawrence Collins (p)	Luxembourg, Sweden	Hydro	05. 2011 and 12. 2011	Final award - 05.08.2020
21	**Cavalum**	31.08.2020	David R. Haigh (c), Daniel Bethlehem (r), Lawrence Collins (p)	Portugal	PV	31.07.2007–08.05.2009	
	Total				PV - 10 cases CSP - 7 cases Wind - 4 cases Hydro - 3 cases		

a - excluding Spain (when local company named as a claimant)
(c) - claimant(s) nominee
(r) - respondent's nominee
(p) - president

CHAPTER 3

Jurisdiction

1 Intra-EU Objection

1.1 *General Comments*

Jurisdiction is understood as the competence to decide a case. In the realm of arbitration, whether commercial or investment, the jurisdiction of tribunals is always based on the consent of the parties to a particular dispute.[1] In treaty-based arbitrations, states provide their consent to arbitrate in their capacity as contracting parties to a particular investment treaty. It is commonly described as an "offer" to arbitrate any future disputes. This offer, contained in a jurisdictional clause of a treaty, is directed to investors with the nationality of another contracting state to that treaty, and covers the defined class of investments set out in the treaty.[2] This means that an entity or individual must meet certain requirements laid down in the applicable treaty to be "eligible" to effectively accept the offer to arbitrate made by the states.[3]

This open offer to arbitrate does not, by itself, constitute a valid basis for the jurisdiction of an arbitral tribunal. An arbitration agreement, and therefore a proper basis for the jurisdiction of arbitral tribunals, is created only when both

1 See for example: Christopher R. Dugan, Don Jr. Wallace, Noah Rubins, Borzu Sabahi, Investor-State Arbitration (Oxford University Press 2019), p. 309, para. 9.01, Ursula Kriebaum, Christoph Schreuer, Rudolf Dolzer, Principles of International Investment Law (Oxford University Press 2022), pp. 360, 366.

2 Dugan, Wallace, Rubins, Sabahi, ibid, p. 310, para. 9.03, Kriebaum, Schreuer, Dolzer, ibid, p. 360. Some describe it as a "standing offer to arbitrate." See for example: Gary B. Born, International Arbitration: Law and Practice (Kluwer Law International 2021) pp. 506, 507, Andrea K. Bjorklund, Waiver and the Exhaustion of Local Remedies Rule in NAFTA Jurisprudence, in: Todd Weiler (ed.), NAFTA Investment Law and Arbitration: Past Issues, Current Practice, Future Prospects (Transnational Publishers 2004), p. 274. It may also be described as a "continuing offer to a class of potential claimants." See: Jack J. Jr. Coe, The Mandate of Chapter 11 Tribunals – Jurisdiction and Related Questions, in: Todd Weiler (ed.), NAFTA Investment Law an Arbitration: Current Practice, Future Prospects (Transnational Publishers 2004), p. 219.

3 Such as the nationality of another contracting state to a treaty, holding an investment in the territory of the respondent state etc.

DOI:10.1163/9789004509344_004

parties to a dispute provide their consent to arbitrate.[4] This means that the offer to arbitrate, expressed by states in investment treaties, must be accepted by an investor. Typically, it materializes when investors initiate arbitrations.[5] However, some treaties require more than an implied consent. For example, Art. 26(4) ECT[6] and Art. 25(1) of the ICSID Convention require investors to provide their consent in writing.[7] However, this requirement is generally met when investors commence arbitrations.[8]

The consent to arbitrate given by the parties to a dispute is not unlimited. Its scope determines the scope of jurisdiction of arbitral tribunals based on such consent.[9] The limitations of the scope of jurisdiction can be classified as: (i) "rationae personae", which refers to the parties to a dispute ("who" falls within the scope of jurisdiction), (ii) "rationae materiae", which concerns subject matter-related issues ("what" falls within the scope of jurisdiction), and (iii) "rationae temporis", which concerns time-related issues ("when" a particular act must have happened to fall within the scope of jurisdiction).[10]

Sometimes (iv) "rationae voluntatis" limitation is added to the above classification (i.e. have the parties validly consented to the arbitration).[11] Since this type of limitation refers to an alleged absence of consent to arbitrate, it touches upon the very essence of arbitration (i.e. the consent to arbitrate), without which there is no jurisdiction at all. This explains why it is not a

4 Christoph H. Schreuer, Loretta Malintoppi, August Reinisch, Anthony Sinclair, The ICSID Convention: A Commentary (Cambridge University Press 2009), p. 202, para. 416, p. 205, para. 427. This type of arbitration, where no contractual relationship exists between the disputing parties, is commonly known as "arbitration without privity". See: Jan Paulsson, Arbitration Without Privity, ICSID Review – Foreign Investment Law Journal, 10:2 (1995).

5 See for example: Generation v. Ukraine, ICSID Case No. ARB/00/9, Award (16.09.2003) [12.2], Parkerings v. Lithuania, ICSID Case No. ARB/05/8, Award (11.09.2007) [246].

6 All abbreviations contained herein are as used in previous Chapters, unless described otherwise.

7 Other such additional requirements may include, for example, an obligation to present a waiver from pursing the claims in another forum. See for example: Art. 14.D.5(1)(e) USMCA, replacing Art. 1121 NAFTA with a similar requirement.

8 Schreuer, Malintoppi, Reinisch, Sinclair, *supra* note 4, p. 212, para. 448. See for example: Abaclat v. Argentina, ICSID Case No. ARB/07/5, Decision on Jurisdiction and Admissibility (04.08.2011) [258]. This is important in the context of enforcement and recognition based on the New York Convention, since Art. II thereof requires an "agreement in writing".

9 Schreuer, Malintoppi, Reinisch, Sinclair, ibid, p. 233, para. 526.

10 See for example: Dugan, Wallace, Rubins, Sabahi, *supra* note 1, p. 412, para. 12.01.

11 See for example: Joseph M. Boddicker, Whose Dictionary Controls?: Recent Challenges to the Term "Investment" in ICSID Arbitration, American University Law Review, 25:5 (2010), p. 1043, Phoenix v. Czech Republic, ICSID Case No. ARB/06/5, Award (15.04.2009) [66].

common position to distinguish this type of limitation to jurisdiction as a separate category, in addition to the classic tripartite division.

Arbitral tribunals themselves decide upon the existence and scope of their own jurisdiction, based on the competence-competence doctrine.[12]

No appeals are available within the legal framework of investment arbitration. It offers, however, certain mechanisms which enable the correction of some errors made by tribunals when assessing the existence and scope of their jurisdiction. In the context of the ICSID Convention, a tribunal's failure to observe its own jurisdictional limits can serve as a basis for a party requesting the annulment of the tribunal's arbitral award, based on the manifest excess of powers argument, pursuant to Art. 52(1)(b) of the ICSID Convention.[13] Outside the ICSID Convention framework, if a tribunal fails to respect the limits of its jurisdiction, a party may file a motion to a common court in the place of the arbitration to set aside the award.[14] Outside the state which was the place of the arbitration, a party may undertake steps before the state courts to deny the recognition and enforcement of the arbitral award.[15]

The Spanish saga cases shed light on several issues related to jurisdiction. Two jurisdictional objections are the most relevant: the intra-EU objection and the tax carve-out clause. They were discussed in each of the analyzed cases and, as such, have the biggest potential to contribute to the lessons learned for

---

12 Gary B. Born, International Commercial Arbitration (Kluwer Law International 2021), pp. 1139–1169, Emmanuel Gaillard, John Savage (eds.), Fouchard, Gaillard, Goldman On International Commercial Arbitration (Kluwer Law International 1999), pp. 395–400, paras. 650–660. See also: Art 41(1) of the ICSID Convention, Art. 21(1) UNCITRAL Rules 1976, Art. 23(1) UNCITRAL Rules 2010. This principle is known under various other names, such as for example "kompetenz-kompetenz" or "jurisdiction to decide jurisdiction".

13 All EU member states except one (Poland) are contracting parties to the ICSID Convention – Brady Gordon, A Sceptical Analysis of the Enforcement of ISDS Awards in the EU Following the Decision of the CJEU on CETA, European Investment Law and Arbitration Review, 5:1 (2021), p. 97. See also: https://icsid.worldbank.org/about/member-states/database-of-member-states.

14 The motion to set aside is based on the domestic law of the place of arbitration. Many countries adopt the UNCITRAL Model Law on International Commercial Arbitration, Art. 34 of which regulates this issue. Typically, a party alleges that a tribunal is considered to have jurisdiction which is too broad. However, the reverse situation may also happen, which justifies state courts' intervening to correct a decision which narrows the scope of jurisdiction – see, for example: GPF v. Poland, Judgment of the English High Court of Justice, Case No. CL-2017-000174 (02.03.2018) [144].

15 The request to refuse recognition and enforcement of an arbitral award is typically based on Art V of the New York Convention, which has almost global nature with 170 contracting parties – https://uncitral.un.org/en/texts/arbitration/conventions/foreign_arbitral_awards/status2.

the future, by enabling patterns to be identified which make it possible to zoom out from the details of each specific dispute to draw general conclusions.[16] This section analyzes the first of those issues, namely the intra-EU objection. The second section focuses on the tax carve-out objection.

In general, the intra-EU objection should be understood as the respondents having argued that the tribunals had no jurisdiction over treaty-based arbitrations commenced by investors from one EU member state against another EU member state.

01.05.2004 is the date on which the genesis of this argument occurred, triggering a debate over the protection of intra-EU foreign investment. Prior to that date, no BITs existed between EU member states.[17] This all changed when, on 01.05.2004, 10 new member states joined the EU (Cyprus, Czech Republic, Estonia, Hungary, Latvia, Lithuania, Malta, Poland, Slovakia and Slovenia), followed by the accession of Bulgaria and Romania on 01.01.2007 and Croatia on 01.07.2013. All but 2 of these 12 states (i.e. all but Cyprus and Malta) were former Communist states.

These accessions to the EU created an (almost) unprecedented situation, in the sense that they led to the existence of intra-EU BITs. The BITs in force at the time of the accessions, which were previously BITs between the EU's member states and non-EU countries, became binding in reciprocal relations between "old" and "new" EU member states.[18] One commentator noted that "it has apparently never occurred to EU member states to enter into a BIT with one another at a time when both had already acceded to the EU".[19]

16 Apart from the issues analyzed in detail in this Chapter, each of the Spanish saga cases contained other considerations on jurisdiction, relevant to the specific facts of each of them. They include objections to jurisdiction based on arguments such as: fork-in-the-road, denial of ECT's protection, abuse of ECT's protection, cooling-off period, shareholders' claims, and state-to-state disputes. They are not, however, as common as the jurisdictional issues discussed in this Chapter. As such, the potential impact of the Spanish saga case law on the future development of case law on these issues is less probable than on the issues analyzed here.

17 With two exceptions, see fn 18 below for more details.

18 Prior to 01.05.2004, only two intra-EU BITs existed – i.e. the Germany-Greece BIT and the Germany-Portugal BIT. Both followed the same pattern, i.e. they were concluded as extra-EU BITs, at a time when neither Greece nor Portugal was an EU Member State. See: Wenhua Shan, Sheng Zhang, The Treaty of Lisbon: Half Way toward a Common Investment Policy, European Journal of International Law, 21:4 (2010), p. 1065, fn 92. As regards numbers, commentators indicate that there were 196 intra-EU BITs – Gordon, *supra* note 13, p. 93.

19 George A. Bermann, ECT and European Union Law, in: Maxi Scherer (ed.), International Arbitration in the Energy Sector (Oxford University Press 2018), p. 204. He continued:

On 01.12.2009, when the Treaty of Lisbon[20] entered into force, the EU's exclusive competence in the field of "common commercial policy" was extended to foreign direct investment.[21]

In a growing number of investment arbitrations based on the intra-EU BITs, the respondent states presented objections to jurisdiction based on the intra-EU arguments.[22] However, in not a single case was such an objection accepted by a tribunal.[23] Similar intra-EU objections were presented in some intra-EU cases brought under the ECT, and they were equally ineffective.[24]

> any such BIT would be regarded as entirely incompatible with the prohibition on nationality discrimination within the EU and more generally as inimical to the European Single Market. The only reason intra-EU BITs even exist is that they were entered into at a time when one of the two parties to the BIT was not yet an EU member state. In effect, what began as an 'extra-EU BIT' was transformed into an 'intra-EU BIT' upon the non-member state's accession to the EU. The situation under the ECT is somewhat more complicated. Many EU member states were already EU member states upon entering into the ECT. Upon entry, they thereby undertook investor protection obligations to one another, and disputes between one such state and a national of another could thus apparently proceed under the ECT. And yet such a dispute may be regarded as, in every sense, an 'intra-EU' dispute.

20 Treaty of Lisbon amending the Treaty on European Union and the Treaty establishing the European Community, signed at Lisbon, 13 December 2007 (OJ C 306, 17.12.2007, pp. 1–271).

21 Art. 1(157) and 1(158) Treaty of Lisbon, amending Arts. 206 and 207 TFEU. Prior to that, this fell within the scope of competence of the EU member states.

22 Chronologically, the first was probably: Eastern Sugar v. Czech Republic, SCC Case No. 088/2004, Partial Award (27.03.2007) [160], [165], [181]. See also for example: Binder v. Czech Republic, UNCITRAL, Award on Jurisdiction (06.06.2007) [66], Oostergetel v. Slovakia, UNCITRAL, Decision on Jurisdiction (30.04.2010) [109], EURAM v. Slovakia, UNCITRAL, Award on Jurisdiction (22.10.2012) [287], WNC v. Czech Republic, PCA Case No. 2014-34, Award (22.02.2017) [311], Anglia Auto v. Czech Republic, SCC Case No. V 2014/181, Final Award (10.03.2017) [118], [128], Busta v. Czech Republic, SCC Case No. V 2015/014, Final Award (10.03.2017) [118], [128]. This has not been argued in each intra-EU case, see for example: Dan Cake v. Hungary, ICSID Case No. ARB/12/9, Decision on Jurisdiction and Liability (24.08.2015) [67].

23 Kaj Hobér, The Energy Charter Treaty. A Commentary (Oxford University Press 2020), p. 405.

24 Chronologically, the first was probably: Electrabel v. Hungary, ICSID Case No. ARB/07/19, Decision on Jurisdiction, Applicable Law and Liability (30.11.2012). In [4.191] the tribunal, after a detailed analysis, concluded that:

> EU law would prevail over the ECT in case of any material inconsistency. That conclusion depends, however, upon the existence of a material inconsistency; and the Tribunal has concluded that none exists for the purpose of deciding the Parties' dispute in this arbitration.

See also for example: Blusun v. Italy, ICSID Case No. ARB/14/3, Award (27.12.2016) [291], [303], Wirtgen v. Czech Republic, PCA Case No. 2014-03, Final Award (11.10.2017)

The European Commission ("EC") considered that intra-EU foreign investment protection based on BITs was incompatible with EU law. In 2015, the EC called for the termination of all intra-EU BITs.[25] It also commenced an infringement action against five EU member states (Austria, the Netherlands, Romania, Slovakia and Sweden) for having failed to terminate the intra-EU BITs between them.[26]

The tensions between the EC's position and the uniform case law of the investor-state arbitral tribunals is best illustrated by the *Micula v. Romania* case.[27] The award rendered in the *Micula* case ordered Romania to pay compensation.[28] The EC decided that the payment of compensation pursuant to an arbitral award constitutes illegal state aid under EU law.[29] The case remains far from being concluded in a final manner.[30]

In this context, on 03.03.2016 a German state court made a request to the CJEU[31] for a preliminary ruling on whether the intra-EU BITs were compatible

---

[266]. These are the only 3 publicly available decisions concerning the intra-EU objection in ECT-based arbitrations prior to the *Achmea* judgment (see fn 44 below).

25 Commission asks Member States to terminate their intra-EU bilateral investment treaties (18.06.2015) available at: https://ec.europa.eu/commission/presscorner/detail/en/IP_15_5198. In 2009 it was reported that the EC had called upon EU member states to terminate intra-EU BITs but faced reluctance from them. See: Damon Vis-Dunbar, EU Member States Reject the Call to Terminate Intra-EU Bilateral Investment Treaties, Investment TreatyNews(10.02.2009),availableat:https://www.iisd.org/itn/en/2009/02/10/eu-member-states-reject-the-call-to-terminate-intra-eu-bilateral-investment-treaties/

26 Commission asks ..., ibid.

27 Micula v. Romania, ICSID Case No. ARB/05/20, Award (11.12.2013).

28 Ibid [1329].

29 Art. 1 of the EC Decision (EU) 2015/1470 of 30.03.2015 on State aid SA.38517 (2014/C) (ex 2014/NN) implemented by Romania – Arbitral award Micula v Romania of 11 December 2013 (OJ L 232, 04.09.2015, pp. 43–70). Art. 2(1) of the decision imposes an obligation on the claimants to repay any sums received under the *Micula* award, as illegal state aid, since part of the award was compensated against taxes owed by one of the claimants – [4].

30 The EC's decision is not final yet and the case remains pending at the CJEU. In its judgment of 25.01.2022, the CJEU's Grand Chamber (ECLI:EU:C:2022:50) set aside the judgment of 18.06.2019 of the General Court of the EU (ECLI:EU:T:2019:423), which annulled the decision. The claimants continue their efforts to enforce the *Micula* award in the US. See for example: US District Court for the District of Columbia, Case No. 17-cv-02332 (APM), Memorandum Opinion and Order (20.11.2020) [25], US Court of Appeals for the District of Columbia, Case No. 20–7116 (24.06.2022).

31 This Chapter continuously refers to the CJEU, even though numerous arbitral tribunals refer to the ECJ (European Court of Justice). Nevertheless, pursuant to Arts. 251–281 TFUE, together with Protocol (No 3) on the Statute of the Court of Justice of the European Union, reference to the CJEU (as encompassing the General Court and the Court of Justice) is more accurate.

with EU law.[32] The national proceedings which led to the request for a preliminary ruling involved a motion to set aside the arbitral award issued in *Achmea v. Slovakia*.[33] The *Achmea* arbitration was based on an intra-EU BIT concluded in 1991 between the Netherlands and the then Czech and Slovak Federative Republic.[34] It was *ad hoc* arbitration under the UNCITRAL Arbitration Rules, with the seat of arbitration in Frankfurt am Main in Germany.[35]

On 19.09.2017, Advocate General Wathelet issued an opinion to the effect that the existence of intra-EU BITs was not incompatible with EU law ("AG Wathelet's opinion").[36] This position was not shared by the CJEU and, in its judgment of 08.03.2018 ("*Achmea* judgment"), the CJEU decided that Arts. 267 and 344 TFEU:

> must be interpreted as precluding a provision in an international agreement concluded between Member States, such as Article 8 of the Agreement on encouragement and reciprocal protection of investments between the Kingdom of the Netherlands and the Czech and Slovak Federative Republic, under which an investor from one of those Member States may, in the event of a dispute concerning investments in the other Member State, bring proceedings against the latter Member State before an arbitral tribunal whose jurisdiction that Member State has undertaken to accept.[37]

The CJEU observed that an arbitral tribunal may be called upon to interpret or apply EU law.[38] However, arbitral tribunals are not courts or tribunals

32 Judgment of the Court (Grand Chamber) of 06.03.2018, Slovakia v. Achmea, Case No. C-284/16 (ECLI:EU:C:2018:158).

33 Achmea v. Slovakia, PCA Case No. 2008-13, Final Award (07.12.2012).

34 *Achmea* judgment, *supra* note 32, [2]–[3].

35 Achmea v. Slovakia, *supra* note 33, [16], Achmea v. Slovakia, PCA Case No. 2008-13, Award on Jurisdiction, Arbitrability and Suspension (26.10.2010) [10], [224].

36 Opinion of Advocate General Wathelet delivered on 19.09.2017, Slovakia v. Achmea, Case No. C-284/16 (ECLI:EU:C:2017:699) [273]:

> I therefore propose that the Court should answer the questions for a preliminary ruling referred to it by the Bundesgerichtshof (Federal Court of Justice, Germany) as follows: Articles 18, 267 and 344 TFEU must be interpreted as not precluding the application of an investor/State dispute settlement mechanism established by means of a bilateral investment agreement concluded before the accession of one of the Contracting States to the European Union and providing that an investor from one Contracting State may, in the case of a dispute relating to investments in the other Contracting State, bring proceedings against the latter State before an arbitral tribunal.

37 *Achmea* judgment, *supra* note 32, operative part.

38 Ibid [42].

within the meaning of Art. 267 TFEU, because they are "not part of the judicial system" of any of the EU member states.[39] Consequently, they cannot request that the CJEU issue a preliminary ruling.[40] The CJEU also underlined the differences between commercial and investment arbitrations.[41] It concluded that the jurisdictional clause in the intra-EU BIT upon which it was ruling had "an adverse effect on the autonomy of EU law".[42]

The *Achmea* judgment did not address the compatibility of the ECT with EU law.[43] The arbitral tribunals constituted under the ECT decided that they had jurisdiction over intra-EU disputes, even after the *Achmea* judgment.[44]

39 Ibid [45]. The CJEU has consistently said that, in order to qualify as a "court or tribunal of a Member State" within the meaning of EU law, the judicial body in question must have certain features, namely it must be established by law, be permanent in nature, have compulsory jurisdiction, apply inter partes procedure, apply rules of law and be independent (see for example: Judgment of the Court of 17.09.1997, Dorsch Consult, Case No. C-54/96 (ECLI:EU:C:1997:413) [23], Judgment of the Court (Fifth Chamber) of 11.06.1987, Pretore di Salò, Case No. 14/86 (ECLI:EU:C:1987:275) [7], Judgment of the Court of 17.10.1989, Danfoss, Case No. 109/88 (ECLI:EU:C:1989:383) [7]-[8], Judgment of the Court of 27.04.1994, Almelo, Case No. C-393/92 (ECLI:EU:C:1994:171) [21]). Whist arbitral tribunals such as those analyzed in the present study would have no difficulty in complying with some of the aforementioned criteria, they would be unable to show that their jurisdiction was compulsory, as consent of the parties is required in order for any arbitration to commence.

40 Ibid [49].

41 Ibid [54]. For the CJEU, while commercial arbitrations "originate in the freely expressed wishes of the parties", investment arbitrations:

> derive from a treaty by which Member States agree to remove from the jurisdiction of their own courts, and hence from the system of judicial remedies which the second subparagraph of Article 19(1) TEU requires them to establish in the fields covered by EU law [...] disputes which may concern the application or interpretation of EU law.

42 Ibid [59].

43 Some describe the *Achmea* judgment as having "laconic reasoning". See for example: Venetia Argyropoulou, Vattenfall in the Aftermath of Achmea: Between a Rock and a Hard Place?, European Investment Law and Arbitration Review, 4:1 (2019), p. 223.

44 See for example: Greentech v. Italy, SCC Case No. V 2015/095, Final Award (23.12.2018) [403], CEF v. Italy, SCC Case No. V 2015/158, Award (16.01.2019) [100], Eskosol v. Italy, ICSID Case No. ARB/15/50, Decision on Italy's Request for Immediate Termination and Italy's Jurisdictional Objection Based on Inapplicability of the Energy Charter Treaty to Intra-EU Disputes (07.05.2019) [177], [186], Voltaic v. Czech Republic, PCA Case No. 2014-20 Award (15.05.2019) [348], I.C.W. v. Czech Republic, PCA Case No. 2014-22, Award (15.05.2019) [396], WA v. Czech Republic, PCA Case No. 2014-19, Award (15.05.2019) [438], Rockhopper v. Italy, ICSID Case No. ARB/17/14, Decision on the Intra-EU Jurisdictional Objection (29.06.2019) [172], [175], Belenergia v. Italy, ICSID Case No. ARB/15/40, Award (06.08.2019) [340], Sun Reserve v. Italy, SCC Case No. V 2016/32, Award (25.03.2020) [464], ESPF v. Italy, ICSID Case No. ARB/16/5, Award (14.09.2020) [336], Festorino v. Poland, SCC Case No. V2018/098, Award (30.06.2021) [473].

The highly commented *Vattenfall v. Germany* case is an illustrative example.[45] What may be more surprising is that, even in the arbitrations based on intra-EU BITs, the tribunals continued to dismiss the intra-EU objections.[46]

This prompted the EC to intensify its efforts to eliminate intra-EU investor-state arbitration.[47] It organized a summit[48] at which, on 15.01.2019, 22 EU member states issued a declaration that the *Achmea* judgment applied to ECT-based arbitrations in the same way as it applied to arbitrations based on intra-EU BITs.[49] However, there was a clear lack of uniformity among the EU member states as regards the consequences of the *Achmea* judgment. 5 member states declared, on the following day, that the *Achmea* judgment concerns the interpretation of EU law solely as regards intra-EU BITs and that it is

45 Vattenfall v. Germany, ICSID Case No. ARB/12/12, Decision on the *Achmea* Issue (31.08.2018). This is probably "the most detailed analysis and discussion of the intra-EU and Achmea issues" – Hobér, *supra* note 23, p. 412.

46 See for example: Marfin v. Cyprus, ICSID Case No. ARB/13/27, Award (26.07.2018) [579]-[580], UP and C.D v. Hungary, ICSID Case No. ARB/13/35, Award (09.10.2018) [252], [267], Tallinn v. Estonia, ICSID Case No. ARB/14/24, Award (21.06.2019) [540], [560], Magyar Farming v. Hungary, ICSID Case No. ARB/17/27, Award (13.11.2019) [207]–[208], [248], Adamakopoulos v. Greece, ICSID Case No. ARB/15/49, Decision on Jurisdiction (07.02.2020) [162], [172], [187], although with a dissenting opinion on this issue – Adamakopoulos v. Greece, ICSID Case No. ARB/15/49, Statement of Dissent of Professor Marcelo Kohen (03.02.2020), GPF v. Poland, SCC Case No. V 2014/168, Award (29.04.2020) [346]–[348], [384]–[385], AMF v. Czech Republic, PCA Case No. 2017-15, Final Award (11.05.2020) [376]–[378], Addiko v. Croatia, ICSID Case No. ARB/17/37, Decision on Croatia's Jurisdictional Objection Related to the Alleged Incompatibility of the BIT with the EU Acquis (12.06.2020) [297], Fynerdale v. Czech Republic, PCA Case No. 2018-18, Award (29.04.2021) [281].

47 Samantha J. Rowe, Nelson Goh, Resolving Perceived Norm Conflict through Principles of Treaty Interpretation. The January 2019 EU Member States' Declarations, European Investment Law and Arbitration Review, 5:1 (2021), p. 173.

48 Rockhopper v. Italy, *supra* note 44 [180]:

> [...] the representatives who signed the Declaration were gathered for that purpose by the EC (the Respondent states as follows: "Commissioner Valdis Dombrovskis invited the Permanent Representatives into the premises of the European [Commission] to sign the Declaration declaring the readiness of the Commission to organize signature in the afternoon of 15 January"), [...]

(footnote omitted).

49 Declaration of the Representatives of the Governments of the Member States on the Legal Consequences of the Judgment of the Court of Justice in *Achmea* and on Investment Protection in the European Union, issued by 22 EU Member States: Austria, Belgium, Bulgaria, Croatia, Cyprus, Czech Republic, Denmark, Estonia, France, Germany, Greece, Ireland, Italy, Latvia, Lithuania, Netherlands, Poland, Portugal, Romania, Slovakia, Spain, and United Kingdom (15.01.2019) (available at: https://commission.europa.eu/system/files/2019-01/190117-bilateral-investment-treaties_en.pdf).

"silent" on the investor-state arbitration clause in the ECT.[50] 1 EU member state went further and declared that the *Achmea* judgment concerns only intra-EU BITs, and that it "does not concern any pending or prospective arbitration proceedings initiated under the ECT"[51] (all three of these declarations are jointly referred to as the "2019 Declarations").

The process of terminating the intra-EU BITs culminated on 05.05.2020, when 23 EU member states concluded the Agreement for the termination of Bilateral Investment Treaties between the member states of the European Union ("Termination Agreement").[52] Apart from terminating the intra-EU BITs, Art. 4(1) of the Termination Agreement "confirms" that jurisdictional

---

50 Declaration of the Representatives of the Governments of the Member States on the Enforcement of the Judgment of the Court of Justice in *Achmea* and on Investment Protection in the European Union, issued by: Finland, Luxembourg, Malta, Slovenia and Sweden (16.01.2019) (available at: https://www.regeringen.se/48ee19/contentassets/d759689c0c80 4a9ea7af6b2de7320128/achmea-declaration.pdf).

51 Declaration of the Representative of the Government of Hungary on the Legal Consequences of the Judgment of the Court of Justice in *Achmea* and on Investment Protection in the European Union (available at: https://commission.europa.eu/system /files/2021-09/190116-bilateral-investment-treaties-hungary_en.pdf). It further added that the "ongoing and future applicability of the ECT in intra-EU relations requires further discussion and individual agreement amongst the Member States".

52 Agreement for the Termination of Bilateral Investment Treaties between the Member States of the European Union (OJ L 169, 29.05.2020, pp. 1–41). 4 EU member states are not parties to this agreement: Austria, Ireland, Finland and Sweden. It entered into force on 29.08.2020 (https://www.consilium.europa.eu/en/documents-publications/treaties -agreements/agreement/?id=2019049&DocLanguage=en). One may have the impression that the Termination Agreement left arbitral tribunals unimpressed, since they continued to dismiss the intra-EU objections. However, this would be a superficial conclusion. This is because the tribunals assess the existence and scope of their jurisdiction at the moment of commencing arbitration, not issuing the award. *Muszynianka v. Slovakia* serves as an example of this. The tribunal stated that:

> jurisdiction is determined at the time of the institution of the proceedings [...]. Thus, if jurisdiction existed on that date (subject to the Respondent's remaining jurisdictional objections), it will remain so regardless of subsequent events, including the termination of the BIT

(footnotes omitted) – Muszynianka v. Slovakia, PCA Case No. 2017-08, Award (07.10.2020) [263]. This suggests that, had the arbitral proceedings been initiated after the entry into force of the Termination Agreement, the decision may have been different. This may, in turn, have triggered a debate on whether the Termination Agreement had unlawfully violated investors' acquired rights, by terminating the sunset clauses in the intra-EU BITs. See for example: Nikos Lavranos, The World after the Termination of Intra-EU BITs, European Investment Law and Arbitration Review, 5:1 (2021), p. 196.

clauses in intra-EU BITS are "inapplicable". The preamble to the Termination Agreement clarifies that the ECT is out of its scope.[53]

2021 brought two new important judgments of the CJEU in this context. On 02.09.2021, the CJEU issued judgment in the *Komstroy* case ("*Komstroy* judgment").[54] This case was initiated by a French court's request for a preliminary ruling in court proceedings initiated by a motion to set aside an ECT arbitral award issued in *Energoalliance v. Moldova, ad hoc* proceedings under the UNCITRAL Arbitration Rules with the seat of arbitration in Paris. The seat of arbitration was the only link of the arbitration with EU law, since the claimant was from Ukraine.[55] The French court asked 3 questions concerning the interpretation of the term "investment" used in Art. 1(6) and 26(1) ECT.[56] In answering these questions, the CJEU aligned the *Achmea* judgment with ECT-based arbitration.[57] It added that "Article 26(2)(c) ECT must be interpreted as not being applicable to disputes between a Member State and an investor of another Member State concerning an investment made by the latter in the first Member State".[58] However, this is not the operative part of the *Komstroy* judgment, but merely part of the CJEU's reasoning. The questions asked by the French court did not concern the intra-EU aspect of the ECT jurisdictional clause.[59]

---

53 "[…] CONSIDERING that this Agreement addresses intra-EU bilateral investment treaties; it does not cover intra-EU proceedings on the basis of Article 26 of the Energy Charter Treaty. The European Union and its Member States will deal with this matter at a later stage, […]".

54 Judgment of the Court (Grand Chamber) of 02.09.2021, Moldova v. Komstroy, Case No. C-741/19 (ECLI:EU:C:2021:655).

55 Energoalliance v. Moldova, UNCITRAL, Arbitral Award (23.10.2013) [1]. The claimant in the arbitral proceedings was a predecessor of Komstroy, the party in the proceedings before the CJEU.

56 *Komstroy* judgment, *supra* note 54 [20].

57 Ibid [52]. In [64] the CJEU added that:

> despite the multilateral nature of the international agreement of which it forms part, a provision such as Article 26 ECT is intended, in reality, to govern bilateral relations between two of the Contracting Parties, in an analogous way to the provision of the bilateral investment treaty at issue in the case giving rise to the *Achmea* judgment.

58 Ibid [66]. Already in 2011 some commentators had highlighted the inevitable conclusion that, from the vantage point of EU law, a cross-border investment between the EU Member States is not a "foreign" investment. See for example: Christer Söderlund, The Future of the Energy Charter Treaty in the context of the Lisbon Treaty, in: Graham Coop (ed.), Energy Dispute Resolution: Investment Protection, Transit and the Energy Charter Treaty (JurisNet 2011), p. 106.

59 The CJEU admitted as much when it noted [41] that:

> although the fact that the dispute at issue in the main proceedings, based on Article 26(2)(c) ECT, is between an operator from one third State and another third State does not preclude, for the reasons stated in paragraphs 22 to 38 of the present judgment, the Court's jurisdiction to answer those questions, it cannot be inferred that that provision of the ECT also applies to a dispute between an operator from one Member

Shortly afterwards, on 26.10.2021, the CJEU issued judgment in the *PL Holdings* case ("*PL Holdings* judgment").[60] This case concerned a motion to set aside the two awards (partial and final) issued in the *PL Holdings v. Poland* case, an SCC arbitration with the seat of arbitration in Stockholm.[61] The Swedish Supreme Court requested a preliminary ruling as to whether EU law permits a "free will" decision of a state not to present intra-EU objections to jurisdiction, which would be understood as being implied consent to arbitrate, substituting an offer to arbitrate in an intra-EU BIT.[62] The CJEU decided that Art. 267 and Art. 344 TFEU preclude:

> national legislation which allows a Member State to conclude an ad hoc arbitration agreement with an investor from another Member State that makes it possible to continue arbitration proceedings initiated on the basis of an arbitration clause whose content is identical to that agreement, where that clause is contained in

an intra-EU BIT.[63]

State and another Member State.

Similar focus on the ECT's intra-EU jurisdictional clause, which was not directly covered by the questions asked by the French state court, can be seen in Advocate General Szpunar's opinion of 03.03.2021, Moldova v. Komstroy, a company the successor in law to the company Energoalians, Case No. C-741/19 (ECLI:EU:C:2021:164). It was described how:

> at the hearing, the European Commission and several EU Member States 'hijacked' the debate and introduced the question of the validity of intra-EU ECT arbitration, even though the dispute at issue involved a non-EU investor and a non-EU Member State

– Clement Fouchard, Vanessa Thieffry, CJEU Ruling in Moldova v. Komstroy: the End of Intra-EU Investment Arbitration Under the Energy Charter Treaty (and a Restrictive Interpretation of the Notion of Protected Investment), Kluwer Arbitration Blog (07.09.2021), available at: http://arbitrationblog.kluwerarbitration.com/2021/09/07/cjeu-ruling-in-moldova-v-komstroy-the-end-of-intra-eu-investment-arbitration-under-the-energy-charter-treaty-and-a-restrictive-interpretation-of-the-notion-of-protected-investment/.

60 Judgment of the Court (Grand Chamber) of 26.10.2021, Poland v. PL Holdings, Case No. C-109/20 (ECLI:EU:C:2021:875).

61 Ibid [22], PL Holdings v. Poland, SCC Case No. V 2014/163, Partial Award (28.06.2017) [30], PL Holdings v. Poland, SCC Case No. V 2014/163, Final Award (28.08.2017).

62 *PL Holdings* judgment, *supra* note 60 [33]:

> Do Articles 267 and 344 TFEU, as interpreted in [the *Achmea* judgment], mean that an arbitration agreement is invalid if it has been concluded between a Member State and an investor – where an investment agreement contains an arbitration clause that is invalid as a result of the fact that the contract was concluded between two Member States – by virtue of the fact that the Member State, after arbitration proceedings were commenced by the investor, refrains, by the free will of the State, from raising objections as to jurisdiction?

63 Ibid, operative part.

1.2 *Spanish Saga Case Law*

In this context, the Spanish saga cases provide a valuable contribution to the analysis of the intersections between investment arbitration tribunals and the EU legal order, as well as the interplay between their case law and the case law of the CJEU.

The chronological order of the Spanish saga cases in the present Chapter differs from the order adopted in the remaining Chapters in this book. The reason is that, in two of the analyzed cases, namely *PV Investors*[64] and *RREEF*,[65] the tribunals bifurcated the proceedings and issued separate decisions on jurisdiction. Thus, the analysis follows the order presented in the table below, which reflects the chronological order of decisions on jurisdiction:

TABLE 3 Decisions on jurisdiction, differentiation between ICSID and non-ICSID arbitrations

No	Case name	Date of award / decision on jurisdiction	Institution	Place of arbitration	Comments
1	PV Investors	13.10.2014	ad hoc (UNCITRAL Rules)	Geneva (Switzerland)	Final award - 28.02.2020
2	Charanne	21.01.2016	SCC	Madrid (Spain)	Limited scope of disputed measures
3	RREEF	06.06.2016	ICSID	N/A	Decision on responsibility and on the principles of quantum - 30.11.2018, final award - 11.12.2019
4	Isolux	12.07.2016	SCC	Stockholm (Sweden)	
5	Eiser	04.05.2017	ICSID	N/A	Award annulled (for reasons related to non-disclosure of an arbitrator)

64 The PV Investors v. Spain, PCA Case No. 2012-14, Preliminary Award on Jurisdiction (13.10.2014).

65 RREEF v. Spain, ICSID Case No. ARB/13/30, Decision on Jurisdiction (06.06.2016).

TABLE 3 Decisions on jurisdiction, differentiation between ICSID and non-ICSID arbitrations (*Cont.*)

No	Case name	Date of award / decision on jurisdiction	Institution	Place of arbitration	Comments
6	**Novenergia**	15.02.2018	SCC	Stockholm (Sweden)	
7	**Masdar**	16.05.2018	ICSID	N/A	
8	**Antin**	15.06.2018	ICSID	N/A	
9	**Foresight**	14.11.2018	SCC	Stockholm (Sweden)	
10	**Cube**	19.02.2019	ICSID	N/A	Final award - 15.07.2019
11	**NextEra**	12.03.2019	ICSID	N/A	Final award - 31.05.2019
12	**9REN**	31.05.2019	ICSID	N/A	
13	**SolEs**	31.07.2019	ICSID	N/A	Rectification - 05.12.2019
14	**InfraRed**	02.08.2019	ICSID	N/A	Rectification - 25.03.2010
15	**OperaFund**	06.09.2019	ICSID	N/A	
16	**BayWa**	02.12.2019	ICSID	N/A	Final award - 25.01.2021
17	**Stadtwerke**	02.12.2019	ICSID	N/A	
18	**RWE**	30.12.2019	ICSID	N/A	Final award - 18.12.2020
19	**Watkins**	21.01.2020	ICSID	N/A	Rectifcation - 13.07.2020
20	**Hydro**	09.03.2020	ICSID	N/A	Final award - 05.08.2020
21	**Cavalum**	31.08.2020	ICSID	N/A	
	Total		ICSID cases - 16 non-ICSID cases - 5		

•••

1.2.1 PV Investors

1.2.1.1 *Nationality/Territorial Diversity*

In *PV Investors*, the tribunal commenced its analysis of the intra-EU jurisdictional objection by considering whether the territorial diversity requirement was met. It analyzed the definition of the "Area" in Art. 1(10) ECT, noting that it covers both the territory of the ECT's contracting parties and that of a Regional Economic Integration Organization ("REIO"), which must be distinguished.[66] The relevant definition depends on the identity of the respondent in any particular dispute. As Spain was the respondent in this case, the territory of Spain (not the territory of the EU) was relevant.[67] If the EU was the respondent, then the territory relevant for assessing jurisdiction would be "the entire EU Area".[68]

1.2.1.2 *Disconnection Clause*

Second, the tribunal found that no disconnection clause was present in the ECT. It defined disconnection clauses as provisions that "ensure that between parties to a multilateral treaty which are also parties to a regional organization, the rules of the regional organization prevail over the treaty".[69] It noted that the EU and its member states had prior experience in disconnection clauses by the time the ECT was concluded, such as the clause in the 1988 Convention on Mutual Administrative Assistance in Tax Matters.[70] The tribunal also noted that the ECT contains a disconnection clause with respect to the Svalbard Treaty.[71] It would be "striking" if the ECT's contracting states had made an express exception for a treaty concerning an archipelago in the Arctic but "somehow omitted to specify that the ECT's dispute settlement system did not apply in all of the EU member states' relations". Therefore, it concluded that the ECT's ordinary meaning precludes the existence of an implied disconnection clause.[72]

1.2.1.3 *EU Law*

Third, the tribunal analyzed whether EU law precluded it from having jurisdiction over intra-EU disputes. It considered it "doubtful" that Art. 344 TFEU

66 The PV Investors v. Spain, *supra* note 64 [178].

67 Ibid [179].

68 Ibid [180].

69 Ibid [169]. This appears to be a definition adopted by the tribunal, even though it is contained in the part of the award which presents the positions of the parties.

70 Ibid [182].

71 Treaty concerning Spitsbergen of 09.02.1920. Annex 2, Decision 1 to the ECT reads as follows:

> In the event of a conflict between the treaty concerning Spitsbergen of 9 February 1920 (the Svalbard Treaty) and the Energy Charter Treaty, the treaty concerning Spitsbergen shall prevail to the extent of the conflict, without prejudice to the positions of the Contracting Parties in respect of the Svalbard Treaty. In the event of such conflict or a dispute as to whether there is such conflict or as to its extent, Article 16 and Part V of the Energy Charter Treaty shall not apply.

72 The PV Investors v. Spain, *supra* note 64 [183].

would bar inter-state arbitration between EU member states in all circumstances. It noted, for example, that the United Nations Convention on the Law of the Sea is not considered to be contrary to the TFEU.[73] In any case, since Art. 344 TFEU applies to state-to-state disputes involving EU member states, it does not prohibit the "submission of disputes between other actors to a different method of settlement not contemplated in the EU Treaties".[74]

In the tribunal's view, there is no "absolute monopoly of the CJEU over the interpretation and application of EU law", which is proven by "numerous instances where EU law is applied outside of the judicial framework of the EU",[75] such as when a non-EU court or arbitral tribunal, hearing a dispute between private parties, applies EU law whilst having no possibility to seek a preliminary ruling from the CJEU. A similar situation would happen in investor-state arbitration commenced by an investor from outside the EU against an EU member state – a possibility which was not questioned by the respondent.[76]

1.2.1.4 *Subsequent Agreement or Practice*

The tribunal considered that no subsequent agreement or practice existed, within the meaning of Art. 31(3)(a) or 31(3)(b) Vienna Convention on the Law of Treaties ("VCLT"), which would result in a different conclusion. It considered that any such subsequent agreement must "regard" the interpretation of the relevant treaty, be purported to clarify the meaning of the treaty and be made between all of the parties to the treaty.[77] Any such subsequent practice must occur "in the application" of the treaty and concern all the parties (even if not all of them participate in the practice, they must have at least acquiesced in the respective interpretation of the treaty).[78] None of the EU legal instruments relied upon by the respondent met these prerequisites.[79] The tribunal considered the *travaux préparatoires* of the ECT to be too "unclear and inconclusive" to encourage it to depart from the meaning at which it had arrived by applying the general rules of treaty interpretation.[80]

Finally, the tribunal observed that the answer did not differ according to whether the host and home states were "old" or "new" EU member states.[81]

---

73 Ibid [187]–[188].
74 Ibid [189].
75 Ibid [191].
76 Ibid.
77 Ibid [193].
78 Ibid [194].
79 Ibid [196]–[199].
80 Ibid [202].
81 Ibid [205].

1.2.1.5 *Achmea Judgment*

After the *Achmea* judgment and the 2019 Declarations were issued, the respondent asked the tribunal to reconsider its decision on jurisdiction, based on these "new facts".[82] The tribunal denied the request, considering this to be an attempt to re-litigate an already decided issue. The tribunal added that, under the law of the place of arbitration, a challenge to an award on jurisdiction must be launched immediately, within 30 days of it having been handed down. Otherwise, the decision has *res judicata* (or comparable) effect.[83] Therefore, the decision on jurisdiction binds the tribunal and cannot be re-opened. For the tribunal, the respondent's intra-EU objection was not altered by the new developments, which simply "added possible legal arguments". The tribunal viewed this as compatible with the principle that the date of initiating the arbitration is the relevant moment for assessing jurisdiction.[84]

The tribunal dismissed the respondent's additional request, filed at the same stage of the proceedings, to seek the views of the 22 EU member states which had signed the first of the 2019 Declarations, to confirm their understanding of the declaration.[85] The tribunal confirmed that it had the authority to do so "under its broad procedural powers", but it saw no reason for doing it.[86] It saw no need to clarify the content of the relevant declaration.[87]

1.2.2 Charanne

1.2.2.1 *Nationality/Territorial Diversity*

In *Charanne*, Spain commenced by arguing that the dispute did not meet the requirement of diversity of territories between the investor and the host state, as required by Art. 26 ECT.[88] Spain argued that the claimants should be considered as EU investors, and not investors from their respective home states. Then, the dispute would concern an investment made by the EU investors within

82 The PV Investors v. Spain, PCA Case No. 2012-14, Final Award (28.02.2020) [151], [538].

83 Ibid [543]. This underlines the differences between various mechanisms of arbitration. In ICSID arbitrations, tribunals have some room to reconsider previous decisions until the final award is issued. In this case, which was *ad hoc* under the UNCITRAL Rules, the law of the place of arbitration determined that the award on jurisdiction had a res judicata effect (or a comparable effect).

84 Ibid [544].

85 Ibid [531].

86 Ibid [546].

87 Ibid [549].

88 Charanne v. Spain, SCC Case No. V 062/2012, Award (21.01.2016) [427].

EU territory. It would mean that there is no diversity of nationality within the meaning of Article 26(1) ECT.[89]

The tribunal considered that the EU member states had not ceased to be contracting parties to the ECT simply because the EU is also a contracting party to the ECT. Consequently, both the EU and its member states may have legal standing as respondents in arbitrations based on the ECT.[90] The tribunal added that the claims did not concern the EU's own actions, but measures adopted by Spain, in the exercise of its national sovereignty. Furthermore, the claimants had not directed the claim against the EU, nor requested that the EU be declared liable for a treaty violation.[91]

1.2.2.2 *Disconnection Clause*

Spain further argued that the ECT contains an implicit disconnection clause for intra-EU relations and that its purpose would be to "unlink" the EU member states of the ECT in their relations with each other.[92] The tribunal considered this to be a matter of interpreting the ECT, which must be done in accordance with Art. 31 VCLT. The tribunal applied the "fundamental rule" of interpreting a treaty's terms in good faith according to their ordinary meaning and in the context of the treaty as a whole, taking into account the ECT's object and purpose. It concluded that the terms of the ECT are clear and do not justify adopting any additional interpretation "that could lead to reading into the ECT an implicit disconnection clause for intra-EU disputes".[93]

1.2.2.3 *EU Law*

The tribunal added that the ECT's contracting parties had no need to agree on a disconnection clause over intra-EU disputes, whether implicit or explicit, because its aim would be to resolve a conflict between the ECT and the TFEU, whilst no such conflict exists.[94] The tribunal identified no rule of EU law that prevents EU Member States from resolving their disputes with investors from other EU Member States through arbitration, nor a rule of EU law that prevents arbitral tribunals from applying EU law to resolve such disputes.[95] It recognized,

89 Ibid [428].
90 Ibid [429].
91 Ibid [431].
92 Ibid [433].
93 Ibid [437].
94 Ibid [438].
95 Ibid.

however, that Art. 267 TFEU prevents EU member states from resolving interstate disputes through arbitration based on Art. 27 ECT.[96]

Spain argued that Art. 344 TFEU does not allow EU member states to resolve disputes about EU law through international arbitration.[97] The tribunal noted that this provision refers to disputes between the EU Member States, not between an EU Member State and a private party.[98] It dismissed the position that this provision also covers other disputes involving an interpretation of EU law and which should therefore "remain within the jurisdiction of the European institutions".[99] For the tribunal, accepting this line of reasoning would mean that no arbitral tribunal "could ever decide any issue that involved an interpretation of the European treaties whenever the responsibility of a Member State would be at stake".[100] Nevertheless, in reality there are many cases in which the EU Member States are respondents in proceedings before national courts, in which the interpretation or application of European treaties may be relevant. In addition, the EU member states can conclude arbitration agreements in disputes that may involve aspects of EU law. For the tribunal "it is today universally accepted that an arbitral tribunal not only has the power, but also the duty to apply EU law".[101] It considered Art. 344 TFEU as a tool to achieve the objective of a harmonious application of EU law and, as such, to ensure that the CJEU has the final word on the interpretation of EU law to achieve its uniform interpretation.[102] This conclusion was reinforced by the fact that the EU had signed the ECT, which does not permit reservations to be made, and therefore the EU itself accepted the jurisdictional clause in Art. 26 ECT.[103] The tribunal also noted that Spain did not allege that the arbitral award could violate the European judicial order.[104]

1.2.3 RREEF

1.2.3.1 *EU Law*

In the *RREEF* case, the tribunal started by observing that the main issue to be decided regarding the intra-EU objection is whether the supremacy of EU law

96 Ibid [436].
97 Ibid [440].
98 Ibid [441].
99 Ibid [442].
100 Ibid [443].
101 Ibid.
102 Ibid [444].
103 Ibid [445].
104 Ibid [448].

prevails over norms of international law.[105] It reaffirmed that EU law prevails "in the relations" between the EU member states "that fall within the scope of the EU constitutional framework", and that EU law is part of international law "outside of the EU legal order".[106] However, the tribunal considered that the ECT was its "constitution" and its basis for exercising jurisdiction, which – in the event of any conflict with other treaties – must find "full application". Any "hierarchy" must be decided based on public international law, not EU law, which would lead to the conclusion that the ECT would prevail over other norms (aside from *ius cogens* norms). Also Art. 16 ECT grants no basis to distinguish EU law from other international agreements.[107] EU law is *res inter alios acta* and non-EU contracting states to the ECT did not accept its alleged supremacy over the ECT.[108]

Regardless of the above, if both the ECT and EU law are to be applied, they must be interpreted in a manner "as not to contradict each other". This interpretative directive is strengthened by the fact that the EU played a significant role in promoting and negotiating the ECT, and therefore it finds support in Art. 207(3) TFEU.[109]

Based on the above, the tribunal decided that there was no contradiction between Art. 344 TFEU and Art. 26 ECT, since these provisions concern the resolution of two different types of disputes.[110] Art. 344 TFEU does not establish an "interpretative monopoly" for the CJEU and there are "a number of contexts" in which other judicial or arbitral bodies interpret and apply EU law.[111]

1.2.3.2 *Disconnection Clause*

The tribunal considered that the purpose of a disconnection clause is to make it clear that the EU Member States apply EU law, as opposed to the ECT, in their relations. In the absence of such a clause, the ECT is intended to be integrally applied by the EU and its Member States.[112] The tribunal underlined that there was no need for a disconnection clause, whether explicit or implicit, as there is no "disharmony or conflict" between EU law and the ECT.[113] Moreover,

105 RREEF v. Spain, *supra* note 65 [71].
106 Ibid [72]–[73].
107 Ibid [75].
108 Ibid [74].
109 Ibid [76].
110 Ibid [79].
111 Ibid [80]. This shows that the tribunal blended the analysis of the arguments put forward by the respondent about the intra-EU nationality and the supremacy of EU law.
112 Ibid [82].
113 Ibid [82]–[83].

it considered it "untenable" to construe an implicit disconnection clause into the ECT, since it would be contrary to the public international law principle of *pacta sunt servanda*. This was clearly true, given that the ECT contains express exceptions to the consent to arbitration (e.g. Annex IA ECT) and that Art. 46 ECT precludes the possibility of making reservations.[114] Interpretating the ECT otherwise "would put into question the function of explicit disconnection clauses when they exist".[115]

Even if a conflict existed between the provisions of the ECT and the TFUE, the public international law obligation of an ECT-based tribunal would be to apply ECT, as the "EU law does not and cannot "trump" public international law".[116] This conclusion was strengthened by the fact that it was in line with all known treaty cases in which the intra-EU objection was raised.[117]

1.2.3.3 *Achmea Judgment*

After the decision on jurisdiction was issued, in March 2018 Spain requested permission to admit the *Achmea* judgment on the record.[118] That request was granted.[119] However, this did not alter the tribunal's decision on jurisdiction. The tribunal considered its previous finding as *res judicata* and incapable of being revisited.[120]

The tribunal added that the *Achmea* judgment was "inapposite" because it had to be distinguished on the facts – it dealt with an intra-EU BIT between two EU countries – whereas the ECT "binds both the EU and its Member States on the one hand and non-EU States on the other hand". The tribunal added that it would be "highly improper to impose a sweeping modification of the ECT on EU non-member States using the pretext that it was eventually considered as being incompatible with EU law".[121]

The tribunal added that international law does not provide a hierarchy to resolve any potential incompatibility between the ECT and EU law. If any

114 Ibid [85].
115 Ibid [86].
116 Ibid [87].
117 Ibid [88].
118 RREEF v. Spain, ICSID Case No. ARB/13/30, Decision on Responsibility and on the Principles of Quantum (30.11.2018) [73].
119 Ibid [75].
120 Ibid [209]. This was even though "these findings do not appear in the operative part of the Decision on Jurisdiction, they constitute the necessary support for it". The tribunal also considered its decision on jurisdiction as *res judicata*, which can be considered as controversial when comparing jurisdiction with admissibility. The tribunal failed to address this issue in more detail.
121 Ibid [211].

conflict exists, this is a matter of negotiation between states. To the extent that the EU or an EU member state violates the law on state responsibility by ratifying incompatible treaties, "that is a matter for it to resolve".[122]

The tribunal disagreed with the CJEU's distinction between commercial and investment treaty arbitration in respect of the relevance of EU law. It considered that, in both types of arbitration, the source of the obligation to arbitrate is based on the consent of the parties. It added that "no post-hoc decision of the CJEU can somehow undo that consent once given".[123]

1.2.4 Isolux

1.2.4.1 *Nationality/Territorial Diversity*

In *Isolux*, Spain also argued that a claimant from an EU member state fails to fulfill the prerequisite of being from "another Contracting Party" within the meaning of Art. 26 ECT.[124] The tribunal looked first at the definition of "Area" found in Art. 1(10) ECT. It noted that both the home state and the host state exercise sovereign rights over their respective territories.[125] In consequence, although the "Area" of the EU, according to Art. 1(10) ECT, covers the territories of the two states, this does not prevent each of them from retaining their own "Areas" within the meaning of that article.[126]

The tribunal added that, pursuant to Art. 31 VCLT, it must interpret Art. 1(10) ECT in the context of the aim pursued by Art. 26(1) ECT.[127] Since the latter refers to disputes between "a Contracting Party and an Investor of another Contracting Party relating to an investment of the latter in the Area of the former", this means that the relevant territory is that of the ECT Contracting Party

122 Ibid [212].

123 Ibid [213]:

> To finish with this discussion concerning the relevance of EU law in the present case, the Tribunal feels obliged to disagree with the assertion of the CJEU concerning the alleged distinction between commercial and investment-treaty arbitration. In both cases, the source of the obligation to arbitrate is based on the consent of the parties to the dispute, whether States or private persons. As this Tribunal's decision in its Decision on jurisdiction made clear, both of the Parties in the present case gave their consent to arbitrate under the relevant documents, for the Respondent that being the ECT. No post-hoc decision of the CJEU can somehow undo that consent once given. If the European Commission considers that an EU Member State has violated EU law in relation to such consent, then that is an internal matter for EU law that does not affect the application of international law by the Tribunal instituted on the basis of the ECT

(footnote omitted).

124 Isolux v. Spain, SCC Case No. V 2013/153, Award (12.07.2016) [630].

125 Ibid [633].

126 Ibid [634].

127 Ibid [635].

against which the investor has filed a claim. Consequently, the territorial diversity requirement was met.[128]

1.2.4.2 *Disconnection Clause*

The tribunal then turned to the alleged existence of an implied disconnection clause, understood as a provision of a multilateral treaty that allows the parties to another treaty or the members of a regional organization to disapply, entirely or partially, such multilateral treaty in their mutual relations.[129] The tribunal decided that nothing in the text of the ECT permits the conclusion that it contains an implicit disconnection clause for the EU's member states.[130]

1.2.4.3 *EU Law*

Next, the tribunal noted that it considered "unlikely" that any incompatibility existed between the ECT and EU law.[131] In any case, even if such an incompatibility existed, it would not affect the tribunal's jurisdiction, but would concern the "substantive rights of the investor" and therefore the choice of law applicable to the merits.[132] These conclusions were unaffected by Art. 344 TFEU, which refers to the EU treaties, but not to other international instruments, such as the ECT. The claims brought by the investor concerned alleged violations of the ECT, not violations of EU law.[133]

The tribunal also noted that arbitral tribunals not only have the power, but also the duty to apply EU law.[134] Consequently, it concluded that EU law does not prohibit the submission of a dispute based on the ECT to arbitration.[135]

1.2.5 Eiser

1.2.5.1 *Treaty Interpretation*

In *Eiser*, the tribunal commenced its analysis of the intra-EU objection by noting that Art. 26 ECT must be interpreted in accordance with Arts. 31 and 32 VCLT.[136] The proper interpretative starting point is the ordinary meaning of the words used in this provision, viewed in their context.[137] The tribunal looked

128 Ibid [636].
129 Ibid [637].
130 Ibid [638].
131 Ibid [645].
132 Ibid [644].
133 Ibid [651].
134 Ibid [654].
135 Ibid [655].
136 Eiser v. Spain, ICSID Case No. ARB/13/36, Award (04.05.2017) [179].
137 Ibid [182].

at the content of the definitions of a "Contracting Party" and of an "Investor", found in Art. 1 ECT, as well as the standards of protection included in Arts. 10 and 13 ECT.[138] It decided that the ordinary meaning of these provisions was consistent with it having jurisdiction over the claims.[139]

1.2.5.2 *Disconnection Clause*

With respect to the argument concerning the existence of an implied disconnection clause, the tribunal noted that it could not disregard the ECT's ordinary meaning in order to introduce a significant, but unstated exception which would bar any claims being made by investors from EU Member States against another EU member state that is party to the ECT. It is a fundamental rule of international law that treaties are to be interpreted in good faith and, in the same vein, that treaty makers should perform their functions in good faith, without "traps for the unwary with hidden meanings and sweeping implied exclusions".[140] The ECT negotiators made use of mechanisms available for treaty makers seeking to limit or exclude the application of particular provisions in particular situations, but solely for issues other than intra-EU ones, such as the Svalbard Treaty and nuclear materials.[141] Moreover, the ECT's purpose did not support the intra-EU arguments presented by Spain.[142]

The tribunal noted that the definition of an REIO in Art. 1(3) ECT contemplates that an REIO's members can transfer competence over certain matters to the REIO. However, this happened only when the Treaty of Lisbon was signed in 2007, so it could not have been communicated to, nor accepted by, the other ECT parties back in 1994.[143]

1.2.5.3 *Nationality/Territorial Diversity*

As regards the nationality argument, the tribunal emphasized that, while the EU is a contracting party to the ECT, so too are the EU member states. In consequence, investors from the latter satisfy the requirement to be an "Investor" of a "Contracting Party" which invests in an "Area" of another Contracting Party.[144] There is no EU law which regulates the organization of companies, as this continues to be regulated at the level of the EU member states' domestic laws. This

138 Ibid [182]–[183].
139 Ibid [184].
140 Ibid [185]–[186].
141 Ibid [187].
142 Ibid [188].
143 Ibid [190].
144 Ibid [194].

led the tribunal to conclude that there is no category of "EU Investors" within the definitions of the ECT.[145]

1.2.5.4 *EU Law*

Spain argued that EU law forms part of the applicable law within the meaning of Art. 26(6) ECT and that consequently, pursuant to Art. 344 TFEU and the "controlling principles of European law" stemming from the CJEU's case law, only European courts, and in particular the CJEU, have jurisdiction to decide on the meaning and content of European law.[146] The tribunal considered this to be an attempt to introduce a major, but unwritten exception to the scope of the ECT.[147] It viewed its jurisdiction as derived from a binding treaty under international law. It also noted that it is not "an institution of the European legal order" and therefore is not "subject to the requirements of that legal order".[148]

The tribunal saw no conflict between its role under the ECT and the European legal order, and therefore no need to address it.[149] It added that, insofar as EU law may provide more favorable protection than that offered by the ECT, Art. 16(2) of the latter makes it clear that they do not "detract from or supersede other ECT provisions, in particular the right to dispute settlement under ECT Part V" and, in consequence, whilst EU law may enhance the protections available under the ECT, it may not lessen the rights or protection under the ECT.[150]

For the tribunal, Art. 344 TFEU was not "implicated here", because the case did not concern a dispute between the EU member states, nor was it about the allocation of competences between the EU and its member states.[151]

The tribunal found nothing ambiguous or obscure in the interpretation of Art. 26 ECT, which rendered it unnecessary to resort to the complementary means of interpretation provided for in Art. 32 VCLT.[152] Even if the circumstances were to justify recourse to such complementary means of interpretation, the respondent had provided no evidence to demonstrate that, at the time of negotiating the ECT, the countries of the European Economic Community

145 Ibid [196].

146 Ibid [197]. In this case, the arguments on the supremacy of EU law appear to be closely linked to the arguments on nationality. The award does not differentiate them into separate subsections.

147 Ibid [198].

148 Ibid [199].

149 Ibid.

150 Ibid [202].

151 Ibid [204].

152 Ibid [205].

(at the relevant time prior to creation of the EU)[153] intended that the ECT would not affect the internal market, nor that such objective was communicated to and accepted by the other contracting parties to the ECT.[154]

1.2.6 Novenergia

1.2.6.1 *Nationality/Territorial Diversity*

In *Novenergia*, the tribunal confirmed the intra-EU objection to be *rationae personae*.[155] In this case, Spain also argued that the investor was not from an "Area" of "another Contracting Party", as required by Art. 26(1) ECT, because both the host and home states were EU member states.[156] The tribunal disagreed, observing that "even though the EU itself is a Contracting Party of the ECT, this does not eliminate the EU Member States' individual standing as respondents under the ECT".[157] Applying the VCLT, the tribunal concluded that it cannot deduce from Art. 26(1) ECT a limitation to the effect that an investor is not a national of an ECT contracting state if this state is also a member of the same REIO (i.e. the EU).[158]

1.2.6.2 *Disconnection Clause*

The tribunal observed that, according to the VCLT, treaties must be interpreted in good faith and that "the terms of the ECT are clear" in providing no basis for implying that a disconnection clause existed.[159]

1.2.6.3 *EU Law*

The respondent also relied on the primacy of EU law in intra-EU relations, arguing that EU law should be given preference over any other law that regulates internal EU relations, including the ECT.[160] It further argued that the case affects EU law as it concerns state aid to the RE sector.[161] The tribunal observed in this context that all of the claims before it were based on the ECT, and none of them was based on EU law. The claimant had not relied upon nor challenged any measures adopted or directed by the EU or its authorities but solely on

153 It was incorporated into the EU, established by the Maastricht Treaty which entered into force on 01.11.1993.
154 Eiser v. Spain, *supra* note 136 [205]–[206].
155 Ibid [455].
156 Novenergia v. Spain, SCC Case No. 2015/063, Final Arbitral Award (15.02.2018) [449].
157 Ibid [453].
158 Ibid [453].
159 Ibid [454].
160 Ibid [456].
161 Ibid [457].

"measures that were of the Respondent's own volition".[162] The tribunal added that it "is not constituted on the basis of the European legal order and it is not subject to any requirements of such legal order",[163] and that no clash between EU law and the ECT has been proven to exist.[164] This led the tribunal to conclude that there was no need "to determine the hierarchy between the ECT and EU law as this issue becomes redundant".[165] The tribunal considered the previous Spanish saga decisions on jurisdiction, *Charanne, Isolux*, RREEF and *Eiser* to be "stable case law" and saw no reason to depart from it.[166]

The tribunal considered that its conclusions were supported by a decision issued in 2017 against Spain in the context of a state aid dispute ("2017 EC Decision").[167] Whilst it recognized that it would have been bound by this decision if it applied EU law, it considered that the dispute did not concern any matters governed by EU law. It further stated that EU law does not "recognize, nor prohibit, a similar right" to the FET under the ECT. As a result, "the two legal orders do not share the same subject matter, but may easily coexist to the extent that they do not interfere with each other".[168]

1.2.7 Masdar

1.2.7.1 *Disconnection Clause*

The tribunal in *Masdar* observed that "one of the principal grounds" of the respondent's jurisdictional objections "appears to have been abandoned".[169] Although this is not entirely clear, it seems that the tribunal was referring to the argument concerning the implied disconnection clause, which had been vigorously argued by Spain in the preceding cases. The tribunal observed that "it is now common ground between the Parties that there is no "disconnect" clause, express or implicit, in Article 26 of the ECT".[170]

1.2.7.2 *Nationality/Territorial Diversity*

As a result, the first part of the intra-EU objection analyzed by the *Masdar* tribunal concerned the nationality argument, i.e. that the parties to the dispute

162 Ibid [460].
163 Ibid [461].
164 Ibid [462].
165 Ibid [463].
166 Ibid [464].
167 Decision C(2017)7384 regarding the Spanish State Aid Framework for Renewable Sources, dated 10.11.2017.
168 Ibid [465].
169 Masdar v. Spain, ICSID Case No. ARB/14/1, Award (16.05.2018) [308].
170 Ibid [312].

were from a "single Contracting Party".[171] Spain argued that the definition of a Contracting Party in Art. 1(2) ECT includes states and REIOs such as the EU, and therefore that the "Area" of the EU, as defined in Art. 1(10) ECT, subsumes the territories of all of the EU's Member States.[172] The tribunal disagreed.[173] It simply quoted relevant passages from the *PV Investors*, *Charanne* and *Isolux* cases, adding that it "sees no reason to depart from the reasoning and the conclusions" stated therein.[174]

1.2.7.3 *EU Law*

Next, the tribunal analyzed the allegation that investment arbitration is incompatible with EU law, based on an argument that Art. 344 TFEU precludes the submission of a dispute of an intra-EU nature pursuant to Art. 26 ECT "because it would require the Tribunal to decide about European investor rights on the Internal Market".[175] The tribunal dismissed this "second prong" of the intra-EU objection.[176] It observed that investor protections under the ECT and judicial remedies afforded by EU law are different.[177] It added that Art. 16 ECT "affords precedence to the more favourable investor-protection provisions of Article 26 of the ECT of which Claimant has availed itself over any conflicting provision of the EU treaties".[178] This is not altered by Art. 36(7) ECT, which simply deals with voting rights in the context of an REIO.[179]

The tribunal considered that Art. 344 TFEU applies solely to state-to-state disputes, rather than to disputes between private parties or to disputes between a private party and a state.[180] The tribunal relied on the *Charanne* and *Isolux* awards in declaring that arbitral tribunals "not only have the power, but the duty, to apply EU law".[181] Given that only the ECT, and not EU law, deals with investor-state arbitration, "nothing in EU law can be interpreted as precluding investor-State arbitration under the ECT and the ICSID Convention".[182]

171 Ibid [315]. This must be understood as referring to the claimant's home state.
172 Ibid [316]–[318].
173 Ibid [324].
174 Ibid [319]–[323].
175 Ibid [333].
176 Ibid [341].
177 Ibid [327].
178 Ibid [332].
179 Ibid [331].
180 Ibid [337].
181 Ibid [338]–[339].
182 Ibid [340].

1.2.7.4 *Achmea Judgment*

The *Masdar* case is the first Spanish saga case when a tribunal decided on jurisdiction following the issuance of the *Achmea* judgment. Spain applied to re-open the proceedings and sought to introduce the *Achmea* judgment onto the record.[183] The tribunal dismissed this application, observing that the *Achmea* judgment "has no bearing upon the present case".[184] In the tribunal's eyes, the *Achmea* judgment related to ISDS provisions in BITs between EU member states, but was silent on multilateral treaties to which the EU itself was a party, such as the ECT.[185] In reaching these conclusions, the tribunal referred to AG Wathelet's opinion, which relied on the fact that no one had requested an opinion from the CJEU on the compatibility of the ECT with EU law because, at the time when ECT was being negotiated, no one had the "slightest suspicion that it might be incompatible".[186] The tribunal added that the *Achmea* judgment "is simply silent on the subject of the ECT" and did not address, much less depart from or reject AG Wathelet's opinion on this issue.[187]

1.2.8 Antin

1.2.8.1 *Treaty Interpretation*

The tribunal in *Antin* commenced its analysis of the intra-EU objection by confirming that Art. 26 ECT must be interpreted in accordance with Arts. 31 and 32 VCLT.[188] It reiterated that Art. 31 VCLT is an "integral single rule", which means that the text, context, object and purpose of the provision being interpreted are not separate elements of interpretation. Art. 32 VCLT is a subsidiary rule, in the sense that it applies either to confirm the interpretative result reached after applying Art. 31 VCLT, or if that result leaves the meaning ambiguous or obscure or leads to a result which is manifestly absurd or unreasonable.[189] The tribunal analyzed the ordinary meaning, in their context, of Arts. 1(2) and 1(7)(a)(II) ECT, which define "Contracting Party" and "Investor". This led to an understanding that the host state and the home states are ECT Contracting Parties, whereas the claimants are "Investors" with investments protected under Arts. 10 and 13 ECT. This sufficed to give the tribunal jurisdiction over the dispute.[190]

---

183 Ibid [669], [683].
184 Ibid [678].
185 Ibid [679].
186 Ibid [680]–[681].
187 Ibid [682].
188 Antin v. Spain, ICSID Case No. ARB/13/31, Award (15.06.2018) [206].
189 Ibid [207].
190 Ibid [208]–[212].

1.2.8.2 *Disconnection Clause*

After these preliminary observations, the tribunal looked at the respondent's objection that the context of the ECT excludes intra-EU investor-state disputes based on the ECT.[191] Spain clarified that it was not arguing that a disconnection clause existed, whether explicit, or implicit.[192]

1.2.8.3 *Nationality/Territorial Diversity*

The tribunal noted that the same objection had been rejected in the *Charanne*, *Isolux* and *Eiser* cases.[193] It added that such a "wide exclusion" would have to be express and clear.[194] It did not find support for the objection in the ECT's purpose, as stated in its Art. 2.[195] Similarly, no specific provisions of the ECT supported this objection. In reaching this conclusion, the tribunal analyzed Arts. 1(3) – definition of an REIO, Art. 36(7) – an REIO's voting rights, and Art. 25 – eliminating the rights under an REIO from the application of the ECT's most-favored nation obligations.[196]

The tribunal observed that its jurisdiction was not barred by the fact that the EU is also a Contracting Party to the ECT. The ordinary meaning of Arts. 1(2), 1(3) and 1(10) ECT means that an REIO, such as the EU, can be an ECT Contracting Party, "Area" of which is also defined in the ECT as including the territories of its constituent member states. This means that claims can be brought against an REIO if a dispute arises in the thus-defined "Area" of the REIO.[197] "Area" is therefore defined depending on who is the respondent – an EU member state, or the EU itself.[198] Therefore, separate ratifications of the ECT result in the simultaneous existence of the home states, the host state and the EU as Contracting Parties, each having its own obligations under the ECT. The EU's consent to arbitration under the ECT "does not supersede or eliminate the specific consent granted by each sovereign EU Member State that is also a Contracting Party to the ECT".[199]

1.2.8.4 *EU Law*

The respondent argued also that EU law forms part of the applicable law, and that it does not allow a mechanism for dispute resolution between the EU's

191 Ibid [213].
192 Ibid [180].
193 Ibid [214].
194 Ibid [215].
195 Ibid [216].
196 Ibid [217].
197 Ibid [218].
198 Ibid [220].
199 Ibid [219], [221].

member states and EU investors other than as provided for in the EU treaties.[200] The tribunal disagreed.[201] It explained that: (i) its jurisdiction is derived from the express terms of a treaty which is binding on the states, (ii) the EU is itself is a party to this treaty, (iii) each EU member state itself granted its consent to arbitrate claims against it, and finally (iv) nothing in the text, context, purpose and object of ECT suggests that reference to "rules and principles of international law" should include EU law in a manner undermining "the prior consents to submit to arbitration under the ECT given by each of the EU Member States and the EU itself".[202] The tribunal noted also the obligation stemming from Art. 32 VCLT to interpret the treaties in good faith. This requires that "a formal warning, or an express exclusion or a reserve" should have been given if one was to accept the respondent's position.[203]

The tribunal shortly referred to the argument concerning Art. 344 TFEU, noting that "the different concepts of substantive protections" available under EU law may apply to the merits if a dispute is "brought under EU law", but concluding that this was irrelevant for the tribunal's jurisdiction.[204]

The tribunal also referred to the argument based on Opinion 1/91 on the Agreement on the Creation of a European Economic Area ("Opinion 1/91"), which had been relied upon by the respondent.[205] The tribunal simply noted that the case at hand, unlike Opinion 1/91, "does not concern the validity of decisions of EU organs and institutions".[206]

1.2.8.5 *Achmea Judgment*

After the *Achmea* judgment was issued, the respondent applied to re-open the proceedings and include it in the record.[207] The tribunal simply noted that it denied this application.[208] It provided no explanation as to the reasons behind this decision.[209]

---

200 Ibid [223].
201 Ibid [226].
202 Ibid [224].
203 Ibid [225].
204 Ibid [228].
205 Opinion 1/91 of the Court (14.12.1991) (ECLI:EU:C:1991:490).
206 Ibid [229].
207 Ibid [56].
208 Ibid [58].
209 In the light of the applicable rules of procedure (in particular Rule 38(2) ICSID Arbitration Rules), the tribunal could have explained in more detail why it considered that the *Achmea* judgment did not constitute a decisive factor for the case, or that there was no vital need to clarify this point. The approach is different to that in the *Masdar* case, where

1.2.9 Foresight

1.2.9.1 *Treaty Interpretation*

In *Foresight*, Spain presented seven different elements of its intra-EU jurisdictional objection.[210] The tribunal analyzed them all together. It commenced by noting that the jurisdictional clause contained in the ECT, "as any other treaty provision" must be interpreted "with the normal canons" of treaty interpretation contained in Arts. 31 and 32 VCLT.[211] It reiterated that Art. 31 VCLT is the primary rule of treaty interpretation, whereas Art. 32 applies "in limited circumstances".[212] The tribunal considered that the "context" of Art. 26 ECT includes Art. 1(2) ECT (i.e. the definition of a "Contracting Party"), Art. 1(7)(a)(ii) ECT (i.e. the definition of an "Investor"), Art. 10(1) and Art. 13 ECT (the applicable standards of protection),[213] whereas its "purpose" is set out in Art. 2 ECT.[214]

1.2.9.2 *Disconnection Clause*

The tribunal also added that the ECT contains no disconnection clause and that it "can discern no attempt in the ECT's provisions to carve-out" intra-EU disputes from the ECT's protection.[215]

1.2.9.3 *Nationality/Territorial Diversity*

Based on the above, the tribunal concluded that it had jurisdiction, "following the textual approach" to interpretation under Art. 31 VCLT.[216] Art. 26 ECT should be given its ordinary meaning in accordance with Art. 31 VCLT.[217] The claimants were investors of "another" Contracting Party, the respondent was a "Contracting Party" and the dispute concerned an investment in the "Area" of the respondent, as defined in the ECT.[218] The tribunal saw no need to resort to the supplementary means of interpretation envisaged in Art. 32 VCLT. It saw

---

the tribunal analyzed the issue and decided that the *Achmea* judgment did not apply to the ECT context and so had no bearing upon the case.

210 Foresight v. Spain, SCC Case No. V 2015/150, Final Award (14.11.2018) [157].
211 Ibid [201].
212 Ibid [202].
213 Ibid [205].
214 Ibid [206].
215 Ibid [207].
216 Ibid [212].
217 Ibid [208].
218 Ibid [209]–[211].

nothing ambiguous or obscure in Art. 26(1) ECT, and it did not perceive the above conclusion as leading to absurd or unreasonable result.[219]

1.2.9.4 *EU Law*

The tribunal analyzed "for completeness" the respondent's arguments based on the alleged primacy of EU law over the ECT.[220] It considered that EU law was not relevant to the question of the tribunal's jurisdiction. In its view, Art 26(6) ECT, which defines the applicable law, applies to the merits of a case, but not to jurisdiction.[221] Thus, jurisdiction must be established solely in accordance with the requirements set forth in the ECT.[222]

1.2.9.5 *Achmea Judgment*

The tribunal considered the *Achmea* judgment as "irrelevant" to the jurisdictional objection, relying extensively the reasoning of the *Masdar* tribunal as a justification.[223] It added that it was "not aware of a single award that has found "intra-EU" disputes to be excluded from the scope of Article 26(1) ECT". On the contrary, it referred to 20 awards where tribunals have upheld jurisdiction over intra-EU investment treaty disputes.[224]

1.2.10 Cube

In the *Cube* case, the intra-EU objection was framed as *rationae personae*.[225] The tribunal noted that it had invited the parties to comment on the *Masdar* award, "the first award in an ECT investment case after the Achmea Judgment of the CJEU".[226] Interestingly, in this case Spain first relied on Opinion 2/13 regarding the EU's planned accession to the ECHR ("Opinion 2/13"),[227] claiming that the CJEU reiterated there that "the autonomy of the EU's legal order

---

219 Ibid [213].

220 Ibid [214]. Analyzing the jurisdictional objections based on the alleged primacy of EU law over the ECT "for completeness" suggests that the tribunal considered them as going beyond the ordinary meaning of the jurisdictional clause, and thus requiring reference of the Art. 32 VCLT.

221 Ibid [218]–[219].

222 Ibid [218].

223 Ibid [220].

224 Ibid [221]. Notably, the tribunal did not refer to the *Antin* award, which was probably not in the public domain at that time.

225 Cube v. Spain, ICSID Case No. ARB/15/20, Decision on Jurisdiction, Liability and Partial Decision on Quantum (19.02.2019) [76].

226 Ibid [82].

227 Opinion 2/13 of the Court (Full Court) (18.12.2014) (ECLI:EU:C:2014:2454).

would be jeopardized if in proceedings before the European Court of Human Rights binding determinations on the scope and meaning of human rights guarantees under EU law could be made".[228]

1.2.10.1 *Nationality/Territorial Diversity*

The tribunal started by clarifying that the presented intra-EU objection requires it to determine whether the dispute was initiated against a Contracting Party by an Investor from another Contracting Party within the meaning of Art. 26(1) ECT.[229] It noted that the general rules of interpretation, as laid down in the VCLT, apply.[230]

First, the tribunal noted that the literal meaning of the provision leaves no doubt that Art. 26(1) ECT does not differentiate between different classes of Contracting Parties (i.e. intra-EU and extra-EU). It added that, if the ECT's drafters had felt it necessary to introduce such a distinction, they could have done so, as was done in the Svalbard Treaty, but they clearly did not.[231]

1.2.10.2 *Disconnection Clause*

The tribunal understood the alleged existence of an implied disconnection clause as an invitation to read Art. 26(1) ECT differently in the light of its "context or the object and purpose" and in the light of Art. 26(6) ECT which regulated the applicable law.[232] The tribunal noted that Art. 26(6) ECT is

> an ancillary norm destined to insert the ECT into the general framework of general international law. No specialized international instrument can stand isolated on its own feet. In order to become operational, the lacunae not covered by the treaty itself must be filled in by recourse to the general rules and principles that make up the legal universe of international law. In this regard, Article 26(6) ECT fulfils a highly desirable auxiliary function.[233]

228 Cube v. Spain, *supra* note 225 [91]. This may be explained by the background of one of the arbitrators – Prof. Tomuschat – who is a leading expert in international human rights law.

229 Ibid [121].

230 Ibid [122].

231 Ibid [124]–[126].

232 Ibid [127].

233 Ibid [129].

It also questioned the practical relevance of this provision, since "normally such recourse to general international law is effected without any specific authorization clause", in accordance with Art. 31(3)(c) VCLT.[234]

1.2.10.3 *EU Law*

The tribunal noted in this context that

> [w]ithin the system of international law, EU law does not have supremacy, and has no hierarchical priority over the laws of non-Member States, or over rules of international law, including the ECT.[235]

The EU treaties are international agreements – binding between their contracting states – but at the same time "function as the constitution of an autonomous community". EU secondary legislation represents a type of supra-national regulations, but it does not form part "of the corpus of international law as such". In this vein, EU law has supremacy over the national laws of the EU member states, but only within the EU legal system, not with respect to international law.[236] The tribunal then noted that Art. 16 ECT confirms this understanding.[237] The tribunal added that "clarity and transparency are guiding criteria" in drafting any legal text. It cannot be assumed that the drafters of the ECT "intended to push aside one of the central pieces of the ECT", i.e. the jurisdictional clause, in a "clandestine fashion without the open knowledge of the participating nations".[238]

The tribunal noticed that one of the reasons underpinning the conclusion of the ECT was the fear that the states of the Central and Eastern Europe might fall back under socialist rule, thereby threatening investments made after the collapse of Communism. In this context, in the early 1990s, the EC saw no obstacle to the EU member states participating in the ECT. No advisory opinion of the CJEU was sought, as no potential for incompatibility was perceived.[239] The EU itself had implicitly recognized the compatibility of the ECT with EU law when it decided not to take any initiative to modify the ECT after most

234 Ibid.
235 Ibid [130].
236 Ibid.
237 Ibid [131]–[132].
238 Ibid [133].
239 Ibid [134]–[136].

countries from the formerly communist eastern bloc became EU member states in 2004.[240]

All of the above led the tribunal to conclude that Art. 26(6) ECT does not reverse the clear meaning of Art. 26(1) ECT.[241]

1.2.10.4 *Achmea Judgment*

The tribunal then analyzed whether its conclusions:

> must be reviewed in light of the supremacy doctrine that assigns paramount importance to any EU law norm vis-à-vis any other legal norm in the same or a neighbouring field ratione materiae.[242]

First, it recalled that the *Achmea* judgment concerned arbitration provided for in a BIT concluded between two Member States of the EU, but without the EU's participation in this treaty.[243] Thus, this case revealed "specificities that make it inapposite as precedent" for the case at hand.[244]

Second, the *Achmea* judgment concerned proceedings which were placed "under the jurisdiction of the EU legal order", because the seat of arbitration was in Germany and therefore German law (and thus EU law) was applicable to the arbitral procedure as the law of the seat.[245] On the contrary, in the *Cube* case, the tribunal's jurisdiction was based on two multilateral treaties extending beyond the EU, i.e. the ECT and the ICSID Convention.[246] No single contracting party to these treaties could "impose specific requirements under its domestic law on those institutions".[247] The tribunal added that it had "consistently operated outside the jurisdiction" of any of the three states involved (i.e. the host state and the two home states) and it "has used as the legal foundation of the present proceedings only the international law rules laid down in those two instruments and deriving therefrom".[248]

Thus, the respondent's objection could be upheld only "if it could be established that the three States involved lacked the legal capacity to conclude a treaty for the establishment of an arbitral body acting outside the EU legal

240 Ibid [137].
241 Ibid [139].
242 Ibid [140].
243 Ibid [141], [153].
244 Ibid [142].
245 Ibid [143].
246 Ibid [144].
247 Ibid [145].
248 Ibid [146].

order". However, there was no evidence that the three states involved had "exceeded the limits of their treaty-making power" by doing so.[249]

The tribunal further noted that the EU had powers conferred upon it in the field of investment protection by virtue of the Treaty of Lisbon. However, that treaty contains no provision to regulate the fate of existing BITs. Thus, in the tribunal's view, "the negotiators were of the view that the system of investment protection, as it had evolved over decades, had stood the test of time and should be transformed only step by step in a process without any disturbing ruptures".[250] The EC initiated infringement procedures concerning the intra-EU BITs only in 2015[251] in an attempt "to push aside a well-established practice of more than one decade".[252]

Finally, the tribunal saw no conflict related to the application of EU law to the dispute. It noted that, in accordance with Art. 42(1) of the ICSID Convention and Art. 26(6) ECT, international law, and particularly the ECT, is the applicable law.[253] Thus, EU law does not form part of the applicable law.[254] The EU treaties are not directly applicable. [255] Spanish law and EU secondary law "are relevant only as facts in the light of which the rights and duties of the Parties under the ECT and international law are to be determined". They are relevant only as "part of the factual matrix".[256]

1.2.10.5 *Treaty Interpretation*

The tribunal reiterated that, under the VCLT, a consistent practice constitutes an element of the context within which the interpretative process shall operate and that, for almost two decades, the EU had "communicated the message to the Contracting Parties of the ECT that the ECT constitutes a crucial building block of the regime of investment protection".[257] It added that the ECT offers a "far more extensive" level of investment protection than EU law, particularly as regards protected assets being threatened by legislative measures.[258]

249 Ibid [147].
250 Ibid [150].
251 Fn 26.
252 Ibid [151].
253 Ibid [156].
254 Ibid [157].
255 Ibid [159].
256 Ibid [160].
257 Ibid [154].
258 Ibid [155].

1.2.11 NextEra

1.2.11.1 *Treaty Interpretation*

The intra-EU objection in *NextEra* was framed as *rationae personae* and, as such, divided into two sub-categories: (i) whether the ECT excludes *inter se* obligations among EU member states and whether (ii) the subsequent overlap between the ECT and EU law rendered Spain's offer to arbitrate invalid.[259]

As a preliminary matter, the tribunal observed that consent to jurisdiction must be "established". As such, the tribunal is not "bounded by the way in which a claimant may decide to frame its claims". The principle of competence-competence requires any tribunal "to establish the extent and limits of its jurisdiction objectively".[260]

The tribunal acknowledged that "the very dynamic nature and rapid evolution" of EU law may "complicate the interpretation of treaties such as the ECT", which makes the harmonious interpretation the most effective in avoiding conflicts between the two sets of norms.[261] Nevertheless, for the purpose of establishing jurisdiction, it felt bounded "by the explicit terms" of the ECT, paying due regard to its object and purpose in line with the VCLT.[262]

1.2.11.2 *Nationality/Territorial Diversity*

The tribunal disagreed with the view that Art. 1(3) or 1(10) ECT constitute a basis for excluding intra-EU disputes from its scope of jurisdiction. It observed that the EU's status as a Contracting Party to the ECT does not deprive the EU Member States of their competence to assume obligations under the ECT. The EU's consent – as an REIO within the ECTs meaning – does not "supersede" the consent to arbitration given by each state individually. On the contrary, a good faith interpretation of the ECT leads to the conclusion that an REIO – and therefore the EU – can have standing in international arbitration under the ECT. There would only be a different conclusion if a disconnection clause existed.[263]

---

259 NextEra v. Spain, ICSID Case No. ARB/14/11, Decision on Jurisdiction, Liability and Quantum Principles (12.03.2019) [338].

260 Ibid [336].

261 Ibid [341].

262 Ibid.

263 Ibid [342].

1.2.11.3 *EU Law*

The tribunal noted that, when concluding the ECT, the EU had shared its competence with its member states.[264] The fact that such competence was later transferred to the EU cannot be an argument to decline jurisdiction.[265]

As regards the second sub-category of the objection, the tribunal started by observing that its task was to determine whether the dispute fell within the provisions of the ECT, and not whether the dispute fell within the scope of Art. 344 TFEU, breached Art. 267 TFEU, or whether the scope of the dispute concerned the application of the TFEU.[266] It added that the EU aspects of the dispute did not make it an internal EU dispute, and that it remained international in nature and fell to be decided under international law.[267] Whether or not EU law might overlap with the respondent's obligations under the ECT is relevant for merits, not for jurisdictional analysis.[268]

1.2.11.4 *Subsequent Agreement or Practice*

The tribunal then decided that there was no reason to apply Art. 30(4)(a) VCLT, which concerns "application of successive treaties relating to the same subject matter", to "the present situation where treaties negotiated by a smaller number of States, i.e., the EU founding Treaties, are claimed to modify a treaty such as the ECT". It added that there is "no evidence placed before it that would demonstrate that the subsequent EU Treaties were amending the ECT" within the meaning of Art. 41(1)(b) VCLT.[269]

1.2.11.5 *Achmea Judgment*

The tribunal then noted that the *Achmea* judgment did not rely on the VCLT.[270] It further stated that "the internal constitutional laws of the EU and its constant changes and interpretations by the CJEU, as the Member States seek to minimize their mutual obligations in another context, are of no relevance for the present Tribunal".[271] It added that Art. 25 ECT specifies that the treatment among the EU member states cannot be extended to non-EU member states via the MFN clause.[272]

---

264 It is implied that it refers to competence over foreign direct investment.

265 NextEra v. Spain, *supra* note 259 [343]. Formally speaking, in 1994 the competence was shared between the EEC and its member states. The phraseology used in the analysis mirrors that used by the tribunals.

266 Ibid [349].

267 Ibid [350].

268 Ibid [351].

269 Ibid [352].

270 Ibid [353].

271 Ibid [354].

272 Ibid [356].

1.2.12 9REN

1.2.12.1 *Nationality/Territorial Diversity*

It seems that in the *9REN* case, the intra-EU nationality argument was not clearly differentiated from the other issues regarding the intra-EU objection.[273] This may be explained by the fact that, in this case, Spain argued that the claimant was only a shell company, whereas the real party was a US-based entity.[274] The respondent presented arguments which were classified by the tribunal into three categories: (i) the governing law argument, (ii) the institutional argument and (iii) the application of EU law argument.[275]

With respect to the first category, the respondent's argument was that EU law governs the determination of the tribunal's jurisdiction under Art. 26(6) ECT and Art. 42(1) of the ICSID Convention.[276] The tribunal simply noted that the "exclusion of intra-EU disputes from the scope of ECT would not be consistent with the plain language of the ECT or the ICSID Convention" and rejected the objection on that basis.[277]

1.2.12.2 *Achmea Judgment*

With respect to the second category, Spain's argument was that EU law does not permit the existence of any institutional dispute mechanism other than an institution established by the EU treaties.[278] Further, it argued that a decision of an arbitral tribunal constituted under the ECT or the ICSID Convention is final (pursuant to Art. 53 of the ICSID Convention), subject only to the possibility of annulment by an *ad hoc* committee falling outside the EU's judicial system. Thus, Spain argued that the *Achmea* judgment precludes jurisdiction of the tribunal since the opposite would "prevent" the CJEU from "exercising its function".[279]

The tribunal started its analysis by presenting a negative perception of the *Achmea* judgment. It commented that it has attempted "to understand the truncated reasoning" therein, and that there "is much to understand".[280] It then noted that whilst the tribunal reached a consensus in rejecting the objection, "it should not be assumed that it's [sic] three members share equally the

273 9REN v. Spain, ICSID Case No. ARB/15/15, Award (31.05.2019) [142], [144].
274 Ibid [125].
275 Ibid [144].
276 Ibid.
277 Ibid [147].
278 Ibid [144].
279 Ibid [148].
280 Ibid [150].

same identical perspective or attach equal importance to the issues raised by the objection".[281]

In this context, the tribunal noted that the *Achmea* judgment itself differentiates between a BIT concluded between two EU member states and a multilateral investment treaty to which the EU itself is a party (together with not only the EU member states, but also non-EU member states). In joining the ECT, the EU itself agreed to submit to the jurisdiction of arbitral tribunals. The *Achmea* judgment confirms the treaty-making authority of the EU, allowing it to enter treaties which include dispute resolutions mechanisms outside the framework of the EU courts. The distinction between using a word "court" and "tribunal" is of no difference to that conclusion.[282] Thus, the *Achmea* judgment itself recognizes that "the EU enjoys no immunity in respect of non-EU dispute resolution mechanisms under the international treaties to which the EU itself has made itself a party, and may therefore be sued as a respondent in an ECT case". For the tribunal, this rebuts the argument that "EU laws exist in a bubble subject to interpretation and consideration only by EU courts (and tribunals)".[283]

The tribunal considered that the ECT text and the *Achmea* judgment gave no basis to conclude that "within the remedial provisions of the ECT there are different categories of members with different access to different remedies", depending on whether a contracting state is a member of the EU or not.[284] The EU member states "are as much parties" to the ECT as the EU itself.[285] The tribunal saw nothing in the *Achmea* judgment to suggest that the CJEU allowed the EU to be the respondent, but "immunized" the EU member states from claims based on the ECT. For the tribunal, "Spain is as firmly bound by the ECT dispute resolution mechanism as is the EU itself".[286]

1.2.12.3 *EU Law*

With respect to the third category, Spain's argument was that the tribunal lacks jurisdiction to apply EU law to determine the rights of intra-EU investors, "including alleged ECT violations arising from Spain's participation in the EU Internal Market in Electricity including rules governing State Aid".[287] This was directly based on the *Achmea* judgment, according to which "the autonomy of

281 Ibid [151]. One can guess that two arbitrators from Canada had a different perspective on these issues than the arbitrator from the United Kingdom.
282 Ibid [152].
283 Ibid [153].
284 Ibid [154].
285 Ibid [156].
286 Ibid [157].
287 Ibid [144].

the EU and its legal order" must be respected.[288] Spain argued that reference to international law as the applicable law includes EU law and that its RE support schemes are not only implementing EU directives, but are also regulated by EU law on state aid.[289]

In this context, the tribunal observed that the claimant's case did not rest on EU law, but on the ECT and case law in respect of rights and obligations under international law. It was the respondent which had invoked EU law as a defense.[290] Thus, the tribunal considered it "misconceived" to argue that only EU judges may apply EU law. When applying international law, it may have regard to national law (for example with respect to the claimant's corporate status) and to EU law (for example when analyzing Spain's justification for its regulatory steps) in the same way as any other international court or tribunal.[291] For the purposes of deciding its jurisdiction, the tribunal accepted that Spain's modifications of the regulatory framework were permitted under both EU law and Spanish law. If this were not the case, the claimant "would more properly be engaged in a Spanish court seeking their annulment", whereas it did not seek their modification in the ECT case. Therefore, this case was not "an attack on Spain's regulatory system".[292]

The tribunal concluded that it was within its jurisdiction "to consider EU law to the extent necessary for the resolution of the dispute under international law" and that EU law is not "materially incompatible" with the applicable international law, including investor-state arbitration.[293]

1.2.13 SolEs

The tribunal in *SolEs* also considered the intra-EU objection as *rationae personae* in nature, even though it identified "two strands": (i) based on investor's nationality (i.e. home and host states being members of the EU), linked to the implied disconnection clause, and (ii) based on the argument that the TFEU takes precedence over the ECT's dispute settlement provisions.[294]

---

288 Ibid [159].

289 Ibid [161]. This appears to be the first case where Spain's defense is directly based on the argument that subsidies to RE facilities constitute state aid under EU law – [162].

290 Ibid [168].

291 Ibid [170].

292 Ibid [171].

293 Ibid [172].

294 SolEs v. Spain, ICSID Case No. ARB/15/38, Award (31.07.2019) [178]–[180].

1.2.13.1 *Nationality/Territorial Diversity*

With respect to the first argument, the tribunal commenced by noting that the ECT should be interpreted in accordance with Art. 31(1) VCLT.[295] It examined the definitions laid down in Art. 1 ECT, used in Art. 26 ECT, and concluded that it had jurisdiction based on the ordinary meaning of the terms "Investor", "Contracting Party" and "Area".[296]

The tribunal then dismissed the respondent's objection that no diversity of "nationality" or "area" occurred if two Contracting Parties to the ECT are also member states of an REIO, namely the EU.[297] It considered that this argument was based on an "implied exception" in the ECT's text, which would be "highly unusual" and "would mean that the negotiators concluded a treaty that was largely inoperable as between EU investors and other EU Member States, but did not indicate that exception in the text".[298]

The tribunal also rejected the suggestion that the jurisdictional objection was grounded in the "context" of the ECT, within the meaning of Art. 31(2)(a) VCLT. The tribunal noted that the European Community was an active participant in negotiations on the ECT, which permits an REIO to become a Contracting Party and which the European Community used to become a Contracting Party. The definition of the "Area", contained in Art. 1(10) of the ECT, "is tailored to the situation of a REIO". The tribunal noted that "negotiators also could have specified that the "Area" of a Contracting Party that is also a Member State of a REIO is deemed to be the entire Area of the REIO", but they did not do so.[299] Similarly, the negotiators could have included an "additional derogation" precluding the operation of the ECT's protections and dispute settlement options to intra-EU investors, for example in Art. 25 ECT, which deals with granting more-favored nation treatment to states that are parties to an economic integration area.[300] The tribunal further noted that the negotiators had explicitly agreed to exceptions included in the Svalbard Treaty.[301]

1.2.13.2 *EU Law*

Finally, the tribunal disagreed that the "principle of EU primacy over non-EU treaties [...] was so obvious in the early 1990s that there was no need for an

295 Ibid [223].
296 Ibid [224]–[225].
297 Ibid [226].
298 Ibid [227].
299 SolEs v. Spain, *supra* note 294 [228]–[229].
300 Ibid [230].
301 Ibid [232].

express exclusion of intra-EU disputes from the investor-State arbitration provisions of the ECT".[302] On the contrary, even decades later, not only arbitral tribunals, but also AG Wathelet's opinion, had concluded that Art. 344 TFEU "does not even address the same subject matter as the investor-State provisions of an investment treaty". Thus, this issue could not have been so obvious earlier that no express exception was needed.[303]

The object and purpose of the ECT did not lead the tribunal to adopt a different outcome. The preamble makes it clear that the ECT's object and purpose was much broader than simply to increase East-West cooperation (as had been alleged by the respondent) but included the "catalysation of economic growth through measures to liberalise investment and trade in energy".[304]

1.2.13.3 *Achmea Judgment*

As regards the second "strand" of the intra-EU objection, the tribunal clarified that, as it is not an EU institution, it "approaches this question from the vantage point of a tribunal established pursuant to the ICSID Convention and the ECT".[305]

First, it analyzed whether Art. 344 TFEU address the same subject matter as Art. 26 ECT. The tribunal noted that some tribunals, and AG Wathelet's opinion, considered that the subject matter is different.[306] It also noted that the CJEU had decided otherwise.[307] The tribunal disagreed with the *Masdar* tribunal's reasoning, which emphasized the difference between the ECT and the BIT considered by the CJEU in the *Achmea* judgment. It doubted that "the bilateral nature of the treaty at issue in Achmea was critical to the reasoning of the CJEU".[308] On this basis, the tribunal considered it "prudent" to assume that the subject-matter scope of Art. 344 TFEU and Art. 26 ECT is the same. Based on that assumption, the tribunal followed the *Achmea* judgment's conclusion that "the consent of EU Member States to investor-State arbitration pursuant to Article 26 of the ECT is in conflict with Article 344 of the TFEU, as the TFEU has been interpreted by the CJEU".[309]

302 Ibid [234].
303 Ibid.
304 Ibid [235].
305 Ibid [238].
306 Ibid [242].
307 Ibid [243].
308 Ibid [244]. The CJEU's reference to past case law, including its Opinion 1/91 which concerned a multilateral treaty, was relevant in coming to this conclusion.
309 Ibid [245].

The tribunal proceeded to analyze which treaty takes precedence in the event of such a conflict.[310] Whilst Art. 30 VCLT provides "residual rules that can be used to determine which treaty has primacy", reference to these rules were unnecessary, because Art. 16 ECT "expressly addresses the relationship between the dispute settlement chapter of the ECT and the provisions of another treaty on that subject matter".[311] In the light of this provision, the TFEU can derogate from an investor's right to resolve a dispute under the ECT only if the TFEU is more favorable to investors than the ECT.[312] This was not the case, since the ECT provides a dispute settlement option which is "additional to those otherwise available" to investors in intra-EU disputes.[313] Consequently, the TFEU cannot "derogate from the dispute settlement provisions of the ECT".[314]

1.2.13.4 *Subsequent Agreement or Practice*

The tribunal was also unconvinced that the EU and its member states had modified the ECT, noting that no notification of any such alleged modification had been filed.[315] The 2019 Declarations did not impact on the tribunal's conclusions.[316]

1.2.14 InfraRed

The tribunal in *InfraRed* perceived the intra-EU objection as consisting of 2 "main themes": (i) that the ECT itself excludes intra-EU disputes from its scope of application (this was considered as a "foreignness criterion"),[317] and that (ii) EU law is supreme and peremptory among the EU member states and, as a result, precludes arbitral tribunals from having jurisdiction over intra-EU investment disputes.[318] The second "theme" reveals a development of the respondent's line of arguing. While "the notion of the supremacy of EU law was not very prominent" in the first two written submissions, it "was principally

---

310 Ibid.

311 Ibid [246].

312 Ibid [247].

313 Ibid [248].

314 Ibid [250].

315 Ibid [251]. This argument was novel and "suggested at the Hearing", not in previous written submissions.

316 Ibid [253].

317 InfraRed v. Spain, ICSID Case No. ARB/14/12, Award (02.08.2019) [206].

318 Ibid [204].

brought forward explicitly and developed as a basis for Respondent's arguments in the latter's Reply on Preliminary Objections".[319]

1.2.14.1 *Treaty Interpretation*

The tribunal commenced by analyzing arbitral awards dealing with the intra-EU objection.[320] It considered that these arbitral awards form *jurisprudence constante* which, even though not binding, provides "a persuasive, reasoned and documented analytical framework that the Tribunal endorses and adopts without the need to spell it out in detail" in its analysis.[321]

The tribunal considered the ECT to be the starting point for analyzing the existence and scope of jurisdiction, being the tribunal's "constitutive treaty" and the only ground of its jurisdiction.[322] Nevertheless, the tribunal recognized that, pursuant to Art. 26(6) ECT, it must consider "applicable rules and principles of international law". EU law is "fundamentally treaty-based law" and, as such, it is "undeniably part of the body of international law that the Tribunal is also bound to apply".[323] Thus, Art. 30 and 31 VCLT apply.[324]

1.2.14.2 *Nationality/Territorial Diversity*

First, the tribunal decided that the ordinary meaning of the used terms does not support the intra-EU objection. Art. 1(10) ECT defines "Area" (a term used in the jurisdictional clause) with respect to a state and with respect to an REIO. These two definitions are not mutually exclusive. Rather, one or the other applies depending on whether the disputed measures were adopted by an REIO or by a state.[325]

1.2.14.3 *EU Law*

Second, the tribunal referred to Art. 16 ECT, which shows that the ECT's contracting parties "intended to safeguard the applicability of the dispute resolution provisions [...] even in case of conflict with another treaty" insofar as the ECT is more favorable. To be successful in its attempts to set aside the application of Art. 26(1) ECT to intra-EU disputes, the respondent has the burden of

319 Ibid fn 209. This can be also seen regarding references to ECJ judgments as, for example, this is probably the first case in which the respondent relied on the Costa v. E.N.E.L. judgment from 1964 (judgment of the Court, of 15.07.1964, Case No. 6–64, ECLI:EU:C:1964:66) – [212].

320 InfraRed v. Spain, ibid [230]–[255].

321 Ibid [260].

322 Ibid [257].

323 Ibid [258].

324 Ibid [259].

325 Ibid [263].

showing that the EU legal system provides a more favorable dispute resolution method, which it failed to do.[326]

Third, the tribunal found no incompatibility between the object and purpose of the ECT and the fact that arbitral tribunals established thereupon may have jurisdiction over intra-EU disputes. Even if one agrees that the integration of former Soviet bloc states into western Europe's energy market was a prominent purpose of the ECT, this purpose is not diminished by ECT tribunals having jurisdiction over intra-EU disputes. On the contrary, the application of the same dispute resolution method to all ECT-related investor-state disputes is in line with this purpose.[327]

1.2.14.4 *Subsequent Agreement or Practice*

Finally, the tribunal considered that the *Achmea* judgment and all of the EC's various decisions, statements and legal positions were adopted "solely within the legal sphere" of the EU. As such, they cannot be qualified as an "instrument", "subsequent agreement" or "subsequent practice" concerning the ECT, within the meaning of Arts. 31(2)(b), 31(3)(a) or 31(3)(b) VCLT.[328]

The tribunal came to similar conclusions with respect to the 2019 Declarations.[329] These were not "adopted within the EU legal order and are not EU legal instruments". Three distinct declarations existed, each of which enounced a distinct legal position on the same legal issues. In the tribunal's opinion, the CJEU,

> which is the highest judicial body in charge of the interpretation of European law, has not taken so far any position as to the applicability of its judgment in the Achmea case to arbitration tribunals the jurisdiction of which is based on the ECT.[330]

Thus, they were simply "declarations by sovereign states made within the framework of the general international legal system" and, as such, were not an authentic interpretation of EU law.[331] In any event, the tribunal considered that the 2019 Declarations exceeded the scope of "interpretative declarations" by stating that a key provision of the ECT – its jurisdictional clause – "is to be

326 Ibid [264].
327 Ibid [266].
328 Ibid [267].
329 Ibid [268].
330 Ibid [269].
331 Ibid.

simply set aside" in the intra-EU context, which comes "very close to introducing a disconnection clause", and brings about an "effect akin to an amendment of the ECT or, at the very least, akin to a reservation by the states that signed it". However, an amendment of the ECT requires the consent of all of the ECT's contracting parties, pursuant to Art. 36(1)(a) ECT, whereas Art. 46 ECT provides that no reservations can be made.[332]

1.2.14.5 *Disconnection Clause*

The tribunal also referred to the *travaux préparatoires* of the ECT, which reveal that a disconnection clause between the ECT and the EU treaties was considered, but was not adopted.[333]

1.2.14.6 *Achmea Judgment*

The tribunal commented that the result of its analysis might have led to a different outcome if the EU member states had withdrawn from the ECT, or at least had activated the procedure for amending the treaty – but this had not happened. Thus, such intra-EU documents could at best qualify as "supplementary means of interpretation" within the meaning of Art. 32 VLCT, pursuant to which the tribunal "can resort at its discretion to either confirm the result of the interpretative exercise above or to infirm it in the limited circumstances set out at Articles 32(a) and (b) VCLT". The tribunal saw no reason to do the latter for three reasons. First, its interpretation of Art. 26(1) ECT was neither "ambiguous or obscure" nor "manifestly absurd or unreasonable". Second, EU law is neither dispositive nor even relevant for the dispute, so the tribunal did not apply or interpret it. Third, the respondent did not demonstrate any incompatibility between a provision of EU law and the ECT applicable in the case at hand, and thus did not demonstrate that arbitration would jeopardize the autonomy of EU law. In the tribunal's view, the CJEU in the *Achmea* judgment "implicitly upheld the validity and applicability of international agreements referring intra-EU disputes to non-EU decision-making bodies "provided that the autonomy of the EU and its legal order are respected"".[334]

1.2.15 OperaFund

In *OperaFund*, Spain presented the intra-EU jurisdictional objection with respect to one of the two claimants.[335] The tribunal observed that there was

332 Ibid [270].

333 Ibid [271].

334 Ibid [272].

335 OperaFund v. Spain, ICSID Case No. ARB/15/36, Award (06.09.2019) [335]. The jurisdictional objection related to the claimant from Malta, and did not concern the second claimant, who was from Switzerland.

no need to "re-invent the wheel" and shared the view of the previous tribunals that also after the *Achmea* judgment, the intra-EU objection is not grounded.[336]

1.2.15.1 *Disconnection Clause*

First, the tribunal considered that the *Achmea* judgment concerned a BIT between two EU member states, and "makes no mention" of the ECT. Nothing in the ECT indicated that the contracting states intended to carve out intra-EU disputes, despite the fact that it would have been "a simple matter" to include such a carve-out. Moreover, the ECT lacks a disconnection clause applicable to relations between the EU member states. The tribunal added that such disconnection clauses are present in other treaties to which the EU is a party, and that the negotiating history reveals that such a disconnection clause was in fact discussed, but it was decided to be excluded from the ECT.[337] The existence of a disconnection clause cannot be presumed, which excludes implicit disconnection clauses.[338]

1.2.15.2 *Achmea Judgment*

The tribunal then observed that the EU member states are not prevented from agreeing on investment arbitration in the framework of the ECT. Such limitation neither flow from the *Achmea* judgment (which is limited in its scope to intra-EU bilateral treaties) nor from Art. 344 TFEU (which is limited in its scope to state-to-state disputes).[339] Malta's accession to the EU was perceived as having no impact on the tribunal's jurisdiction, since the TFEU has a different subject matter to the ECT. Moreover, the ECT provides for different remedies, namely access to an investment arbitration, and contains guarantees against uncompensated expropriation and against violations of other standards of protection, which are not present in the TFEU.[340]

Second, the *Achmea* judgment concerned arbitration pursuant to the UNCITRAL arbitration rules, which is different from the ICSID arbitration, which places the tribunal "in a public international law context and not in a national or regional context".[341] The tribunal underlined that the CJEU analyzed arbitration: (i) with the place of arbitration in Germany and German law applicable to arbitration proceedings, (ii) where the German courts were competent for judicial review of the validity of the award and (iii) in this review process

336 Ibid [380].
337 Ibid [381].
338 Ibid [383].
339 Ibid [382].
340 Ibid [383].
341 Ibid [384].

the court submitted the preliminary questions to the CJEU.[342] The tribunal differentiated these factors from the ICSID arbitration, with respect to which (i) no national law applies to the proceedings regardless of the place of arbitration, (ii) no national court is competent to review the validity of the award (which is subject solely to the ICSID annulment procedure) and (iii) the annulment procedure leads to a final decision by an international *ad hoc* committee, which again – is not subject to review by any national court.[343] Moreover, in light of Art. 53 and 54 of the ICSID Convention, Spain "is expressly bound" by the award and

> has no option of appeal outside the ICSID system, and has to recognize the present Award as binding and enforce the pecuniary obligations imposed by this Award within its territory as if it were a final judgment of a court in Spain.[344]

1.2.16 BayWa

In *BayWa*, after the *Achmea* judgment was issued, the tribunal scheduled separate (second) hearings, devoted primarily to the issue of the impact of the *Achmea* judgment and other EU law aspects on its jurisdiction.[345] The tribunal noted that, prior to the *Achmea* judgment, intra-EU objections had been "repeatedly raised" and "repeatedly rejected" by arbitral tribunals, and that this position was shared in AG Wathelet's opinion.[346] It then divided its intra-EU objection's analysis into two parts: (i) whether the ECT applied to intra-EU disputes prior to the adoption of the TFEU and (ii) whether the TFEU changed anything in this regard (the *Achmea* judgment being principally relevant to the second issue).[347]

1.2.16.1 *Disconnection Clause*

On the first issue, the tribunal saw nothing in the ECT's text to exclude issues arising between the EU member states. No contrary indication could be found in the preamble nor in the definition of a "Contracting Party" in Art. 1(2) ECT and it would require an "express provision or clear understanding" in the form

---

342 Ibid.

343 Ibid [385].

344 Ibid [387].

345 BayWa v. Spain, ICSID Case No. ARB/15/16, Decision on Jurisdiction, Liability and Directions on Quantum (02.12.2019) [40], [55].

346 Ibid [244].

347 Ibid [245].

of a disconnection clause, which the ECT lacked. The tribunal noted that this was confirmed in the ECT's *travaux préparatoires,* which noted that a disconnection clause was discussed during the negotiations of the ECT, but was rejected.[348]

1.2.16.2 *Nationality/Territorial Diversity*

The mere fact that the EU is one of the contracting parties to the ECT did not change this conclusion. On the contrary, the definition of an REIO and the "Area" thereof suggest that the ECT contemplates "that there would be overlapping competences".[349]

The tribunal noted that, under international law, a state cannot invoke its domestic law concerning its competence to conclude treaties to invalidate a treaty "unless it was a manifest violation of a rule of fundamental importance". This follows from the principle of *pacta sunt servanda* and is expressed in Art. 46 VCLT. A similar principle must apply to the EU, even though it operates on both, an internal and international levels.[350] The tribunal added that, when the ECT was signed, "matters of internal investment" were a shared competence between the European Communities (i.e. the EU's predecessor) and its member states. However, even assuming otherwise, the EU member states had signed the ECT without "qualification or reservation".[351]

1.2.16.3 *EU Law*

The tribunal then proceeded to the second issue, i.e. whether the TFEU had an impact on the above conclusions. In the beginning, it noted that the ECT constitutes the source of the tribunal's competence. Rules of international law on the relations between successive treaties govern the impact, if any, of subsequent developments at the EU level.[352]

It then analyzed the law applicable to jurisdiction. It noted that, even though the *Vattenfall* tribunal decided that Art. 26(6) of the ECT applies to the merits of the case, but not to the tribunal's jurisdiction, what it "excluded via the front door" of Art. 26(6)ECT, it then "substantially brought back in as treaty law independently" of this provision.[353] The *BayWa* tribunal perceived Art. 26(6) ECT as "an unexceptionable provision, which would have had to be

348 Ibid [247].
349 Ibid [248].
350 Ibid [249].
351 Ibid.
352 Ibid [262].
353 Ibid [265].

implied if it had not been expressed".[354] In its view, the relevant provisions of EU law (i.e. Arts. 107, 108, 267 and 344 TFEU) apply as treaty provisions and are not merely part of the EU's "internal legal order".[355] The crucial question was what the rules of international law say about the application of those TFEU provisions.[356]

The tribunal looked at Art. 16 ECT, which gives priority to Parts III and V of the ECT under two conditions: (i) the other treaty concerns the same subject matter and (ii) the other treaty is less favorable to the investor or the investment.[357] The tribunal assessed that the first condition was not met, as the TFEU does not concern the same subject matter as the ECT. As a result, Art. 16 ECT did not help to resolve the potential conflict between the ECT and the TFEU. As to the second condition, the tribunal "would be inclined, if necessary" to decide that it was met. Art. 10 ECT is more favorable, as the TFEU does not allow for a direct challenge against state measure on the grounds specified in Art. 10 ECT (nor on any other, more favorable, grounds) and does not contain any provisions on the resolution of disputes between an investor and a state by an international tribunal.[358]

1.2.16.4 *Subsequent Agreement or Practice*

The tribunal decided that Art. 30 VCLT did not apply for the same reason (i.e. given the different subject matters of the treaties in question).[359] Whilst it considered Art. 41 VCLT to be relevant, since it is not limited to treaties sharing the same subject matter, it found that the conditions laid down in this provision were not met. First, the alleged modification would be contrary to the object and purpose of the ECT. Second, no notification was made.[360]

1.2.16.5 *Achmea Judgment*

For the above reasons, "if it were free to do so", the tribunal would have dismissed the jurisdictional objection. Nevertheless, it observed that international law allows states to establish "their own international courts with jurisdiction over and authority to bind the Member States on issues of international law affecting them" and to establish "the priority of the regime treaty over other sources of international law, at least so long as peremptory norms are not

354 Ibid [267].
355 Ibid [266].
356 Ibid [268].
357 Ibid [270].
358 Ibid [271].
359 Ibid [273].
360 Ibid [276].

implicated". The CJEU is such a type of court.[361] If the *Achmea* judgment was to be applied to the ECT, it would "authoritatively establish", as between the home state and the host state in the case at hand, "that the TFEU modifies Article 16 of the ECT on an inter se basis".[362] Nevertheless, the tribunal considered the *Achmea* judgment to be irrelevant, as it concerned (i) a bilateral, not a multilateral treaty, and (ii) an agreement concluded by the EU member states, not by the EU itself.[363]

1.2.17 Stadtwerke

In *Stadtwerke* the intra-EU objection was again considered as *rationae personae*.[364] The tribunal noted that the core of the objection related to the proper interpretation of Art. 26 ECT.[365] It also underlined that in its analysis and interpretation, it must be guided by Arts. 31 and 32 VCLT.[366]

1.2.17.1 *Nationality/Territorial Diversity*

In the tribunal's view, the term "another Contracting Party" used in Art. 26(1) ECT means a "Contracting Party different from the Contracting Party mentioned at the beginning of Article 26(1)", which would have meant, in the present case, that an investor from Spain could not be a claimant.[367] This prerequisite was met.[368] This provision refers to investors "organized", not "operating" or "functioning" under a particular state's law. Therefore, even though, to a certain degree, the claimants operate under EU law, they are not organized under EU law, but under the law of a particular EU member state. This precludes a conclusion that they are investors of both the EU and an EU member state.[369]

The tribunal also noted that the ECT neither distinguishes between Contracting States nor expressly carves out disputes between an investor from an EU member state against another EU member state from the consent to

361 Ibid [280].

362 Ibid [282]. The tribunal referred to Art. 16 ECT. This seems to be a typographical error. The correct reference should be to the jurisdictional clause – Art. 26 ECT.

363 Ibid.

364 Stadtwerke v. Spain, ICSID Case No. ARB/15/1, Award (02.12.2019) [101].

365 Ibid [124].

366 Ibid [125].

367 Ibid [126].

368 Ibid [127]. All of the claimants, except for one, were established under the laws of the home state (Germany), whereas the Spanish SPV was controlled by them, thus falling within the definition of an investor of another state.

369 Ibid [128].

arbitrate given in Art. 26(1) ECT.[370] In addition, nothing suggests that a preference should be given to the protection granted by EU law over that granted by the ECT. Such a conclusion cannot be derived from the definition of an REIO in Art. 1(2) ECT, and an "express stipulation" in the text of the ECT would be necessary to conclude otherwise.[371] Similarly, Art. 25 ECT does not suggest that EU law prevails over ECT. It simply eliminates the possibility that a state which is not an EU member state may benefit from the EU's treaties.[372]

1.2.17.2 *EU Law*

The tribunal decided that, as one of the claimants was wholly owned by a public authority of the home state, this meant that the claimant was a state-owned company.[373] However, this did not mean that the dispute fell within Art. 344 TFEU. In addition, the ECT does not differentiate between state-owned and private-owned entities, and both groups fall within the definition of an "investor" under the ECT.[374] Moreover, Art. 344 TFEU refers only to inter-state disputes between EU member states, and only those related to such "treaties" as are defined in Art. 1(2) TFEU (i.e. the TFEU and TEU), not to other treaties such as ECT.[375]

The tribunal observed that Art. 26(6) ECT refers solely to the law applicable to the merits of a dispute, not to the question of jurisdiction. Thus, it cannot serve as the gateway for incorporating Arts. 267 and 344 TFEU into the analysis of the tribunal's jurisdiction.[376] This does not, however, mean that EU law is irrelevant to the jurisdiction question. EU law, "including the findings of the CJEU in the Achmea case, can be characterized as international law" for the purposes of Art. 31(3)(c) VCLT and, as a result, be relevant when interpreting Art. 26(1) ECT.[377]

1.2.17.3 *Achmea Judgment*

Nevertheless, the tribunal's analysis of Arts. 267 and 344 TFEU, interpreted in line with the *Achmea* judgment, did not support the jurisdictional objection.[378] The tribunal viewed the *Achmea* judgment as concerning only a BIT

370 Ibid [129].
371 Ibid [131].
372 Ibid [132].
373 Ibid [134]. One of the claimants was owned by the Council of the City of Munich.
374 Ibid [133]–[134].
375 Ibid [135].
376 Ibid [137].
377 Ibid [138].
378 Ibid.

concluded between two EU member states, whereas the ECT was a multilateral treaty being a "mixed agreement", i.e. one to which not only the EU itself and its member states are parties, but also other states.[379] In its view, the CJEU confirmed this in the *Achmea* judgment by differentiating between arbitral tribunals established on the basis of a BIT and courts or tribunals which adjudicate disputes on the basis of a treaty to which the EU itself is a party.[380]

Finally, the tribunal considered that, even if it agreed that Art. 344 TFEU has the same subject matter as Art. 26 ECT, any conflict would be resolved in favor of the ECT based on Art. 16 ECT, as it is more favorable to investors, in the sense that it allows them to submit a dispute to an arbitral tribunal, whereas the TFEU does not envisage it.[381]

1.2.18 RWE

1.2.18.1 *EU Law*

In *RWE*, the intra-EU objection was again framed as *rationae personae* in nature.[382] The tribunal first looked at the applicable law.[383] It rejected the applicability of EU law via local law, stating that, in ICSID arbitration, the tribunal is not bound by the law of the place of arbitration.[384] The tribunal also rejected the applicability of EU law via Art. 26(6) ECT, considering that this article only regulates the law applicable to the merits. The term "dispute" used in this provision refers to an alleged breach of the substantive provisions of Part III of the ECT, and the function of Art. 26(6) ECT is "functionally equivalent" to Art. 42(1) of the ICSID Convention.[385] The tribunal added that only some of EU law can be considered as international law. It considered it "unusual" for an international tribunal examining its own jurisdiction to apply any law beyond the treaty upon which jurisdiction was based, together with the rules on treaty interpretation in accordance with the VCLT.[386]

---

379 Ibid [142].
380 Ibid [143].
381 Ibid [145].
382 RWE v. Spain, ICSID Case No. ARB/14/34, Decision on Jurisdiction, Liability, and Certain Issues of Quantum (30.12.2019) [237].
383 Ibid [310]. The tribunal framed it under a heading "the law applicable to the intra-EU objection", but it can be understood as the law applicable to jurisdiction.
384 Ibid: "It follows from the fact that this is an ICSID arbitration that the Tribunal is not concerned with the application of a curial law (unlike in the Achmea case, for example), which might bring into play EU law as a matter of that curial law".
385 Ibid [315]. Moreover, it is understood to have the same effect as Art 27(3)(g) ECT.
386 Ibid [316].

The tribunal then observed that, even if Art. 26(6) ECT mandates the application of EU law to the jurisdiction question, the intra-EU objection would still fail.[387] It considered that only such rules as are established by treaty exist within, and are governed by, international law, whereas secondary EU law operates "only within the internal legal order of the EU".[388]

1.2.18.2 *Nationality/Territorial Diversity*

The tribunal dismissed the argument that the investments had not been made in the area of another contracting party, as required by Art. 26(1) ECT. It noted that the definition of an REIO's "Area" is "predicated on individual States that are Contracting Parties having their own Areas".[389] The ECT does not indicate that, if the two relevant states are simultaneously members of the REIO, they should be regarded as "ceasing to have their own Areas as States and Contracting Parties to the ECT or that the relevant Area becomes the Area of the EU (and exclusively so)".[390] The tribunal recognized that, if a claim is brought against the EU, then the EU is a contracting party and the definition of its area becomes relevant.[391] Denying access to arbitration in intra-EU disputes would require "some form of disconnection clause or declaration of competencies".[392] Art. 25 ECT does not change this conclusion. It says nothing about the primacy of EU law, but simply states that a party to an Economic Integration Agreement is not required to extend any preferential treatment under MFN clauses.[393]

1.2.18.3 *Treaty Interpretation*

The tribunal applied customary international law ("CIL") to confirm the above conclusions. First, it noted that Art. 30 VCLT offers a "default rule" with respect to the rules on conflict of treaties, which cannot prevail over any specific conflict provisions contained in the relevant treaty.[394] Art. 16 ECT contains such a rule in favor of the investor.[395] Even if one assumes that the TFEU and the TEU have the same subject matter as the ECT, Part III and V of the ECT were considered as being more favorable to claimants.[396] Second, even though Art. 16 ECT

---

387 Ibid [318]. See analysis in the following paragraphs.
388 Ibid [314].
389 Ibid [326].
390 Ibid [327].
391 Ibid [328].
392 Ibid [330], [331].
393 Ibid [336].
394 Ibid [338].
395 Ibid [339].
396 Ibid [340].

can be displaced by the express provisions of a subsequent treaty, no such provision existed. In any case, such a subsequent modification would need to be approved by all contracting states to the ECT.[397] For the same reason (i.e. that a subsequent treaty must be concluded by all of the ECT's contracting states) Art. 59 VCLT was also deemed irrelevant for the intra-EU objection. Moreover, no notification of suspension had been given, within the meaning of Art. 65 VCLT.[398]

The tribunal concluded that, pursuant to Art. 31(3)(c) VCLT, a treaty interpretation cannot result in "re-writing" the ECT's explicit provisions in a manner contrary to their ordinary meaning so as to result in different meanings of the same provision for different parties to the same treaty.[399] Rejection of the intra-EU objection was also confirmed by reference to the *pacta sunt servanda* principle.[400]

The tribunal added that, even if the above conclusions were wrong, it would still arrive at the same result via the application of EU law.[401] First, the claims concerned an alleged breach of the ECT, not EU law. The ECT grants investors rights that are "additional to any other rights provided by the internal market" and there is no inconsistency between EU law and the ECT.[402] No incompatibility between the two regimes could be said to exist merely because an EU internal market in electricity existed and EU directives on RE had been adopted.[403]

The tribunal did not consider the 2019 Declarations to be an authentic interpretation of Art. 26 ECT but, rather, as a statement as to how this provision "is received and applied (or misapplied) in EU law".[404] Likewise, it did not consider it as constituting a subsequent practice or subsequent agreement between the parties within the meaning of Art. 31(3)(a) VCLT. First, it pointed to the internal disagreement among the EU member states regarding the *Achmea* judgment's impact on the ECT. Second, it noted the lack of any consensus among the ECT's contracting parties, other than the EU member states.[405]

---

397 Ibid [341].
398 Ibid [343].
399 Ibid [345].
400 Ibid [347]–[348].
401 Ibid [350].
402 Ibid [354].
403 Ibid [355].
404 Ibid [369].
405 Ibid [371]–[372].

1.2.18.4 *State Aid*

The tribunal rejected the argument that the dispute affected essential elements of EU law on state aid. The Disputed Measures were not motivated by concerns over state aid. Moreover, the EC's investigation and the 2017 EC Decision concerned the New Regime only, not the Special Regime.[406] In any case, the mere fact that the 2017 EC Decision found the New Regime to be lawful under Art. 107(3)(c) TFEU (albeit also unlawful under Art. 108(3) TFEU) cannot determine whether or not it breaches the ECT.[407] Also, the fact that a subsidy to the RE sector may constitute a form of state aid under EU law does not mean that EU law on state aid applies.[408]

The tribunal added that the protections granted in Part III of the ECT are consistent with, albeit different from, the EU's rules on free movement of capital and freedom of establishment. It added that:

> nothing in the ECT that suggests that the EU saw the Part III protections as falling within an area of its exclusive competence and, even if Article 3(2) TFEU were engaged, it has not been demonstrated to the Tribunal how or why this would override the jurisdiction.[409]

1.2.18.5 *Achmea Judgment*

The tribunal then analyzed the impact of the *Achmea* judgment. It noted that this judgment can be distinguished from the case at hand for several reasons. In particular, the *Achmea* judgment was "predicated on the EU not being a party to the BIT then at issue", as opposed to the EU being a contracting party to the ECT.[410] The tribunal considered that Arts. 267 and 344 TFEU were not implicated in the case at hand, because the tribunal did not need to resolve any issues under EU law.[411] Even though the *Achmea* judgment suggests, on the one hand, that "the potential for the application of EU law appears to have been sufficient", on the other hand it "appears to have been fundamental to the reasoning that the EU itself was not a party to the relevant investment treaty".[412] The tribunal rejected the suggestion that Art. 26 ECT may adversely affect the autonomy of EU law if a claim is brought against an EU member state in a situation when, in the same treaty, the EU itself accepted the possibility that claims

406 Ibid [356], [357]–[358].
407 Ibid [359].
408 Ibid [360].
409 Ibid [361].
410 Ibid [363].
411 Ibid [364].
412 Ibid [365].

may be brought against it. In the latter scenario, EU law would apply to the merits of such a dispute insofar as such EU law qualifies as international law.[413]

The tribunal rejected the suggestion that it should refer the matter to the CJEU "through a juge d'appui", considering that it had no "general power of delegation" to "refer the matter" to the CJEU under the ECT or the ICSID Convention without the consent of the parties before it (which had not been given).[414]

Finally, the tribunal concluded that it could not decide jurisdiction by reference to the future enforceability of the award. Even though it was "naturally concerned" about enforcement, it is ultimately a matter for the state courts to implement a state's obligations, pursuant to Art. 54 of the ICSID Convention.[415]

1.2.19 Watkins

In *Watkins*, the intra-EU objection was also characterized as *rationae personae*.[416] The tribunal started its analysis by referring to Arts. 31 and 32 VCLT.[417] It identified four sub-divisions of the objection, based on the arguments that it lacked jurisdiction as: (i) the claimants were not investors "of another Contracting Party" under Article 26 ECT, (ii) the relationship between EU law and the ECT, (iii) the existence of an implicit disconnection clause within the ECT, and (iv) the impact of the *Achmea* judgment.[418]

1.2.19.1 *Nationality/Territorial Diversity*

Referring to the first line of argument, the tribunal noted that the ECT defined the "Area" of an REIO, such as the EU, as constituting the areas of the REIO's member states.[419] Thus, the EU's member states preserved their own "Areas" within the ECT meaning, notwithstanding the EU's accession to the ECT.[420] The tribunal also noted that, in the CJEU's own case law, "European citizenship is based on superimposition on the nationality of a Member State" because the EU member states' domestic laws define the acquisition and loss of nationality. Consequently, European citizenship does not remove a foreign element from intra-EU disputes based on the ECT.[421]

---

413 Ibid [366].
414 Ibid [373].
415 Ibid [374].
416 Watkins v. Spain, ICSID Case No. ARB/15/44, Award (21.01.2020) [141].
417 Ibid [183].
418 Ibid [180].
419 Ibid [185].
420 Ibid [186].
421 Ibid [188]. The tribunal did not explain why European citizenship rules (which apply to natural persons only pursuant to Art. 20 TFEU) would have any bearing on the issue of nationality of legal persons.

1.2.19.2 *EU Law*

Regarding the second issue, whilst the tribunal doubted that EU law prohibits dispute settlement systems other than those established in the EU treaties, it concluded that this was irrelevant to an assessment of its jurisdiction.[422] This was because international law is "the sole body of law governing its jurisdiction", and it "derives its jurisdictional power exclusively from the ECT".[423] It added that the dispute concerned no question of the hierarchy between EU law and international law since it did not require any assessment of the validity of EU law.[424]

The tribunal noted that, according to the *Achmea* judgment, arbitral tribunals are not tribunals within the meaning of Art. 267 TFEU, and therefore they do not operate "stricto sensu within the EU judicial system". Such "dualist reasoning reinforces the idea that ICSID tribunals are located in a legal space solely governed by international law that is the only source of jurisdiction".[425]

1.2.19.3 *Disconnection Clause*

With respect to the third line of argument, the tribunal rejected to suggestion that an implicit disconnection clause existed.[426] It noted that "some European treaty practice" developed disconnection clauses in favor of EU law, but had been criticized.[427] In its view, the idea of an implicit disconnection clause would be against the international law principle of *pacta sunt servanda*.[428] An implicit modification of such magnitude would not only be contrary to the international law of treaties but also to "EU constitutional law" (i.e. Art. 3(5) TEU), which requires a consistent and harmonious interpretation of European treaty practice with international law.[429]

1.2.19.4 *Achmea Judgment*

Finally, the tribunal turned to the implications of the *Achmea* judgment. It identified three patterns of reasoning that other tribunals had adopted

422 Ibid [191].
423 Ibid [193].
424 Ibid [195].
425 Ibid.
426 Ibid [197].
427 Ibid [198]. See, for example, the commentary of the ILC Study Group and the Parliamentary Assembly of the Council of Europe.
428 Ibid [200].
429 Ibid [202], relying on CJEU judgment in the *Western Sahara* case – Judgment of the Court (Grand Chamber) of 27.02.2018, Western Sahara Case No. C-266/16 (ECLI:EU:C:2018).

regarding this judgment's impact on arbitral proceedings.[430] The first group had adopted the position that no incompatibility existed between the two regimes and that the *Achmea* judgment was "ill-grounded".[431] The second group considered the position taken in the *Achmea* judgment as irrelevant to a multilateral, as opposed to a bilateral, investment treaty.[432] The third group took the position that the *Achmea* judgment had no bearing in another legal order, and that a parallelism of treaties exists, with a clear distinction between the EU legal order, on the one hand, and the international law legal order, on the other hand. Both legal orders are distinct, but should be considered as operating in harmony, not in conflict. However, if indeed some conflict exists and creates the need to determine the hierarchy between the two, this must be resolved from the perspective of public international law.[433]

The tribunal did not explicitly endorse the position of any of these three groups. However, it impliedly accepted the reasoning of the second and the third groups. First, it noted that the *Achmea* judgment is silent on the ECT.[434] Then it added that, when determining jurisdiction, it must rely solely on the ECT because of the "fundamental principle" of "treaty parallelism".[435]

1.2.20 Hydro

In *Hydro*, the tribunal considered that the "obvious starting point" for analyzing the intra-EU objection was the wording of the relevant provisions of the relevant treaties.[436] The tribunal looked at Arts. 26(1)–(3), 1(2), 1(3), 16 ECT, as well as Art. 25(1), 41(1) of the ICSID Convention.[437] The "combined effect of these provisions on the face of their wording" was that the tribunal had jurisdiction.[438]

1.2.20.1 *Nationality/Territorial Diversity*

The respondent argued that, as both claimants were nationals of EU member states, they held EU nationality, which precluded them from commencing arbitration against an EU member state.[439] The tribunal disagreed and noted that, while Art. 20 TFEU establishes a "separate category of EU citizenship", it

430 Ibid [207].
431 Ibid [208]–[211].
432 Ibid [212]–[214].
433 Ibid [215]–[220].
434 Ibid [221].
435 Ibid [223].
436 Hydro v. Spain, ICSID Case No. ARB/15/42, Decision on Jurisdiction, Liability and Directions on Quantum (09.03.2020) [455].
437 Ibid [456]–[461].
438 Ibid [462].
439 Ibid [463].

does not a "create dual nationality". In addition, Art. 25(2)(a) of the ICSID Convention applies to natural persons only, not to legal persons.[440]

The tribunal noted that merely because the EU is a contracting party to the ECT does not mean that, in the context of Art. 26(1) ECT, the relevant "Area" is the territory of the EU as a whole, and not its individual member states. A contrary conclusion "would simply make no sense".[441] This conclusion remains unaltered despite the possibility for the REIO to vote instead of its member states in certain circumstances.[442]

1.2.20.2 *Disconnection Clause*

The tribunal rejected the possibility that a disconnection clause may exist, either explicit or implied, understood as a provision that "disapplies certain provisions of a treaty in mutual relations between certain parties".[443]

1.2.20.3 *Achmea Judgment*

The next and final issue in the intra-EU objection concerned the *Achmea* judgment. The tribunal noted that both parties relied on the VCLT, even though not all of the ECT's contracting parties (including the EU) are parties to the VCLT. Nevertheless, the tribunal did not hesitate to rely on the VCLT, given that its relevant provisions – Arts. 30 and 31 – codify CIL on the interpretation of international treaties.[444]

A "preliminary point" of the tribunal's analysis was whether the *Achmea* judgment applies to multilateral treaties, such as the ECT.[445] The tribunal understood the CJEU's position as being that it is "not in principle incompatible with EU law, provided that the autonomy of the EU and its legal order is respected" for the EU to enter into an international agreement establishing a court to interpret and apply the agreement's provisions and whose decisions would be binding on the institutions, including on the CJEU.[446]

The tribunal then identified two reasons to justify why, in its view, the scope of the *Achmea* judgment covers investor-state arbitration based on a multilateral treaty. First, it read the *Achmea* judgment as suggesting that the CJEU "was mainly directing itself to agreements with third States". Second, the CJEU relied on its Opinion 1/91 and Opinion 2/13, concerning treaties concluded by

440 Ibid [464]. It is worth noting that Art. 20 TFEU also applies to natural persons only.
441 Ibid [470].
442 Ibid.
443 Ibid [471].
444 Ibid [474], [510], [540].
445 Ibid [486].
446 Ibid [489].

the EU with third states, and on Opinion 1/09[447] concerning the draft Agreement creating a unified patent litigation system.[448] In the latter, the CJEU ruled that the EU member states cannot confer jurisdiction to resolve patent disputes concerning direct actions between individuals to a court created by such international agreement, which would deprive the EU member states' court of their task to implement EU law and of "the power or obligation" in Art. 267 TFEU to refer questions for a preliminary ruling in the concerned field.[449] The tribunal also noted that the CJEU used the term "international agreement" in the operative part of the *Achmea* judgment, as opposed to the term "bilateral investment protection agreement" used in the question asked by the domestic court.[450]

The above led the tribunal to conclude that there is "at least the possibility, and perhaps the probability" that "if the compatibility of the ECT with the TFEU arose before the CJEU, it would apply the Achmea ruling to the dispute resolution mechanism under the ECT".[451]

The tribunal then noted that EU law is international law, since "the corpus of EU law derives from treaties". Likewise, it also considered the CJEU's judgments which interpret the EU treaties as being part of international law.[452] This did not answer, however, whether EU law is part of the international law which must be applied when determining jurisdiction.[453] The tribunal added that the principle of EU law supremacy concerns EU law's relationship with national law, but not international law – regardless of whether customary or treaty law.[454]

The tribunal then observed that "although phrased in terms of interpretation of two provisions of the TFEU, it is hard to read the Achmea ruling as a normal case of treaty interpretation" because Art. 267 TFEU "is simply the latest iteration [...] of the power (and in some cases the duty) of national courts to make references" to the CJEU, whereas Art. 344 TFEU "simply prevents Member States from submitting disputes concerning the interpretation or application of the Treaties to any method of settlement other than those provided for in the Treaties".[455] In the tribunal's view, the "residual remedy" for a national

447 Opinion 1/09 of the Court (Full Court) (08.03.2011) (ECLI:EU:C:2011:123).
448 Hydro v. Spain, *supra* note 436 [490], [492].
449 Ibid [491].
450 Ibid [493].
451 Ibid.
452 Ibid [494].
453 Ibid [495]. This question was left unanswered – [502(16)].
454 Ibid [502(17)].
455 Ibid [498].

of an EU member state who alleges that another EU member state has violated the ECT is to commence arbitration. The domestic courts are engaged only at the enforcement stage. Thus, the tribunal did not consider Art. 26(3) ECT to be contrary to the aforementioned understanding of Art. 267 or 344 TFEU.[456]

The tribunal added that the *Achmea* judgment is "entitled to the greatest respect", being a "decision on the constitutional order of the EU in support of the policy of European integration", but it is not "an orthodox application of the rules of treaty interpretation".[457] Accordingly, it decided that it was not bound by the *Achmea* judgment.[458]

It further stated that, under the *Achmea* judgment, the agreement to arbitrate in an investment treaty is "precluded" by EU law, not that it is void or incompatible with the TFEU. The CJEU was silent on the effect of such preclusion. Thus, it is unclear whether the provision ceased to have legal effect, or whether the consequence is that the EU member states should modify or abrogate investment treaties between them.[459]

1.2.20.4 *Subsequent Agreement or Practice*

In the tribunal's view, there is no conflict between the provisions requiring application of the principles codified in Art. 30 VCLT.[460] This rendered it unnecessary to decide upon the effects of Art. 16 ECT.[461] It added that the 2019 Declarations are political in nature and lack any legal force. Since they were not signed by all of the ECT's contracting parties, they do not constitute a "subsequent agreement" within the meaning of Art. 31 VCLT.[462]

Thus, the tribunal concluded that it is a "creature of international law" and that neither its inability to make a reference to the CJEU, nor the CJEU's interpretation of EU law, deprived it of jurisdiction under international law.[463]

1.2.21 Cavalum

In *Cavalum*, the tribunal's analysis of the intra-EU objection was essentially the same as in the *Hydro* case.[464] The tribunal added a few observations.

---

456 Ibid [499].
457 Ibid [500].
458 Ibid.
459 Ibid [501].
460 Ibid [502(11)].
461 Ibid [502(12)].
462 Ibid [502(15)].
463 Ibid [502(14)].
464 Cavalum v. Spain, ICSID Case No. ARB/15/34, Decision on Jurisdiction, Liability and Directions on Quantum (31.08.2020) [328]–[371], repeating Hydro v. Spain, *supra* note 436

In its view, even if the final determination of EU law's content is reserved for the CJEU, this does not mean that non-EU courts and tribunals are precluded from deciding issues of EU law. It would produce "absurd" results if a court in a third state, having jurisdiction over a dispute (and similarly an arbitral tribunal in such a state or an international arbitral tribunal) must refrain from dealing with issues of EU law raised by a party simply because it is incapable of making a reference to the CJEU.[465] Thus, even if the principles set out in the *Achmea* judgment apply to the ECT as a matter of EU law, this does not affect the jurisdiction under the applicable international law (i.e. the ECT and the ICSID Convention in this case).[466]

Moreover, no conflict exists between Art. 26(1)–(3) ECT and Art. 267 and 344 TFEU which would bring into play the principles reflected in Art. 30 or 41 VCLT. In addition, even if one agreed that EU law created a right to dispute resolution regarding the subject matter of Part III (investment protection) and Part V (dispute settlement) of the ECT, Part V of the ECT would still operate pursuant to Art. 16 ECT, since the ECT is more favorable to the investor.[467]

Finally, the mere fact that an award may not be effectively enforced in the EU Member States does not affect the tribunal's jurisdiction.[468] While it is the tribunal's duty to issue an enforceable award, this duty is outweighed by its duty to perform its mandate under the ECT.[469]

1.3 *Lessons Learned*

The modern reality is that the *Achmea* judgment has existed for long enough to be firmly rooted in the mindsets of everyone dealing with investor-state arbitration. However, the Spanish saga cases date back to the "pre-Achmea era". The first 6 decisions on jurisdiction, issued in *PV Investors, Charanne, RREEF, Isolux, Eiser* and *Novenergia*, pre-date the *Achmea* judgment.

Regardless of whether the tribunals in the Spanish saga cases issued their jurisdiction decisions before or after the *Achmea* judgment was handed down, they were unanimous in dismissing the intra-EU objection.[470] Furthermore,

---

[470]–[502]. There are some minor amendments in the text of some of the provisions and additional headings.

465 Cavalum v. Spain, ibid [362].

466 Ibid [370(9)].

467 Ibid [367].

468 Ibid [370(18)].

469 Ibid [369].

470 An important development occurred when this book was already in the production process, with a groundbreaking decision of the first tribunal to ever uphold the intra-EU jurisdictional objection – Green Power v. Spain, SCC Case No. V 2016/135, Award (16.06.2022).

this was unanimous approach of all of the arbitrators on each tribunal. None of the dissenting opinions concerned the jurisdictional issues analyzed in the present Chapter.[471] This is in line with the general investor-state arbitration.[472]

The Spanish saga cases must be read *vis-à-vis* a notable "recalibration" of the perspective of the EU, its institutions, and its member states. For many years the EC lobbied against intra-EU investment arbitration and encouraged EU member states to terminate any intra-EU BITs.[473] In virtually all of the Spanish saga cases, the EC sought permission to file *amicus curiae* submissions in support of the respondent's intra-EU objection.[474] The *Achmea* judgment

---

Keeping in mind the time constraints and the analysis here, which focuses on the first 21 Spanish saga cases (see Introduction for detailed explanation of the adopted methodology), this cannot be dealt with in more detail in the first edition of this book.

471 The only dissenting opinion concerning jurisdiction was issued in the *PV Investors* case, but it did not concern any of the issues analyzed in this Chapter. It concerned the majority's decision that the local companies under the control of foreign investors lacked standing (the tribunal declined jurisdiction over legal entities incorporated in Spain, but wholly owned by foreign investors, and as a result it retained jurisdiction over 26 of the 88 initial claimants). See: The PV Investors v. Spain, PCA Case No. 2012-14, Concurring and Dissenting Opinion of Judge Charles N. Brower (10.10.2014) [1].

472 Fn 44-46. See also for example: Tim Maxian Rusche, How to Enforce the Achmea Judgment – Tools for EU Member States before, during and after Investment Arbitration Proceedings Brought by an Investor from Another EU Member State, European Investment Law and Arbitration Review, 6:1 (2022), p. 327, David Sandberg, Jacob Rosell Svensson, Achmea and the Implications for Challenge Proceedings before National Courts, European Investment Law and Arbitration Review, 5:1 (2021), p. 148, Lavranos, *supra* note 52, p. 198.

473 See for example: Marc Bungenberg, The Multilateral Investment Court – Royal Road Or Dead End for the EU Legal Order, International Business Law Journal, 5 (2019), p. 471: "Hardly any other area of European economic law has been exposed in recent years to such strong attacks as EU investment protection law". See also for example: Deyan Draguiev, 2018 In Review: The Achmea Decision and Its Reverberations in the World of Arbitration, Kluwer Arbitration Blog (16.01.2019), available at: http://arbitrationblog.kluwerarbitration.com/2019/01/16/2018-in-review-the-achmea-decision-and-its-reverberations-in-the-world-of-arbitration/. See also for example the EC's position from 2018 that:

> for the Commission, investor-to-State arbitration in EU trade and investment agreements is a thing of the past and has been replaced by the Investment Court System (ICS), already included in CETA, the EU-Singapore, EU-Viet Nam and EU-Mexico agreements and the negotiation basis for negotiations with 3rd countries

– Commission provides guidance on protection of cross-border EU investments – Questions and Answers (19.07.2018), available at: https://ec.europa.eu/commission/presscorner/detail/fi/MEMO_18_4529.

474 See for example: Nikos Lavranos, Regime Interaction in Investment Arbitration: EU Law; From Peaceful Co-Existence to Permanent Conflict, Kluwer Arbitration Blog (13.01.2022), available at: http://arbitrationblog.kluwerarbitration.com/2022/01/13/regime-interaction-in-investment-arbitration-eu-law-from-peaceful-co-existence-to-permanent-conflict/,

represented a significant milestone in these efforts.[475] From the perspective of interpreting EU law, it put an end to the debate as to whether a conflict exists between Arts. 267 and 344 TFEU and intra-EU investor-state arbitration.[476] The CJEU took a clear position that there is a conflict, and that EU law "precludes" intra-EU BITS' jurisdictional provisions which provide for investor-state arbitrations.[477] This could have been considered as a *Roma locuta, causa finita* type of judgment. Even if one had doubts on this issue earlier, the *Achmea* judgment was supposed to resolve them.

It is indisputable that the *Achmea* judgment had a serious impact.[478] For example, it rendered it effectively impossible to attract any third-party funding for intra-EU disputes based on a BIT. The Spanish saga cases prove, however, that the reality of the *Achmea* judgment's impact on the case law of arbitral tribunals did not meet the EC's high expectations, nor of those EU member states which welcomed the *Achmea* judgment as a positive development.[479] There continued to be a significant number of investor-state arbitrations which continued to dismiss the intra-EU jurisdictional objections. This triggered the 2019 Declarations which, again, failed to meet the high expectations

---

where he claims that the EC "continued to escalate the conflict by intervening in practically all intra-EU disputes (both based on intra-EU BITS and the ECT) as amicus curiae before arbitral tribunals as well as before domestic courts". This can be seen in the examples of *Blusun v. Italy* and *Wirtgen v. Czech Republic*, where the EC's *amicus curiae* triggered an analysis of the intra-EU objection. See: Blusun v. Italy, *supra* note 24 [231], Wirtgen v. Czech Republic, *supra* note 24 [250]. Detailed analysis of the EC's interventions in the Spanish saga cases is outside of the scope of this Chapter.

475 "[...] the Achmea decision is the flag that the EU Commission needed to reinvigorate its campaign against intra-EU" investor-state arbitration – Draguiev, *supra* note 473.

476 Sandberg, Svensson, *supra* note 472, p. 164.

477 Fn 37.

478 One commentator described how "the commotion Achmea provoked in the investment arbitration community came close to pandemonium" – Crawford Jamieson, Assessing the CJEU's Decisions in *Achmea* and Opinion 1/17 in Light of the Proposed Multilateral Investment Court – Winner of the Essay Competition 2020, European Investment Law and Arbitration Review, 5:1 (2021), p. 216. Some authors picture it as having "already put the final nail in the coffin of intra-EU investment arbitration" – Rusche, *supra* note 472, p. 335.

479 See for example the EC's statement that "following the Achmea judgment, the Commission has intensified its dialogue with all Member States, calling on them to take action to terminate the intra-EU BITS, given their incontestable incompatibility with EU law", which described the intra-EU BITS as "a parallel treaty system overlapping with single market rules, thereby preventing the full application of EU law" – Communication from the Commission to the European Parliament and the Council, Protection of intra-EU investment, COM(2018) 547 (19.07.2018), p. 2.

insofar as their impact on arbitration reality.[480] It was only in 2020, when the Termination Agreement entered into force, that intra-EU arbitrations based on BITs were effectively brought to an end, at least as regards new cases commenced thereafter.[481] Again, however, this development did not apply to the ECT.[482]

Within this context, 4 lessons can be learned for the future from the intra-EU objections to jurisdiction discussed in the Spanish saga cases.

1.3.1 First Lesson Learned – the Spanish Saga Cases Were an Important Contribution to the Factual Matrix Which Led to the 2021 Komstroy Judgment

The *Komstroy* judgment was a direct reaction to the uniform case law of the investor-state arbitral tribunals having confirmed their jurisdiction in intra-EU disputes based on the ECT.[483] The Spanish saga cases form a major part of this case law. This can be seen merely from the simple fact that no other EU member state has had a comparable total number of cases brought against it. As noted in the Introduction, publicly available information shows that Spain has faced at least 49 investor-state arbitrations triggered by its reforms to RE regulations.[484] Accordingly, the Spanish saga cases represent approximately 80% of all investor-state arbitrations in the RE sector,[485] approximately 60%

480 Fn 316, 329, 404-405, 462.

481 See for example: Muszynianka v. Slovakia, *supra* note 52. Some commentators acknowledge the fact of eliminating the intra-EU BIT protection, but with critical assessment, noting for example that the CJEU "even itself subject to similar legitimization challenges as a supranational governmental body, has adopted elements of the democratic-legitimacy critique of ISA when effectively eliminating" the intra-EU BITs – Alexander W. Resar, Tai-Heng Cheng, Investor State Arbitration in a Changing World Order (Brill 2021), p. 50. Others welcomed this development and underlined that it is not limited to intra-EU BITs but covers the intra-EU aspect of the ECT as well – see for example: Rusche, *supra* note 472, p. 326.

482 Fn 53.

483 Fn 24, 44.

484 Based on publicly available information as of 15.04.2022 (https://www.energychartertreaty.org/cases/list-of-cases/). The actual number may be higher, given the confidentiality of potential cases based on treaties other than the ECT.

485 According to Viñuales:

> between 1972 and 2020, at least 178 foreign investment claims with environmental components were filed. [...] Approximately 80% (143) of these disputes have been brought after 2008, and over half of them (76) concern the energy transition, mostly (61) modern renewable energy projects (solar, wind and geothermal)

– Jorge E. Viñuales, Geopolitics of the Energy Transformation, Revue Européenne du Droit (Governing Globalization), 2 (2020), pp. 148–155, available at: https://geopolitique.eu/en/articles/geopolitics-of-the-energy-transformation/.

of intra-EU investor-state arbitrations under the ECT[486] and ⅓ of the total number of 145 cases brought under the ECT since it entered into force in 1998.[487] As such, the cases against Spain can be understood as having best illustrated a problem which permanently attracted attention, like a lighthouse on a seacoast and, at least from the EU's perspective, called for a solution.

This allows one to legitimately assume that the Spanish saga cases serious impacted on the deliberations of the CJEU judges in the *Komstroy* judgment. It goes without saying that there is no documentary evidence to directly support this assumption. The CJEU's deliberations take place behind the closed doors,[488] and no dissenting or concurring opinions exists so as to enable an additional layer of analysis, supplementing a reading of the judgment itself.[489] Nevertheless, the detailed analysis of the cases presented in this Chapter permits this assumption and the conclusion in the form of the first lesson learned presented above.

Of course, the impact of the Spanish saga cases cannot be considered in isolation. These cases must be assessed not only alongside other RE cases initiated against EU member states, but also in the light of all other intra-EU cases, particularly high-profile cases such as *Vattenfall v. Germany*.[490] In all of these cases, arbitral tribunals constituted on the basis of the ECT confirmed that they enjoyed jurisdiction over the relevant dispute, notwithstanding the intra-EU objections vigorously argued by the respondent EU member states and supported by the EC's *amicus curiae* submissions. Nevertheless, the number of cases, combined with the uniformity of arguments and conclusions on the legal issues and factual background makes the RE cases, and the Spanish saga in particular, the most visible, repetitive and therefore the most relevant element of the factual matrix which pathed the way for the *Komstroy* judgment.

The CJEU must have considered itself duty-bound to react at the earliest opportunity to this undesired development in the case law, which was steadily growing in numbers, as arbitral tribunals continued to manifestly declare that

486 https://www.energychartertreaty.org/fileadmin/DocumentsMedia/Statistics/All_statistics_-_1_December_2021_Rev.pdf, p. 4, understanding that intra-EU cases are the only "intra-REIO" cases presented in the statistics.

487 Ibid, p. 1.

488 Art. 35 of the Statute of the CJEU: "The deliberations of the Court of Justice shall be and shall remain secret".

489 Michal Bobek, The Court of Justice of the European Union, in: Anthony Arnull, Damian Chalmers (eds.), The Oxford Handbook of European Union Law (Oxford University Press 2015), p. 169.

490 Some authors underline that the EU member states faced more than 100 intra-EU arbitrations, based on both intra-EU BITs and the ECT, noting that "this state of affairs is surprising" after the *Achmea* judgment – Rusche, *supra* note 472, p. 311.

EU law, including CJEU case law, was irrelevant in cases brought against the EU member states. The *NextEra* tribunal made it clear that "the internal constitutional laws of the EU and its constant changes and interpretations by the CJEU, as the Member States seek to minimize their mutual obligations in another context, are of no relevance for the present Tribunal".[491]

The above finds further support in cases where the arbitral tribunals openly criticized the "truncated reasoning" of the *Achmea* judgment, to borrow the colorful description of the *9REN* tribunal.[492] Other examples are the *Hydro* and *Cavalum* tribunals, which were more diplomatic by underlining, firstly, that the *Achmea* judgment is "entitled to the greatest respect", but then noting that it was not "an orthodox application of the rules of treaty interpretation" because it disregarded the VCLT rules of treaty interpretation.[493]

It would be unreasonable to assume that the EU institutions, including the CJEU, turned a blind eye to the growth of high-profile cases in which arbitrators openly criticized the CJEU's reasoning.[494] Some authors confirm that, prior to issuing the *Komstroy* judgment, the CJEU was "under increasing pressure from Member States and EU organs to put an end to the uncertainty caused by the unresolved issued brought about in the wake of the Achmea decision".[495] This refers mainly to the *Achmea* judgment's silence about intra-EU investor-state arbitration under the ECT. This silence may be explained by the fact that, until the *Achmea* judgment, there were only 3 publicly known decisions dismissing the intra-EU objection in investor-state arbitrations under the ECT.[496] This number increased rapidly after the *Achmea* judgment was issued.[497]

---

491 Fn 271.

492 Fn 280.

493 Fn 457, 464. It was noted that:

> arbitral tribunals tend to approach the issue through the lens of public international law, applying, for example the VCLT and rules of treaty conflict. The CJEU could have similarly approached the issue as one of treaty interpretation, engaging in a dialogue with other international dispute settlement bodies and using reasoning that would resonate with arbitral tribunals deciding on their jurisdiction

– Jed Odermatt, Is EU Law International? Case C-741/19 Republic of Moldova v Komstroy LLC and the Autonomy of the EU Legal Order, European Papers – A Journal on Law and Integration, 6:3 (2021), p. 1268.

494 Some authors describe arguments relied upon by the arbitral tribunals as "legal gymnastics" – see for example: Ahmad Ghouri, Interaction and Conflict of Treaties in Investment Arbitration (Kluwer Law International 2015), p. 167.

495 Auriane Negret, Opinion of Advocate General Saugmandsgaard Øe in *Anie and Others v. Italy* – End of the Road for intra-EU ECT Arbitration?, European Investment Law and Arbitration Review, 6:1 (2022), p. 268.

496 Fn 24.

497 Apart from the Spanish saga, see cases listed in fn 44.

Indeed, many Spanish saga tribunals relied on a reading that the *Achmea* judgment was limited to intra-EU BITs. They adopted a position, to use the *Masdar* tribunal's words, that the *Achmea* judgment "is simply silent on the subject of the ECT".[498] This was the position taken in the *RREEF*,[499] *Masdar*,[500] *Foresight*,[501] *Cube*,[502] *9REN*,[503] *SolEs*,[504] *InfraRed*,[505] *OperaFund*,[506] *BayWa*,[507] *Stadtwerke*,[508] *RWE*[509] and *Watkins*[510] cases. These tribunals underlined that, in the *Achmea* judgment, the CJEU had analyzed a bilateral treaty concluded between two EU member states, to which the EU itself was not a contracting party. They distinguished this from the ECT, which was a multilateral treaty to which the EU itself was a contracting party. This allowed them to wash their hands of the impact of the *Achmea* judgment on arbitral proceedings, and to continue with the narrative that no conflict exists between EU law and the jurisdiction of arbitral tribunals in intra-EU cases based on the ECT.

The following passage from the *InfraRed* award serves as an illustration of nothing short of an explicit call to action for the CJEU. The tribunal stated that the CJEU:

> which is the highest judicial body in charge of the interpretation of European law, has not taken *so far* any position as to the applicability of its judgment in the Achmea case to arbitration tribunals the jurisdiction of which is based on the ECT" (emphasis added).[511]

498 Fn 187.

499 Fn 121.

500 Fn 187.

501 Fn 223.

502 Fn 243–244.

503 Fn 282–283.

504 Fn 308, however having noted this silence, this tribunal assumed that the subject-matter scope of Art. 344 TFEU and Art. 26 ECT is the same – fn 309.

505 Fn 330.

506 Fn 339.

507 Fn 363.

508 Fn 379–380.

509 Fn 410.

510 Fn 434.

511 Fn 330. Similar observation could be made as regards the case law concerning intra-EU BITs which pre-dates the *Achmea* judgment. See for example *Oostergetel v. Slovakia*, where the tribunal decided that an intra-EU BIT was not terminated when Slovakia joined the EU, and the conclusion was "especially so considering the absence of any conclusive position of the EC or the ECJ on this question" – Oostergetel v. Slovakia, *supra* note 22 [109]. *WNC v. Czech Republic* is another example, where the tribunal stated:

> [...] EU law was modified by the Treaty of Lisbon, and the EC has been developing its views of the legal questions involved with intra-EU investment treaties; the European Court of Justice has also expressed views about related questions of competence and

Even when tribunals declared that they felt bound by the *Achmea* judgment, as in *BayWa*,[512] they subsequently upheld their jurisdiction by differentiating ECT-based arbitration from arbitration based on an intra-EU BIT, considering that only the latter was the subject of the *Achmea* judgment.[513] Only two of the Spanish saga tribunals which ruled on the intra-EU objection after the *Achmea* judgment had been issued, *Hydro* and *Cavalum*, noted that there is "at least the possibility, and perhaps the probability" that "if the compatibility of the ECT with the TFEU arose before the CJEU, it would apply the Achmea ruling to the dispute resolution mechanism under the ECT".[514] This did not prevent them, however, from dismissing the intra-EU objection.[515]

This must have been received by the CJEU like a ceaseless call for intervention. That call was heard and replied to at the earliest opportunity – in the guise of the *Komstroy* judgment.

This conclusion is further supported by the fact that the preliminary question asked by the French state court, which led to the *Komstroy* judgment, made no mention of the jurisdiction of arbitral tribunals in ECT-based, intra-EU arbitrations. This is not surprising. There was no room for such a question in this case, since the *Energoalliance v. Moldova* arbitration, which formed the backdrop to the set aside proceedings, was not an intra-EU arbitration. This case's only link to EU law was via the domestic law of the place of arbitration.

Only with this context in mind it is possible to understand why a major part of the *Komstroy* judgment's reasoning refers to issues of intra-EU arbitration, which is only remotely (if at all) related to the preliminary questions asked by the French court. This shows that the CJEU clearly intended to put an end to the debate as to how to read its 2018 *Achmea* judgment and, in particular, whether it should be understood as relevant for ECT-based, intra-EU investor-state arbitrations. This goal was achieved, even if only in the form of *obiter dictum*, and not in the operative part of the *Komstroy* judgment.[516]

> will no doubt define its position more precisely in due course. The Tribunal recognizes that a different view may eventually prevail. [...]
>
> – WNC v. Czech Republic, *supra* note 22 [311].

512 Fn 361.

513 Fn 362–363.

514 Fn 451, 464.

515 Ibid.

516 Some authors note that "since the issue is far too important to be clarified by way of obiter dictum", the CJEU should have issued an opinion in the proceedings triggered by Belgium, which asked questions concerning the modernization of the ECT – see: Julian Scheu, Petyo Nikolov, AG Szpunar's Opinion in Case C-741/19: Preparing the End of Intra-EU Investment Arbitration Under the Energy Charter Treaty?, Kluwer Arbitration Blog (25.05.2021), available at: http://arbitrationblog.kluwerarbitration.com/2021/05/25/ag

1.3.2 Second Lesson Learned – the Tensions between EU Law and Protection under the ECT Are Far from Being Resolved in a Final Manner, and the Main Points of the Debate Have Evolved over Time

This section's preceding analysis of the Spanish saga cases show that the respondent presented several arguments which can be classified under the broad umbrella of the intra-EU objection. The analysis reveals a significant development in the respondent's line of arguments over time. In the chronologically first cases, Spain placed most emphasis on the intra-EU nationality and the implied disconnection clause arguments. The natural consequence of the *Achmea* judgment was that the focus of the objection shifted to arguments based on the supremacy of EU law.[517] The *Masdar* tribunal confirmed that "one of the principal grounds" of the intra-EU objection "appears to have been abandoned", and added that "it is now common ground between the Parties that there is no "disconnect" clause, express or implicit, in Article 26 of the ECT".[518] The same was true in *Antin*, when Spain confirmed that it was no longer arguing in favor of the existence of an implied disconnection clause.[519] In a similar vein, the *InfraRed* tribunal commented that "the notion of the supremacy of EU law was not very prominent" in the first two written submissions, but it "was principally brought forward explicitly and developed as a basis for Respondent's arguments in the latter's Reply on Preliminary Objections".[520]

The above confirms that the intra-EU objections pre-dating the *Achmea* judgment had the same legal nature as those made after the judgment. The CJEU's judgment added legal arguments to support the objection, but did not alter its fundamental nature.

As noted above, during the Spanish saga the focus of the debate drifted away from the first two issues: the EU nationality and the implied disconnection clause. Indeed, there is little scope for arriving at any conclusion other than the Spanish saga tribunals' views on these two fronts.

-szpunars-opinion-in-case-c-741-19-preparing-the-end-of-intra-eu-investment-arbitration-under-the-energy-charter-treaty/. The CJEU considered the request inadmissible – Opinion 1/20 of the Court (Fourth Chamber) of 16.06.2022, ECLI:EU:C:2022:485. Similarly: Fouchard, Thieffry, *supra* note 59, noting that the *Komstroy* judgment "raises a question of legitimacy. Was the CJEU competent to rule on the validity of ECT arbitration in intra-EU disputes? The case at hand was arguably not the best to extend the Achmea solution to ECT arbitration".

517 See for example the *InfraRed* tribunal's comments on this evolution – fn 319.

518 Fn 169, 170.

519 Fn 192.

520 Fn 319.

The EU nationality (or territorial diversity) argument is based on a presumption that the territory of the whole EU is the "area" of the REIO within the meaning of the ECT, and therefore that no diversity of areas exists between the home state and the host state, provided that both are EU member states. The Spanish saga tribunals uniformly disagreed with this view. The *PV Investors*,[521] *Charanne*,[522] *Isolux*,[523] *Novenergia*,[524] *Masdar*,[525] *Antin*,[526] *Foresight*,[527] *NextEra*,[528] SolEs,[529] *BayWa*,[530] *Stadtwerke*,[531] *RWE*,[532] *Watkins*,[533] *Hydro*[534] and *Cavalum*[535] tribunals underlined that the mere fact that the EU has its own "area" within the ECT meaning does not prevent its member states from retaining their own "areas". The *SolEs* tribunal observed that this "would mean that the negotiators concluded a treaty that was largely inoperable as between EU investors and other EU Member States, but did not indicate that exception in the text".[536] The *Eiser*,[537] *Stadtwerke*[538] and *Watkins*[539] tribunals relied on the fact that EU law does not regulate the creation of legal persons nor the acquisition of nationality by individuals. Thus, "European" citizenship exists in addition to the national citizenship of each EU member state, and is therefore subsidiary in nature. Nonetheless, the *PV Investors*,[540] *Charanne*,[541] *Antin*,[542] *InfraRed*[543] and *RWE*[544] tribunals recognized that different conclusions would apply if the EU itself, as opposed to its member states, was named as the respondent in a particular dispute. In such a situation, if an investor presented ECT claims

521 Fn 66.
522 Fn 90.
523 Fn 126.
524 Fn 157–158.
525 Fn 174.
526 Fn 199.
527 Fn 218.
528 Fn 263.
529 Fn 297.
530 Fn 349.
531 Fn 367.
532 Fn 390.
533 Fn 420.
534 Fn 441.
535 Fn 464.
536 Fn 298.
537 Fn 145.
538 Fn 369.
539 Fn 421.
540 Fn 68.
541 Fn 91, *a contrario*.
542 Fn 197–198.
543 Fn 325.
544 Fn 391.

concerning measures undertaken by the EU, the nationality requirement would indeed require that the home state of the investor was different to an EU member state.[545]

The existence of a disconnection clause would mean that, to use the *Hydro* tribunal's words, it "disapplies certain provisions of a treaty in mutual relations between certain parties", namely the jurisdictional clause to intra-EU investor-state disputes.[546] Since it is undisputed that the text of the ECT does not contain such an explicit disconnection clause, Spain argued that an implied one existed. The tribunals unanimously rejected this argument. First, as noted by the *InfraRed*,[547] *OperaFund*[548] and *BayWa*[549] tribunals, the ECT negotiators had discussed an explicit intra-EU disconnection clause, but subsequently decided not to include it in the ECT text. Second, the *Charanne*,[550] *Eiser*,[551] *RREEF*[552] and *Watkins*[553] tribunals underlined that an implied disconnection clause would be contrary to good faith negotiations and the *pacta sunt servanda* principle. Using the *Eiser* tribunal's illustrative description, treaty makers should perform their function without "traps for the unwary with

545 It remains to be seen how the EU will react when faced with such a claim. On the one hand, it stated that "the European Communities have not given their unconditional consent to the submission of a dispute to international arbitration or conciliation". On the other hand, it recognized that it would need to implement non-ICSID arbitral awards. It stated that:

> as far as international arbitration is concerned, it should be stated that the provisions of the ICSID Convention do not allow the European Communities to become parties to it. The provisions of the ICSID Additional Facility also do not allow the Communities to make use of them. Any arbitral award against the European Communities will be implemented by the Communities' institutions, in accordance with their obligation under Article 26(8) of the Energy Charter Treaty

– "Statement submitted by the European Communities to the Secretariat of the Energy Charter pursuant to Article 26(3)(b)(II) of the Energy Charter Treaty made on 17/11/1997" (OJ L 69/115 09.03.1998). It was replaced by "Statement submitted to the Energy Charter Treaty (ECT) Secretariat pursuant to Article 26(3)(b)(II) ECT replacing the statement made on 17 November 1997 on behalf of the European Communities" (OJ L 115/1, 02.05.2019), which is essentially the same as regards the quoted part, with the only difference being substitution of the "European Communities" by "the European Union and Euratom", reflecting the changes introduced by the Treaty of Lisbon.

546 Fn 443. The same wording was used in *Cavalum* – see fn 464. See also the definition given by the *Isolux* tribunal – fn 129 and by the *PV Investors* tribunal – fn 69.

547 Fn 333.

548 Fn 337.

549 Fn 348.

550 Fn 93.

551 Fn 140.

552 Fn 114.

553 Fn 428.

hidden meanings and sweeping implied exclusions".[554] Third, as underlined by the *Isolux*,[555] *Novenergia*,[556] *Antin*[557] and *Foresight*[558] tribunals, interpretative diversion from a treaty text of such magnitude was not supported by any evidence. On the contrary, as noted by the *PV Investors*[559] and *Watkins*[560] tribunals, the EU's treaty practice demonstrated that explicit disconnection clauses had been adopted in treaties to which both the EU and its member states are contracting parties. The *PV Investors*,[561] *Cube*[562] and *SolEs*[563] tribunals also noted that the ECT contains an explicit disconnection clause applicable to the Svalbard Treaty. As the *PV Investors* tribunal explained, it would be "striking" that the ECT contains an explicit disconnection clause concerning an archipelago in the Arctic, but "somehow omitted to specify that the ECT's dispute settlement system did not apply in all of the EU member states' relations".[564]

The most recent line of argumentation underpinning the intra-EU objection has shifted to the conflict between intra-EU investor-state arbitration and EU law, with the argument being that the latter prevails over the ECT (and intra-EU BITs) in the event of any such conflict. The existence of such a conflict, from an EU law perspective, was confirmed by the *Achmea* judgment, followed by the *Komstroy* judgment and the *PL Holdings* judgment. This position is based on two main assumptions.

First, the sole fact that an arbitral tribunal, which "may be called on to interpret or indeed to apply" EU law,[565] cannot ask request a preliminary ruling from the CJEU on the interpretation of EU law[566] has "an adverse effect on the autonomy of EU law".[567]

Second, this threat to the autonomy of EU law is different when one considers an offer to arbitrate given by states in investment treaties, when compared to commercial arbitration based on consent given in contracts. Whilst, in the latter scenario, arbitral tribunals may equally interpret and apply EU law and

554 Fn 140.
555 Fn 130.
556 Fn 159.
557 Fn 194.
558 Fn 215.
559 Fn 70.
560 Fn 427.
561 Fn 71.
562 Fn 231.
563 Fn 301.
564 Fn 72.
565 *Achmea* judgment, *supra* note 32 [42], similarly: *Komstroy* judgment, *supra* note 54 [50].
566 *Achmea* judgment, ibid [49], *Komstroy* judgment, ibid [53].
567 *Achmea* judgment, ibid [59].

be equally unable to request a preliminary ruling from the CJEU, the CJEU did not consider that this threatened the autonomy of EU law.[568]

These assumptions suggest that the debate over the intra-EU dispute is far from over, at least at the level of academic discussion.

If EU law autonomy is the genuine reason for the CJEU's incompatibility finding, why would it be a lesser threat to the autonomy of EU law when a tribunal interprets and applies EU law in a horizontal relationship between private parties (including state-owned entities), and a more significant threat when it does the same in a vertical relationship between a private party and a state? The CJEU remains silent on that issue. The justification appears to be rooted in the CJEU's differentiation between commercial arbitration (based on consent to arbitrate derived from "the freely expressed wishes of the parties") and treaty-based arbitration (based on a "treaty by which Member States agree to remove from the jurisdiction of their own courts" certain disputes).[569] This implies, in turn, that the offers to arbitrate included by states in investment treaties are not given "freely". This underlying assumption is contrary to the wording of the very same sentence in which the CJEU presented it, where the CJEU confirmed that states "agree" to remove certain disputed from the jurisdiction of their domestic courts. If states "agree", this means that they have a choice and consciously take a certain decision. It contravenes the very essence of the principles of public international law, which governs the actions of sovereign states which may, but have no obligation to, negotiate, sign and ratify international treaties. The *RREEF* tribunal correctly emphasized that, regardless of the type of arbitration, whether commercial or investment, arbitration is always based on the consent of the parties.[570]

The *PL Holdings* judgment may shed additional light on the CJEU's reasoning. It suggests that, in reality, the EU member states are not "free" to enter

568 *Achmea* judgment, ibid [55], *Komstroy* judgment, *supra* note 54 [59].

569 *Achmea* judgment, ibid [55]:

> However, arbitration proceedings such as those referred to in Article 8 of the BIT are different from commercial arbitration proceedings. While the latter originate in the freely expressed wishes of the parties, the former derive from a treaty by which Member States agree to remove from the jurisdiction of their own courts, and hence from the system of judicial remedies which the second subparagraph of Article 19(1) TEU requires them to establish in the fields covered by EU law [...], disputes which may concern the application or interpretation of EU law. In those circumstances, the considerations set out in the preceding paragraph relating to commercial arbitration cannot be applied to arbitration proceedings such as those referred to in Article 8 of the BIT.

Similarly: *Komstroy* judgment, ibid [59].

570 Fn 123. See also the general comments as the introduction to this section, fn 1–9.

into *ad hoc* arbitration agreements with investors if they have content which mirrors a BITs' jurisdictional clause, because it "would in fact entail a circumvention of the obligations arising for that Member State under the Treaties and, specifically, under Article 4(3) TEU and Articles 267 and 344 TFEU, as interpreted in" the *Achmea* judgment.[571]

Additionally, the analyzed assumption provides no clear answer as to why the CJEU did not perceive a threat to EU law's autonomy in the jurisdictional provision contained in the CETA, whereas it perceives such a threat in the intra-EU application of the ECT and in intra-EU BITs.[572] The CJEU's approach to the EU's ratification of the ECHR illustrates how the CJEU jealously protects its superiority over other adjudicatory bodies.[573] This may suggest that the "new generation" treaties, which contain a modern approach to numerous issues regulated therein, are perceived as "new quality" treaties, which do not pose a threat comparable to that posed by "old generation" treaties. An important factor in this context may have been that a tribunal under the CETA "will have to confine itself to an examination of EU law as a matter of fact and will not be able to engage in interpretation of points of law".[574] This may also shed light on why some ECT tribunals, such as the *Cube* tribunal, emphasized that EU law is not the applicable law and should, rather, be treated as a fact.[575]

Moreover, this assumption is based on an understanding that EU law is superior to the ECT, and that a conflict exists between Arts. 267 and 344 TFEU, on the one hand, and Art. 26 ECT, on the other hand. Whilst the *Achmea* judgment, read in conjunction with the *Komstroy* judgment, puts an end to any doubts about this, that case merely reflects developments from the perspective of EU law. This limitation is an obvious consequence of the CJEU being a supreme court with competence for interpreting EU law. However, as noted by the *NextEra*,[576] *Hydro*[577] and *Cavalum*[578] tribunals, the CJEU remained silent on how to interpret this same issue from the perspective of public international law. This prompted the criticism of the tribunals, which concerned themselves to be "creatures of international law", to borrow the *Hydro* tribunal's

571 *PL Holdings* judgment, *supra* note 60 [47].
572 Opinion 1/17 of the Court (Full Court) (30.04.2019) (ECLI:EU:C:2019:341).
573 Opinion 2/13, *supra* note 227.
574 Opinion 1/17, *supra* note 572 [76].
575 See for example fn 254–256.
576 Fn 270.
577 Fn 457.
578 Fn 464.

phraseology.[579] The *RREEF*,[580] *Cube*[581] and *Watkins*[582] tribunals underlined that any "hierarchy" for resolving such a conflict must be decided based on public international law, and not EU law.

This shows that the tribunals considered the issue from the perspective of international law and only applied EU law insofar as they considered it to form part of international law.[583] When adopting this perspective, the Spanish saga tribunals doubted whether EU law regulates the same subject matter as Art. 26 ECT which, in turn, means that there is no conflict which needs to be solved. However, even if an opposite approach were to be adopted and it were to be recognized, or at least assumed, that such a conflict exists, the *RREEF*,[584] *Eiser*,[585] *Masdar*,[586] *Cube*,[587] *SolEs*,[588] *InfraRed*,[589] *BayWa*,[590] *Stadtwerke*,[591] *RWE*[592] and *Cavalum*[593] tribunals referred to Art. 16 ECT, which stipulates that those provisions which are more favorable to investors shall apply. For these tribunals, treaty provisions have priority over the CIL principles codified in the VCLT, which regulate the conflict of treaties. They considered that the ECT's standards of protection, and the ability to initiate a claim before an international tribunal instead of merely before domestic courts, were more favorable for investors and therefore prevailed.

579 Fn 463.
580 Fn 107, 122.
581 Fn 235.
582 Fn 433.
583 See for example: Brigitte Stern, 2019 Freshfields Lecture: Investment Arbitration and State Sovereignty, ICSID Review - Foreign Investment Law Journal, 35:3 (2020), p. 452:

> [...] EU law is international law; the interpretation of the ECT has to take into account 'relevant rules of international law'. It seems to result from these two statements, taken together, that tribunals should apply EU law as international law. This is, however, too simple, and is not the end of the matter, because international law is not a uniform body of law. It is indeed of the utmost importance to understand that the international legal system is a general system without any central authority and a hierarchical organization of the law, as in national systems where everything flows from the constitution [...].

584 Fn 107.
585 Fn 150.
586 Fn 178.
587 Fn 237.
588 Fn 311–313.
589 Fn 326.
590 Fn 357–358.
591 Fn 381.
592 Fn 395-397.
593 Fn 467.

In addition, the *RREEF*[594] and *BayWa*[595] tribunals underlined that EU law should not be superior to the EU member states' international obligations. From this perspective, the argument that EU law invalidates the intra-EU consent to arbitrate, included in the ECT, could be compared to arguing that internal law can invalidate such consent. This has been considered as tantamount to saying that domestic law can justify a breach of an international law obligation, which contravenes the principle expressed in Art. 46 VCLT.[596]

All of the above confirms that the tensions between EU law and protection under the ECT are far from being resolved in a final manner. It may be expected that arbitral tribunals will continue to critically assess the CJEU's reasoning. This leads invariably to the next lesson learned.

1.3.3 Third Lesson Learned – the Differences between ICSID and Non-ICSID Arbitrations Have Become More Important Than Ever Before

Many of the Spanish saga tribunals underlined the international nature of the ICSID regime, which is detached from the impact of the domestic law of the state of the place of arbitration. In the words of the *OperaFund* tribunal, ICSID arbitration places the tribunal "in a public international law context and not in a national or regional context".[597]

Paradoxically, this reasoning finds support in the *Achmea* judgment itself, as the CJEU considered arbitral tribunals to not be tribunals within the meaning of Art. 267 TFEU, and therefore to represent "a body which is not part of the judicial system of the EU".[598] This made the *Achmea* judgment a double-edged sword from the EC's perspective of seeking to invalidate intra-EU investor-state arbitrations. To use the words of the *Watkins* tribunal, the CJEU's "dualist reasoning reinforces the idea that ICSID tribunals are located in a legal space

594 Fn 116.

595 Fn 350.

596 See for example, although in the context of substantive law: Bermann, *supra* note 19, p. 215: "It is awkward, to say the least, for the internal law of some members of a multilateral treaty system, but not others, to operate as an affirmative defence to a treaty violation". This may explain reluctancy to follow the CJEU's reasoning, in particular by those arbitrators who come from jurisdictions other than the EU-member states. Similarly, for example: "Indeed, it would undermine the whole purpose of establishing an international investment regime if ultimately jurisdiction could be defeated by provisions of the domestic law of one or both of the parties". – Adamakopoulos v. Greece, *supra* note 46 [158].

597 Fn 341. The same wording was used for example in UP and C.D v. Hungary, *supra* note 46 [253].

598 *Achmea* judgment, *supra* note 32 [58].

solely governed by international law that is the only source of jurisdiction".[599] In the same vein, the *SolEs* tribunal stated that, as it is not institution of the EU, it "approaches this question from the vantage point of a tribunal established pursuant to the ICSID Convention and the ECT".[600] That different perspectives (as the "departure points" for the analysis) may explain the different outcomes in the analyzes of the ECT tribunals and of the CJEU.

The significance of the ICSID regime in the Spanish saga cases cannot be overestimated. 16 of the 21 cases analyzed in this book were ICSID cases, and all EU member states except one (Poland) are contracting parties to the ICSID Convention.[601] In non-ICSID arbitration, the seat of arbitration may be in an EU member state, as actually occurred in 4 of the 21 analyzed cases. Only 1 of the analyzed cases was a non-ICSID arbitration with the seat of arbitration outside the EU (see Table 3, Page 91).

As underlined by the *OperaFund* tribunal, there is no seat of arbitration in ICSID arbitrations, and national courts play no role in verifying the validity of ICSID awards.[602] The situation is different in non-ICSID arbitrations. As correctly noted by the *RWE*[603] and *OperaFund*[604] tribunals, this opens the door for EU law to apply regardless of the debate concerning its applicability from the perspective of public international law, as discussed above.[605] It can be expected that, after the CJEU judgments, Spain (and other EU member states being respondents in investor-state arbitrations) will attempt to set-aside arbitral awards which uphold jurisdiction in intra-EU, non-ICSID arbitrations which have a seat of arbitration in an EU member state.[606]

The domestic law of the place of arbitration applies to such motions. Thus, it may be expected that the case law of EU member states' domestic courts may evolve in the direction of upholding such motions. All 3 of the CJEU's judgments discussed here (i.e. the *Achmea*, *Komstroy* and *PL Holdings* judgments) are relevant in this context. All 3 concerned proceedings before the domestic

---

599 Fn 425.

600 Fn 305.

601 Fn 13.

602 Fn 343. See also for example Belenergia v. Italy, *supra* note 44 [339], noting that "the ICSID Convention, which establishes a self-contained system independent from national legal systems". Similarly, for example: Eskosol v. Italy, *supra* note 44 [231].

603 Fn 384.

604 Fn 342.

605 For similar understanding see for example: Voltaic v. Czech Republic, *supra* note 44 [349]–[350], I.C.W. v. Czech Republic, *supra* note 44 [397]–[398], WA v. Czech Republic, *supra* note 44 [439]–[440].

606 Fn 14.

courts of an EU member states, namely Germany, France and Sweden, respectively. All 3 were initiated by motions to set aside arbitral awards in non-ICSID arbitrations. This shows that the non-ICSID Spanish saga cases in which the seat of arbitration is located in an EU member state will most certainly give rise to further legal battles initiated by motions to set aside the arbitral awards. This has already materialized in both non-ICSID Spanish saga cases having their seat of arbitration in Stockholm, in which the tribunals found violations of the ECT: *Novenergia* and *Foresight*.[607] The same pattern can also be observed for example in the Italian RE cases: *Greentech v. Italy* and *CEF v. Italy*.[608]

Similar developments can be expected regarding attempts to enforce arbitral awards before the national courts in EU member states.[609] The EC had already made it clear that, from an EU law perspective, not only are "national courts are under the obligation to annul any arbitral award rendered on" the basis of intra-EU BITs and the ECT, but also that they have a duty "to refuse to enforce it".[610]

---

607 Anina Liebkind, Fredrik Norburg, Ossian Dittmer Hvarfner, The ECT, Achmea and Intra-EU Arbitration – Swedish Court Requests Preliminary Ruling from the CJEU, European Investment Law and Arbitration Review, 6:1 (2022), p. 243. Motion to set aside the award rendered in the *Novenergia* case has been registered by the Svea Court of Appeal under the case no. T 4658–18, whereas the motion to set aside the award rendered in the *Foresight* case by the same court under the case no T 1626–19. No publicly available information suggests that similar motions were filed in the *Charanne* and *Isolux* cases, in which the tribunals dismissed the claims on their merits.

608 Liebkind, Norburg, Hvarfner, ibid, p. 245. The cases were registered by the Svea Court of Appeal under the case nos. T 3229–19 and T 4236–19, respectively.

609 Fn 15. For similar observations see for example: Marek Anderle, Andrej Leontiev, Here Comes Doomsday ... Or Does It? – Implications of Achmea on Intra-EU Investment Arbitration in Light of Recent Case Law, European Investment Law and Arbitration Review, 6:1 (2022), pp. 158–159. Some note that when tribunals issue awards in intra-EU arbitrations, they "knowingly deliver an award, which is unenforceable in the Respondent States and the entirety of the EU" – Szilárd Gáspár-Szilágyi, Maxim Usynin, The Uneasy Relationship between Intra-EU Investment Tribunals and the Court of Justice's Achmea Judgment, European Investment Law and Arbitration Review, 4:1 (2019), p. 29.

610 Communication, *supra* note 479, pp. 3–4:

> In the Achmea judgment the Court of Justice ruled that the investor-to-State arbitration clauses laid down in intra-EU BITs undermine the system of legal remedies provided for in the EU Treaties and thus jeopardise the autonomy, effectiveness, primacy and direct effect of Union law and the principle of mutual trust between the Member States. Recourse to such clauses undermines the preliminary ruling procedure provided for in Article 267 TFEU, and is not compatible with the principle of sincere cooperation. This implies that all investor-State arbitration clauses in intra-EU BITs are inapplicable and that any arbitration tribunal established on the basis of such clauses lacks jurisdiction due to the absence of a valid arbitration agreement. As a consequence, national courts are under the obligation to annul any arbitral award

The overall impact of the CJEU's 3 judgments may even mean that the battle before the domestic courts occurs at an earlier time. A German state court (which had jurisdiction because the parties had agreed that the place of arbitration would be in Frankfurt am Main) recently upheld Croatia's motion to declare a pending UNCITRAL arbitration "inadmissible" because of the invalidity of the consent to arbitrate given by two EU member states acting as contracting parties to an intra-EU BIT.[611] After the *Komstroy* judgment, similar developments in the EU member states' domestic courts can also be expected as regards ECT arbitrations.

An open issue is to what extent the EU member states and the EU institutions will attempt to extend this approach to ICSID arbitrations. On the one hand, the legal nature of ICISD arbitration, and in particular the absence of a seat of arbitration in any state, may suggest that such attempts would be unfounded.[612] However, the EC seems to take an opposite view and makes no

---

rendered on that basis and to refuse to enforce it. [...] The Achmea judgment is also relevant for the investor-State arbitration mechanism established in Article 26 of the Energy Charter Treaty as regards intra-EU relations. This provision, if interpreted correctly, does not provide for an investor-State arbitration clause applicable between investors from a Member States of the EU and another Member States of the EU. Given the primacy of Union law, that clause, if interpreted as applying intra-EU, is incompatible with EU primary law and thus inapplicable.

611 "Lack of effective arbitration agreement" in words of Stompfe – Philipp Stompfe, The Higher Regional Court of Frankfurt am Main Is the First European Court to Declare the *Achmea* Case a Landmark Decision with Significance for All Intra-EU BITs, European Investment Law and Arbitration Review, 6:1 (2022), p. 273. The case concerned the Austria-Croatia BIT. See: judgment of the German Higher Regional Court in Frankfurt, of 11.02.2021, Case No. 26 SchH 2/20 (unofficial translation available at: https://www.italaw.com/sites/default/files/case-documents/italaw12018.pdf). The judgment was upheld by the Federal Court of Justice, in its judgment of 17.11.2021, Case No. I ZB 16/21 (unofficial translation available at: https://www.italaw.com/sites/default/files/case-documents/italaw20000_0.pdf). Croatia's motion was possible based on the German Code of Civil Procedure, which allows such a motion to be filed until the arbitral tribunal is constituted: "Until the arbitral tribunal has been formed, a petition may be filed with the courts to have it determine the admissibility or inadmissibility of arbitration proceedings" (translation as in: https://www.iareporter.com/articles/now-public-judgment-reveals-reasons-why-german-courts-upheld-croatias-achmea-objection-and-declared-a-treaty-based-arbitration-inadmissible/).

612 See for example: Anderle, Leontiev, *supra* note 609, pp. 161–162, Sahra Arif, The Future of Intra-EU Investment Arbitration: Intra-EU Investment Arbitration under the ECT post Achmea, European Investment Law and Arbitration Review, 4:1 (2019), pp. 174–175, Christian Tietje, Darius Ruff, Mathea Schmitt, Final Countdown in EU Investment Protection Law: Does the ECJ's Komstroy Ruling also Apply in intra-EU ICSID Proceedings?, Beiträge zum Transnationalen Wirtschaftsrecht (2022), available at: https://opendata.uni-halle.de/bitstream/1981185920/80384/1/BeitraegeTWR_178.pdf, p. 23.

distinction between ICSID and non-ICSID awards.[613] Some scholars share the EC's position, at least insofar as concerns the rules on enforcing ICSID arbitral awards.[614]

A second open issue is to what extent the division between ICSID and non-ICSID arbitrations will result in creating divisions in the otherwise uniform conclusions arrived at by arbitrators on the intra-EU jurisdictional objection.[615] Until now, arbitrators recognized it as their duty to issue an enforceable award, whilst considering this duty to be outweighed by their duty to perform their mandate under the ECT, as the *Cavalum* tribunal noted.[616] Referring to the *RWE* tribunal's words, whilst arbitrators were "naturally concerned" about the future enforcement of the award, they considered this to be a matter for the state courts to apply the states' international obligations.[617] This suggests that the tribunals considered future enforcement as too hypothetical and/or beyond their powers. A similar approach can be seen beyond the scope of the Spanish saga.[618] *Micula v. Romania* is probably the most high-profile example of this

613 See for example: the EC's decision (10.11.2017), case no C(2017) 7384, State Aid SA.40348 (2015/NN) – Spain [165], in which the EC specifically refers to the *Eiser* award, which was an ICSID case, as an example of an obligation to pay compensation treated by the EC as notifiable public aid, "subject to the standstill obligation". In the EC's decision (28.11.2016), case no C(2016) 7827, State Aid SA.40171 (2015/NN) – Czech Republic [150], it takes the position that an award of compensation would not be enforceable, as Art. 108(3) TFEU regulating state aid "is part of the public order", without differentiating between ICSID and non-ICSID awards. The EC also initiated state aid proceedings against Spain, concerning enforcement of the ICSID award issued in the *Antin* case, on the basis that the award "constitutes aid because it has the effect of compensating for the withdrawal of unlawful aid, i.e. of the 2007 scheme" – State Aid SA.54155 (2021/NN) – Arbitration award to Antin – Spain, Invitation to submit comments pursuant to Article 108(2) of the Treaty on the Functioning of the European Union (OJ C 450, 5.11.2021, pp. 5–25) [88]. All of this suggests that the EC intends to continue its efforts to ensure the non-enforcement of all intra-EU awards, as known from the *Micula* legal odyssey, regardless of whether they are ICSID or non-ICSID awards.

614 See for example: Rusche, *supra* note 472, pp. 329–333, Anna Bilanova, Jaroslav Kudrna, The End of Investment Arbitration as We Know It, European Investment Law and Arbitration Review 3:1 (2018) pp. 266–267.

615 See fn 470 concerning *Green Power v. Spain*, which appears to confirm that the first exception was driven by the non-ICSID nature of the arbitral proceedings and related consequences as to the role of EU law in the set-aside and enforcement proceedings. See also the dissenting opinion in Adamakopoulos v. Greece, *supra* note 46, which was the first crack, although driven by reasons other than related to enforcement.

616 Fn 469.

617 Fn 415.

618 Vattenfall v. Germany, *supra* note 45 [230]: "While the Tribunal is mindful of the duty to render an enforceable decision and ultimately an enforceable award, the Tribunal is equally conscious of its duty to perform its mandate granted under the ECT". In *Tallinn*

approach,[619] and its possible consequences.[620] This is in line with the general perception that, although "the ultimate purpose of an arbitration tribunal is to render an enforceable award",[621] this "does not mean that the arbitrator is under an obligation to render an award which is enforceable in all conceivable circumstances. Rather, the obligation is only to try one's best to render an enforceable award".[622]

However, some arbitrators may consider that the intra-EU objection requires more emphasis to be placed of the duty to render an enforceable award,[623]

---

v. Estonia the tribunal stated that "it will be up to the courts at the enforcement stage, if called upon, to draw the necessary consequences from the Achmea judgment and their national laws with respect to the enforceability of this Award" – Tallinn v. Estonia, *supra* note 46 [541]. The same wording was used in Marfin v. Cyprus, *supra* note 46 [596]. In *Fynerdale v. Czech Republic* the tribunal observed that "enforceability cannot dominate jurisdiction since this would, in violation of the independent existence of the Tribunal, render the jurisdiction of the latter dependent upon national law" – Fynerdale v. Czech Republic, *supra* note 46 [351].

619 Micula v. Romania, *supra* note 27 [340]:

> The Tribunal finds that it is not desirable to embark on predictions as to the possible conduct of various persons and authorities after the Award has been rendered, especially but not exclusively when it comes to enforcement matters. It is thus inappropriate for the Tribunal to base its decisions in this case on matters of EU law that may come to apply after the Award has been rendered. It will thus not address the Parties' and the Commission's arguments on enforceability of the Award.

620 See fn 29-30 for more information on the ongoing legal battles concerning enforcement.

621 Julian Lew, The Law Applicable to the Form and Substance of the Arbitration Clause, in: Albert Jan van den Berg (ed.), Improving the Efficiency of Arbitration Agreements and Awards: 40 Years of Application of the New York Convention (Kluwer Law International 1999), p. 119. Some consider the arbitrators' duty to render an enforceable award "equivalent to the Hippocratic Oath (primum non nocere, or "above all else, don't render an unenforceable award") [...]" – Gunther J. Horvath, The Duty of the Tribunal to Render an Enforceable Award, Journal of International Arbitration, 18:2 (2001), p. 136.

622 Martin Platte, An Arbitrator's Duty to Render Enforceable Awards, Journal of International Arbitration, 20:3 (2003), p. 309. On pp. 312–313 he concludes:

> It is well established that an international arbitrator is under the obligation to render an enforceable award. An enforceable award is the raison d'etre, the ultimate purpose, of an arbitration. The arbitrator's subsequent duty to bear this in mind when making the award is undisputable, However, there is no obligation to render an award which is enforceable always and everywhere. The arbitrator's duty is better characterised as a best efforts commitment; in other words, the arbitrator's duty is to "make every effort to make sure" that the award is enforceable at law

(footnote omitted).

623 By way of example, the tribunal in AMF *v. Czech Republic* recognized that:

> enforcement of the Arbitral Tribunal's award might be challenging or create further disputes. However, this does not make the award unenforceable. A truly unenforceable award can only exist if it is rendered in violation of Article 190 of the PILA governing

rather than considering the setting aside and/or enforcement stages as independent from the arbitral proceedings.[624] In this context, it is worth noting that the tribunal in *Belenergia v. Italy* considered the arguments on non-recognition and non-enforcement as "unfounded in relation to award recognition and hypothetical in relation to award enforcement" given the nature of ICSID arbitration.[625] This suggests that the same arbitrators may have reached a different conclusion in non-ICSID arbitration. Relevant factors will include the place of arbitration (whether it is in an EU member state), the relevant arbitral institution (unless it is *ad hoc* arbitration) and the applicable arbitration rules.[626] For example, 4 of the analyzed cases were SCC arbitrations, meaning that the arbitrators had a duty to "make every reasonable effort to ensure that any award is legally enforceable".[627]

---

the setting aside of awards rendered by arbitral tribunals seated in Switzerland – AMF v. Czech Republic, *supra* note 46 [393]. However, in [395] it considered that upholding jurisdiction in an intra-EU case was not contrary to Swiss international public policy.

624 The latter approach can be deduced, for example, from the award rendered in *Silver Ridge v. Italy*, where the tribunal noted that "neither the ICSID Convention nor the ECT contain a rule analogous to Article 40 of the ICC Rules of Arbitration, according to which arbitral tribunals "shall make every effort to make sure that the award is enforceable at law"" (footnote omitted) – Silver Ridge v. Italy, ICSID Case No. ARB/15/37, Award (26.02.2021) [233].

625 Belenergia v. Italy, *supra* note 44 [339]. Similarly non-ICSID tribunal in *Sun Reserve v. Italy*, which commented that it:

> is mindful of its duty to render an enforceable Award. In the present situation, the Tribunal does not foresee any hindrances to the validity or enforceability of this Award. In any event, at this stage, the Tribunal is not in a place to predict the future validity or enforceability of its Award before Swedish courts or other enforcing courts

– Sun Reserve v. Italy, *supra* note 44 [371].

626 Horvath, *supra* note 621, p. 157.

627 This obligation is imposed not only on the tribunals, but also on the parties. Art. 2(2) of the SCC Arbitration Rules (2017) reads as follows:

> In all matters not expressly provided for in these Rules, the SCC, the Arbitral Tribunal and the parties shall act in the spirit of these Rules and shall make every reasonable effort to ensure that any award is legally enforceable.

A similar approach can be seen for example in Art. 42 of the ICC Arbitration Rules (2021): "In all matters not expressly provided for in the Rules, the Court and the arbitral tribunal shall act in the spirit of the Rules and shall make every effort to make sure that the award is enforceable at law" and likewise in Art. 32(2) of the LCIA Arbitration Rules (2020):

> For all matters not expressly provided in the Arbitration Agreement, the LCIA, the LCIA Court, the Registrar, the Arbitral Tribunal, any tribunal secretary and each of the parties shall act at all times in good faith, respecting the spirit of the Arbitration Agreement, and shall make every reasonable effort to ensure that any award is legally recognised and enforceable at the arbitral seat.

1.3.4 Fourth Lesson Learned – the Nature of the Intra-EU Objection Can Be Classified as Rationae Personae

Apart from the issues analyzed above, the Spanish saga cases constitute a valuable contribution to a debate on how to classify the intra-EU objection from the perspective of the limitations to jurisdiction of arbitral tribunals.[628]

Although some of the tribunals remained silent on how to classify the intra-EU jurisdictional objection, the *Novenergia*,[629] *NextEra*,[630] *Cube*,[631] *SolEs*,[632] *Stadtwerke*,[633] *RWE*[634] and *Watkins*[635] tribunals presented a uniform confirmation that this objection can be classified as *ratione personae*.

The classification accepted by the Spanish saga tribunals was based on how the respondent framed the intra-EU jurisdictional objection. This, in turn, was related to the evolution of the intra-EU argument over time. As noted above, in the second lesson learned, Spain initially emphasized arguments concerning intra-EU nationality and the existence of an implied disconnection clause, which explains this approach. The evolution of the intra-EU arguments may also be expected to impact on this classification. For those who differentiate the *rationae voluntatis* limits of jurisdiction as a separate category, in addition to the classic tripartite division,[636] the intra-EU jurisdictional objection may fall within this category.

This depends largely upon how to understand the *Achmea* judgment's comments that jurisdictional clauses in investment treaties are "precluded" by EU law in intra-EU relations.[637] Whilst initially this may have given rise to doubts, the CJEU clarified those doubts in the *Komstroy* judgment, by stating that the ECT jurisdictional clause "must be interpreted as not being applicable" to intra-EU investment disputes.[638] In short, EU law "precludes" the offer to arbitrate, granted by the states in Art. 26 ECT (and similarly intra-EU BITs), by rendering this offer inapplicable to disputes initiated by an investor from one EU member state against another EU member state. Consequently, from an EU law perspective, there is no consent to arbitrate (an investor from an EU member state cannot validly accept this offer) and therefore a tribunal has no

628 Fn 9–11.
629 Fn 155.
630 Fn 259.
631 Fn 225.
632 Fn 294.
633 Fn 364.
634 Fn 382.
635 Fn 416.
636 Fn 9–11.
637 Fn 37.
638 Fn 58.

jurisdiction. This line of reasoning has been confirmed by the German court which had requested, and ultimately applied, the CJEU's *Achmea* preliminary ruling.[639]

Nevertheless, in the ECT context, the above conclusion would only apply to a group of investors which was differentiated according to their nationality. The same offer to arbitrate, granted by the EU member states, would continue to be applicable *vis-à-vis* investors from non-EU member states. This confirms that the classification observed in the Spanish saga cases stands up to scrutiny.

2 Tax Carve-Out Objection

2.1 *General Comments*

The power to tax is an essential element of state sovereignty.[640] As noted by the *El Paso v. Argentina* tribunal, "the tax policy of a country is a matter relating to the sovereign power of the State and its power to impose taxes on its territory".[641] Naturally, tax policies change over time. These changes may take various forms, such as introducing new taxes, modifying existing taxes or cancelling tax incentives. Inevitably, such changes may produce tax-related disputes.[642] In this context, it is unsurprising that states resist any external limitations on their power to tax.[643] This is "reflected in many treaties by the exclusion from their coverage of matters of taxation, sometimes with exceptions to that exclusion, for instance when taxation measures amount to an expropriation".[644]

639 Order of the German Federal Court of Justice, Case No. I ZB 2/15 (31.10.2018) [25]–[26]:

> Thus, if Art. 8(2) BIT contradicts Art. 267 and Art. 344 TFEU, the provision is inapplicable [...] and no valid arbitration agreement has been concluded between the parties. [...] [...] There thus was never an offer by the Applicant to conclude an arbitration agreement with the investors from the Netherlands which the Respondent could have accepted

(unofficial translation, available at: https://jusmundi.com/en/document/decision/en-achmea-b-v-formerly-eureko-b-v-v-the-slovak-republic-i-decision-of-the-federal-court-of-justice-of-germany-wednesday-31st-october-2018).

640 For example: Burlington v. Ecuador, ICSID Case No. ARB/08/5, Decision on Liability (14.12.2012) [391]: "Taxation is an essential prerogative of State sovereignty. By virtue of this sovereign prerogative, States may tax not only their own nationals but also aliens, including foreign investors, if they effectuate investments in those States".

641 El Paso v. Argentina, ICSID Case No. ARB/03/15, Award (31.10.2011) [290].

642 See for example: Markus Burgstaller, Agnieszka Zarowna, The Growing Importance of Investment Arbitration in Relation to Tax Measures in the Energy and Natural Resources Sectors, Turkish Commercial Law Review, 4:1 (2018), p. 81.

643 Hobér, *supra* note 23, pp. 656–657.

644 ConocoPhillips v. Venezuela, ICSID Case No. ARB/07/30, Decision on Jurisdiction and the Merits (03.09.2013) [313].

The ECT is an example of a treaty which contains a so-called "tax carve-out".[645] Pursuant to Art. 21(1) ECT "[e]xcept as otherwise provided in this Article, nothing in this Treaty shall create rights or impose obligations with respect to Taxation Measures of the Contracting Parties. [...]".[646] Art. 21(7)(a) ECT defines the term "taxation measures", albeit by referring to "taxes" without any definition of the latter term.[647]

The tax carve-out clause limits arbitral tribunals' jurisdiction by excluding from its scope taxation measures adopted by the states. As such, it falls within *rationae materiae* scope of jurisdiction and its limits, concerning the permissible subject-matter of a dispute.[648]

The ECT provides for two relevant so-called "claw-back" clauses, which are themselves exceptions to the tax carve-out clause exception.[649] The first is contained in Art. 21(5)(a), which stipulates that Art. 13 ECT regulating expropriation "shall apply to taxes". The second is contained in Art. 21(3) ECT, which states that the standards of protection guaranteed in Art. 10(2) and 10(7) ECT (i.e. the Most-Favored Nation and National Treatment standards) shall apply to taxation measures "other than those on income or on capital".[650]

Only a few cases exist in which tribunals have looked beyond the label of a tax and concluded that the disputed measures were not taxes within the meaning of CIL. Until now, the most famous examples are the various cases

645 Uğur Erman Özgür, Taxation of Foreign Investments under International Law: Article 21 of the Energy Charter Treaty (Energy Charter Secretariat 2015), p. 16.

646 It continues: "In the event of any inconsistency between this Article and any other provision of the Treaty, this Article shall prevail to the extent of the inconsistency".

647 "The term "Taxation Measure" includes: (i) any provision relating to taxes of the domestic law of the Contracting Party or of a political subdivision thereof or a local authority therein; and (ii) any provision relating to taxes of any convention for the avoidance of double taxation or of any other international agreement or arrangement by which the Contracting Party is bound".

648 Fn 9-11. See for example: EnCana v. Ecuador, LCIA Case No. UN3481, Award (03.02.2006) [110], [149].

649 Hobér, *supra* note 23, p. 358. He differentiates two additional claw-back clauses, contained in Arts. 21(2) and 21(4) ECT, but these are not relevant for this book.

650 "Article 10(2) and (7) shall apply to Taxation Measures of the Contracting Parties other than those on income or on capital, except that such provisions shall not apply to: (a) impose most favoured nation obligations with respect to advantages accorded by a Contracting Party pursuant to the tax provisions of any convention, agreement or arrangement described in subparagraph (7)(a)(II) or resulting from membership of any Regional Economic Integration Organisation; or (b) any Taxation Measure aimed at ensuring the effective collection of taxes, except where the measure arbitrarily discriminates against an Investor of another Contracting Party or arbitrarily restricts benefits accorded under the Investment provisions of this Treaty".

concerning *Yukos*. What mattered there was the state's bad faith in having imposed various taxation measures to destroy a political opponent.[651]

2.2 *Spanish Saga Case Law*

Except for the first two cases, in all of the other analyzed cases Spain objected to jurisdiction over taxes introduced by Law 15/2012. This concerned all of the claims other than claims for expropriation.[652] Majority of the cases focused on IVPEE, although the Water Levy was also discussed in the *Masdar, Cube, RWE, Hydro* cases.[653] In addition, the "claw-back" clause contained in Art. 21(3) ECT became relevant in some cases. Spain was successful on each occasion that it presented the tax carve-out jurisdictional objection.

The following analysis follows the chronological order adopted in the previous section, which differs from the order adopted in the remaining Chapters of this book. As explained earlier, the reason for this is that, in two of the analyzed cases, the tribunals bifurcated the proceedings and issued separate decisions on jurisdiction.

•••

2.2.1 PV Investors

In *PV Investors*, the claimants did not present claims with respect to damages suffered by the IVPEE but treated it merely as part of the factual background.[654] Thus, the respondent did not present any jurisdictional objection concerning the tax carve-out.

2.2.2 Charanne

Also in *Charanne*, the tribunal was not faced with any jurisdictional objection to the tax carve-out. This is because the case only concerned the 2010 Disputed Measures, i.e. those pre-dating Law 15/2012.[655]

---

651 Yukos v. Russia, UNCITRAL, PCA Case No. 2005-04/AA227, Final Award (18.07.2014) [1407], Hulley v. Russia, UNCITRAL, PCA Case No. 2005-03/AA226, Final Award (18.07.2014) [1407], Veteran v. Russia, UNCITRAL, PCA Case No. 2005-05/AA228, Final Award (18.07.2014) [1407]. Similarly: RosInvestCo v. Russia, SCC Case No. V079/2005, Final Award (12.09.2010) [628], Renta 4 v. Russia, SCC No. 24/2007, Award (20.07.2012) [179].

652 Which, as noted above, falls within the scope of jurisdiction even as regards taxation measures pursuant to Art. 21(5)(a) ECT.

653 For details about the IVPEE and the Water Levy, see Chapter 2.

654 The PV Investors v. Spain, *supra* note 82 [274], [427].

655 Charanne v. Spain, *supra* note 88 [395].

2.2.3 RREEF

In the *RREEF* case, the tribunal felt that the tax carve-out jurisdictional objection went to the heart of the dispute and was one which could not be decided on a preliminary basis in bifurcated proceedings.[656] It then unanimously concluded that the IVPEE was a "tax" within the meaning of Art. 21(7)(a)(I) ECT. As such, it was carved out of the dispute resolution provisions of the ECT.[657]

The tribunal noted that there is no need to decide whether a "presumption" exists that a tax is *bona fide*.[658] It quoted the ICJ that "the applicant must establish its case and [...] a party asserting a fact must establish it" to justify its conclusion that the claimants bore the burden of providing evidence of bad faith.[659] It then observed that the IVPEE was part of Spain's global policy on the protection of the environment, and that the law which introduced the IVPEE had also introduced two other new taxes and modified special taxes on natural gas supplies.[660] Moreover, the IVPEE had been considered lawful by both, the Spanish Constitutional court and the EC.[661] The tribunal considered it irrelevant that alternative methods may have existed to achieve the policy objectives underlying the IVPEE.[662]

Although the tribunal decided that it lacked jurisdiction to "take a decision over the legality of the levy", it considered that the IVPEE was "a cost impacting the return to the Claimants" in relation to their investments, "which must be taken into consideration for the global assessment of the reasonable return to which the Claimants are entitled".[663]

2.2.4 Isolux

In *Isolux*, the parties agreed that IVPEE has a "tax nature".[664] The tribunal considered that, in order to apply the tax carve-out clause, a taxation measure must be adopted in good faith.[665] This required the claimants to prove that the measure was not adopted in good faith, which required evidence that it was adopted for a purpose other than to generate income for the state.[666] The

656 RREEF v. Spain, *supra* note 65 [195], [197].
657 RREEF v. Spain, *supra* note 118 [185].
658 Ibid [188].
659 Ibid [187].
660 Ibid [188].
661 Ibid [189].
662 Ibid [190].
663 Ibid [191].
664 Isolux v. Spain, *supra* note 124 [722].
665 Ibid [729], [733].
666 Ibid [734].

claimants failed to fulfil the burden of proof.[667] The mere fact that the economic consequences of the measure could be "obscure and debatable" was insufficient to establish the existence of bad faith.[668] For the tribunal, it was irrelevant whether the tax had a positive environmental effect, as it is nothing extraordinary that the only reason for imposing a tax is to raise state revenue.[669]

2.2.5 Eiser

In *Eiser*, the parties agreed that the IVPEE "has characteristics typically associated with a legitimate tax", i.e. (i) it was established by law, (ii) it imposed obligations on a defined class of persons, (iii) it generated state revenues used for public purposes.[670] The tribunal avoided answering whether the tax carve-out clause applies only to good faith taxation. It noted that bad faith could be established if the respondent had "knowingly violated" its obligations under the ECT by introducing the tax, but that this was not the situation at hand.[671] In the tribunal's view, taxes are the "core of sovereign power", so they can be questioned only "in carefully limited circumstances", for example when they seek to destroy the claimants.[672] No such "abusive or improper" use of tax was proven in this case.[673]

2.2.6 Novenergia

In *Novenergia*, the tribunal had no doubt that the provisions of Law 15/2012 fell within the definition of a "taxation measure", as defined in Art. 21(7)(a)(I) ECT.[674] Consequently, the tribunal deemed it necessary to review whether the regulation's objective "is truly taxation, i.e. whether Law 15/2012 was enacted in good faith".[675] In the tribunal's view, the taxation measure must have been adopted in good faith in order for it to benefit from the tax carve-out clause. However, good faith is assumed and the burden of proving otherwise lies on the claimant.[676] The evidential threshold is high.[677] It is "not easy to overthrow

667 Ibid [735].
668 Ibid [739].
669 Ibid [740].
670 Eiser v. Spain, *supra* note 136 [266].
671 Ibid [269].
672 Ibid [270].
673 Ibid [271].
674 Novenergia v. Spain, *supra* note 156 [519].
675 Ibid [520].
676 Ibid [521].
677 Ibid [522].

the presumption" and the IVPEE fell "short of the extreme actions" as seen in the cases initiated against Russia by shareholders of the Yukos company.[678]

2.2.7 Masdar

The tribunal in *Masdar* underlined that the purpose of Art. 21(1) ECT is that "the prerogative of a State to raise taxes should not be subject to review by a tribunal seized of a dispute under the ECT".[679] The tribunal then distinguished the *Masdar* case from the *Yukos* cases, which it considered as "on any view, an extreme case", dealing with "measures which were egregious and which, in reality, had little, if anything, to do with the bona fide raising of tax revenues for public purposes".[680]

The tribunal acknowledged that the IVPEE must be assessed as one of many elements in the dispute, in the context of measures affecting the RE sector, described by the claimant as a "regulatory rollercoaster".[681] However, the circumstances of the case did not "reach the high bar" to justify a state losing the benefit of the tax carve-out clause included in Art. 21(1) ECT.[682] In the tribunal's view, the IVPEE fell far short of being part of a pattern of behavior aimed at destroying the claimant, and there had been no improper or abusive use of the power to tax. The tribunal considered its task as being to assess the actual purpose of the measure, not the way in which it had been presented as a political issue. The real purpose of the measure was to raise funds, which is a legitimate purpose of any tax.[683]

2.2.8 Antin

In the *Antin* case, the tribunal applied a three-part test regarding the characteristics of a tax under international law. It stated that a tax must (i) be laid-down by law, (ii) impose an obligation on a class of people and (iii) entail an obligation to pay money to the state for public purposes. All of these elements were met by the IVPEE.[684]

The tribunal then assessed an additional element, i.e. whether the IVPEE was a *bona fide* taxation measure. It noted, however, that if the above three-stage test was fulfilled, it would be "very likely" that the tax carve-out clause would apply and that the burden of proving the absence of good faith lay on

678 Ibid [524].
679 Masdar v. Spain, *supra* note 169 [281].
680 Ibid [284].
681 Ibid [288].
682 Ibid [291].
683 Ibid [293]–[294].
684 Antin v. Spain, *supra* note 188 [313].

the claimant.[685] The tribunal applied "the general principle of good faith", understood as an element of international law, according to which the parties are not allowed to abuse their rights.[686] It considered whether an abuse of rights had materialized when adopting the IVPEE "with the precise aim of abusing its rights under the ECT, by strategically creating" the IVPEE "to curtail the investors' alleged rights under the Treaty, in a manner that abusively sought to employ the taxation exclusion". This "high threshold of proof" was not met by the claimant.[687] In the tribunal's view, the evidence presented was not "even a close call" that the IVPEE was part of a "scheme" to deprive the claimants of their rights and preclude the tribunal from examining the measure by virtue of Art. 21 ECT.[688] Thus, the IVPEE was not merely "labelled" as a taxation measure.[689] The tribunal contrasted the facts of the case with the "extraordinary circumstances" found in the *Yukos* cases and noted a "strong contrast" between them. Here, the law introducing the IVPEE was "designed with a general public purpose, rather than with the aim of employing a tax for the entirely unrelated purpose of destroying the Claimants' investments".[690]

2.2.9 Foresight

The *Foresight* tribunal noted that the tax carve-out jurisdictional objection refers to the meaning of the term "tax", which is left undefined in the ECT.[691] It agreed that it could look "behind the label" and assess whether "a taxation measure is truly what it says it is".[692] The characteristics to be met are that the measure: (i) is imposed by law, (ii) imposes an obligation on a broad class of persons, and (iii) entails the payment of money to the state for public purposes.[693] The tribunal decided that these characteristics were met by the IVPEE.[694] In reaching this conclusion it relied on judgments of the Spanish domestic courts and tax authorities, and also the fact that the IVPEE had been declared to be a tax in conformity with EU law.[695] In its view, an economic analysis of a measure cannot displace the conclusion as to whether the measure is a tax,

685 Ibid [314].
686 Ibid [316].
687 Ibid [317].
688 Ibid [319].
689 Ibid [320].
690 Ibid [321].
691 Foresight v. Spain, *supra* note 210 [252]–[253].
692 Ibid [255].
693 Ibid.
694 Ibid [256].
695 Ibid [256].

from a legal-definitional standpoint.[696] The tribunal did not decide whether a taxation must be *bona fide*. It simply noted that no bad faith had been proven by the claimant.[697]

2.2.10 Cube

The *Cube* tribunal analyzed whether the IVPEE and Water Levy were *bona fide* taxation measures, given that they appeared to be a tax. The tribunal decided that there was no evidence that the respondent's motive was to reduce the value of the subsidy. Virtually any tax has the commercial effect of reducing revenue, which meant that the claimant's allegations were "flimsy" in suggesting that such an impact of the tax could demonstrate the absence of good faith.[698] The tribunal applied the "three-prong test", according to which a measure is a tax if: (i) it is imposed by law, (ii) upon a class of persons, and (iii) it entails an obligation to pay money to the State for public purposes and without any benefit to the taxpayer.[699] It considered the reduction of the tariff deficit to be a public purpose. This conclusion was unaltered by the fact that other measures of achieving the same purpose may have been available.[700]

In its further analysis, the tribunal considered that its decision on jurisdiction "requires it to take no account whatever" of the impact of the taxation measures, which "precludes consideration of the impact of tax measures as a fact".[701]

2.2.11 NextEra

In the *NextEra* case, the tribunal decided that the IVPEE had all of the necessary attributes of a tax, i.e. (i) it was established by law, (ii) it imposed an obligation on a class of people, and (iii) this obligation was to "pay money to the State for public purposes".[702] The IVPEE's economic effect, i.e. whether the tax was "functionally a tariff cut", was irrelevant.[703] The tribunal also decided that the IVPEE was a tax on gross income within the meaning of Art. 21(3) ECT, as it applied to revenue derived from the supply of electricity into the grid.[704]

---

696 Ibid [257]–[258].
697 Ibid [259].
698 Cube v. Spain, *supra* note 225 [224].
699 Ibid [229].
700 Ibid [231].
701 Ibid [362].
702 NextEra v. Spain, *supra* note 259 [372].
703 Ibid.
704 Ibid [383].

2.2.12 9REN

In contrast to the earlier cases, in *9REN* the claimant argued that it was unnecessary to look at whether the IVPEE had been adopted in "bad faith". It focused on "the prior question" of whether the IVPEE satisfies the "four traditional tests" of a tax, namely whether the measure: (i) is a levy established by law, (ii) imposes obligations on a defined class of persons, (iii) generates revenues which go to the state and (iv) generates revenues used for public purposes.[705] The tribunal had no doubt that the IVPEE was established by law[706] and that it was imposed on a "defined group of persons".[707] The tribunal also saw "nothing objectionable" in concluding that the IVPEE was a tax on revenue rather than on profit. This feature alone did not deprive the IVPEE of its status as a tax. The tribunal noted that corporations "can structure themselves to allocate profits to different jurisdictions to suit their corporate purposes, which may not align with the legitimate interest of the host country". It also referred to the examples of Amazon and Google which caused controversies in the EU concerning the transfer of profits.[708] The tribunal also noted that the revenue from the IVPEE went to the Spanish state. It saw nothing extraordinary in the fact that it was then redirected for a specific purpose. Reduction of the tariff deficit was capable of being classified as a "public purpose" and it was not the tribunal's task to "micromanage" the state's tax policy.[709]

For the tribunal, in the absence of bad faith, there was also nothing extraordinary in the fact that some taxpayers were able to pass on the costs of this fiscal charge to their consumers, whereas other taxpayers were not. It considered that this state of affairs aligned with an established division between a direct and an indirect tax.[710] The tribunal added that Art. 21 ECT "manifests a deliberate policy decision not to limit a State's taxation power".[711]

2.2.13 SolEs

In *SolEs*, the tribunal agreed that the IVPEE had the characteristics of a taxation measure, because it: (i) was imposed on a large class of persons, (ii) was enacted as a law and (iii) generated revenue for the state.[712] In the tribunal's view, the ECT's explicit tax carve-out clause could only be overridden in "extraordinary circumstances", such as those present in the *Yukos* cases.[713] The

705 9REN v. Spain, *supra* note 273 [195].
706 Ibid [196].
707 Ibid [197].
708 Ibid [201].
709 Ibid [203].
710 Ibid [204].
711 Ibid [205].
712 SolEs v. Spain, *supra* note 294 [272].
713 Ibid [276].

tribunal was unimpressed by the allegation that the IVPEE was a "tariff cut which dares not speak its name", adopted in this way so as to escape liability under the ECT. The fact that legislation was "informed" by the state's treaty obligations was insufficient to establish a lack of good faith.[714]

2.2.14 InfraRed

In *InfraRed*, the claimants' arguments regarding bad faith related to the economic effect of the IVPEE, understood independently of its legal operation.[715] This differs from the *Yukos* disputes, where the bad faith resulted from the state's motivation, which was entirely unrelated to any desire to raise general revenue and independent of the effects of the taxation measure.[716] The tribunal observed that the economic effects of a measure "were only secondarily relevant" for assessing whether it is a taxation measure. The most relevant is the legal operation of the measure, i.e. whether: (i) it was established by law, and (ii) imposed liability on classes of persons (iii) to pay funds to the state for public purposes.[717] The IVPEE had "the nature" of a taxation measure, as the proceeds of the IVPEE were payable directly to Spain and formed part of its budget.[718] The IVPEE targeted RE and non-RE producers alike, whereas its ultimate economic effects on RE producers were viewed as irrelevant to whether or not to categorize it as a taxation measure.[719] Consequently, the tribunal decided that the claimants had failed to discharge their burden of proving the existence of bad faith.[720]

The tribunal emphasized that the broad and general terms used to describe the tax carve-out exception were "in furtherance of the principle of state sovereignty enshrined (in its application to state energy resources) at Article 18 ECT".[721] When looking at the claw-back clause, the tribunal analyzed whether the IVPEE was a tax "on income or on capital", which would have meant that the tax fell outside the scope of the claw-back clause.[722] The definition of "taxes on income" in Art. 21(7)(b) of the ECT is broad and intended to restrict the scope of the claw-back clause, which is in line with the principle

714 Ibid [275].
715 InfraRed v. Spain, *supra* note 317 [297], [304].
716 Ibid [298].
717 Ibid [299].
718 Ibid [301].
719 Ibid [307].
720 Ibid [308].
721 Ibid [309].
722 Ibid [310].

of state sovereignty.[723] Thus, the tribunal viewed the IVPEE as a tax on gross income, "substantially similar" – if not "squarely identical" – to a tax on income or on capital as defined in the ECT.[724]

2.2.15 OperaFund

In *OperaFund*, the tribunal also considered that the IVPEE was a tax within the meaning of international law, because it: (i) was established by law, (ii) imposed obligations on a class of people and (iii) entailed paying money to the state for public purposes.[725] The tribunal found no reason to call into question the nature of the IVPEE. The IVPEE supported the electricity system and had an "environmental nature", and therefore served a public purpose. Moreover, it applied to income and was therefore related to economic capacity. The tribunal did not view the IVPEE as discriminating against the RE producers "in terms of repercussion, whether legal or economic".[726]

In the context of the claw-back provision, the tribunal simply noted that the IVPEE was a "tax on income" within the meaning of the ECT. In conclusion, it declined to apply the claw-back provision.[727]

2.2.16 BayWa

The *BayWa* tribunal noted that the term "taxation measure" is not defined in the ECT. Accordingly, it should be given its "normal meaning" within the context of the ECT.[728] This means that a tax is a "compulsory exaction of money by law for public purposes".[729] The IVPEE was *prima facie* a tax, as it was upheld as such by the Spanish courts.[730] The tribunal saw no evidence of bad faith by Spain, as opposed to in the *Yukos* disputes. The tariff deficit was viewed a legitimate concern to justify the imposition of a new fiscal burden on the energy sector.[731] The fact that the charge may have obscure or debatable economic repercussions is insufficient to conclude that a tax is not *bona fide*.[732]

The tribunal distinguished the IVPEE from the tax in the *Antaris v. Czech Republic* case, based on two reasons. First, the purpose of the Czech measure in

723 Ibid [316]–[317].
724 Ibid [318].
725 OperaFund v. Spain, *supra* note 335 [404].
726 Ibid.
727 Ibid [415].
728 BayWa v. Spain, *supra* note 345 [298]–[299].
729 Ibid [300].
730 Ibid [301].
731 Ibid [306].
732 Ibid [305].

the latter case was to reduce the feed-in tariffs for certain investors, as opposed to raising budget revenue. Second, the Czech courts had decided that it was not a tax for the purposes of double taxation treaties.[733]

Finally, the IVPEE was imposed at least on "elements of income".[734] This precluded the application of the claw-back clause, which applied only to taxes that are not imposed on income or capital.[735]

2.2.17 Stadtwerke

The *Stadtwerke* tribunal started by noting that the term "taxation measures", used in Art. 21(7) ECT, can be broader than the term "tax".[736] However, as the IVPEE was found to be a "tax", the tribunal did not define the scope of a "taxation measure".[737]

The tribunal looked at the ordinary meaning of the word tax, pursuant to Art. 31(1) VCLT.[738] This allowed it to identify three basic elements of a tax: (i) it is a compulsory payment obligation, (ii) it is imposed by the state on a defined class of persons, and (iii) its aim is to generate revenues for the state to be used for public purposes. In the ECT's context, these three elements were supplemented by a fourth one, stemming directly from Art. 21(7) ECT, according to which (iv) it must be imposed in accordance with the state's law. The IVPEE met all four of these requirements.[739]

The tribunal noted that neither the ECT's text nor the ordinary meaning "that the Tribunal has gleaned from various dictionaries" required that a tax must be *bona fide*.[740] It underlined that "the power to tax is a fundamental sovereign right". States have a wide discretion in exercising this right, which provides them with the necessary means to "carry out their governmental functions". In consequence, states "jealously protect the power to tax and strongly resist any external limitations on it". The last sentence of Art. 21(1) ECT proves that the contracting states intended to leave themselves free to use their discretion.[741]

The tribunal recognized that, despite the above, some limitations on the states' power to tax exist under CIL, as a tax cannot be either confiscatory or

733 Ibid [306].
734 Ibid [313].
735 Ibid [311].
736 Stadtwerke v. Spain, *supra* note 364 [161].
737 Ibid [162], [171].
738 Ibid [162]–[165].
739 Ibid [166].
740 Ibid [167].
741 Ibid [169].

discriminatory.[742] These limits are reflected in Art. 21 ECT, read in conjunction with Arts. 10(2), 10(7) and 13 ECT. The tribunal regarded itself as having no mandate to "graft further limitations", which were not reflected in the ECT's text.[743] In its view, this conclusion was supported by the ECT's preparatory works, which are relevant according to Art. 32 VCLT.[744] It noted that Art. 21 ECT, contrary to other ECT provisions, was negotiated by officials of the states' ministries of finance, "a group of persons who by position and inclination would resist as far as possible any limitations on their countries' power to tax".[745]

The tribunal observed that sometimes governments "may abuse their power to tax in order to injure an investor for political reasons or to seize its property to satisfy the corrupt ambitions of a country's rulers", which may have been the situation in the *Yukos* disputes. However, no circumstances comparable to those present in *Yukos* were proven to exist in the dispute at hand. A decision to impose a tax "may have been wise or unwise", but it applied to all producers of electricity and targeted neither the claimants specifically nor foreign investors generally.[746]

2.2.18 RWE

In *RWE*, the tribunal commenced its analysis of the tax carve-out objection by noting that, on a plain reading, the IVPEE and Water Levy fell within the "broad definition of Taxation Measures" found in Art. 21(7) ECT. In addition, it had no doubt that they were valid taxes under Spanish law.[747] The tribunal also found that they fell within the various descriptions of taxation measures found in investor-state arbitral case law, understood as measures: (i) established by law, (ii) imposing an obligation on a class of people (iii) to pay money to the state for public purposes.[748]

The tribunal refrained from expressing a position as to whether only *bona fide* taxation measures fall within the scope of the tax carve-out clause. It simply noted that the claimants had not established any bad faith by the respondent.[749] Even if the measures were disguised tariff cuts, this alone was insufficient for the tribunal to find the existence of any bad faith.[750] The claimants had not

742 Ibid [170].
743 Ibid.
744 Ibid [172].
745 Ibid [173].
746 Ibid [174].
747 RWE v. Spain, *supra* note 382 [385].
748 Ibid [386].
749 Ibid [389].
750 Ibid [390].

proved that the measures targeted the RE installations, as opposed to simply having a greater impact on them when compared to other energy producers.[751]

2.2.19 Watkins

In *Watkins*, the claimants did not dispute that the IVPEE should be qualified as a "tax".[752] Referring to the *Yukos* cases, the tribunal understood its mandate as being to apply a "standard of review" by controlling whether there has been an "egregious abuse of tax power".[753] In its view, the burden of proof that the IVPEE was not a *bona fide* taxation measure is "particularly demanding" and fell upon the claimants.[754] Even if the IVPEE was a "mere tariff cut", it would still coincide with the aim of a taxation measure to raise money for the state, and therefore this alone would not suffice to establish bad faith.[755]

2.2.20 Hydro

In *Hydro*, the tribunal started by analyzing whether the IVPEE and Water Levy were "taxation measures" within the meaning of Art. 21 ECT.[756] First, the measures must be qualified as taxes under domestic law. It was undisputed that this was the situation under Spanish law.[757] Second, they must meet the definition under international law, which encompasses two elements: (i) being imposed by law, as part of a tax regime and (ii) creating "a liability on classes of persons to pay money to the State for public purposes".[758] Both elements of the definition were met.[759]

The tribunal recognized that a measure may fall outside the scope of the tax carve-out clause if it was "imposed in bad faith for other reasons". A tribunal can look beyond the form and analyze the reality of a measure.[760] Nevertheless, the required standard of proof is high and rests on the claimants. The tribunal saw no evidence that the Disputed Measures had any "illegitimate ulterior purpose". The respondent's stated purpose of this measure, and the actual purpose, was to raise revenue for the electricity system and to create a balanced budget.

751 Ibid [391].
752 Watkins v. Spain, *supra* note 416 [267].
753 Ibid [269], [272].
754 Ibid [270].
755 Ibid [273].
756 Hydro v. Spain, *supra* note 436 [509].
757 Ibid [511], [513].
758 Ibid [514].
759 Ibid [515].
760 Ibid [516].

A mandatory allocation of revenue received from a tax does not change the nature of the measure.[761]

The tribunal declined to apply the ECT's claw-back clause, noting that it does not apply to taxation measures on "income or on capital".[762] It was irrelevant that the IVPEE and Water Levy were imposed on gross revenues.[763] The exclusion extended beyond "net income" and covered "total income", as well as even "elements of income". The purpose of the claw-back provision was to exclude indirect taxes from the tax carve-out clause, whereas the IVPEE and Water Levy were direct taxes.[764]

2.2.21 Cavalum

In *Cavalum*, the tribunal's analysis of the taxation carve-out objection was essentially the same as in the *Hydro* case, with a few modifications relating to the fact that the *Cavalum* case concerned the IVPEE only, whereas the *Hydro* case also concerned the Water Levy.[765] The tribunal added that, although the existence of possible discrimination and a lack of proportionality do not automatically negate the conclusion that a measure constitutes a tax, they can be relevant to the bad faith analysis.[766] However, the allegations of bad faith were considered as "equivocal" and unevidenced in this case.[767]

2.3 *Lessons Learned*

Whereas the case law analyzed above concerns Art. 21 ECT and is rooted in its wording, the conclusions which can be derived from it extend beyond the ECT. Many BITs contain tax carve-outs, which provide for similar limits of the scope of jurisdiction as those found in the ECT. Typically, expropriation is the only type of claim which remains within the scope of jurisdiction in disputes concerning taxes.[768]

---

761 Ibid [518].

762 Ibid [519].

763 Ibid [520].

764 Ibid [521].

765 Cavalum v. Spain, *supra* note 464 [382]–[396], repeating *Hydro v. Spain*, ibid [509]–[518]. This may be explained by the fact that they were issued by tribunals which had the same presiding arbitrator. There are some minor differences in the text of some of the repeated paragraphs.

766 Cavalum v. Spain, ibid [387].

767 Ibid [394]–[395].

768 See for example: Art. XII Canada – Ecuador BIT, Art. XII US – Argentina BIT or Art. VI Poland – US BIT. This does not apply, however, to differentiation between a "tax" and a "taxation measure", which results from the definition included in ECT and which is generally irrelevant for other treaties.

This comes as no surprise. As the tribunal in *Stadtwerke* correctly noted, CIL imposes certain limitations on a state's power to tax, in the sense that taxes cannot be confiscatory or discriminatory.[769] Thus, tax carve-outs such as Art. 21 ECT are in line with the limits under CIL.

It is notable that Spain was successful on each occasion that it presented the tax carve-out jurisdictional objection. All of the tribunals perceived the IVPEE, and the Water Levy when relevant, as genuine taxes, which fell outside of the scope of their jurisdiction. Their analysis of this issue allows two lessons to be learned for the future.

2.3.1 First Lesson Learned – Arbitral Tribunals Not Only Can, but Must, Commence Their Analysis by Looking beyond the "Label" of a Tax, to Decide Whether a Disputed Measure Fulfils CIL's Prerequisites

Tribunals must verify whether a particular measure – named as a "tax" by a state – falls within the definition of a tax under CIL.[770] This is correct whenever no definition of a "tax" can be found in the relevant, applicable international treaty, as was the situation in the ECT.

The considerations of the tribunals in *Eiser*,[771] *Antin*,[772] *Foresight*,[773] *NextEra*,[774] *Cube*,[775] *SolEs*,[776] *InfraRed*,[777] *OperaFund*,[778] *BayWa*,[779] *Stadtwerke*[780] and *RWE*[781] confirm that, in order to comply with the definition of a tax under CIL, a measure must: (i) be established by law, (ii) impose an obligation on a class of people and (iii) involve paying money to the state for public purposes. All of these prerequisites must be met cumulatively.

The *9REN* tribunal divided the third prerequisite into two separate ones,[782] whereas the tribunals in *Hydro* and *Cavalum* merged the last two prerequisites

769 Fn 742.
770 Some of the Spanish saga tribunals referred simply to international law, rather than to CIL.
771 Fn 670.
772 Fn 684.
773 Fn 693.
774 Fn 702.
775 Fn 699.
776 Fn 712.
777 Fn 717.
778 Fn 725.
779 Fn 729.
780 Fn 739.
781 Fn 748.
782 Fn 705.

into one.[783] This can be considered as a technical differentiation, entailing no difference in substance. Consequently, these 3 tribunals also confirmed the aforementioned elements which make up the definition of a tax under CIL. In addition, the *Stadtwerke* tribunal identified an additional prerequisite, namely that a tax must be imposed in accordance with the host state's law. This stems from the wording of Art. 21(7) ECT.[784] However, this requirement can be considered as subsumed by the first element of the CIL definition of a tax, namely that it must be imposed by law. If a measure is adopted in violation of domestic law, it will not fulfill the first prerequisite for being a tax.

The first element of the definition requires that a measure is established by law and within the limits of domestic law. This will hardly be a contentious issue in investor-state arbitrations, where disputes concern alleged abuses of taxation, which essentially means using the tax label as a disguise for measures having a different nature. Nevertheless, it became a relevant factor in the RE cases initiated against the Czech Republic, which ultimately resulted in decisions that the ECT tax carve-out clause was inapplicable.[785]

The second element requires the measure to impose an obligation on a class of people. Accordingly, a measure which targets a particular investor, being legislation which applies in reality to an individual entity, notwithstanding that it is theoretically of general applicability, would not meet this prerequisite. As such, this element relates to one of the CIL limits of a state's tax powers, namely that a tax cannot be discriminatory.[786]

The third element is that the measure must require payments to the state for public purposes. This refers to the very essence of a tax, but it is also related to the CIL limitations of a state's tax powers, in the sense that taxes cannot be confiscatory.[787] This was yet another reason in the RE cases initiated against the Czech Republic which resulted in the inapplicability of the ECT's tax carve-out clause. The tribunal in *Antaris v. Czech Republic* recognized that, although the contested measure generated revenue for the respondent state, "the principal purpose was to reduce the FiT for certain investors".[788] Similarly the tribunals in the *I.C.W. v. Czech Republic*, *Voltaic v. Czech Republic* and *WA v. Czech Republic* cases noted that "the main objective" of the disputed measures "was other

783 Fn 758, 765.

784 Fn 739.

785 I.C.W. v. Czech Republic, *supra* note 44 [307], Voltaic v. Czech Republic, *supra* note 44 [250], WA v. Czech Republic, *supra* note 44 [317], Antaris v. Czech Republic, PCA Case No. 2014-01, Award (02.05.2018) [233], [242].

786 Fn 742.

787 Ibid.

788 Antaris v. Czech Republic, *supra* note 785 [250].

than that of the raising of general revenue for the State, and which were formulated and structured as taxation measures for a particular ulterior reason (such as, here, reducing the risk of legal challenges)".[789] The same approach can be seen in *Horthel v. Poland*, where the tribunal decided that, although a disputed measure "was a taxation measure on its face, it was not in fact aimed at increasing the state's revenues".[790] Consequently, it was not considered to be a genuine tax.

If any of the aforementioned characteristics of a tax are missing, a disputed measure will not be deemed to be a genuine tax and will therefore not fall within the tax carve-out clause. This was not the case in the Spanish saga, as the tribunals unanimously decided that the IVPEE and Water Levy fulfilled all 3 of these requirements. However, the various tribunals' analysis is often blended with discussion on whether the state adopted a tax in good faith, which leads to the second lesson learned.

2.3.2 Second Lesson Learned – Tax Carve-Out Clauses Do Not Apply to Mala Fide Measures

The Spanish saga tribunals confirmed that they are entitled to assess whether or not a tax was adopted in bad faith. Some tribunals, such as those in *RREEF*,[791] *Foresight*,[792] *Cube*,[793] *SolEs*,[794] *InfraRed*,[795] *BayWa*,[796] *Watkins*,[797] *Hydro*[798] and *Cavalum*[799] simply observed that the claimants had failed to prove the existence of bad faith. Others, such as those in *Isolux*,[800] *Novenergia*[801] and *Antin*[802] suggested that a tax must be adopted in good faith. Sometimes, as in *Eiser*[803] and *RWE*,[804] the tribunals preferred to limit themselves to commenting that

789 I.C.W. v. Czech Republic, *supra* note 44 [313], Voltaic v. Czech Republic, *supra* note 44 [265], WA v. Czech Republic, *supra* note 44 [332].

790 Horthel v. Poland, PCA Case No. 2014-31, Final Award (16.02.2017) [256]. This case does not, however, concern the scope of the ECT tax carve-out.

791 Fn 659.

792 Fn 697.

793 Fn 698.

794 Fn 714.

795 Fn 720.

796 Fn 731.

797 Fn 755.

798 Fn 760.

799 Fn 765.

800 Fn 665.

801 Fn 675–676.

802 Fn 685.

803 Fn 671.

804 Fn 749.

bad faith had not proven, whilst avoiding expressing a clear position on this issue.[805]

The tribunals in *Eiser*,[806] *Masdar*,[807] *Antin*,[808] *Stadtwerke*[809] and *Watkins*[810] related bad faith to the prohibition on abusing the power to tax, which in turn was perceived as being the "core of sovereign power"[811] or "a fundamental sovereign right".[812]

This is in line with the general case law. The most famous examples of inapplicable taxation carve-outs concern the *Yukos* disputes, where the disputed measures in reality aimed to achieve an "entirely unrelated purpose", i.e. the destruction of a company and the elimination of a political opponent.[813] Against the same factual background, the tribunal in *RosInvest* confirmed that the taxation carve-out provision does not apply to an abuse of a state's tax powers.[814] The tribunal in *Renta 4* stated that, otherwise, treaty protection would become illusory, as states would "dress up" all adverse measures as taxation.[815]

However, the standard of evidence required to prove that a state has acted in bad faith is high, and the burden of proof rests on the claimants. Whenever claimants argue that a tax was adopted in bad faith, the facts of the particular dispute will inevitably be compared to the *Yukos* dispute. The Spanish saga cases confirm that a state measure which is labelled as a tax but is, in reality, designed to destroy a particular investment or investor, would amount to an abuse of right and fall outside the scope of the tax carve-out. However, such a state-designed scheme is an example of the extraordinary circumstances which must be proven by the party alleging the existence of bad faith. None of the claimants in the Spanish saga cases was able to meet this high threshold of

805 However, even this reasoning allows the same conclusion that bad faith taxation precludes application of the taxation carve-out clause. Otherwise, these tribunals would have refrained from such comments and adopted a different approach.

806 Fn 673.

807 Fn 683.

808 Fn 686–687.

809 Fn 746.

810 Fn 753.

811 Fn 672.

812 Fn 741. Similarly fn 723.

813 Fn 651.

814 RosInvestCo v. Russia, *supra* note 651 [628].

815 Renta 4 v. Russia, *supra* note 651 [179]:

> […] If that were enough, investment protection through international law would likely become an illusion, as states would quickly learn to avoid responsibility by dressing up all adverse measures, perhaps expropriation first of all, as taxation. When agreeing to the jurisdiction of international tribunals, states perforce accept that those jurisdictions will exercise their judgment, and not be stumped by the use of labels.

establishing bad faith.[816] Even if they were able to prove that certain political statements suggested an alternative rationale behind the disputed taxes, such as environmental protection, which were shown to be untrue, and the only real purpose of the measure was shown to be to raise funds for the budget, this was still insufficient to meet this high threshold.

It is notable that the discussion assumes a dichotomy between two scenarios, namely that a tax is either adopted in good faith or in bad faith. However, the high threshold required in order to prove bad faith suggests that a lack of good faith should not automatically be equated with the existence of bad faith. The *SolEs* and *Watkins* tribunals noted that, even if the tax was a "mere tariff cut", which is arguably not a good faith measure, given that it was adopted as "informed" by the respondent's investment treaty obligations, this would be insufficient to establish bad faith.[817]

The Spanish saga cases leave unanswered the question of whether a good faith requirement represents an additional element of the definition of a tax or, rather, a factor which precludes the application of a tax carve-out to a tax. From a theoretical perspective, the difference is visible. In the first approach, a bad faith measure would not be a tax. In the second approach, it would be a tax, but a tax carve-out provision would be inapplicable. From a practical perspective, however, this is of little relevance. Within both understandings, the consequence of bad faith would be that a tribunal has jurisdiction over the contested measure.

The analysis above reveals an inconsistency in the consequences of the tribunals having declined jurisdiction over the disputes taxes. Despite making

816 Novenergia v. Spain, *supra* note 156 [525], Masdar v. Spain, *supra* note 169 [295], Foresight v. Spain, *supra* note 210 [247], [260], SolEs v. Spain, *supra* note 294 [277], OperaFund v. Spain, *supra* note 335 [405], BayWa v. Spain, *supra* note 345 [297], Watkins v. Spain, *supra* note 416 [274], Hydro v. Spain, *supra* note 436 [522], Isolux v. Spain, *supra* note 124 [741], Eiser v. Spain, *supra* note 136 [271].

817 Watkins v. Spain, ibid [273], SolEs v. Spain, ibid 296 [275]. Against a different factual background, the tribunal in *Antaris v. Czech Republic* noted that the structure of the disputed measure adopted by the respondent "principally for the purpose of taking the reduction in the FiTs outside the protections accorded by several international investment treaties, including the ECT [...] does not imply that the Respondent was acting in bad faith" – Antaris v. Czech Republic, *supra* note fn 785 [253]. This did not preclude the tribunal from finding that the ECT tax carve-out clause did not apply, because the disputed measure failed to meet all of the elements of genuine tax. Similarly, the tribunals in the *I.C.W.*, *Voltaic* and *WA* cases, which also decided that the disputed measures lacked two of the three definitional characteristics of a tax, noted that this conclusion was nevertheless "not dependent upon a finding of bad faith" – I.C.W. v. Czech Republic, *supra* note 44 [314], Voltaic v. Czech Republic, *supra* note 44 [266], WA v. Czech Republic, *supra* note 44 [333].

this decision, some tribunals considered the IVPEE to be an element of the relevant factual background, i.e. a "cost impacting the return to the Claimants".[818] Others took the opposite approach.[819] The first approach diminishes the practical relevance of a decision to decline jurisdiction over the disputed taxes, if they are later to be treated as a relevant factor and taken into account when calculating damages.

Finally, the *NextEra*,[820] *InfraRed*,[821] *OperaFund*,[822] *BayWa*,[823] *Hydro*[824] and *Cavalum*[825] tribunals consistently decided that the claw-back clause in Art. 21(3) ECT was inapplicable. This is, however, of little relevance for the future, as it is a fact-specific issue regarding the particular characteristics of the IVPEE and the Water Levy.

---

818 RREEF v. Spain, *supra* note 118 [191].
819 Cube v. Spain, *supra* note 225 [362].
820 Fn 704.
821 Fn 724.
822 Fn 727.
823 Fn 735.
824 Fn 764.
825 Fn 765.

CHAPTER 4

Liability

1 Fair and Equitable Treatment

1.1 *General Comments*

The FET[1] is the most frequently invoked standard of protection and of the "highest practical relevance" in investment disputes.[2] It has been described as "the grundnorm or basic norm of the investment treaty system".[3]

It is one of the "absolute" standards.[4] This means that it establishes a certain standard of conduct required from the state, regardless of how the state treats its own nationals or the nationals of third states.[5]

Some investment treaties simply guarantee the FET, whilst others link it with the protection guaranteed by (customary) international law or with general principles of international law.[6] The starting point for assessing whether the FET is an independent standard one or one which is tied to CIL is the wording of the relevant treaty provision. However, whilst the issue of the relationship between the FET and CIL remains debated, it is of limited practical

1 All abbreviations contained herein are as used in previous Chapters, unless described otherwise.

2 Rudolf Dolzer, Ursula Kriebaum, Christoph Schreuer, Principles of International Investment Law (Oxford University Press 2022), p. 186. See also: Christoph H. Schreuer, Fair and Equitable Treatment (FET): Interactions with Other Standards, in: Graham Coop, Clarisse Ribeiro (eds.), Investment Protection and the Energy Charter Treaty (JurisNet 2008), p. 65, Peter D. Cameron, International Energy Investment Law: The Pursuit of Stability (Oxford University Press 2010), p. 169.

3 Jeswald W. Salacuse, The Law of Investment Treaties (Oxford University Press 2021), p. 291.

4 Garanti v. Turkmenistan, ICSID Case No. ARB/11/20, Award (19.12.2016) [380].

5 Joshua P. Meltzer, Investment, in: Simon Lester, Bryan Mercurio (eds.), Bilateral and Regional Trade Agreements. Commentary and Analysis (Cambridge University Press 2015), p. 265, UNCTAD, Fair and Equitable Treatment. UNCTAD Series on Issues in International Investment Agreements II (United Nations 2012), available at: https://unctad.org/system/files/official-document/unctaddiaeia2011d5_en.pdf, p. 6, Todd J. Grierson-Weiler, Ian A. Laird, Standards of Treatment, in: Peter T. Muchlinski, Federico Ortino, Christoph Schreuer (eds.), The Oxford Handbook of International Investment Law (Oxford University Press 2008), p. 262. See also: Kaj Hobér, The Energy Charter Treaty. A Commentary (Oxford University Press 2020), p. 188, which describes it as an "objective" standard when compared, for example, to national treatment, which requires a comparator.

6 Salacuse, *supra* note 3, p. 291. See for example: Art. III(1) BIT Poland – Canada, Art. 14.6(1) USMCA, Art. 1105(1) NAFTA.

relevance.[7] Many tribunals perceive it as "more apparent than real",[8] "more theoretical than real"[9] or "more theoretical than substantial".[10]

There is no single, commonly accepted abstract definition of the FET.[11] Arbitral tribunals underline that the plain meaning of the terms "fair" and "equitable" provide little assistance.[12] Thus, tribunals typically look at several non-cumulative criteria to determine whether a state has violated the FET. These include, among others, whether the state has: (i) breached the investor's legitimate expectations, (ii) acted in proportionate manner, (iii) acted in an arbitrary or discriminatory manner, (iv) acted in good faith, (v) violated due process, or (vi) acted in a transparent manner.[13]

---

7 See for example: Rusoro v. Venezuela, ICSID Case No. ARB(AF)/12/5, Award (22.08.2016) [520]–[521], Gosling v. Mauritius, ICSID Case No. ARB/16/32, Award (18.02.2020) [243], Merrill & Ring v. Canada, ICSID Case No. UNCT/07/1, Award (31.03.2010) [210], CC/Devas v. India, PCA Case No. 2013-09, Award on Jurisdiction and Merits (25.07.2016) [457], Azurix v. Argentina, ICSID Case No. ARB/01/12, Award (14.07.2006) [361], Rumeli v. Kazakhstan, ICSID Case No. ARB/05/16, Award (29.07.2008) [609].

8 Saluka v. Czech Republic, UNCITRAL, Partial Award (17.03.2006) [291].

9 Rumeli v. Kazakhstan, *supra* note 7 [611].

10 Murphy v. Ecuador, PCA Case No. 2012-16, Partial Final Award (06.05.2016) [206].

11 Hobér, *supra* note 5, p. 187. See the general description of the FET presented, for example, by the tribunals in: Tecmed v. Mexico, ICSID Case No. ARB (AF)/00/2, Award (29.05.2003) [154], MTD v. Chile, ICSID Case No. ARB/01/7, Award (25.05.2004) [113], Waste Management v. Mexico, ICSID Case No. ARB(AF)/00/3, Award (30.04.2004) [98], S.D. Myers v Canada, UNCITRAL, Partial Award (13.11.2000) [263], Saluka v. Czech Republic, *supra* note 8 [309].

12 See for example: GPF v. Poland, SCC Case No. V 2014/168, Award (29.04.2020) [539], Micula v. Romania, ICSID Case No. ARB/05/20, Award (11.12.2013) [504].

13 See for example: GPF v. Poland, *supra* note 12 [543], Rumeli v. Kazakhstan, *supra* note 7 [609], Philip Morris v. Uruguay, ICSID Case No. ARB/10/7, Award (08.07.2016) [320], Marfin v. Cyprus, ICSID Case No. ARB/13/27, Award (26.07.2018) [1211], Biwater v. Tanzania, ICSID Case No. ARB/05/22, Award (24.07.2008) [602], Rudolf Dolzer, Fair and Equitable Treatment: Today's Contours, Santa Clara Journal of International Law, 12:1 (2014), p. 15, Salacuse, *supra* note 3, p. 304. Art. 4(1) BIT France-Colombia is an example when a treaty itself lists some of the elements of the FET . It is not always possible to draw a clear line between the specific elements of the FET due to a degree of overlap which exists between these elements. Some inspirations about the "undisputed" elements of the FET can be found in the most recent investment treaties, which provide for the more detailed definitions of the FET. See for example: Art. 8.10(2) CETA:

> A Party breaches the obligation of fair and equitable treatment referenced in paragraph 1 if a measure or series of measures constitutes: (a) denial of justice in criminal, civil or administrative proceedings; (b) fundamental breach of due process, including a fundamental breach of transparency, in judicial and administrative proceedings; (c) manifest arbitrariness; (d) targeted discrimination on manifestly wrongful grounds, such as gender, race or religious belief; (e) abusive treatment of investors, such as coercion, duress and harassment; or (f) a breach of any further elements of the fair and equitable treatment obligation adopted by the Parties in accordance with paragraph 3 of this Article.

The first of the listed elements, legitimate expectations and their protection, has "emerged as the most significant element of the FET standard".[14] Arbitral tribunals have consistently found that the protection of legitimate expectations constitutes an element of the FET.[15] By way of example, the *Electrabel* tribunal described the protection of legitimate expectations as "the most important function" of the FET.[16] However, critical voices exist and some commentators consider that the protection of legitimate expectations favors investors at the expense of host states.[17]

Whilst subjective perception is insufficient to create legally protected expectations, it is necessary.[18] The FET protects only those legitimate expectations

---

It remains to be seen how the FET will be interpreted as part of these "new generation" definitions. Their silence on the protection of legitimate expectations is particularly notable.

14 Jonathan Bonnitcha, Substantive Protection under Investment Treaties: a Legal and Economic Analysis (Cambridge University Press 2014), p. 161. For example the *Saluka* tribunal described legitimate expectations as "the dominant element" of the FET – Saluka v. Czech Republic, *supra* note 8 [302].

15 For example: Flemingo v. Poland, UNCITRAL, Award (12.08.2016) [534], Unión Fenosa v. Egypt, ICSID Case No. ARB/14/4, Award (31.08.2018) [9.52], EDF v. Romania, ICSID Case No. ARB/05/13, Award (08.10.2009) [216].

16 Electrabel v. Hungary, ICSID Case No. ARB/07/19, Decision on Jurisdiction, Applicable Law and Liability (30.11.2012) [7.75].

17 See for example: Suez v. Argentina, ICSID Case No. ARB/03/19, Separate Opinion of Arbitrator Pedro Nikken (30.07.2010) [3]. See also: Emmanuel T. Laryea, Legitimate Expectations in Investment Treaty Law: Concept and Scope of Application, in: Julien Chaisse, Leïla Choukroune, Sufian Jusoh (eds.), Handbook of International Investment Law and Policy (Springer 2021), p. 113:

> Application of the legitimate expectation concept overwhelmingly benefits investors. Considering that developing countries are mostly the respondents in investor-State arbitration cases, it stands to reason that they suffer the most from the application of the legitimate expectation principle, at least to the extent that the principle disadvantages host-States.

Also in this vein see for example: Muthucumaraswamy Sornarajah, Resistance and Change in the International Law on Foreign Investment (Cambridge University Press 2015), pp. 256–299, Christopher Campbell, House of Cards: the Relevance of Legitimate Expectations under Fair and Equitable Treatment Provisions in Investment Treaty Law, Journal of International Arbitration, 30:4 (2013), pp. 361–380. On the other hand, concept of legitimate expectations is present in many other legal systems, including domestic legal systems, the EU law and case law of the ECtHR. See for example: Thunderbird v. Mexico, UNCITRAL, Separate Opinion (01.12.2005) [27].

18 Elizabeth Snodgrass, Protecting Investors' Legitimate Expectations: Recognizing and Delimiting a General Principle, ICSID Review – Foreign Investment Law Journal, 21:1 (2006), p. 41. See also for example: Micula v. Romania, *supra* note 12 [671].

that were "relied upon by the investor when deciding to invest".[19] In other words, they must be a relevant factor in the decision-making process on whether to make an investment.

The particular legitimate expectations relied upon must be assessed objectively.[20] Their assessment must "take into account all circumstances, including not only the facts surrounding the investment, but also the political, socioeconomic, cultural and historical conditions prevailing in the host State".[21] The relevant threshold is at the level of expectations of a "prudent investor".[22]

Investors' due diligence, prior to deciding whether to invest, is a relevant factor when assessing whether expectations are objectively reasonable.[23] Sometimes it is taken into account by a tribunal implicitly.[24] However, the precise relevance of this factor and the consequences which result if due diligence is lacking remain unclear.

In order to be protected, the relevant legitimate expectations must exist at the moment of making the investment.[25] This aspect is often more complex than may appear at first glance. Many investments comprise a series of decisions, taken over a period of time. On the one hand, as the tribunal in *Horthel v. Poland* noted:

19 Enron v. Argentina, ICSID Case No. ARB/01/3, Award (22.05.2007) [262]. Similarly, for example: Biwater v. Tanzania, *supra* note 13 [602], Micula v. Romania, *supra* note 12 [722], Olin v. Libya, ICC Case No. 20355/MCP, Final Award (25.05.2018) [307], GPF v. Poland, *supra* note 12 [545], Crystallex v. Venezuela, ICSID Case No. ARB(AF)11/2, Award (04.04.2016) [557].

20 National Grid v. Argentina, UNCITRAL, Award (3.11.2008) [173].

21 Duke Energy v. Ecuador, ICSID Case No. ARB/04/19, Award (18.08.2008) [340].

22 Dolzer, Kriebaum, Schreuer, *supra* note 2, p. 209.

23 See for example: Biwater v. Tanzania, *supra* note 13 [601], Mamidoil v. Albania, ICSID Case No. ARB/11/24, Award (30.03.2015) [634], Gavrilovic v. Croatia, ICSID Case No. ARB/12/39, Award (25.08.2018) [986], Lemire v. Ukraine, ICSID Case No. ARB/06/18, Decision on Jurisdiction and Liability (14.01.2010) [285], Invesmart v. Czech Republic, UNCITRAL, Award (26.06.2009) [254], MTD v. Chile, *supra* note 11 [117], Parkerings v. Lithuania, ICSID Case No. ARB/05/8, Award (11.09.2007) [333], South American Silver v. Bolivia, PCA Case No. 2013-5, Award (22.11.2018) [648], Unglaube v. Costa Rica, ICSID Case No. ARB/08/1 and ICSID Case No. ARB/09/20 (consolidated cases), Award (16.05.2012) [258]. See also: Yulia Levashova, Fair and Equitable Treatment and Investor's Due Diligence Under International Investment Law, Netherlands International Law Review, 67:2 (2020).

24 Jorge E. Viñuales, Investor Diligence in Investment Arbitration: Sources and Arguments, ICSID Review – Foreign Investment Law Journal, 32:2 (2017), p. 362.

25 Parkerings v. Lithuania, *supra* note 23 [331], National Grid v. Argentina, *supra* note 20 [173], Duke Energy v. Ecuador, *supra* note 21 [340], [347], [365], Bayindir v. Pakistan, ICSID Case No. ARB/03/29, Award (27.08.2009) [190].

> legitimate expectations should be related to the investment and not to each and every decision concerning the implementation of the investment. That being said, it is impossible to point to a specific moment of making of one or more investments which are a result of multiple decisions and transactions.[26]

On the other hand, as explained by the tribunal in *Frontier v. Czech Republic,* when "investments are made through several steps, spread over a period of time, legitimate expectations must be examined for each stage at which a decisive step is taken towards the creation, expansion, development, or reorganisation of the investment".[27]

Legitimate expectations include the expectation of the "presumed stability of the overall legal framework".[28] Stability has been described as "the holy grail of every investor in every sector".[29] It relates to the host states' legal framework. It is often considered together with consistency, understood as concerning the application of the legal framework by domestic administrative and judicial authorities.[30] The *Suez* tribunal recognized that "a host government through its laws, regulations, declared policies, and statements creates in the investor certain expectations about the nature of the treatment that it may anticipate from the host State".[31] The *Duke Energy* tribunal confirmed that

26 Horthel v. Poland, PCA Case No. 2014-31, Final Award (16.02.2017) [244]. A similar approach can be seen, for example, in: Mamidoil v. Albania, *supra* note 23 [695].

27 Frontier v. Czech Republic, UNCITRAL, Final Award (12.11.2010) [287]. See also for example: Christoph Schreuer, Ursula Kriebaum, At What Time Must Legitimate Expectations Exist?, in: Jacques Werner, Arif Hyder Ali (eds.), A Liber Amicorum: Thomas Walde - Law Beyond Conventional Thoughts (Cameron May 2009).

28 Roland Kläger, Fair and Equitable Treatment in International Investment Agreements (Oxford University Press 2011), p. 164. Some authors consider an interpretation of the FET which encompasses regulatory stability to be "expansive". See for example: Ely Caetano Xavier Junior, Fabio Costa Morosini, El Estándar de Trato Justo y Equitativo, in: José Manuel Álvarez Zárate, Maciej Żenkiewicz (eds.), El Derecho Internacional de las Inversiones. Desarrollo Actual de Normas y Principios (Universidad Externado de Colombia 2021), p. 449. See also for example: Sempra v. Argentina, ICSID Case No. ARB/02/16, Award (28.09.2007) [300], Plama v. Bulgaria, ICSID Case No. ARB/03/24, Award (27.08.2008) [173], [219].

29 Giuseppe Bellantuono, The Misguided Quest for Regulatory Stability in the Renewable Energy Sector, Journal of World Energy Law & Business, 10:4 (2017), p. 274.

30 Kriebaum, Schreuer, *supra* note 2, p. 205, August Reinisch, Christoph Schreuer, International Protection of Investments. The Substantive Standards (Cambridge University Press 2020), p. 468. Whereas some BITs explicitly list stability together with the FET, even without such an explicit reference stability is considered to be an element of the FET.

31 Suez v. Argentina, ICSID Case No. ARB/03/19, Decision on Liability (30.07.2010) [222].

legitimate expectations protect "the stability of the legal and business environment".[32] The *Mamidoil* tribunal observed that "even when legislative changes seem legitimate, they must not have the character of a continuous oscillation and unpredictability".[33] The LG&E tribunal described that the FET "consists of the host State's consistent and transparent behavior, free of ambiguity that involves the obligation to grant and maintain a stable and predictable legal framework necessary to fulfill the justified expectations of the foreign investor".[34] Sometimes, however, the stability of the legal framework is perceived as a separate element of the FET, rather than merely in the context of legitimate expectations.[35]

The above does not mean that the FET is equivalent to a stabilization clause.[36] A legitimate expectation of stability and consistency does not amount to "the virtual freezing of the legal regulation of economic activities" or "a kind of insurance policy against the risk of any changes in the host State's legal and economic framework".[37] It is often balanced with a state's right to regulate.[38]

32 Duke Energy v. Ecuador, *supra* note 21 [340].

33 Mamidoil v. Albania, *supra* note 23 [621].

34 LG&E v. Argentina, ICSID Case No. ARB/02/1, Decision on Liability (3.10.2006) [311].

35 Reinisch, Schreuer, *supra* note 30, p. 462, Simon Maynard, Legitimate Expectations and the Interpretation of the Legal Stability Obligation, European Investment Law and Arbitration Review, 1:1 (2016), pp. 106–107, 111–112. See also for example: Merrill & Ring v. Canada, *supra* note 7 [232], Lemire v. Ukraine, *supra* note 23 [284].

36 Moshe Hirsch, Between Fair and Equitable Treatment and Stabilization Clause: Stable Legal Environment and Regulatory Change in International Investment Law, Journal of World Investment & Trade, 12:6 (2011), p. 802.

37 EDF v. Romania, *supra* note 15 [217]. Similarly, for example: Electrabel v. Hungary, *supra* note 16 [7.77]:

> the host State is entitled to maintain a reasonable degree of regulatory flexibility to respond to changing circumstances in the public interest. Consequently, the requirement of fairness must not be understood as the immutability of the legal framework, but as implying that subsequent changes should be made fairly, consistently and predictably, taking into account the circumstances of the investment.

Similarly: Levy v. Peru, ICSID Case No. ARB/10/17, Award (26.02.2014) [319]: "[…] stability does not mean a freezing of the legal system or making it impossible for the State to reform laws and other regulations in force at the time the investor made the investment". See also: Teinver v. Argentina, ICSID Case No. ARB/09/1, Award (21.07.2017) [668], BG v. Argentina, UNCITRAL, Final Award (24.12.2007) [298], Impregilo v. Argentina, ICSID Case No. ARB/07/17, Award (21.06.2011) [290]–[291], Ulysseas v. Ecuador, UNCITRAL, Final Award (12.06.2012) [249], Glamis Gold v. US, UNCITRAL, Award (08.06.2009) [813], Micula v. Romania, *supra* note 12 [673], AES v. Hungary, ICSID Case No. ARB/07/22, Award (23.09.2010) [9.3.29].

38 See for example: Total v. Argentina, ICSID Case No. ARB/04/01, Decision on Liability (27.12.2010) [123], UAB E energija v. Latvia, ICSID Case No. ARB/12/33, Award (22.12.2017) [836], South American Silver v. Bolivia, *supra* note 23 [649], Saluka v. Czech Republic, *supra* note 8 [255], [305]–[306], Arif v. Moldova, ICSID Case No. ARB/11/23, Award

The question often faced by tribunals is whether a disputed measure fundamentally modifies the regulatory framework applicable to the investment beyond an "acceptable margin of change".[39] For this reason, the exact scope of necessary stability and consistency remains controversial.[40] This is also where proportionality, mentioned earlier as one of the elements of the FET, becomes relevant.[41]

It is uncontroversial that legitimate expectations can be based on "specific and unambiguous" representations.[42] These representations may be explicit or implicit.[43] In the words of the *Micula* tribunal:

> There must be a promise, assurance or representation attributable to a competent organ or representative of the state, which may be explicit or implicit. The crucial point is whether the state, through statements

---

(08.04.2013) [537], Perenco v. Ecuador, ICSID Case No. ARB/08/6, Decision on Remaining Issues of Jurisdiction and Liability (12.09.2014) [560], Plama v. Bulgaria, *supra* note 28 [177]. Resar and Cheng identify a:

> transition from early ISA tribunals, which neglected regulatory concerns in their single-minded efforts to enforce an investor's rights under an investment agreement, to modern ISA tribunals that consider a state's "right to regulate" increasingly required arbitral awards to openly resolve questions of public law

– Alexander W. Resar, Tai-Heng Cheng, Investor State Arbitration in a Changing World Order (Brill 2021), pp. 46–47. This is in line with Schreuer's description that "in the early years of investment protection, as we know it, there was a certain euphoria for the rights of investors" – Christoph Schreuer, Evolution of Investment Law in Treaty Making and Arbitral Practice, in: Stephan Hobbe, Julian Scheu (eds.), Evolution, Evaluation and Future Developments in International Investment Law. Proceedings of the 10 Year Anniversary Conference of the International Investment Law Centre Cologne (Nomos 2021), p. 43.

39 See for example: El Paso v. Argentina, ICSID Case No. ARB/03/15, Award (31.10.2011) [402], Philip Morris v. Uruguay, *supra* note 13 [423].

40 Roland Kläger, *supra* note 28, p. 166, argues that, beside the prohibition of retroactivity, legitimate expectations do not "usually impose any restrictions that would delimit the legislator's ability to pursue or change certain economy-related laws or policies".

41 See for example: Occidental v. Ecuador, ICSID Case No. ARB/06/11, Award (05.10.2012) [404].

42 Andrew Newcombe, Lluís Paradell, Law and Practice of Investment Treaties: Standards of Treatment (Kluwer Law International 2009), pp. 281–282, explicitly relied upon by the tribunal in White Industries v. India, UNCITRAL, Final Award (30.11.2011) [10.3.7]. See also for example: Saint-Gobain v. Venezuela, ICSID Case No. ARB/12/13, Decision on Liability and the Principles of Quantum (30.12.2016) [531], OKO v. Estonia, ICSID Case No. ARB/04/6, Award (19.11.2007) [247], Gavrilovic v. Croatia, *supra* note 23 [984], Crystallex v. Venezuela, *supra* note 19 [547].

43 For example: Gold Reserve v. Venezuela, ICSID Case No. ARB(AF)/09/1, Award (22.09.2014) [571], United Utilities v. Estonia, ICSID Case No. ARB/14/24, Award (21.06.2019) [576], Parkerings v. Lithuania, *supra* note 23 [331], Toto v. Lebanon, ICSID Case No. ARB/07/12, Award (07.06.2012) [159].

> or conduct, has contributed to the creation of a reasonable expectation, in this case, a representation of regulatory stability. It is irrelevant whether the state in fact wished to commit itself; it is sufficient that it acted in a manner that would reasonably be understood to create such an appearance. The element of reasonableness cannot be separated from the promise, assurance or representation, in particular if the promise is not contained in a contract or is otherwise stated explicitly.[44]

What remains controversial is whether the legitimate expectation of stability and consistency can be rooted exclusively in general regulatory framework, without additional representations from the state. On the one hand, some tribunals accepted this position.[45] Others adopted a similar position, but based on "both the contractual and the regulatory framework".[46]

On the other hand, some tribunals recognized that the protection of legitimate expectations requires specific representations, and is available only insofar as "the host State has explicitly assumed a specific legal obligation for the future, such as by contracts, concessions or stabilisation clauses on which the investor is therefore entitled to rely as a matter of law", or at least "when public authorities of the host country have made the private investor believe that such an obligation existed through conduct or by a declaration".[47] For the *Philip Morris* tribunal, "no undertaking or representation may have been grounded on legal rules of general application".[48] The *Manchester* tribunal observed that for an expectation "to be considered as a legitimate expectation protected by international law, something more than the existence of a

44 Micula v. Romania, *supra* note 12 [669].

45 See for example: CMS v. Argentina, ICSID Case No. ARB/01/8, Award (12.05.2005) [275], LG&E v. Argentina, *supra* note 34 [133], BG v. Argentina, *supra* note 37 [310], National Grid v. Argentina, *supra* note 20 [178], Electrabel v. Hungary, *supra* note 16 [7.78], Frontier v. Czech Republic, *supra* note 27 [285], Enron v. Argentina, *supra* note 19 [265], Tecmed v. Mexico, *supra* note 11 [154].

46 Tethyan v. Pakistan, ICSID Case No. ARB/12/1, Decision on Jurisdiction and Liability (10.11.2017) [958]. Similarly, for example: Duke Energy v. Ecuador, *supra* note 21 [360].

47 Total v. Argentina, *supra* note 38 [117]–[118] (however, in [122] the tribunal sems to recognize that the legitimate expectations can be based also on general legislation). In the words of the *Glamis Gold* tribunal, "investment-backed expectation requires, as a threshold circumstance, at least a quasi-contractual relationship between the State and the investor, whereby the State has purposely and specifically induced the investment" – Glamis Gold v. US, *supra* note 37 [766]. See also: Continental Casualty v. Argentina, ICSID Case No. ARB/03/9, Award (05.09.2008) [259], Metalpar v. Argentina, ICSID Case No. ARB/03/5, Award on the Merits (06.06.2008) [185]–[186]. See also for example: Art. 8.10(4) CETA, underlying the relevance of a "specific representation to an investor to induce a covered investment".

48 Philip Morris v. Uruguay, *supra* note 13 [431].

general legal framework is needed".[49] Similarly the *Horthel* tribunal, which commented that "general statutory norms thus do not give rise to legitimate expectations unless they contain a specific commitment of stability",[50] adding that "general rules of law do not generate legitimate expectations because they can be repealed or amended by the state".[51]

This position is closely related to another unresolved issue – namely, whether generally applicable legislation can amount to a specific commitment to something more than stability and consistency, protected as an investor's legitimate expectation.

1.2 *Spanish Saga Case Law*

The Spanish saga cases are an important contribution to the development of international investment law on the issues identified above. A violation of the FET was alleged in all of the Spanish saga cases.

The FET applied in the Spanish saga cases is envisaged in the second sentence of Art. 10(1) ECT and closely linked with the first sentence of the same provision. The relevant part reads as follows:

> Each Contracting Party shall, in accordance with the provisions of this Treaty, encourage and create stable, equitable, favourable and transparent

---

49 Manchester v. Poland, UNCITRAL, Award (07.12.2018) [495], although this comment was made outside the context of regulatory stability. See also for example the *El Paso* tribunal, which observed that:

> in order to prevent a change in regulations being applied to an investor or certain behaviour of the State, there can indeed exist specific commitments directly made to the investor – for example in a contract or in a letter of intent, or even through a specific promise in a person-to-person business meeting – and not simply general statements in treaties or legislation which, because of their nature of general regulations, can evolve. The important aspect of the commitment is not so much that it is legally binding – which usually gives rise to some sort of responsibility if it is violated without a need to refer to FET – but that it contains a specific commitment directly made to the investor, on which the latter has relied.

In the following paragraph, the tribunal recognized, however, that in limited circumstances, general legislation can create legitimate expectations:

> Second, a commitment can be considered specific if its precise object was to give a real guarantee of stability to the investor. Usually general texts cannot contain such commitments, as there is no guarantee that they will not be modified in due course. However, a reiteration of the same type of commitment in different types of general statements could, considering the circumstances, amount to a specific behaviour of the State, the object and purpose of which is to give the investor a guarantee on which it can justifiably rely

– El Paso v. Argentina, *supra* note 39 [376], [377].

50 Horthel v. Poland, *supra* note 26 [240].

51 Ibid [248].

> conditions for Investors of other Contracting Parties to make Investments in its Area. Such conditions shall include a commitment to accord at all times to Investments of Investors of other Contracting Parties fair and equitable treatment. […]

On its surface, the case law appears to be uniform that – after the initial *Charanne* and *Isolux* awards and with the sole exception of the *Stadtwerke* award – the FET was violated. This would, however, be an over-simplification. Part of the awards indeed declares that a violation of the FET occurred, caused by radical alterations to the applicable regulatory framework: *Eiser, Novenergia, Masdar, Antin, Foresight, Cube, NextEra, 9REN, SolEs, InfraRed, OperaFund, Watkins.* Other awards linked the violation of the FET with shortages of the New Regime, limiting compensation to the difference between the RRR as regulated by the respondent and any actual RRR below this threshold: *RREEF, BayWa, Stadtwerke* (although dismissing the claim, since all of the plants were above the RRR), *RWE, PV Investors, Hydro* and *Cavalum.*

Despite years of growth of investor-state dispute settlement ("ISDS") case law, as one arbitrator recently noted, "[t]he jurisprudence concerning specific commitments and fair and equitable treatment is, to say the least, inconsistent".[52] The Spanish saga cases contribute to the discussions concerning (i) the possibility of rooting legitimate expectations solely in general legislation, without any additional specific commitments, (ii) stability, (iii) the relevance of due diligence and (iv) the right to regulate and its limits.

•••

1.2.1 Charanne

The *Charanne* tribunal decided that 2010 legislation did not violate "regulatory stability", understood as an element of FET.[53] However, it clarified that this was not intended to "prejudice" the conclusions of any another tribunals concerning subsequent (post-2010) legislative amendments.[54] No post-2010 measures were disputed in this case.

---

52 Silver Ridge v. Italy, ICSID Case No. ARB/15/37, Dissenting Opinion of Judge O. Thomas Johnson (24.02.2021) [12].

53 Charanne v. Spain, SCC Case No. V 062/2012, Award (21.01.2016) [484].

54 Ibid [542].

TABLE 4 Fair and equitable treatment

No	Case name	Claim for FET	Outcome	Basis of violation
1	Charanne	Yes	Dismissed	N/A
2	Isolux	Yes	Dismissed	N/A
3	Eiser	Yes	Violation found	Regulatory stability
4	Novenergia	Yes	Violation found	Regulatory stability
5	Masdar	Yes	Violation found	Specific commitment + Regulatory stability
6	Antin	Yes	Violation found	Regulatory stability
7	Foresight	Yes	Violation found	Regulatory stability
8	RREEF	Yes	Violation found	Reasonable Rate of Return
9	Cube	Yes	Violation found	Regulatory stability
10	NextEra	Yes	Violation found	Regulatory stability
11	9REN	Yes	Violation found	Regulatory stability
12	SolEs	Yes	Violation found	Regulatory stability
13	InfraRed	Yes	Violation found	Specific commitment + Regulatory stability
14	OperaFund	Yes	Violation found	Regulatory stability
15	BayWa	Yes	Violation found	Reasonable Rate of Return
16	Stadtwerke	Yes	Dismissed	N/A (recognized Resonable Rate of Return)
17	RWE	Yes	Violation found	Reasonable Rate of Return
18	Watkins	Yes	Violation found	Regulatory stability
19	PV Investors	Yes	Violation found	Reasonable Rate of Return
20	Hydro	Yes	Violation found	Reasonable Rate of Return
21	Cavalum	Yes	Violation found	Reasonable Rate of Return
	Total	Yes - 21 No - 0	Dismissed - 3 Upheld - 18	

1.2.1.1 *Stability*

The tribunal considered that the FET is "included in the more general obligation to create stable, equitable, favourable and transparent conditions".[55] It then recognized a "good faith principle of customary international law", according to which a state cannot induce an investor to make an investment and generate legitimate expectations, only to subsequently ignore the commitments generated by these expectations.[56] However, in its view, there was no specific commitment *vis-à-vis* the claimants.[57] A set of legal norms – even if directed to a specific, limited group of investors – does not amount to "specific commitments" which give rise to legitimate expectations.[58] A different view would be an excessive limitation of a state's right to regulate its economy in accordance with the public interest.[59]

1.2.1.2 *Legitimate Expectations*

The tribunal did not adopt a clear position on whether a legal order *per se* can create legitimate expectations.[60] Instead, it concluded that a regulatory framework cannot generate legitimate expectations that its rules will never be modified.[61] The tribunal analyzed not only the regulatory framework itself, but also Spain's activities to promote investments in RE in Spain. It concluded that these activities were not "specific enough" to generate legitimate expectations.[62] It added that the contrary conclusion would mean "freezing" the regulatory framework, which would be equivalent to a stabilization clause.[63]

In the tribunal's view, registration in the RAIPRE was simply an administrative requirement, necessary to sell energy. As such, it did not create any legitimate expectation.[64]

55 Ibid [477].
56 Ibid [486].
57 Ibid [490].
58 Ibid [492].
59 Ibid [493].
60 Ibid [494]. However, the dissenting opinion suggests that the majority dismissed this possibility. Charanne v. Spain, SCC Case No. V 062/2012, Dissenting Opinion of Prof. Guido Santiago Tawil (21.12.2015) [5].
61 Ibid [499].
62 Ibid [496]–[497].
63 Ibid [503].
64 Ibid [510].

1.2.1.3 *Domestic Courts*

The tribunal reinforced this conclusion by referring to case law of the Spanish Supreme Court, which established that the domestic law allowed changes to the applicable regulations.[65] In light of this, the claimants could have "easily foreseen possible adjustments" to the regulatory framework.[66]

1.2.1.4 *Due Diligence*

For the tribunal, "preliminary and comprehensive" due diligence is required from foreign investors in a "highly regulated sector" such as energy.[67]

1.2.1.5 *Reasonableness and Proportionality*

The tribunal confirmed the existence of legitimate expectations that a state, when it modifies the regulatory framework which underpinned an investment, cannot act unreasonably, disproportionately, or contrary to the public interest.[68] Such expectations are based on the regulatory framework itself.[69] In the tribunal's view, the 2010 Disputed Measures were not unreasonable, disproportionate or contrary to the public interest and therefore did not violate legitimate expectations which existed.[70]

1.2.1.6 *Discrimination*

Moreover, the tribunal did not consider it discriminatory that the 2010 Disputed Measures applied to the PV sector, but not to the Wind energy sector. It considered them to be different sectors of the economy and recognized that states have freedom to apply different rules to such different sectors.[71]

1.2.1.7 *Retroactivity*

It also added that the 2010 Disputed Measures applied to operating power plants immediately after they entered into force, but did not apply retrospectively. In its view, nothing in international law prohibits states from adopting such immediately effective measures which apply prospectively.[72]

65 Ibid [504].
66 Ibid [505].
67 Ibid [507].
68 Ibid [514].
69 Ibid [515].
70 Ibid [536]–[537].
71 Ibid [538].
72 Ibid [548].

1.2.2 Charanne – Dissenting Opinion

1.2.2.1 *Legitimate Expectations*

In a dissenting opinion, one of the arbitrators stressed that legitimate expectations can be based on the legal order in force when an investment is made.[73] In his view, RD 661/2007 and RD 1578/08 created a "regime of promotion" and incentives to direct private capital in a determined direction, an objective which most probably could not have been achieved otherwise.[74] He considered these two regulations to be decisive for the claimants to make the investment in the PV plants. As a result, they could have legitimately expected that the tariff regime would be maintained unaltered.[75] This regime was not addressed to an undefined audience or an indefinite number of addressees but, rather, to a limited number of defined potential beneficiaries who had the capital required to invest in the PV sector.[76]

In his view, it is unacceptable to think that there will not be legal consequences when a state modifies and eliminates the expected benefit after the investments were made and all the requirements under the applicable regulations were complied with.[77] Whilst there is no acquired right to the maintenance of a particular general legal regime, the state is obliged to pay compensation if it affects acquired rights or legitimate expectations.[78]

1.2.3 Isolux

1.2.3.1 *Stability*

In *Isolux*, the tribunal recognized that the obligation to create stable and favorable conditions, envisaged in the first sentence of Art. 10(1) ECT, are not stand-alone obligations, but form part of the FET.[79] It continued its analysis by determining whether the alleged legitimate expectations were reasonable. The analysis is based on what any prudent investor should know and effectively knows about the regulatory framework prior to making the investment. At the

---

73 Charanne v. Spain, Dissenting opinion, *supra* note 60 [5]:

> the creation of legitimate expectations for an investor is not solely limited to the existence of a "specific commitment" – whether of a contractual nature or based on statements or specific terms granted by the host State – but can also originate or be based on the legal order in force when the investment is made

(unofficial translation).

74 Ibid [7].

75 Ibid [6].

76 Ibid [8].

77 Ibid [10].

78 Ibid [11].

79 Isolux v. Spain, SCC Case No. V 2013/153, Award (12.07.2016) [764]–[766].

same time, this does not mean that an investor must undertake "extensive" legal due diligence.[80] However, the absence of a due diligence requirement is irrelevant if, prior to making the investment, the investor has personal knowledge which allows him to anticipate an unfavorable evolution of the regulatory framework. Thus, if new legislation is to be found to have violated legitimate expectations, it cannot have been foreseeable either by a prudent investor, or by the particular investor.[81]

1.2.3.2 *Legitimate Expectations*

The tribunal did not disagree that legitimate expectations can be based on general legislation, but it found this conclusion unjustified on the facts of the particular case.[82] The disputed investment was made on 29.10.2012.[83] In the tribunal's view, at that time, the regulatory framework was no longer capable of generating legitimate expectations that it will not be modified.[84] Several regulatory changes had taken place prior to that time, and further changes were inevitable.[85] The tribunal observed that, as of October 2012, "all the investors knew or should have known that the system was going to be modified" and "each investor could anticipate, not only a fundamental modification of the content of the Special Regime, but also cancellation of the regime, as long as the principle of the reasonable return guaranteed in the LSE is respected".[86]

1.2.3.3 *Domestic Courts*

The tribunal referred to the Spanish Supreme Court judgments, issued before the disputed investment was made. It was clear that, under Spanish law, the only limit on the government's ability to alter the regulatory framework was the LSE's concept of the RRR.[87] Therefore, any investor should have been aware that modifications to the regulatory framework were legal under Spanish law. The tribunal recognized that, whilst Supreme Court judgments do not formally bind it, they form part of the relevant factual matrix. As such, they inform the analysis of legitimate expectations.[88]

80 Ibid [781].
81 Ibid [781].
82 Ibid [784]–[785].
83 Ibid [784]. Although the decision to invest was taken earlier, in June, until this date it could have been revoked.
84 Ibid [784]–[785].
85 Ibid [787]–[788].
86 Ibid [803]–[804].
87 Ibid [789]–[792].
88 Ibid [793].

1.2.3.4 *Due Diligence*

In this dispute, it was established that the claimant had "perfectly known" the case law of the Spanish Supreme Court.[89] The local company (before the investment was made) had itself applied to the Spanish Supreme Court to complain about numerous reforms of the domestic laws.[90] Nonetheless, the tribunal stressed that it would have reached the same conclusion even without this contributing factor. In its view, one must assume the knowledge about the existence of important decisions of the supreme judicial authority about the regulatory framework of the investment, even in the absence of a requirement to conduct "extensive" legal due diligence.[91]

The tribunal distinguished between retroactivity and the immediate application of the new legislation, which in this case "does not revoke acquired rights" regarding the operation of the plants.[92]

1.2.4 Isolux – Dissenting Opinion

1.2.4.1 *Legitimate Expectations*

In his dissenting opinion, one of the arbitrators disagreed with the majority's "vision" of legitimate expectations. He underlined that general legislation could create a "commitment" and that those legitimate expectations can be created by a regulatory framework, particularly if it is designed to attract foreign investment.[93] Until this moment, he seems to be in line with the majority's view. The diverging conclusions are most probably explained by a different assessment of the date of the disputed investment. The dissenter considered 29.06.2012 to be the relevant date, as opposed to 29.10.2012 which was applied by the majority.[94] The dissenter considered that, when the investment was made, the claimant could not have known that Spain would remove the FITs.[95]

The dissenter underlined the states' right to modify any law for public interest reasons and that there is no acquired right to expect the maintenance of a particular general legal regime. However, a state is obliged to pay compensation if such reform adversely affects acquired rights or legitimate expectations. He considered this to be a "typical event of states' responsibility for legal activity,

89 Ibid [795].
90 Ibid [818].
91 Ibid [794].
92 Ibid [814].
93 Isolux v. Spain, SCC Case No. V 2013/153, Dissenting Opinion of Prof. Guido Santiago Tawil (06.07.2016) [3]–[4].
94 Ibid [5].
95 Ibid [8].

broadly recognized" in academic writings and comparative law and also recognized in Spanish law since at least the middle of the twentieth century.[96]

The dissenter added that there is no difference between the removal of FITs (granted in RDs) and removing the RRR (granted in the LSE). If it were permissible to cancel the FIT system without compensation, this should make it possible by analogy to cancel the guarantee of RRR contained in Art. 30(4) LSE.[97]

1.2.5 Eiser

1.2.5.1 *Stability*

In *Eiser*, the tribunal observed that the FET protects investors "from a fundamental change to the regulatory regime in a manner that does not take account of the circumstances of existing investments made in reliance on the prior regime" and "against the total and unreasonable change".[98] It recognized that investment treaties do not eliminate a state's right to modify its regulatory regime to respond to "evolving circumstances and public needs", absent "explicit undertakings directly extended to investors". Whilst the FET does not give "a right to regulatory stability per se", the question is whether compensation is due as a result of a state exercising its right to regulate.[99] While Spain was entitled to address the public policy problem of tariff deficit, it was obliged to adopt reasonable measures and to respect its obligations under the ECT.[100]

1.2.5.2 *Domestic Courts*

In the tribunal's view, the Spanish Supreme Court's judgments are irrelevant, because they do not address the conformity of Spain's measures with the ECT.[101]

1.2.5.3 *Treaty Interpretation*

The tribunal confirmed that the ECT must be applied in accordance with the VCLT (to which the host state and both home states are parties)[102] and that the FET must be interpreted "in the context of a particular treaty in which it is found, not on some Platonic plane".[103] The tribunal looked at the purpose of the ECT, its objectives and principles, and the concepts of legal stability

96 Ibid [9].
97 Ibid [12].
98 Eiser v. Spain, ICSID Case No. ARB/13/36, Award (04.05.2017) [363].
99 Ibid [362].
100 Ibid [371].
101 Ibid [373].
102 Ibid [375].
103 Ibid [376].

and transparency.[104] It also noted that the first sentence of Art. 10(1) ECT reinforces the emphasis on ensuring the stability of the legal regime.[105] All of this led the tribunal to conclude that the FET "embraces an obligation to provide fundamental stability in the essential characteristics of the legal regime" relied upon by investors when making long-term investments.[106] Whereas regulatory regimes can evolve, they "cannot be radically altered as applied to existing investments in ways that deprive investors who invested in reliance on those regimes of their investment's value".[107] Investors must have expected "some changes" to their "regulated investment", they were entitled to expect that the host state "would not drastically and abruptly revise the regime, on which their investment depended, in a way that destroyed its value".[108]

1.2.5.4 *Regulatory Revolution*

Having made these general comments on the stability of the regulatory framework, the tribunal turned to the changes introduced by Spain. It noted that the New Regime reduced the revenues of one disputed plant by 66% when compared to the projections under the Special Regime.[109] The New Regime provided for a reduced target rate, based on a hypothetical "efficient" plant. It ignored the real return obtained by each of the plants, whilst the claimants incurred higher initial construction and financing costs than in a standard installation, with the goal of increasing its production.[110] The Spanish officials performed an "idealized" RRR, calculated on the basis of estimates of the asset values and costs of a hypothetical "standard installation".[111] However, the respondent did not explain the reasons behind its change of opinion between 2007 and 2013 as to what constituted an RRR.[112] The New Regime pays no regard to actual costs (including loan servicing) or to the actual efficiencies of specific, existing power plants.[113] Moreover, Spain "retroactively" applied these "one size fits all" standards to existing plants that were designed, financed and constructed based on the "very different" Special Regime.[114] The claimants

104 Ibid [377]–[380].
105 Ibid [380].
106 Ibid [382].
107 Ibid.
108 Ibid [387].
109 Ibid [389].
110 Ibid [393].
111 Ibid [397].
112 Ibid [394].
113 Ibid [398].
114 Ibid [400].

proved that they paid EUR 12 million in local taxes, outside the New Regime's assumptions, and that their actual costs were higher because their plants were located on owned, rather than rented, real estate.[115]

The tribunal underlined that the level of subsidy rests upon officials' estimates of a hypothetical installation, based on "their review of professional literature and studies and other "relevant" information". Two groups of private consultants were engaged. One withdrew (the reasons underpinning this decision were disputed), whereas the second issued a report after the regulators had already announced their decision.[116] The evidence about the reasons underlying the disputed measures "largely rested upon the written and oral testimony of Mr. Carlos Montoya, head of the solar department at IDAE". He acknowledged that they were not "based on a rigorous mathematical analysis of data" and, although he:

> expressed confidence that he knew "exactly" the costs required to construct a CSP plant anywhere in Spain, he was less informative or informed regarding the financing of such plants. When asked if such plants were usually constructed with project financing, he disavowed knowledge of the subject, saying "it's not something that I have analysed".[117]

As a result, the New Regime "deprived Claimants of substantially the total value of their investment", because the new, hypothetical standard plant used in the new calculations did not take into account the disputed plants' actual characteristics. They were designed to achieve higher production, but their

115 Ibid [406].

116 Ibid [403].

117 Ibid [404]. The tribunal's reasoning reveals its negative assessment of the respondent's approach, that all of the regulatory changes were based on one individual's personal knowledge. Even if his expertise covered technical issues, he affirmed that it did not extend to financial issues. It was also important that the claimant proved that some financially significant characteristics of their plants did not conform to the hypothetical costs standards of a hypothetical standard installation, for example the acquisition (as opposed to the lease) costs of real property. Yet another important aspect was that the respondent's own authorities, besides the Ministry's officials, and the CSP industry expressed reservations and disputed many assumptions underlying the New Regime, none of which altered the course of its implementation – [407]. Even the Spanish authorities (IDAE) estimated that about 77% of such projects would be debt financed – [411]. This was ignored by the official who designed the New Regime. It is notable that, in subsequent cases, Spain changed its strategy and stopped calling Mr. Carlos Montoya as a witness. It remains a question whether a causal link exists between this decision and the absence of any similar assessment of facts (or at least similar comments) in the subsequent cases.

capital costs were "about 40% higher" and their operation and management costs ranged from 13% to 18% higher than those of an "efficient" plant under the New Regime.[118]

1.2.5.5 *Retroactivity*

The tribunal did not isolate the prohibition of retroactivity as a separate element of the FET. However, the New Regime:

> in effect retroactively prescribe[d] design and investment choices that in regulators' view should have been incorporated in plants designed and built some years before. Such design choices – for example, to design higher cost plants capable of higher annual production and therefore of generating higher revenues under the RD 661/2007 regime – are retroactively condemned as inefficient and undeserving of subsidy.[119]

1.2.5.6 *RRR*

The revenues under the New Regime were far below the level required to cover the plants' actual financing and operating costs.[120] Forced rescheduling negotiations meant that, for the next several years, any revenues above operating costs went to external lenders, leaving nothing to repay the investors' loans or as part of a return of capital.[121] The value of the investment fell from 125 million Euro to 4 million Euro, which amounted to "deprivation of essentially all of the value of" the investment and therefore violated the FET.[122] The tribunal added that Art. 10(1) ECT does not entitle investors to an RRR at any given level, but it does guarantee them the FET.[123]

1.2.6 Novenergia

1.2.6.1 *Legitimate Expectations*

In *Novenergia*, the tribunal carefully considered the date on which the disputed investment was made, as this is an important factor when assessing the

118 Ibid [413]. The tribunal's observation on the substantial deprivation of the value of the investment fits more properly to an analysis of expropriation, rather than the FET. A violation of the FET can be found to have taken place without finding that a substantial deprivation has occurred. This comment stems most probably from the blended arguments presented by the parties during the proceedings and the tribunal's decision, based on judicial economy, to refrain from commenting on claims unless necessary.

119 Ibid [414].

120 Ibid [416].

121 Ibid [417].

122 Ibid [418].

123 Ibid [434].

existence of legitimate expectations.[124] It recognized that legitimate expectations can be "grounded in the legal order of the host State as it stands at the time the investor acquires or makes the investment".[125] They should be assessed at the time the claimant made its investment in the host state.[126]

The tribunal defined the moment the investment was made as the time of the "decision to invest" (13.09.2007 in that case), i.e. when the claimant acquired a 100% interest in the local company which owned a PV plant. This was considered as the relevant date even though, subsequently, the claimant made further investments to develop other disputed PV plants.[127] The tribunal determined that all of the plants in which the claimant had an interest were registered in the Special Regime in 2008, long before any of the disputed measures were adopted.[128]

1.2.6.2 *Stability*

The tribunal considered that Art. 10(1) ECT does not envisage a separate obligation for a state to create stable and transparent conditions for investors, but rather than these are "an illustration" of the obligation to respect legitimate expectations.[129] It then observed that legitimate expectations are the primary element of the FET.[130] Specific assurances underlying legitimate expectations can be explicit or implicit.[131] Moreover, an expectation that the regulatory framework will be stable "can arise from, or be strengthened by, state conduct or statements".[132] It is not necessary that the host state actually intended to create legitimate expectations. The question is merely whether a statement or conduct "objectively suffices" to create legitimate expectations for the recipient.[133]

1.2.6.3 *Regulatory Revolution*

The tribunal also recognized that investors must expect legislative reforms. Nevertheless, the FET protects them from "a radical or fundamental change to legislation or other relevant assurances by a state that do not adequately consider the interests of existing investments already made on the basis of

124 Novenergia v. Spain, SCC Case No. 2015/063, Final Arbitral Award (15.02.2018) [531].
125 Ibid [532].
126 Ibid [535].
127 Ibid [539].
128 Ibid [540].
129 Ibid [646].
130 Ibid [648].
131 Ibid [650].
132 Ibid [651].
133 Ibid [652].

such legislation".[134] Although regulatory regimes may evolve, a state's measures should not fall outside "the acceptable range of legislative and regulatory behaviour".[135] Consequently, an assessment of the FET "allows for a balancing exercise",[136] and the burden of proof is on the claimant.[137]

The tribunal then assessed whether the claimant's expectations were legitimate and reasonable in the present case. It looked at the Spanish regulatory framework and all of the surrounding statements made by the Spanish authorities, seeking to incentivize companies to invest heavily in the Spanish electricity sector. It concluded that the respondent's commitment "could not have been clearer".[138] This led it to conclude that the claimant had a legitimate expectation that there would not be "any radical or fundamental changes to the Special Regime".[139]

1.2.6.4 *Due Diligence*

The tribunal did not consider it necessary for the investor to conduct due diligence because RD 661/2007 "was so adamantly clear" that it did not require a "particularly sophisticated analysis".[140]

Based on this conclusion, the tribunal distinguished the facts of this case from previous cases. It observed that the *Charanne* case was different because it concerned only legislation enacted by Spain until 2010.[141] The *Isolux* case concerned an investment made in 2012, when it was clear that changes were being made to the Special Regime.[142] The facts of this case were similar to those in *Eiser*, although the impact of the regulatory changes was different.[143]

1.2.6.5 *Balancing Exercise*

In the tribunal's view, the 2010 Disputed Measures did not violate the FET. They limited the number of years and the number of hours of the energy production which benefitted from the Special Regime, but investors could not reasonably have expected that there would be no changes whatsoever to the regulatory regime. Moreover, in its balancing exercise, the tribunal paid attention to the

134 Ibid [654].
135 Ibid [655].
136 Ibid [657].
137 Ibid [660].
138 Ibid [667].
139 Ibid [681].
140 Ibid [679].
141 Ibid [685].
142 Ibid [686].
143 Ibid [687].

legitimate purpose underpinning the measures, understood as the need to address a tariff deficit. Spain had "a regulatory right" to react to the tariff deficit, albeit not an "unfettered right". At the time the tribunal analyzed, Spain had not crossed the line.[144] The same conclusion applied to RD 2/2013.[145]

In the tribunal's view, analyzing the FET involves "a balancing exercise, where the state's regulatory interests are weighed against the investors' legitimate expectations and reliance". The effect of destroying the value of an investment is only "one of several factors" to be taken into account in this exercise. However, it is a relevant factor, as it can prove the existence of a "change in the essential characteristics of the legal regime relied upon by investors in making long-term investments". [146]

The tribunal concluded that the 2013–2014 Disputed Measures were "radical and unexpected". The manner in which they were adopted fell "outside the acceptable range of legislative and regulatory behaviour" and "entirely transform[ed] and alter[ed] the legal and business environment under which the investment was decided and made".[147] Moreover, those measures had a significant damaging economic effect, causing decreased revenues of between 24% and 32%. This amounted to a "substantial deprivation" and violated the FET.[148] The tribunal concluded that the measures "have definitely abolished the fixed long-term FIT and have done so retroactively" (although it did not explain how it came to the conclusion on retroactivity).[149]

1.2.7 Masdar

In *Masdar*, the tribunal emphasized that the purpose of the FET is to ensure that the legal framework (i) is not to be subject to unreasonable or unjustified modification and (ii) is not modified in a manner contrary to specific commitments made to the investor.[150]

1.2.7.1 *Legitimate Expectations*

The tribunal underlined the states' freedom to amend their legislations.[151] However, this freedom is not "unfettered" and cannot go against specific

144 Ibid [688].
145 Ibid [689].
146 Ibid [694].
147 Ibid [695].
148 Ibid.
149 Ibid [697].
150 Masdar v. Spain, ICSID Case No. ARB/14/1, Award (16.05.2018) [484].
151 Ibid [485].

commitments given to investors.[152] Different types of specific commitments can create legitimate expectations.[153] The tribunal identified two "schools of thought" on specific commitments, according to which (i) commitments can arise from general statements contained in general laws, and conversely (ii) such commitments must be specific.[154]

1.2.7.2 *Due Diligence*

When analyzing the first school of thought, the starting point to determine legitimate expectations is the "legal order" of the host state at the time when the investment was made.[155] Within this approach, legitimate expectations require that "appropriate due diligence" is exercised regarding the existing laws.[156] They must be assessed on the basis of the "information that the investor knew and should reasonably have known" at the time of the investment.[157]

In this particular case, the claimant knew that (i) the respondent encouraged investments in the RE sector, (ii) the respondent adopted RD 661/2007 to increase incentives "beyond the mere prospect of a reasonable return", (iii) no Supreme Court authority had questioned the legality or validity of RD 661/2007 and (iv) an installation which complied with certain registration requirements within specified time limits would acquire the right to receive the FIT or a Premium.[158] In addition, the claimant performed "substantial due diligence", which included legal advice on the regulatory regime. The due diligence did not reveal "the slightest possibility" that the RD 661/2007 regime which applied to existing installations registered with RAIPRE would be swept away, but also that "any reasonable investor might foresee that they might be".[159] This satisfied the tribunal that the claimant "believed" it had legitimate expectation "that the laws would not be modified, as they included stabilisation clauses".[160]

Thus, if the first school of thought was to be followed, Art. 44(3) RD 661/2007, supplemented by Art. 4 RD 1614/2010, would be considered as a stabilization

152 Ibid [486]–[488].
153 Ibid [489].
154 Ibid [490].
155 Ibid [491]. In [492]–[493] the tribunal noted in this respect the dissenting opinions of arbitrator Tawil in the *Charanne* and *Isolux* cases.
156 Ibid [492]–[493].
157 Ibid [494].
158 Ibid [496].
159 Ibid [497], [498].
160 Ibid [499].

clause.[161] They would prohibit "any modification of the law, so far as investors, which had made investments in reliance upon its terms, were concerned".[162]

The tribunal then analyzed the second school of thought, according to which legitimate expectations cannot result from general regulations and that "something more is needed", as a stabilization clause included in law "is just as much subject to change as all the other dispositions of the law in question" and a limitation on legislative power "can only be derived from constitutional principles in the internal legal order and possibly rules of *jus cogens* in the international legal order".[163] Thus, if one adopts this approach, legitimate expectations cannot be created by stabilization clauses in general legislation.[164]

1.2.7.3 *Specific Commitments*

The tribunal avoided endorsing any particular school of thought. It concluded that, regardless of the approach, the claimants received specific commitments that RD 661/2007 would remain unaltered.[165] This resulted in finding that the FET had been violated.[166]

161 Ibid [500]–[502].

162 Ibid [503].

163 Ibid [504].

164 Ibid [505]–[507].

165 Ibid [521]. The tribunal refrained from expressing its view on whether a stabilization clause, contained in generally applicable law, is sufficient to create legitimate expectations that a regulatory regime will remain unchanged. The award suggests that the answer would be positive if this were the case. However, the tribunal chose not to take a firm position by referring to the facts of the present case which, in its view, sufficiently distinguished it from other cases and allowed it to conclude that a "specific commitment" had been made. One can guess that this approach allowed the tribunal to reach a unanimous decision and issue an award without a dissenting opinion (as occurred in relation to its conclusions on remedies, where the tribunal noted that it "has been unable to reach an overall consensus as to its conclusions" and emphasized that the relevant parts of the award "largely reflect the view of a majority of the Tribunal" – [547]). If these assumptions are true, the approach may be considered reasonable. However, looking at this approach from outside the arbitrators' deliberations, the approach seems controversial. The first element which supposedly distinguishes the case – the written resolutions of registration – were typical and nothing extraordinary. Although in the letters sent to the authorities, the investor requested confirmation of the economic conditions for the whole operational life of the CSP plants, the replies do not confirm it. Rather, they confirmed that "currently", i.e. as of the date of their issuance, the applicable regime was that arising from RD 661/2007. Thus, the "distinguishing factors" are actually not distinguishing at all. They can be considered as an "excuse", allowing the majority of the tribunal to avoid stating that the stabilization clause in Art. 44(3) RD 661/2007 was capable of generating legitimate expectations under Art. 10(1) ECT.

166 Ibid [522].

In the tribunal's view, the whole procedure required to benefit from the tariffs granted by RD 661/2007 constituted a "very specific unilateral offer from the State". The state "guaranteed the stability of the benefits, if the investors fulfilled a certain number of conditions, both procedural and substantial, during a certain window of time". This offer was accepted by the investor by constructing plants and formally registering them in the RAPIRE within a prescribed timeframe.[167]

The tribunal noted that, in the *Charanne* case, registration with RAPIRE was considered to be "a mere administrative requirement with no specific consequences".[168] It arrived at a different conclusion on the facts of the *Masdar* case.[169] At the pre-registration phase, each of the three CSP plants received a letter entitled "resolution", confirming that registration and that the economic regime regulated in RD 661/2007 had been granted.[170] The letter confirmed that "the economic regimen for the facilities [...] will be as foreseen in" RD 661/2007.[171] Later, the claimants sent three letters to the Spanish authorities, each one on behalf of each of the CPS plant, requesting that: "[...] the compensation conditions for the facility throughout its operating life be communicated".[172] The authority replied to each of the three letters, in which it "communicated" that "currently" the applicable retribution "consists of the tariffs, premiums, upper and lower limits and supplements established in" RD 661/2007.[173] As a result, the tribunal concluded that the RAPIRE registration

167 Ibid [512]–[513].

168 Ibid [514].

169 Ibid [515].

170 Ibid [516]: "Resolution of the Directorate General for Energy Policy and Mines, through which the [relevant Plant], is registered in the Pre-Allocation Registry for Compensation and to which to economic regime regulated in Royal Decree 661/2007, dated 25 May, is granted".

171 Ibid [517], the relevant part of the letters:

> In accordance with the provisions of Section 1 of the Fifth Temporary Provision of the aforementioned Royal Decree Law, the economic regimen for the facilities that are registered in the Pre- Allocation Registry for Compensation, in application of the provisions of the Fourth Temporary Provisions of the same, will be as foreseen in Royal Decree 661/2007, dated 26 September

(without emphasis of the tribunal).

172 Ibid [518].

173 Ibid [519], full quotation of the relevant part of the replies:

> [c]ommunicates that, currently, and by virtue of the provisions of section 1 of the fifth transitional provision of Royal-Decree-law 6/2009, dated 30 April, the retribution applicable to the installations consists of the tariffs, premiums, upper and lower limits and supplements established in Royal Decree 661/2007, dated 25 May [...]

(without emphasis of the tribunal).

resulted in Spain providing written assurances that the plants would benefit from the RD 661/2007 regime for their operational lifetime. It "would be difficult to conceive of a more specific commitment" confirming that each of the CSP plants in question qualified under the RD 661/2007 economic regime for their "operational lifetime".[174]

1.2.7.4 *Retroactivity*

The tribunal did not refer to retroactivity in its analysis of liability. However, in its analysis of the amount of compensation it noted that the New Regime "had retroactive effect", which justified including lost historical cash flows in the compensation assessment.[175]

1.2.8 Antin

1.2.8.1 *Stability*

In the *Antin* case, the tribunal started its analysis by noting that Art. 10(1) ECT is to be applied in accordance with Art. 31 VCLT.[176] The tribunal looked at the ordinary meaning of the words "fair" and "equitable". It added that they cannot be interpreted in isolation of the context, object and purpose of the ECT.[177] It looked at Art. 2 ECT and noted that the purposes stated in this provision emphasize the ECT's role in providing a legal framework to promote long-term cooperation, "suggesting that the ECT is conceived as enhancing the stability required for such cooperation".[178] This is confirmed also in the objectives and principles of the European Energy Charter which, in turn, refers to the "formulation of stable and transparent legal frameworks creating conditions for the development of energy resources".[179] The tribunal concluded that Art. 2 ECT refers to a legal framework that is "stable, transparent, and compliant with international legal standards".[180] It then added that the stability of the legal regime is reinforced in Art. 10(1) ECT, which uses "shall" and therefore is not "merely a suggestion or a recommendation", but an obligation to "create stable, equitable, favourable and transparent conditions".[181] In fact, it understood that "stability of the conditions" is a "leitmotiv" of the ECT.[182]

174 Ibid [520].
175 Ibid [651].
176 Antin v. Spain, ICSID Case No. ARB/13/31, Award (15.06.2018) [517].
177 Ibid [518].
178 Ibid [520].
179 Ibid [521]–[522].
180 Ibid [523].
181 Ibid [524]–[525].
182 Ibid [526].

In the light of the text and context of the ECT, the stability requirement neither cancels nor "extremely limits" the states' regulatory powers. The limits on regulatory powers imposed by the ECT are higher than those under the minimum standard of international law, as the ECT lays down specific obligations on that issue.[183] These limits do not prevent states from amending their legislation, provided that the given state does not "suddenly and unexpectedly eliminate the essential features of the regulatory framework in place". [184] The tribunal interpreted Art. 10(1) ECT as containing an obligation to afford "fundamental stability" with regard to the "essential characteristics of the legal regime relied upon by the investors in making long-term investments". This allows for the evolution of legal frameworks and for states to use their regulatory powers to adapt their legal frameworks to changing circumstances in the public interest. It prohibits, however, radical alterations – understood as stripping the legal framework of its key features – as applied to existing investments made in reliance on the hitherto legal framework.[185]

Within the context of the ECT, the tribunal viewed the obligation to provide a stable and predictable legal framework as not being a separate obligation but, rather, one which is inherent in the FET.[186]

1.2.8.2 *Legitimate Expectations*

Regarding legitimate expectations, the tribunal first reiterated that they must be based on an objective standard and analyzed on a case-by-case basis.[187] Second, they must be assessed as of the moment of making the investment. Attention must be paid to circumstances which existed at that moment in time and "information that the investor had or should reasonably have had, had it acted with the requisite degree of diligence (considering its expertise)", without the benefit of hindsight.[188] Third, an "affirmative action" from the state is needed for legitimate expectations to arise. This can take the form of specific commitments or by way of representations, for example with respect to "certain features of a regulation aimed at encouraging investments in a specific sector".[189]

The tribunal observed that, through the Special Regime, the respondent "sought to encourage further investments in its RE sector to meet the targeted

183 Ibid [530].
184 Ibid [531].
185 Ibid [532], [555].
186 Ibid [533].
187 Ibid [536].
188 Ibid [537].
189 Ibid [538].

growth in certain technologies".[190] The tribunal referred to the CNE report and the 2007 Press release, PER 2005–2010 as well as express references to the principles of stability and predictability referred to in the preambles of RD 661/2007 and RD 1614/2010.[191] It noted that the preamble of RD 1614/2010 recognized that "the stability and predictability of the regime were key to attaining Spain's policy goals regarding RE technologies and further provides that any changes to the regime must ensure the legal security of the investments".[192] It also underlined that the reasoning of an administrative act, as expressed in its preamble, "exposes the motives" of the state's actions. Here, they expressed the respondent's intention to guarantee the stability of the legal and economic regime which applied to RE investments. The tribunal concluded that "the stability of the regulatory regime for investments in the RE sector was thus the leitmotiv of Spain's acts" at the relevant time.[193]

It considered registration with the RAIPRE to be more than merely an administrative requirement. Given the precision and detail of the regulatory framework, particularly in Arts. 44(3) RD 661/2007 and 4 RD 1614/2010, Spain's conduct "falls squarely" into the type of acts intended to give rise to investors' legitimate expectations.[194] The tribunal added that, even if one disagreed with that conclusion, these provisions of local law reflect a "commitment to ensuring the stability and predictability of the existing economic regime".[195]

1.2.8.3 *Regulatory Revolution*

The tribunal recognized that legitimate expectations do not entitle an investor to assume that the legislative framework will be frozen in time. They do not equate to the immutability of the legal framework.[196] It then analyzed whether the exercise of the state's regulatory powers altered the "essential features" of the framework relied on by the investor.[197] It noted that the essential features were considered by the tribunal in *Charanne* to be not only the FIT,

190 Ibid [540].
191 Ibid [541]–[546].
192 Ibid [547].
193 Ibid [548].
194 Ibid [552]:

> Given the precision and detail exhibited in the royal decrees, particularly the contemplation that the treatment would be accorded for a defined period of time, the Tribunal has no difficulty in concluding that this falls squarely into the type of State conduct that was intended to, and did, give rise to legitimate expectations of the Claimants.

195 Ibid [553].
196 Ibid [555].
197 Ibid [556]–[557].

but also privileged access to the electricity transmission and distribution grid. The tribunal concluded that, regardless of whether it adopted this approach or alternatively concluded that only the FIT constituted an essential feature of the regime, Spain had violated Art. 10(1) ECT.[198]

1.2.8.4 *RRR*

The tribunal rejected the respondent's RRR argument. The methodology for determining payments to RE producers "must be based on identifiable criteria" to comply with the stability and predictability requirements under the ECT. As a result, the question is not whether the new regime provides an RRR, but how this RRR is calculated.[199] The tribunal concluded that the manner in which Spain determined the RRR under the New Regime (i) was not based on "identifiable criteria", but depended on the government's discretion, and (ii) was inconsistent with the representations on stability historically made by Spain to attract investments, which were based on objective and identifiable criteria.[200]

This conclusion was very evidence-driven, in particular by (i) witness testimony of an official who "conveyed that the 3% adjustment is simply what he considered to be an appropriate spread", (ii) the Spain's inability to present any studies (technical, financial or other) to support the parameters used to determine the features of a standard installation under the New Regime, and (iii) the lack of an "identifiable set of criteria for the revision of the remuneration for RE installations" scheduled under the New Regime.[201]

1.2.8.5 *Tariff Deficit*

Based on the evidence on the record, the tribunal concluded that the incentives under the Special Regime for the CSP plants (the plants in dispute) did not play a significant role in the accumulation of the tariff deficit. Therefore, the tariff deficit argument could not justify the elimination of the essential

198 Ibid [560]. Different outcome in the *Charanne* case resulted from the limited scope of regulatory changes considered by the tribunal in that case.

199 Ibid [562].

200 Ibid [568].

201 Ibid [564–566]. The "criticism" of the New Regime did not concern the amendment of the regulatory framework itself – which in theory could be based on the approach of "standard installations". It would have to be based, however, on identifiable criteria. The tribunal's decision seems to be heavily influenced by witness testimony given by a Spanish official, who appears to confirm that he determined the new levels of incentives based on his own assessment, with no studies having been conducted to inform decision makers. See a similar comment in the *Eiser* case in fn 117.

characteristics of RD 661/2007 and its replacement by a wholly new regime, lacking any identifiable criteria.[202]

1.2.9 Foresight

1.2.9.1 *Stability*

In *Foresight*, the tribunal reiterated that Art. 10(1) ECT must be interpreted in accordance with the VCLT.[203] Whilst Art. 31 VCLT is the primary rule of treaty interpretation, its Art. 32 applies "in limited circumstances".[204] The tribunal looked at the "context" of the ECT within the meaning of Art. 31(2) VCLT, concluding that the relevant context for the FET interpretation is the ECT's purpose to ensure that the national legal frameworks are "stable, transparent, and compliant with international legal standards".[205]

The tribunal added that, under the ECT, the obligation to ensure a stable regulatory framework is part of the FET.[206] It arises when the state has created legitimate expectations of such stability on the side of the investors.[207] Such legitimate expectations may be explicit or implicit, but they must be reasonable and objective.[208] There are limits to the degree of legal stability which can be legitimately expected. Investors cannot expect that regulatory frameworks will be frozen in time (unless a specific commitment to the contrary is made). This leaves enough space for states to reasonably modify their legislation without breaching legitimate expectations.[209] However, the FET precludes "a radical or fundamental change" in the regulatory framework.[210] A state's right to regulate in the public interest has limits, as otherwise investors' protection would be meaningless.[211]

---

202 Ibid [569–572]. The tribunal did not reject the theoretical possibility that the existence of a tariff deficit could constitute a reason to eliminate the essential characteristics of the Special Regime. It simply found that this as not proved by the evidence on the record. The tribunal seems willing to accept that such a public concern could justify more drastic changes to a regulatory framework, although probably only if the new regime was based on objective criteria and not governmental discretion.

203 Foresight v. Spain, SCC Case No. V 2015/150, Final Award (14.11.2018) [343].

204 Ibid [344].

205 Ibid [350].

206 Ibid [351].

207 Ibid [352].

208 Ibid [353]–[355].

209 Ibid [356]–[358].

210 Ibid [359].

211 Ibid [363]–[364].

1.2.9.2 *Legitimate Expectations*

The tribunal decided that the claimants lacked any legitimate expectations to receive the FIT specified in RD 661/2007 for the entire lifetime of their PV plants.[212] This was based on regular amendments of the Special Regime prior the enactment of RD 661/2007[213] and the Spanish Supreme Court's judgments rejecting challenges to these amendments.[214] The tribunal differentiated the facts of this case from those in *Masdar*, where the claimants "sought and received" specific clarification from the Spanish authorities.[215] The claimants had, however, legitimate expectations that the regulatory framework "would not be fundamentally and abruptly altered, thereby depriving investors of a significant part of their projected revenues".[216] They were based on the "express language" of RD 661/2007, "reinforced" by surrounding statements of Spanish officials, emphasizing the stability of the Special Regime for registered facilities.[217]

1.2.9.3 *Domestic Courts*

The tribunal added that a reasonable investor could not have interpreted the Spanish Supreme Court's case law as "a warning that Spain had the power to abrogate RD 661/2007 and replace it with a radically different support scheme".[218]

1.2.9.4 *Due Diligence*

The claimants did not conduct any due diligence analysis on the stability of the regulatory framework. Even though the legal report prepared by a Spanish law firm was "rather vague" on the issue, it was considered as sufficient. In the tribunal's view, a law firm "would have raised a red flag" if any risk of fundamental change to the regulatory regime was identified.[219]

---

212 Ibid [365].

213 Ibid [369].

214 Ibid [370]–[376].

215 Ibid [367].

216 Ibid [365], [377].

217 Ibid [378]:

> The Claimants' legitimate expectation that the remuneration and benefits their PV facilities received would not be radically changed were based foremost on the express language of RD 661/2007, which sets out fixed FiTs to be paid for entire operating life of a PV facility. This expectation was reinforced by statements of Spanish officials emphasizing the stability of the remuneration regime for PV facilities registered under RD 661/2007 and promoting the possibility of returns for investors well above 7%

(footnotes omitted).

218 Ibid.

219 Ibid [380].

1.2.9.5 *State Aid*

The tribunal considered the 2017 EC Decision as having "no bearing" on legitimate expectations, since the EC decision did not assess the Special Regime, within which the claimants had made their investment.[220]

1.2.9.6 *Regulatory Revolution*

The tribunal decided that the initial measures, from 2010 until the first 2013 measure, did not breach the FET. The claimants should reasonably have expected some changes to the regime, since there had been changes to the regime earlier, prior to their investment.[221] However, the measures which introduced the New Regime fundamentally altered the applicable legal regime. They did not "merely modify" the FIT promised to investors under RD 661/2007, but introduced a "number of fundamental changes" to the support scheme.[222] The majority agreed with the *Eiser* and *Novenergia* tribunals that, by adopting these measures, the respondent "crossed the line from a non-compensable regulatory measure to a compensable breach of the FET standard".[223]

This conclusion was based on a number of factors, in particular that the New Regime (i) switched the support scheme from an "at risk" model to a "regulated return" model, (ii) raised the bar for a "standard plant" to earn the target under the New Regime, (iii) based remuneration on capacity rather than production, adding an applicable cap of "maximum operating hours" cut off, (iv) is linked with market interest rates when compared to the previous fixed remuneration (indexed only to inflation).[224] In addition, the retroactive effect of the New Regime was relevant (i.e. the claw-back applicable to returns earned prior to the entry into force of the New Regime).[225] The New Regime reduced the RRR of the disputed facility from "between 7% and 9.5%" to 5.9% post-tax (7.398% pre-tax).[226]

---

220 Ibid [381].

221 Ibid [383]–[388].

222 Ibid [390].

223 Ibid [397]–[398].

224 Ibid [391], [393]–[394], [396].

225 Ibid [395].

226 Ibid [392]. The majority seems to accept the position which becomes more important for the awards rendered later in time with respect to the RRR. In [392] it notices that the RRR was reduced "from between 7% and 9.5% post-tax under RD 661/2007 to 7.398% pre-tax (5.9% post-tax) under the New Regulatory Regime". This change is considered as one of six considerations which led the majority to conclude that the new regime altered the fundamental characteristics of the scheme and that the respondent had "crossed the line". However, the majority fails to address how such a difference (and reliance on the concept of the RRR at all) justifies its conclusion. It is actually in line with the dissenter's view, that

1.2.10 Foresight – Dissenting Opinion

1.2.10.1 *Due Diligence*

In a dissenting opinion, one of the arbitrators disagreed on the limited relevance of due diligence analyses. In his view, the claimants could only have acquired legitimate expectations if they had conducted thorough due diligence on Spanish law and EU state aid law. He underlined that due diligence is a "prerequisite for the viability of a legitimate expectation's claim", particularly for investments in a "highly regulated activity".[227] He noted that the majority also commented that due diligence was "... in fact rather vague" on the issue of possible reforms to the regulatory framework.[228] He also referred to the Spanish Supreme Court judgments, which clarified that variations to regulated incentives are "regulatory risks".[229]

The dissenter concluded that failing to conduct due diligence was "negligent behavior" which did not justify the majority's "assumptions concerning Claimants' due diligence oversights and omissions".[230] As a result, he disagreed on the findings on liability and, consequently, on damages.[231]

1.2.11 RREEF

The tribunal in *RREEF* was the first to apply the RRR threshold for determining a violation of the FET.[232]

1.2.11.1 *Treaty Interpretation*

It commenced by underlining the role played by Art. 31 VCLT on the ECT interpretation.[233] It noted that the purpose of the ECT, expressed in its Art. 2, refers to the European Energy Charter, which therefore forms part of the "context" relevant for the ECT interpretation.[234] In the tribunal's view, the parties to the

---

the PV facilities in this case "continue to obtain a reasonable rate of return" – Foresight v. Spain, SCC Case No. V 2015/150, Partial Dissenting Opinion (30.10.2018) [48].

227 Foresight v. Spain, Partial Dissenting ..., ibid [40]–[41].

228 Ibid [42]–[44], [47].

229 Ibid [49].

230 Ibid [50]–[51].

231 Ibid [52]–[53].

232 RREEF v. Spain, ICSID Case No. ARB/13/30, Decision on Responsibility and on the Principles of Quantum (30.11.2018) [589].

233 Ibid [237].

234 Ibid [238], in particular its Title I:

> Within the framework of State sovereignty and sovereign rights over energy resources and in a spirit of political and economic co-operation, [the signatories] undertake to promote the development of an efficient energy market throughout Europe, and a better functioning global market, in both cases based on the principle of

ECT aimed "at realizing a balance between the sovereign rights of the State over energy resources and the creation of a climate favourable to the flow of investments on the basis of market principles in this field".[235]

The tribunal noted that the ECT does not regulate "fully and integrally" all possibly relevant matters and therefore "other applicable rules and principles of international law" may apply. Despite being silent on these matters, the ECT does not exclude concepts such as the states' right to regulate or the margin of appreciation.[236] Any potential waiver of exercise of a state's regulatory power is an extraordinary act, which must "emerge from an unequivocal commitment".[237] States enjoy a margin of appreciation in public international law, which must be recognized when applying the ECT.[238] It is not, however, unlimited, and can only be exercised insofar as it does not violate "the special legal regime, established by the ECT itself".[239]

1.2.11.2 *Legitimate Expectations*

The tribunal noted that the FET goes beyond the minimum standard of protection under the CIL.[240] Instead of trying to define the FET, the tribunal focused on identifying its elements: (i) transparency, (ii) constant protection and security, (iii) non-impairment including (iv) non-discrimination and (v) proportionality and reasonableness, as well as (vi) respect for the legitimate expectations of the investor.[241] Assessing legitimacy is an objective task, whereas "expectation" is assessed subjectively.[242] The "threshold of proof as to the legitimacy of any expectation is high and only measures taken in clear violation of the FET will be declared unlawful", because states "are in charge of the general interest and, as such, enjoy a margin of appreciation in the field of economic regulations".[243] An investor cannot legitimately expect that the

---

non-discrimination and on market-oriented price formation, taking due account of environmental concerns. They are determined to create a climate favourable to the operation of enterprises and to the flow of investments and technologies by implementing market principles in the field of energy.

235 Ibid [239].
236 Ibid [241].
237 Ibid [244].
238 Ibid [242].
239 Ibid [243].
240 Ibid [263].
241 Ibid [260].
242 Ibid [261].
243 Ibid [262].

conditions of its investment will be "immutable", and reasonableness is the main criterion in interpreting the FET.[244]

1.2.11.3 *Stability*

The tribunal then opined that the "stability" principle contained in Art. 10(1) ECT cannot be read in isolation and forms part of the FET.[245] In this sense, stability "is not an absolute concept" and "absent a clear stabilization clause, it does not equate with immutability". It does, however, exclude "any unpredictable radical transformation in the conditions of the investments".[246] The tribunal looked at Art. 44(3) RD 661/2007 and Arts. 4 and 5 RD 1614/2010 and observed that "adjustments" to the legal regime "were to be envisaged".[247] The tribunal acknowledged that undertakings and assurances given by States can be explicit or implicit.[248] It considered, however, that no representation invoked by the claimants could be considered as a "pledge" neutralizing the "clear possibility" of modifications stemming from the provisions of legal acts. Absent a specific commitment, there could be no legitimate expectations that the legal regime would remain unchanged.[249]

Based on the above, the tribunal considered that its task was to "determine whether the changes in the regulations equate to a substantial change to the legal framework applicable to investors".[250] It also concluded that the claimants had "an acquired right to a general regime guaranteeing the essential advantages they could reasonably expect when they made their investments".[251]

The tribunal considered that, before deciding whether the respondent had violated the ECT, it must analyze the scope and content of the claimant's legitimate expectations at the moment of making the investment, and ask whether the changes to the regulatory regime were "reasonable and proportionate".[252]

1.2.11.4 *Retroactivity*

The tribunal had no doubt, however, as to the existence of one violation of the "principle of stability", resulting from the retroactivity of the New Regime.[253]

244 Ibid [263].
245 Ibid [314].
246 Ibid [315].
247 Ibid [319].
248 Ibid [320].
249 Ibid [321].
250 Ibid.
251 Ibid [322].
252 Ibid [324].
253 Ibid [325]–[326].

Even though the New Regime "applies only for future remuneration", it "subtracts past remuneration (remuneration that was due under the previous regime) from the future remunerations". The tribunal agreed that this had the effect of clawing-back past remuneration, understood as shareholders' acquired rights at the moment when this remuneration was realized.[254] The tribunal compared this to dividends, to which shareholders have an acquired right once they are paid, which must be preserved not only in the past, but also for the future.[255]

1.2.11.5 *RRR*

The tribunal's focus then returned to legitimate expectations and the crucial question of whether the regulatory changes introduced by Spain were "a drastic and radical change".[256] In this context, the "reasonable return or profitability" was part of the guarantees given by Spain and, thus, part of the claimants' legitimate expectations.[257] Based on Art. 30(4) LSE and the preamble to RD 661/2007, the tribunal concluded that the guarantee of "reasonable return" or "reasonable profitability" was "the main specific commitment of Spain vis-à-vis the investors in the Special Regime".[258] Even though legitimate expectations did not extend to the right to receive the FIT, they entailed:

> a return for their investment at a reasonable rate which implies significantly above a mere absence of financial loss, the precise average rate taking into account the actual cost of money on capital markets for such investments as well as other objectives.[259]

The majority considered this was the only legitimate expectation the claimants had.

The tribunal identified four issues to be considered when deciding is legitimate expectations existed: (i) whether the state's conduct and representations gave rise to these expectations, (ii) whether the expectations are legitimate and reasonable, which must be assessed objectively (iii) whether the investor relied on the state's conduct or representations, and (iv) whether these expectations were frustrated by the disputed measures.[260]

254 Ibid [328].
255 Ibid [329].
256 Ibid [379].
257 Ibid [381], [386].
258 Ibid [384].
259 Ibid [387].
260 Ibid [388].

The tribunal considered it necessary to globally assess the situation that resulted from the reforms made by the respondent and the extent of the loss suffered by the claimants. Only within such a context was it possible to assess whether the measures were proportionate and reasonable.[261]

1.2.11.6 *Due Diligence*

The tribunal also noted that registration in the RAIPRE did not generate stronger or different expectations.[262] In the light the tribunal's determinations as to the context of legitimate expectations, the tribunal also did not consider it relevant whether the claimants had undertaken a due diligence analysis, since they were aware that the legal regime could be reformed in the future.[263]

The tribunal was also faced with an allegation of discrimination, as the IVPEE targeted RE generators which were incapable of passing-on the levy to the final consumers.[264] Before noting that it lacked jurisdiction over the IVPEE, the tribunal observed that the prohibition of discrimination is an inherent part of the FET and that, even if were not, it would be still applicable on the basis of CIL.[265]

1.2.11.7 *Reasonableness and Proportionality*

The tribunal then analyzed proportionality and reasonableness. These are intertwined, and "the breach of one of them normally entails the breach of the other one".[266] Reasonableness, in the context of a state's regulatory powers, includes factors such as: (i) legitimacy of purpose, "inasmuch as it represents interests of the society as a whole and does not alter the substance of the rights affected by the regulation", (ii) necessity, which implies a "pressing social need", with a threshold higher than being "useful" or "desirable", and (iii) "suitability", i.e. the measure must make it possible to achieve the objective.[267] Proportionality, in turn:

> is a weighing mechanism that seeks a fair balance between competing interests and/or principles affected by the regulation, taking into account all relevant circumstances. The regulation must be closely adjusted to the

261 Ibid [399].
262 Ibid [396].
263 Ibid [398].
264 Ibid [431].
265 Ibid [428].
266 Ibid [463].
267 Ibid [464].

> attainment of its legitimate objective, interfering as little as possible with the effective exercise of the affected rights.[268]

Reasonableness and proportionality enable a "global view of the situation".[269] It is, however, inseparable from the assessment of damages (if any).[270]

In this sense, the tribunal blended its analysis of liability with an analysis of the extent of loss suffered, in order to determine whether the state's measures were reasonable and proportional.

1.2.11.8 *Level of the RRR*

On the relevant facts, the tribunal decided that the claimants' legitimate expectations were limited to an RRR, i.e. that the IRR would exceed 6.86% post tax.[271] The RRR targeted by Spanish law corresponded to the IRR of a project, understood as the average annual returns of a project based on cash flows generated over the project's entire lifespan. Therefore, the tribunal considered the IRR as an indicator of the project's profitability.[272] The tribunal did not decide whether there exists a "general principle" defining the RRR. It decided that, in this case, it must be defined in accordance with Spanish law, and thus based on the LSE.[273]

With respect to the disputed CSP plants, the actual return earned, after the disputed measures entered into force, fell short of legitimate expectations. It fell below the RRR as calculated by the tribunal (though the actual IRR could not be determined). Consequently, the tribunal decided that Spain had violated its obligation to ensure an RRR, which in turn triggered an obligation to pay compensation calculated as the difference between the actual return and a reasonable return.[274] Compensation thus calculated would include compensation for the retroactivity of the New Regime.[275]

With respect to the disputed Wind energy plants, the actual IRR after the disputed measures entered into force was considered reasonable (13% pre-tax compared to the 7.398% after-tax target under the New Regime).[276] Neverthe-

---

268 Ibid [465].
269 Ibid [467].
270 Ibid [472], [475], [476].
271 Ibid [588]–[589].
272 Ibid [520]–[521].
273 Ibid [524].
274 Ibid [589].
275 Ibid [590].
276 Ibid [569].

less, the compensation was to be determined for the retroactive application of the New Regime also in this context.[277]

This is the first case in which the tribunal found that an investor's legitimate expectations were limited to expectations regarding an RRR. This had crucial consequences when calculating damages. The tribunal applied the concept of a legitimate expectation to a RRR to the full extent, i.e. not only when considering whether the violation of the ECT took place, but also when calculating the amount of compensation. In previous cases, if violations were found, the tribunals awarded compensation corresponding to the amounts of lost profits, comparing the Special Regime with the New Regime. Here, the tribunal considered this approach inappropriate. It decided that compensation should be calculated as to the difference between actual profits under the New Regime and the RRR guaranteed by the Special Regime.

The tribunal blended its analysis of the merits with damages, by postponing its decision regarding the reasonableness and proportionality of Spain's measures until actually calculating the claimants' loss.

1.2.12 RREEF – Dissenting Opinion

1.2.12.1 *Legitimate Expectations*

In a partially dissenting opinion, one of the arbitrators disagreed (i) that there were no other ECT violations and (ii) with the method of calculating compensation.[278] He further disagreed that (iii) the claimants had only one legitimate expectation, (iv) the change in regime did not constitute a breach of that expectation and (v) the determination of what constitutes an RRR in this case.[279]

The dissenter considered that Spain had admitted that one of the reasons for the change in regime was to reduce the claimants' profits, which he considered as "fatal" to Spain's case theory.[280] He viewed Spain's actions as a "bait-and-switch" pattern of behavior, i.e. that Spain initially sought to (and did) attract investments (the "bait"), and later – due to Financial Crisis and EC's requests to "to deal with its budget deficit" – Spain changed the levels of remuneration and profit capable of being achieved by the claimants (the "switch").[281] For him, this meant that the measures fell outside the state's margin of appreciation, because the profits they sought to reduce were the very profits that

277 Ibid [591].

278 RREEF v. Spain, ICSID Case No. ARB/13/30, Partially Dissenting Opinion of Professor Robert Volterra to the Decision on Responsibility and the Principles of Quantum (30.11.2018) [9].

279 Ibid [19].

280 Ibid [28].

281 Ibid [26].

the respondent had used to entice the claimants to invest.[282] He found it particularly convincing given that the respondent admitted in its pleadings that "its actions have not eliminated its tariff deficit but that its actions have extinguished the hopes of investors in the renewable energy sector for above-average profits".[283]

He also noted that the respondent's expert did not know whether the cost of capital had increased or decreased between 2007 and 2013. He understood that one of the reasons for changing the regime was due to the cost of capital. In fact, the evidence on the record proved that the cost of capital had remained stable during the relevant period.[284]

1.2.13 Cube

1.2.13.1 *Specific Commitments*

In *Cube*, the tribunal recognized that any legislation is susceptible to being amended. This is the reason why states can give assurances "that are set out or are implicit in legislation".[285] It decided that Spain made such an assurance with respect to RD 661/2007, that the regulated tariff regime "would continue to apply to power plants that opted for that regime and were registered as having been accepted into that regime".[286] This was a "sophisticated, carefully planned and durable regulatory regime designed to attract investments in renewable energy".[287] This representation on non-retroactivity concerns an issue over which Spain had control – its approach to future reforms of the regulatory system. Such a "grandfathering" provision leaves a wide range of possible responses to future developments, even though it excludes certain possibilities.[288]

The 2007 Press release accompanying the adoption of RD 661/2007 explained the reasons behind the government's approach as being: (i) to provide legal safety, (ii) to provide stability to the sector and (iii) to foster its development.[289] It was seen as "an explanatory statement by the Government as

282 Ibid [29].
283 Ibid [30].
284 Ibid [31], [33]–[35]. The dissenter's description of the shortages of Spain's expert suggests that he believed the New Regime was introduced capriciously, without proper analysis and preparation.
285 Cube v. Spain, ICSID Case No. ARB/15/20, Decision on Jurisdiction, Liability and Partial Decision on Quantum (19.02.2019) [275].
286 Ibid [276].
287 Ibid [282].
288 Ibid [278], [411].
289 Ibid [279].

to what the meaning and effect of RD 661/2007 was".[290] It was attributable to Spain, as it was published on the website of the competent ministry on the date of adopting RD 661/2007.[291]

The tribunal acknowledged that Art. 44(3) RD 661/2007 did not specifically exclude the possibility of being repealed by a later law. But it stated, as well as the mentioned 2007 Press release, that there will be no retrospective alteration of the regime applicable to existing facilities, registered under the Special Regime. If such a commitment could be repealed by later law, "it would be practically impossible for a State ever to give an undertaking upon which anyone could rely, or for legitimate expectations ever to arise".[292]

1.2.13.2 *RRR*

The tribunal noted that an attractive regulatory regime must be addressed to both greenfield investors, who construct plants, and to brownfield investors, who invest in plants that are already constructed by other investors and who wish to release and redeploy their capital. For a brownfield investor, the rate of return on the original investment is irrelevant. What matters is the predicted future income flows at the moment of acquisition. The ECT protects both.[293] The respondent's position on the RRR concerns only greenfield investors and ignores brownfield investors, so it was dismissed.[294]

1.2.13.3 *Domestic Courts*

The tribunal considered the case law of the Spanish Supreme Court to be irrelevant. First, the cases were resolved under domestic law, not under the ECT. Second, they concerned legal measures that preceded RD 661/2007, whereas this regulation aimed to alter the expectations operating under the earlier regimes.[295] On the contrary, the tribunal considered that the government was fully aware of the Supreme Court's case law and deliberately decided to introduce the Special Regime "for a long duration in order to attract sufficient investment that otherwise could not have been obtained".[296]

---

290 Ibid [273].

291 Ibid [277]. Whilst this reinforced the tribunal's analysis of RD 661/2007, most probably the same conclusions would have been reached even without the press release.

292 Ibid [289].

293 Ibid [285], [475].

294 Ibid [286]–[287].

295 Ibid [300].

296 Ibid [305].

1.2.13.4 *State Aid*

Finally, the tribunal rejected the argument that the Special Regime was unlawful state aid within the meaning of EU law. The obligations regarding state aid applied to Spain, and investors were entitled to assume that they had been considered when the legislation was drafted. They were not obliged to "second-guess the Respondent's legislature". Moreover, at the relevant period, when the investments were made, it was unclear that the tariff regime should have been regarded as state aid *per se*, let alone unlawful state aid.[297]

1.2.13.5 *Legitimate Expectations*

The tribunal then analyzed the disputed Hydro energy investments, which differed from the PV plants analyzed above because they were made later, in 2011 and 2012.[298] It observed that, at that time the regulatory regime was "largely the same" as that applicable when the PV investments were made, although with one important difference – namely, that Spain had already adopted certain regulatory changes "with retroactive effect". There were already signs that Spain would adjust the periods for which incentives were payable and the levels of the price incentives in order to address its tariff deficit.[299] In these circumstances:

> any reasonable investor would have taken a much more cautious view of the extent to which the continuation of the existing legal regime could be relied on, but would not have had reason to expect the complete abandonment of the Special Regime.[300]

This actually happened, when the investment committee of one of the claimants noted that there was a "real possibility" of "non-dramatic" changes in the regulated tariffs for Hydro energy plants, and even a "remote possibility" of "dramatic" changes.[301]

The tribunal decided that at this stage, changes to the Special Regime should have been reasonably anticipated.[302] However, this did not mean an anticipation of a "radical change in the nature of the Special Regime [...] amounting to an abandonment of the commitment to stability given in RD 661/2007". The

297 Ibid [306].
298 Ibid [272], [327].
299 Ibid [330].
300 Ibid [333].
301 Ibid [338]–[339].
302 Ibid [353].

ECT protects against such "fundamental changes".[303] Such protection does not amount to "petrification" of the legal regime, since the investors' financial interests can be protected in many ways.[304] Radical changes can happen, as long as they do not produce harmful effects for investors.[305] Since, at the relevant time, there was "evidently a climate of change", the tribunal applied the discount for regulatory risk at the quantum phase.[306]

The tribunal observed that the ECT does not protect legitimate expectations as a free-standing right, but only as part of the FET.[307] It added that a violation of legitimate expectations does not necessarily imply that there has been a breach of the FET.[308]

In the tribunal's view, a specific commitment is needed to create legitimate expectations. It found such a commitment included in the regulatory framework. In

> a highly-regulated industry, and provided that the representations are sufficiently clear and unequivocal, it is enough that a regulatory regime be established with the overt aim of attracting investments by holding out to potential investors the prospect that the investments will be subject to a set of specific regulatory principles that will, as a matter of deliberate policy, be maintained in force for a finite length of time. Such regimes are plainly intended to create expectations upon which investors will rely; and to the extent that those expectations are objectively reasonable, they give rise to legitimate expectations when investments are in fact made in reliance upon them.[309]

Such "promised stability" extends also to new owners of facilities if they are sold.[310] Based on this, the tribunal decided that, regarding the PV installations, the claimants had legitimate expectations that the relevant tariffs and premiums would be maintained.[311]

With respect to investments in Hydro energy installations, the claimants' legitimate expectations were limited to expecting a lack of "dramatic" or "fundamental" changes' in the Special Regime, and in particular that due remuneration would not be reduced to the RRR, as this would result in a material

303 Ibid [354].
304 Ibid [408].
305 Ibid [355].
306 Ibid [356]–[357].
307 Ibid [386].
308 Ibid [387].
309 Ibid [388].
310 Ibid [389].
311 Ibid [390], [311].

alteration of "the economic balance of the project" relied upon at the moment of making the investments.[312]

1.2.13.6 *Due Diligence*

With respect to due diligence, it was sufficient that the claimants "took professional advice on the matter and took it into consideration in making their investments", even without a "detailed written analysis".[313] The tribunal explained that if legitimate expectations are created by legislation, their justification is often grounded in legal due diligence reports. But the form of such due diligence is of "secondary significance". What is relevant is that legitimate expectations are based "upon a proper and thorough understanding of the nature and scope of the representation that is relied upon".[314]

In this case, the "documentary evidence" of legal due diligence was "very thin", with no record of detailed legal advice to affirm that no regulatory risk existed.[315] One of the claimants did not perform any due diligence by itself, but instead relied on the other claimant's due diligence.[316]

The tribunal considered that no evidence of "any particular form or scale of legal due diligence by external advisors" was required.[317] This was because (i) the text of RD 661/2007 "was itself clear and specific", (ii) the regulatory representations were reinforced by their clear and specific restatement in the 2007 Press release (iii) the respondent has not proven that "any more exhaustive legal analysis would have produced any different understanding of the Spanish measures" and (iv) the significance of the representations is not a matter of Spanish law, but of international law.[318]

1.2.13.7 *Regulatory Revolution*

The tribunal decided that the 2010 and first of the 2013–2014 Disputed Measures did not amount to a violation of the ECT.[319] RDL 9/2013 was the measure which initiated "a radical and decisive break with the earlier regime".[320] The tribunal concluded that Spain moved away "from a regime based on what were at the time of the investments 'promised' tariffs and premiums, to a regime based

312 Ibid [391], [440].
313 Ibid [304].
314 Ibid [393].
315 Ibid [394].
316 Ibid [406].
317 Ibid [396].
318 Ibid [401].
319 Ibid [419], [424].
320 Ibid [425].

on capped 'reasonable returns', and that this move represented a fundamental change in the economic basis of the relationship" between the investors and the host state.[321] Even though both regulatory regimes might by themselves be "reasonable and fair", it was:

> an unanticipated shift from one to the other in the face of an express statement that the tariff regime applicable to existing plants registered under the Special Regime would not be withdrawn, and after investments had been made with a view to profitability over a long term, steps over the line drawn

in Art. 10 ECT.[322] For these reasons, it was irrelevant that the tribunal found "nothing inherently improper" in the respondent's conduct.[323] The mere fact that an action was taken in good faith does not mean that it cannot breach the FET. Moreover, a lack of good faith does not automatically mean that there was bad faith, and no evidence of bad faith existed on Spain's part.[324]

Thus, the tribunal found that a violation of legitimate expectations had occurred with respect to the PV facilities[325] and with respect to Hydro energy plants, even though the latter were "narrower in scope and less well-defined, and less firm".[326]

1.2.14 Cube – Dissenting Opinion

1.2.14.1 *Legitimate Expectations*

In a dissenting opinion, one of the arbitrators disagreed with decision that there was a violation of legitimate expectations with respect to the Hydro energy plants. In his view, in 2011 and 2012 (when the Hydro energy investments were made), the conditions of the Spanish electricity regime had already "changed significantly".[327] It was already clear that the system "needed some re-equilibration".[328] The new regulations adopted prior to the Hydro energy

321 Ibid [427].
322 Ibid [428].
323 Ibid [430].
324 Ibid [446].
325 Ibid [432].
326 Ibid [440], [442].
327 Cube v. Spain, ICSID Case No. ARB/15/20, Separate and Partial Dissenting Opinion (19.02.2019) [7].
328 Ibid [9].

investments "must have put on alert every investor" and recognized that the Special Regime "was at the brink of failure".[329]

1.2.14.2 *Due Diligence*

In his view, the majority's explanation of its decision on this point is not persuasive.[330] First, even if it is true that the text of RDL 661/2007 was "clear and specific", 4 years had passed and "time had begun to dismantle the original factual framework".[331] Second, as professional investors, the claimants were "clearly negligent in assessing the regulatory risks" by not conducting proper due diligence.[332] Third, the majority's conclusion that such due diligence would probably not have led to another result is speculative and "grants too easily a blessing to a major management failure".[333] Fourth, even though legitimate expectations arise under the ECT, as opposed to domestic law, the factual circumstances in the host country are relevant.[334]

He explained that the above would not have deprived the investors of any protection as regards their Hydro energy plants. He referred to the concept of the RRR as the leitmotiv of the Spanish legislation.[335] Thus, the right to compensation would arise, but only if the New Regime violated the guarantee of the RRR.[336]

1.2.15 NextEra

In *NextEra*, the tribunal noted that Art. 10 ECT, as any treaty provision, is to be interpreted in accordance with Arts. 31 and 32 VCLT. As such, it found it unnecessary to analyze an "overall perspective" of the ECT's objectives.[337]

1.2.15.1 *Legitimate Expectations*

The tribunal affirmed that legitimate expectations are an "essential element" of the FET.[338] In this context, the regulatory framework by itself "in the circumstances

---

329 Ibid [14]. The dissenter presented this point of view only with respect to the investments made during the regulatory changes. He did not question the tribunal's approach with respect to the previous investments.

330 Ibid [18].

331 Ibid [19].

332 Ibid [20].

333 Ibid [21].

334 Ibid [22].

335 Ibid [23].

336 Ibid [24]–[25].

337 NextEra v. Spain, ICSID Case No. ARB/14/11, Decision on Jurisdiction, Liability and Quantum Principles (12.03.2019) [580].

338 Ibid [582].

of the present case" was insufficient to give rise to legitimate expectations that the investors would be "guaranteed" the terms of the Special Regime, as "legislation can be changed".[339] RD 661/2007 did not contain a stabilization clause and no legitimate expectations could be based on later regulations that merely confirmed the provisions of RD 661/2007.[340] Similarly, registrations in the Pre-RAIPRE and in the RAIPRE were a necessary part of the process for obtaining the benefits of the regulatory regime. As such, they were only administrative requirements and did not grant any right *per se*.[341]

However, the above was merely a context for analyzing the written reassurances received from the Spanish authorities, a central piece of the claimants' legitimate expectations argument.[342] The tribunal differentiated 5 categories of relevant statements: (i) statements made in writing by Spanish officials to the claimants, (ii) statements made in writing by the claimant's representatives to Spanish officials, which were not explicitly contradicted or disagreed with by the Spanish officials (notwithstanding that they were also not responded to or agreed with), (iii) the claimants' internal memoranda reporting on meetings with the Spanish officials, (iv) witness statements indicating the claimants' understanding of the Spanish position, as well as (v) statements made to industry.[343]

Each of the categories had a different "level of probity".[344] The first category could "reasonably be taken as statements that the Spanish government had no intention of making significant changes to the investment regime set out in RD 661/2007 and that this could be relied on by an investor".[345] The tribunal observed that, although they contained no clear commitment to stability, these letters could still form the basis of legitimate expectations of certainty and security.[346] With respect to the third and fourth categories, the respondent did not deny that such statements had been made and decided not to cross-examine relevant witnesses on what they said they had been told by the Spanish officials. As a result, the tribunal relied upon this evidence.[347]

339 Ibid [584].
340 Ibid [586].
341 Ibid [585].
342 Ibid [587].
343 Ibid [588].
344 Ibid [589].
345 Ibid [592].
346 Ibid [593]. These letters are incomparable to those analyzed in the *Masdar* case. See: fn 170–172.
347 Ibid [590].

The claimants' legitimate expectation that there would be no radical changes made to the economic regime based on RD 661/2007 was "reinforced" by the manner in which RD 1614/2010 was adopted i.e. extensive consultations with industry had taken place, with amendments proposed by the claimants' (among others) being accepted by the government.[348] Thus, the claimants had legitimate expectations that the applicable legal regime would not be "changed in a way that would undermine the security and viability of their investment".[349]

1.2.15.2 *Regulatory Revolution*

The tribunal decided that the claimants' legitimate expectations in this regard were breached when Spain's regulatory "regime was fundamentally and radically changed", and its reforms introduced changes that "went beyond anything that might have been reasonably expected by Claimants when they undertook their investment".[350] Even though individually, the changes might not have violated the FET, collectively they made the regulatory regime applicable to the investment "substantially different".[351]

1.2.15.3 *Due Diligence*

The tribunal rejected the argument that the claimants had failed to carry out due diligence. The fact that the claimants refused to disclose the legal advice they obtained did not entitle the tribunal to draw adverse inferences. The mere fact that the claimants received legal advice on the regulatory regime was sufficient to satisfy the due diligence requirement.[352]

1.2.15.4 *RRR*

The respondent's argument that legitimate expectations were limited to an RRR and that both legal regimes (i.e. both before and after the disputed reforms) aimed to deliver the RRR did not convince the tribunal. It viewed the assurances made by the Spanish authorities as concerning regulatory certainty and stability, not an RRR. These legitimate expectations were violated by a

348 Ibid [594].

349 Ibid [596].

350 Ibid [599].

351 Ibid [598].

352 Ibid [595]. This is interesting also from the perspective of adverse inferences drawn from the non-disclosure of documents. The tribunal did not draw any adverse inferences from the fact that the claimants did not produce the legal opinions they received as part of their due diligence, probably relying on client-attorney privilege.

failure to provide such certainty and security when fundamental changes were made to the regime.[353]

1.2.16 9REN

In *9REN*, the tribunal commenced by defining the "threshold issue" to be decided – whether the facts created legitimate expectations that the benefits set out in the Special Regime were irrevocable.[354]

1.2.16.1 *Domestic Courts*

The tribunal analyzed the Spanish Supreme Court's case law and its impact on the existence of legitimate expectations. Whilst this case law "is entitled to great respect", it addresses a different issue than the issue before the tribunal, which was concerned only with international law obligations (as opposed to domestic law, addressed by the Spanish Supreme Court).[355] It was unsurprising for the tribunal that, under domestic law, the Spanish Supreme Court affirmed that regulatory measures may be modified by the exercise of Spain's sovereignty. But the tribunal's task was to decide "whether such changes can be made by Spain without financial consequences under the ECT".[356] The tribunal then referred to Art. 27 VCLT to reiterate that a state cannot rely on provisions of internal law to justify its failure to perform a treaty.[357]

The tribunal then analyzed the argument that Spain had not only a right but also a duty to regulate its energy sector. In this context, the tribunal had no doubt that Spain possessed the requisite constitutional authority "to evolve its regulatory system to keep abreast of changing circumstances". The question is, however, "whether under the ECT the cost of such changes should fall on the investors who were attracted to Spain's renewable energy by specific promises of stability rather than fall on Spanish consumers or Spanish taxpayers generally".[358] For the tribunal, a decision in favour of the claimant would not question the validity of the disputed measures under Spanish law, but its effect would simply transfer their cost back to Spain.[359]

---

353 Ibid [600].

354 9REN v. Spain, ICSID Case No. ARB/15/15, Award (31.05.2019) [214].

355 Ibid [242].

356 Ibid [243].

357 Ibid [244].

358 Ibid [253]. The tribunal explicitly departed from the approach adopted by the *Charanne* tribunal, which – in its view – placed too much emphasis on the case law of the Spanish Supreme Court. It considered as irrelevant to assessing whether a violation of the ECT had occurred.

359 Ibid [258].

1.2.16.2 *Specific Commitments*

The tribunal then considered Art. 44(3) RD 661/2007 as a "specific undertaking", which can be made in legislation provided that its addressees are identifiable. A promise is specific if it is addressed to an identifiable class of persons, namely prospective investors whose money was solicited by Spain's FIT program.[360] This particular provision "created legitimate expectations of stability in accordance with its terms".[361] Even though the existence of legitimate expectations requires "a clear and specific commitment", in the tribunal's view such a commitment can be contained in legislation provided that it is adopted to induce investment, succeeds in attracting investment and then results in a loss for the investor.[362]

In this context, the tribunal referred to the legal analysis of this issue in the *Masdar* case, which identifies:

> a spectrum of situations where a claimant relies only on a bare regulatory measure addressed to the entire world, which lies at the weaker end of the spectrum, to clear and specific undertakings to a particular investor, which lies at the strongest end.

This did not change its assessment. Even though, in this case, the claimant did not obtain specific letters of commitment, such letters present in the *Masdar* case "simply confirmed what was already in RD 661/2007 and were issued after not before the claimant in that case made its investment".[363]

The tribunal referred to the 2007 Press release which accompanied the adoption of RD 661/2007, in which the Spanish government "affirmed with crystal clarity" that it assured investors of the stability guarantee.[364] "Clear and obvious paramount purpose" of Art. 44 RD 661/2007 was "the inducement of investment in renewable energy that Spain's earlier incentives had failed to attract".[365] In the tribunal's view, Spain was under time pressure from the EU to meet its RE targets, and in 2007 it recognized that its offer to potential investors needed to be dramatically improved. This materialized in RD 661/2007.[366]

360 Ibid [257].
361 Ibid [259].
362 Ibid [295].
363 Ibid [299].
364 Ibid [265].
365 Ibid [266].
366 Ibid [267].

The tribunal concluded that the claimant relied on the guarantee provided in RD 661/2007 at the moment of making the investment. The claimant's plain reading of the text of the regulation was reinforced by a due diligence report prepared by a law firm.[367] There was a "regulatory guarantee of price stability".[368]

1.2.16.3 *Legitimate Expectations*

The tribunal differentiated between Art. 44(3) RD 661/2007 and the text of RD 1578/2008, which contained no explicit "grandfathering" of existing RE facilities. This made it critical to identify the date of the investment.[369] Spain's argument was that the investment was made in stages, from 2008 to 2011.[370] The tribunal decided that an assessment of the reasonableness and legitimacy of the expectations must take place in connection with the date when the investment was made, which was decided to be 23.04.2008 – i.e. when the claimant acquired a Spanish company which developed the projects.[371] The fact that one of the disputed plants was registered later, not under RD 661/2007 but under RD 1578/2008 (which did not contain the same stability guarantee), was irrelevant to the question of whether legitimate expectations had arisen (although it was relevant for quantum).[372]

The tribunal then noted that legitimate expectations based upon a specific representation are only one factor in deciding whether there was a violation of the FET.[373] It concluded that there had been a violation of the FET with respect to all but one plant (which was not registered until 11.03.2011).[374] The tribunal reiterated that:

> the financial vulnerability of renewable energy projects is the heavy up-front capital costs. Once money is "sunk" in the PV facilities, the funds of the developer (and its bankers) are locked into the FIT contracts with their investments effectively (as the Claimant put it) long-term hostages.

---

367 Ibid [270]–[272].
368 Ibid [311].
369 Ibid [274].
370 Ibid [275].
371 Ibid [289]–[290]. In that way, the tribunal placed less emphasis on the moment when the projects were developed, but focused on when the SPV was acquired (treating this as the relevant moment for the assessment of legitimate expectations).
372 Ibid [291].
373 Ibid [308].
374 Ibid [309]–[310]. An important difference from the earlier cases is that both the 2013–2014 Disputed Measures and earlier measures were viewed as violations (although no emphasis was put on that issue).

It understood Spain's position to be that "it alone should benefit from rising prices, but the burden of falling prices is to be off-loaded onto investors". Even if such an approach is constitutional under Spanish domestic law, "such one-sided treatment is neither fair nor equitable".[375]

1.2.17 SolEs

1.2.17.1 *Legitimate Expectations*

The *SolEs* tribunal agreed with the parties that (i) the ECT should be interpreted in accordance with the VCLT, (ii) legitimate expectations are to be assessed as of the date of the investment, and (iii) subjective expectations are not enough, since they must be assessed on an objective basis, i.e. with reference to the expectations of a prudent investor.[376]

Then, the tribunal decided that specific commitments are not necessary to create legitimate expectations, which can "arise from provisions of law and regulations and from statements made by or on behalf of the State for the purpose of inducing investment by class of investors".[377]

The tribunal underlined that the FET includes an obligation not to "radically alter" the legal and regulatory framework on which investors had relied. It then confirmed that the FET protects against "disproportionate" changes that remove "the essential features of the regulatory regime".[378] It noted that "proportionality" is relevant for an analysis of the changes of the regulatory framework in the context of legitimate expectations.[379] This is because the FET "does not operate as a stabilization provision". Thus, the tribunal needs to weigh the investor's legitimate expectations against the state's legitimate regulatory interests, "in light of any undertakings of stability that are contained in the laws, regulations and authoritative pronouncements of the host State, upon which the investor relied when it made its investment".[380]

The tribunal noted that Spain "provided public aid to the renewable energy sector in order to meet its objectives for renewable energy, which it has set against the backdrop of EU targets", which included subsidies to the PV plants, of which FIT were the key instrument.[381] By creating this regime, Spain encouraged investments in RE, with the aim of addressing shortfalls in meeting its RE

375 Ibid [311].
376 SolEs v. Spain, ICSID Case No. ARB/15/38, Award (31.07.2019) [312].
377 Ibid [313].
378 Ibid [315]–[316].
379 Ibid [317].
380 Ibid [318].
381 Ibid [420].

targets.[382] This conclusion was strengthened by the 2007 Press release and by other statements given by state officials in the context of promoting investment in RE.[383] Once the policy set in RD 661/2007 generated more investment than had been expected, Spain introduced adjustments to address the new situation.[384]

1.2.17.2 *Stability*

The claimant made its investments in March 2010. For the tribunal, at that time "the stability of a FIT assigned to a particular plant was a fundamental aspect of the design of the regulatory regime that was in place" and that the applicable regulations indicated that any adjustments going beyond annual adjustments for inflation would apply only to new facilities.[385] Thus, at that time, based on RD 1578/2008, any PV investor had a legitimate expectation to "receive a FIT that was stable, once assigned to a PV plant, for the 25-year period" and that "stable FIT was an essential element of the regulatory regime".[386]

This conclusion was unaltered by the fifth additional provision of RD 1578/2008, which provided for "modification" of the economic regime "downward, following the expected evolution of the technology". The tribunal opined that a prudent investor could reasonably have understood this provision as applying only to new plants, since existing PV plants cannot benefit from the technological evolution.[387]

1.2.17.3 *Domestic Courts*

The tribunal considered the Spanish Supreme Court's case law as operating only as a fact, not as law. Only judgments issued prior to the investment were relevant when assessing the claimant's legitimate expectations.[388] For the tribunal, a prudent investor is expected "to have a general awareness of recent decisions of the highest court of the host State that interpret provisions regulatory regime on which the investor would rely". The evidence on the record indicated that participants in the RE sector were following developments in the Supreme Court's case law and the claimant's representatives had "at least a general appreciation" of this case law.[389] However, the tribunal approached

382 Ibid [421].
383 Ibid [426].
384 Ibid [422].
385 Ibid [423]–[424].
386 Ibid [444].
387 Ibid [425].
388 Ibid [428].
389 Ibid [429].

this issue "with caution", as the Supreme Court had applied Spanish law, not the ECT, and since each judgment addresses specific facts and provisions of law. In addition, the relevant case law did not address "changes in the remuneration of an existing plant that are comparable in significance to the abolition of the Special Regime".[390] The tribunal concluded that, in March 2010, a prudent investor would have expected "modest changes to the remuneration regime applicable to an existing plant", and the expectation was not limited to receiving an RRR.[391]

1.2.17.4 *Tariff Deficit*

The tribunal then analyzed the relevance of the tariff deficit. It noted that the tariff deficit in Spain had been large for several years prior to the Financial Crisis, which led to a decline in demand for electricity and caused further increases in the tariff deficit.[392] At the same time, Spain's own policy choices determined many of the key variables that gave rise to the tariff deficit. Spain was aware of the magnitude of the tariff deficit already in 2008, when it adopted RD 1578/2008 and revised the FIT for new PV plants, which applied to the claimant's 2010 investment.[393] Thus, there were "warning signs" that Spain would act to correct the tariff deficit. However, a prudent PV investor in March 2010 could not have expected a reduction of the FITs for existing plants and the abolition the Special Regime. Even if Spain had contemplated doing so at the relevant period, its intentions were not transparent to investors, whereas legitimate expectations are based solely on available information.[394]

Moreover, the tribunal found no basis to conclude that, as of March 2010, an investor should have anticipated that the Special Regime would eventually have been found to be inconsistent with EU requirements on state aid.[395]

1.2.17.5 *Due Diligence*

The tribunal put little emphasis on due diligence, considering that "a formal due diligence process is not a precondition to a successful claim of legitimate expectations". However, legitimate expectations are "measured with reference to the knowledge that a hypothetical prudent investor is deemed to have had

390 Ibid [430].
391 Ibid [432]–[433].
392 Ibid [434].
393 Ibid [438].
394 Ibid [439]–[440].
395 Ibid [442].

as of the date of the investment", so investors cannot benefit from gaps in their subjective knowledge.[396]

1.2.17.6 *Regulatory Revolution*

Based on the above, the tribunal decided that 2010 and first of the 2013–2014 Disputed Measures did not violate legitimate expectations. Even though they reduced the claimant's revenue, these measures "did not remove the essential features of the regulatory regime in place when Claimant invested".[397] They were also proportionate.[398]

The conclusion was different with respect to the New Regime. First, the remuneration received by the claimant under the New Regime was "considerably lower". The original IRR was "around 7% after taxes", compared to 5.9% under the New Regime.[399] Second, the tribunal noted that the claim is not about a particular IRR, but about a stable remuneration in the form of the FIT set for each plant.[400] Under the Special Regime, the claimant was entitled to receive the FIT for all energy produced during a particular year, creating an "efficiency reward" for plants that were more efficient than standard plants. The New Regime introduced a cap on the number of hours, which impacted the claimant, since its plants reached the cap around September or October each year.[401] Moreover, the FIT applicable under the New Regime was subjected to periodic revision and Spain was not transparent on how the FIT would be calculated for the next periods. This risked further reductions during the life of the relevant PV plants.[402]

The tribunal concluded that the disputed measures were disproportionate. They "suddenly and unexpectedly removed the essential features of the regime in place" and the "severity of the impact of those measures" on the value of the disputed investment exceeded "that which a prudent investor could have reasonably anticipated in light of the stability that inhered" in the Special Regime.[403]

---

396 Ibid [331].
397 Ibid [450].
398 Ibid [451].
399 Ibid [456].
400 Ibid [458].
401 Ibid [459].
402 Ibid [460]–[461].
403 Ibid [462].

1.2.18 InfraRed

1.2.18.1 *Legitimate Expectations*

In *InfraRed*, the tribunal dismissed the argument that the FET is limited to non-discrimination. It recognized that the legitimate expectations of investors also require protection.[404] It distinguished between two types of legitimate expectations, of (i) stability and of (ii) consistency. Stability was understood as a synonym of immutability. Expectations of immutability require a "specific commitment tendered directly to the investor or industry sector at issue". This is in line with the principle of state sovereignty, as any other approach would result in a significant limitation on the state's "sovereign legislative powers".[405] The expectation of consistency is different, meaning "that the regulatory framework will not be radically or fundamentally changed".[406] It may arise even in the absence of any specific commitment. This type of the legitimate expectation requires a balancing exercise between itself and the state's inherent sovereignty to modify its laws and regulations.[407]

1.2.18.2 *Specific Commitments*

The tribunal considered that, at a general level, neither the Spanish legislative acts nor the surrounding press releases could reasonably be interpreted as creating a specific commitment giving grounds to legitimate expectations of stability (or immutability).[408] The same conclusion applied to the registration in the RAIPRE and the pre-allocation register.[409]

The tribunal concluded, however, that all the facts concerning the specific situation of the claimant amounted to a specific commitment given to this

---

404 InfraRed v. Spain, ICSID Case No. ARB/14/12, Award (02.08.2019) [365].

405 Ibid [366].

406 In that sense, the tribunal understood "consistency" differently than an obligation on the administrative and judicial authorities to apply local law in a consistent manner, as defined in the general comments – fn 30.

407 InfraRed v. Spain, *supra* note 404 [368]:

> A valid public policy purpose does not automatically foreclose a finding of breach of the FET standard since – in the balancing exercise that tribunals are called upon to carry out – the consideration of a legitimate legislative objective may be outweighed by the radical nature of the changes to the legislative framework at issue. Although a host state enjoys the sovereignty to modify its laws and regulations, its liability towards investors may be engaged (again, depending on the facts) if, in doing so, it fundamentally or radically alters a regulatory framework upon which the investors legitimately relied to invest

(footnotes omitted).

408 Ibid [407], [441].

409 Ibid [408].

particular investor. This perception was grounded in "purported agreement" (i.e. 2010 Agreement), RD 1614/2010 itself, and the exchange of letters of waiver and "December resolutions" concerning the disputed plants. This grounded a:

> legitimate expectation that CSP plants registered on the Pre-allocation Register would be shielded from subsequent regulatory changes to three specific elements of the Original Regulatory Framework, and that this expectation was violated by Spain.[410]

These shielded elements were (i) future revisions of tariffs, (ii) the pool price premium and the (iii) applicable lower and upper price limits.[411] The tribunal underlined that this cannot be understood as a promise or a commitment of "freezing" the Special Regime by maintaining all its elements, but is limited to "certain elements" of the Special Regime.[412]

The tribunal noted that the 2010 Agreement – even if it had no binding effect under the domestic law – stated unequivocally that any future revisions of the premiums will not affect existing facilities. This language was subsequently reflected in the text of Art. 4 RD 1614/2010, which specifically "targets" the CSP sector, involved in the 2010 Agreement.[413] This provision, which reiterated the "guarantee" from Art. 44(3) RD 661/2007 with respect to the CSP plants, suggested that Spain intended "to shield CSP plants registered on the Pre-allocation Register from future revisions of the tariffs, premiums and lower and upper limits that were in effect" when the disputed investments were made.[414]

Art. 4 RD 1614/2010 moreover "enshrined in law" many of the elements of the 2010 Agreement.[415] Even understanding it as "legally cognizable fact", and not a source of binding contractual obligations under the local law, it showed that Spain "intended to grant the CSP sector a distinct and privileged status in the context of future regulatory revisions and to extend to CSP producers specific assurances in that regard", when compared to other RE producers.[416]

It was crucial that Spain issued a resolution directly concerning each of the disputed plants, in which it "specifically represented" that "at present … the remuneration applicable to the facility is made up of the tariffs, premiums,

410 Ibid [410].
411 Ibid [418], [451].
412 Ibid [406].
413 Ibid [413]–[415].
414 Ibid [418], [421].
415 Ibid [422].
416 Ibid [426]–[427].

upper and lower limits and supplements established by RD 661/2007 (…)".[417] They were issued in reply to the letters of waiver, in which the investors agreed to postpone the date of commencement of operations of the CSP plants, but requested to "[…] to have the remuneration conditions for the facility during its operational lifespan communicated" to them.[418]

These resolutions were a "key particularity" of this case.[419] In isolation and out of the context, they could have been read simply as referring to the regime applicable on the date of their issuance.[420] However, these two sets of documents read together constituted a specific commitment that the claimants' plants "would be shielded from any revisions" to the "tariffs, premiums and lower and upper limits" during their operation lifetime.[421] This was a specific commitment made not for the whole CSP sector, but directly to the two disputed CSP plants, although the fact that it confirmed the clear terms of RD 1614/2010 and the related press release helped the tribunal to achieve this reading.[422] The claimants could have relied on this specific commitment, received 6 months prior to their investment, and the expectation on its basis was reasonable and legitimate.[423] In this sense, the tribunal followed the approach of the *Masdar* tribunal.[424]

As noted earlier, the tribunal considered that the specific commitments shielded against any future revisions of tariffs, the pool price premium and the applicable lower and upper price limits.[425] They did not cover other elements of the Special Regime, such as the right to sell the full net amount of electricity produced, to obtain remuneration for electricity produced using non-renewable back-up fuel, the way of updating the FIT based on the IPC, a

417 Ibid [428]–[429].
418 Ibid [431].
419 Ibid [428].
420 Ibid [430].
421 Ibid [433].
422 Ibid [434]. Nevertheless, it seems that the tribunal somewhat "tailored" its decision on facts of the case to find a way to distinguish it from other cases and escape saying that the specific commitment was given to the whole CSP sector based on more general documents. This is particularly grounded given that, in some parts of the awards, such statements blending the specific commitment with an obligation towards the CSP sector can be found – [443], [449], [451].
423 Ibid [435]–[436].
424 This is the author's conclusion. The award rendered in *Masdar* (as well as in *Antin*) was presented too late and the tribunal decided not to consider them in its analysis – ibid, [fn 761]. *NextEra* was not mentioned at all. Whilst this cannot be clearly determined without access to the case files, the resolutions analyzed by *InfraRed* and *Masdar* tribunals appear to be comparable – fn 170–172.
425 InfraRed v. Spain, *supra* note 404 [418], [451].

right to priority access to transmission and distribution gird, or finally a right to receive a supplement for "reactive energy".[426]

1.2.18.3 *Stability*

The tribunal found that Spain had violated legitimate expectations of stability by abrogating the FITs and Premiums and replacing them with a system based on a remuneration per unit of installed capacity, calculated according to an "efficient" standard plant.[427]

1.2.18.4 *Due Diligence*

With respect to the due diligence, the tribunal paid attention to two factors: (i) the nature of the sector, which is heavily regulated, and (ii) the main source of profit (i.e. state subsidies). They require a "stricter due diligence standard", i.e. including an "adequate review" of the applicable regulatory framework and the case law of the Supreme Court. In this context, the issue to be decided was whether the disputed measures "were foreseeable to a reasonably prudent investor with the benefit of an adequate due diligence".[428] The tribunal did not decide whether the claimants carried out sufficient due diligence. Instead, it observed that, even if it were to accept the opposite conclusion, "this would not undermine the legitimacy" of the claimants' legitimate expectation defined earlier.[429]

1.2.18.5 *Domestic Courts*

All of the Supreme Court's cases, the Spanish and EU laws and regulations as well as other factors relied upon by the respondent were issued prior to Spain's specific commitment of stability "crystallized" in December 2010, when the resolutions were issued. As such, the tribunal considered them irrelevant.[430] Even a more thorough due diligence analysis would not have made the disputed measures "reasonably foreseeable" to the claimants and would have confirmed that Spain specifically committed to shield the CSP registered in the Pre-RAIPRE from future revisions of the "tariffs, premiums and lower and upper limits" of the Special Regime.[431]

426 Ibid [452].
427 Ibid [453].
428 Ibid [370]–[371].
429 Ibid [438].
430 Ibid [439]–[440].
431 Ibid [441].

1.2.18.6 *State Aid*

The tribunal was "prepared to accept" that remuneration under the Special Regime could have been considered as "state aid" within the meaning of the EU law, but considered it irrelevant as to whether Spain had violated its specific commitment.[432]

1.2.18.7 *Transparency*

The tribunal recognized that the FET also encompassed a duty of transparency and due process, requiring the state to be "forthcoming with information about intended changes in policy and regulations that may significantly affect investments [...]".[433] In its view, the reform was "announced sufficiently in advance to allow the CSP sector investor and actors to react".[434] The outcome of the process was contrary to the claimants' hopes and violated their legitimate expectations of stability. Moreover, Spain could have provided for greater participation of the industry in the reform process. This does not mean, however, that the duty of transparency and due process was breached.[435]

1.2.19 OperaFund

1.2.19.1 *Legitimate Expectations*

In *OperaFund*, the tribunal observed that, as the FET is explicitly mentioned in Art. 10(1) ECT, it is autonomous and goes beyond the minimum standard of treatment under CIL.[436] One of its elements is to protect legitimate expectations.[437] They require "reasonable reliance of investors on host state acts". The more specifically they are directed towards investors, the more likely they can be considered as "reasonable".[438]

The tribunal considered that "it is hard to imagine a more explicit stabilization assurance" than Art. 44(3) RD 661/2007, which "contained an express stability commitment that served its purpose of inducing investment in part by shielding investors in Claimants' position from legislative or regulatory change".[439] Whilst changes of regulations occurred in the past and would happen in the future, Art. 44(3) RD 661/2007 "laid out the consequences of such

432 Ibid [443]–[444].
433 Ibid [469].
434 Ibid [470].
435 Ibid [472].
436 OperaFund v. Spain, ICSID Case No. ARB/15/36, Award (06.09.2019) [425].
437 Ibid [426].
438 Ibid [481].
439 Ibid [485].

changes". The tribunal viewed its position as one that "respects the legislative authority" of the states and their right to regulate.[440]

Registration in the RAIPRE was an "important additional element" for the tribunal, which allowed for these conclusions.[441]

1.2.19.2 *Due Diligence*

In view of the applicability of the Special Regime to the disputed investments, the tribunal found it "not determinative" how relevant the claimants' reliance was on a due diligence report from 2007. The tribunal observed that RD 661/2007 was the only regulation analyzed by that report, and it was in the claimants' possession even though it was mandated by a third party. It then agreed that an adequate due diligence is required, and that the absence of any "real due diligence" would vitiate a claim based on legitimate expectations.[442] The tribunal decided that the claimants "did what could be expected under the circumstances and at the time of their investments by a prudent investor". Relying on the above-mentioned opinion was sufficient "at least in confirming their expectations". The tribunal decided that any further steps to achieve information on whether Spain would "fundamentally withdraw the assurance and benefits" provided in RD 661/2007 would not have resulted in the claimants expecting such changes. Moreover, in the light of clear wording of the relevant provision, the majority saw no need to make inquiries about possible "future changes of the regulations".[443]

1.2.19.3 *Regulatory Revolution*

The tribunal also agreed that the FET protects against changes in the "essential characteristics of the regulatory regime relied upon by investors".[444] Reiterating that states are "free to change their regulatory framework for various business sectors", the tribunal considered it critical "whether and to what extent

440 Ibid.

441 Ibid [483]–[484].

442 Ibid [486].

443 Ibid [487]. The tribunals' analysis of the due diligence requirement seems to blend the issue of a specific commitment given in a stabilization clause (Art. 44(3) RD 661/2007 understood as being one) and the possibility of becoming informed that "future changes of the regulations" could happen. It can only be explained if the latter referred to "fundamental withdrawal of the assurance and benefits", but this is not clear from the majority's analysis.

444 Ibid [508].

the degree of the regulatory change was so radical that it amounts to a breach of the FET-inherent stability requirement".[445]

In this context, the tribunal was unconvinced that the disputed measures were a reasonable response to the tariff deficit. It recognized that, whilst states "retain much leeway in deciding on reasonable measures", this discretion does not mean that a state "is free to change the rules of the game" it adopted to such an extent as to burden "particularly the investors who have already made investments and are unable to exit the regulatory framework".[446] Adopting a regulatory framework aiming at attracting investors in certain sectors is commonplace, as is dismantling such incentives for future investments.[447] However, it is unreasonable to do this in respect of pre-existing investments which exist precisely due to the past incentives. This is even less reasonable in the light of "the legislator's express statement that the old regime should continue to apply to existing registered investments in spite of possible future changes".[448] RD 661/2007 was a "regulatory offer" of FITs, by which Spain "assumed an obligation of regulatory stability" and which boosted investments in RE.[449]

The tribunal concluded that the disputed measures amounted to a fundamental change of the regulatory framework, violating "legitimate expectations of stability".[450]

1.2.19.4 *Proportionality*

The tribunal recognized proportionality "as an inherent element when balancing regulatory state interests and investor interests in assessing stability obligations as well as legitimate expectations". It had, however, "some doubts as to whether proportionality should be accepted as a separate element of FET". It saw no need to decide this issue in the light of its previous findings that the FET had been violated.[451]

---

445 Ibid [509].
446 Ibid [510].
447 Ibid.
448 Ibid [511].
449 Ibid [512]:

> Respondent put into place a regime defining and fixing feed-in values according to the cost of money on capital markets at that point in time, and provided that those values would be updated annually according to inflation. RD 661/2007 set remuneration for the lifetime of the plant. Through its regulatory offer, Respondent assumed an obligation of regulatory stability, which resulted in the boosting of renewable investments in Spain and gave rise to legitimate expectations of stability under the ECT.

450 Ibid [512]–[513].
451 Ibid [555].

1.2.20 OperaFund – Dissenting Opinion

In the dissenting opinion, one of the arbitrators described the award as based on three findings of facts which were "entirely unsupported by evidence on the record, and reached without reasoning or explanation". These alleged facts were as follows: (i) an expectation existed that the tariff regime established by RD 661/2007 was immutable during the reasonable life of investments, (ii) the claimants had relied on that expectation at the time when they made their investments, and (iii) the claimants had exercised the necessary due diligence.[452]

The dissenting opinion is strongly-worded and reveals major disagreement with the majority's position regarding the violation of Art. 10 ECT and, as a result, on quantum.[453]

1.2.20.1 *Legitimacy of ISDS*

In the dissenter's view, the majority devoted only one single page of the 273-page award to the "central issue", i.e. the legal standard applicable to legitimate expectations, and gave "no real response" to the issues referred to by the dissenter.[454]

Three times he referred to the damaging effect of the majority's approach to the legitimacy of the whole ISDS system. First, it considered the system as a "fragile creature" and one that attracts an "increasingly critical eye", and the award as a threat to the ISDS system, as it does not "enhance confidence in the system, or a sense of its legitimacy".[455] Second, in his view the "unreasoned" conclusion of the majority on the interpretation of RD 661/2007 is apt to "undermine the legitimacy of, and trust in" the ISDS system. In the context of assessing the Spanish Supreme Court's judgments, arbitrators have a vital responsibility to exercise caution if they "substitute their views for those of a country's highest court". This may be justified, but requires "full and complete reasons", not present in the award.[456] Third, in the context of the conflict of interest of the claimants' counsel team (who had in the past prepared an opinion on the regulatory framework, analyzed in the context of due diligence and who could have been called as a witness during the proceedings), he noted that, "it is imperative that the very strictest standards are applied in the

452 OperaFund v. Spain, ICSID Case No. ARB/15/36, Dissent on Liability and Quantum (13.08.2019) [2].

453 Ibid. The dissenter agreed, however, on the decision on jurisdiction, including the intra-EU objection.

454 Ibid [3].

455 Ibid.

456 Ibid [23].

quest to avoid perceptions of conflict" if the ISDS system is to "retain" or even "regain" legitimacy.[457]

1.2.20.2 *Due Diligence*

The dissenter agreed that, whilst legitimate expectations can be based on "legal and business stability, or the legal framework", or "specific guarantee in legislation", it is relevant to determine the source and scope of this expectations, which must be based on "some degree" of due diligence.[458]

The dissenter did not agree that RD 661/2007 contained an "explicit stabilization assurance".[459] In his view, it could be amended or replaced as any general legislative act.[460] A "reasonable and diligent investor" would have been aware that the regulatory framework had been changed in the past. The regularity of such changes requires investors to inform themselves as to the risk of future changes, but the dissenter saw no due diligence carried out on this issue.[461] He also considered relevant that the immutability of tariffs and related regimes had been ruled upon by the Spanish courts prior to the claimants' investments. The majority passed "in total silence on the substance of these judgments on Spanish law, taking refuge in the claim that they are of no relevance". By doing so, the majority substituted its own interpretation of whether a Spanish RD provides an expectation for the one adopted by the Spanish courts. The majority's judgment entailed a "grave" failure to provide an explanation of that.[462]

The dissenter interpreted RD 661/2007 in line with the judgments of the Spanish Supreme Court. Because RD 661/2007 did not provide for an immutable

---

457 Ibid [47]. The dissenter placed great emphasis on the arbitrators' duty to act in a way that protects the legitimacy of the ISDS system. Interestingly, he did not present a similar critique with respect to the jurisdiction decision. Even though the award was drafted in a similar manner, with the tribunal's analysis being drafted in a concise manner when compared to the parties' arguments, he did not consider that this put at risk the legitimacy of the system.

458 Ibid [16]–[17].

459 Ibid [18].

460 Ibid [19].

461 Ibid [20].

462 Ibid [21]. What seems striking in the dissenting opinion is the implicit conclusion that the existence of past changes to the regulatory framework justify future changes. This would render ineffective any legislative incentives introduced by almost any state in the world (we must remember that this conclusion was found in the context of an EU member state) as, from the perspective of international law, they would lack relevance and could be changed at any time. Perhaps, however, the dissenter would have "softened" his dissent had the claimants' undertaken any due diligence prior to making decision to invest.

regime, no expectation could have arisen on its basis. However, the dissenter analyzed the hypothetical contrary scenario, for which the claimants must had demonstrated a "minimum exercise of due diligence".[463] The dissenter would have required an "inquiry in advance" regarding the prospects of change in the regulatory framework. Even though this is not a high standard, for him the record showed that it was not met by the claimants.[464] A proper and reasonable assessment of evidence is part of the reasoning process by the arbitrators. He considered the majority's conclusion as contrary to the evidence.[465] In his view, the two legal opinions issued in 2006 and 2007 were not helpful. First, they were addressed to a third party, not to the claimants, and contained a disclaimer excluding its use by any other entity. Second, they "say nothing" about the risk of changes to the regulatory framework resulting from RD 661/2007. Thus, "a reasonable reader would conclude that what has happened before – regulatory change – could happen again, as it did".[466]

1.2.20.3 *Balancing Exercise*

The dissenter added that the disputed investments continued to be profitable after the adoption of the disputed measures. The new rate of return was "aligned" with those granted by other EU member states.[467] Spain was faced with a "delicate balancing act". On the one hand, it had to reduce public expenditures without imposing excessive burdens on consumers. On the other hand, it had to continue to encourage environmental protection and the RE sector, including the legitimate rights of existing investors in the sector.[468] The FET allows for such a balancing exercise and does not require that the interests of investors are elevated above all other considerations.[469] In the dissenter's view, Spain adopted a "balanced approach" which fell within "the acceptable margin of change".[470] In the absence of evidence, the award prioritizes the interests of investors over those of other social actors, treating the ECT as "akin to an insurance mechanism".[471]

463 Ibid [24].
464 Ibid [26]–[27].
465 Ibid [37].
466 Ibid [31].
467 Ibid [38].
468 Ibid [39].
469 Ibid [40].
470 Ibid [42].
471 Ibid [44].

1.2.20.4 *The Majority's Reply*

The majority replied to the dissenting opinion. It clarified that its approach was to address only the determinative factors required to decide on the requests of the parties, without repeating all the arguments advanced by the parties. It commented that many of the dissenter's observations "are incorrect, out of context, or misleading". It then clarified that the award refers to "by now many awards issued in the parallel Spanish renewable energy cases" based on almost the same factual and legal scenarios, whereas the dissenter "relies on cases dealing with very different factual and legal scenarios without explaining why these should nevertheless be more relevant for and prevail for the present case over the awards in the Spanish cases". It then clarified where it analyzes issues which the dissenter claimed had not been analyzed. It also commented on the dissenter's allegation of not respecting judgments of the Spanish courts, suggesting that the dissenter had failed to explain why these should impact the majority's reasoning, given that it "need not and does not take any view as to the correctness of the decisions of the Spanish Supreme Court, which the Parties agree the Tribunal must accept as fact". It then commented that the Spanish Supreme Court's judgments pre-dating the claimants' investments concerned irrelevant issues and laws (i.e. they did not concern RD 661/2007), whereas later judgments are irrelevant to the question of the claimants' expectations at the time of investment.[472]

1.2.21 BayWa

In *BayWa*, the tribunal noted that the first phrase of Art. 10(1) ECT (referring to "stable, equitable, favourable and transparent" conditions) cannot be interpreted in isolation from the second sentence, embodying the FET.[473] The tribunal divided its FET analysis into five issues.[474]

1.2.21.1 *Specific Commitments*

First, the tribunal determined that no specific commitments were made. This was in line with the claimants' position, who did not argue in favour of the "freezing of a particular royal decree".[475]

472 OperaFund v. Spain, *supra* note 436 [491].

473 BayWa v. Spain, ICSID Case No. ARB/15/16, Decision on Jurisdiction, Liability and Directions on Quantum (02.12.2019) [458].

474 Ibid [463].

475 Ibid [463], [465]–[466].

1.2.21.2 *Legitimate Expectations*

Second, the tribunal decided that the claimants had legitimate expectations of the "continuation of subsidies in some substantial form", but not that that the Special Regime subsidies "would be maintained unchanged for the life of the investment".[476] Thus, the tribunal did not agree that legitimate expectations extended to total energy production for the lifetime of the disputed plants regulated by the Special Regime.[477] Therefore, the legitimate expectations were that of the RRR regulated in Art. 30(4) LSE.[478]

The tribunal observed that Spain's RE policy was implemented through RDs, which "would naturally change, and did change, and not in any uniform direction favouring the recipients".[479] Thus, the relevant legislation was Art. 30(4) LSE, not the RDs, as it established the general principle, which was to be given effect by regulations. The regulations cannot commit the state "to more than the legislative framework allows", which imposes "some limits on what can be done".[480] The tribunal also acknowledged that the case law of the Spanish Supreme Court from 2005 onwards denied the position that subsidies were "intangible". This led to a conclusion that there could be no legitimate expectation that subsidies would never be reduced or capped.[481]

The tribunal noted that as to legitimate expectations based on general legislation, its conclusions are the same as in *NextEra*, although in the other case the tribunal found the existence of legitimate expectations based on additional, specific assurances given to the investor.[482] The tribunal referred also to the *9REN* and *Cube* awards, recalling their different conclusions, but did not comment in detail on how to reconcile those diverging positions.[483]

1.2.21.3 *Proportionality*

Third, the tribunal considered that the disputed measures were proportionate in the circumstances they were adopted, except for the claw-back of previously paid benefits.[484] In this context, the tribunal referred to the test laid down in *Blusun v. Italy* (much relied upon by the parties in their pleadings), focusing on

476 Ibid [463].
477 Ibid [467].
478 Ibid [498].
479 Ibid [471].
480 Ibid [473].
481 Ibid [472].
482 Ibid [474].
483 Ibid [475]–[476].
484 Ibid [463].

proportionality and "the reasonable reliance interests of recipients who may have committed substantial resources on the basis of the earlier regime".[485]

In the tribunal's view, an assessment of proportionality does not involve second-guessing the alternative measures available to address the tariff deficit.[486] Already at this stage, the tribunal analyzed the appropriate regulatory life for Wind energy plants, finding that 25-years was appropriate.[487] Similarly, there was nothing unreasonable to calculate subsidies, "at least for the future", based on standard facilities. For the tribunal, earlier legislation also contained elements of calculations based on standard facilities.[488] Also, the estimated costs as an element of the disputed measures were considered proportionate. In fact, there was no claim concerning the OPEX, whereas the difference in CAPEX was "relatively slight".[489]

1.2.21.4 *Retroactivity*

The tribunal then focused on the "retrospectivity" of the disputed measures, which considered subsidies paid in the past for the purpose of assessing future payments. This resulted in no entitlements for the disputed facilities for the future, based on their historical performance. The tribunal considered this as a "weaker form of retrospectivity, but the label 'retrospective' is not crucial: what matters is the substance".[490] The tribunal differentiated between amending future payments with immediate effect from reducing payments "that would have otherwise been made by reference to payments lawfully made in the past in respect of past production".[491] It highlighted that it is far from simple to differentiate between immediately operative and retrospective measures.[492]

The tribunal followed the *RREEF* tribunal and decided that deducting from future subsidies the amounts historically earned in excess of a newly-introduced threshold amounted to penalizing the relevant Wind energy plants for their successful operations in the past. To claw-back past profits based on a subsequent judgment that such profits were "excessive" violated the FET, in particular given that the disputed measures would have solved the tariff deficit problem without this measure.[493]

485 Ibid [460]–[462], [478].
486 Ibid [480].
487 Ibid [484].
488 Ibid [485].
489 Ibid [486].
490 Ibid [488].
491 Ibid [490].
492 Ibid [492].
493 Ibid [495]–[496].

1.2.21.5 *RRR*

Fourth, the tribunal decided that if the disputed measures had been applied without the claw-back, *pro futuro* only, due regard to the reasonable interests of recipients would have been respected.[494] In this context, the tribunal criticized the approach adopted by the tribunal in the *RREEF* case, where the proportionality analysis was performed as part of the damages analysis. In that tribunal's view, the question of proportionality pertains to the merits (being necessary to determine whether there has been a breach at all), not to the quantum (which is consequential).[495]

Having said this, the tribunal followed the *RREEF* award that the relevant measure was the IRR.[496] Thus, the RRR equates to the IRR. The IRR is compared to the weighted average cost of capital and if it exceeds the latter, the cash flows will cover the costs of the project.[497] The projects' (not the shareholders') IRR over the lifetime of the plants was relevant.[498] The tribunal held that there was no need to decide the exact amount of the RRR, as this is a dynamic concept and can change over time, to accommodate changing circumstances. It observed that the actual IRR, in any case, exceeded the 7.398% pre-tax, envisaged in the New Regime, as well as the 6.86% adopted by the tribunal in the *RREEF* case.[499] Therefore, the claimants' legitimate expectation to an RRR for the future had not been violated.[500] This would have resulted in there being no breach of the FET, but for the retroactive nature of the New Regime, discussed earlier.

1.2.21.6 *State Aid*

Fifth, the tribunal turned its attention to the impact of EU law on the merits. It started by analyzing the content of EU state aid law, based on Arts. 107 and 108 TFEU.[501] It noted that, under EU law, state aid is unlawful if it is not notified, or if it is implemented before it is authorized. The EC may require the

494 Ibid [463], [497].
495 Ibid [500].
496 Ibid [503].
497 Ibid [504].
498 Ibid [505].
499 Ibid [507]–[508], [514].
500 Ibid [515].
501 Ibid [553]–[557]. This case is notable for the weight placed on EU state aid law. This is the first award to consider this issue as relevant and potentially important for the outcome of the case, even though it did not actually impact on this final decision (with the exception of the dissenting opinion in *Foresight* – Foresight v. Spain, Partial Dissenting ..., *supra* note 226 [34]–[38]).

recipients of unlawful state aid to repay the granting state. However, in the case lacking notification, the EC may subsequently find that the state aid is compatible with the internal market (which actually happened with the New Regime, notified "only some time after their implementation").[502] Recipients of such state aid can easily verify whether it was notified by consulting the online register.[503] In the EU law context, legitimate expectations can sometimes "constitute a defence to a claim for repayment of aid".[504]

In the tribunal's view, the Special Regime potentially constituted state aid and should have been notified.[505] The 2001 Directive and 2009 Directive expressly referred to the relevant provisions on the state aid, and the EC approved many subsidies schemes for RE. The EC adopted a "rather generous" approach to their approvals in the relevant period and it apparently approved all green energy support schemes at the relevant time.[506] The tribunal also noted that the 2017 EC Decision considered that the New Regime introduced state aid, which was unlawful from 2014 until 2017 for lack of notification, but otherwise compatible with the internal market. At the same time, it was "not relevant for the scope of this decision to assess whether the originally foreseen payments under the previous schemes would have been compatible or not".[507]

The tribunal then followed the approach of the *Vattenfall* tribunal and considered that even if the "damages award would by itself constitute notifiable state aid", the enforceability of the award is a separate matter.[508] The tribunal has a duty to decide a case in accordance with the applicable law. While it disagreed with the EC's decision to "block" payment of compensation awarded by arbitral tribunals, it considered this as an issue to be dealt with in the subsequent proceedings.[509]

The EU law was relevant as part of Spanish law, which in turn was considered as a fact, rather than as the applicable law. The tribunal clarified that it "does not interpret EU law as such, but accepts the consistent interpretation of EU law as applied by the relevant institutions".[510] Nevertheless, it later

502 Ibid [558], [567].
503 Ibid [559].
504 Ibid [561].
505 Ibid [565].
506 Ibid [567].
507 Ibid [567]. See also: [562]–[564], [569.h].
508 Ibid [568].
509 Ibid [569.f], [536].
510 Ibid [569.b]. Most probably, this was an attempt to escape the reasons underlying the *Achmea* judgment.

commented that the "European state aid regime" applies concurrently with the ECT and forms part of the applicable law.[511]

The tribunal took into consideration a number of factors, including that (i) the claimants' due diligence process paid no regard to EU state aid law, (ii) the EC was well-informed about the Special Regime but took no action with respect to it, (iii) Spain ought to have been aware of its duty to notify the Special Regime to the EC and (iv) there was no causal link between the lack of notification and the discontinuance of subsidies under the Special Regime.[512]

Because the claimants should have been aware of the lack of notification and approval of the subsidies under the Special Regime, they could have no legitimate expectations that the Special Regime subsidies were lawful and that the amount of state aid granted under the Special Regime would be paid for the lifetime of the plants.[513] This was in line with the tribunal's finding that, under the ECT, no compensation is due for a failure to continue the level of state aid which was in force under the Special Regime. Nevertheless, this did not alter the decision on a violation of Art. 10(1) ECT as regards the retroactivity, i.e. claimants being entitled to the benefit of a stable regime with respect to subsidies received in the past. This was confirmed by the fact that no recovery measures were initiated under EU law to order repayment of the subsidies received under the Special Regime by all its recipients.[514] Thus, an alternative conclusion would unjustifiably differentiate investors such as the claimants from investors who sold their investments (and retained the subsidies received under the Special Regime).[515]

The tribunal's conclusion on the merits took into account the timing of the investment (i.e. in 2009 the economic situation in Spain was already "problematic"), the fact that the due diligence conducted was limited (and did not cover EU state aid law) that there were no specific representations (either prior to or after making the investment) and that under the New Regime, substantial support system survived, guaranteeing an IRR of 7.98%.[516]

1.2.22 BayWa – Dissenting Opinion

1.2.22.1 *Balancing Exercise*

In view of one of the arbitrators who issued a dissenting opinion, the claimants were entitled to full compensation.[517] The FET analysis "requires a balancing

511 Ibid [591.a].
512 Ibid [569.c–569.e].
513 Ibid [569.g].
514 Ibid [569.i].
515 Ibid [570].
516 Ibid [590].
517 BayWa v. Spain, ICSID Case No. ARB/15/16, Dissenting Opinion (02.12.2019) [1], [43].

exercise" between the rights granted, and "accompanying expectations of stability, gain and profit through concrete and specific provisions under the Special Regime and the New Regime regulations curtailing or eliminating such rights or baffling those expectations".[518] This balancing must be based upon notions of reasonableness and proportionality.[519]

1.2.22.2 *Regulatory Revolution*

The dissenter favored the possibility of legitimate expectations based on the regulatory framework. A contrary view would defeat the "very function of rules of law", which is to create "areas of predictability and security orienting human action".[520]

For the dissenter, the New Regime drastically put an end to and "erased" the Special Regime.[521]

He noted that – unlike other RE facilities, such as the PV plants – the measures taken by the government until the disputed measures aimed to preserve the Special Regime for Wind energy plants.[522] Even though the Special Regime was changed across time, previous changes were not a "radical innovation" or a "Copernican modification going to the roots of the Special Regime, and could not be deemed to have been the harbinger of the radical new model introduced through the New Regime as far as the Wind Farms are concerned".[523]

The dissenter underlined the relevance of the 2007 Press release.[524] He also highlighted that the tariff deficit originated in 2000, well before the RDs from 2004 and 2007 (being core to the claimants' rights and expectations) were enacted.[525]

All of this led him to conclude that the New Regime imposed a "disproportionate, unreasonable and unexpected economic burden" on the claimants, which "suppressed the legal and economic substance of the regulatory framework they relied upon when investing, and thus defeated their legitimate expectations".[526] This suppression should be compensated, not a suppression

518 Ibid [3]–[4].
519 Ibid [4].
520 Ibid [6].
521 Ibid [17].
522 Ibid [18].
523 Ibid [26]. This was much fact-driven, given the timing of the claimants' investment in this case (2009–2012).
524 Ibid [20]–[22].
525 Ibid [25].
526 Ibid [28].

of the RRR, which he considered as an "open-textured and undefined" term of the LSE.[527]

1.2.22.3 *State Aid*

The dissenter also had a different view on the relevance of the EU law on state aid. First, because of the date on which it was adopted, the 2017 EC Decision could not have been relevant to the assessment of the claimant's legitimate expectations.[528] Second, it was Spain's failure to notify the Special Regime to the EC. This "essential failure" was invoked for the first time in the arbitration to reduce the respondent's obligations under the ECT. This was contrary to the principle *nemo turpitudem suam allegarem potest* and the principle of good faith under international law.[529] It was even more reprehensible in the light of the fact that Spain had relied heavily on the Special Regime in 1997–2013 to attract RE investments.[530]

1.2.22.4 *Due Diligence*

In the dissenter's view, there is no requirement of a particular form of legal due diligence. Even if the due diligence did not extend to issues of state aid, this was irrelevant when an investor "is confronted with a drastic suppression of the very legal regime enticing its investment which could not be reasonably anticipated by the due diligence exercise".[531] Given that EU law on state aid forms part of Spanish law, more extensive due diligence cannot be expected from foreign investors than from Spain itself in enforcing EU law (and failing to notify it to the EC).[532]

1.2.23 Stadtwerke

In *Stadtwerke*, the tribunal followed the framework adopted by the parties, which consisted in identifying five elements of the FET: (i) to afford the investor a stable regulatory regime, (ii) not to frustrate the investor's legitimate and reasonable expectations arising at the time of making the investment, (iii) to act transparently towards an investor and/or investment, (iv) to avoid taking unreasonable, abusive or discriminatory actions and (v) to avoid taking disproportionate actions.[533] The tribunal considered each of these in turn.

527 Ibid [49]–[50].
528 Ibid [31].
529 Ibid [33], [36].
530 Ibid [34].
531 Ibid [35].
532 Ibid [41].
533 Stadtwerke v. Spain, ICSID Case No. ARB/15/1, Award (02.12.2019) [256].

1.2.23.1 *Stability*

With respect to the obligation to afford the investor a stable regulatory regime, the tribunal considered that the first sentence of Art. 10(1) ECT does not contain an independent obligation but should be analyzed in the context of the FET.[534] It then noted that:

> just as a merchant who makes a contract or agreement with the intent not to perform would normally be considered to be acting unfairly, a Government deliberately inducing a foreign company to invest by promising certain benefits which it intended to cancel once the investment had been made might also be found to be acting unfairly, and thus to violate the FET standard of protection in an applicable investment treaty.[535]

The tribunal saw no evidence to support the position that Spain had developed its RE policy with the intention of drastically modifying it once it achieved the desired level of investments. In the tribunal's view, Spain had no ulterior motive for its reforms, which were undertaken in good faith to eliminate the negative consequences of imbalances in the Spanish electricity system at a time of Financial Crisis.[536] Thus, the tribunal disagreed with an allegation that Spain adopted a "bait and switch" strategy, understood as a situation that "a person offers or advertises goods or services at an apparent bargain price with the intention of substituting inferior or more expensive goods and services once a buyer becomes committed".[537] Rather, it considered Spain's development of its RE policy as "the law of unintended consequences", understood as a situation when purposeful actions undertaken with good intentions result in undesirable outcomes and the need for policy makers to take what they perceive as necessary corrective actions to remedy an undesirable situation.[538] This was even more the fact, given that Spain retained its sovereign right to enact laws and regulations and to amend or cancel those in force.[539]

1.2.23.2 *Legitimate Expectations*

The tribunal then looked at the second element of the FET, the obligation not to frustrate the investor's legitimate expectations which existed at the time of

534 Ibid [195].
535 Ibid [257].
536 Ibid [258].
537 Ibid [258].
538 Ibid [259]–[260].
539 Ibid [261].

making the investment. In this context, the tribunal first recognized that investors' expectations are fundamental to the investment process, being a crucial element of their decision whether to invest. A state can create certain expectations "through its laws, regulations, or other acts that has caused the investor to invest", including policy statements. Subsequent states' actions that "fundamentally deny or frustrate" those expectations can result in a violation of the FET.[540] Such expectations do not, however, shield an investor from "any and all changes". If there is no contractual specific commitment assumed by the state, the tribunal must objectively examine the legislation and the facts surrounding the investment in order to determine whether a "prudent and experienced investor could have reasonably formed a legitimate and justifiable expectation of the immutability of such legislation". This requires "rigorous" due diligence. In any case, such expectations do not preclude reforms to "safeguard the public interest to address a change of circumstances".[541]

The tribunal then turned to legitimate expectations based on Art. 44(3) RD 661/2007, which in its view must be read against the background of Art. 30(3) and (4) LSE.[542] This is because the LSE "was the legal foundation" of the regulatory framework for electricity production at the time the claimants made their investment, and an "umbrella legislation" for RD 661/2007. Based on the hierarchy of norms, RD 661/2007 cannot contradict the LSE.[543] The LSE was clear that the RDs will fix the precise terms of remuneration for RE producers, according to an "overriding principle" of the RRR and by taking into account,

540 Ibid [263]:

> The actions of host State governments through their laws, regulations, policy statements and contracts, among others, often influence the investment expectations of investors that cause them to invest. Thus, when a State that has created certain investor expectations through its laws, regulations, or other acts that has caused the investor to invest, it is often considered unfair for a State to take subsequent actions that fundamentally deny or frustrate those expectations and cause disappointed investors to seek compensation by invoking investment treaties, like the ECT, in which States have promised investors "fair and equitable treatment".

541 Ibid [264]:

> […] In the absence of a specific commitment contractually assumed by a State to freeze its legislation in favor of an investor, when an investor argues – as is the case here – that such expectation is rooted, among others, in the host State's legislation, the Tribunal is required to conduct an objective examination of the legislation and the facts surrounding the making of the investment to assess whether a prudent and experienced investor could have reasonably formed a legitimate and justifiable expectation of the immutability of such legislation. For such an expectation to be reasonable, it must also arise from a rigorous due diligence process carried out by the investor.

542 Ibid [274].

543 Ibid [273].

among others, investment costs that have been incurred and the cost of money in the capital market.[544] The tribunal observed that Art. 44(3) RD 661/2007 was "almost identical" to the text of the previously applicable Art. 40(3) RD 436/2004, and yet RD 436/2004 was repealed and replaced by RD 661/2007. The Spanish Supreme Court rejected an argument that RD 436/2004 created a "stabilized regime immune to revision".[545] This judgment was available in the public domain and any prudent investor would have been aware of it, understood its implications and adjusted its expectations accordingly.[546] The tribunal added that the preamble to RD 661/2007 refers to the need of "recalibration" when calculating compensation, to ensure that the underlying principles set up in the LSE are respected.[547]

1.2.23.3 *Due Diligence*

For the tribunal, an investor who had engaged in an "appropriate due diligence" would have been aware of the above.[548] Against this background, it would be unreasonable for the claimants to interpret Art. 44(3) RD 661/2007 "as constituting a stabilized regime for the calculation of the premium". Any such interpretation would be contrary to the established hierarchy of norms in the Spanish legal system.[549]

The tribunal reaffirmed that legitimate expectations can be grounded in the law, but it dismissed the relevance of "promotional literature about what the law says".[550] It considered irrelevant PowerPoint presentations emanating from various Spanish agencies, such as the CNE and InvestInSpain. The former had no authority to enact rules or regulations. The latter was merely a private enterprise, despite being owned by state agencies, with powers restricted to attracting foreign investments.[551]

Other developments relied upon by the claimants were irrelevant for assessing legitimate expectations because they took place after the investment was made.[552] Similarly, registration in the Pre-RAIPRE could not have created more extensive rights than those which already existed under RD 661/2007. They cannot constitute the source of an independent expectation of a stabilized

544 Ibid [275].
545 Ibid [277].
546 Ibid [278].
547 Ibid [280].
548 Ibid [281].
549 Ibid [282].
550 Ibid [287].
551 Ibid [284]–[286].
552 Ibid [290], [293], [296], [300], [306].

remuneration regime or confirmation of the same.[553] Similarly, registration in the RAIPRE, did not purport to create additional rights to a stabilized regime.[554]

The tribunal referred again to the absence of any contractual commitment by Spain which would govern the plant's provision of electricity to state entities. Such a contract – a Power Purchase Agreement ("PPA") – is common in comparable power projects. It stipulates the pricing and operational conditions for the provision of power to the national grid, as well as the amendment procedure to be followed to change those conditions during the life of the PPA. The aim of a PPA is to "reduce the regulatory risk that the investor would otherwise bear". Absent such a PPA, "reasonable investors would not have had expectations, as they might have had with a PPA, that Spain's regulatory regime was immutable". This is because expectations are created not only by positive actions of states, but also by actions which states choose not to take.[555]

This led to a conclusion that a prudent investor, having conducted appropriate due diligence, would not have reasonably formed an expectation of receiving a stable income stream for the life of the disputed plant.[556]

1.2.23.4 *Transparency*

The tribunal then looked at the third element of the FET, the obligation to act transparently towards an investor and/or the investment. It concluded that a lack of transparency could be sufficiently extreme that it constitutes a violation of the FET. However, this would require a "continuing pattern of non-transparent actions" over time, which had not been proven to exist in this case.[557] The claim particularly alleged that it took over eleven months to develop the remuneration parameters announced in RDL 9/2013. In the tribunal's view, given the complexities associated with elaborating a compensation scheme, such a period was within "the bounds of reasonable administrative practice".[558] The length of time it takes to legislate is not a conclusive factor.[559]

1.2.23.5 *Reasonableness*

The tribunal then looked at the fourth element of the FET, the obligation to avoid taking unreasonable, abusive or discriminatory actions. Based on the dictionary definition of "reasonable", the tribunal considered Spain's

553 Ibid [300].
554 Ibid [306].
555 Ibid [307].
556 Ibid [308].
557 Ibid [311], [315].
558 Ibid [313].
559 Ibid [314].

measures as "within the bounds of reason" and rational.[560] Then the tribunal adopted the analysis from *AES v. Hungary*, i.e. existence of a rational public policy and the reasonableness of a state measure in relation to that policy.[561] It found that Spain's measures met this test.[562] Spain was not required to exempt investors from its policies to remedy the tariff deficit merely because investors were not responsible for this deficit.[563] Spain already had increased consumer prices for electricity over 80% during the period 2003–2009, which were already among the highest in Europe. Thus, it was reasonable to choose a policy to protect consumers and require energy producers to bear additional costs.[564]

1.2.23.6 *Proportionality*

Finally, the tribunal looked at the fifth and final element of the FET, the obligation to avoid taking disproportionate actions. First, it noted that the ECT does not mention proportionality and in fact, the claim was "another way of making an argument" already rejected, concerning reasonableness.[565] Nevertheless the tribunal looked at the ordinary meaning of the word "proportionate", which "is normally used to describe a relationship, often in quantitative terms, between the whole of an entity or situation and a part of that whole".[566] To assess it, the tribunal assessed the rate of return earned by the claimants before and after the disputed measures.[567]

1.2.23.7 *RRR*

The tribunal reasoned that, in several publications and the claimants own contemporaneous documents, the estimated rate of return under the Special Regime ranged from 7.5% to 8%.[568] Thus, in the tribunal's view, the RRR was around 7% post-tax, prior financing.[569] Under the New Regime, the IRR was set at the level of 7.4% pre-tax.[570] The claimants argued that this equals 5.9%

560 Ibid [317].
561 Ibid [316].
562 Ibid [319].
563 Ibid [320].
564 Ibid [319].
565 Ibid [325]–[326].
566 Ibid [325].
567 Ibid [327].
568 Ibid [331]–[335].
569 Ibid [337].
570 This is probably a simplification in light of uniform description in other cases that the pre-tax IRR was 7.398%.

post-tax, whereas the respondent argued that it is 7% post-tax.[571] The tribunal sided with the respondent's position, considering that the claimants had failed to meet the evidential burden of proof on this point.[572] Based on the record, the tribunal considered it "reasonable to infer" that at the time of issuing the award, the claimants were achieving a return in excess of 7% post-tax. The exact number was not disclosed by the claimants.[573]

Thus, in "absolute terms", the tribunal considered the disputed measures proportionate, in the sense that they did not have a "significant negative effect" on the claimants' investment. The same conclusion applied when considering the proportionality from a "relative" analysis, i.e. whether there was a "reasonable relationship between the burden placed on the foreign investor by the contested measures and the aim sought to be realized by those same State measures". The "shared sacrifice" approach, requiring those who benefit from the system to contribute to its continued operation and financial stability, justified requiring the claimants to "forego a modest amount of revenue" to preserve the electricity system. Thus, the aim, the method and the effect of the State measures were reasonable.[574]

1.2.24 Stadtwerke – Dissenting Opinion

1.2.24.1 *Regulatory Revolution*

One of the arbitrators issued a dissenting opinion.[575] He agreed with the majority's analysis and conclusions on jurisdiction, but disagreed on the liability issue and considered that the claimants were entitled to full compensation.[576] In his view, even if one agrees that the reference to "stable" conditions in the first sentence of Art. 10(1) ECT does not constitute a separate obligation, it constitutes a "context" for the purposes of interpretating the FET, pursuant to Art. 31(1) VCLT.[577] Thus, the FET includes "stable and equitable conditions", which allows to legitimate expectations of "fundamental stability with respect to the main characteristics of the legal and regulatory regime" which exists at the time of making the investment.[578] They preclude fundamental and radical

571 Ibid [338].

572 Ibid [339]–[343].

573 Ibid [353].

574 Ibid [354].

575 Stadtwerke v. Spain, ICSID Case No. ARB/15/1, Dissenting Opinion (02.12.2019). Formally, the document does not stipulate the date on which it was issued. The date is that on which it was dispatched to the parties together with the award.

576 Ibid [1]–[2].

577 Ibid [6].

578 Ibid [7].

changes being made to this regime.[579] This is notwithstanding that states retain a power to regulate their economies, including by making reforms and amendments to the legal and regulatory regime (unless agreed otherwise).[580]

Although legitimate expectations are "more than a hope", they can be based on the legal and regulatory framework in the host state, which exists at the time of making the investment, "in combination with statements by and conduct of the host State and its representatives concerning the legal and regulatory framework, as well as concerning the investment in question".[581] The claimants' expectations based on RD 661/2007 were reinforced by several publications issued by the Spanish ministry, the CNE and by InvestInSpain. In the dissenter's view, all of these statements were not about an RRR, but about regulatory certainty and stability.[582] The dissenter also found the 2011 resolution to be a confirmation that the RD 661/2007 regime would apply to the disputed plant for its entire operational life.[583]

For the dissenter, the disputed measures fundamentally and radically changed the regulatory regime which existed when the investment was made, and therefore breached legitimate expectations.[584] For reasons of judicial economy, he focused on RDL 9/2013, "which was the straw that broke the camel's back".[585] He emphasized that the power plants were no longer paid on the basis of the electricity produced but, rather, on the regulator's estimates concerning a hypothetical standard installation. Moreover, the regulated FITs were abolished, remuneration was no longer provided for the lifetime of the plant but limited to 25 years and natural gas as a support fuel was restricted.[586] Furthermore, the New Regime ignored actual costs, which was intended to significantly reduce the subsidies to existing plants, as it was "applied retroactively to all existing facilities", including the claimants' plant.[587] Even though the New Regime states that it applies with respect to future remuneration only, it subtracts past remuneration from future remuneration, which has retroactive effect.[588]

579 Ibid [9].
580 Ibid [8].
581 Ibid [10].
582 Ibid [12], [15], [16].
583 Ibid [13].
584 Ibid [23].
585 Ibid [18].
586 Ibid [20].
587 Ibid [21].
588 Ibid [22].

1.2.25 RWE

1.2.25.1 *Stability*

In *RWE*, the tribunal observed that the obligation included in the first sentence of Art. 10(1) ECT on stable conditions concerns only the initial conditions at the moment of making the investment, not an "ongoing obligation of stability".[589] An obligation to ensure "ongoing regulatory stability" exists only insofar as it forms part of the FET. As such, the first sentence of Art. 10(1) ECT "does not add materially" to the FET enshrined in the second sentence.[590] When interpreting it, the tribunal looked at the object and purpose of the ECT, which calls for a balanced approach.[591] It also noted that the ordinary meaning of the used wording was not helpful in interpreting the FET.[592]

The tribunal recognized that regulations change over time and that the FET offers protection from "certain forms of fundamental regulatory change".[593] Absent specific commitments, a breach of the FET may occur if "there has been some form of total or unreasonable change to, or subversion of, the legal regime". This is so regardless of whether the FET is understood as autonomous, or as arising from CIL.[594] The tribunal noted earlier, however, that the FET should be approached based on CIL, and the term was not used in the ECT in a "legal vacuum", but against a backdrop of the formula being used for many decades and tied closely to CIL.[595]

1.2.25.2 *Specific Commitments*

The tribunal then analyzed whether legislation can contain specific commitments.[596] It noted the *Masdar* tribunal's comment about two opposing schools of thought.[597] The tribunal was unconvinced that domestic law had the same effect as a contractual stabilization clause or some more specific commitment.[598] It sided with those tribunals which did not "sanctify laws as promises".[599] Nevertheless, the claimants' reliance on a given tariff at the moment of making the investments was a relevant factor in assessing whether

589 RWE v. Spain, ICSID Case No. ARB/14/34, Decision on Jurisdiction, Liability, and Certain Issues of Quantum (30.12.2019) [426].
590 Ibid [429].
591 Ibid [439].
592 Ibid [440].
593 Ibid [448]–[449].
594 Ibid [451].
595 Ibid [447].
596 Ibid [452].
597 Ibid [453]–[457].
598 Ibid [458], [461].
599 Ibid [459]–[460].

a tariff regime change was "disproportionate", particularly given that they were "invited and encouraged" to invest in Spain through a number of factors, including "a very attractive regime of remuneration".[600]

The tribunal denied that Art. 44(3) RD 661/2007 included a specific commitment to legislative stability. This provision could be "readily understood" in such a way that future revisions would be made as regulated in the said provision.[601] However, it was included in a regulation of general application, which is itself susceptible to change.[602] This was strengthened by the fact that Art. 40(3) RD 436/2004, with almost identical wording, "had not lasted unchanged for more than around two years".[603]

Registration in the RAIPRE and related registration certificate also did not constitute any specific commitment. They were seen as fulfilment of administrative requirements, not as a source of independent obligations.[604] Similarly, no specific commitments were considered to have been made in the 2010 Agreement, as even the claimants themselves did not perceive it in this manner.[605]

1.2.25.3 *Legitimate Expectations*

The tribunal looked at the issue of legitimate expectations. First, it underlined the relevance of the timing, as in this case the claimants made a number of investments over a period of 12 years.[606] With respect to the first group of investments – made under RD 2818/1998 – the tribunal relied on that the fact that the previous regime did not contain a promise that future revisions would not affect registered plants. Thus, it found no legitimate expectations with respect to investments made prior to 2004.[607]

The tribunal then turned to the second group, i.e. a major investment made in 2008 and a few minor investments made in 2008 and 2009. Based on the evidence, it considered that the claimants relied on a "stable and predictable regime", rather than on a specific understanding of the relevant provisions of RD 661/2007.[608]

600 Ibid [462].
601 Ibid [537], [542].
602 Ibid [538].
603 Ibid [539].
604 Ibid [544].
605 Ibid [546].
606 Ibid [483].
607 Ibid [484]–[488].
608 Ibid [491]–[497]. The relevant evidence, included witness testimony, confirmed that the claimants did not rely on any particular wording of the RDs, but on the general stability of the regime.

With respect to the third group, i.e. investments made after 2010, the tribunal assessed that the claimants did not rely on a stable and predictable legal environment, as by then they were already informed of the possibility of changes in the incentives scheme.[609]

1.2.25.4 *Due Diligence*

The tribunal then looked at the relevance of the due diligence. The claimants presented a "rather confused picture as to the due diligence that was carried out" prior to making their investments, which focused on the economics rather than on the regulatory framework.[610] However, in the tribunal's view, at least starting with the investments made in 2008 there was "ample reason" for due diligence focused on the regulatory framework. The lawyers could not have been expected to advise on that issue without being explicitly requested to perform a specific, regulatory due diligence.[611] Since there was "plainly visible regulatory instability", the tribunal regarded as "incumbent" on the claimants "to have performed some discrete due diligence exercise on the applicable law and regulations", which they failed to do.[612]

1.2.25.5 *Domestic Courts*

The tribunal observed that, when analyzing legitimate expectations, it must take into account all statements, reports and legal decisions that would have been covered by the regulatory due diligence, and in particular the relevant case law of the Spanish Supreme Court.[613] However, the tribunal also observed that the relevant judgments were not made "in a sufficiently analogous context" to be directly relevant, because those existing at the relevant time concerned prior regimes and transitional provisions of RD 436/2004, not Art. 40(3).[614] The relevant case law of the Spanish Supreme Court was handed down after the investments were made. On the one hand, it confirms the meaning of the relevant provisions under Spanish law, done by the "ultimate arbiter in domestic law".[615] On the other hand, this is not what a diligent investor could have concluded when making the investment.[616] The tribunal took note of the 2007 Press release made by the Spanish government, as well as

609 Ibid [498]–[506].
610 Ibid [508].
611 Ibid [510].
612 Ibid [513].
613 Ibid [514].
614 Ibid [518]–[519].
615 Ibid [524]–[525].
616 Ibid [534].

presentations of InvestInSpain and CNE, confirming that Spain itself had understood Art. 44(3) RD 661/2007 to protect existing plants against any future tariff revisions.[617]

1.2.25.6 *Proportionality*

The tribunal then observed that regulatory changes must be proportionate even in absence of a specific commitment. It assessed proportionality insofar as whether the disputed measures were (i) necessary, (ii) suitable, and (iii) proportionality *sensu stricto*, i.e. whether they placed an excessive financial burden upon the claimants.[618] It also recognized the state's margin of appreciation, noting that the tribunal itself as simultaneously in a better (having the benefit of hindsight and experts) and in a worse (having narrower perspective) position to assess proportionality than the state was.[619]

The tribunal found the disputed measures suitable, understood as a establishing an appropriate relationship between the measures and their objective.[620] They were directly aimed at reducing the tariff deficit and their implementation achieved this goal.[621] The tribunal did not agree that the tariff deficit was a problem prior to enactment of RD 661/2007. The Special Regime was grounded in the macroeconomic data forecast from 2005–2010 Plan, whereas the tariff deficit was caused by the electricity consumption decrease caused by the Financial Crisis.[622]

The disputed measures were also found to be necessary, which implies an analysis of whether less restrictive means were reasonably available to achieve the objective. If other, less restrictive measures were available, any more restrictive measure is unnecessary.[623] The tribunal was unconvinced that the same result could have been achieved by increasing taxes and electricity charges.[624] The claimants did not meet the burden of proof that other, less restrictive measures were available.[625]

The tribunal then analyzed the third element of proportionality, i.e. proportionality *sensu stricto*. It stressed that a measure lacks proportionality if an

617 Ibid [533].
618 Ibid [550]–[551], [569].
619 Ibid [553].
620 Ibid [554].
621 Ibid [560].
622 Ibid [559].
623 Ibid [554].
624 Ibid [562].
625 Ibid [567].

investor "bears an individual and excessive burden".[626] This requires a balancing exercise. However, the tribunal considered that "a particularly wide margin" of appreciation was inappropriate in the context of the case, where the Special Regime was established "with the aim of attracting investors into an industry that requires a large up-front investment" and where the respondent was speaking of a "guarantee" back in 2007.[627]

The tribunal also considered whether the respondent paid attention to the impact its decision-making process had on investors. It noted that Spain mandated: (i) the BCG report, which was never prepared for an unknown reason and (ii) the Roland Berger report, which was finished several months after the Order IET/1045/2014 was published and for which Spain did not wait before adopting the New Regime.[628] Recognizing that Spain was not obliged to follow or to wait for these reports, failing to do resulted in it putting itself at greater risk of an unintended or disproportionate impact of the disputed measures.[629]

1.2.25.7 *RRR*

As an element of this analysis, the tribunal looked at the RRR. It agreed that an IRR of 7.398%, as introduced in the New Regime, is "an appropriate minimum figure" in the circumstances of the case to protect against placing an excessive and disproportionate burden on the claimants.[630] However, it preferred to examine the IRR achieved individually by each of the claimants' plants by reference to the actual costs of these plants, rather than the costs of a hypothetical standard installation as regulated in the New Regime.[631] Of a total number of 24 disputed plants, 6 Wind energy plants and 1 Hydro energy plant achieved IRR calculated based on the actual costs below the benchmark level of 7.398%.[632] This led the tribunal to conclude that it was an excessive and disproportionate burden borne by the claimants with respect to the investments in those plants, in the context of an overall impact of the disputed measures, which reduced the claimants' overall returns by approx. 54%.[633] The FET was violated to that extent.[634]

626 Ibid [569].
627 Ibid [571].
628 Ibid [595], [596].
629 Ibid [597], [599].
630 Ibid [599].
631 Ibid [586].
632 Ibid [587].
633 Ibid [589], [599]
634 Ibid [600]

1.2.25.8 *Regulatory Revolution*

The tribunal then turned back to the issue of stability, understood as an element of the FET, and noted that this prohibited a "total and unreasonable change to, or subversion of, the legal regime".[635] Whilst there was a radical change in the method of calculating remuneration, the claimants remained entitled to subsidies and "other key elements of the prior regime have remained substantially unchanged".[636] Moreover, the history of the Spanish RE regulatory regime "has been of regulatory change", with numerous important changes taking place historically.

1.2.25.9 *Retroactivity*

A key question for the stability analysis was alleged the "impermissible retroactive effect" of the disputed measures.[637] Plants which, under the Special Regime, had previously received payments that were subsequently viewed as excessive under the New Regime, were now "brought back into account". This resulted in lower subsidies under the New Regime, and even the absence of any subsidies for 10 of the claimants' plants. The tribunal considered that these measures had a "retrospective", but not an "impermissible retroactive effect".[638] Thus, making deductions from future payments was found to be consistent with Art. 10(1) ECT.[639]

Nevertheless, the tribunal concluded differently on the obligation to repay approx. 19.4 million Euro as a reimbursement of subsidies received in the period between the adoption of RDL 9/2013 and the Order IET/1045/2014 by the mentioned 10 plants (which were not eligible for subsidies under the New Regime).[640] This was "a subversion of the prior legal regime" which resulted in a violation of the FET.[641]

The tribunal concluded that the respondent violated the FET, but only through: (i) procuring the repayment of sums that had already been paid to the claimants in 2013 and 2014 (i.e. until the Order IET/1045/2014 was adopted) and (ii) the disproportionate (but otherwise necessary, reasonable

635 Ibid [610].

636 Ibid [612].

637 Ibid [613]. In other words, even though the tribunal agreed that the FET protects against a wholesale reform of the regulatory regime, it concluded that this had not occurred in this case. It considered that many elements of the Special Regime were included in the New Regime, even if they did not include FITs or Premiums.

638 Ibid [617].

639 Ibid [619].

640 Ibid [620].

641 Ibid [621].

and non-discriminatory) impact of the disputed measures with respect to some of the claimants' plants.[642]

1.2.26 RWE – Dissenting Opinion

One of the arbitrators issued a dissenting opinion.[643] He agreed with the majority in issuing the award because to do otherwise would "potentially weaken or undercut our years of common effort". He also recognized the tribunal's obligation to produce a coherent award that will be enforceable.[644] He drafted his opinion inspired by Thomas Wälde's separate opinion in *Thunderbird v. Mexico*, with the intention to influence future tribunals.[645]

The dissenter weighed the facts differently and would have reached a different outcome regarding virtually everything except the finding of a breach that necessitated paying compensation.[646] He would have found more extensive breaches of the FET and awarded a higher amount of compensation.[647]

1.2.26.1 *Schools of Thought regarding ISDS*

The dissenter analyzed the two main "schools of legal thought" regarding ISDS.[648] One school is rooted in the origins of investment arbitration, a reply to an urgent need to increase the flow of private investment resources to developing nations after World War II.[649] It focuses on the rights of foreign investors, and the perception of the business community after World War II that private foreign investment needed to be protected from political and other non-commercial risks in developing states with legal systems perceived as weak and unreliable.[650] By entering into investment treaties, governments agreed to "honor such treaty obligations and commitments as part of their domestic law – even if such commitments were understood to include standards that are

642 Ibid [729].
643 RWE v. Spain, ICSID Case No. ARB/14/34, Separate Opinion of Mr. Judd L. Kessler (01.12.2020).
644 Ibid [2].
645 Ibid [3].
646 Ibid [4].
647 Ibid [5].
648 Even if one disagrees with the description or with a division drew by the dissenter, this may contribute to the ongoing debate concerning the "pro-investor" and "pro-state" bias of arbitrators and the ISDS system as a whole. This view suggests that this is not necessarily a "bias", but a different conceptual framework applied by some of the arbitrators.
649 RWE v. Spain, Separate opinion ..., *supra* note 643 [7].
650 Ibid [10].

more demanding than those normally applied in domestic law".[651] He leaned towards the first school.[652]

The second school of thought reacts to the insufficient structurization of the ISDS system and the call to be more deferential to decisions adopted by governments, particularly in democratic states.[653] It is closely related to the critique of investment arbitration over the past 20 years, linked to concerns over its legitimacy. The critique is "predominantly from Europe" and calls for a greater use of proportionality analyses, understood as a gateway for non-investment principles to enter the arbitration framework, thus avoiding the fragmentation of international law.[654]

The dissenter then analyzed the main aspects and the predominant logic behind the majority's decision. He disagreed that the ECT is "relatively neutral regarding the protection of foreign investment". Such an approach pays insufficient attention to the context and origin of the ECT, which must be perceived from the perspective of the fall of the Berlin Wall in 1989.[655] In his view, the language adopted in the ECT was by no means novel. By 1998, more than 1.700 investment treaties existed.[656] Nothing in the ECT suggests any particular "generous deference" granted to governmental decisions or national laws, "much less the former Communist bloc nations".[657]

1.2.26.2 *Right to Regulate*

The dissenter noted that Spain recognized that its industrial competitiveness was impacted by reliance on imported petroleum-based energy resources, which caused a shift towards RE, which was particularly attractive given Spain's geography.[658]

He also recognized that each state can have a different view of the role of the private sector in its economy. There is no obligation under international law to seek foreign investment, and if a state decides to do so – there is no fixed formula of how to do so. However, when a state chooses to seek foreign investment, then international law becomes relevant. This is what happened when Spain deliberately sought foreign investment in the RE sector. By doing so, Spain made a number of relevant policy choices. First, it could have established

651 Ibid [15].
652 Ibid [19].
653 Ibid [7].
654 Ibid [16]–[18].
655 Ibid [23].
656 Ibid [25].
657 Ibid [26].
658 Ibid [29].

incentives which applied solely to Spanish nationals, but it decided to extend these to foreigners as well. Second, it could have limited the Special Regime to greenfield investments, but it decided to include brownfield investments as well. Third, Spain decided to provide incentives for the operational life of each plant, to incentivize investments at a time when the costs of RE plants were too high to make unassisted private investment viable.[659] These were all the respondent's own choices.[660]

As to Art. 30(4) LSE, the dissenter paid more attention to the passage "shall be supplemented by the payment of a premium under statutory terms set out in regulations" rather than "reasonable profitability rates with reference to the cost of money on capital markets".[661]

For him, Spain "for its own good and sufficient reasons", had created a sophisticated invitation to long-term RE investors, recognizing that RE at that time used technologies "involving higher costs that do not allow them to compete in the free market".[662] It was a "clear and unmistakable message". If the investor considered the Spanish incentives were sufficient to earn an acceptable profit and decided to make the investment, "Spain would welcome this investment and Spain would do its best to maintain stability over the long term".[663] The legal framework had no particular regard for the compensation earned by investors, since returns depended on the efficiency of each plant.[664] Benefits and responsibilities of the Special Regime flowed in both directions for many years, until 2013/2014. Investors operated RE plants, delivered power to the grid and paid their taxes, whereas Spain lowered its quantities of imported petroleum products and improved its carbon footprint.[665] The dissenter summarized this as "the history of a highly successful campaign by the Respondent to attract billions of Euros in RE investment in Spain; as well as to comply with the ambitions and binding Directives of the EU regarding increased RE generation capacity".[666]

Thus, he did not consider that the dispute concerned Spain's sovereign right to regulate or the need to exercise broad discretion when addressing issues of public interest.[667] He noted that the tariff deficit started to grow from 2000

659 Ibid [31].
660 Ibid [32].
661 Ibid [34].
662 Ibid [38].
663 Ibid [39].
664 Ibid [40].
665 Ibid [41].
666 Ibid [43].
667 Ibid [48]–[49].

onwards, even though Spain did not address it before the Financial Crisis.[668] The required balancing exercise depends on when it takes place, when different elements of weight are involved in the imagined scales.[669] There were numerous changes to the Special Regime that Spain could have introduced at various times, which would not have triggered the obligation to compensate and would have stopped the tariff deficit worsening. However, these would probably also have halted the large flows of new RE investments, which was not desired and would have meant that Spain would fail to meet its obligations under EU law.[670] He compared his understanding of the right to regulate in this case to a hypothetical situation whereby, instead of financing the Special Regime as it did, Spain took out a loan at an international bank to cover the tariff deficit and later refused to repay it, justifying such refusal on its right to regulate.[671]

1.2.26.3 *Domestic Courts*

The dissenter also commented on the Spanish Supreme Court's judgments. Even though he approached them with "appropriate respect", he was "struck" that they were silent on the lack of any discussion concerning the role of international law arising from treaties to which Spain is a party, including the ECT, since they form part of Spanish law pursuant to Art. 96 of the Spanish Constitution.[672]

1.2.26.4 *Proportionality*

Finally, he disagreed with the majority's decision on proportionality. First, the disputed measures were not "necessary", as he considered that other methods were available to obtain funds during the Financial Crisis.[673] Second, a 54%

---

668 Ibid [53]. Apart from the different perspective (the dissenter leaning towards the first school of thought, whilst the majority probably leaned towards the second, albeit not expressly stating this), it seems that a fundamental difference existed between the dissenter and the majority in terms of their perception of the tariff deficit. Whereas the majority considered that this was caused by the Financial Crisis, the dissenter considered that it had already begun in 2000 and that Spain had simply decided to leave it unaddressed for a number of years.

669 Ibid [53]:

> [...] If one is to balance public and private investor interests, a lot may depend on when the balancing takes place. As will be seen below, there were many significant moments during the period 2004 to 2013–14. A snapshot taken in 2006, 2008 or 2010 would involve different elements of weight in the imagined scales.

670 Ibid [66], [67].

671 Ibid [74].

672 Ibid [67]–[69].

673 Ibid [79].

reduction of expected cash flows is disproportionate.[674] Proportionality cannot simply weigh Spain's need to regulate against investors' interests. Prior policy decisions, taken by Spain to attract foreign investment should also be given weight.[675] Otherwise, the proportionality analysis "points in a rather dangerous direction", that states can shift all negative consequences of macroeconomic crisis onto investors. This would negatively impact on the ability to attract and maintain investments.[676]

1.2.26.5 *Retroactivity*

The dissenter stressed that an arbitrator's function is to play a part in an institution based on the rule of law. This makes it impossible for him to accept the majority's view on the claw-back provision, that after operating for 10 years the claimants were subjected to a "time machine" introduced by the New Regime. He considered it as "the fundamental inequity of a State inviting and accepting investment on one set of conditions and then, for its own reasons, establishing new rules to be applied "as if" they had been in force in the first place".[677] This is contrary to due process and, as such, it violates the FET.[678]

1.2.27 Watkins

In *Watkins*, the tribunal started with a general observation that Art. 10(1) ECT contains a number of obligations: (i) to encourage and create suitable,[679] equitable, favorable and transparent investment conditions, (ii) the FET, (iii) constant protection and security, (iv) the non-impairment standard, (v) non-discrimination obligations and (vi) an umbrella clause.[680] The tribunal identified the violation of the FET as the "primary claim", which requires analysis of the FET and the stable, equitable, favorable and transparent conditions together.[681] It understood the FET as autonomous standard, which goes beyond the minimum standard of treatment under international law and does not require bad faith or any "ulterior motive".[682]

---

674 Ibid [80].
675 Ibid.
676 Ibid [84].
677 Ibid [81].
678 Ibid [82].
679 Instead of "stable" as in the text of Art. 10(1) ECT.
680 Watkins v. Spain, ICSID Case No. ARB/15/44, Award (21.01.2020) [482].
681 Ibid [483]–[484].
682 Ibid [511]–[513], [516].

1.2.27.1 *Specific Commitments*

The tribunal then observed that specific commitments were made by the relevant legislation, and that there is no need to anchor them in contractual obligations.[683] It underlined that Spanish law cannot be used as a tool to override international law, which is why Spanish law was seen as irrelevant when assessing the commitments and obligations made to the claimants.[684] The tribunal observed that the balancing exercise conducted in *Electrabel v. Hungary* is irrelevant, because it was accepted by the parties to this case. It also found no place for the concept of the "so called right to regulate" in the context of Art 10(1) ECT.[685]

1.2.27.2 *RRR*

It then disagreed with the RRR concept, preferring "the persuasive views" set out in the *Eiser*, *Novenergia*, *Antin* and *Masdar* cases in reference to the view expressed in the *RREEF* case.[686] It added that the methodology for determining the RRR was not based on any identifiable criteria.[687]

1.2.27.3 *Legitimate Expectations*

The tribunal confirmed that legitimate expectations must be viewed objectively, assessed at the moment when the investment was made. They must originate from some "affirmative action".[688] They could be based upon "any undertakings and representations made explicitly or implicitly by the host State".[689] An important element of legitimate expectations is to protect from measures which threaten "the stability of the legal and business framework" relied upon by an investor when making the investment.[690]

The tribunal acknowledged the state's right to amend the regulatory regime, which is nonetheless limited by the ECT. It does not cover "fundamental and radical changes" which are unfair, unreasonable and inequitable or undermine an investor's legitimate expectations.[691]

In the tribunal's view, Art. 44(3) RD 661/2007, reiterated by Art. 5(3) RD 1614/2010, contained a "stabilization commitment" and explicitly promised

683 Ibid [495].
684 Ibid [505].
685 Ibid [496].
686 Ibid [500].
687 Ibid [504].
688 Ibid [517].
689 Ibid [518].
690 Ibid [522].
691 Ibid [521].

that future revisions would not affect duly-registered existing installations.[692] A number of factors supported this conclusion, particularly the specific language of RD 661/2007, representations made by the CNE (i.e. that the economic regime of RD 661/2007 was "part of a wider international and domestic policy to develop RE power generation infrastructure and to specifically encourage and attract the necessary investments") and that the purpose of RD 661/2007 was to attract the necessary investment in RE, without which such investments would not have been attractive or able to compete with conventional power plants.[693] Moreover, Spain had no obligation to make such a commitment, but it chose to.[694] The tribunal also noted that the 2010 Agreement and various representations, including presentations in foreign countries designed to attract foreign investments, support the view that the claimants' expectations were reasonable.[695]

The tribunal found that the claimants' legitimate expectations were frustrated.[696] Spain wiped out the Special Regime and substituted it by an "entirely different" regime.[697]

1.2.27.4 *Stability*

The tribunal then looked at the obligation to provide a "stable and predictable regulatory regime", stemming from the first sentence of Art. 10(1) ECT.[698] The tribunal noted that Spain was under an obligation to "provide long term stability".[699] It differentiated the ECT from BITs which do not contain a similar obligation, particularly in the RE sector, which requires a substantial initial capital investment and offers return on long-term basis.[700]

1.2.27.5 *Regulatory Revolution*

In the tribunal's view, Spain created stable conditions for investments when the disputed investment was made and its intention was to provide long term stability.[701] This was supported by several official statements made by the CNE,

692 Ibid [526].
693 Ibid [527].
694 Ibid [528].
695 Ibid [531]–[532].
696 Ibid [538].
697 Ibid [534].
698 Ibid [539].
699 Ibid [540]. Although this is not unambiguous from the text of the award, it seems that the tribunal read the first sentence of Art. 10(1) ECT as containing as enabling a separate cause of action related to violation of an obligation to "provide long term stability".
700 Ibid [541].
701 Ibid [553].

the 2007 Press release, as well as various presentations made by InvestIn-Spain.[702] Such stability was "taken away" by the disputed measures.[703] The tribunal recognized that Spain has a sovereign right to regulate but if the exercise of this sovereign right results in a violation of Art. 10(1) ECT, Spain would be required to pay compensation.[704] Here, the Special Regime was "radically altered", which resulted in a violation of the ECT.[705]

In the tribunal's view, there was a "retroactive overhaul" of the Special Regime.[706] The tribunal did not explain this conclusion in more detail. It simply relied on other cases, which allowed it to conclude that this refers to the claw-back provision of the New Regime, pursuant to which past remuneration was subtracted from future remunerations.[707]

1.2.27.6 *Due Diligence*

Based on two memorandums and a report, the tribunal was persuaded that the claimants exercised proper due diligence.[708]

1.2.27.7 *Transparency*

The tribunal held moreover that Spain's conduct was not transparent.[709] It noted that Spain "dismantled" the Special Regime even though there was "no urgent need" for it to be modified. Moreover, (i) there was an 11-month period during which the new remuneration system remained uncertain, (ii) the disputed measures did not provide "any analysis explaining the underlying reasons behind" the New Regime, (iii) there was a "lack of visibility and predictability" under the New Regime, (iv) there was no clear time frame during which the new Special Payment would apply and (v) the CNE was replaced by another institution after the CNE criticized the New Regime.[710]

1.2.27.8 *Reasonableness and Proportionality*

The tribunal also opined that the disputed measures were unreasonable.[711] There must be a reasonable relationship to some rational policy goal.[712] Addressing the

702 Ibid [551]–[552].
703 Ibid [554].
704 Ibid [560].
705 Ibid [562]–[563].
706 Ibid [569].
707 Ibid [566]–[567].
708 Ibid [588]–[589].
709 Ibid [594].
710 Ibid [593].
711 Ibid [600].
712 Ibid [595]–[596].

tariff deficit was not such a goal. It "had existed long before" the relevant plants were developed and was a result of Spain's "own regulatory conduct".[713]

The disputed measures were also found to be disproportionate.[714] First, the FIT for Wind energy plants played a limited role in the accumulation of the tariff deficit, which meant that the disputed measures were unsuitable from the perspective of the proportionality test.[715] Second, the disputed measures were unnecessary, because other, less intrusive means were available and had been identified by the respondent's authorities (e.g. imposing a tax on all CO_2 emissions).[716]

The tribunal found that the disputed measures also impaired the claimants' investment, since the tariff deficit, which Spain relied upon to justify its measures, was a result of Spain's own regulatory failures to set proper consumer prices.[717]

As described above, the tribunal examined the claim from the perspective of a number of concepts, such as legitimate expectations, retroactivity, transparency, reasonableness, proportionality and non-impairment. It remains unclear whether this forms part of the tribunal's reasoning on legitimate expectations as an element of the FET, of a broader reasoning on the FET, or of an even broader test interpretation of Art. 10(1) ECT as a whole. On the one hand, this appears to be explained in the tribunal's words that it found not "only" a violation of the FET, but "that Spain also violated its obligations under Article 10(1)".[718] When one compares this to the introductory analysis, it seems that the tribunal found a violation of the FET, the obligation to provide stable and transparent investment conditions and the non-impairment standard.[719] On the other hand, when the tribunal relied on the judicial economy to escape analysis of the umbrella clause, it mentioned that it found violation of the FET only.[720] A similar conclusion stems from the operational part of the award.[721] The tribunal did not explain whether the violation of the stability requirement was, therefore, an element of the FET, or a separate cause of action. In any case, it remains unexplained whether the violation was found to exist merely

713 Ibid [599].
714 Ibid [603].
715 Ibid [601].
716 Ibid [602].
717 Ibid [604].
718 Ibid [606].
719 Ibid [482].
720 Ibid [629].
721 Ibid [775.c)].

by virtue of the fact that the Special Regime was altered, or only because that alteration was "radical".

1.2.28 Watkins – Dissenting Opinion

In a dissenting opinion, one of the arbitrators explained that she only supported the majority's conclusions on jurisdiction and on tax gross-up.[722]

1.2.28.1 *Prior Cases*

In her view, the dispute was located within the broader context of a series of cases regarding the Spanish saga. When numerous parallel cases stem from the same general measures, "the clarity of the reasoning is especially important", but she did not consider that the *Watkins* award brings clarity to the discussion.[723] The majority did not sufficiently justify its reasoning, whereas any tribunal has a "duty of legal reasoning that goes far beyond the exercise of qualifying certain awards as convincing or discarding the reasons of others as non-satisfactory".[724] A tribunal must develop its own argumentation and pay due attention to the evidence put before it. And yet, the majority failed to explain whether it considered the peculiarity of the case concerning Wind energy plants, as opposed to PV or CSP plants in all of the other cases it referred to, with the exception of *RREEF*.[725]

In cases concerning a sovereign right to legislate, the FET requires a "fine-tuned balance" which implies an in-depth analysis of what commitments were made by the state and whether it overstepped the permissible boundaries.[726]

1.2.28.2 *Legitimate Expectations*

The dissenter noted that in a recent judgment, ICJ dismissed an argument that the doctrine of legitimate expectations exists in general international law, outside the FET context. She regretted that the majority did not rebut the

---

722 Watkins v. Spain, ICSID Case No. ARB/15/44, Dissent on Liability and Quantum (09.01.2020) [1], Watkins v. Spain, *supra* note 680 [671], Watkins v. Spain, ICSID Case No. ARB/15/44, Decision on Spain's Request for Rectification of the Award (13.07.2020) [fn 50].

723 Watkins v. Spain, Dissent ..., *supra* note 722, [3]. The dissenter's criticism towards lack of clarity of the award seems to be justified. From the awards rendered in the Spanish saga, this is probably the one which is the most difficult to follow in terms of the tribunal's reasoning.

724 Ibid [4].

725 Ibid [4].

726 Ibid [5]: "[...] a fine-tuned balance should be found between the protection of the investment, especially the legitimate expectations of the investor, and the sovereign prerogatives of the State to legislate for purposes in the general interest" (footnote omitted).

argument that Art. 10(1) ECT provides an autonomous standard of stability, independent from the FET.[727]

In her view, the FET's protection has variable intensity, depending on whether there was a stabilization clause or specific commitments, or legitimate expectations stemming from the general regulatory framework.[728] She identified three different approaches adopted by the tribunals in the previous Spanish saga cases: (i) some tribunals found that specific commitments, equivalent to a stabilization clause, existed in the regulatory framework (ii) others found that individual representations had been made to the relevant investors and (iii) in the absence of any of the above, the tribunals assessed whether legitimate expectations based on the regulatory framework entailed an expectation that the normative framework will not change, by assessing a balance based on a proportionality control, between a state's regulatory margin of discretion and the legal security which investors are entitled to expect.[729]

She recognized that the majority adopted the first approach. However, even under this approach, she disagreed with the majority's conclusion.[730] First, it requires an in-depth analysis of Art. 44(3) RD 661/2007, which was absent in the award.[731] Second, the majority failed to properly consider the date of the investment, and how this affected the "intensity" of the claimants' legitimate expectations.[732] She noted that the disputed investment was made in 2011, whereas the tribunal in *Cube* considered that in 2010 a "climate of change" was already visible.[733]

1.2.28.3 *Reasonableness and Proportionality*

The dissenter also disagreed with the majority's approach on reasonableness and its failure to identify the proper parameters adopted in the proportionality analysis and its conclusion that other, less intrusive means were available, without having verified them and without even acknowledging the existence of the Financial Crisis.[734]

Finally, she disagreed that the investment was "destroyed". She noted that the claimants bought the investment for 91 million Euro in 2011, it was valued

727 Ibid [7].
728 Ibid [8].
729 Ibid [9].
730 Ibid [10].
731 Ibid [11].
732 Ibid [12].
733 Ibid [13].
734 Ibid [14].

at 98 million Euro in 2014 and the claimants sold it for 133 million Euro in 2016. She saw no loss to be repaired in such circumstances.[735]

1.2.29 PV Investors

In *PV Investors*, the claim concerned the regulatory stability requirement and the "stabilization commitment".[736] The respondent's primary defense was based on the RRR theory, i.e. that the claimants could have expected a subsidized remuneration and the right to sell their energy on a priority basis and to achieve reasonable profitability.[737] Faced with this defense, the claimants presented an alternative claim.[738] The proceedings were initiated in 2011. However, the claimants were allowed to amend their claims, which covered all of the disputed measures, including those adopted when the arbitration was already pending.[739]

1.2.29.1 *Prior Cases*

The tribunal started its analysis by noting the three main groups of cases in the Spanish saga, i.e. in which the tribunals: (i) upheld claims similar to the primary claim (naming *Eiser, Masdar* and *Novenergia*), (ii) dismissed such claims (naming *Charanne, Isolux* and *Stadtwerke*) and (iii) upheld claims similar to the alternative claim (naming *RREEF* and *BayWa*). It noted that "the picture is thus by far not unanimous and rather shows a diversity of views between arbitral tribunals".[740] The tribunal followed the approach of the third group of cases. It identified several factors which explained the discrepancies. It noted that *Charanne* concerned only some of the disputed measures, *Isloux* concerned investments made late in 2012, whereas *Masdar* and *NextEra* included specific individual confirmations. Moreover, in its view, the tribunals from the first group were not presented with claims equivalent to the alternative claim in this arbitration.[741] It also noted that one of the main reasons for the diverging

---

735 Ibid [16]. In addition, she criticized the failure to properly consider the regulatory risk in the DCF analysis – [15]. Even if one accepts the decision on the merits, the dissenter rightly points out that no loss was suffered by the claimants. This is a situation which qualifies for a declaratory award, but no compensation.

736 The PV Investors v. Spain, PCA Case No. 2012-14, Final Award (28.02.2020) [213], [550].

737 Ibid [419].

738 Ibid [216], [481]–[482].

739 Ibid [15].

740 Ibid [553].

741 Ibid [554]: "[…] the Tribunal's assessment of the expectations which investors could derive from the regulatory framework and the reasonableness of Spain's changes to such framework lead it to dismiss the Primary Claim and thus move to assess the Alternative Claim […]".

case law is the assessment of expectations which can be derived from the regulatory framework. It noted that "it is not entirely unsurprising, and indeed to some extent to be expected in a system based on ad hoc adjudication, that arbitral tribunals may assess relevant circumstances in different ways".[742]

The tribunal identified the FET's content as encompassing the protection of legitimate expectations, the protection against arbitrary, unreasonable, and disproportionate conduct, and transparency.[743]

1.2.29.2 *Stability*

It rejected an argument that the first sentence of Art. 10(1) ECT represents a stand-alone or absolute standard of treatment. Rather, it considered this provision to be "intertwined with and closely linked to FET".[744] Having said so, the ECT "provides for the creation and maintenance of stable conditions as part of FET within well-defined limits which derive from the object and purpose" of the ECT.[745] The object and purpose is to be assessed in the light of the European Energy Charter, referred to in Art. 2 of the ECT.[746] In its view, the ECT's contracting parties sought to achieve a balance between "the sovereign rights of the State over energy resources and the creation of a climate favorable to the flow of investments on the basis of market principles". This shows that the purpose of "promoting long term cooperation in the energy field", as contained in Art. 2 ECT, may be facilitated by the stability of regulatory framework, but this requirement is not absolute and has to be balanced with state sovereignty.[747]

1.2.29.3 *Legitimate Expectations*

The tribunal then focused on the relevant legitimate expectations, reiterating that the standard of protection is objective and that they must be assessed as of the time of making the investment.[748] It also reiterated that specific

742 Ibid [555]. The tribunal's reasoning is self-contradictory when compared to its observation that it must strengthen the consistency of ISDS case law (and follow established case law), i.e. "to contribute to the harmonious development of international investment law, with a view to meeting the legitimate expectations of the community of States and investors towards the certainty of the rule of law" – [521]. See also: The PV Investors v. Spain, PCA Case No. 2012-14, Preliminary Award on Jurisdiction (13.10.2014) [53].

743 The PV Investors v. Spain, *supra* note 736 [565].

744 Ibid [567].

745 Ibid [568].

746 Ibid [568]–[569].

747 Ibid [570].

748 Ibid [573], [575].

representations may become relevant, that changes to the regulatory framework must be "unreasonable" in order to trigger a FET violation and that legitimate expectations must be balanced with the right to regulate in the public interest.[749] The tribunal also recognized the state's margin of appreciation. It viewed its task not as being to evaluate the policy choices behind the state's economic decisions, or to second-guess the state's choices, or review *de novo* whether they were well-founded or to assess the availability of alternative solutions. At the same time, the margin of appreciation is limited by the principles of reasonableness and proportionality, as otherwise it would render the substantive treaty protections "wholly nugatory".[750]

The tribunal added that the above considerations on legitimate expectations apply *mutatis mutandis* to its analysis of other elements of the FET and other standards of protection found in the ECT.[751]

1.2.29.4 *RRR*

The tribunal analyzed the disputed measures in the context of the general legal framework, rather than in isolation.[752] After looking at the evolution of the Spanish RE regulations, the tribunal concluded that the LSE "established the principle of reasonable profitability or reasonable rate of return as general rule leaving it to the implementing regulation, to establish the means ensuring such reasonable profitability".[753]

The tribunal dismissed the claim based on a legitimate expectation regarding an immutable FIT.[754] The "systemic interpretation" of Art. 44(3) RD 661/2007 "in its proper context" led it to conclude that this was not a stabilization commitment.[755] First, it was "an act of general regulation", subject to changes by the Spanish authorities.[756] Second, a reasonable investor must have been aware of the "propensity of change" of the Spanish regulatory framework. Since the LSE was adopted in 1997, it was "subject to continuous changes aimed at adapting it to the constantly evolving technological and economic circumstances".[757]

---

749 Ibid [577]–[582]. In [577]: "[...] in what can be seen as an over-arching requirement (in line with the interplay between stability and FET highlighted above), an investor's legitimate expectations must be balanced with the State's right to regulate in the public interest".

750 Ibid [583].

751 Ibid [584].

752 Ibid [588].

753 Ibid [596].

754 Ibid [620].

755 Ibid [600].

756 Ibid [601].

757 Ibid [602].

In particular, RD 436/2004 contained a provision analogous to Art. 44(3) RD 661/2007, but this did not preclude the respondent from repealing its previous regulation.[758] Third, the Spanish Supreme Court consistently held that an investor should have reasonably expected possible changes to the regulatory framework. The domestic judgments were considered as "facts", and as such those which predated the disputed investments were relevant to the analysis of legitimate expectations.[759] For the tribunal, these judgments made it clear that the government can amend the system of RE remuneration, provide that the system stayed within the scope of the general framework established by the LSE based on the guarantee of reasonable profitability.[760] Even though these judgments concerned previous regulations, and not RD 661/2007, they "sent a clear message that the remuneration offered to any kind of installations under the Special Regime could be amended".[761] The Spanish Supreme Court's case law developed in the years following the disputed investments confirmed the principles set in the earlier judgments and created a "consistent jurisprudence".[762]

The tribunal was unconvinced that there were any specific representations or assurances to the contrary. Whilst Spain indeed launched a campaign to promote its RE regulations and attract investments in the sector, they did not contain promises not to change RD 661/2007. The 2007 Press release simply reiterated the content of RD 661/2007, whereas presentations by IDAE, InvestInSpain and the CNE were "too general". In any case, these entities had no authority to enact rules or regulations and therefore could not change or interpret the clear content of legal provisions.[763]

Thus, the RRR "was the regulatory framework's leitmotiv, the essential feature underpinning all of the instruments that were enacted through the years". It restricted Spain's power to amend the framework and guaranteed a level of stability of the conditions in which investors operated, ensuring the existence of "stable conditions" pursuant to Art. 10(1) ECT.[764] More specifically, pursuant to Art. 30(4) LSE, the investors were entitled to make a profit after having paid

758 Ibid [602].
759 Ibid [603], [604].
760 Ibid [605]–[606].
761 Ibid [608].
762 Ibid [610].
763 Ibid [615].
764 Ibid [616].

their capital and operating expenses, whereas the reasonability of profit was to be measured by reference to the cost of money in financial matters.[765]

The tribunal considered that the RRR on investments was a key element of the RD 661/2007 regime and that it served to limit ECT-compliant regulatory changes. Only if the changes cross the "reasonable return" line would there be a violation of the ECT.[766] This "strikes the right balance" between the protection of investors, on the one hand, and the right to regulate and to adapt regulatory framework to changing circumstances, on the other hand.[767]

Given its decision that no legitimate expectation existed regarding an immutable FIT, the mere elimination of RD 661/2007 was not considered to be unreasonable, disproportionate, arbitrary, or otherwise contrary to the FET.[768]

The tribunal proceeded to analyze the secondary claim, based on a premise that the respondent failed to provide the RRR promised under the Special Regime.[769]

The tribunal noted that its considerations on quantification of the harm (if any) informed its findings on liability and both elements of the analysis are "intimately intertwined". The assessment of the harm suffered was "necessarily linked to the reasonableness, non-arbitrariness, proportionality, etc".[770] This was because the tribunal felt unable to verify whether the guarantee of reasonable profitability had been observed without considering the economic impact of the disputed measures.[771] Thus, it proceeded based on the understanding

765 Ibid [617].

766 Ibid [638]. The tribunal acknowledged that the Special Regime did not impose any cap and allowed efficient installations to make profits above the reasonable return target – [618].

767 Ibid [639]:

> [...] This approach strikes the right balance between, on the one hand, the protection of investors who have committed substantial resources in a sector which continues to provide Spain with the environmental benefits of clean solar power, and, on the other hand, Spain's right to regulate and adapt its framework to changed circumstances, provided that right is exercised in a manner that is proportionate, reasonable, and non-arbitrary manner.

768 Ibid [619].

769 Ibid [641].

770 Ibid [648].

771 Ibid [647]:

> The guarantee provided by Spain in the 1997 Electricity Law (the "reasonable return" or "reasonable profitability") is economic in nature. This being so, the Tribunal cannot verify whether or not such guarantee was observed without considering the economic impact of the Disputed Measures on the Claimants' investment. Only once it has ascertained such impact will the Tribunal be able to determine whether or not there is a breach of the Treaty

(footnote omitted).

that if it concludes the claimants suffered harm under the alternative claim, it can issue an award on both liability and damages.[772] The tribunal's reasoning on this issue is described in detail in the Chapter 5. It suffices to say here that the tribunal concluded that the disputed measures meant that 10 of the 19 claimants had a rate of return which fell below 7%, which violated the FET and triggered a compensatory obligation.[773]

1.2.29.5 *Due Diligence*

The question of due diligence was considered irrelevant because of the tribunal's conclusion on the foreseeability of changes.[774]

1.2.29.6 *Reasonableness and Proportionality*

The tribunal acknowledged that the changes could violate the FET by being unreasonable, disproportionate, or arbitrary, but it added that such a conclusion could not be arrived at merely because the reforms put the claimants in a worse position than they were earlier.[775] The regulatory changes were prompted by a number of factors, such as a negative GDP, unemployment rate growth, a substantial reduction of demand for electricity and the related tariff deficit.[776] The choices made by Spain represented "a middle course", consisting of reducing RE producers' rate of return, but still guaranteeing a reasonable profit at a level comparable to that available in other EU member states.[777]

1.2.29.7 *Transparency*

The tribunal did not find a violation of the transparency obligation. There was no evidence that the claimants were "left in the dark" for 11 months and in any case, any such violation would not have caused any harm to the claimants.[778]

1.2.29.8 *State Aid*

The tribunal explained why it considered its approach as compatible with the 2017 EC Decision on state aid. First, it noted that the decision concerns the New Regime, not the Special Regime.[779] Second, it noted the EC's position that awarding compensation for modifying RD 661/2007 would itself constitute

772 Ibid [659].
773 Ibid [847].
774 Ibid [613].
775 Ibid [630].
776 Ibid [627].
777 Ibid [628].
778 Ibid [632].
779 Ibid [635].

state aid.[780] In its view, this appears to be premised on compensation having been awarded along the lines of the primary claim, but there was no suggestion that the same conclusion applies to any compensation awarded based on the secondary claim, in line with Spain's position that the claimants could legitimately expect the RRR.[781]

1.2.29.9 *Retroactivity*

The tribunal also noted that, under RD 661/2007, efficient installations could outperform the reasonable return target and were entitled to keep the profits which the system allowed them to make. The claw-back provisions in New Regime were considered as retroactive. This was not altered by the fact that the claimants did not have to repay sums received earlier, because they were treated as offsetting the total amount payable under the New Regime. The tribunal had "no hesitation to find that it is correct not to take past profits into account when calculating an investor's remuneration going forward".[782]

1.2.30 PV Investors – Dissenting Opinion

A dissenting opinion was delivered, agreeing that Spain had violated the ECT, but disagreeing with the dismissal of the primary claim. Upholding the primary claim would have resulted in compensation of approx. 540.9 million Euro higher than what was actually awarded.[783]

1.2.30.1 *Prior Cases*

The dissenter saw no reason to depart from the established line of case law issued "in like circumstances".[784] He identified 18 cases decided ahead of the one at hand, of which 15 were decided in favor of the claimants, 11 of which upheld claims comparable to the primary claim in this dispute, that the claimants were entitled to the FIT which existed at the time of making the investments.[785] He disagreed with the majority's view that in these cases, the tribunals were not presented claims comparable to the alternative claim in this case, noting that the claimants pleaded such claims in 5 cases and that in 2 more they were presented to the tribunals by damages experts.[786]

---

780 Ibid [636].
781 Ibid [637].
782 Ibid [813].
783 The PV Investors v. Spain, PCA Case No. 2012-14, Concurring and Dissenting Opinion of Charles N. Brower (28.02.2020) [1], [17].
784 Ibid [2].
785 Ibid [3], [8].
786 Ibid [3].

The dissenter then analyzed each of the 11 cases which upheld claims comparable to the primary claim, which he would have preferred to follow: *Eiser, Novenergia, Masdar, Antin, Foresight, SolEs, 9Ren, Cube, OperaFund, InfraRed* and *Watkins*.[787]

He then analyzed 4 cases decided in favor of the claimants, but based on the alternative claim – the RRR. In each of them, he identified relevant factual differences when compared to the case at hand. These cases involved CSP, Wind energy and Hydro energy plants, "each of which was governed by different regulations and was the object of different representations". None of them involved PV plants and every single previous case concerning PV plants had upheld the primary claim.[788] Moreover, timing was critical in these cases. The disputed investments in these cases either pre-dated the Special Regime or were made when the regulatory changes had already materialized, which impacted on the assessment of legitimate expectations in these cases.[789] In *RREEF*, the investments were made between December 2010 and 2012, when "the regulatory changes of 2010 already had foreshadowed alteration of the FiT regime". In *BayWa*, the original investment was made in 1997, long before the Special Regime was put in place, whereas 2011 was fixed by the claimants as the relevant date for their legitimate expectations. Moreover, the case concerned Wind energy plants, which rendered irrelevant any specific representations concerning solar energy. Similarly in *RWE*, the claimants started investing in Spain in 2001, before the Special Regime was put in place. The second tranche of investments was made in 2010, at the time when the tribunal considered that the claimants should have been alerted about the changes. Also in this case, representations about solar energy were irrelevant, as the case concerned Hydro energy and Wind energy plants. Finally, the dissenter commented that, in *NextEra*, registration in the RAIPRE occurred at a time when changes to the regulatory framework were already underway.[790]

The dissenter also noted that RAIPRE registration in the *PV Investors* case happened before the deadline expired on 29.09.2008, and that 4 previous cases considered this to be not merely an administrative requirement, but a fact which created legitimate expectations.[791]

787 Ibid [5], naming *Foresight* as *Greentech*, as it is sometimes referred to.

788 Ibid [11].

789 Ibid [14].

790 Ibid [6]. The dissenter considered the *NextEra* award as falling with this group, contrary to this author's classification of this case. The difference is explained by the dissenter's reliance on the *NextEra* tribunal's dismissal of the DCF methodology when calculating compensation.

791 Ibid [14], with reference to *Antin, Masdar, Novenergia*, and *OperaFund*.

The dissenter then looked at 3 awards that dismissed such claims. In his view, none of these cases was analogous to *PV Investors*, given the different timing of the disputed investments and its impact on the respective claimants' legitimate expectations.[792] In *Charanne,* the scope of the dispute was limited to 2010 Disputed Measures. In *Isolux,* the investment was made on 29.10.2012, when reform of the regulatory framework was "inevitable". In *Stadtwerke,* the CSP plants in question were registered in the RAIPRE in April 2012.[793]

He concluded that the majority should follow the reasoning of the cases decided before it:

> PV Investors, Novenergia, Cube, 9Ren, and OperaFund all have involved the same technology, close timing of investments, the same incentives, the same compliance with RAIPRE registration deadline, the same assurances, the same regulations, the same investment treaty, the same host State, and the same measures in dispute. Logic dictates that the PV Investors would harbor the same expectations and that this sub-category of the eleven cases be followed absent compelling contrary reasons.

He also noted that the majority's observation that discrepancy is "expected" in a system of *ad hoc* adjudication is "intellectually disingenuous".[794]

1.2.31 Hydro

In *Hydro,* the disputed investments had been commissioned and were in full operation when the claimants invested in them in 2011, with most of their installed capacity being operational since 1950.[795] All qualified for the Special Regime and were duly registered in the RAIPRE.[796]

The tribunal distinguished two main themes of the claim. The first was whether RD 661/2007 amounted to a specific commitment that the Hydro energy plants will receive FITs for electricity produced throughout the entire operational lifetime.[797] The second was whether the key terms of the investments and the stability of the host state's legal and business framework are protected as legitimate expectations.[798]

792 Ibid [9].
793 Ibid [7].
794 Ibid [16].
795 Hydro v. Spain, ICSID Case No. ARB/15/42, Decision on Jurisdiction, Liability and Directions on Quantum (09.03.2020) [436].
796 Ibid [435].
797 Ibid [441].
798 Ibid [443].

1.2.31.1 *Stability*

The tribunal began with an observation that the VCLT requires a treaty to be interpreted with regard to its purpose.[799] Art. 2 ECT, read together with the European Energy Charter, reveals that the ECT's purpose is to "establish a legal framework in order to promote long-term cooperation", balanced with state sovereignty and responsibility "to create an adapted and evolutionary framework for the development of economic activities and the necessity to protect foreign investment and its continuing flow".[800] For the tribunal, Art. 10(1) ECT establishes a separate obligation of stability and transparency. They are not merely an illustration of the FET, even though they form part of the FET and legitimate expectations as well.[801]

The meaning of stability is linked to legitimate expectations that the legal framework will not be arbitrarily changed and that commitments will be observed. However, it does preclude the existence of any change whatsoever. It has a "relatively high threshold, and the emphasis is on the subversion of the legal regime".[802] Moreover, states maintain their right to regulate.[803] Transparency is "plainly linked" with stability, as it enables investors to be shielded against arbitrary changes made to the legal framework and against the frustration of legitimate expectations.[804]

1.2.31.2 *Reasonableness and Proportionality*

Whilst the prohibition of unreasonable and discriminatory measures are free-standing obligations, the FET also contains the same obligation.[805] A state is not obliged to grant subsidies, nor to maintain them unchanged if they exist. However, if the state lawfully grants such subsidies and then it becomes necessary to modify them, this must be done in a manner which is proportionate to the aim of the legislative amendment and should have due regard to the reasonable reliance interests of recipients, taking into consideration that they committed substantial resources based on the earlier regime.[806] Reasonableness requires a relationship to some rational policy.[807] However, the concept

799 Ibid [540].
800 Ibid [543].
801 Ibid [547]–[549], [552].
802 Ibid [553].
803 Ibid [555].
804 Ibid [557].
805 Ibid [567].
806 Ibid [568].
807 Ibid [569].

cannot be used as an open-ended mandate to second guess the state's policies.[808] The tribunal recalled that measures are unreasonable or discriminatory when they (i) inflict damage on investors without serving any apparent legitimate purpose, (ii) are based on discretion, prejudice or personal preference rather than on legal standards, (iii) are taken for other reasons than those put forward by the decision-maker and (iv) are taken in willful disregard of due process and proper procedure.[809]

In the tribunal's eyes, proportionality forms part of the reasonableness standard, as well as being an inherent part of the FET.[810] It requires a measure to be (i) suitable (to achieve a legitimate policy objective), (ii) necessary (for that objective) and (iii) not excessive (proportional) when balancing each interest involved.[811]

Retroactivity is relevant in the context of reasonableness, legitimate expectations and destruction of acquired rights. There is, however, no general principle which *per se* prohibits retroactive legislation.[812]

The tribunal noted that legally protected legitimate expectations are not synonymous with reasonable business judgments, not all of which are protected.[813]

1.2.31.3 *Right to Regulate*

The tribunal recognized the sovereign right to regulate and noted that this is not affected by the FET.[814] The FET does not freeze the legal regulation of economic activities, it requires weighing investors' expectations against states' regulatory interests.[815] Unless specific promises were made, investment treaties are not "a kind of insurance policy against the risk of any changes in the host State's legal and economic framework".[816] The tribunal observed that the risk of regulatory change is "for entrepreneurs to assess and assume".[817] It added that "economic, social, environmental and legal circumstances and problems are by their nature evolutionary, dynamic and bound to constant change, and

808 Ibid [570].
809 Ibid [571].
810 Ibid [573].
811 Ibid [574].
812 Ibid [578].
813 Ibid [580].
814 Ibid [582].
815 Ibid [583]: "There has to be a weighing of an investor's expectations and the State's regulatory interests".
816 Ibid [584].
817 Ibid [586].

it is indispensable for successful public infrastructure and public services to be adaptable to change in evolving circumstances".[818]

The tribunal agreed that states enjoy a wide margin of appreciation when making use of their right to regulate.[819] Thus, reforming a regulatory framework can violate legitimate expectations only if a specific commitment existed that it would not be changed.[820] General legal texts do not contain such stability commitments.[821] Whilst some case law adopts a view that "legitimate expectations may be engendered by the legal framework at the time of the investment", in particular if "reiteration of the same type of commitment in different types of general statements" is present, the tribunal considered this to be an aspect which was relevant to stability, rather than being an example of a specific commitment.[822]

1.2.31.4 *Due Diligence*

The tribunal recognized the importance of due diligence in creating legitimate expectations. In its view, the "fairness and consistency" of the legal framework "must be assessed against the background of information that the investor knew and should reasonably have known at the time of the investment".[823]

1.2.31.5 *Specific Commitments*

Based on the above general considerations, the tribunal turned to the first of the two main themes of the claim – i.e. whether there was a legislative commitment in RD 661/2007 on which the claimants were entitled to rely. In this context, the tribunal referred back to the due diligence. It noted that the claimants (and related companies from the group) had received legal advice from three eminent law firms.[824] Nevertheless, they "never sought, nor received, advice on regulatory risk" from them.[825] The tribunal understood that the reason for this was that all parties were aware of the regulatory risk. This led the tribunal to conclude that the claimants "deliberately avoided being advised that regulatory changes could be made".[826] Moreover, the share purchase and option agreement included a provision that the repeal or change of the Special

818 Ibid [587].
819 Ibid [589].
820 Ibid [592].
821 Ibid [594].
822 Ibid [596].
823 Ibid [599].
824 Ibid [611]–[615].
825 Ibid [616].
826 Ibid [617].

Regime was not a ground for its termination or damages, whereas financing agreements provided that such a change was a material adverse effect and a ground for early repayment.[827]

The tribunal also concluded that the claimants must have been advised on the hierarchical superiority of the LSE, which guaranteed reasonable profitability, and that Art. 44(3) RD 661/2007 concerned only a revision of specific premiums contained in the relevant part of the regulation.[828]

The tribunal added that the claimants' capital group knew about the 2010 Disputed Measures (the disputed investments were made later, in 2011). The claimants had failed to disclose that the group was one of the claimants in the *PV Investors* case.[829]

The claimants argued that they took comfort from the 2010 Disputed Measures, as they affected PV, CSP and Wind energy, leaving Hydro energy installations outside the scope of their regulation.[830] The tribunal was unconvinced. It viewed this as further evidence that the claimants knew that RD 661/2007 was not "immune" from reform, as long as it was within the LSE's framework and that there changes could be made to the Special Regime – even though this showed nothing about the anticipated scale of the changes, their lawfulness or whether they would also apply to Hydro energy plants.[831] Thus, the claimants should have been aware that the changes in the Special Regime could have gone beyond the revisions regulated in Art. 44(3) RD 661/2007.[832]

The tribunal then analyzed whether the claimants received any specific commitments that there would be no changes made to the Special Regime. Based on the evidence, it was "probable" that the claimants met with the director of IDAE.[833] He did not provide witness testimony, because his new employer refused permission for this. The tribunal assessed the record that he "gave the impression" that, in his view, there would be no substantial regulatory changes made to the regime in so far as Hydro energy plants were concerned.[834] Nevertheless, this was not a commitment or assurance made on behalf of Spain.[835] This individual had no authority to make such commitments nor to give assurances on behalf of Spain since IDAE was "merely technical and

827 Ibid [617].
828 Ibid [618].
829 Ibid [619], [628].
830 Ibid [621].
831 Ibid [629].
832 Ibid [630].
833 Ibid [643].
834 Ibid [658].
835 Ibid [660].

advisory, and that it had no authority to regulate the Special Regime" – which every rational investor knew.[836]

The tribunal also rejected the arguments that specific commitments could be derived from the 2007 Press release (having been issued by a press office and with no suggestion that the claimants took it into account), presentations and reports made by the CNE (being outside the scope of its duties) or presentations by InvestInSpain (which the claimants did not attend).[837]

This led the tribunal to conclude that the claimants did not receive any specific commitments or assurances, either in legislation or otherwise, that there would be no change of RD 661/2007. On the contrary, the tribunal considered that the claimants must have known that change was legally and politically possible, even though in their commercial assessment the regulatory risk was low, especially for Hydro energy plants.[838]

1.2.31.6 *Regulatory Revolution*

Nonetheless, Spain was not "free to make radical changes" to the Special Regime without incurring liability under the ECT. The claimants had acquired legitimate expectations which required protection.[839]

The tribunal understood that the "overall effect" of the disputed measures resulted in eliminating the regulated tariff available under the Special Regime.[840] The result was "a radical change in the renewable regime as to breach the FET obligation of stability (or the legitimate expectation of stability) of the overall legal framework, by dismantling the entire legal framework going back in different forms to 1998".[841] This was because: (i) the Special Regime was based on maximizing production and the volume of electricity produced, whereas the New Regime introduced a remuneration framework which was not production-oriented and was based on hypothetical standard installations, (ii) the Special Regime was not subject to a cap on remuneration, whereas the Special Regime's remuneration is capped by reference to a "target rate of return", (iii) in calculating the cap, the New Regime takes into account past remuneration, (iv) the Special Regime entitled Hydro energy plants to receive remuneration for their entire operational life, as opposed to the 25 years offered by the New Regime, (v) the New Regime entitles Spain to vary the *ex-post* target return

836 Ibid [663].
837 Ibid [668].
838 Ibid [673].
839 Ibid [675].
840 Ibid [678].
841 Ibid [682].

and modify the remuneration parameters with limited scrutiny.[842] Moreover, the CNE recognized that the change was "unprecedented internationally" and proposed alternative measures.[843]

1.2.31.7 *RRR*

In this context, however, the tribunal considered that compensation must take into account that, even without the disputed measures, Spain would still have adopted other measures to address its tariff deficit.[844] The "essence" of the Special Regime was to "promote, and ensure the continuance of, renewables having a reasonable rate of return for their future lifetime balanced against the cost to the consumer".[845] This conclusion was based, among others, on the LSE, the preambles of RD 436/2004 and RD 661/207 and the case law of the Spanish Supreme Court.[846] Compensation was payable only as regards the difference between the actual scenario and the RRR for each individual plant (and not as if the Special Regime remained in place).

1.2.31.8 *Retroactivity*

The tribunal also considered the claw-back of past remuneration, that under the New Regime, if the return obtained by a facility prior to July 2013 exceeded the new target return, the facility was no longer entitled to a regulated revenue and could only sell electricity on the market without any subsidy.[847] It concluded that this violated the FET obligation to take into account past remuneration when calculating an RRR for the future. No reference to the concept of acquired rights was needed to arrive at this conclusion.[848]

1.2.31.9 *Legitimate Expectations*

The tribunal then identified the scope of the claimants' legitimate expectations, following the approach adopted by the *RREEF* tribunal. This covered legitimate expectations that: (i) they would receive "a reasonable return for

842 Ibid [681].
843 Ibid [683].
844 Ibid [687]–[688].
845 Ibid [690].
846 Ibid.
847 Ibid [691].
848 Ibid [694]. The tribunal did not clarify whether the final answer as to whether there was a violation of the FET – deferred for a later stage – also included its decision on the claw-back of past remunerations. It seems that the tribunal considered it as a separate violation of the FET but then ordered that it be taken into consideration when calculating the projected rate of return (i.e. excluding it from these calculations).

their investment through special means such as the FiT, designed to attract investments in a sector which was unattractive at market prices", (ii) the RRR was "significantly above a mere absence of financial loss", taking into account the cost of money on capital markets for this type of investments and other objectives, (iii) Spain "would not significantly modify the legal framework applicable to the investors as provided for in Spanish law when the investments were made", although not for their operational lifetimes, and (iv) any such modifications would be reasonable and equitable.[849]

The tribunal observed that there was a close connection between the issues of liability and damages.[850] The tribunal again mirrored the *RREEF* tribunal that a final answer on whether the FET was violated cannot be given until it is decided whether the projected rate of return under the New Regime is unreasonable.[851] The "real question" was whether the remuneration for the facilities going forward and without the claw-back provision accords with the RRR.[852] The tribunal concluded that it does not, and awarded compensation.[853]

1.2.32 Cavalum

Most of the *Cavalum* tribunal's analysis on liability is the same as in the *Hydro* case, with only a few modifications.[854]

1.2.32.1 *Balancing Exercise*

First, the tribunal underlined that the ECT does not protect against "any and all changes" in the regulatory framework.[855] Circumstances change, and entrepreneurs must assess and assume the risk of change of the regulatory framework, unless there are some specific commitments.[856] The FET may involve a balancing or weighing exercise.[857]

849 Ibid [695].
850 Ibid [685].
851 Ibid [696].
852 Ibid [697], [717].
853 Hydro v. Spain, ICSID Case No. ARB/15/42, Award (05.08.2020) [123]–[124], [162].
854 Cavalum v. Spain, ICSID Case No. ARB/15/34, Decision on Jurisdiction, Liability and Directions on Quantum (31.08.2020) [400]–[449], repeating Hydro v. Spain, *supra* note 795 [547]–[550], [552]–[553], [555], [578], [567]–[570], [573]–[574], [577]–[578], [580], [583]–[585], [587]–[589], [591]–[594], [596], [599], [600]. There are some minor amendments in the text of some of the provisions. This results from the fact that the presiding arbitrator was the same in both cases, which concluded around same time.
855 Cavalum v. Spain, ibid [420].
856 Ibid [422].
857 Ibid [423]: "An FET standard may legitimately involve a balancing or weighing exercise by the host State".

1.2.32.2 *Legitimate Expectations*

Second, legitimate expectations must be based on a promise, assurance or representation, which may be explicit or implicit.[858] Explicit promises "can be made through statutory commitments or through conduct, or in the legal or regulatory framework of the host State at the time the investor made its investment".[859] A "reiteration" of the same type of commitment, even if in different types of general statements, as well as a specific entitlement to incentives may amount to specific state behavior and thereby create legitimate expectations.[860] However, in general, legislation does not give rise to legitimate expectations regarding the stability of that legislation.[861]

1.2.32.3 *Due Diligence*

Third, the tribunal underlined that legitimate expectations must be objectively reasonable and consider all relevant circumstances.[862] This means that an investor who invests in a "highly regulated sector" must perform due diligence of the relevant legal regime.[863] When analyzing whether an investor was aware of possible changes that could be made to the regulatory framework, judgments handed down by the host state's courts should be taken into account. They are "factually relevant" to verify whether, at the time of making the investment, an investor could expect that the law would not be modified.[864] A foreign investor is "expected" to perform due diligence.[865] Normally, it lacks detailed knowledge of the host state's legal system and knows only the "essential commercial characteristic" of the law.[866] Any detailed knowledge lies with the investor's legal, commercial, and financial advisers. Therefore the extent and quality of the due diligence is relevant in determining legitimate expectations.[867]

The tribunal's analysis of the consistent case law of the Spanish Supreme Court pre-dating the Special Regime was that the domestic law allowed the government to modify a specific remuneration system provided that it remains within the framework of the LSE. Under the domestic law, electricity producers "do not have an inalienable right to an unchanged economic regime". Whilst

858 Ibid [431].
859 Ibid [432].
860 Ibid [433]–[434].
861 Ibid [439].
862 Ibid [443].
863 Ibid [444].
864 Ibid [446].
865 Ibid [470].
866 Ibid [471].
867 Ibid [472], similarly [531].

they have "an expectation that they will obtain reasonable rates of return with reference to the cost of money in the capital market", they have no guarantee that there would be no change of level of profits or revenues or that there would be no change in methods for fixing the applicable premiums.[868]

In this case, the claimant relied on the advice of a local counsel.[869] Moreover, it requested a due diligence report from another law firm and was aware that two other law firms had provided legal due diligence to banks involved in the project financing. None of the advisors mentioned the risk of regulatory changes.[870] However, they were not asked to provide an opinion on such risk.[871] The tribunal noted "a striking fact" that, in the awards on the record concerning the Spanish saga, many of the claimants had obtained due diligence advice from leading law firms, either directly or indirectly through the financing banks, and yet in most cases the claimants did not enquire about and did not receive advice on possible regulatory change – despite the Supreme Court's case being the subject of wide discussion in the industry.[872] In its view, investors should ask their lawyers "about ministerial or legislative power to amend the incentive regime", and not about the validity of Art. 44(3) RD 661/2007 or the possibility that it may be amended.[873]

1.2.32.4 *Domestic Courts*

The tribunal considered the Supreme Court decisions to be "highly relevant" in determining the claimant's expectations at the time of making the investments.[874] It made it clear that a change to the Special Regime within the scope of the LSE was potentially lawful and that the LSE did not guarantee complete immunity from reforms, since the government had a discretionary power to determine remuneration within its regulatory power and in the general interest. There was "no unalterable right to the maintenance of the remuneration framework", provided that the LSE's principles of the RRR were respected.[875] Thus, the claimant knew, or should have known, that the Special Regime could be amended or replaced, as long as it was within the scope of the LSE, particularly given that RD 436/2004 had been replaced by RD 661/2007.[876]

868 Ibid [515].
869 Ibid [516].
870 Ibid [517].
871 Ibid [529].
872 Ibid [fn 390].
873 Ibid [fn 392].
874 Ibid [532].
875 Ibid [533].
876 Ibid [534]–[535].

1.2.32.5 *Specific Commitments*

The above led to the conclusion that any legitimate expectations which existed were limited to an expectation that changes would not be made "radically and fundamentally without notice".[877] The tribunal found no specific commitments in the wording of Art. 44(3) RD 661/2007.[878] Similarly, registration in the RAIPRE neither amounted to a specific commitment nor created vested rights. It was merely an administrative requirement.[879]

The tribunal found statements made by ministers and officials irrelevant, because the claimant did not rely on any such statements. In any case, they would not form the basis for legally protected legitimate expectations but, at most, may impact on a "reasonable business decision".[880]

The tribunal assessed that the 2010 Disputed Measures did not alter the essential elements of the Special Regime. They were not radical and were within the state's margin of appreciation.[881]

1.2.32.6 *RRR*

The tribunal then sought to answer which – if any – legitimate expectations were engendered by the Spanish regulatory regime.[882] It agreed with Spain's argument that "the cornerstone" of the incentive regime and the only legitimate expectation concerned the RRR.[883] This was based on the wording of Art. 30(4) LSE.[884] The LSE was, at all material times, the "relevant controlling legislation" in the Spanish legislative system, and as such, superior to the RDs.[885] This was a legislative "umbrella".[886]

1.2.32.7 *State Aid*

The tribunal found Spain's arguments on state aid misplaced, as neither Spain nor the EC ever had any concern about the lawfulness of RD 661/2007 from the perspective of state aid rules. This was confirmed by the 2017 EC Decision. This conclusion would remain unaltered even assuming differently. First, the tribunal saw no "necessary connection" between a failure to notify state aid and

877 Ibid [538].
878 Ibid [547].
879 Ibid [550].
880 Ibid [556].
881 Ibid [564].
882 Ibid [598].
883 Ibid [601].
884 Ibid [603].
885 Ibid [602].
886 Ibid [612].

any legitimate expectations regarding an RRR. Second, Spain's prior conduct precluded it from relying on this argument.[887]

The tribunal observed that the New Regime had been adopted in the public interest.[888] In the tariff deficit context, the tribunal deemed it unnecessary to assess whether Spain had properly managed the costs and benefits of the electricity system.[889]

The tribunal decided that the New Regime totally dismantled and replaced the previous incentive system.[890] The new remuneration capable of being achieved was unrelated to operating performance, whereas the Special Regime was based on the installed capacity of the plants.[891] Thus, insofar as the New Regime did not adhere to the principle of the RRR, it breached the FET.[892]

The tribunal observed that the claimant did not frame its claim based on a legitimate expectation to the RRR, and even "expressly disavowed" such a position.[893] This did not preclude the tribunal from finding that it had such a legitimate expectation. First, the case was based on legitimate expectations theory. Second, the claimant argued for legitimate expectations regarding the return expected on its investments. Third, the return was rooted in the disputed measures and regulatory framework at the heart of the dispute. Fourth, the claimant's experts produced alternative calculations, based on the RRR.[894]

1.2.32.8 *Stability*

Similarly, the claw-back provision of the New Regime was not "at the forefront" of the claimant's submissions, but its experts "squarely put it" in their submissions.[895] Relying on the *RREEF* award, the tribunal considered that the subtraction of past remuneration (received under the Special Regime) from future remuneration was contrary to the stability obligation in Art. 10(1) ECT.[896]

887 Ibid [611].
888 Ibid [615].
889 Ibid [619].
890 Ibid [614].
891 Ibid [624].
892 Ibid [625], [631].
893 Ibid [627].
894 Ibid [629], [658]. The tribunal's acceptance of the possibility that a legitimate expectation as regards receiving the RRR may have been violated, despite the claimant's express position that this was not how it chose to frame its claim, may raise concerns regarding the *ne ultra petita* principle. This contrasts with the findings in the *PV Investors* case, where the majority found the similar position of the claimants to justify the decision of some tribunals – not faced with alternative claims – to uphold primary claims.
895 Ibid [634].
896 Ibid [636]–[637].

The tribunal did not clearly state whether this violated the FET, or whether stability was a separate obligation, but its wording suggests the second approach. The tribunal simply noted that there is a "plain overlap" between the two.[897]

As the New Regime is "opaque", it was "not easy" to determine whether it provides the RRR.[898]

1.2.33 Cavalum – Dissenting Opinion

One of the arbitrators issued a dissenting opinion.[899] Whilst he agreed on findings on jurisdiction, expropriation, the claw-back provision and the distinction between the 2010 and 2013–2014 Disputed Measures, he disagreed with "some of the basic determinations" on the FET.[900]

1.2.33.1 *Specific Commitments*

Based on a "plain reading" of Art. 44(3) RD 661/2007, read together with Art. 36 RD 661/2007, he understood it as an "express promise of stability for the feed-in tariffs for these facilities". At the same time, other elements of the Special Regime (e.g. the consumer price index, taxes, access to the grid, or the amount of production), were not included in the promise and could be changed, "as long as that was done proportionally".[901] The dissenter followed the *Novenergia* and *Masdar* reasoning.[902] He observed that the Special Regime "could not have been clearer" and that the claimant "undoubtedly relied on the straightforward and plain reading of" the above provisions. They guaranteed FIT and its duration. The wording of these provisions was "as explicit as possible".[903] Thus, he concluded that the claimant "financed, developed, built, commissioned and registered its long-term facilities in a timely way in RAIPRE" relying on the plain language of RD 661/2007.[904] The dissenter took a similar position with respect to RD 1578/2008, which applied to some of the disputed investments.[905]

In his view, Spain emphasized the stability of the Special Regime through a "full objective panoply of inducements", created in the form of the two RDs,

897 Ibid [639].
898 Ibid [632].
899 Cavalum v. Spain, ICSID Case No. ARB/15/34, Dissenting Opinion of David R. Haigh Q.C. (31.08.2020) [4].
900 Ibid [1].
901 Ibid [8], [8(t)], [8(u)].
902 Ibid [9], [11].
903 Ibid [10].
904 Ibid [12].
905 Ibid [13]–[22].

press releases, Ministerial statements, and statements made by the CNE, IDAE and InvestInSpain.[906] These were "specific promises" and "clear and robust representations" that Spain will provide FIT for at least 25 years.[907] The promises were not only explicit, but also surrounded by circumstances which made them "even more compelling".[908] This includes the press releases.[909] Even assuming that no specific promises were made, he would identify the existence of "implicit undertakings and assurances" made by or on behalf of the respondent.[910]

1.2.33.2 *Domestic Courts*

The dissenter disagreed with the majority's understanding and relevance of the Spanish Supreme Court's judgments. He considered that only judgments pre-dating the disputed investments were relevant to the claimant's legitimate expectations.[911] These judgments did not relate to the "sort of stability provisions" found in RD 661/2007 and 1578/2008.[912] Such provisions did not exist in previous RDs, which contained other incentives for the RE sector and were not even close to achieving Spain's goals. These circumstances form the context of the stability provisions, included for the first time in RD 661/2007 and RD 1578/2008. As such, they were not reviewed by the Supreme Court in its prior judgments.[913] Thus, even a most careful analysis of the relevant Supreme Court judgments would not have forewarned any reasonable investor that the Special Regime could be "destroyed and replaced", on the grounds of applying "another version of" the RRR.[914] Thus, these judgments were incapable of warning anyone that the respondent would not "keep its word" that future amendments of the FIT would not affect pre-constructed and registered PV facilities.[915] He then quoted *Novenergia* that the wording of the relevant provisions was "adamantly clear" and that to understand its wording did not require

906 Ibid [23].
907 Ibid [24]–[25].
908 Ibid [27].
909 Ibid [28]–[30].
910 Ibid [33].
911 Ibid [39].
912 Ibid [40].
913 Ibid [41].
914 Ibid [42].
915 Ibid [49].

a "particularly sophisticated analysis".[916] Thus, he considered the claimant's due diligence as sufficiently reasonable.[917]

While acknowledging the state's right to regulate in the public interest, the dissenter underlined that this general right does not preclude a state from being liable under international law for unlawfully infringing vested rights.[918] He considered that the promises of stability had become a vested right.[919] This happened when the PV facilities were registered in the RAIPRE. This was not merely an administrative act. Registration "crystallized" the vested right, by changing the relationship "from one that was executory to one that had become executed".[920]

1.2.33.3 *RRR*

The dissenter noted that the RRR is not a standalone element of Art. 30(4) LSE. Several other references must also be considered when setting the remuneration of RE producers.[921] He did not "fundamentally disagree" that the RRR can be characterized as "a cornerstone" of the various regimes enacted under the LSE. However, for him, such a "broad statement of policy" is irrelevant in the specific circumstances of the case. First, Spain voluntarily limited its regulatory discretion to attract large amounts of capital to meet targets set by the EU.[922] Second, RD 661/2007 expressly stated that it fulfilled the objective of the RRR under the LSE.[923] Third, Spain's understanding of the RRR would result in applying an "after-the-fact" general principle of RRR, which would result in "perpetual, practically ad hoc" right of resetting remuneration in the future.[924]

The dissenter distinguished this case from *RREEF*, which concerned investments made in 2011 (whereas the *Cavalum* investments were made in 2008).[925] He also criticized the *RREEF* tribunal for not fully analyzing the language of Art. 44(3) RD 661/2007.[926]

916 Ibid [44].
917 Ibid [46].
918 Ibid [43].
919 Ibid [49].
920 Ibid [52].
921 Ibid [59].
922 Ibid [61].
923 Ibid [62].
924 Ibid [63].
925 Ibid [65].
926 Ibid [66]–[67], [69]–[72].

As a result, the dissenter was inclined to order compensation based on the difference in the value of the investments under the Special Regime and after the introducing the New Regime.[927] He argued that it is improper for the tribunal to analyze whether the New Regime fell short of the objective of the RRR. This would be an after-the-fact assessment which would substitute the tribunal's decision for that of the respondent. It is not the task of the tribunal to determine what the RRR is in any particular case. This is "far afield from assessing what the state explicitly promised and the investor relied upon".[928]

Finally, the dissenter referred to the dissenting opinion in the *PV Investors* case and concurred that there no reason existed to depart from the reasoning repeatedly adopted by 11 other tribunals in similar circumstances, all of which awarded compensation at a level which exceeded the RRR.[929] Even though the principle of *stare decisis* does not apply to the tribunal, it should pay attention to earlier tribunals' decisions.[930] He also agreed with the dissenting opinion issued in the *Stadtwerke* case.[931]

1.3 *Lessons Learned*

The above review of the Spanish saga case law provides a detailed analysis of how each tribunal approached the FET and reached its decision. They can be summarized in Table 4 (see page 197).

One may now zoom out from a detailed analysis of each individual tribunal's approach and adopt a "helicopter view", allowing general conclusions to be drawn, which are of general applicability, outside the Spanish context. In this sense, they are "lessons learned" for the future and general case law, not limited to Spain or the ECT.

The FET is discussed in each of the Spanish saga cases. These cases are important, given their discussion on (i) the possibility to ground legitimate expectations solely in general legislation, without any additional specific commitments having been made, (ii) stability, (iii) the relevance of due diligence, and (iv) the right to regulate and the limits thereupon. In this sense, the analysis contributes to a discussion on how states' actions are scrutinized during a dispute – not only when adopting specific legislation, but also when public officials make statements and other activities form the backdrop to the adoption of new legislation.

927 Ibid [4(k)], [79].
928 Ibid [77].
929 Ibid [81]–[82], [84].
930 Ibid [83].
931 Ibid [85]–[87].

These cases may sometimes appear contradictory. However, the discrepancies are mostly apparent. They do not concern general issues of law but, rather, how to understand the facts against the backdrop of the same legal concepts. This allows a number of lessons to be learned for the future.

1.3.1 First Lesson Learned – Regulatory Frameworks Can Create Legitimate Expectations That Are Protected by International Investment Treaties

The Spanish saga cases allow the conclusion that general legislation (the regulatory framework) can create legitimate expectations that are protected by international investment treaties.[932]

The tribunals adopted different positions on whether the legitimate expectations that existed in the Spanish saga protected against any drastic changes being made to the regulatory framework or only if such changes failed to include the RRR. To consider these two groups of cases uniform is unrealistic. However, an important lesson is learned when one takes a step back and adopts a more general perspective. Once a "helicopter view" is adopted, it becomes irrelevant what a particular tribunal decided regarding the scope of legitimate expectations considered to exist in the particular case. What matters is that all of the tribunals confirmed that the investors had legitimate expectations based on the regulatory framework – either as regards the RRR, stability and/or protection against fundamental change of the regulatory framework, or even as regards a particular remuneration scheme. This wider perspective allows uniformity to be perceived in the case law.

In this sense, each of the Spanish saga cases confirms that legitimate expectations can be based on general legislation.[933] They concur with academic

932 Similarly, based on the analysis of Spanish, Italian and Czech RE cases: Rahmi Kopar, Stability and Legitimate Expectations in International Energy Investments (Hart 2021), p. 210, Jack Biggs, The Scope of Investors' Legitimate Expectations under the FET Standard in the European Renewable Energy Cases, ICSID Review - Foreign Investment Law Journal, 36:1 (2021), p. 107.

933 Fn 45. For a similar conclusion, see: Amélie Noilhac, Renewable Energy Investment Cases Against Spain and the Quest for Regulatory Consistency, Questions of International Law (Zoom-In), 71 (2020), p. 38:

> Accordingly, and despite the fact that only three cases out of twenty published decisions decided in favor of Spain, tribunals did in fact follow a consistent approach regarding legitimate expectations claims. Indeed, tribunals focused on (i) establishing a specific commitment from the State, which would crystallize into a strict obligation of stability of the legal framework; (ii), in the absence of such a commitment, article 10(1) of the ECT was interpreted to bestow upon the State an obligation of consistency of the legal framework, that would generate a legitimate expectation for the investor; (iii) the tribunals would then assess whether the modification of the legal framework was radical or disproportionate in order to find a breach of article 10(1).

writings which consider that "when a state has created certain expectations through its laws and acts that have led the investor to invest, it is generally considered unfair for the state to take subsequent actions that fundamentally deny or frustrate those expectations".[934]

It is notable that this consistent approach of the tribunals at least partially resulted from Spain's litigation strategy. Spain continuously argued that, in broad terms, legitimate expectations should be limited to the RRR, since they were grounded on a hierarchically superior norm (i.e. the LSE, which was an Act of Parliament) as opposed to a hierarchically lower norm (i.e. an RD, which is an act adopted by the government and merely implements a legislative concept). Thus, whereas Spain argued that the scope of legislation-based legitimate expectations differed, it did not challenge the fundamental foundation of the cases that its legislation had created legitimate expectations that were protected under international law.[935] By way of example, the dissenter in the *Cavalum* case quoted Spain's post-hearing brief, in which Spain submitted that "Spanish legislation does contain a general commitment to investors investing in renewables in Spain, but it is not the commitment that Claimant claims".[936]

934 Salacuse, *supra* note 3, p. 305.

935 A question may arise as to why Spain chose to adopt such a strategy. One possible answer is that it would be virtually impossible to prove that Spain did not intend to encourage investments in RE by adopting the Special Regime. As such, the Special Regime can be classified as legislation that it intended to attract capital to a specific sector. Some authors describe such legislation as creating legitimate expectations "by induction" – Fulvio Maria Palombino, Fair and Equitable Treatment and the Fabric of General Principles (Springer 2018), p. 115.

936 The submission continued:

> The Commitment that Spanish legislation contained at the time of Claimant's investment and that is maintained in the Spanish legislation currently in force, after the disputed measures, is that investors obtain a reasonable return to their investment in accordance with the cost of money in the capital markets

– see: Cavalum v. Spain, Dissenting ..., *supra* note 899, [53]. The claimant's rebuttal of the respondent's position is described by the *Cavalum* majority in the following manner:

> Lastly, it is worth noting that Spain does not dispute that legitimate expectations can arise from its regulatory framework. In fact, Spain contends that investors did have legitimate expectations that they would receive a reasonable rate of return on their investments (which is an assurance that Spain made, if at all, only in the regulatory regime and not in a contract or some more specific context directed to investors). Rather, the crux of Spain's case challenges what the regulatory regime assured to investors

– see: Cavalum v. Spain, *supra* note 854 [229]. Similar conclusion can be drawn from the awards even when there is no such direct quotation, and even though written submissions and minutes from the hearings are not publicly available. However, some parts suggest

This justifies the first lesson learned from the Spanish saga cases. In the words of *Novenergia* tribunal, legitimate expectations can "be grounded in the legal order of the host State as it stands at the time the investor acquires or makes the investment".[937] The *Masdar* tribunal described it as one of two schools of thought, which "considers that such commitments [specific commitments – author's note] can result from general statements in general laws of regulations".[938] The *Antin* tribunal concluded that:

> given the precision and detail exhibited in the royal decrees, particularly the contemplation that the treatment would be accorded for a defined period of time, the Tribunal has no difficulty in concluding that this falls squarely into the type of State conduct that was intended to, and did, give rise to legitimate expectations of the Claimants.[939]

The *Foresight* tribunal also recognized that the investors':

> legitimate expectation that the remuneration and benefits their PV facilities received would not be radically changed were based foremost on the express language of RD 661/2007, which sets out fixed FiTs to be paid for entire operating life of a PV facility.[940]

The *Cube* tribunal decided that in:

> a highly-regulated industry, and provided that the representations are sufficiently clear and unequivocal, it is enough that a regulatory regime be established with the overt aim of attracting investments by holding out to potential investors the prospect that the investments will be subject to a set of specific regulatory principles that will, as a matter of deliberate policy, be maintained in force for a finite length of time. Such regimes are plainly intended to create expectations upon which investors will rely; and to the extent that those expectations are objectively reasonable, they give rise to legitimate expectations when investments are in fact made in reliance upon them.[941]

---

that the position evolved over time, and the primary defense was based on reference to lack of specific commitments – see: SolEs v. Spain, *supra* note 376 [313].

937 Fn 125.

938 Masdar v. Spain, *supra* note 150 [490].

939 Fn 194.

940 Fn 217.

941 Fn 309.

According to the *9REN* tribunal:

> there is no doubt that an enforceable "legitimate expectation" requires a clear and specific commitment, but in the view of this Tribunal there is no reason in principle why such a commitment of the requisite clarity and specificity cannot be made in the regulation itself where (as here) such a commitment is made for the purpose of inducing investment, which succeeded in attracting the Claimant's investment and once made resulted in losses to the Claimant.[942]

The *SolEs* tribunal confirmed that legitimate expectations can "arise from provisions of law and regulations and from statements made by or on behalf of the State for the purpose of inducing investment by class of investors".[943] The *OperaFund* tribunal acknowledged that:

> RD 661/2007 set remuneration for the lifetime of the plant. Through its regulatory offer, Respondent assumed an obligation of regulatory stability, which resulted in the boosting of renewable investments in Spain and gave rise to legitimate expectations of stability under the ECT.[944]

The *Stadtwerke* tribunal observed that:

> when a State that has created certain investor expectations through its laws, regulations, or other acts that has caused the investor to invest, it is often considered unfair for a State to take subsequent actions that fundamentally deny or frustrate those expectations.[945]

The *Watkins* tribunal stated that:

> Spain had promised explicitly that the economic regime for the qualifying Special Regime installation would remain stable under RD 661/2007 which contained the stabilisation commitment in Article 44(3)607 and reiterated in RD 1614/2010 that any revisions to the fixed tariff and

942 9REN v Spain, *supra* note 354 [295].
943 Fn 377.
944 Fn 449.
945 Fn 540.

premium pursuant to Article 44(3) of RD 661/2007, would not affect duly registered existing installations.[946]

The *Hydro* and *Cavalum* tribunals also agreed that, in the context of stability, "legitimate expectations may be engendered by the legal framework at the time of the investment".[947]

Not all of the Spanish saga tribunals explicitly recognized the existence of legitimate expectations based on the regulatory framework. However, even if this was not explicitly articulated, each tribunal's acceptance of this position is implied in its reasoning. The *Eiser* tribunal implicitly agreed with this position when analyzing the "obligation to provide fundamental stability in the essential characteristics of the legal regime".[948] The *RREEF* tribunal seems to recognize it when finding the existence of legitimate expectations to the RRR based on the "relevant applicable texts" in Spanish law (simultaneously avoiding the need to determine whether a "general principle" defining an RRR exists in international law).[949] The *InfraRed* tribunal implicitly shared this view when it agreed that no specific commitment is needed to create legitimate expectations "that the regulatory framework will not be radically or fundamentally changed".[950] Likewise, the *RWE* tribunal did so when analyzing the proportionality of the disputed regulatory measures.[951] The *PV Investors* tribunal also implicitly confirmed this when upholding the "alternative claim" based on the RRR derived from the legislation.[952]

It may appear that two tribunals expressed a different view. The *NextEra* tribunal "in the circumstances of the present case" dismissed the possibility that legitimate expectations could be created by the regulatory framework.[953] This approach seemed to be followed by the *BayWa* tribunal.[954] Nevertheless, the *NextEra* tribunal's comment was made solely in the context of analyzing written reassurances received from the Spanish authorities, which was a central piece of the claimants' legitimate expectations argument.[955]

946 Fn 692.
947 Fn 822, repeated in Cavalum v. Spain, *supra* note 854 – fn 863.
948 Fn 106.
949 Fn 273.
950 Fn 407.
951 Fn 618.
952 Fn 741, 771.
953 Fn 339.
954 Fn 481.
955 Fn 342.

The *BayWa* tribunal's comment quoted above referred to a "freezing" of legislation, but the tribunal recognized later the existence of legitimate expectations based on Art. 30(4) LSE.[956]

The first lesson learned is also confirmed by those Spanish saga cases which dismissed claims that the FET had been violated. The *Charanne* tribunal admitted that a regulatory framework can generate legitimate expectations. The scope of such expectations is not that the relevant legislation will not be amended but, rather, that any such amendment will be reasonable, proportional and done in the public interest.[957] Similarly, the *Isolux* tribunal confirmed that legitimate expectations can be based on a regulatory framework, whilst concluding that no such expectations were created on the facts of this particular case. At the time the disputed investment was made, prior regulatory changes had already taken place and further changes were inevitable.[958] The *Stadtwerke* tribunal also agreed that legitimate expectations can be based on a regulatory framework and can arise even in the absence of any specific commitment having been made to a particular investor. However, such an expectation does not entitle an investor to conclude that there will not be "any" change to the regulatory framework. In this case, the tribunal found that the legitimate expectation could have been based on the LSE having provided for the RRR, rather than based on the RDs (which, although they developed the RRR concept, had an inferior legislative status to the LSE as an Act of Parliament).

Legitimate expectations based on a regulatory framework have a different scope to those based on specific commitments. Most of the tribunals differentiated between these two types of legitimate expectations and clearly stated that legislation does not amount to a specific commitment. Only the *OperaFund, Watkins, 9REN* and *Cube* tribunals accepted, at least theoretically, that legislation itself can amount to a specific commitment. The *OperaFund* and *Watkins* tribunals perceived Art. 44(3) RD 661/2007 as a stabilization clause.[959] The *Cube* tribunal explicitly linked this conclusion with the specificity of

956 Fn 480.

957 Fn 68–69. See also the dissenting opinion, explicitly confirming that legitimate expectations can "originate or be based on the legal order in force when the investment is made" – fn 73.

958 Fn 79–86. Similarly the dissenting opinion, recognizing that legitimate expectations can be created by regulatory framework, in particular if it is designed to attract foreign investment – fn 93.

959 Fn 439, fn 692. Also *Masdar* tribunal recognized this as theoretical possibility if "first school of thought" was to be applied – fn 161.

the RE cases, which concern investments made in highly regulated sectors of the economy.[960] The fact that the Special Regime was a sophisticated, carefully-designed regime which sought to attract (and did attract) investments was also a relevant fact for this tribunal when reaching this conclusion. For the *9REN* tribunal, a specific commitment can "be made in the regulation itself where (as here) such a commitment is made for the purpose of inducing investment".[961] This is, however, a minority view – not only when compared to the other Spanish saga awards, but also to the general case law.[962]

The division between legitimate expectations based on specific commitments and those based on a regulatory framework has a material impact on their content. Legitimate expectations based on a regulatory framework concern protection from radical changes being made to that framework.[963] They do not entail an expectation that the legislation will not be amended at all, but merely that such amendments will be reasonable, proportional and done in the public interest. They recognize that states – as sovereigns – have a right to regulate. However, if – when exercising this right – certain limits (imposed by the ECT or other investment treaties) are exceeded, it may trigger an obligation to pay compensation. This is analyzed further below, as the fourth lesson learned.

The first lesson learned from the Spanish saga case law is confirmed by recent cases concerning RE disputes outside the Spanish context.[964] The tribunal in *Blusun v. Italy* confirmed that "a representation as to future conduct of the state could be made in the form of a law, sufficiently clearly expressed", although it drew attention to "a clear distinction between a law, i.e. a norm of greater or lesser generality creating rights and obligations while it remains in force, and a promise or contractual commitment".[965] The *ESPF v. Italy* tribunal decided that:

---

960 Fn 309.

961 Fn 942.

962 Fn 37. However, some authors argue that this minority view should prevail in the RE cases. This is because the regulatory frameworks relied upon by the investors are "deliberately and clearly designed to attract foreign investment" in this sector. See: Biggs, *supra* note 932, p. 123.

963 Fn 28–35 for authorities on general scope, unlimited to the RE sector.

964 However, contrary positions were also presented. See, for example: Belenergia v. Italy, ICSID Case No. ARB/15/40, Award (06.08.2019) [580], [583], Wirtgen v. Czech Republic, PCA Case No. 2014-03, Final Award (11.10.2017) [417].

965 Blusun v. Italy, ICSID Case No. ARB/14/3, Award (27.12.2016) [371].

> explicit promises or guarantees can be given in the legislative and regulatory framework of a state at the time an investor makes its investment when the purpose of that framework is to guarantee stability to investors upon which they can rely when deciding to invest.[966]

The *Silver Ridge v. Italy* tribunal similarly recognized that states "may make specific commitments to investors also by virtue of legislative or regulatory acts which are not addressed to particular individuals, provided that these acts are sufficiently specific regarding their content and their object and purpose".[967] The tribunal in *Antaris v. Czech* Republic recognized that "an expectation may arise from what are construed as specific guarantees in legislation".[968]

A question arises regarding the extent to which the above conclusions stemming from the Spanish saga cases can become relevant outside the scope of the ECT. A doubt in this regard arises from the specific wording of Art. 10(1) ECT. Its first sentence speaks about stability, whereas the FET is included in its second sentence:

> Each Contracting Party shall, in accordance with the provisions of this Treaty, encourage and create stable, equitable, favourable and transparent conditions for Investors of other Contracting Parties to make Investments in its Area. Such conditions shall include a commitment to accord at all times to Investments of Investors of other Contracting Parties fair and equitable treatment.

---

966 ESPF v. Italy, ICSID Case No. ARB/16/5, Award (14.09.2020) [530]. Similarly [512]:

> [...] there is no reason in principle why such a commitment of the requisite clarity and specificity cannot be made in the regulation itself where (as here) such a commitment is made for the purpose of inducing investment, which succeeded in attracting the Claimants' investments and, once made, resulted in losses to the Claimants. In these circumstances, there is no principled reason to deny that the investor's expectations of performance by the state are legitimate [...].

967 Silver Ridge v. Italy, ICSID Case No. ARB/15/37, Award (26.02.2021) [408], adding that: "In this context, the Tribunal considers the creation of legitimate expectations more likely where a State has adopted legislative or regulatory acts "with a specific aim to induce [...] investments"" (footnotes omitted).

968 Antaris v. Czech Republic, PCA Case No. 2014-01, Award (02.05.2018) [360(4)], [360.(6)], adding that:

> provisions of general legislation applicable to a plurality of persons or a category of persons, do not create legitimate expectations that there will be no change in the law; and given the State's regulatory powers, in order to rely on legitimate expectations the investor should inquire in advance regarding the prospects of a change in the regulatory framework in light of the then prevailing or reasonably to be expected changes in the economic and social conditions of the host State.

Most of the arbitral tribunals (*Isolux*,[969] *Eiser*,[970] *Novenergia*,[971] *Antin*,[972] *Foresight*,[973] *RREEF*,[974] *BayWa*,[975] *Stadtwerke*,[976] *RWE*,[977] *PV Investors*,[978] *Hydro*[979]) considered that the first sentence does not create a separate obligation to provide regulatory stability, but that this should be read into the FET. Some tribunals failed to adopt a clear position on this question (*NextEra, 9REN, Cube, InfraRed, OperaFund*), whereas the *Cavalum* tribunal simply observed that there is a "plain overlap" between the two.[980] Only the *Watkins* tribunal interpreted the first sentence of Art. 10(1) ECT as creating a separate obligation, albeit one which remains closely linked to the FET.[981] The *Charanne* tribunal took a different perspective and considered the FET to be "included in the more general obligation to create stable, equitable, favourable and transparent conditions".[982]

As such, the Spanish saga cases confirm the prevailing view that the first sentence of Art. 10(1) ECT does not contain a stand-alone standard for protecting investments which are already made.[983] It relates to "best efforts" during the pre-investment phase.[984]

Nevertheless, one must remember that the Spanish saga tribunals' interpretation of the FET is driven by the wording of the applicable treaty. This is understood as forming the "context" of the FET within the meaning of Art. 31 VCLT.[985] Additionally, Art. 2 ECT and the European Energy Charter forms part of the object and purpose of the ECT, which was taken into account by the Spanish

969 Fn 79.
970 Fn 106.
971 Fn 129.
972 Fn 186.
973 Fn 206.
974 Fn 245.
975 Fn 473.
976 Fn 534.
977 Fn 589, 590. In *RWE*, the tribunal considered that it is a separate obligation, but concerning only conditions in which the investment is made, and not an ongoing obligation of stability.
978 Fn 744.
979 Fn 801.
980 Fn 897.
981 Fn 698–699, although with a strong dissent – fn 727.
982 Fn 55.
983 Niclas Landmann, Legitimate Expectations and Fair-and-Equitable-Treatment under the Energy Charter Treaty. A Comparative Analysis of the Renewable Energy Cases (Nomos 2022), p. 67.
984 Hobér, *supra* note 5, p. 185.
985 Ibid, p. 190. Similarly awards in *Eiser* – fn 104 and *PV Investors* award – fn 745, and dissenting opinion in *Stadtwerke* – fn 577.

saga tribunals.[986] This must be kept in mind when relying on these cases in the future, outside of the ECT context. Whilst some investment treaties contain a comparable "context" of references to legal stability,[987] others do not.[988]

Bearing in mind the above reservation, the Spanish saga cases can be expected to impact on future case law, by creating an important contribution to developing our understanding of the FET as encompassing legitimate expectations regarding "stable and equitable conditions".[989]

In summary, the first lesson learned is that legitimate expectations can be based on general legislation. However, the scope of such expectations is not equal to a specific commitment that a regulatory framework will remain frozen in time.[990] They are legitimate expectations "to stability".[991] They protect against revolutionary changes to the regulatory framework (see the following lessons learned). This is particularly relevant in the RE sector, which concerns long-term investments that are closely aligned to state policies which, with the minor exceptions of household installations, cannot exist independently from the state's infrastructure and legislation.[992]

---

986 Fn 178, 179, 746, 800. See also: Reinisch, Schreuer, *supra* note 30, p. 290.

987 See, for example BIT Poland-US, BIT Argentina-US, BIT Pakistan-Turkey and BIT Jordan-Turkey, which in their preambles recognize, among others, that "fair and equitable treatment of investment is desirable in order to maintain a stable framework for investment and maximum effective utilization of economic resources". This exact wording of a preamble led the *Occidental* tribunal to observe that: "[t]he stability of the legal and business framework is thus an essential element of fair and equitable treatment" (Occidental v. Ecuador, UNCITRAL, LCIA Case No. UN 3467, Final Award (01.07.2004) [183]). Similarly the *LG&E* tribunal, which observed in the context of this wording of a preamble:

> In light of these stated objectives, this Tribunal must conclude that stability of the legal and business framework is an essential element of fair and equitable treatment in this case, provided that they do not pose any danger for the existence of the host State itself

– LG&E v Argentina, *supra* note 34 [124].

988 See, for example BIT Poland – Malaysia, which in its preamble and Art. II refers to encouragement and creation of "favourable conditions", but is silent on their "stability".

989 Fn 28, 35.

990 See also: fn 37.

991 For a discussion of legitimate expectations "to" stability, as opposed as "from" stability, see: Kopar, *supra* note 932, pp. 193–203.

992 See, for example: Deyan Draguiev, Investment Treaty Arbitration in the Renewable Energy Sector: Overview of Arbitral Case Law on Legitimate Expectations in the Light of Policy, Transnational Dispute Management, 7 (2018), pp. 4–5, 12.

1.3.2 Second Lesson Learned – the Content of Domestic Law Is Crucial to Determine the Scope of Legitimate Expectations Based on a Regulatory Framework

The scope of legitimate expectations based on a regulatory framework may encompass more than merely an expectation to stability, as discussed above. This depends on the precise content of the domestic law.

This is clearly visible in the *Cube* example. Whereas, as regards PV investments made by 2009, the tribunal understood Spanish law as justifying legitimate expectations regarding specific FITs, the Hydro energy investments made in 2011 and 2012, after new legislation had already been introduced, limited the scope of legitimate expectations to those concerning stability only.[993]

The second lesson is confirmed also by those cases which found that the investors' legitimate expectations were limited to expecting the RRR. They were created by Spanish law and their scope was determined by Spanish law.

This explains the attention paid by the tribunals to the: (i) the wording of Spain's relevant legal acts, (ii) the case law of the Spanish courts, particularly the Supreme Court, and (iii) Spain's activities surrounding the adoption of the relevant legislation.

With respect to the first issue, any general conclusion on the specific wording and/or interpretation of legal acts will be of limited usefulness outside the Spanish context. Moreover, the interpretation could differ between RD 661/2007 and RD 1578/2008, since the latter contained no explicit "grandfathering" provision of existing RE facilities comparable to Art. 44(3) of the former.[994] For these reasons, it is pointless to try to distil a lesson learned regarding the "correct" interpretation of Spanish domestic law provisions, which are no longer binding.

Nevertheless, a lesson can be still learned for the future also in this context. One cannot look at a particular legislative provision in isolation, ignoring the domestic legal system as a whole. Due attention must be paid to the hierarchy of legal acts, pursuant to the domestic law legal order, together with the case law of domestic courts which apply these acts and any other specific features of the relevant legal system.[995] When analyzing an EU member state, this includes the EU law. It is particularly relevant in the RE sector (and, indeed, the energy

993 Fn 311, 312.

994 See, for example 9REN v. Spain, *supra* note 354 [274].

995 This is part of the assessment of facts which shows that legitimate expectations have (or have not) come into existence. As such, it does not contravene the position of those who do not consider international arbitrators to be formally bound by the local law. See, for example: Horacio A. Grigera Naón, Should International Commercial Arbitrators Declare a Law Unconstitutional, in: David D. Caron, Stephan W. Schill, Abby Cohen Smutny,

sector as a whole) because this is a highly regulated sector which typically has various aspects regulated at different levels of the legal system. Consequently, if there is no specific commitment, legitimate expectations "might be created from cumulative legal sources" within the domestic legal system.[996] Reading them in isolation will be appropriate in rare circumstances only.

The varying weight placed by different tribunals on the interpretation of Spanish law sheds light on why divergent views were reached on the conclusions that: (i) there is no difference between removing FITs and Premiums (as guaranteed in RDs) and removing the RRR (as guaranteed in the LSE), i.e. allowing the FIT and Premiums system to be revoked without compensation means that the guarantee of the RRR contained in Art. 30(4) LSE could be similarly removed,[997] as opposed to the view that (ii) RDs are subordinate to the LSE and only a violation of the RRR would result in the a violation of the FET.[998]

Those Spanish saga tribunals which concluded that the FET had been violated only insofar as the New Regime did not meet the threshold of the RRR decided that investors had no "vested rights" to a specific remuneration scheme. This is not to say that such a right could never exist. It possibly could, even based on general legislation, and not being rooted in specific commitments. These conclusions were driven by these tribunals' understanding that the Spanish RDs (regulations adopted by the government) were subordinate to the LSE (Act of Parliament). The latter was not only superior in the hierarchy of legal norms, but also consisted of provisions that were worded in a more general manner, thereby creating more flexibility, but also needing to be specified by regulations capable of being applied in practice.[999]

The conclusion on this point is, however, straightforward: legitimate expectations can be based on general legislation (first lesson learned), and that legislation frames the content of those expectations (second lesson learned).

Epaminontas E. Triantafilou (eds.), Practising Virtue: Inside International Arbitration (Oxford University Press 2015), p. 314:

> international arbitrators are not necessarily bound by the hierarchy of norms or legal sources spelled out in any national constitution or legal system. Although such hierarchy may certainly be considered in their analysis, it will not necessarily have preponderant or decisive weight in the decision-making process or its outcome.

996 Kopar, *supra* note 932, pp. 156–157.

997 Fn 97.

998 Fn 480, 543, 549.

999 Some commentators observe that tribunals "did not explain why investors could rely on a general legislative representation guaranteeing a reasonable rate of return but not on a specific legislative representation regarding guaranteed FiT rates" – see: Biggs, *supra* note 932, p. 110. However, this understanding explains such differences, even if they were not directly addressed in the written reasoning in the awards.

The Spanish saga cases do not provide grounds to conclude that, outside their context, at a general level, a violation of legitimate expectations can be claimed only if a state's measures prevent investors from receiving the RRR.[1000] Consequently, they provide no grounds to determine that the level of return guaranteed by the New Regime – applied as the threshold in the analyses of those tribunals which concluded that legitimate expectations existed regarding the RRR – can be simply transposed to other cases. Similarly, the concept of "fair return" or "fair remuneration" in the Italian RE cases is rooted in Italian legislation which has a different meaning, determined by Italian law.[1001] This is confirmed also by the Czech cases, where domestic legislation also set a minimal annual return that served as a benchmark for the respective tribunals' analysis.[1002]

As regards the second issue – the case law of domestic courts – the Spanish saga awards are uniform in treating the case law of the Spanish Supreme Court as part of factual background of those disputes. Being considered as a fact, this case law was a factor in informing the content of legitimate expectations. A natural consequence of this is that, in assessing legitimate expectations, only such case law as existed at the time of making the investment was relevant. This was explicitly confirmed in *Isolux*,[1003] *SolEs*,[1004] *OperaFund*,[1005] *PV Investors*[1006] and *Cavalum*.[1007]

Nevertheless, Spanish Supreme Court judgments issued after investments had occurred were also relevant. They were a factor confirming the interpretation of domestic law.[1008] As such, they played a role in the first issue, identified above.

1000 A contrary conclusion was reached by Landmann, based on the Spanish, Italian and Czech cases – Landmann, *supra* note 983, p. 333.

1001 See, for example: Greentech v. Italy, SCC Case No. V 2015/095, Final Award (23.12.2018) [108], CEF v. Italy, SCC Case No. V 2015/158, Award (16.01.2019) [241], Sun Reserve v. Italy, SCC Case No. V 2016/32, Award (25.03.2020) [843], Eskosol v. Italy, ICSID Case No. ARB/15/50, Award (04.09.2020) [414].

1002 Antaris v. Czech Republic, *supra* note 968 [440], Wirtgen v. Czech Republic, *supra* note 964 [369], [416], WA v. Czech Republic, PCA Case No. 2014-19, Award (15.05.2019) [548], [549], Voltaic v. Czech Republic, PCA Case No. 2014-20 Award (15.05.2019) [462], [463], I.C.W. v. Czech Republic, PCA Case No. 2014-22, Award (15.05.2019) [504], [505].

1003 Fn 88.

1004 Fn 388.

1005 Fn 462, 472.

1006 Fn 759.

1007 Fn 874.

1008 Fn 615.

Some tribunals (*Eiser*,[1009] *9REN*,[1010] *Cube*[1011] and *SolEs*[1012]) paid little attention to the Spanish Supreme Court's case law because it did not apply the ECT.[1013] Whilst formally this approach could be correct and justify why the tribunals were not formally "bound" by the relevant domestic judgments, this should not be used as a reason to disregard these judgments' impact on the scope of legitimate expectations, as commented above.

Finally, with respect to the third issue – state activities surrounding the adoption of the relevant legislation – legitimate expectations can be strengthened by different activities undertaken by a state when adopting the relevant legislation, such as press releases, "roadshows" promoting regulations incentivizing investments, public statements etc. An important element of the Spanish saga analysis was the respondent's emphasis, made earlier, underlying the stability of the Special Regime. This was specifically intended to encourage foreign investment. The *Antin* tribunal noted that the "leitmotiv" of all these actions was to guarantee the stability of the then-applicable regulations.[1014] By way of example, the *Cube* tribunal paid special attention to the 2007 Press release – attributable to Spain – which was posted on the official webpage of the competent ministry on the adoption date of RD 661/2007, confirming how the legislation was understood at that time.[1015]

In summary, the second lesson learned for the future is that the scope of legitimate expectations based on a regulatory framework may encompass more than merely an expectation of stability. The content of domestic law determines whether this is relevant to a particular investment.

1.3.3 Third Lesson Learned – Legal Due Diligence Is Essential to Ensuring the Existence of Legitimate Expectations to Regulatory Stability in Highly Regulated Sectors

At first, it seems that the Spanish saga tribunals lacked conformity on whether detailed legal due diligence must take place before legitimate expectations can arise. The threshold question is how detailed such due diligence must be in order to inform investors' expectations that no regulatory changes will be made for the period of their investments.

Some tribunals underlined that detailed legal due diligence is required in order for legitimate expectations to exist concerning investments in "highly

1009 Fn 101.
1010 Fn 355, 356.
1011 Fn 295.
1012 Fn 390.
1013 Similarly dissenter in RWE – fn 672.
1014 Fn 190–193.
1015 Fn 291.

regulated sectors". This was the approach taken by the tribunals in *Charanne*,[1016] *Masdar* (in its description of the first school of thought),[1017] *Stadtwerke*,[1018] *RWE*,[1019] *Watkins*,[1020] *Cavalum*[1021] and the dissenter in *Foresight*.[1022]

Other tribunals, in *Isolux*,[1023] *Antin*,[1024] *Foresight*,[1025] *Cube*,[1026] *SolEs*,[1027] *OperaFund*[1028] and *Hydro*,[1029] saw no need for extensive due diligence to have taken place. They applied the threshold of knowledge possessed by a prudent investor, explaining that because legitimate expectations are measured against an objective standard, investors cannot benefit from their own ignorance. The *Foresight* tribunal went so far as to be satisfied that, as the investors had received legal advice, this was sufficient to conclude that legal due diligence had taken place. It was irrelevant to analyze the detailed content of that advice.[1030]

The *InfraRed* tribunal struck a balance between the two approaches. One the one hand, it underlined the requirement of the "stricter due diligence standard" in highly regulated sectors. However, it applied the threshold of the foreseeability of legislative changes "to a reasonably prudent investor with the benefit of an adequate due diligence".[1031]

The tribunal in *Novenergia*[1032] saw no need for any due diligence to have taken place, provide that the relevant legislation is clear on its wording.

1016 Fn 67.
1017 Fn 156.
1018 Fn 541.
1019 Fn 610–612.
1020 Fn 708, although here the discussion was short, since the claimants undertook "an appropriate fact-finding mission in Spain with a view to their investments in RE".
1021 Fn 863, 867.
1022 Fn 227.
1023 Fn 80, 91.
1024 Fn 188.
1025 Fn 352.
1026 Fn 317, 318.
1027 Fn 396.
1028 Fn 443.
1029 Fn 823.
1030 Fn 352, in particular the following part of the tribunal's analysis:

> The fact that Claimants refused to waive their privilege in respect those legal opinions should not lead to any adverse inferences. Nondisclosure means that Respondent and the Tribunal have not had access to the content of those opinions, but the fact that Claimants received legal advice is not really contested. In short, the Tribunal does not consider that the assertion that there was a lack of due diligence on the part of Claimants has been established.

1031 Fn 428.
1032 Fn 140.

Some tribunals did not consider due diligence as relevant and remained silent on the issue.[1033]

This can be summarized by table below.

TABLE 5 Due diligence in highly regulated sectors

No	Case name	Detailed DD	Threshold of a prudent investor	DD unnecessary	Not adressed by tribunal
1	Charanne	✓			
2	Isolux		✓		
3	Eiser				✓[a]
4	Novenergia			✓	
5	Masdar	✓			
6	Antin		✓		
7	Foresight	(dissent)	✓		
8	RREEF			✓	
9	Cube	(dissent)	✓		
10	NextEra		✓		
11	9REN				✓[b]
12	SolEs		✓		
13	InfraRed		✓		
14	OperaFund		✓		
15	BayWa				✓
16	Stadtwerke	✓			
17	RWE	✓			
18	Watkins	✓			
19	PV Investors				✓
20	Hydro		✓		
21	Cavalum	✓			
	Total	Yes - 6 Dissent - 2	Yes - 9	Yes - 2	Yes - 4

a DD was relevant for damages (when analyzing the expected life-time of a plant)

b DD was present and uncontested

1033 See, for example fn 774.

Thus, in general, the Spanish saga cases recognize the fact of legal due diligence as relevant to forming the content of legitimate expectations. This aligns with general investor-state arbitration case law, which often refers to the requirement of due diligence.[1034] It is closely related to an analysis of whether, when making the investments, investors have relied upon the expectations which they subsequently seek to protect in arbitration. As recently noted in the context of RE cases, "in order to grant a legitimate expectations protection based on a stability provision under the domestic legislation, tribunals seek additional requirements and elaborate more on the reliance aspect".[1035]

The discussion on due diligence, and in particular the relevance of the Spanish Supreme Court's case law on legitimate expectations, must be read in the light of Art. 1(6) Spanish Civil Code, which states that: "Case law shall complement the legal system by means of the doctrine repeatedly upheld by the Supreme Court in its interpretation and application of statutes, customs and general legal principles". It places due diligence analysis in its proper context in the Spanish saga cases. However, one can expect that, typically, domestic legal systems envisage a similar role for the case law of their supreme courts, regardless of how this outcome is achieved, i.e. the precise wording of a particular provision. It may also be an implicit principle which is not envisaged *expressis verbis* in any local law provision.

The real discrepancy between the first and the second group of cases is not whether due diligence is required but, rather, what are the consequences if an investor fails to conduct sufficiently detailed due diligence.

This question unanswered in the first group of cases.[1036] However, the second group of cases provides a clear answer – tribunals must assess the objectively available knowledge, accessible by a prudent investor at the relevant time, who would have performed the legal due diligence.[1037] In the words of the *SolEs* tribunal:

1034 See case law in fn 23.

1035 Kopar, *supra* note 932, p. 190.

1036 Only the *RWE* tribunal clarified that all statements, reports and legal decisions that would have been covered by the regulatory due diligence must be taken into account in such a situation – fn 613.

1037 This finds support also in other cases. For example the *Electrabel* tribunal observed that "fairness and consistency must be assessed against the background of information that the investor knew and should reasonably have known at the time of the investment and of the conduct of the host State" – Electrabel v. Hungary, *supra* note 16 [7.78].

> an investor cannot benefit from gaps in its subjective knowledge of the regulatory environment because, under an objective standard, the investor's legitimate expectations are measured with reference to the knowledge that a hypothetical prudent investor is deemed to have had as of the date of the investment.[1038]

In short, ignorance cannot shield the investor.

This allows the conclusion that the discrepancy is apparent if the consequences of failing to perform proper due diligence in the first group of cases would be the same, i.e. if the same test of a prudent investor shall apply.[1039]

On the contrary, the discrepancy between the two identified groups would become real only if one concluded otherwise, i.e. that a lack of detailed due diligence should automatically preclude the possible existence of legitimate expectations of regulatory stability. This conclusion is, however, less convincing for two reasons. First, it would lead to a formalistic approach, according to which any claim based on legitimate expectations to regulatory stability should be dismissed even if the due diligence would not have impacted on the investors' behavior. Second, it would produce an unexplainable gap between the two groups of cases, which can otherwise be read as a consistent body of case law.

The conclusion on the applicability of the "prudent investor test" is in line with other recent RE cases. This was explicitly confirmed in *Belenergia v. Italy*, where the tribunal analyzed the reasonableness of legitimate expectations "considering the information that a "prudent" investor had to know about Italian PV regulatory framework at the time of the investment".[1040] Similarly, the *Sun Reserve v. Italy* tribunal observed that "the standard of due diligence that investors are expected to adhere to should meet the threshold of what a "prudent investor" would "reasonably" do to know about regulatory framework

---

1038 Fn 396.

1039 See also, for example, Kopar, *supra* note 932, p. 153:

> what is required here is not an in-depth and extensive legal inquiry into the legal framework of the host state, but rather a certain level of knowledge about the existing laws. [...] a breach of legitimate expectations claim cannot be asserted if the investor has not undertaken any kind of legal survey regarding the laws of the host state. However, it should also be noted that if the modifications were not foreseeable regardless of due diligence, then the investor should not be refused protection solely on the basis of its lack of conducting due diligence.

1040 Belenergia v. Italy, *supra* note 964, [584], adding: "In other words, an investor cannot legitimately expect that the legal and regulatory framework will not change when any prudent investor could have anticipated this change before making its investment". See also: [587], [600].

in question".[1041] The tribunal in *Antaris v. Czech Republic* applied the view of "an informed investor who had undertaken proper diligence".[1042] As was recently concluded in academic writings, the Spanish, Italian and Czech RE disputes "demonstrate the trend that there is no requirement for a particularly sophisticated analysis, if the underlying norms are so adamantly clear that they can be easily understood by common readers".[1043]

This is not to deny the importance of conducting due diligence. The tribunal in *Antaris v. Czech Republic* perceived the lack of "real due diligence" as a crucial factor in concluding that the claimant had no internationally-protected legitimate expectations but, rather, an unprotected "speculative hope".[1044]

If this approach prevails in the future case law, once an investor proves that it has undertaken some legal due diligence, this may shift the burden of proof to the respondent, who would then be required to prove that the regulatory changes would have been foreseeable to other, prudent investors.

This conclusion on the relevance of detailed legal due diligence cannot be over-exaggerated for future case law and cannot be understood as requiring such due diligence to have taken place in each single case concerning an alleged FET violation. First, this conclusion applies only to legitimate expectations, i.e. to one of the constituent elements of the FET. The FET may be violated even if no legitimate expectations have been breached.[1045] Second, due diligence is relevant to creating legitimate expectations only as regards (i) regulatory stability rooted in the regulatory framework (not based on specific representations *vis-à-vis* a particular investor) and (ii) only in "highly regulated sectors", such as the subsidized RE sector.[1046]

1041 Sun Reserve v. Italy, *supra* note 1001 [714].

1042 Antaris v. Czech Republic, *supra* note 968 [440].

1043 Landmann, *supra* note 983, p. 251.

1044 Antaris v. Czech Republic, *supra* note 968 [432]–[435].

1045 Even if typically they are considered as its core element – fn 14–16.

1046 See, for example the following summary of *Charanne v. Spain* and *Blusun v. Italy*: "Two recently issued awards pertaining to renewable energy procurement in Europe have generalized this analysis: sophisticated investors in a highly regulated industry are reasonably anticipated to conduct legal diligence and thus cannot expect zero regulatory changes" – Matthew A. J. Levine, Emerging Practice on Investor Diligence: Jurisdiction, Admissibility, and Merits, in: Julien Chaisse, Leïla Choukroune, Sufian Jusoh (eds.), Handbook of International Investment Law and Policy (Springer 2021), p. 1096. Similarly, the *InfraRed* tribunal, referring to "stricter due diligence standard" in highly regulated sectors – fn 428. Also Landmann, *supra* note 992, p. 267:

> [...] the level of due diligence is strongly influenced by the legal framework regulating the investment. In a highly regulated field, such as the renewable energy sector, diligent investors are expected to conduct an extensive legal analysis of the law of the courts, in which they plan to invest

(footnote omitted).

Regarding point (i) above, it must be also differentiated from an expectation of consistency, understood in terms of how the domestic law is applied by the administrative and judicial authorities.[1047] This expectation is not necessarily grounded in a due diligence analysis, as long as the investment is made in a developed state, for example in an EU member state.

As regards point (ii) above, other examples of such "highly regulated sectors" include: financial services, extraction of natural resources, crop protection, production and/or sale of tobacco or alcohol, utilities etc.[1048] The specific requirement of legal due diligence applicable to these sectors only is based on the understanding that foreign investors who decide to invest in such sectors of the economy must be aware of the high level of regulation which applies to them.[1049] In the words of the *Grand River* tribunal, "an investor entering an area traditionally subject to extensive regulation must do so with awareness of the regulatory situation".[1050] Some sectors are extensively regulated, given their importance for the host state.

1.3.4 Fourth Lesson Learned – the Sovereign Right to Regulate Has Its Limits, Which Is Related to the Rule of Law

It is undisputed that states have a right to regulate.[1051] However, sometimes the exercise of this right may trigger an obligation to compensate investors, which can happen if changes in the regulatory framework are revolutionary, rather evolutionary.[1052] The former can be considered to violate legitimate

1047 Fn 30.

1048 See, for example: Invesmart v. Czech Republic, *supra* note 23 [254], Chemtura v. Canada, UNCITRAL, Award (02.08.2010) [9], [149].

1049 Filip Balcerzak, Investor – State Arbitration and Human Rights (Brill 2017), p. 181.

1050 Grand River v. US, UNCITRAL, Award (12.01.2011) [144]. Although this observation was made with reference to legitimate expectations when considering the expropriation claim, the tribunal indicated in [218] that its analysis has relevance also for the FET analysis.

1051 Only the *Watkins* tribunal disagreed with this – fn 685. This has been confirmed not only by the Spanish cases, but similarly in the Italian and Czech RE disputes: Landmann, *supra* note 983, p. 181: "[…] the states' right to regulate has been uniformly acknowledged and taken into consideration by arbitral tribunals assessing the legitimacy of expectations".

1052 See, for example AES v. Hungary, *supra* note 37 [9.3.34]: "[…] any reasonably informed business person or investor knows that laws can evolve in accordance with the perceived political or policy dictates of the times". Similarly: Mamidoil v. Albania, *supra* note 23 [617]:

> Economic, social, environmental and legal circumstances and problems are by their nature dynamic and bound to constant change. It is indispensable for successful public infrastructure and public services to exist that they are adaptable to these changes. Accordingly, State policy must be able to evolve in order to guarantee adequate infrastructure and services in time and thereby the fair and equitable treatment of investments. The legal framework makes no exception.

expectations as an element of the FET, being "regulatory revolution", if the disputed measures may be described as "total and unreasonable change",[1053] "radical and unexpected" measures,[1054] "fundamental changes",[1055] which "suddenly and unexpectedly eliminate the essential features of the regulatory framework in place",[1056] alter the "essential features" of the regulatory framework,[1057] are "a radical or fundamental change",[1058] do not "merely modify" but introduce a "number of fundamental changes" to the regulatory framework,[1059] or "undermine the security and viability" of the investments.[1060]

In other words, if a state exercises its right to regulate and, in doing so, violates legitimate expectations to stability (as described in the first lesson learned), the state's obligations arising from investment treaties may require it to pay compensation.

Until this point, the Spanish saga awards are consistent. They are also in line with the prevailing case law.[1061] The threshold is high, and it "grants States discretion to regulate in the public interest without generating liability for breaching the FET standard".[1062] However, in some circumstances even a "roller-coaster" of legislative changes can violate legitimate expectations regarding the stability of the regulatory framework.[1063] The question is

---

The tribunal in *El Paso v. Argentina* underlined that "[e]conomic and legal life is by nature evolutionary and in consequence" and "[t]he State has to be able to make the reasonable changes called for by the circumstances and cannot be considered to have accepted a freeze on the evolution of its legal system" – El Paso v. Argentina, *supra* note 39 [351], [371]. See also for example: Yulia S. Selivanova, Changes in Renewables Support Policy and Investment Protection under the Energy Charter Treaty: Analysis of Jurisprudence and Outlook for the Current Arbitration Cases, ICSID Review – Foreign Investment Law Journal, 33:2 (2018), p. 452: "Regulatory regimes can evolve. It is a legitimate expectation of any investor to foresee the potential for reasonable changes in the limits of the law".

1053 Fn 98.

1054 Fn 147.

1055 Fn 303.

1056 Fn 184.

1057 Fn 197.

1058 Fn 210.

1059 Fn 222.

1060 Fn 349.

1061 See, for example: TECO v. Guatemala, ICSID Case No. ARB/10/23, Award (19.12.2013) [619], Toto v. Lebanon, *supra* note 43 [244], BG v. Argentina, *supra* note 37 [307]. See also cases referred to in Fn 37. Some authors perceive this "regulatory fairness" and "predicable regulatory environment" as closely linked to states' obligation to act in good faith, common to all members of the international community – Grierson-Weiler, Laird, *supra* note 5, p. 277.

1062 Biggs, *supra* note 932, p. 109.

1063 PSEG v. Turkey, ICSID Case No. ARB/02/5, Award (19.01.2007) [250]. This illustrative comparison was relied upon in the Spanish context – NextEra v. Spain, *supra* note 337 [519].

when a state crosses the boundary dividing a legitimate exercise of the right to regulate from an activity which triggers the compensatory obligation. Using the words of the *Foresight* tribunal, it is a question about "the circumstances in which a State will be found to have violated its obligations under the ECT as a consequence of the exercise by that State of its inherent right to regulate in the public interest".[1064]

A classic example of crossing the line is if legislation targets a specific, individual investor.[1065] This is not, however, relevant in the Spanish saga cases, which concerned general legislation adopted for a public purpose (i.e. to reduce the tariff deficit).

The Spanish saga case law is divided on identifying the location of the "red line". Some tribunals considered that Spain crossed this line by quashing the Special Regime. Others considered that the line was not crossed merely by revoking the Special Regime, but only insofar as a particular investment was unable to achieve the RRR under the New Regime.

Thus, determining the exact location of the boundary between a measure which triggers responsibility and one which does not is directly related to another question, asked one step earlier – i.e. what scope of legitimate expectations arose from the regulatory framework? In most cases, however, radical changes to the regulatory framework resulted in a violation of the FET: (i) either by the mere fact of quashing the Special Regime, or (ii) by causing a situation that the investments did not meet the RRR – the threshold of the general provision grandfathering the New Regime. In that sense, the Spanish saga cases confirm that legitimate expectations, and the FET, are violated by radical reforms made to the regulatory framework (i.e. by revolutionary rather than evolutionary reform).

The Spanish saga tribunals almost unanimously confirmed also that the retroactivity of the new regulations involved crossing the "red line". This was expressly recognized by the *Eiser*,[1066] *Novenergia*,[1067] *Foresight*,[1068] *RREEF*,[1069] *BayWa*,[1070] *RWE*,[1071] *Watkins*,[1072] *PV Investors*[1073] and *Hydro*[1074] tribunals. In

1064 Foresight v. Spain, *supra* note 203 [340].
1065 See, for example: Plama v. Bulgaria, *supra* note 28 [218].
1066 Fn 119.
1067 Fn 149.
1068 Fn 225.
1069 Fn 253–255, 277.
1070 Fn 493.
1071 Fn 641.
1072 Fn 706.
1073 Fn 782.
1074 Fn 848.

the words of *BayWa* tribunal, there is a difference between amending future payments with immediate effect and reducing payments "that would have otherwise been made by reference to payments lawfully made in the past in respect of past production", even if it is far from simple to differentiate between them.[1075]

Thc *Charanne*,[1076] *Isolux*[1077] and RWE[1078] tribunals recognized, however, that the application of the New Regime to ongoing projects – solely for future periods, without looking back to the past – is not equivalent to retroactivity. The difference stems from a different understanding of the concept of retroactivity – i.e. whether this involves applying the New Regime to power plants which operated at the time it was introduced, or only to the claw-back provision that required plants to repay subsidies they had received prior to that moment.

This confirms the case law in the general context, which often considers the retroactive application of new regulations to violate the FET.[1079] Retroactive regulatory changes have been illustratively described as "investors' nightmare".[1080] States assumed in investment treaties an obligation to ensure that any reform of their laws does not disrupt ongoing investments.

In this sense, the Spanish saga cases can be considered as a timid step towards recognizing the close relationship between the FET and the rule of law, since legal certainty and legal security are central elements of the rule of law concept.[1081]

Some consider that the FET (or even investment treaties in general) can be perceived as embodying the rule of law.[1082] This conclusion stems from

1075 Fn 491, 492.

1076 Fn 72.

1077 Fn 92.

1078 Fn 639.

1079 See, for example: ATA v. Jordan, ICSID Case No. ARB/08/2, Award (18.05.2010) [128]. This comes as no surprise, since legitimate expectations are considered to be rooted in the good faith and *venire contra factum propium* principles – Landmann, *supra* note 983, p. 283.

1080 Bellantuono, *supra* note 29, p. 292.

1081 Stephan W. Schill, Fair and Equitable Treatment under Investment Treaties as an Embodiment of the Rule of Law, Institute for International Law and Justice, IILJ Working Paper 2006/6, available at: https://iilj.org/wp-content/uploads/2016/08/Schill-Fair-and-Equitable-Treatment-under-Investment-Treaties-as-an-Embodiment-of-the-Rule-of-Law-2006-2.pdf, p. 12.

1082 For example: ibid, Stephan W. Schill, International Investment Law and the Rule of Law, Amsterdam Law School Legal Studies Research Paper No. 2017-18, Amsterdam Center for International Law No. 2017-15, available at: https://papers.ssrn.com/sol3/papers.cfm?abstract_id=2932153, David W. Rivkin, Sophie J. Lamb, Nicola K. Leslie, The Future of Investor-State Dispute Settlement in the Energy Sector: Engaging with Climate Change, Human Rights and the Rule of Law, Journal of World Energy Law & Business, 8:2 (2015), pp. 150–151, Kenneth J. Vandevelde, A Unified Theory of Fair and Equitable Treatment, New York University Journal of International Law & Politics, 43:1 (2010) 43–106, available at http://ssrn.com/abstract=2357642 and http://nyujilp.org/print-edition/#43, pp. 49–53, 104–106.

an overall analysis of the approaches of various tribunals, viewed as "rule of law-inspired" decisions, with arbitrators pursuing the "paradigm" of the rule of law and applying "distilled rule of law precepts".[1083] Similar views have been expressed with respect to the ECT.[1084]

The dissenter in *RWE v. Spain* underlined that the retroactive application of the disputed measures were "impossible to accept, in terms of any understanding of the rule of law".[1085] She considered them as contrary to due process of law and, as such, as violating the FET.[1086] This is in line with the position taken by the tribunal in *ADC v. Hungary*, which observed that the rule of law includes obligations stemming from investment treaties and, as such, imposes boundaries on a state's right to regulate.[1087] This as re-affirmed by the tribunal in

---

Vandevelde considers that BITs in general, not only the FET, promote the rule of law. See, for example: Kenneth J. Vandevelde, Bilateral Investment Treaties: History, Policy, and Interpretation (Oxford University Press 2010), Kenneth J. Vandevelde, Rebalancing Through Exceptions, Lewis & Clark Law Review, 17:2 (2013), p. 458, Kenneth J. Vandevelde, The Liberal Vision of the International Law on Foreign Investment, [in:] C. L. Lim (ed.), Alternative Visions of the International Law on Foreign Investment. Essays in Honour of Muthucumaraswamy Sornarajah (Cambridge University Press 2016), pp. 61–62. In his view, this can be traced back to the Friendship, Commerce and Navigation Treaties, which preceded the BITs, and similarly aimed at, among others, promoting the rule of law. See: Kenneth J. Vandevelde, The First Bilateral Investment Treaties: U.S. Postwar Friendship, Commerce, and Navigation Treaties (Oxford University Press 2017). For an opposite view, see for example: Bartosz Soloch, International Investment Law: A Self-Proclaimed Ally in Commission's Rule of Law Endeavors, in: Julien Chaisse, Leïla Choukroune, Sufian Jusoh (eds.), Handbook of International Investment Law and Policy (Springer 2021) 1653.

1083 Velimir Živković, Fair and Equitable Treatment Between the International and National Rule of Law, Journal of World Investment & Trade, 20:4 (2019), pp. 525, 526. Vandevelde points out that the tribunals "implicitly have interpreted the fair and equitable treatment standard as requiring treatment in accordance with the concept of the rule of law", to "embrace five principles that are elements of the procedural and substantive dimensions of the rule of law: reasonableness, consistency, nondiscrimination, transparency, and due process" – Vandevelde, A Unified Theory …, ibid, pp. 49, 104. See also: Reinisch, Schreuer, *supra* note 30, pp. 342–344.

1084 "The fundamental aim of the Energy Charter Treaty is to strengthen the rule of law on energy issues, by creating a level playing field of rules to be observed by all participating governments, thereby mitigating risks associated with energy-related investment and trade" – https://www.energycharter.org/process/overview/. See also for example: Ernesto Bonafé, Natasha A. Georgiou, The New International Energy Charter and the Rule of Law in the Global Energy Architecture, European Energy Law Report, 11 (2017).

1085 RWE v. Spain, Separate opinion …, *supra* note 643 [81].

1086 Ibid [82]. The dissenter also considered that she served as "an arbitrator functioning as part of an institution based on the rule of law" – [81].

1087 ADC v. Hungary, ICSID Case No. ARB/03/16, Award (02.10.2006) [423]:

> […] while a sovereign State possesses the inherent right to regulate its domestic affairs, the exercise of such right is not unlimited and must have its boundaries. As

Horthel v. Poland, which explicitly linked the FET with "certainty and the rule of law".[1088] A dissenter in *Philip Morris v. Uruguay* linked the FET with the rule of law, which "serves to ensure predictability, stability", among others (albeit in the context of domestic law being applied by the judiciary, not in the context of regulatory changes).[1089]

If this understanding of an existing relationship between the FET and the rule of law finds broader recognition, the Spanish saga cases experience would be even more relevant in guiding the future development of international investment law, including outside the ECT context.

In addition, this understanding reaffirms that a state's sovereignty is unaffected by determining where that border exists between measures which fall within its right to regulate and those which trigger international responsibility. States remain entitled to regulate, and can do so. As correctly noted, "the Spanish government maintains that it had the authority to modify the regulations under the circumstances".[1090] This is undoubted. However, both concepts – the rule of law and the FET – require a state to pay compensation if it decides to exercise its authority in such a way that it crosses certain legal limits. This was explicitly recognized by the *9REN* tribunal, which underlined that it:

> does not doubt the constitutional authority of Spain to evolve its regulatory system to keep abreast of changing circumstances. The question is whether under the ECT the cost of such changes should fall on the investors who were attracted to Spain's renewable energy [...].[1091]

> rightly pointed out by the Claimants, the rule of law, which includes treaty obligations, provides such boundaries.

Similar approach can be read from Wirtgen v. Czech Republic, PCA Case No. 2014-03, Dissenting Opinion of Arbitrator Gary Born (11.10.2017) [110]–[111].

1088 Horthel v. Poland, *supra* note 26 [296]:

> It is undisputed that the FET standard guarantees legal certainty and the rule of law. This entails that executive organs should not withhold benefits contemplated by the applicable legal regime. This does not mean that any violation of domestic law will amount to a breach of the FET standard. However, when an administrative organ deliberately refuses to act in accordance with the existing legal regime, the principle of legality and the rule of law are implicated and the conduct can be found to constitute a Treaty violation.

1089 Philip Morris v. Uruguay, ICSID Case No. ARB/10/7, Concurring and Dissenting Opinion (08.07.2016) [42], [51], [133].

1090 Carmen Otero García Castrillón, Spain and Investment Arbitration: the Renewable Energy Explosion, Investor-State Arbitration Series Paper no. 17, Centre for International Governance (2016), available at: https://eprints.ucm.es/id/eprint/40105/1/ISA%20Paper%20No.17.pdf, p. 18.

1091 Fn 358.

1.3.5 Fifth Lesson Learned – the FET Involves a Balancing Exercise

This lesson is linked with the previous one, as the balancing exercise is closely related to determining the limits of the right to regulate. The Spanish saga cases confirm the widely accepted position that the FET "by its very nature requires a balancing of interests".[1092] It is no less relevant in the context of legitimate expectations in RE disputes, which must be "assessed on a case-by-case basis, through an act of balancing".[1093]

Some tribunals explicitly recognized the above. The *Novenergia* tribunal observed that the application of the FET is "a balancing exercise, where the state's regulatory interests are weighed against the investors' legitimate expectations and reliance".[1094] The *InfraRed* tribunal indicated that it is "called upon to carry out" the balancing exercise in its analysis of the FET.[1095] The *OperaFund* tribunal commented on "balancing regulatory state interests and investor interests in assessing stability obligations as well as legitimate expectations".[1096] The *PV Investors* tribunal noted that "an investor's legitimate expectations must be balanced with the State's right to regulate in the public interest",[1097] which requires striking "the right balance".[1098] The *Hydro* tribunal added that "there has to be a weighing of an investor's expectations and the State's regulatory interests".[1099] Similar approach was adopted by the dissenters in *BayWa* – who considered that the FET "requires a balancing exercise",[1100] in RWE – who underlined that "a lot may depend on when the balancing takes place",[1101] and in *Watkins* – who drew

1092 Aikaterini Titi, The Right to Regulate in International Investment Law (Nomos/Hart 2014), p. 277. Similarly, for example: Graham Coop, Isabella Seif, ECT and States' Right to Regulate, in: Maxi Scherer (ed.), International Arbitration in the Energy Sector (Oxford University Press 2018), p. 234. In the words of Muchlinski:

> For if 'equity' means anything it suggests a balancing process and weighing up of what is right in all the circumstances. It is, after all, a word related to the idea of 'equilibrium' defined as 'a state of physical balance'

(footnote omitted) – Peter Muchlinski, Caveat Investor – The Relevance of the Conduct of the Investor under the Fair and Equitable Treatment Standard, International and Comparative Law Quarterly, 55:3 (2006), p. 532.

1093 Landmann, *supra* note 983, pp. 101–102. In general on RE disputes, see also for example: Selivanova, *supra* note 1052, pp. 445–447.

1094 Fn 146. See also: fn 136.

1095 Fn 407.

1096 Fn 451.

1097 Fn 749.

1098 Fn 767.

1099 Fn 815.

1100 Fn 518.

1101 Fn 669.

attention to a "fine-tuned balance".[1102] Some tribunals considered that this balancing exercise constitutes an element of proportionality (*SolEs*,[1103] *RWE*,[1104] *Watkins*,[1105] *Hydro*[1106] and *Cavalum*[1107]). However, a similar balancing can be seen even in those Spanish saga awards which remained silent on this issue.[1108]

In this sense, the Spanish cases confirm general investor-state arbitration case law, which recognizes that applying the FET involves a "balancing exercise"[1109] or "weighing of the legitimate interests of the foreign investor with the legitimate interests of the host State and others, including (in particular) its own citizens and residents".[1110] As summarized by the *9REN* tribunal, other

1102 Fn 726.

1103 Fn 379. The tribunal did not apply a "proportionality test", but "proportionality" played a key role in its analysis. Its finding of violation of the FET was not based on decrease of revenue, but on disproportionate lack of stability together with a sudden and unexpected revocation of the legal regime relied upon by the investor at the moment of making the investment.

1104 Fn 626.

1105 This dichotomy reflects similar dichotomy in the general case law. It was commented that:

> as with the inherent tension between stability and the right to regulate, tribunals have emphasized that they need to balance the investors' legitimate expectations and the host states' right to regulate. This balancing is often conducted with express or implied reference to a proportionality analysis

– Reinisch, Schreuer, *supra* note 30, p. 524.

1106 Fn 811.

1107 Fn 854.

1108 See also for example in the general RE context – Draguiev, *supra* note 992, p. 20: "The balance between state regulatory interests and regulatory stability interests of the investors is a cornerstone that all tribunals agree upon". The *Stadtwerke* tribunal looked at proportionality as an element of the FET, closely linked to reasonableness – fn 566, 574.

1109 Copper Mesa v. Ecuador, PCA Case No. 2012-2, Award (15.03.2016) [6.81], Electrabel v. Hungary, ICSID Case No. ARB/07/19, Award (25.11.2015) [165], [180]. The approach is described in different manners, for examples as "balanced application of the standard to the circumstances of the case" (Mamidoil v. Albania, *supra* note 23 [622]), "a balancing or weighing exercise" (Antaris v. Czech Republic, *supra* note 968 [360.9]), "balanced approach" (Perenco v. Ecuador, *supra* note 38 [560]) or interpretation in a "balanced manner" (Gosling v. Mauritius, *supra* note 7 [245]).

1110 South American Silver v. Bolivia, *supra* note 23 [649]. See also cases referred to in Fn 38. It has been also described as "balancing of interests" in the academic literature. See, for example: Rivkin, Lamb, Leslie, *supra* note 1082, p. 140, Virginie Colaiuta, When Does a Violation of the Domestic Law of the Host State Amount to a Violation of a Public International Law Principle in Determining Protection of Investors' Claims?, in: Graham Coop (ed.), Energy Dispute Resolution: Investment Protection, Transit and the Energy Charter Treaty (JurisNet 2011), p. 22, Benedict Kingsbury, Stephan Schill, Investor-State Arbitration as a Governance: Fair and Equitable Treatment, Proportionality and the Emerging Global Administrative Law, in: Albert Jan van den Berg (ed.), 50 years of the New York Convention

tribunals in general case law "have been quite consistent on the need to balance a State's regulatory autonomy against international obligations freely undertaken".[1111]

Beyond any doubt, such a balancing act does not relate to "ordinary business risks".[1112] The whole purpose of investment treaties is to provide protection from non-commercial risks, i.e. political risks.[1113] Regulatory risks are one category of such political risks.[1114]

The Spanish saga cases are also aligned with views that the proportionality analysis is well embedded in investor-state arbitration.[1115] According to some, "while the introduction of the proportionality test into investment law was controversial in the beginning, it is recognized as a part of the FET standard today".[1116] The *RREEF*,[1117] *RWE*,[1118] *Watkins*,[1119] *Hydro*[1120] and *Cavalum*[1121] awards show that the balancing exercise can be performed in a "structured" manner,

(Wolters Kluwer 2009), p. 31, Benedict Kingsbury, Stephan W. Schill, Public Law Concepts to Balance Investors' Rights with State Regulatory Actions in the Public Interest – the Concept of Proportionality, in: Stephan W. Schill (ed.), International Investment Law and Comparative Public Law (Oxford University Press 2010), p. 78. McLachlan perceives the "core task" of the whole investor-state arbitration as "the enduring one of finding a proper balance between two equally valid and important interests: the protection of private rights of the investor and the legitimate public interest of the host state" – Campbell McLachlan, Investment Treaty Arbitration: The Legal Framework, in: Albert Jan van den Berg (ed.), 50 Years of the New York Convention (Wolters Kluwer 2009), p. 101.

1111 9REN v. Spain, *supra* note 354 [254].

1112 Salacuse, *supra* note 3, p. 312.

1113 Kopar, *supra* note 932, p. 88.

1114 Ibid, pp. 41–44, N. Stephan Kinsella, Noah D. Rubins, International Investment, Political Risk, and Dispute Resolution: A Practitioner's Guide (Oceana Publications 2005), pp. 11–17.

1115 The proportionality analysis itself has been theme of numerous studies focused exclusively on this issue. See, for example: Caroline Henckels, Proportionality and Deference in Investor-State Arbitration. Balancing Investment Protection and Regulatory Autonomy (Cambridge University Press 2015). There are, however, also views which oppose applying the proportionality test as part of international investment law. See, for example: N. Jansen Calamita, The Principle of Proportionality and the Problem of Indeterminacy in International Investment Treaties, Yearbook on International Investment Law & Policy (2013–2014), pp. 157–200, Federico Ortino, Investment Treaties, Sustainable Development and Reasonableness Review: A Case Against Strict Proportionality Balancing, Leiden Journal of International Law, 30:1 (2017), pp. 71–91.

1116 Landmann, *supra* note 983, pp. 122–123.

1117 Fn 267–268, although this tribunal blended the proportionality and reasonableness analyses, considering them as separated, but intertwined concepts.

1118 Fn 618.

1119 Fn 714–716.

1120 Fn 811.

1121 Fn 854.

being anchored in the three-steps proportionality test.[1122] The proportionality test has been applied by other arbitral tribunals, outside the Spanish context.[1123] It consists in assessing (i) suitability, i.e. whether a measure objectively allows to achieve the legitimate government purpose, (ii) necessity, i.e. whether the measure is the least restrictive from those available, and (iii) proportionality *sensu stricto*, i.e. a balancing between the affected rights and the public purpose.[1124]

The third step of the proportionality test is "crucial for the weighing of competing interests".[1125] It:

> requires taking into account all relevant factors such as cost benefit analysis, the importance of the right affected, the importance of the right or interest protected, the degree of interference (minor versus major interference), the length of interference (permanent versus temporary), the availability of alternative measures that might be less effective, but are proportionally less restrictive for the right affected, and so on.[1126]

1122 This is the concept anchored in the EU law, case law of the ECtHR, as well as in many domestic constitutional laws. See, for example: Occidental v. Ecuador, *supra* note 41 [403], Electrabel v. Hungary, Award, *supra* note 1109 [179], EDF v. Romania, *supra* note 15 [293], Azurix v. Argentina, *supra* note 7 [311] (although in the context of expropriation). The *Tecmed* tribunal explicitly relied on the ECtHR's case law on proportionality, albeit in the expropriation context – Tecmed v. Mexico, *supra* note 11 [122]. For examples of criticism of the proportionality in the FET context, see: Muthucumaraswamy Sornarajah, Developing Countries in the Investment Treaty System: A Law for Need or a Law for Greed?, in: Stephan W. Schill, Christian J. Tams, Rainer Hofmann (eds.), International Investment Law and Development. Bridging the Gap (Edward Elgar 2015), p. 64:

> The reaction of arbitrators has been the discovery of the proportionality rule, picked out of the air without any basis in treaty language [...] The proportionality test reserves some power in the arbitrator to determine whether the measure taken was proportionate to the end achieved by the state. The domestic courts give a large margin of appreciation to the state in these matters. Arbitrators, hardly qualified to perform such an exercise as they are by no means acquainted with the internal situation of the state within its political and social context, have arrogated unto themselves the power of performing such a function. They will only alienate states further from investment arbitration.

1123 Ibid.

1124 Fn 267, 618, 620–626. For a detailed analysis of the three stages of the proportionality test see, for example: Henckels, *supra* note 1115, pp. 45–68, Kingsbury, Schill, Investor-State ..., *supra* note 1110, pp. 38–40, Kingsbury, Schill, Public ..., *supra* note 1110, pp. 85–88.

1125 Reinisch, Schreuer, *supra* note 30, p. 345, 446.

1126 Kingsbury, Schill, Public ..., *supra* note 1110, p. 87.

In this sense, the RREEF, RWE, *Watkins*, *Hydro* and *Cavalum* tribunals' application of the proportionality test does not contradict other Spanish saga tribunals, which simply jumped into "balancing".

The Spanish saga cases are also uniform in recognizing a wide margin of discretion when exercising the balancing and/or proportionality tests. At a general level, it is uncontroversial that arbitral tribunals must adopt a degree of deference towards states when they act as sovereigns and determine their public policies. Generally, this is uncontroversial.[1127] It is rooted already in early investor-state arbitration case law, with the *S.D. Myers* tribunal recognizing that application of the FET does not create an:

> open-ended mandate to second-guess government decision-making. Governments have to make many potentially controversial choices. In doing so, they may appear to have made mistakes, to have misjudged the facts, proceeded on the basis of a misguided economic or sociological theory, placed too much emphasis on some social values over others and adopted solutions that are ultimately ineffective or counterproductive.[1128]

Some of the Spanish saga tribunals deemed this to be a "margin of appreciation". This is a concept which is anchored in the case law of the European Court of Human Rights ("ECtHR"), understood as:

1127 See, for example: Horthel v. Poland, *supra* note 26 [268]: "policy-making and choosing between conflicting or competing demands, often in situations of less-than-perfect information, is an inherent function of the government and except in clear cases of abuse, treaty tribunals ought to respect the government's policy preferences". Similarly, for example: Vestey v. Venezuela, ICSID Case No. ARB/06/4, Award (15.04.2016) [294]–[296]. See also for example: Julian Arato, The Margin of Appreciation in International Investment Law, Virginia Journal of International Law, 54:3 (2014), who considers that the margin of appreciation is improper for investment disputes, but makes it clear that the applicable standard of review of the state actions must observe a certain the degree of deference. For example, on p. 548 he comments:

> In the arbitral context, the margin of appreciation acts as little more than a pseudo-standard. While appearing to connote a coherent doctrine of deference, the invocation of the margin tends to obscure the reasoning behind tribunals' determination of the appropriate degree of deference in particular disputes, and obstruct dialogue among tribunals across cases.

1128 S.D. Myers v. Canada, *supra* note 11 [263]. It has been cited with approval for example in: Saluka v. Czech Republic, *supra* note 8 [284], Cargill v. Mexico, ICSID Case No. ARB(AF)/05/2, Award (18.09.2009) [292], Gemplus v. Mexico, ICSID Case No. ARB(AF)/04/3 and Talsud v. Mexico, ICSID Case No. ARB(AF)/04/4 (conjoined arbitrations), Award (16.06.2010) [6]–[26].

> freedom to act; maneuvering, breathing or "elbow" room; or the latitude of deference or error which the Strasbourg organs will allow to national legislative, executive, administrative and judicial bodies [...]. It has been defined as the line at which international supervision should give away to a State Party's discretion in enacting or enforcing its laws.[1129]

Nevertheless, it has been relied upon by some tribunals adjudicating treaty based, investor-state disputes.[1130]

In the Spanish saga context, the *RREEF*,[1131] *RWE*,[1132] *PV Investors*,[1133] *Hydro*[1134] and *Cavalum*[1135] tribunals referred to the margin of appreciation, not to more generic notion of the margin of discretion. The *9REN* tribunal also referred to the margin of appreciation, but in the context of the valuation method.[1136] *OperaFund* requested the parties to elaborate on how the margin of appreciation should be applied, but procedural economy led it to consider it unnecessary to adopt a position on that issue.[1137]

In this sense, the Spanish saga adds to the debate on whether concepts developed by a human rights court can (or should) be directly transposed into international investment law. The analyzed cases either remain silent, or side with the case law which accept this possibility.[1138] None of the cases endorsed case law which refutes this possibility.[1139] It may be related to the European context of the analyzed cases. All EU member states are also contracting parties

1129 Howard Charles Yourow, The Margin of Appreciation Doctrine in the Dynamics of European Human Rights Jurisprudence (Brill 1996), p. 13 (footnotes omitted).

1130 See, for example: Electrabel v. Hungary, *supra* note 16 [6.92], [8.35], Philip Morris v. Uruguay, *supra* note 13 [399], Micula v. Romania, ICSID Case No. ARB/05/20, Decision on Jurisdiction and Admissibility (24.09.2008) [94], Continental Casualty v. Argentina, *supra* note 47 [181], Frontier v. Czech Republic, *supra* note 27 [527]. In the literature see, for example: Valentina Vadi, Proportionality, Reasonableness and Standards of Review in International Investment Law and Arbitration (Edward Elgar 2018), pp. 210–225.

1131 Fn 238, 243, 282.

1132 Fn 619, 627.

1133 Fn 750.

1134 Fn 819.

1135 Fn 881.

1136 9REN v. Spain, *supra* note 354 [411].

1137 "What, if any, is the application and effect in this case, situated as it is in the field of environmental protection, of the "margin of appreciation enjoyed by national regulatory agencies when dealing with public policy determinations [...]"" – OperaFund v. Spain, *supra* note 436 [83], [555].

1138 See, for examples: fn 1130.

1139 See, for example: Renta 4 v. Russia, SCC Case No. 24/2007, Award (20.07.2012) [22], Siemens v. Argentina, ICSID Case No. ARB/02/8, Award (06.02.2007) [354], Chemtura v.

to the European Convention on Human Rights ("ECHR"). This eliminated the doubt indicated by many scholars, as to why the case law of the ECtHR should apply in disputes involving states that are not parties to the ECHR.[1140]

Unfortunately, the Spanish saga cases are of little help when attempting to draw a general conclusion on where to place the red line in the balancing exercise, the crossing of which triggers a state's liability (or, when applying the proportionality test *sensu stricto*, if the three-stages approach is followed). By way of example, the *RWE* tribunal considered the overall 54% reduction of the future cash flow as insufficient to amount to a violation of the FET for this sole reason, whereas the dissenter had a contrary opinion.[1141]

Some authors arrive at different conclusions, and consider the Spanish and Italian cases to indicate that "in case of legitimate expectations arising out of a general regulation the threshold of the impact needed for a finding of a breach of the FET standard seems to be set in the fair remuneration".[1142] This is, however, redundant, as it raises the immediate question of how to define "fair remuneration". The answer to this follow-up question would again depend on the applicable domestic regulations which shaped the legitimate expectation, as described above, in the second lesson learned. Others, in turn, have concluded that "the interest of the PV investors outweighs the regulatory interest of the Spanish State and the revocation measures constitute a breach of legitimate expectations and, hence, a violation of FET".[1143] This, in turn, would be an oversimplification and is not supported by the overall tenor of the Spanish saga cases.

This hardly comes as a surprise. It is a truism to say that the FET is fact driven. Diverging outcomes of the balancing exercise in the Spanish saga cases may be explained, at least to a certain degree, by this factor and by the different evidence on record in those cases and even a different assessment of the same evidence. This is particularly notable regarding the assessment of when

Canada, *supra* note 1048 [123], von Pezold v. Zimbabwe, ICSID Case No. ARB/10/15, Award (28.07.2015) [456]–[466].

1140 See, for example: José E. Alvarez, The Boundaries of Investment Arbitration. The Use of Trade and European Human Rights Law in Investor-State Disputes (JurisNet 2018), pp. 109–113.

1141 Fn 633, 674.

1142 Sondra Faccio, The Assessment of the FET Standard between Legitimate Expectations and Economic Impact in the Italian Solar Energy Investment Case Law, Questions of International Law (Zoom-In), 71 (2020), p. 20.

1143 Thomas Dromgool, Daniel Ybarra Enguix, The Fair and Equitable Treatment Standard and the Revocation of Feed in Tariffs – Foreign Renewable Energy Investments in Crisis-Struck Spain, in: Voler Mauerhofer (ed.) Legal Aspects of Sustainable Development (Springer 2016), p. 414.

the tariff deficit problem arose in Spain. On the one hand, the *SolEs* tribunal is an example of a tribunal which assessed that the tariff deficit was already large several years prior to the Financial Crisis.[1144] Similarly the *Watkins* tribunal considered the tariff deficit to exist "long before" and even to have resulted from Spain's "own regulatory conduct".[1145] On the other hand, the *RWE* tribunal dismissed the argument that the tariff deficit was a problem prior to enactment of RD 661/2007 and considered that it was caused by the electricity consumption decrease triggered by the Financial Crisis.[1146]

A particular output is always fact-driven and evidence-based, since the input required for the balancing exercise must take into account "all circumstances, including not only the facts surrounding the investment, but also the political, socioeconomic, cultural and historical conditions prevailing in the host State".[1147] However, on that point, the Spanish saga cases confirm that the balancing exercise must be exercised in a manner which guarantees sufficient space for host states to react in times of crises.[1148]

In that sense, the analyzed cases confirm that the state's changes in policy when reacting to changing reality are a legitimate public purpose to be taken into account during the proportionality analysis/balancing exercise. In the analyzed cases, this purpose was defined as reducing the tariff deficit. However, other reasons in future cases may relate to countless situations which require a governmental reaction. By way of example, RE disputes can concern state measures to reduce the costs of green certificates or consumer energy prices.[1149]

An unexplored aspect of the balancing exercise in RE disputes concerns the relationship between investments in this sector and the fight against climate change and sustainable development. The Spanish saga cases did not balance investors' protection against the state's right to pursue its agenda on fighting climate change and/or encouraging sustainable development. Rather, the public interests taken into account were those involved in recalibrating state public spending and the budget deficit. The weight of the balanced public

---

1144 Fn 392. See also for example: ibid, pp. 393, 413.

1145 Fn 713.

1146 Fn 622. It is notable that arbitrators in the *RWE* case were divided on this issue even when faced with the same evidence. The dissenter came to the opposite conclusion, and recognized that the tariff deficit began in 2000 – fn 668.

1147 Duke Energy v. Ecuador, *supra* note 21 [340].

1148 See, for example EDF v. Argentina, ICSID Case No. ARB/03/23, Award (11.06.2012) [1005], El Paso v. Argentina, *supra* note 39 [374], Continental Casualty v. Argentina, *supra* note 47 [258].

1149 Faccio, *supra* note 1142, pp. 7–8.

interest would be increased if it concerned issues related to maintaining and/or developing the energy system, such as efforts undertaken to balance the state energy system.[1150] Similarly, the weight of private interests would increase if they included legitimate expectations backed by previous commitments of the state to meet its international climate agenda if the state then reduced its support for reasons unrelated to this agenda.[1151]

There is room in future case law to further explore these interests and to assess whether they will tip the weighting of interests in favor of investment protection or, rather, towards governmental action aimed at further fostering the desired actions. As the *PV Investors* tribunal reiterated, the ECT contracting parties sought to achieve a balance between "the sovereign rights of the State over energy resources and the creation of a climate favorable to the flow of investments on the basis of market principles".[1152]

In this context, brief reference may be made to the ongoing works to reform the ISDS. UNCITRAL Working Group III, which commenced its work on this issue in 2017, has *inter alia* debated reforms regarding the creation of the Multilateral Investment Court ("MIC").[1153] The proponents of such a reform argue that the MIC may bring more uniformity to the ISDS case law.[1154] With this objective in mind, if the MIC already existed, one could assume that it would have two instances and would be composed of full-time adjudicators with no "outside activities".[1155]

Given these two important features, the MIC could potentially have a positive impact on (i) unifying the currently divergent theoretical approaches to conducting the "balancing exercise" during adjudications (and placing that

1150 Such problems would be related to the nature of solar and wind RE, which may cause oversupply and shortages of supplies of energy, depending on changing weather conditions. This, in turn, requires states not only to balance various sources of energy production, but also to safeguard sustainability of the grid. In this context, Hydro energy is distinct, as it allows to constant energy production and even to store water in the dams to supply energy in the peaks in demand – see: Attila Tanzi, International Law and Foreign Investment in Hydroelectric Industry: A Multidimensional Analysis, in: Eric De Brabandere, Tarcisio Gazzini (eds.), Foreign Investment in the Energy Sector. Balancing Private and Public Interests (Brill 2014), p. 62.

1151 See, for example: Hui Helen Pang, The Role of Investor-State Arbitration in Promoting Climate Change Mitigation: from "Shield" to "Sword" through Renewable Energy Disputes?, Academy of European Law, European Society of International Law Paper, AEL 2022/05 (2022), available at: http://hdl.handle.net/1814/74450.

1152 Fn 747.

1153 Possible reform of investor-State dispute settlement (ISDS). Submission from the European Union and its Member States (A/CN.9/WG.III/WP.159/Add.1).

1154 Ibid, p. 6, para. 6(I).

1155 Ibid, p. 4–5, paras. 13–17.

exercise more firmly within, or altogether outside, the three-steps proportionality test); and (ii) unifying the approach regarding the extent, if at all, to which the case law of other adjudicatory bodies and concepts developed thereby – such as the ECtHR's margin of appreciation concept – should be transposed to the ISDS. Additionally, the MIC might be encouraged to openly recognize the relationship between the FET and the rule of law (as discussed in the fourth lesson learned).

If the MIC already existed, it could also have had a broader positive impact on the uniformity of the outcomes of the Spanish saga cases. Whereas the conclusions presented earlier suggest that the Spanish saga tribunals were consistent in their interpretation of international law (the first lesson learned), they diverged when assessing the scope of Spanish law (the second lesson learned). This affected the tribunals' assessment of whether a "full" violation of the FET had taken place, or merely one limited to the RRR. This resulted in different amounts of compensation being awarded by different tribunals. One might expect that the MIC would be capable of providing a more uniform answer to the question of whether legitimate expectations grounded in Spanish law were limited to the RRR, or were broader. However, diverging outcomes would be inevitable even if all of the Spanish saga cases were to be decided by the MIC. This is because the outcomes would have differed depending upon the moment at which the disputed investments were made, which is a relevant factor when assessing legitimate expectations, just as it was in the disputes resolved by the arbitral tribunals analyzed here.

Regardless of whether a future dispute is adjudicated by an arbitral tribunal or by the MIC, it will arise out of measures adopted by a state. In that sense, the form of dispute resolution mechanism (whether arbitral proceedings or MIC proceedings) does not directly impact on the number of cases that will arise. However, one criticized aspect of investor-state arbitrations is the expense of such proceedings. If access to the MIC proved to be cheaper than investor-state arbitrations, this could result in more cases being initiated before the MIC forum than before arbitral tribunals.

1.3.6 Sixth Lesson Learned – Contractual Obligations Can Be Game Changers

A final lesson for the future can be learned from what is missing in the Spanish saga cases – PPAs.[1156]

1156 This is an issue which differentiates the RE sector from the energy sector in general, where such contracts are more common. See, for example: Electrabel v. Hungary, *supra* note 16 [5.56], AES v. Hungary, *supra* note 37 [4.4], El Paso v. Argentina, *supra* note 39 [405].

Much attention given to the Spanish saga awards is devoted to whether general legislation can be read as a stabilization commitment – a position which was dismissed by most of the tribunals (see the first lesson learned for more details). The tribunals recognized that stabilization clauses may be included in the contracts, but typically cannot be interpreted as having arisen from general legislation.

The absence of any contractual obligations entered into by the Spanish authorities with RE producers formed an important element of the factual matrix in the analyzed cases. This explains why contractual commitments – an important element relevant in many other jurisdictions, but missing in the factual matrix of the Spanish cases – was left unanalyzed by most of the Spanish saga tribunals. Only the *Stadtwerke* tribunal referred in its analysis to such contractual commitments, potentially included in PPAs – contracts governing plants' provision of electricity to state entities.[1157] If such PPAs are present, they could add two relevant layers of legal analysis. First would be the extent to which a host state is responsible for the actions of state entities acting as the buyer side in PPAs.[1158] Second would be consequences of the early termination of such agreements.

The Spanish saga cases could be a reference point on how such PPAs can impact the scope of legitimate expectations created by a regulatory framework. PPAs would most probably strengthen such legitimate expectations. This is because a state-owned enterprise would conclude a long-term contract based on the applicable regulatory framework. This would confirm the understanding of the regulatory framework and its applicability for a specified, lengthy period. In many states, the buyer in a PPA is a state-owned company.[1159] In this sense, PPAs could be understood as "investment contracts" between a foreign investor and a state.[1160]

Such reinforcement of legitimate expectations could potentially reach a level of shifting them from those based on a regulatory framework to those based on a specific commitment. This would, in turn, impact on the balancing

---

1157 Fn 555.

1158 This relates to the issue of attribution. It is, however, not uncommon to attribute the actions of a state-owned company to the state. See, for example: Flemingo v. Poland, *supra* note 15 [435].

1159 This tendency is "more common in emerging economies" – see: Emma Johnson, Lucy McKenzie, Matthew Saunders, International Arbitration of Renewable Energy Disputes (Globe Law and Business 2021), p. 15.

1160 Ibid, p. 29.

exercise and the final decision as to whether a state crossed the "red line" of regulatory changes.[1161]

This is not a hypothetical issue. The publicly known example of *Invenergy v. Poland* concerns PPAs concluded with state owned enterprises, which declared their contractual obligation to be invalid.[1162]

Based on domestic law regulations, some tribunals have recognized a category of "administrative contracts", which go beyond a mere contractual relationships between the parties, but play a role "within a broader framework of law".[1163] The Italian RE awards recognized "accessory" contracts, which simply "replicated from the relevant legislation"[1164] and "only reflect a legal relationship whose existence and essential features have been determined before", in the applicable regulations.[1165] This type of an agreement is defined in domestic law as one that preserves the vertical relationship between the state and the other party.[1166] PPAs can potentially fall within a comparable category of contracts, to which this reasoning would apply *mutatis mutandis* even in the absence of such a category within the domestic law.

2 Expropriation

2.1 *General Comments*

States are entitled to expropriate. It is an aspect of their sovereignty.[1167] On the one hand, expropriation is considered as "the most serious threat to a foreign investment".[1168] On the other hand, generally investment treaties do not prohibit expropriation, provided that certain conditions are satisfied.[1169] Instead,

---

1161 Faccio, *supra* note 1142, p. 20.

1162 https://invenergy.com/news/invenergy-submits-notification-of-dispute-to-polish-government-under-bilateral-investment-and-energy-charter-treaties.

1163 Perenco v. Ecuador, *supra* note 38 [561].

1164 Belenergia v. Italy, *supra* note 964 [615].

1165 Silver Ridge v. Italy, *supra* note 967 [376], [379]–[380]. As such, they were not considered as "autonomous" from the applicable regulations – [383]. Similarly: Sun Reserve v. Italy, *supra* note 1001 [1002].

1166 CEF v. Italy, *supra* note 1001 [251].

1167 Maciej Żenkiewicz, Interferencia y Privación a la Propiedad y los Derechos, in: José Manuel Álvarez Zárate, Maciej Żenkiewicz (eds.), El Derecho Internacional de las Inversiones. Desarrollo Actual de Normas y Principios (Universidad Externado de Colombia 2021), p. 346.

1168 Hobér, *supra* note 5, p. 260. Similarly, as "an age-old, overriding concern": Salacuse, *supra* note 3, p. 380.

1169 Dolzer, Kriebaum, Schreuer, *supra* note 2, p. 147.

in the event of an expropriation (or nationalisation), investment treaties entitle investors to receive market value compensation.[1170] The ECT is no exception to this. Art. 13(1) ECT lays down four prerequisites of a legal expropriation: (i) public purpose, (ii) non-discrimination, (iii) due process of law and (iv) prompt, adequate and effective compensation. An expropriation can only be considered as legal (lawful) if all of these criteria are met cumulatively. Otherwise, an expropriation is illegal (unlawful).

The protection extends to indirect expropriation, which can occur through "a measure or measures having effect equivalent to nationalisation or expropriation".[1171] As the tribunal in *Biwater v. Tanzania* explained, indirect expropriations do "not involve actual takings of title but nonetheless result in the effective loss of management, use or control, or a significant depreciation of the value, of the assets of a foreign investor".[1172] In the words of the *Metalclad* tribunal, it is:

> covert or incidental interference with the use of property which has the effect of depriving the owner, in whole or in significant part, of the use or reasonably-to-be-expected economic benefit of property even if not necessarily to the obvious benefit of the host State.[1173]

Most tribunals in the early ISDS cases considered that a loss of value of an investment was in and of itself sufficient to establish indirect expropriation.[1174]

Indirect expropriation can take the form of a "creeping expropriation", consisting in a series of measures. Although none of these measures, taken alone and in isolation, would amount to expropriation, taken together and as a whole they have an expropriatory effect. It "may be defined as the slow and incremental encroachment on one or more of the ownership rights of a foreign investor that diminishes the value of its investment".[1175] The tribunal in *Generation v. Ukraine* defined creeping expropriation as:

> a form of indirect expropriation with a distinctive temporal quality in the sense that it encapsulates the situation whereby a series of acts

1170 See for example: Art. 7 Australia – Poland BIT, Art. 5 Malaysia – Poland BIT, Art. 6 Singapore – Poland BIT, Art. VI Canada-Poland BIT.

1171 Art. 13(1) ECT.

1172 Biwater v. Tanzania, *supra* note 13 [452].

1173 Metalclad v. Mexico, ICSID Case No. ARB(AF)/97/1, Award (30.08.2000) [103].

1174 See, for example: ibid, Tecmed v. Mexico, *supra* note 11 [115].

1175 UNCTAD, Taking of Property. UNCTAD Series on issues in international investment agreements (United Nations 2000), p. 10.

attributable to the State over a period of time culminate in the expropriatory taking of such property.[1176]

The crucial factor to determine whether an indirect expropriation has occurred is whether the disputed measure(s) has/have caused a "substantial deprivation" of the investor's asset(s).[1177] This means "the interference with the investor's rights must be such as substantially to deprive the investor of the economic value, use or enjoyment of its investment".[1178] By way of example, a tribunal found that indirect expropriation had occurred when a state "radically deprived [the investor] of the economic use and enjoyment of their concessionary rights", which "had the effect of putting an end to the investment".[1179]

In order to reach the level of an indirect expropriation, there must be a substantial loss of the investment's economic value or loss of control over the investment.[1180] Some tribunals continue to focus on the loss of value.[1181] Others require deprivation not merely of "benefits", but also of the "use" of an investment.[1182]

It is irrelevant whether or not the state intended to expropriate the investment by implementing the disputed measures.[1183] However, tribunals sometimes take into consideration additional circumstances, such as the proportionality of the respondent state's measures.[1184]

Thus, the crucial issue for indirect expropriation is whether an investor maintains control and can effectively benefit from the investment after the disputed measures were adopted. Whether a deprivation is "substantial" is determined on a case-by-case basis. While tribunals "have consistently held

1176 Generation v. Ukraine, ICSID Case No. ARB/00/9, Award (16.09.2003) [20.22]. See also for example: Tradex v. Albania, ICSID Case No. ARB/94/2, Award (29.04.1999) [191], Siemens v. Argentina, *supra* note 1139 [263].

1177 Dolzer, Kriebaum, Schreuer, *supra* note 2, pp. 157, 163.

1178 Telenor v. Hungary, ICSID Case No. ARB/04/15, Award (13.09.2006) [65]. See also for example: Alpha Projektholding v. Ukraine, ICSID Case No. ARB/07/16, Award (8.11.2010) [408]: "in order to establish an indirect expropriation of this sort, it is necessary to demonstrate that the investment has been deprived of a significant part of its value".

1179 Compañía de Aguas v. Argentina, ICSID Case No ARB/97/3, Award (20.08.2007) [7.5.29].

1180 Archer Daniels v. Mexico, ICSID Case No. ARB(AF)/04/05, Award (21.11.2007) [242].

1181 See for example: RosInvestCo v. Russia, SCC Case No. V 079/2005, Final Award (12.09.2010) [624], Rumeli v. Kazakhstan, *supra* note 7 [701], Alpha Projektholding v. Ukraine, *supra* note 1178 [408]–[410].

1182 El Paso v. Argentina, *supra* note 39 [256].

1183 See for example: Siemens v. Argentina, *supra* note 1139 [270], Metalclad v. Mexico, *supra* note 1173 [111].

1184 See for example: Tecmed v. Mexico, *supra* note 11 [122].

that the deprivation must be severe and not ephemeral", they have "eschewed numerical thresholds".[1185]

2.2 *Spanish Saga Case Law*

Allegations of expropriation were made in 12 of the analyzed Spanish saga cases (i.e. *Charanne, Isolux, Eiser, Novenergia, Foresight, 9REN, Cube, SolEs, InfraRed, BayWa, Hydro* and *Cavalum*). Not a single tribunal upheld those allegations. Some tribunals invoked the concept of judicial economy to justify leaving the issue unaddressed (*Eiser, Cube, SolEs*). This is in line with the approach of numerous other tribunals hearing ECT claims.[1186] The Spanish saga cases only concerned indirect expropriation. Not a single investor alleged that direct expropriation had occurred.

The claimants decided not to argue that expropriation had occurred in the remaining 9 cases (i.e. *Masdar, Antin, RREEF, NextEra, OperaFund, Stadtwerke, RWE, Watkins* and *PV Investors*).[1187]

Expropriation analyzed in the Spanish saga cases is regulated in Art. 13 ECT, of the following wording:

> 1. Investments of Investors of a Contracting Party in the Area of any other Contracting Party shall not be nationalised, expropriated or subjected to a measure or measures having effect equivalent to nationalisation or expropriation (hereinafter referred to as "Expropriation") except where such Expropriation is:
> a. for a purpose which is in the public interest;
> b. not discriminatory;
> c. carried out under due process of law; and
> d. accompanied by the payment of prompt, adequate and effective compensation.
>
> Such compensation shall amount to the fair market value of the Investment expropriated at the time immediately before the Expropriation or impending Expropriation became known in such a way as to affect the value of the Investment (hereinafter referred to as the "Valuation Date").
>
> Such fair market value shall at the request of the Investor be expressed in a Freely Convertible Currency on the basis of the market rate of exchange existing for that currency on the Valuation Date. Compensation

---

1185 Newcombe, Paradell, *supra* note 42, p. 344.

1186 See for example: Stati v. Kazakhstan, SCC Case No. V 116/2010, Award (19.12.2013) [1205]–[1206].

1187 Masdar v. Spain, *supra* note 150 [138], Antin v. Spain, *supra* note 176 [360], RREEF v. Spain, *supra* note 232 [12], NextEra v. Spain, *supra* note 337 [391], Stadtwerke v. Spain, *supra* note 533 [96], RWE v. Spain, *supra* note 589 [395], Watkins v. Spain, *supra* note 680 [65], The PV Investors v. Spain, *supra* note 736 [219].

shall also include interest at a commercial rate established on a market basis from the date of Expropriation until the date of payment. [...]

2. For the avoidance of doubt, Expropriation shall include situations where a Contracting Party expropriates the assets of a company or enterprise in its Area in which an Investor of any other Contracting Party has an Investment, including through the ownership of shares.

The table below summarizes the Spanish saga case law on expropriation.

TABLE 6 Expropriation

No	Case name	Expropriation Alleged?	Outcome
1	Charanne	Yes	Dismissed
2	Isolux	Yes	Dismissed
3	Eiser	Yes	Not decided (judicial economy)
4	Novenergia	Yes	Dismissed
5	Masdar	No	N/A
6	Antin	No	N/A
7	Foresight	Yes	Dismissed
8	RREEF	No	N/A
9	Cube	Yes	Not decided (judicial economy)
10	NextEra	No	N/A
11	9REN	Yes	Dismissed
12	SolEs	Yes	Not decided (judicial economy)
13	InfraRed	Yes	Dismissed
14	OperaFund	No	N/A
15	BayWa	Yes	Dismissed
16	Stadtwerke	No	N/A
17	RWE	No	N/A
18	Watkins	No	N/A
19	PV Investors	No	N/A
20	Hydro	Yes	Dismissed
21	Cavalum	Yes	Dismissed
	Total	Yes - 12 No - 9	Dismissed - 9 Not decided (judicial economy) - 3

•••

2.2.1 Charanne

In *Charanne*, the tribunal analyzed whether state measures had totally or partially deprived investors of their rights in the shares of local companies.[1188] The tribunal assessed whether the shares themselves, not the "returns" thereupon, had been expropriated.[1189] Although the dispute was limited to the 2010 Disputed Measures of a transitory character, such measures were found to be capable of violating the investors' rights.[1190]

The tribunal observed that the investors remained as shareholders in the local company, which continued to operate and generate profits.[1191] Whilst a decrease in a company's rentability and related decrease in share value can, as such, amount to indirect expropriation, this will only be the case if the effect is equivalent to a deprivation of property.[1192] That threshold was not met in this case.[1193]

Unfortunately, the publicly available and redacted version of the award does not reveal the tribunal's assessment of the percentage by which the local company's rentability had been reduced, nor the related decrease in share value. It is only known that the tribunal reached its conclusions based on evidence that "the rentability of the plants continued to be positive".[1194]

2.2.2 Isolux

In *Isolux*, the disputed investment was also defined as shares in local companies which controlled power plants. The tribunal noted that protecting this shareholding extended to both the ownership of the shares and their value.[1195] Decreased returns can be equivalent to a decrease in the investment's economic value. In such a situation, the object of the alleged expropriation is not the returns themselves, but the assets that produce such returns and lose their economic value.[1196] Based on the above, the tribunal applied the substantial deprivation test and analyzed whether the extent to which the returns had decreased met the required threshold.[1197] The tribunal considered that the claimant had not proved substantial deprivation of its control over the shares,

1188 Charanne v. Spain, *supra* note 53 [460].
1189 Ibid [458]–[459].
1190 Ibid [452], [454].
1191 Ibid [462].
1192 Ibid [463]–[464].
1193 Ibid [465].
1194 Ibid [466].
1195 Isolux v. Spain, *supra* note 79 [834].
1196 Ibid [835].
1197 Ibid [836]–[837].

nor the power plants' profitability.[1198] This conclusion was fact-driven as, at the moment the investment was made, the claimant relied on estimations of 6.19% IRR, whilst after the legislative amendments this exceeded 7.398%.[1199] Therefore, no loss could be shown to exist and, consequently, no expropriation.[1200] This surprising conclusion (i.e. that the disputed measures resulted in increased value, rather than a loss) most probably arose due to the methodology applied by the experts.[1201]

2.2.3 Eiser

For reasons relate to "jurisprudential and financial" judicial economy, the tribunal in *Eiser* decided not to address the expropriation claim (and certain other claims). It viewed them as non-essential, as it had already concluded that a violation of the FET had occurred.[1202] Such additional analysis would not "alter the outcome or affect the damages".[1203]

2.2.4 Novenergia

In *Novenergia*, the tribunal concluded that no expropriation had taken place, because the disputed legislation "left unaffected the Claimant's proprietary rights".[1204] The tribunal considered that the assets capable of being expropriated were the claimant's industrial properties (plants and related facilities) and the shares of companies involved in the investment, directly or indirectly owned and controlled by the claimant. However, the claimant was left "untouched" insofar as its plants and the shares in those companies were concerned.[1205] The tribunal also concluded that, although the value of these assets had been diminished, they had not been expropriated nor affected by measures having an effect equivalent to expropriation.[1206]

This observation appears to contradict the tribunal's own conclusions on the FET, where it found that the 2013–2014 Disputed Measures had a significantly harmful economic effect, amounting to a "substantial deprivation" caused by a decrease in revenues between 24% and 32%.[1207] The tribunal failed to explain

---

1198 Ibid [839]–[840].
1199 Ibid [846]–[849].
1200 Ibid [852]–[853].
1201 Ibid [842].
1202 Eiser v. Spain, *supra* note 98 [354].
1203 Ibid [353].
1204 Novenergia v. Spain, *supra* note 124 [761].
1205 Ibid [762].
1206 Ibid [762].
1207 Ibid [695].

how its view differed between the concept of substantial deprivation in the FET context when compared to its conclusions on the expropriation claim. This was probably a fact specific conclusion since the claimant – surprisingly – had calculated the compensation due for expropriation at a lower level than the compensation envisaged in the FET.[1208]

2.2.5 Foresight

In the *Foresight* case, the disputed investment consisted of shares in companies that owned power plants, and legal title to those shares remained with the claimants, notwithstanding the Disputed Measures.[1209] As regards indirect expropriation, the tribunal decided that no substantial deprivation of the value of the disputed investment had occurred. Although the claimants had suffered serious losses, this was insufficient to lead to the conclusion that the investments had been expropriated.[1210] This was based on the conclusion that the claimants remained the "untouched" owners of the disputed power plants and continued to make profit on them, albeit at a lower rate than initially expected. The precise details of the new profit level were contentious. However, even assuming the claimants' position to have been correct, the post-tax IRR was 5.5%.[1211]

2.2.6 Cube

In *Cube*, the tribunal relied on judicial economy to avoid analyzing an expropriation claim. It explained that, even if the claim was upheld, it would not result in a different outcome "in terms of liability, quantum or otherwise".[1212]

2.2.7 9REN

In *9REN*, the disputed investment was also defined as shares held in local companies. This meant that the claimant did not directly have a "right to the income stream", although the shares' value "was directly or indirectly impacted by a modification of the income stream".[1213] The tribunal considered the "fate" of the shares, noting that the claimant maintained control over them until the moment that it voluntarily chose to sell them.[1214] The tribunal concluded that, even though the regulatory modifications "significantly reduced

1208 Ibid [759].
1209 Foresight v. Spain, *supra* note 203 [426]–[427].
1210 Ibid [430]–[431].
1211 Ibid [429].
1212 Cube v. Spain, *supra* note 285 [457].
1213 9REN v. Spain, *supra* note 354 [369].
1214 Ibid [369].

the share value", this was "better analyzed" from the perspective of a violation of legitimate expectations (which, earlier in the award, the tribunal had concluded were infringed).[1215] It added that the respondent never denied payments and that the income stream, even after the reduction, still represented a return "in the order of 7.9%".[1216]

2.2.8 SolEs

A similar approach was adopted in *SolEs*. Apart from the FET claim, the claimant alleged unlawful expropriation and a violation of the umbrella clause. The tribunal considered that all three claims arose "from the same facts", and that the parties did not differentiate between the three claims in their arguments regarding compensation. It stated that its earlier finding, that the FET had been infringed, "fully disposes of the matter of liability in this case".[1217]

2.2.9 InfraRed

The *InfraRed* tribunal took a different view and did not seek to rely on procedural economy to avoid analyzing the expropriation claim. It reasoned that, if the expropriation were upheld, this may affect the quantum of damages. This was because the IVPEE fell outside the tribunal's jurisdiction over the FET claim, but was within its jurisdiction regarding expropriation.[1218]

The tribunal reiterated that the substantial deprivation test determines whether an expropriation has occurred.[1219] The disputed investment was defined as the claimants' rights as shareholders and debt holders in certain power plants.[1220] The tribunal decided that the claimants "clearly maintained control" over their investment and that the disputed plants remained operational.[1221] Moreover, the claimants would continue to benefit from their investment, even if "only marginally so". The power plants in question retained "some value" and provided for "some measure of free cash flows" throughout their operational life.[1222] The tribunal concluded that their decreased value could constitute a violation of legitimate expectations, but did not amount to the expropriation of the claimant's shareholding or debt interest.[1223]

1215 Ibid [370].
1216 Ibid [371].
1217 SolEs v. Spain, *supra* note 376 [466].
1218 InfraRed v. Spain, *supra* note 404 [479].
1219 Ibid [504].
1220 Ibid [503].
1221 Ibid [507]–[508].
1222 Ibid [509].
1223 Ibid [506], [509].

2.2.10 BayWa

In *BayWa*, the expropriation claim was argued half-heartedly. Even though not "formally dropped", it was not argued during the hearing.[1224] The tribunal reiterated that expropriation of any type, whether direct or indirect, requires the substantial deprivation of the asset in question.[1225] It considered that the claimants' indirect stake in the Spanish projects remained unaffected, as the project companies were "still intact and operating under the Claimants' ultimate control and continued oversight, although their value is impaired".[1226] The tribunal observed that, before it can be concluded that an expropriation of intangible rights has occurred, such rights must exist under the relevant legal system.[1227] It was clear from the Spanish Supreme Court's case law that under the Spanish law, the claimants had no right to receive subsidies. Accordingly, this right could not have been expropriated.[1228]

2.2.11 Hydro

In *Hydro*, the disputed investments were defined as the equity and debt interest held by the claimants in local companies.[1229] The claimants argued that the disputed measures reduced the fair market value of their investments by 85%, which led to the disappearance of these investments' economic benefits and rendered them essentially worthless.[1230] The tribunal first analyzed the "basic principles" underlying expropriation.[1231] It noted the four conditions of a lawful expropriation: (i) public purpose, (ii) non-discrimination, (iii) due process of law and (iv) compensation.[1232] It also repeated that expropriation, whether direct or indirect, entails a substantial deprivation (i.e. a loss of significant economic value comparable to the deprivation of property or the loss of "all attributes of ownership").[1233] A mere loss in value does not amount to indirect expropriation until it is so severe as to be equivalent to a deprivation of the investment.[1234] The tribunal added that regulatory measures can be an indirect

1224 BayWa v. Spain, *supra* note 473 [420].
1225 Ibid [422].
1226 Ibid [430].
1227 Ibid [428].
1228 Ibid [424]–[427].
1229 Hydro v. Spain, *supra* note 795 [287].
1230 Ibid [291], [561]. The value of the claimants' equity investments was reduced from 130.2 million Euro to 19 million Euro and the value of their debt investments was reduced from 9.4 million Euro to 1.8 million Euro.
1231 Ibid [527].
1232 Ibid [528].
1233 Ibid [531], [536].
1234 Ibid [532], [536].

expropriation when their negative economic impact is "sufficient to neutralize in full the value, or economic or commercial use of its investment" without compensation. However, no compensation is due if the regulatory measures are non-discriminatory and protect legitimate public welfare objectives.[1235]

Based on these considerations, the tribunal dismissed the expropriation claim. It found that the disputed measures neither intended to expropriate nor had that effect. The claimants still held their shares in the Spanish companies which owned the Hydro energy plants, and those plants continued to operate, albeit that there "may have been a substantial reduction" in their value.[1236]

2.2.12 Cavalum

The *Cavalum* tribunal repeated most of the *Hydro* tribunal's analysis, with a few modifications.[1237] First, the tribunal explicitly recognized that the property subject to expropriation may be intangible. This can include financial commitments if they amount to "a vested property right" under the domestic law of the host state. Thus, a legislative act which "cancels" a state's liability can amount to expropriation.[1238]

Second, the tribunal rephrased some of the reasons why it dismissed the expropriation claim. It noted that the disputed measures did not "unlawfully deprive" the claimant of its investments or "to so denude them of value such that the loss can be said to be equivalent to a taking of the investments or of the core attributes of ownership of the investments".[1239] The tribunal considered the disputed measures as "lawful regulatory measures for the public good" which did not amount to a deprivation of the investment. The tribunal noted that the claimant continued to own shares in the local companies, and that the plants continued to operate and generate revenue.[1240] This conclusion was reinforced by the tribunal's decision on the FET, that the claimant did not have a "vested right to the tariff incentives" under Spanish law. Accordingly, there could be no "taking" of these rights.[1241]

1235 Ibid [533].

1236 Ibid [537].

1237 Cavalum v. Spain, *supra* note 854 [646]–[652], repeating *Hydro v. Spain*, *supra* note 795 [527]–[529], [532]–[533], [536]. Some minor amendments exist in the text regarding some of the provisions.

1238 Ibid [650].

1239 Ibid [653].

1240 Ibid [653].

1241 Ibid [654].

2.3 *Lessons Learned*

As noted earlier, expropriation claims were made in 12 cases, from which 3 tribunals relied on the concept of judicial economy to avoid expressing a view on this issue. However, notwithstanding that this was a limited number of cases based on similar facts and the same applicable treaty, these cases allow us to zoom out from each specific dispute and present some general conclusions. The wording of Art. 13(1) ECT is comparable to provisions in numerous other investment treaties, which contain similar wording regulating lawful expropriation.[1242] This confirms that the conclusions from the Spanish saga cases are potentially relevant to the future development of the case law.

2.3.1 First Lesson Learned – the Impact of the State's Measures on Attributes of Ownership and/or Control Are Relevant Factors in Assessing Whether a Substantial Deprivation Occurred, and Continued Ownership and/or Control of Investments Elevates the Threshold to Be Met by the Economic Impact of the Disputed Measures

The Spanish saga cases confirm the prevailing position in the general case law on expropriation.[1243] The decisive factor when analyzing expropriation is the substantial deprivation test. It determines whether expropriation has occurred or not. None of the tribunals denied the relevance of this factor. Even if a tribunal did not explicitly refer to this test, as happened in *9REN*, its analysis remained fully consistent with the test. Unfortunately, the cases fail to add much clear guidance on identifying the dividing line between non-expropriatory measures an expropriatory ones.

The *Novenergia* tribunal considered that a decrease of revenues between 24% and 32% amounted to a "substantial deprivation" in the FET context, but not as regards expropriation. It failed to explain, however, the differences between the concept of substantial deprivation in both settings. It can be understood – although it was not explicitly stated – that (i) in the FET context, the level of decreased revenues was one of many elements used in the "balancing" exercise, whereas (ii) as regards expropriation, it is the sole determinant of whether the disputed measure is tantamount to expropriation.

The *Hydro* tribunal acknowledged that there "may have been" a substantial reduction in the investments' value, which was approximately 85% in this case. The tribunal was unclear whether the 85% reduction in value fell short of the high threshold required to pass the "substantial deprivation" test or,

1242 See for example treaties referred to in fn 1170.

1243 Fn 1177–1179.

alternatively, whether the decisive factor in the tribunal's decision was that the claimants were not deprived of attributes of ownership of the asset.

Unfortunately, the Spanish cases add little to define a substantial deprivation test threshold *in abstracto*, which could apply in future cases. Thus, despite the passing years, "what was and remains contentious is the line between non-compensable regulatory and other governmental activity and measures amounting to indirect, compensable expropriation".[1244] They do, however, confirm the observation that the concept of substantial deprivation is not "a mathematical exercise but a question of reasonableness".[1245] In this context, the oft-cited passage from *Tokios Tokeles v. Ukraine* remains valid, namely that "one can reasonably infer that a diminution of 5% of the investment's value will not be enough for a finding of expropriation, while a diminution of 95% would likely be sufficient".[1246]

The Spanish saga cases do not support the most elevated thresholds, perceived as around 99%. Such conclusions arose in the context of cases brought against Ecuador, concerning a 99% "windfall profit tax" on oil revenues above a low reference price.[1247] The tribunal in *Burlington v. Ecuador* considered that this was not substantial enough to amount to expropriation, since "the investment preserved its capacity to generate a commercial return".[1248] Similarly the tribunal in *Perenco v. Ecuador* considered that the state measure "came close to, but did not cross the line", as the investment continued to operate and "was not effectively taken away".[1249] However, an important aspect of these cases is the nature of the disputed measure. The 99% tax applied not to "the investment as a whole, but only on a portion of the profits".[1250] The low reference price,

1244 Dolzer, Kriebaum, Schreuer, *supra* note 2, p. 154. Similarly, for example: Jan H. Dalhuisen, Andrew T. Guzman, Expropriatory and Non-Expropriatory Takings Under International Investment Law, UC Berkeley Public Law Research Paper No. 2137107 (2013), available at: http://ssrn.com/abstract=2137107, p. 9. This situation is unfortunate. Some authors perceive this to favour states, giving them greater space and flexibility when using their right to regulate. See for example: Salacuse, *supra* note 3, p. 396: "This lack of a clear line between valid regulation and illegal indirect expropriation may lead governments to use their regulatory power more aggressively against foreign investments than they would otherwise, when they deem it in the public interest".

1245 Burlington v. Ecuador, ICSID Case No. ARB/08/5, Dissenting Opinion of Arbitrator Orrego Vicuña (08.11.2012) [26].

1246 Tokios Tokeles v. Ukraine, ICSID Case No. ARB/02/18, Award (26.07.2007) [120].

1247 Burlington v. Ecuador, ICSID Case No. ARB/08/5, Decision on Liability (14.12.2012) [404].

1248 Ibid [456].

1249 Perenco v. Ecuador, *supra* note 38 [684], [687].

1250 Burlington v. Ecuador, *supra* note 1247 [404].

unaffected by the tax, allowed the claimants to achieve a return at the level they had anticipated prior to making the investment.[1251]

The duration of the disputed measure is also a relevant factor when analyzing expropriation claims.[1252] However, the Spanish saga adds little to this aspect of the analysis, since the disputed measures were permanent in nature.

These cases do, however, support the visible trend that the impact of the disputed measures on attributes of ownership and/or control are relevant factors, and that continued ownership and/or control militates against a finding that expropriation has occurred.[1253] The tribunals paid attention to the fact that the disputed measures neither deprived the investors of their shareholding (and related rights) in the local companies nor of their ability to control the relevant power plants. The absence of such effects elevated the threshold needing to be met by the economic impact of the disputed measures. *A contrario*, if such effects were present and would not, in themselves, amount to expropriation, they would lower the percentage threshold required from an economic perspective when calculating the effect of the measure.

The Spanish cases uniformly paid no attention to the intention behind the disputed measures. Not a single tribunal rejected the possibility that general legislation can be an expropriatory measure even if adopted within the scope of a sovereign state's prerogative and where no bad faith can be proved in relation to its adoption. As such, the cases side with the "sole effects" approach found in the general case law.[1254]

1251 Perenco v. Ecuador, *supra* note 38 [681].

1252 See for example: LG&E v. Argentina, *supra* note 34 [193], Biwater v. Tanzania, *supra* note 13 [463], Telenor v. Hungary, *supra* note 1178 [70].

1253 See for example: AES v. Hungary, *supra* note 37 [14.3.2], Sempra v. Argentina, *supra* note 28 [285], PSEG v. Turkey, *supra* note 1063 [278], Enron v. Argentina, *supra* note 19 [245], Feldman v. Mexico, ICSID Case No. ARB(AF)/99/1, Award (16.12.2002) [142], [152], Nykomb v. Latvia, SCC Case No. 118/2001, Arbitral Award (16.12.2003) [4.3.1.], Perenco v. Ecuador, *supra* note 38 [681], Mamidoil v. Albania, *supra* note 23 [566]–[569].

1254 See for example: Tecmed v. Mexico, *supra* note 11 [116], Siemens v Argentina, *supra* note 1139 [270], Santa Elena v. Costa Rica, ICSID Case No. ARB/96/1, Final Award (17.02.2000) [72], Spyridon v. Romania, ICSID Case No. ARB/06/1, Award (07.12.2011) [330]. This approach is often considered as "favouring interests of investors" – see for example: Sebastián López Escarcena, La Expropriación Condicionada en los Tratados de Invesrsion, in: José Manuel Álvarez Zárate, Maciej Żenkiewicz (eds.), El Derecho Internacional de las Inversiones. Desarrollo Actual de Normas y Principios (Universidad Externado de Colombia 2021), p. 381. However, this approach will most probably be revisited in cases based on new generation treaties, which recognize the relevance of the intent underlying the measures, such as Art. 5 of the India-Latvia BIT, concluded in 2010, as supplemented by a protocol which states that:

2.3.2 Second Lesson Learned – General Regulatory Measures Can Result in Indirect Expropriation

The Spanish cases are also uniform in confirming that general regulatory measures can result in indirect expropriation. This "subtle way" of states using their regulatory power has replaced direct expropriations, which were common until the 1980s, but are rare nowadays.[1255] As such, states do not have an absolute right to regulate and legislation may result in an indirect, regulatory form of expropriation.[1256] This is of crucial importance for RE cases, which often involve taxation issues.[1257] Taxes are introduced by regulations and, as such, may fall within the category of indirect expropriation. The importance of this cannot be overstated as, typically, if an investment treaty contains a taxation carve-out clause, expropriation is exempted from the scope of such carve-out.[1258]

In that sense, the Spanish saga cases fall within the group of cases which do not recognize the "police powers" doctrine as precluding a finding of indirect expropriation.[1259] Whilst they acknowledge that states are entitled to regulate, they also recognize that indirect expropriation can occur if a substantial deprivation has taken place, and that compensation may be necessary.

The cases also reveal the importance of how a protected investment is defined. If the investment is defined as shareholding in local companies, any substantial deprivation must relate to this asset. The tribunals had no difficulty in identifying a causal link between the decreased value of a particular power plant and the decreased value of shares, owned by foreign investors, in the local company that owned the plant. Although the Spanish cases made no specific reference to the concept of reflective loss, they remain fully inline with it.

> [a]ctions by a Government or Government controlled bodies, taken as a part of normal business activities, will not constitute indirect expropriation unless it is prima facie apparent that it was taken with an intent to create an adverse impact on the economic value of an investment.

1255 Salacuse, *supra* note 3, pp. 381, 395–396.

1256 This is in line with for example: ADC v. Hungary, *supra* note 1087 [423]–[424], Azurix v. Argentina, *supra* note 7 [310]–[311], Telenor v. Hungary, *supra* note 1178 [64]–[65].

1257 Also, in a broader sense, in all energy cases which often involve a combination of taxes imposed at various levels (federal, regional and local/municipal).

1258 As is the case in the ECT – Art. 21(5).

1259 For details of the police powers doctrine in this context see, for example: Methanex v. US, UNCITRAL, Final Award (03.08.2005) [Part IV, chapter D, para 7], Saluka v. Czech Republic, *supra* note 8 [262].

They also confirm that the question of whether an acquired right exists (i.e. the right which was "taken" and thereby fulfilled a precondition for a successful expropriation claim) will be decided in accordance with the domestic law:

> [...] the nature and scope of property rights are determined by the law of the state in which the property is located (the lex situs). Conceptually, property can only be expropriated if it exists. If a right was never acquired or has been otherwise extinguished under local law, it cannot be expropriated.[1260]

In the words of the *Cavalum* tribunal, as the claimants had no right to the tariff incentives, no such right could have been expropriated.[1261]

Sometimes, however, the analysis was blurred. Some tribunals equated the claimants' shareholding with ownership of the power plants themselves, despite the fact that the plants were assets owned by local companies. For example, in *9REN* the tribunal assessed expropriation in relation to the claimants' shareholding and debt interest, but its decision was based on the decreased value of the power plants. Thus, the definition of the investment was a fusion of the shareholding and debt interest, on the one hand, and the indirect investment in the power plants, on the other hand.

3 tribunals relied on judicial economy to avoid stating any conclusion on expropriation claims. They failed, however, to explain their viewpoint that a ruling on those expropriation claims would not impact on the available remedies. It is uncontroversial that the same principles apply to compensation, regardless of the nature of an internationally wrongful act. Therefore, the same principles apply to indirect expropriation (being unlawful expropriation) as apply to a violation of the FET, which these tribunals identified as having taken place. However, this is inconsistent with the same tribunals' decisions to decline jurisdiction over the IVPEE regarding non-expropriation claims. They omit an important element – i.e. that, if indirect expropriation were found to have taken place, the IVPEE would be relevant when calculating remedies. The *InfraRed* tribunal noted this and, for this very reason, felt obliged to analyze the expropriation claim.

Another issue missing from the tribunals' explanations is that, under CIL, compensation is one of 3 types of remedies available following an internationally wrongful act. As recognized in Arts. 34 and 47 of the ILC Articles, remedies can include the satisfaction derived from having a tribunal formally

1260 Newcombe, Paradell, *supra* note 42, p. 351.
1261 Fn 1241.

declare that a treaty was violated. Whilst this was not necessarily the remedy sought by the claimants in these cases, the failure to take this into account is notable.

A final noteworthy aspect is how the tribunals differentiated between judicial and financial economy. The tribunals used the former concept to avoid stating a view on an issue which had been fully pleaded by the parties. Accordingly, this did not save the parties' costs, but it allowed to arbitrators to save time in drafting their award. In this sense, judicial economy justifies the approach adopted by the tribunals, as it accelerates the issuance of their awards. However, financial economy is not always a valid reason for this approach. Each of the tribunals which relied upon the judicial economy concept to avoid addressing an expropriation claim had been constituted under the ICSID Convention and pursuant to the ICSID Arbitration Rules. Therefore, a causal link existed between the arbitrators' remuneration and the number of hours they worked in these cases.[1262] This is, however, not always the case. Financial economy would be irrelevant in situations when remuneration is fixed by the value of the dispute, such as in SCC arbitrations.[1263]

3 Umbrella Clause

3.1 *General Comments*

Numerous arbitral tribunals have taken the position that umbrella clauses elevate the protection of contractual obligations to an international level.[1264] The tribunal in *Eureko v. Poland* considered the detailed history of umbrella clauses, going back to as early as 1954, before concluding that the purpose of

---

1262 2020 ICSID Schedule of Fees and 2005 ICSID Memorandum on the Fees and Expenses.

1263 Art. 2 Appendix IV Schedule of Costs to the 2017 Arbitration Rules of the Arbitration Institute of the Stockholm Chamber of Commerce.

1264 For example: SGS v. Philippines, ICSID Case No. ARB/02/6, Decision of the Tribunal on Objections to Jurisdiction (29.01.2004) [121], [127], Noble Ventures v. Romania, ICSID Case No. ARB/01/11, Award (12.10.2005) [51], [60], BIVAC v. Paraguay, ICSID Case No. ARB/07/9, Decision of the Tribunal on Objections to Jurisdiction (29.05.2009) [141], Garanti v. Turkmenistan, *supra* note 4 [330], Gavrilovic v. Croatia, *supra* note 23 [420]–[421], Strabag v. Libya, ICSID Case No. ARB(AF)/15/1, Award (29.06.2020) [165], Nissan v. India, PCA Case No. 2017-37, Decision on Jurisdiction (29.04.2019) [277], ICS v. Argentina, PCA Case No. 2015-12, Award on Jurisdiction (08.07.2019) [337], [343]–[346]. See also: SGS v. Paraguay, ICSID Case No. ARB/07/29, Award (10.02.2012) [90], although this tribunal apparently would be willing to apply a broader interpretation, which may go beyond contractual commitments and "encompass host State commitments of all kinds, including contractual commitments" – SGS v. Paraguay, ICSID Case No. ARB/07/29, Decision on Jurisdiction (12.02.2010) [170].

umbrella clauses is to protect contractual obligations.[1265] Some tribunals, however, have required a link between contractual and treaty obligations.[1266] In particular, some have required that the state acts "as a sovereign", and not as a "merchant".[1267]

At a general level, no uniform position exists on whether umbrella clauses apply to obligations stemming from host states' legislation. Some tribunals have explicitly denied the possibility that umbrella clauses apply to commitments contained in "municipal legislative or administrative or other unilateral measures of a Contracting Party".[1268] Other tribunals have accepted that umbrella clauses also apply to obligations assumed by host states via their legislation.[1269]

1265 Eureko v. Poland, Ad Hoc, Partial Award (19.08.2005) [251]. For history of umbrella clauses see: Anthony C. Sinclair, The Origins of the Umbrella Clause in the International Law of Investment Protection, Arbitration International, 20:4 (2004), pp. 411–434.

1266 Joy Machinery v. Egypt, ICSID Case No. ARB/03/11, Award on Jurisdiction (06.08.2004) [81], El Paso v. Argentina, *supra* note 39 [532], Pan American v. Argentina, ICSID Case No. ARB/03/13, Decision on Preliminary Objections (27.07.2006) [91], [109]–[110], Hamester v. Ghana, ICSID Case No. ARB/07/24, Award (18.06.2010) [349], Supervision v. Costa Rica, ICSID Case No. ARB/12/4, Final Award (18.01.2017) [284].

1267 Pan American v. Argentina, *supra* note 1266 [108]. This refers to differentiation between acts of a state taken "jure gestionis" and "jure imperii" – Rodrigo Polanco, Jorge Luis Manrique de Lara Seminario, Cláusulas Paraguas, in: José Manuel Álvarez Zárate, Maciej Żenkiewicz (eds.), El Derecho Internacional de las Inversiones. Desarrollo Actual de Normas y Principios (Universidad Externado de Colombia 2021), p. 487.

1268 SGS v. Pakistan, ICSID Case No. ARB/01/13, Decision on Objections to Jurisdiction (06.08.2003) [166]. See also: CMS v. Argentina, ICSID Case No. ARB/01/8, Decision on Annulment (25.09.2007) [95.a], Al-Bahloul v. Tajikistan, SCC Case No. V 064/2008, Partial Award on Jurisdiction and Liability (02.09.2009) [257], Eskosol v. Italy, *supra* note 1001 [462]. See also: James Crawford, Treaty and Contract in Investment Arbitration, Arbitration International, 24 (2008), p. 370:

> But it is a confusion to equate a state law or regulation with an obligation entered into by the state, or to regard an umbrella clause as implicitly freezing the laws of the state as at the date of admission of an investment. The enactment of a law by a state, whether it is specific or general, is not the entry by the state into an obligation distinct from the law itself. No doubt a state is obliged by its own laws, but only for so long as they are in force. In the absence of express stabilisation, investors take the risk that the obligations of the host state under its own law may change, and the umbrella clause makes no difference to this basic proposition.

1269 Enron v. Argentina, *supra* note 19 [274–277], LG&E v. Argentina, *supra* note 34 [172–175], Continental Casualty v. Argentina, *supra* note 47 [301], Khan v. Mongolia, PCA Case No. 2011-09, Decision on Jurisdiction (25.07.2012) [438], Oxus Gold v. Uzbekistan, UNCITRAL, Award (17.12.2015) [368]–[371], Philip Morris v. Uruguay, *supra* note 13 [478], Greentech v. Italy, *supra* note 1001 [464], ESPF v. Italy, *supra* note 966 [787], [792], [823]. In similar vein, although without taking a clear position for example: Plama v. Bulgaria, *supra* note 28 [186], Noble Energy v. Ecuador, ICSID Case No. ARB/05/12, Decision on Jurisdiction (05.03.2008) [159]. See also: Craig S. Miles, Where's My Umbrella? An "Ordinary Meaning"

Some tribunals adopt the stance that they even apply to "obligations of any nature, regardless of their source, provided that they are indeed "obligations" entered into with a particular investor with regard to his or her investment".[1270] Thus, it remains true that "[t]he jurisprudence with respect to umbrella clauses and their effect is still developing, characterized primarily by attempts to limit their scope of application".[1271]

The last sentence of Art. 10(1) ECT contains an umbrella clause. It specifies that "[e]ach Contracting Party shall observe any obligations it has entered into with an Investor or an Investment of an Investor of any other Contracting Party" ("Umbrella Clause"). The wording of the ECT's Umbrella Clause is comparable to many other umbrella clauses, found in numerous investment treaties.[1272] This confirms the potential applicability of the conclusions from the Spanish saga cases for the future development of the general ISDS case law. It is estimated that approximately 1000 investment treaties contain an umbrella clause.[1273] This is approx. 40% of the existing BITs.[1274]

3.2 *Spanish Saga Case Law*

Whilst a violation of the Umbrella Clause was alleged in all but 3 of the analyzed Spanish saga cases, not a single tribunal upheld that allegation. In 10 cases, the tribunals dismissed the claims: *Isolux, Novenergia, Foresight, RREEF, 9REN, Cube, BayWa, Stadtwerke, RWE, Cavalum*. In 8 cases, the tribunals left the issue unaddressed for reasons of judicial economy, considering it unnecessary to state their conclusions on this issue given their findings on other issues of liability: *Eiser, Masdar, NextEra, SolEs, InfraRed, OperaFund, Watkins,* as well as *Antin* (although no explicit reference to judicial economy was made in

Approach to Answering Three Key Questions That Have Emerged from the "Umbrella Clause" Debate, in: Todd J. Grierson Weiler (ed.), Investment Treaty Arbitration and International Law (JurisNet 2008), pp. 16–20, María Cristina Gritón Salias, Do Umbrella Clauses Apply to Unilateral Undertakings?, in: Christina Binder, Ursula Kriebaum, August Reinisch, Stephan Wittich (eds.), International Investment Law for the 21st Century: Essays in Honour of Christoph Schreuer (Oxford University Press 2009), pp. 495–496.

1270 Micula v. Romania, *supra* note 12 [415].

1271 Hobér, *supra* note 5, p. 239.

1272 See for example: Art. 11 Switzerland – Pakistan BIT, Art. 3(4) Netherlands – Paraguay BIT, Art. II.2(c) US – Argentina BIT, last sentence of Art. II(6) US – Poland BIT, among many others.

1273 Salacuse, *supra* note 3, pp. 366–367.

1274 Olga Boltenko, The Umbrella Revolution: State Contracts and Umbrella Clauses in Contemporary Investment Law, in: Julien Chaisse, Leïla Choukroune, Sufian Jusoh (eds.), Handbook of International Investment Law and Policy (Springer 2021), p. 411.

this case). In 3 cases, the claimants did not allege a violation of the Umbrella Clause: *Charanne, PV Investors, Hydro.*

Despite the limited number of awards which discussed the claim, all of which were based on similar facts and the same applicable treaty, the awards allow us to zoom out from each specific dispute and to draw some more general conclusions. There is certainly room for improvement in terms of the consistency of general case law on umbrella clauses. Despite the significant development of ISDS case law in recent years, it is still far from being uniform.[1275]

•••

3.2.1 Isolux

In *Isolux*, the tribunal understood the Umbrella Clause as requiring commitments "entered into" by a state.[1276] Since no such commitments were present in the case, it was not possible for them to have been violated.[1277] For the tribunal, legislation can create such commitments only in "special cases". This may happen in particular if a legal act is directed exclusively at foreign investors.[1278]

3.2.2 Eiser

In *Eiser*, the tribunal relied on the judicial economy argument to avoid deciding issues which it considered "extraneous to those essential to its decision".[1279] This included the Umbrella Clause claim, since the decision on the FET "fully resolves" the case.[1280]

3.2.3 Novenergia

The *Novenergia* tribunal noted that the Umbrella Clause requires a host state to either conclude a specific contract with an investor or make "a specific personal promise" to the investor. These types of commitments cannot be equated with rights "founded in general regulatory acts".[1281]

1275 Hobér, *supra* note 5, p. 239.
1276 Isolux v. Spain, *supra* note 79 [769].
1277 Ibid [772].
1278 Ibid [771].
1279 Eiser v. Spain, *supra* note 98 [354].
1280 Ibid [352]–[353].
1281 Novenergia v. Spain, *supra* note 124 [715].

3.2.4 Masdar

In the *Masdar* case, the tribunal observed that judicial economy meant that it did not need to consider the claimant's other claims, including the Umbrella Clause.[1282] It added that, even if that claim had been decided in favor of the claimant, it would have had no impact on the tribunal's assessment of damages.[1283]

3.2.5 Antin

Although the parties in the *Antin* case also argued the Umbrella Clause, the tribunal's analysis devoted no attention to it and focused instead on the violation of the FET.[1284]

3.2.6 Foresight

In *Foresight*, the tribunal noted that the Umbrella Clause applies to specific commitments (absent in the circumstances of the case), and not to "general regulatory acts".[1285]

3.2.7 RREEF

In the *RREEF* case, the tribunal declined to engage in an "intellectually interesting but practically fruitless discussion concerning the definition and scope of an umbrella clause".[1286] It observed that the respondent had an obligation to comply with Art. 10(1) ECT and that this obligation applies to specific contractual obligations entered into with a particular investor.[1287] The tribunal noted that registration in the RAIPRE did not create a contractual obligation, and that the respective certificates simply manifest registration in the registry, but do not generate specific commitments.[1288] While the Umbrella Clause had "no particular role to play" in this case, Spain was expected to observe and enforce domestic law as part of the FET.[1289]

3.2.8 Cube

According to the *Cube* tribunal, the Umbrella Clause "points to a specific engagement entered into" by the host state with "a specific claimant or a

1282 Masdar v. Spain, *supra* note 150 [666]–[668].
1283 Ibid [667].
1284 Antin v. Spain, *supra* note 176 [573].
1285 Foresight v. Spain, *supra* note 203 [413].
1286 RREEF v. Spain, *supra* note 232 [283].
1287 Ibid [283]–[284].
1288 Ibid [285].
1289 Ibid [287].

specific group of claimants". General legislative measures are not engagements of this kind.[1290] Registration with the RAIPRE was irrelevant in this context. It was merely an administrative measure required by law as a prerequisite for benefitting from the Special Regime.[1291]

3.2.9 NextEra

After finding a violation of the FET, the *NextEra* tribunal also referred to judicial economy to avoid taking a position on the Umbrella Clause.[1292]

3.2.10 9REN

In *9REN*, the tribunal commented that it was "sensitive" to the implications of the Spain's "floodgates" arguments. It interpreted the term "any obligation" used in Art. 10(1) ECT in the context of an obligation "entered into" by the state "with an Investor". This can cover a "bilateral contract, such as a concession or licence agreement", but not a state's public legislation or administrative regulations.[1293] Since the claimant pleaded its case based on the legitimate expectations argument, the tribunal considered that it would be "both problematic and superfluous" to uphold the claimant's position on the Umbrella Clause: (i) problematic because it would "conflate" the claimant's protection under the FET with protection under the Umbrella Clause and "twist the latter out of shape", and (ii) superfluous because finding a violation of the Umbrella Clause would add "nothing in the way of relief to what has already been granted under FET".[1294] In this context, the tribunal added that the RAIPRE registration is an administrative precondition to receiving Special Regime benefits, not a source of those benefits.[1295]

3.2.11 SolEs

The *SolEs* tribunal considered that all of the claims presented by the claimant (expropriation, violation of the FET and violation of the Umbrella Clause) arose "from the same facts", and that the parties did not differentiate between the three claims in their arguments on compensation. It concluded that its decision (i.e. that a violation of the FET had occurred) "fully disposes of the matter of liability in this case".[1296]

1290 Cube v. Spain, *supra* note 285 [452].
1291 Ibid [453].
1292 NextEra v. Spain, *supra* note 337 [602].
1293 9REN v. Spain, *supra* note 354 [342].
1294 Ibid [345].
1295 Ibid [346].
1296 SolEs v. Spain, *supra* note 376 [466].

3.2.12 InfraRed

Based on procedural economy, the *InfraRed* tribunal also refrained from deciding whether the Umbrella Clause had been violated. It decided that this claim – together with other claims based on Art. 10 ECT – effectively sought relief for the same measures as in the FET context, whilst also being a "less suitable approach" for the "overall case" when compared to the FET analysis.[1297]

Nonetheless, the tribunal commented that any violation of the Umbrella Clause requires "a personal obligation entered into" by the state. In this case, the respondent's "actions, enactments and representations were directed generally at the entire Spanish CSP sector, not directly or personally towards Claimants or their investments".[1298]

This is somewhat surprising given that, in its analysis of the legitimate expectations claim, the tribunal based its decision on specific commitments made to the claimants, and not to the CSP sector as a whole.[1299] This may suggest that the tribunal somewhat "tailored" its decision on the facts of the case to find a way to distinguish it from other cases and escape from saying that the specific commitment was given to the whole CSP sector based on more general documents. This seems to be particularly grounded in some parts of the awards, which contain statements that blend the specific commitment with an obligation towards the CSP sector.[1300]

3.2.13 OperaFund

The *OperaFund* tribunal also saw no need to decide on the Umbrella Clause claim, since the parties' requested reliefs did not differentiate between the consequences or damages arising from claims other than those concerning violations of the FET, which the tribunal had already upheld.[1301] The tribunal commented, however, that it considered the interpretations of the tribunals in *Isolux* and *Novenergia* as "more convincing" than that in *Greentech v. Italy*. In the former cases, the Umbrella Clause claim was said to be limited to contractual obligations because it refers to obligations "entered into", whereas the latter case found that the Umbrella Clause claim could encompasses certain legislative and regulatory instruments.[1302]

1297 InfraRed v. Spain, *supra* note 404 [477].
1298 Ibid [478].
1299 Ibid [434].
1300 Ibid [443], [449], [451].
1301 OperaFund v. Spain, *supra* note 436 [568].
1302 Ibid [569].

3.2.14 BayWa

In *BayWa*, the tribunal commenced by observing that the Umbrella Clause apply to "obligations generally", but only those which the state has "specifically entered into with" an investor.[1303] "The paradigm case" is an investment contract "duly entered into". Obligations arising under the general law are beyond the scope of the Umbrella Clause. When enacting legislation, a state:

> establishes binding rules of conduct, but it does not make specific promises to each person entitled to claim under the law, nor does it enter into obligations to specific investors or their investments even when these entities are numbered among the beneficiaries of the law. A general law is not a promise.[1304]

The tribunal also analyzed the opposite approach. However, even then, the promises created by a legislative act would still be considered under Spanish law, according to which such obligations could be lawfully amended or repealed (as confirmed by the Spanish courts), unless they had already created "vested rights".[1305]

The investors relied on several cases to argue that the umbrella clauses apply to general legislation. However, the tribunal considered that none of them actually supported the claimant's position. The tribunal was unaware of a single case in which a general law provision comparable to the Spanish disputed measures had been enforced under the ECT's (or equivalent) Umbrella Clause.[1306] This conclusion was unchanged even in the light of Spain's other actions, including official press releases, which do not create "obligations specifically entered into" within the meaning of the Umbrella Clause.[1307]

Additionally, the tribunal analyzed whether the claimants could rely on the doctrine of binding unilateral statements under international law (as embodied in the ILC's Guiding Principles applicable to unilateral declarations of States capable of creating legal obligations). It decided, however, that this doctrine is inapplicable to "statements made vis-à-vis private parties in a domestic context".[1308]

1303 BayWa v. Spain, *supra* note 473 [434], [442].
1304 Ibid [442].
1305 Ibid [443].
1306 Ibid [445]–[446].
1307 Ibid [445]–[446].
1308 Ibid [447].

3.2.15 Stadtwerke

In *Stadtwerke*, the tribunal answered the "threshold question" by stating that the Umbrella Clause applies only to "contractual obligations or obligations made vis-à-vis a specific investor or investment" (i.e. "contractual-like" obligations assumed in respect of a particular individual or legal person), and not to "all types of obligations undertaken by Spain, however created".[1309] This conclusion was based on a literal interpretation of Art. 10(1) ECT, which uses the phrase "entered into with", and not a broader term, such as for example "assuming".[1310] The tribunal noted that this conclusion is confirmed by the Spanish and French language versions of the ECT. Both are authentic languages and use verbs which could be better translated as "contracted".[1311] The tribunal was unable, on the facts, to identify any contract which could fall within the Umbrella Clause.[1312]

3.2.16 RWE

In *RWE*, the tribunal observed that the Umbrella Clause requires "some form of specific consensual obligation". This was again based on the wording of Art. 10(1) ECT, which applies to obligations that a state "has entered into" with an investor.[1313] Spanish law applies to determine whether a certificate of registration in the RAIPRE created such consensual obligations, and the Claimants failed to convince the tribunal that this was the case.[1314] Given the absence of such an obligation, the tribunal concluded that no violation of the Umbrella Clause had occurred.[1315]

3.2.17 Watkins

Relying on the judicial economy explanation, the *Watkins* tribunal found it unnecessary to address the claim concerning the Umbrella Clause in the light of its decision that the FET had been violated.[1316]

1309 Stadtwerke v. Spain, *supra* note 533 [379], [380], [384].
1310 Ibid [380].
1311 Ibid [381]–[382].
1312 Ibid [383].
1313 RWE v. Spain, *supra* note 589 [677].
1314 Ibid [679].
1315 Ibid [680].
1316 Watkins v. Spain, *supra* note 680 [629].

3.2.18 Cavalum

The *Cavalum* tribunal shortly noted that there was no "specific regulatory or other governmental commitments or obligations" and that, therefore, the Umbrella Clause claim added nothing to the FET claim.[1317]

3.3 *Lessons Learned*

The Spanish saga cases are an important contribution to the future development of case law on this issue. Not a single tribunal accepted the claim that the Umbrella Clause had been violated. On this legal point, the Spanish saga cases can be considered as *jurisprudence constante.*

3.3.1 First Lesson Learned – General Legislation, Directed at a Broad Class of Addressees, Falls outside the Scope of the Umbrella Clause

Pursuant to the interpretation adopted by the Spanish saga tribunals, the Umbrella Clause applies solely to contractual commitments, entered into by a host state with an investor. General legislation, directed at a broad class of addressees, falls outside the scope of the Umbrella Clause.[1318] In other words, commitments stemming from regulatory frameworks do not qualify as obligations covered by the Umbrella Clause, the scope of which is limited to agreements entered into by states with contractual counterparty, i.e. when acting as a merchant (*jure gestionis*) rather than as a sovereign (*jure imperii*).

The position taken by the *Isolux* tribunal is noteworthy, as it permitted a potential exception whereby umbrella clauses may also apply to obligations anchored in general legislation. This may happen, the tribunal suggested, if particular legislation creates "an abstract unilateral promise" directed solely to a defined class of foreign investors.[1319] This position has already been explicitly relied upon by other tribunals, outside of the Spanish saga context.[1320]

The comment made by the tribunal in *Stadtwerke* is also notable. It suggests that some umbrella clauses may allow for a broader interpretation, depending on the wording of the particular treaty provision. The Spanish saga tribunals analyzed the ECT's Umbrella Clause, which uses the term "entered into" with

1317 Cavalum v. Spain, *supra* note 854 [641].

1318 For similar conclusions see for example: Salacuse, *supra* note 3, p. 377.

1319 Fn 1278, Liman v. Kazakhstan, ICSID Case No. ARB/07/14, Excerpts of the Award (22.06.2010) [448]. In this vein see for example: Laura Halonen, Containing the Scope of the Umbrella Clause, in: Todd J. Grierson Weiler (ed.), Investment Treaty Arbitration and International Law (JurisNet 2008), p. 35, who refers to legislative acts "aimed at specific investors", making such obligations "quasi-contractual".

1320 Sun Reserve v. Italy, *supra* note 1001 [993], Belenergia v. Italy, *supra* note 964 [617].

respect to the obligations to be observed by the host states. However, some other treaties use broader terms, such as referring to obligations that are “assumed”.[1321] Such wording may lead to a different conclusion and allow legislation to fall within the scope of application of such broadly worded umbrella clauses.

If one agrees with this position, the scope of the obligation to which the Umbrella Clause applies is determined by the applicable domestic law, typically the law of the host state.[1322] The *BayWa* and *RWE* awards confirm that.[1323]

3.3.2 Second Lesson Learned – the Umbrella Clause May Apply Provided That a PPA Is Concluded between the Investor and an Agency Whose Actions Are Attributable to the State

Sometimes the applicable legislation will envisage the conclusion of a contract to create certain rights in a relationship between an investor and a host state.[1324] This is the situation, for example, in relation to the PPAs. It has already been referred to above in the Sixth Lesson Learned in the context of the FET. The Spanish saga cases allow an *a contrario* conclusion that, in such situations when PPAs are concluded, investors can succeed with the Umbrella Clause claims, since such situations entail a contractual relationship with the state or an authority whose acts are attributable to the state.[1325]

This explains why, in some Italian RE cases, the tribunals concluded that the Umbrella Clause had been violated. The tribunal in *ESPF v. Italy* decided that, whilst the regulatory regime itself was insufficient to create obligations for the host state, protected obligations were created when a state-owned company sent a letter confirming the applicable tariffs and, subsequently, when it entered into an agreement with the respective power plants.[1326] A similar conclusion was reached by the tribunal in *Greentech v. Italy*.[1327] However, this tribunal leaned towards an even broader interpretation of the Umbrella Clause, which would extend its protection to “certain legislative and regulatory instruments that are specific enough to qualify as commitments to identifiable investments or investors”.[1328]

1321 For example Art. X(2) Switzerland-Philippines BIT.

1322 Micula v. Romania, *supra* note 12 [418], Burlington v. Ecuador, *supra* note 1247 [214], Silver Ridge v. Italy, *supra* note 967 [371].

1323 BayWa v. Spain, *supra* note 473 [443], RWE v. Spain, *supra* note 589 [679].

1324 Burlington v. Ecuador, *supra* note 1247 [207].

1325 A fact-specific issue of attribution becomes relevant in this context.

1326 ESPF v. Italy, *supra* note 966 [755]–[758], [791]–[793], [811]–[816].

1327 Greentech v. Italy, *supra* note 1001 [466].

1328 Ibid [464].

This remains very much dependent on the content of the domestic law, which determines the content of the legislation and any contract linked with such legislation. This reason led other Italian RE cases to opposite conclusions. In *Belenergia*, the tribunal differed in its assessment of the domestic law and dismissed the Umbrella Clause claim.[1329] It concluded that the FIT was regulated by legislation and was not "personally addressed" to the investor, whereas a subsequent agreement with the state-owned company simply "replicated" the FIT amount and duration "from the relevant legislation".[1330] Similar conclusions were reached by the tribunal in *Silver Ridge v. Italy*, which observed that these agreements are "accessory" to and "only reflect a legal relationship whose existence and essential features have been determined before", in the applicable regulations.[1331] As such, they were not considered as "autonomous" from the applicable regulations.[1332] Similar conclusions on the "accessory" nature of these agreements were reached in the *Sun Reserve* case.[1333] The *CEF v. Italy* tribunal explained that the category of "accessory agreements" is, according to Italian law, a type of agreement which preserves the vertical relationship between the state and the other party.[1334]

These issues are relevant to the development of investor-state arbitration case law on RE. By way of example, *Invenergy v. Poland* concerns the early termination of agreements concluded by state-owned companies.[1335] This, in turn, is closely linked to issues of attribution and state responsibility for the conduct of state-owned or state-controlled companies.

To conclude, where no PPA exists, the Umbrella Clause will not protect investors in circumstances such as those analyzed above. If such an agreement exists, the Umbrella Clause may apply provided that the agreement itself creates a legal relationship between the investor and an agency whose actions are attributable to the state.

1329 Belenergia v. Italy, *supra* note 964 [619].
1330 Ibid [615].
1331 Silver Ridge v. Italy, *supra* note 967 [376], [379]–[380].
1332 Ibid [383].
1333 Sun Reserve v. Italy, *supra* note 1001 [1002].
1334 CEF v. Italy, *supra* note 1001 [254].
1335 https://invenergy.com/news/invenergy-files-for-international-arbitration-against-the-republic-of-poland-for-violations-of-the-united-states-poland-bilateral-investment-treaty.

CHAPTER 5

Remedies

1 Restitution

1.1 *General Comments*

It goes without saying that the starting point for determining the remedies available in each case is always the text of the applicable investment treaty.[1] Typically, however, BITs[2] remain silent on the issue of remedies following their breach. Generally, the only type of compensation which is regulated is that which is payable following a lawful expropriation. The ECT is no exception in this regard. Art. 13(1) ECT regulates exclusively the standard of "prompt, adequate and effective" compensation payable in the event of a lawful expropriation, which:

> shall amount to the fair market value of the Investment expropriated at the time immediately before the Expropriation or impending Expropriation became known in such a way as to affect the value of the Investment (hereinafter referred to as the "Valuation Date").[3]

Consequently, when concluding that respondents have violated their obligations stemming from the underlying investment treaties, tribunals often make explicit reference to the judgment of the Permanent Court of International Justice ("PCIJ"), issued on 13.09.1928 ("*Chorzów Factory* judgment"). In that case, the PCIJ observed as follows:

> The essential principle contained in the actual notion of an illegal act – a principle which seems to be established by international practice and in particular by the decisions of arbitral tribunals – is that reparation must, as far as possible, wipe out all the consequences of the illegal act and

1 See for example Art. 55 of the ILC Articles.

2 All abbreviations contained herein are as used in previous Chapters, unless described otherwise.

3 The provision continues:

> [s]uch fair market value shall at the request of the Investor be expressed in a Freely Convertible Currency on the basis of the market rate of exchange existing for that currency on the Valuation Date. Compensation shall also include interest at a commercial rate established on a market basis from the date of Expropriation until the date of payment.

DOI:10.1163/9789004509344_006

> reestablish the situation which would, in all probability, have existed if that act had not been committed. Restitution in kind, or, if this is not possible, payment of a sum corresponding to the value which a restitution in kind would bear; the award, if need be, of damages for loss sustained which would not be covered by restitution in kind or payment in place of it – such are the principles which should serve to determine the amount of compensation due for an act contrary to international law.[4]

Even in 1928, the principle expressed in the passage quoted above was viewed as "established by international practice".[5] In 1987, the US-Iran Claims Tribunal noted that "in spite of the fact that it is nearly sixty years old, this judgment is widely regarded as the most authoritative exposition of the principles applicable in this field, and is still valid today".[6] The situation remains unchanged. The *Chorzów Factory* judgment has been confirmed on uncountable occasions.[7] Nowadays, it is reflected in the ILC Articles[8]. Even though the ILC Articles "seek to formulate, by way of codification and progressive development, the basic rules of international law concerning the responsibility of States for their internationally wrongful acts", their respective provisions codify, as opposed to progressively developing, the principle reflected in the *Chorzów Factory* judgment.[9]

---

4 Case Concerning the Factory at Chorzów (Germany v. Poland) (Merits), Judgment (13.09.1928).

5 Ibid.

6 Amoco v. Iran , Case No. 56, Partial Award (Award No. 310-56-3) (14.07.1987) [191].

7 For example: Case Concerning the Gabčíkovo-Nagymaros Project (Hungary v. Slovakia), Judgment (15.09.1997) [149], Case Concerning the Arrest Warrant of 11 April 2000 (Democratic Republic of the Congo v. Belgium), Judgment (14.02.2002) [76], Case Concerning Avena and Other Mexican Nationals (Mexico v. US), Judgment (31.03.2004) [119], Legal Consequences of the Construction of a Wall in the Occupied Palestinian Territories, Advisory Opinion (09.07.2004) [152]. In investor-state arbitrations see for example: Unglaube v. Costa Rica, ICSID Case No. ARB/08/1 and ICSID Case No. ARB/09/20 (consolidated cases), Award (16.05.2012) [306], ADC v. Hungary, ICSID Case No. ARB/03/16, Award (02.10.2006) [484]–[485].

8 Eric De Brabandere, Investment Treaty Arbitration as Public International Law (Cambridge University Press 2014) p. 177.

9 James R. Crawford, State Responsibility, in: Rüdiger Wolfrum (ed.), Max Planck Encyclopedia of Public International Law (online access) [31], Noah Rubins, Vasuda Sinha, Baxter Roberts, Approaches to Valuation in Investment Treaty Arbitration, in: Christina L. Beharry (ed.), Contemporary and Emerging Issues on the Law of Damages and Valuation in International Investment Arbitration (Brill 2018), p. 172, Eric De Brabandere, *supra* note 8, p. 178, Sergey Ripinsky, Kevin Williams, Damages in International Investment Law (British Institute of International and Comparative Law 2008) p. 32, Nykomb v. Latvia, SCC Case No. 118/2001, Arbitral Award (16.12.2003) [38], LG&E v. Argentina, ICSID Case No. ARB/02/1, Award (25.07.2007) [31], Siemens v. Argentina, ICSID Case No. ARB/02/8, Award (06.02.2007) [350], Biwater v. Tanzania, ICSID Case No. ARB/05/22, Award (24.07.2008) [773], Tza Yap Shum v. Peru, ICSID Case No. ARB/07/6, Award (07.07.2011) [253]–[254].

This is the starting point for analyzing the remedies discussions which occurred in the Spanish saga cases. This section focuses on restitution. The claimants sought restitution in 8 of the analyzed cases: *Eiser, Masdar, Antin, RREEF, Stadtwerke, RWE, Watkins, PV Investors* (although the latter request was ultimately withdrawn).[10] The requests were framed in different ways, with some claimants requesting that the tribunal issue an order to repeal "the relevant articles" of the disputed measures[11] and others seeking repeal of "all the harmful laws and regulations complained of [...] and placing Claimants under the same legal and regulatory framework that existed at the time they made the investments".[12]

The claimants primarily sought restitution by way of requiring Spain to restore the Special Regime. They sought compensation only if restitution was not awarded. This approach is unsurprising as the ECT specifies that arbitral awards "shall provide that the Contracting Party may pay monetary damages in lieu of any other remedy granted".[13]

Ultimately, not a single tribunal awarded restitution.

1.2 *Spanish Saga Case Law*

1.2.1 Charanne and Isolux

The *Charanne*[14] and *Isolux*[15] tribunals, having dismissed the claims on their merits, did not analyze the standard which would apply if a violation had been found. No request for restitution was filed in these two cases.

1.2.2 Eiser

In *Eiser*, the tribunal commenced by recognizing that Art. 10 ECT does not lay down any standard of compensation to be paid following a violation. Therefore, the ECT's provision on expropriation served as a reference point, although

---

10 Notably, claimants in all these cases were represented by the same law firm.

11 Masdar v. Spain, ICSID Case No. ARB/14/1, Award (16.05.2018) [526], [554].

12 Antin v. Spain, ICSID Case No. ARB/13/31, Award (15.06.2018) [632], similarly: RWE v. Spain, ICSID Case No. ARB/14/34, Decision on Jurisdiction, Liability, and Certain Issues of Quantum (30.12.2019) [681].

13 Art. 26(8) ECT:

> The awards of arbitration, which may include an award of interest, shall be final and binding upon the parties to the dispute. An award of arbitration concerning a measure of a sub-national government or authority of the disputing Contracting Party shall provide that the Contracting Party may pay monetary damages in lieu of any other remedy granted. Each Contracting Party shall carry out without delay any such award and shall make provision for the effective enforcement in its Area of such awards.

14 Charanne v. Spain, SCC Case No. V 062/2012, Award (21.01.2016).

15 Isolux v. Spain, SCC Case No. V 2013/153, Award (12.07.2016).

TABLE 7 Restitution

No	Case name	Restitution claimed?	Outcome
1	Charanne	No	N/A
2	Isolux	No	N/A
3	Eiser	Yes	Dismissed
4	Novenergia	No	N/A
5	Masdar	Yes	Dismissed
6	Antin	Yes	Dismissed
7	Foresight	No	N/A
8	RREEF	Yes	Dismissed
9	Cube	No	N/A
10	NextEra	No	N/A
11	9REN	No	N/A
12	SolEs	No	N/A
13	InfraRed	No	N/A
14	OperaFund	No	N/A
15	BayWa	No	N/A
16	Stadtwerke	Yes	N/A (no treaty violation)
17	RWE	Yes	Dismissed
18	Watkins	Yes	Dismissed
19	PV Investors	Yes	N/A (withdrawn)
20	Hydro	No	N/A
21	Cavalum	No	N/A
	Total	Yes - 8 No - 13	Dismissed - 6

the tribunal observed that "while tribunals sometimes apply principles relevant to compensation for expropriation to other treaty violations without comment, fuller consideration of the issue is necessary".[16] For the tribunal, the starting point for the analysis was the *Chorzów Factory* judgment.[17] The

16 Eiser v. Spain, ICSID Case No. ARB/13/36, Award (04.05.2017) [420].

17 Ibid [421]–[422]. The tribunal referred to the PCIJ judgment from 1927 on jurisdiction as well: Case Concerning the Factory at Chorzów (Germany v. Poland) (Jurisdiction), Judgment (26.07.1927).

principles set out in this judgment were accepted and then reflected in the ILC Articles.[18] Art. 31 ILC Articles "reflects" the applicable "international law rules".[19]

When faced with a request for restitution, the tribunal considered this remedy to be inappropriate on the facts of that case. Ordering restitution would "question Respondent's sovereign right to take appropriate regulatory measures to meet public needs".[20]

1.2.3 Novenergia

The tribunal in *Novenergia* noted that a violation of the FET "calls for a different assessment of damages" than in a case when unlawful expropriation has occurred.[21] It added that the "compensation formula" in Art. 13 ECT "has at times served as guidance for relevant compensation in relation to breaches of the ECT other than unlawful expropriation", but a more "nuanced assessment" was required, particularly given that it dismissed the claim for expropriation.[22]

As the ECT has no provisions that regulate compensation for treaty violations other than expropriation, the general principles of CIL must be applied.[23] The starting point is Art. 31 of the ILC Articles.[24] It codifies "the best practice set out by many arbitral tribunals over a significant period of time, but stems primarily from" the *Chorzów Factory* judgment.[25] Thus, the tribunal applied the CIL principle of full reparation. This requires that the aggrieved investor be awarded an amount of monetary compensation which will put it in the position it would have been in but for the breaches, including compensation for losses already sustained and loss of profits.[26] Interestingly, the value of the expropriation claim was lower than the claim made regarding the FET.[27]

No claim for restitution was made in this case.

1.2.4 Masdar

The *Masdar* tribunal observed that Art. 10 ECT contains no provisions "regarding remedies or reparations" following a breach of the ECT. In light of this silence, "the default standard provided by customary international law" is to

18 Eiser v. Spain, *supra* note 16 [423].
19 Ibid [424].
20 Ibid [425].
21 Novenergia v. Spain, SCC Case No. 2015/063, Final Arbitral Award (15.02.2018) [699].
22 Ibid [804].
23 Ibid [805].
24 Ibid [806].
25 Ibid [807].
26 Ibid [808].
27 Ibid [810].

be applied.[28] The applicable standard is "full reparation", as expressed in the *Chorzów Factory* judgment.[29] The tribunal observed that "international arbitral tribunals have treated this principle as reflecting customary international law and consistently applied it to investor-State disputes". It added that art. 31 of the ILC Articles codified the *Chorzów Factory* judgment.[30] It further stated that the drafting history of the ILC Articles indicates that "these provisions reflect a general consensus on international principles of State responsibility". As a result, the tribunal applied the principles on reparation set out in the ILC Articles in order to determine the applicable remedies.[31]

It relied on Art. 35 of the ILC Articles and noted that restitution is the primary remedy for the reparation of wrongful acts under international law. It also noted that compensation is the appropriate remedy "where restitution appears materially impossible or disproportionally burdensome". The choice between restitution and compensation involves balancing private and public interests and "is based on considerations of equity and reasonableness".[32]

The tribunal decided that, in this particular case, restitution would "unduly burden Respondent's legislative and regulatory autonomy, and would potentially benefit numerous parties not protected by the ECT (or otherwise)".[33] It added that restitution would be disproportionately burdensome when compared to the potential benefits for the claimants.[34] The balancing process favored the respondent's ability to exercise its legislative and regulatory autonomy and to address public needs.[35] Moreover, the tribunal noted that restitution could face "obvious practical and enforcement obstacles".[36] In the tribunal's view, its decision was justified in the light of Art. 35(b) of the ILC Articles.[37]

28 Masdar v. Spain, *supra* note 11 (16.05.2018) [548]. The tribunal "has been unable to reach an overall consensus as to its conclusions" with respect to remedies, and the relevant parts of the award "largely reflect the view of a majority of the Tribunal" – [547]. The respondent's nominee, Prof. Brigitte Stern, issued a dissenting opinion, which is not, however, in the public domain.

29 Ibid [549], [552].

30 Ibid [550].

31 Ibid [551].

32 Ibid [558].

33 Ibid [559].

34 Ibid [562].

35 Ibid [563].

36 Ibid.

37 Ibid [562].

1.2.5 Antin

In *Antin*, the tribunal also observed that neither Art. 10 ECT nor any other ECT provision lays down a standard for compensating violations.[38] It noted that compensation is regulated only in Art. 13 ECT, with respect to lawful expropriation.[39] Therefore, the tribunal noted that the standard for compensation "should be based on international law" and referred to the *Chorzów Factory* judgment and to Art. 31 of the ILC Articles.[40] It considered them "as reflecting the international law rules that are to be applied", entitling the claimants to full reparation for damages caused by the breach of the ECT, "so as to remove the consequences of the wrongful act".[41]

In this case a request for restitution had been made, albeit in a half-hearted manner. The claimants "merely devoted two paragraphs" of their memorial to this issue, which was not "fully discussed" in the subsequent pleadings.[42] The tribunal referred to Art. 35 of the ILC Articles and considered restitution to be "disproportional to its interference with the sovereignty of the State" when compared to compensation.[43] The tribunal underlined the state's right to:

> exercise its sovereign power to amend its regulations to respond to changing circumstances in the public interest, to the extent that any such amendments are consistent with the assurances on the stability of the regulatory framework provided by the State and required by the ECT.[44]

Non-observance of these commitments triggers an obligation to pay compensation.[45]

1.2.6 Foresight

The tribunal in the *Foresight* case noted that it had to look at CIL in order to find the applicable standard of compensation, which provides for full reparation for any damage caused by an illegal act. The standard articulated by the PCIJ in the *Chorzów Factory* judgment is "reflected" in Art. 31 of the ILC Articles.[46] It added that "the principle of full reparation is generally accepted

38 Antin v. Spain, *supra* note 12 [659].
39 Ibid [660].
40 Ibid [662]–[663].
41 Ibid [664].
42 Ibid [634].
43 Ibid [636].
44 Ibid [637].
45 Ibid [637].
46 Foresight v. Spain, SCC Case No. V 2015/150, Final Award (14.11.2018) [432]–[435].

in international investment law".[47] The tribunal underlined the "discretion in determining the approach to damages".[48] It then concluded that the claimants "are in principle entitled to full compensation" and proceeded to calculate the quantum.[49]

No claim for restitution was made in this case.

1.2.7 RREEF

Likewise, the *RREEF* tribunal did not analyze the standard applicable to remedies, but simply noted that it agreed with the "assumptions" that the principle of full reparation in accordance with CIL applies, as codified in the ILC Articles.[50]

The tribunal accepted that restitution was theoretically available. However, it explained that it had "some doubts that, in a case like this, implying repealing laws and regulations as requested by the Claimants, restitutio in integrum would be an appropriate remedy".[51]

1.2.8 Cube

In the *Cube* case, the tribunal also commenced with a reference to the *Chorzów Factory* judgment. It observed the existence of "the well-established proposition that the function of an award of damages is to compensate for damage caused by internationally wrongful acts, in so far as such damage is not made good by restitution".[52] No request for restitution had been made in this case and both of the parties considered compensation as the appropriate remedy if the ECT was found to have been violated.[53] Nevertheless, the tribunal commented that states have the right to determine their own regulatory regimes.

---

47 Ibid [436].

48 Ibid [437]. Such discretion was discussed and emphasized further in [487]. One arbitrator disagreed. However, this was a consequence of his different conclusions on liability, which resulted in different conclusions on compensation. He noted that "the inexistence of a violation attributable to Respondent, determines the inexistence of an obligation to repair hypothetical damages" – Foresight v. Spain, SCC Case No. V 2015/150, Partial Dissenting Opinion (30.10.2018) [53].

49 Ibid [438]: "In conclusion, the Tribunal, by a majority, has decided that the Claimants are in principle entitled to full compensation for Spain's violation of Article 10(1) ECT. The Tribunal shall now turn to the Parties' respective submissions on quantum".

50 RREEF v. Spain, ICSID Case No. ARB/13/30, Decision on Responsibility and on the Principles of Quantum (30.11.2018) [473].

51 Ibid.

52 Cube v. Spain, ICSID Case No. ARB/15/20, Decision on Jurisdiction, Liability and Partial Decision on Quantum (19.02.2019) [459].

53 Ibid.

Restitution, understood as ordering the respondent to restore "at least the main bases of the original regulatory framework in relation to the Claimants, is beyond the proper scope of the powers of the Tribunal and is moreover plainly materially impossible and disproportionately burdensome".[54]

1.2.9 NextEra

As regards the applicable standard, the *NextEra* tribunal simply noted that the principles "set out" in the *Chorzów Factory* judgment and in Art. 31 of the ILC Articles apply "to the measurement of damages".[55] It was not faced with a claim for restitution.

1.2.10 9REN

In *9REN*, the tribunal noted that the only explicit guidance to quantum contained in the ECT is in its Art. 13, which concerns expropriation, whereas "[i]n the case of other violations of the ECT, resort is had to the customary international law principle of full compensation".[56] The tribunal noted that there was "no real dispute about the measure of applicable compensation" and referred to the *Chorzów Factory* judgment and Art. 31 of the ILC Articles as the applicable standard in this regard.[57] It added that this "customary international law principle" is regularly applied by arbitral tribunals.[58] It also underlined the general principle that the burden of proof regarding compensation is on the claimants.[59]

No claim for restitution was made in this case.

1.2.11 SolEs

The *SolEs* tribunal noted that the ECT does not specify the manner in which compensation is to be determined following a violation of its Art. 10(1).[60] Accordingly, this issue remains governed by CIL. The "essential principle" is, as stated in the *Chorzów Factory* judgment, that reparation must "as far as possible, wipe out all the consequences of the illegal act". Art. 31(1) of the ILC

---

54 Ibid [460].

55 NextEra v. Spain, ICSID Case No. ARB/14/11, Decision on Jurisdiction, Liability and Quantum Principles (12.03.2019) [642].

56 9REN v. Spain, ICSID Case No. ARB/15/15, Award (31.05.2019) [373]. The tribunal seems not to differentiate between lawful and unlawful expropriation, which may be explained by little focus on that issue, since no expropriation was found to take place.

57 Ibid [373], [376].

58 Ibid [377].

59 Ibid [405].

60 SolEs v. Spain, ICSID Case No. ARB/15/38, Award (31.07.2019) [475].

Articles is "to the same effect". Consequently, the respondent is obliged to compensate the claimant "for the reduction in the fair market value of its investment that was caused by the Disputed Measures".[61] The burden of proof rests on the claimant.[62]

No claim for restitution was made in this case.[63]

1.2.12 InfraRed

The *InfraRed* tribunal simply agreed with the parties that the "principle of full compensation set forth" in the *Chorzów Factory* judgment applies to determine the level of compensation.[64] It was not faced with a claim for restitution.

1.2.13 OperaFund

In *OperaFund*, the tribunal observed that once a violation of international law has been identified, this entails an obligation to put the claimants "in the same position they would have found themselves, had Respondent not breached the ECT".[65] CIL applies when the applicable treaty fails to specify the consequences of the violation. "A long tradition of international jurisprudence" establishes that the relevant principles of CIL, which "are derived from the PCIJ Judgment in the Chorzów Factory Case and are recorded" in Articles 31–38 of the ILC Articles.[66]

Likewise, no claim for restitution was made in this case.

1.2.14 BayWa

The *BayWa* tribunal did not analyze the standard applicable to compensation, and simply proceeded to calculate how much compensation should be awarded.[67]

1.2.15 Stadtwerke

The *Stadtwerke* tribunal dismissed the claims on their merits and, consequently, did not analyze the request for restitution which had been made by the claimants.[68]

61 Ibid [476].

62 Ibid [478].

63 Ibid [475].

64 InfraRed v. Spain, ICSID Case No. ARB/14/12, Award (02.08.2019) [510].

65 OperaFund v. Spain, ICSID Case No. ARB/15/36, Award (06.09.2019) [609].

66 Ibid.

67 BayWa v. Spain, ICSID Case No. ARB/15/16, Decision on Jurisdiction, Liability and Directions on Quantum (02.12.2019) [615]: "The Tribunal has held that the breach of Article 10.1, first and second sentences, of the ECT is limited to the retroactive reduction in the allowed return. The question is how to value that amount".

68 Stadtwerke v. Spain, ICSID Case No. ARB/15/1, Award (02.12.2019) [96].

1.2.16 RWE

The *RWE* tribunal did not discuss the applicable standard of compensation and simply quoted the *Chorzów Factory* judgment and Art. 31 of the ILC Articles.[69] It also considered that it faced "plainly not an appropriate case for restitution", as it "would obviously involve a burden to the Respondent out of all proportion to the benefit to the Claimants".[70] The tribunal identified two relevant factors which led it to reach this conclusion. First, the case concerned regulations of general applicability in an important sector for the Spanish economy.[71] Second, its findings on liability were limited to a violation of the FET only in connection with some of the disputed plants, not all of them.[72]

1.2.17 Watkins

The *Watkins* tribunal noted that the ECT is silent on the remedies available following a violation of the FET.[73] Thus, the tribunal applied the standard of reparation found in CIL, which is the "full reparation standard" articulated in the *Chorzów Factory* judgment.[74]

This tribunal also considered restitution to be inappropriate in the circumstances of the case. It said that Spain "has a sovereign right to take appropriate legislative and regulatory measures to meet public interests". The tribunal referred to similar conclusions reached in earlier Spanish saga cases.[75]

1.2.18 PV Investors

The *PV Investors* tribunal simply noted that there was no disagreement between the parties as to the general principles which govern reparation for acts that violate international law, particularly as regards the principle of full reparation for harm caused by an internationally wrongful act.[76]

The claimants in this case had initially requested restitution.[77] However, this request was abandoned during the proceedings.[78] This happened after the quantum phase, once the tribunal had requested the experts' joint model on

69 RWE v. Spain, *supra* note 12 [685].

70 Ibid.

71 Ibid: "This case involves State regulation that is generally applicable across a very important sector in Spain i.e. the RE sector whereas, by contrast, the Claimants can very readily be afforded full reparation through compensation".

72 Ibid.

73 Watkins v. Spain, ICSID Case No. ARB/15/44, Award (21.01.2020) [672].

74 Ibid [673], [676], [677].

75 Ibid [674].

76 The PV Investors v. Spain, PCA Case No. 2012-14, Final Award (28.02.2020) [669].

77 Ibid [219].

78 Ibid [220].

the alternative claim based on the RRR.[79] The tribunal noted that in any case, it would not order restitution given its decision to dismiss the primary claim.[80]

1.2.19 Hydro

In the *Hydro* case, the tribunal simply noted that the parties accepted, "as they must", the principle enshrined in the *Chorzów Factory* judgment.[81]

The claimants explained that they did not seek restitution, which they considered "impracticable" in this particular case.[82]

1.2.20 Cavalum

In *Cavalum*, the tribunal briefly explained that it "had in mind the long-settled principle" enshrined in the *Chorzów Factory* judgment, which is "now commonly accepted to be applicable beyond inter-State disputes".[83]

No claim for restitution was presented in this case.

1.3 *Lessons Learned*

The Spanish saga cases confirm a trend which is visible in general investor-state arbitration case law, namely that of referring to the *Chorzów Factory* judgment as articulating the relevant principle of CIL. As such, this principle governs issues that are not regulated in an applicable international treaty and plays a pivotal role in determining the remedies available in ISDS.[84]

The *Chorzów Factory* principle "is precise, strict, and unchangeable as a principle, but flexible and useful in a myriad of different scenarios".[85] Its biggest advantage, however, sometimes transpires to be a disadvantage. Tribunals

---

79 Ibid [665].

80 Ibid.

81 Hydro v. Spain, ICSID Case No. ARB/15/42, Decision on Jurisdiction, Liability and Directions on Quantum (09.03.2020) [686].

82 Ibid [702].

83 Cavalum v. Spain, ICSID Case No. ARB/15/34, Decision on Jurisdiction, Liability and Directions on Quantum (31.08.2020) [659].

84 For example, the final sentence of the preamble to the VCLT: "Affirming that the rules of customary international law will continue to govern questions not regulated by the provisions of the present Convention".

85 Irmgard Marboe, Assessing Compensation and Damages in Expropriation versus Non-expropriation Cases, in: Christina L. Beharry (ed.), Contemporary and Emerging Issues on the Law of Damages and Valuation in International Investment Arbitration (Brill 2018), pp. 134-135. It is "a double-edged sword in the sense that it not only enables flexibility when responding to the variety of factual situations but also introduces subjectivity and discretion in the application of the legal principles" – Ripinsky, Williams, *supra* note 9, p. 21.

tend to simply refer briefly to the application of this CIL principle, using it as a "shortcut" which enables them to proceed to the calculation of compensation, having observed nothing more than that this is "consistent with the principles set forth" in the *Chorzów Factory* judgment.[86] This is confirmed in the cases analyzed here. In particular, the tribunals in *Foresight, RREEF, NextEra, InfraRed, BayWa, RWE, PV Investors, Hydro* and *Cavalum* seem to have taken this "shortcut" and made only a symbolic reference to the standard applicable to remedies and its content.

Nevertheless, the Spanish saga cases are a timid contribution to the debate on whether the ILC Articles apply in investor-state arbitrations. On the one hand, Part Two of the ILC Articles, relevant for remedies, "does not apply to obligations of reparation to the extent that these arise towards or are invoked by a person or entity other than a State".[87] This "is without prejudice to any right, arising from the international responsibility of a State, which may accrue directly to any person or entity other than a State".[88] On the other hand, the ILC Articles have been continuously relied upon by parties and tribunals in investor-state arbitrations.[89] This typically happens without much analysis of their direct applicability in cases other than inter-state disputes.

The analyzed cases are silent as to the theoretical justification for directly applying the ILC Articles in investor-state arbitration. Nevertheless, they support the view that the ILC Articles can be applied *mutatis mutandis*.[90] The Spanish saga tribunals had no doubt that the ILC Articles codify, rather than progressively develop, the CIL principle reflected in the *Chorzów Factory* judgment.[91] This was explicitly confirmed by the tribunals in *Eiser*,[92] *Novenergia*,[93]

---

86 As *per* the tribunal in Metaclad v. Mexico, ICSID Case No. ARB(AF)/97/1, Award (30.08.2000) [122].

87 ILC Articles, commentary to art. 28, para. 3, pp. 87–88, in similar vein: commentary to art. 33, para. 4, p. 95.

88 Art. 33(2) of the ILC Articles.

89 For example: S.D. Myers v. Canada, UNCITRAL, Partial Award (13.11.2000) [312]–[315], CME v. Czech Republic, UNCITRAL, Partial Award (13.01.2001) [583], Arif v. Moldova, ICSID Case No. ARB/11/23, Award (08.04.2013) [559].

90 De Brabandere describes that "the rules and principles relating to the forms of reparation [reflected in the *Chorzów Factory* judgment – author's note] are, however, similar when it is a nonstate entity that is entitled to invoke the responsibility of a state" – Eric De Brabandere, *supra* note 8, p. 178, fn 12. For broader considerations see: Filip Balcerzak, Investor – State Arbitration and Human Rights (Brill 2017), pp. 236–238.

91 Fn 9.

92 Fn 18, 19.

93 Fn 25.

Masdar,[94] *Antin*,[95] *Foresight*,[96] *RREEF*,[97] *OperaFund*.[98] The remaining cases simply took it for granted that the CIL principle is the same as the ILC Articles on that issue. In the words of the *SolEs* tribunal, Art. 31(1) of the ILC Articles is "to the same effect" as the *Chorzów Factory* judgment.[99]

1.3.1 First Lesson Learned – Restitution May Be Awarded in Investor-State Arbitrations, Although It Is Inappropriate in Cases concerning Violations of Investment Treaties Caused by Regulatory Changes, Given the Disproportionate Impact on a Sovereign State's Legislative Autonomy

The Spanish saga cases confirm that the CIL principle of full reparation, as enshrined in the *Chorzów Factory* judgment, serves as the starting point for analyzing remedies in investor-state arbitrations. Consequently, they also confirm the availability of restitution as the primary remedy in investor-state arbitrations.

This may be a surprising conclusion given that, in general, investor-state arbitral awards almost always comprise a compensation payment.[100] This was also the case in the Spanish saga cases, with the tribunals either awarding compensation or dismissing the claims altogether (see Chapter 4).

The above conclusion is not contradicted by the fact that none of the tribunals ordered restitution in any of these cases. Those tribunals which received requests for restitution confirmed that, at a general level, it fell within their mandate to order restitution. None of the tribunals which received requests for restitution denied the theoretical possibility of awarding restitution.

This is in line with the general case law. From a theoretical perspective, the availability of restitution in investor-state arbitration has been recognized for

94 Fn 30.

95 Fn 41.

96 Fn 46.

97 Fn 50.

98 Fn 66.

99 Fn 61.

100 Carole Malinvaud, Non-pecuniary Remedies in Investment Treaty and Commercial Arbitration, in: Albert Jan van den Berg (ed.), 50 Years of the New York Convention (Wolters Kluwer 2009), p. 210. Compensation is "perhaps the most commonly sought in international practice" in general, not only in investor-state arbitration See: ILC Articles, commentary to art. 36, para. 2, p. 99.

many years.[101] The tribunal in *von Pezold* actually ordered restitution.[102] Other tribunals, such as in the *Enron, Micula* and *Al-Bahloul* cases, confirmed that restitution is theoretically possible, even though they decided not to order restitution based on the facts of those cases.[103]

This should not come as a surprise, given the standard applicable to remedies under CIL. Pursuant to the *Chorzów Factory* judgment, restitution is the default remedy for any violation of a state's international obligations.[104] The "payment of a sum corresponding to the value which a restitution in kind would bear" should be awarded when restitution "is not possible", as is expressly stated in the *Chorzów Factory* judgment and recognized in Art. 35 of the ILC Articles, but also if restitution is "unavailable" or "inadequate".[105]

The tribunals considered restitution as inappropriate in the circumstances of the Spanish saga. This conclusion was arrived at mainly due to the nature of the Disputed Measures,[106] which concerned the legislative powers of a sovereign state. The *Eiser, Antin* and *Watkins* tribunals explicitly referred to their doubts concerning state sovereignty.[107]

The tribunals in *Masdar* and *Antin* expressly analyzed Art. 35 of the ILC Articles, which provides that restitution should be ordered unless it is not

101 For example: Christoph Schreuer, Non-Pecuniary Remedies in ICSID Arbitration, Arbitration International, 20:4 (2004), pp. 331–332. Resar and Cheng rightly argue that restitution becomes relevant even if compensation is awarded in a particular case, which however can open the gate for similar claims brought by other investors in the future – Alexander W. Resar, Tai-Heng Cheng, Investor State Arbitration in a Changing World Order (Brill 2021), pp. 46–47 (on p. 47 in particular: "a respondent state subject to an adverse award would face a decision to either make significant payments to multiple similarly-situated investors, or to modify/repeal the challenged state action").

102 Von Pezold v. Zimbabwe, ICSID Case No. ARB/10/15, Award (28.08.2015) [700], [723], in [1020.1] ordering restitution.

103 Enron v. Argentina, ICSID Case No. ARB/01/3, Decision on Jurisdiction (14.01.2004) [79, 81], Micula v. Romania, ICSID Case No. ARB/05/20, Award (11.12.2013) [1309]–[1311], Micula v. Romania, ICSID Case No. ARB/05/20, Decision on Jurisdiction and Admissibility (24.09.2008) [166]–[168], Al-Bahloul v. Tajikistan, SCC Case No. V 064/2008, Final Award (08.06.2010) [63].

104 There is a "primacy of restitution" – ILC Articles, commentary to art. 35, para. 3, p. 96. It is a "first-ranked" remedy – Thomas W. Wälde, Borzu Sabahi, Compensation, Damages and Valuation, in: Peter Muchlinski, Federico Ortino, Christoph Schreuer (eds.), The Oxford Handbook of International Investment Law (Oxford University Press 2008), p. 1057.

105 ILC Articles, commentary to art. 36, para. 3, p. 99.

106 In this Chapter, the term "Disputed Measures" refers jointly to: 2010 Disputed Measures, 2012 Disputed Measures and 2013–2014 Disputed Measures, as defined in Chapter 2.

107 Fn 20, 43, 75.

"materially impossible" or "does not involve a burden out of all proportion to the benefit deriving from restitution instead of compensation". However, even the other tribunals, which did not refer to Art. 35 of the ILC Articles, underlined that restitution was inappropriate given the nature of the disputed measures at hand. As correctly observed by the *Masdar* tribunal, it would be either impossible or at least extremely difficult to comply with an award that ordered restitution of previously applicable laws and regulations.[108]

Cube is the only of the analyzed cases where the tribunal arrived at a different conclusion, namely that restitution "is beyond the proper scope of the powers of the Tribunal".[109] However, this was stated by the tribunal which was not faced with a request for restitution and without the benefit of having heard the parties' arguments on that issue. Whilst, on its surface, it appears that the tribunal denied even the theoretical possibility of ordering restitution in investor-state arbitrations, a more careful reading suggests otherwise. The tribunal's conclusion was made in the context of restitution narrowed down to specific performance in the form of an order on how to shape a state's regulatory regime. This is, in fact, in line with all of the other cases, which concluded that specific performance on such terms should not be ordered. However, this does not preclude the general possibility of restitution in other, more appropriate circumstances.

The Spanish cases constitute an important contribution to the development of the case law, confirming that claimants can consider restitution as the primary remedy available. In some cases, involving the specific targeting of an individual investor, restitution may be awarded. This requires, however, that the claimants request restitution in the first place. The way in which claims are framed binds the tribunals, as they cannot go beyond the remedies actually sought by the claimants.[110]

All of the Spanish saga tribunals shared a similar concern about the interaction between state sovereignty and restitution sought in the context of treaty violations caused by changes to a generally applicable regulatory framework. Their decisions to dismiss requests for restitution were significantly influenced by concerns regarding state sovereignty. Indeed, such a concern weighs in favor of awarding compensation, as opposed to restitution. The *Masdar* tribunal explained that it undertook a balancing act between private and public interests when deciding on the appropriate remedy.

108 Fn 36.

109 Fn 54.

110 Wälde, Sabahi, *supra* note 104, p. 1059. This principle is expressed in the Latin maxim *non ultra petita*.

1.3.2 Second Lesson Learned – If Restitution Is Awarded, Art. 26(8) ECT Requires to Enable the Respondent to "Pay Monetary Damages in Lieu of" Restitution. It Is Recommended That, Even outside the ECT Context, Similar Reservations Are Made in the Operative Parts of Arbitral Awards in Order to Respect State Sovereignty

The "sovereignty concern" indeed cannot be ignored in the context of treaty violations caused by changes made to regulatory frameworks of general application, as occurred in the Spanish saga cases. It is reasonable to conclude that, when measures of such a nature are disputed, restitution can only become relevant in exceptional circumstances, when measures which operate under the guise of generally applicable legislation are actually implemented to target a specific, individual investor. In such a scenario, the ECT specifically provides a solution on how to mitigate the sovereignty concern. Art. 26(8) ECT provides that the respondent "may pay monetary damages in lieu of any other remedy granted".[111]

This should be reflected in the operative parts of arbitral awards that award restitution. This possibility not only responds to the need to respect state sovereignty, but it also mitigates the difficulty in executing awards that have ordered restitution. Whilst it would be either impossible, or at least extremely difficult, to execute an award that ordered restitution to be made by a sovereign state, any compensation awards for non-compliance with a restitution order are capable of being executed in other jurisdictions if necessary.

This is without prejudice to the fact that restitution may be awarded alongside compensation, not merely as an exclusive alternative.[112] This is particularly relevant in the analyzed context of RE. With respect to an income-generating business, such as RE power plants, restitution alone would not fully restore the claimants to their pre-infringement position, as it would fail to compensate for any income lost during the intervening period.[113] Restitution could then take place "in combination" with compensation, as is explicitly stated in Art. 34 of the ILC Articles. In some cases, this would be necessary to meet the CIL principle of full reparation, as found in the *Chorzów Factory* judgment.[114] Similarly, restitution should take place "in combination" with compensation if an expropriated asset has lost value since it was confiscated. Otherwise, returning the

---

111 Art. 26(8) ECT. Similar solution can be found for example in Art. 14.D.13(1)(b) USMCA, which replaced Art. 1135(1)(b) NAFTA worded similarly.

112 Von Pezold v. Zimbabwe, *supra* note 102 [925], [1020.2].

113 Rubins, Sinha, Roberts, *supra* note 9, pp. 172–173.

114 ILC Articles, commentary to art. 34, para. 2, p. 95.

asset to the claimant would place him in a worse position than if compensation was awarded.[115]

The availability of restitution as a remedy can potentially become relevant for yet another reason. The EC sought to actively participate in the Spanish saga cases. It argued, among others, that any compensation awarded by tribunals constitutes state aid. As such, it must be notified to the EC and may be found to be illegal under EU law, in which case Spain would be precluded from paying it.[116] In this context, restitution could be a factor which allows voluntary compliance with arbitral awards. The Special Regime was never found to constitute illegal state aid under EU law. Thus, restitution may provide a solution to the dilemma as to whether to pay an arbitral award, thereby violating EU state aid regulations, or to face attempts to execute the award in different jurisdiction around the globe.

2 Compensation

2.1 *General Comments*

Typically, BITs regulate the issue of compensation due for lawful expropriation. The level is frequently linked with the "fair market value" of the expropriated object, with the valuation date set immediately prior to expropriation and increased by the applicable interest rate. The ECT is no exception in this respect and contains precisely such a rule in Art. 13(1). However, this applies solely to lawful expropriation, and is inapplicable if the loss occurs as a result of treaty breaches. The CIL principles framed in the *Chorzów Factory* judgment apply where international law has been infringed, including any violation of the ECT and BITs. The CIL concept of "reparation" is divided into three subcategories: restitution (discussed earlier), compensation and satisfaction.[117] This section focuses on the Spanish saga tribunals' reasoning on the second form of reparation, namely compensation for treaty violations. Satisfaction has little, if any, relevance in the practice of investor-state arbitrations.[118]

The principle of full reparation does not provide guidelines on how to calculate compensation due following a treaty violation. It simply requires that

115 Rubins, Sinha, Roberts, *supra* note 9, pp. 172–173.

116 *Micula v. Romania* is notable for the enforcement issues related to the state aid.

117 Art. 34 of the ILC Articles.

118 A declaratory award is typically considered as a "paper victory" and as a *de facto* loss of a case, rather than obtaining a meaningful form of reparation. This is easily understandable considering the average costs of pursuing claims in investor-state arbitrations.

the claimant be put in the same situation as would have existed "but for" the breach.[119] This necessitates a comparison between the real-world situation ("actual scenario") and an alternative, counter-factual scenario ("but-for scenario"), which would have existed if no violation of international law had occurred.

Within this legal framework, arbitral tribunals are required to choose which methodology to apply when valuing compensation. Whilst this choice is largely fact-driven, some general comments can be made on the methodologies typically available in investor-state arbitrations. They are helpful to understand the foregoing analysis.

From a theoretical perspective, the valuation methodologies can be divided into: (i) backward-looking, and (ii) forward-looking.[120]

As regards the first group, the most common methodology is based on amounts actually invested ("sunk costs"), with the aim being to restore these amounts to the investor.[121] The obvious advantage of this method is its certainty and the absence of any element of speculation, since the valuation is based on actual figures.[122] The disadvantage is that awarding sunk costs fails to compensate for lost profits.[123] As such, it may be questioned whether it achieves the goal required under CIL, namely to place the claimant in the situation it would have been in "but for" the treaty breach. It is unlikely that a reasonable business actor would decide to make an investment with the aim of merely receiving back the amounts actually invested, generally after some considerable delay.

119 Marboe, *supra* note 85, pp. 126–127.

120 Rubins, Sinha, Roberts, *supra* note 9, p. 185, Ripinsky, Williams, *supra* note 9, pp.193, 214.

121 See for example: Bear Creek v. Peru, ICSID Case No. ARB/14/21, Award (30.11.2017) [604], South American Silver v. Bolivia, PCA Case No. 2013-5, Award (22.11.2018) [866], Caratube v. Kazakhstan, ICSID Case No. ARB/13/13, Award (27.09.2017) [1164].

122 Wälde, Sabahi, *supra* note 104, pp. 1072–1073.

123 Ibid, p. 1066, in the context of the backward-looking methodologies and the classic division between *damnum emergens* and *lucrum cessans*. On p. 1073 they present an example of investment in searching for petroleum. Whereas most exploration wells are unsuccessful (dry), they:

> get compensated by the few successful results of a drilling campaign. This means that the value of the successful exploration is – often by a multiple – much more than the expenditures incurred. In essence, expenses have either to be multiplied by the exploration risk (historic method) or in this situation (and other comparable situations where a particular high risk is overcome) one needs to look at comparable transactions and forecasts of future income. A combination of historic cost (adjusted by exploration risk), future income, and market-value-based valuations is here called for.

This disadvantage of the sunk costs can be potentially mitigated by pre-award interest.[124] As stipulated in Art. 38 of the ILC Articles, interest may be "necessary in order to ensure full reparation".[125] Pre-award interest "should compensate a claimant for the deprivation of money owed to it between the date of the harm suffered and the award"[126] and should reflect the "cost of money that a lender is willing to be paid to part with his money for a given period of time".[127] Therefore, pre-award interest reflects the time value of money and the decreasing purchasing power of money over time, but it still fails to account for situations where profits are either reduced or non-existent.

Other backward-looking methodologies entail asset-based valuations. This consists in applying book value, replacement value and liquidation value methodologies. A common feature of these methodologies is that they value investments by summing-up their individual assets.[128] The first of these can easily be classified as a backward-looking methodology.[129] Whereas classification of the remaining two asset-based methodologies is less clear, they can also be perceived as backward-looking.[130]

As regards the second group, forward-looking valuation methodologies are typically divided between: (i) income-based and (ii) market-based.[131]

The first of these is often described as the Discounted Cash Flow ("DCF") method. It determines the present value of anticipated future cash flows of an

124 For example, their purpose has been described as being to "ensure full reparation in accordance with the Chorzów principle" – Inna Uchkunova, Oleg Temnikov, A Procrustean Bed: Pre- and Post-award Interest in ICSID Arbitration ICSID Review – Foreign Investment Law Journal, 29:3 (2014), p. 651. See also for example: Occidental v. Ecuador, ICSID Case No. ARB/06/11, Award (05.10.2012) [834], Vivendi v. Argentina, ICSID Case No. ARB/97/3, Award (20.08.2007) [9.2.6].

125 ILC Articles, commentary to art. 38, para. 7, p. 108, *a contrario* commentary to art. 36, para. 33, p. 105.

126 Christina L. Beharry, Prejudgment Interest Rates in International Investment Arbitration, Journal of International Dispute Settlement 8:1 (2016), pp. 56–57. Gotanda defines interest as compensation "for the temporary withholding of money" or "for the loss of the use of money". See: John Y. Gotanda, Compound interest in international disputes, Law and Policy in International Business, 34:2 (2003), pp. 395–396.

127 Beharry, ibid, p. 61. In words of the tribunal in *Quiborax v. Bolivia*, it compensates for that the claimants "were not in possession of the funds to which they were entitled and thus had either to borrow funds at a cost or were deprived of the opportunity of investing these funds at a profit" – Quiborax v. Bolivia, ICSID Case No. ARB/06/2, Award (16.09.2015) [513].

128 Ripinsky, Williams, *supra* note 9, pp. 218–222.

129 Rubins, Sinha, Roberts, *supra* note 9, p. 198.

130 Ibid, p. 199.

131 Some have expressed the opinion that the market-based methodology should be classified as backward-looking – Wälde, Sabahi, *supra* note 104, pp. 1070–1071, 1074.

investment during its operational lifetime.[132] It values the fair market value of a "going concern".[133] As such, DCF requires an ability to forecast future earnings based on past performance. It calculates lost profits which were expected to be generated, but which failed to materialize due to the treaty violation.[134]

Whilst DCF "computes the present value of the business's future earnings" in a direct manner, the market-based methodology does so indirectly, by incorporating "market values of comparable businesses".[135] It determines the value of the disputed investment by comparing it to similar investments, traded on the open market. As such, the obvious condition of its applicability is that comparable transactions exist. They can concern similar projects or even companies, if they refer to SPVs.[136]

There is a degree of subjectivity in forward-looking methodologies, but this does not preclude their application.[137] They are commonly used in business reality, outside the context of litigation or arbitration.[138] By way of example, natural resources industry standards for the valuation of mineral properties foresee the application of both the DCF and the market-based methodology in relation to projects at a certain stage of development.[139]

---

132 Ripinsky, Williams, *supra* note 9, p. 195. See also for example: Garrett Rush, Kiran Sequeira, Matthew Shopp, Valuation Techniques for Early-Stage Businesses in Investor-State Arbitration, in: Christina L. Beharry (ed.), Contemporary and Emerging Issues on the Law of Damages and Valuation in International Investment Arbitration (Brill 2018), p. 273.

133 Whilst this seems to be the prevailing approach of tribunals in investor-state arbitrations, it is not necessarily a pre-condition of the DCF from the financial perspective – Kai F. Schumacher, Henner Klönne, Discounted Cash Flow Method, in: Christina L. Beharry (ed.), Contemporary and Emerging Issues on the Law of Damages and Valuation in International Investment Arbitration (Brill 2018), p. 212.

134 Ripinsky, Williams, *supra* note 9, pp. 279, 289.

135 Ibid, p. 212.

136 "Market capitalization", based on shares price on the stock market, could also be classified as a market-based methodology – Rubins, Sinha, Roberts, *supra* note 9, p. 190.

137 Ibid, p. 200.

138 Rush, Sequeira, Shopp, *supra* note 132, pp. 262, 288, Schumacher, Klönne, *supra* note 133, p. 207.

139 For example, the CIMVal Standards and Guidelines 2003 provide that income-based and market-based methodologies can be applied to any type of mineral property save for an exploration property (Standards and Guidelines for Valuation of Mineral Properties issued by the Special Committee of the Canadian Institute of Mining, Metallurgy and Petroleum on Valuation of Mineral Properties, available at: https://mrmr.cim.org/media/1020/cimval-standards-guidelines.pdf, p. 22). This was confirmed in the CIMVal Code 2019 (The CIMVal Code for the Valuation of Mineral Properties, available at: https://mrmr.cim.org/media/1135/cimval-code-november2019.pdf, p. 16). The same approach has been adopted, for example, in the Polish Code for the Valuation of Mineral Assets (the POLVAL Code

There is a visible reluctancy within arbitral tribunals to apply forward-looking methodologies to early-stage projects. This is notable in particular regarding attempts to apply the DCF to investments which have a short or no operating history and, as a result, a short or no track record of generating income. By way of example, when faced with requests to apply the DCF to investments that had no track record, the DCF was perceived as "too speculative and uncertain",[140] "unattractive and speculative",[141] or as requiring "too many unsubstantiated assumptions" and being "overly speculative".[142] The tribunal in *Caratube v. Kazakhstan* underlined that the DCF requires that the investment be "a going concern with a proven record of profitability".[143]

In similar circumstances, the market-based methodology is also repeatedly considered inappropriate. Often, the identified comparable transactions are considered to be too remote to justify its application. They may be "not sufficiently comparable",[144] but also may not "support a clear conclusion" that they are comparable.[145]

2.2 *Spanish Saga Case Law*

As analyzed in Chapter 4, the tribunals varied in their conclusions on whether the legitimate expectations that existed in the Spanish saga protected against any drastic changes being made to the regulatory framework, or only if such reforms failed to maintain the RRR. This, in turn, had a direct impact on the analysis of compensation in the cases.

…

2.2.1 Charanne and Isolux

The *Charanne*[146] and *Isolux*[147] tribunals, having dismissed the claims on the merits, did not analyze the issue of compensation.

2008, available at: http://polval.org.pl/wp-content/uploads/2019/05/1-wersja-angielska.pdf, p. A-30).

140 Bear Creek v. Peru, *supra* note 121 [604].

141 Khan v. Mongolia, PCA Case No.2011-09, Award on the Merits (02.03.2015) [392].

142 Al-Bahloul v. Tajikistan, *supra* note 103 [96]–[97].

143 Caratube v. Kazakhstan, *supra* note 121 [1094]–[1095].

144 Khan v. Mongolia, *supra* note 141 [398].

145 South American Silver v. Bolivia, *supra* note 121 [838], similarly: Caratube v. Kazakhstan, *supra* note 121 [1133].

146 Charanne v. Spain, *supra* note 14.

147 Isolux v. Spain, *supra* note 15.

2.2.2 Eiser

2.2.2.1 *Methodology and Calculations*

In *Eiser*, the tribunal decided that the appropriate method to determine the amount of compensation is to assess "the reduction of the fair market value of its investment by calculating the present value of cash flows said to have been lost on account of the disputed measures".[148] The respondent's objection to the DCF was "unwarranted". For the tribunal, DCF was an appropriate and effective method in valuating a "business operating as a going concern prior to adverse government actions".[149] It added that, even if no expropriation was found to have taken place, "the calculation of damages involves a comparable assessment of potential future revenues of a going concern with predictable capital and operating costs and cash flows".[150]

The calculations of experts relied upon by both parties "involved relatively similar projected future cashflows".[151] The tribunal then analyzed three inputs that were relevant for the calculations.[152] As regards the operational life of the CSP plants in question, the claimants did not discharge the burden of proof that it extended to 40 years. The tribunal applied a 25-year period instead.[153] As regards loss from regulatory changes prior to June 2014, the tribunal ruled that its decision on liability does not encompass these claims and that the respondent "crossed the line" in June 2014.[154] This decision was in line with the tribunal's decision that it lacked jurisdiction over claims involving the IVPEE.[155] The claim for lost future cash flows (for the period after June 2014) was upheld.[156]

The tribunal added that "in a case of such scope and complexity damages cannot be determined with mechanical precision".[157] The reasonableness of the conclusions based on DCF was confirmed by a "reality check" involving a comparison with the amounts actually invested (sunk costs).[158]

The disputed CSP plants started generating electricity in 2012.[159] The award does not suggest that the short (under 2.5 years) track record of

148 Eiser v. Spain, *supra* note 16 [441].
149 Ibid [465].
150 Ibid.
151 Ibid [439].
152 Ibid [442].
153 Ibid [446], [451], [452].
154 Ibid [457]–[458].
155 Ibid [459].
156 Ibid [460].
157 Ibid [473].
158 Ibid [474].
159 Ibid [229].

generating energy prior to the valuation date was argued against applying the DCF.

2.2.2.2 *Tax Gross-Up*

As regards the tax gross-up claim, the claimants argued that the recovery should be "net of taxes", such as income tax in the home state. However, they failed to provide evidence "establishing the nature, rate or amount of any tax that might be due".[160] The tribunal decided that the burden of proof was not met, so it "can make no decision as to whether or not" the claim for the tax gross-up "might be appropriate".[161]

2.2.3 Novenergia

2.2.3.1 *Methodology and Calculations*

In the *Novenergia* case, the tribunal applied the DCF, considering it as "generally an appropriate starting point",[162] which "is based on fundamental principles of economic and finance and is regarded by many as the preferred method for valuation of income-earning assets".[163] The DCF was well-suited because the cash flow capabilities of the PV plants affected by the violations of the ECT had a track record of 8 years (2008–2016, i.e. since they commenced operations until the date of issuing the award).[164] Moreover, the tribunal considered the DCF as particularly suitable for valuating income-streams regarding regulated, as opposed to unregulated, businesses which are more exposed to market fluctuations.[165]

The DCF calculation revealed two figures: historical damages from the date of the ECT breach until 15.09.2016 (the date of the DCF valuation, based on the estimated foregone cash flow from 01.2011 to 09.2016) and the fair market value of the investment on 15.09.2016 (based on its estimated value to its shareholders on 15.09.2016).[166]

The tribunal analyzed and dismissed all of the corrections suggested by the respondent's experts to the claimant's experts' DCF calculations. The tribunal saw no reason to include a risk premium, to add an illiquidity discount

---

160 Ibid [453].
161 Ibid [456].
162 Novenergia v. Spain, *supra* note 21 [821].
163 Ibid [818].
164 Ibid [820].
165 Ibid.
166 Ibid [814]–[815].

(considering the exit times as normal) or to assume operating costs other than actual costs.[167]

From the overall outcome of the DCF calculations, the tribunal deducted compensation corresponding to IVPEE (which was outside the scope of the tribunal's jurisdiction) and to periods prior to 2013 (i.e. the date on which the tribunal determined as the date of the ECT violation).[168]

2.2.4 Masdar

2.2.4.1 *Methodology and Calculations*

The *Masdar* tribunal relied on Art. 36(1) of the ILC Articles and noted that the principle of full reparation requires putting the claimant "into a position that would have existed but for the breach". Only damages which are not "financially assessable", such as moral damages, remain outside this scope.[169] Thus, compensation should reflect the reduction in the fair market value of the investment which resulted from the ECT violation.[170]

The tribunal rejected objections to applying the DCF. It underlined that both the DCF and the asset-based valuation (argued for by Spain) "are widely accepted in valuation theory" and used by tribunals in investor-state arbitrations. There is no presumption against applying the DCF (or disfavoring DCF). On the contrary, "the DCF valuation method is presumptively appropriate, absent persuasive reasons making it inappropriate in particular cases".[171] This conclusion remains valid even though the DCF implies more complex calculations than the asset-based methods. It is to be decided on a case-by-case basis, depending on the circumstances of each case, whether the DCF method is appropriate.[172] In this sense, tribunals "enjoy a wide margin of discretion" as to which valuation method they adopt to quantify the compensation which seeks to provide full reparation.[173]

The tribunal underlined that there is always uncertainty associated with valuation "and that it is unrealistic to expect or demand absolute certainty".[174] It quoted the *Eiser* tribunal's comment that "in a case of such scope and complexity damages cannot be determined with mechanical precision".[175] It then

167 Ibid [832]–[836].
168 Ibid [838]–[841].
169 Masdar v. Spain, *supra* note 11 [565].
170 Ibid [566].
171 Ibid [575].
172 Ibid [577].
173 Ibid [578].
174 Ibid [576].
175 Ibid [653].

dismissed the respondent's argument that the benchmark for damage valuation should be "confidence approaching absolute certainty".[176] Certainty or standards of proof which apply to issues of liability are inapplicable to valuations of compensation, which involve assumptions about events that did not occur.[177]

The tribunal explained that the standard of compensation for a violation of the ECT, as well as the method of quantifying such compensation, are prescribed by international law. As such, they are independent of domestic case law, in which the Spanish judiciary rejected the DCF method.[178]

The tribunal applied the DCF to assess the fair market value of the claimant's investments.[179] It decided that the disputed CSP plants were "going concerns" for the purposes of the DCF method, even though they had only for operated for a "relatively short period of time" prior to the Disputed Measures.[180] In this case, it was just over 1 year since the plants first supplied electricity into the grid until the moment the notice of dispute was filed,[181] and 2.5 years until the valuation date set by the tribunal.[182] This operating period was sufficient for the tribunal to generate adequate information to calculate future income with reasonable certainty.[183] The tribunal observed that the power plants "rely on a relatively simple business model – limited only to generating electricity, pursuant to generally stable parameters. Both income generated and costs incurred are relatively predictable in the renewable energy sector".[184]

None of other objections raised by the respondent (such as the fact that the claimant's investments are capital intensive, "supposedly" financed with "excessive leverage", the alleged disproportionality between sunk costs and the level of claimed damages, the long time frame of predictions, fluctuations in production, the need for estimations and predictions regarding future assets) precluded the application of the DCF method.[185] The respondent's experts

176 Ibid [576].

177 Ibid [577].

178 Ibid [579]–[580].

179 Ibid [581], [587].

180 Ibid [581].

181 Ibid [96], [98]–[100]. One of the three CSP plants was registered in the RAIPRE on 29.04.2011 and started supplying electricity to the grid on 01.05.2011, whereas the other two were registered in the RAIPRE on 23.12.2011 and started supplying electricity to the grid on 01.01.2012. The claimant filed the notice of dispute on 19.02.2013, following the entry into force of Law 15/2012 on 01.01.2013.

182 Ibid [608]. The valuation date was established as 20.06.2014.

183 Ibid [581].

184 Ibid [582].

185 Ibid [583]–[585].

presented their own DCF calculations, which, in the tribunal's assessment, evidenced that "the DCF method does not necessarily yield inflated valuations, but rather requires a careful analysis of the reasonableness of the factual assumptions and estimates used for such a calculation".[186]

The tribunal analyzed the assumptions underpinning the DCF calculations and rejected some of them.[187] It rejected the claimant's position that the operational life of the CSP plants is 40 years and reduced the assumed operational life to 25 years.[188] It also removed the impact of the IVPEE from the calculations, given its decision on jurisdiction,[189] and modified the assumption about the choice between the FIT and Premium.[190]

In line with its decision on liability, the tribunal dismissed alternative damage calculations (i.e. limiting compensation to the RRR) as "misplaced" because Art. 10(1) ECT does not entitle the claimant to the RRR, but to the FET.[191]

The valuation date, which "determines the point in time relative to which the fair market value of an asset is assessed" and "generally limits information to be taken into account to that available at that date", was established as 20.06.2014, namely the publication date of Order IET/1045/2014.[192]

2.2.5 Antin

2.2.5.1 *Methodology and Calculations*

In the *Antin* case, the tribunal agreed that the DCF method was appropriate.[193] It observed that "there are no right or wrong valuation methods", and that different methods may be appropriate due to the specific circumstances of a particular case. It added that "the DCF method is one of the most commonly used methods to value businesses and companies".[194]

It rejected the respondent's objection to using the DCF and arguments in favor of applying an asset-based valuation.[195] First, 5 years of operation of the power plants in question sufficed to dismiss the objection to the DCF applying to projects "that are not in operation or at very early stages of operation

186 Ibid [586].
187 Ibid [588], [599].
188 Ibid [618].
189 Ibid [621].
190 Ibid [632]. "FIT" and "Premium" as defined in Chapter 2.
191 Ibid [591].
192 Ibid [601], [605].
193 Antin v. Spain, *supra* note 12 [675], [691].
194 Ibid [688].
195 Ibid [654], [688].

and therefore lack a suitable track record of their performance".[196] Second, RE power plants (similarly as conventional ones) "have a relatively simple business, producing electricity, whose demand and long-run value can be analysed and modelled in detail, based on readily available data".[197] This led the tribunal to decide that the disputed plants were not "business concerns having a short performance record and subject to several variables that are difficult to forecast".[198] The tribunal added that the DCF has many variables and some of them, such as inflation or interest rates, may be difficult to predict in the long term. However, this applies to any forecast, not only to the DCF, and does not preclude the application of the DCF.[199]

The tribunal essentially followed the calculations submitted by the claimants' experts, albeit after introducing some corrections.[200] The respondent's expert reports were very much tied to its position on the merits and failed when the tribunal rejected it.[201] As regards the corrections, first the tribunal rejected the claim for "historic losses" (for the period prior to June 2014) because the valuation date was established as June 2014.[202] Second, it rejected the claim for a "tax gross up" given the lack of evidence on the record to prove the type and amount of taxes that may be due on the compensation award.[203] Third, it reduced the operational lifetime of the plants to 25 years (instead of 40 years), noting that the claimants had not discharged the burden of proof on that issue.[204]

2.2.6 Foresight

2.2.6.1 *Methodology and Calculations*

In *Foresight*, the claimants sought compensation representing "the diminution in the fair market value of their equity in the PV facilities" resulting from the violation of the ECT.[205] The tribunal also decided that the DCF was appropriate.[206] However, it quoted the reservation made by the *Eiser* tribunal that

196 Ibid [689].
197 Ibid, quoting an expert report on this issue.
198 Ibid.
199 Ibid [690].
200 Ibid [724].
201 Ibid [690], [723].
202 Ibid [667].
203 Ibid [673].
204 Ibid [707], [713].
205 Foresight v. Spain, *supra* note 46 [473].
206 Ibid [474].

"in a case of such scope and complexity damages cannot be determined with mechanical precision".[207]

The tribunal disagreed with the respondent's arguments that the DCF was "too speculative".[208] It observed that this method "is routinely used in the PV industry because of the predictability of PV facilities".[209] The tribunal observed that "up to five years of operating history" was sufficient to apply the DCF.[210] However, the track record of 4 years was actually used in the calculations.[211]

Thus, the tribunal compared the hypothetical market value of the claimants' equity interest in the but-for scenario with the market value in the actual scenario.[212] For the actual scenario, the "arms' length sales prices" were used, given that the claimants' sold their investments during the arbitration.[213]

The valuation date was established as 30.06.2014, namely at "the end of the quarter in which the New Regulatory Regime was finalized".[214]

The tribunal based its decision on the claimants' expert DCF calculations, although it modified some of the underlying assumptions.[215] First, it reduced the expected operational lifetime of the plants from 35 years to 30 years.[216] Second, it excluded the taxation measures from the calculations. Third, it eliminated from its calculations the Disputed Measures that predated the valuation date. Even though some retroactive effect of the Disputed Measures was not compensated as a result, this was a "direct consequence" of the claimants' decision not to present a break-down of losses caused separately by each Disputed Measure.[217] Interestingly, the tribunal accepted calculations with reduced corporate income tax, i.e. applicable as per the changes introduced in November 2014, "shortly after" the valuation date.[218]

The tribunal dismissed the respondent's argument that the regulatory risk was lower after the Disputed Measures were introduced.[219] Similarly, it disagreed with the argument that the claimants should receive no compensation

207 Ibid [530].
208 Ibid [477].
209 Ibid [478], [480].
210 Ibid [478].
211 Ibid [490]: "[…] based on each company's average historical production in each full year from 2011 through the end of 2014. […]".
212 Ibid [489].
213 Ibid [492], [513].
214 Ibid [489].
215 Ibid [506].
216 Ibid [517], [539].
217 Ibid [536], [538].
218 Ibid [522].
219 Ibid [525]–[526].

because the PV plants in question remained profitable even after the Disputed Measures were adopted. To give no compensation "misses the point" since the purpose of damages is to "eliminate the consequences of the Respondent's breach".[220]

The tribunal agreed that the sunk costs may serve as a useful "reality check" as to whether or not the damages sought are reasonable. The difference in amounts was considered to be reasonable in this case. However, the tribunal compared not the actually paid amounts, but rather the value of the acquired equity on the valuation date, which increased over time.[221]

2.2.7 RREEF

The *RREEF* tribunal made it clear that compensation for the retroactive application of the New Regime must be evaluated autonomously, as otherwise this would result in double-compensation.[222]

2.2.7.1 *Methodology and Calculations*

The tribunal's approach to damages departed from the previous awards rendered in the Spanish saga. In those previous cases, the tribunals had adopted an "either/or" approach to damages. If a tribunal concluded that a violation of the ECT had occurred, it awarded "full reparation of the losses suffered", whereas if no violation was found, no compensation was awarded. The *RREEF* tribunal adopted an alternative approach, explained by its decision on liability. The claimants were not "immune" from reasonable changes being made to the regulatory framework, and compensation was due only for reforms that went beyond what was reasonable.[223] It disagreed with the *Eiser* award, in which the investors were "integrally compensated" for losses caused by the New Regime, even though the tribunal in that case shared the view that they could not have reasonably expected the regulatory regime to remain completely unchanged.[224] Thus, compensation was calculated as the decreased threshold of the RRR, and not the total decrease of profits resulting from adoption of the New Regime.[225]

The RRR targeted by Spanish law corresponded to the IRR, understood as the average annual returns of a project based on cash flows generated by the project over its entire lifespan. Therefore, the tribunal considered the IRR as an

---

220 Ibid [533].
221 Ibid [534]–[535].
222 RREEF v. Spain, *supra* note 50 [483].
223 Ibid [515].
224 Ibid [517].
225 Ibid [523].

indicator of the project's profitability.[226] The tribunal did not decide whether there exists a "general principle" defining a RRR. It decided that, in this case, "this rule must be applied since it is consecrated in the relevant applicable texts". As such, it must be defined in accordance with Spanish law, and therefore based on the LSE.[227] The tribunal clarified that this is the project's, and not the shareholders', IRR.[228] This excluded from the analysis any premium paid by the claimants to acquire the investments.[229] Therefore, the fact that the plants were sold during the arbitral proceedings did not affect the calculations, although it was a factual element which could be useful in assessing the market value of the investment and the reasonableness of the return.[230] The lifespan of the disputed plants was decided to be 25 years.[231]

Even though the IRR under the Special Regime was higher than under the New Regime, the tribunal considered this this fact alone was insufficient to find the Disputed Measures unreasonable. What is reasonable may vary over time and reasonableness is not an absolute notion in this context.[232]

In its calculations of the IRR, the tribunal included the IVPEE, even though it lacked jurisdiction to assess the validity of the 7% levy *per se*. The levy constituted a cost which impacted the IRR.[233]

In its calculations, the tribunal referred to the weighted average cost of capital ("WACC"), since the LSE referred to the cost of money in the capital market.[234]

The tribunal determined the date relevant for WACC calculations, financial structure (debt/equity), country risk premium, market risk premium and the risk-free rate linked to Spanish bonds.[235] Based on these assumptions, the tribunal calculated the WACC as 5.86%.[236] The tribunal decided that, based on the facts of this particular case, the claimants had a legitimate expectation that the return on their investment would exceed the basic WACC level, as Spain had attracted RE investments by raising hope of above-average profits.[237] It

226 Ibid [520]–[521].
227 Ibid [524].
228 Ibid [545].
229 Ibid [546].
230 Ibid [550], [573].
231 Ibid [549].
232 Ibid [567].
233 Ibid [571].
234 Ibid [574].
235 Ibid [576]–[585].
236 Ibid [586].
237 Ibid [587].

considered 1% as a "fair addition" to the WACC and determined that the RRR could not fall below 6.86% post-tax.[238]

The tribunal differentiated between the CSP plants and Wind energy plants in which the claimants had invested. With respect to the CSP plants, the actual return earned under the New Regime did not meet the RRR threshold. Consequently, the tribunal decided that Spain had violated its obligation to ensure the RRR, which in turn triggered an obligation to pay compensation amounting to the difference between the actual return and the RRR.[239] This calculation included compensation for the New Regime's retroactivity.[240]

With respect to the Wind energy plants, the new IRR was considered reasonable (13% pre-tax compared to the 7.398% post-tax target under the New Regime).[241] As a result, the compensation covered only the loss caused by the New Regime's retroactivity.[242]

2.2.7.2 *Joint Experts' Report*

The tribunal decided that it was unable to make the calculations necessary to determine the actual IRR for each of the disputed CSP plants investments, and for the impact of the retroactive application of the New Regime to the Wind energy plants.[243] It invited the parties to seek an agreement on the calculations, failing which the tribunal itself would appoint an expert.[244] The tribunal received mutually agreed models prepared by the parties' experts, which allowed it to determine the amounts due.[245]

2.2.7.3 *Tax Gross-Up*

The tribunal rejected the claim for a tax gross-up. It observed that any profits under the Special Regime would be subject to taxation, such as awarded compensation.[246] It added that the claim was uncertain and hypothetical, as insufficient evidence had been provided by the claimants.[247]

238 Ibid [588]–[589].
239 Ibid [589].
240 Ibid [590].
241 Ibid [569].
242 Ibid [591].
243 Ibid [592].
244 Ibid [597].
245 RREEF v. Spain, ICSID Case No. ARB/13/30, Award (11.12.2019) [13].
246 Ibid [54].
247 Ibid [55].

2.2.8 RREEF – Dissenting Opinion

In a dissenting opinion, one arbitrator disagreed with the approach to calculating damages. He did not endorse the majority's criticism of the approach to compensation adopted by previous tribunals. Even though he agreed with the majority that "it is only to the extent that the modifications would have exceeded the limits of what is reasonable that compensation would be due and should be calculated", it was logical to follow the previous pattern of awarding the difference of profits under the Special Regime and the New Regime, because at the relevant time the cost of capital had not changed, whilst such change was necessary to justify changes to the RRR level.[248] This would have allowed due compensation to be calculated without the additional stage and for a joint model to be prepared by the experts.[249]

2.2.9 Cube

2.2.9.1 *Methodology and Calculations*

The tribunal in *Cube* accepted the DCF and rejected the argument that the cost-based approach is more appropriate.[250] The tribunal viewed the DCF as "now well established in the practice of international investment tribunals".[251] This case concerned "performance of specific plants which had an operating history, even if relatively short, in a highly-regulated industry" and it "addresses the specific impact of the disputed measures in terms of the loss of cash flows to those plants".[252] The essence of the dispute related to the difference between the cash flows under the two regimes, both of which set-up detailed formulas applicable for many years, which provided a basis for estimating cash flows.[253]

The tribunal viewed its task as being to estimate the harm caused by the violation of the ECT, which did not mean that the but-for scenario should be one where no regulatory changes were ever made. Some adjustment to the Special Regime was inevitable and would not have amounted to a violation of

248 RREEF v. Spain, ICSID Case No. ARB/13/30, Partially Dissenting Opinion of Professor Robert Volterra to the Decision on Responsibility and the Principles of Quantum (30.11.2018) [42]–[44].

249 Ibid [49]. He distinguished situations when additional fact-finding is necessary, from merely calculating damages.

250 Cube v. Spain, *supra* note 52 [473]–[474].

251 Ibid [478].

252 Ibid.

253 Ibid.

the ECT.[254] The tribunal did not intend to second-guess how the government might alternatively have constructed its national regulatory system so as to comply with the ECT.[255] Instead, it applied a discounted rate, by adjusting the projected cash flows to take account of regulatory risk.[256] The loss suffered was understood as the difference in the cash flows that the claimants reasonably expected under the Special Regime with those reasonably expected under the New Regime.

The tribunal noted that the respondent's RRR-based arguments referred to the original cost of the investment by the greenfield investor. Even if one agreed that the RRR on that investment materialized, it was received by the previous owners (who developed the project), rather than the claimants, who acquired it later, once it was already operational. The tribunal had no doubt that the ECT's protection extends over "brownfield investors for the actual investment they made", and is not limited to greenfield investors.[257]

The valuation date was established as 20.06.2014.[258] When calculating compensation, the tribunal rejected claims related to measures before that date and those related to taxes (which fell outside its scope of jurisdiction).[259] With respect to the disputed PV plants, it shortened the estimated operational life of these plants to 30 years, as opposed to 35 years.[260]

The tribunal adopted a different approach with respect to calculations concerning the disputed Hydro energy plants. The lifetime of such plants is different, as the durations of the respective concessions ranged from 25 to 75 years, with the average being approximately 45 years.[261] Thus, the tribunal considered it necessary to reflect the fact that a reasonable investor, when investing in 2011–2012 in Hydro energy plants, would have had a certain "apprehension" that the regulatory regime might change. However, the tribunal decided to take a different approach and, rather than simply reducing the operational life expectations of the plants, it chose to apply an additional discount to reflect the existence of regulatory risk.[262] This was "of a different order of magnitude" than the reduction of the operational lifetime expectations related to the PV

254 Ibid [464].
255 Ibid [465].
256 Ibid [466]–[467].
257 Ibid [475].
258 Ibid [477], [489].
259 Ibid [482].
260 Ibid [493]–[495].
261 Ibid [505].
262 Ibid [507], [509].

plants.[263] The tribunal did not accept that the regulatory changes "conferred a net benefit on investors". It considered those changes as being so radical that the investor's trust was adversely affected.[264] It acknowledged that the regulatory changes "offered the prospect of a more stable regime for electricity pricing and, in consequence, less pressure to amend the regime further", although not to such an extent that it would lower the regulatory risk in the actual scenario below that which existed in the but-for scenario.[265]

2.2.9.2 *Joint Experts' Report*

Consequently, as regards the disputed Hydro energy plants, the tribunal applied the "revenue haircut" by reducing the amount of compensation by 40%.[266] It ordered the parties' experts to implement this decision by submitting a joint report reflecting this reduction.[267] Initially, the experts were unable to agree on how to apply this adjustment.[268] After the tribunal's clarifications, the experts ultimately submitted a joint report.[269]

2.2.10 NextEra

2.2.10.1 *Methodology and Calculations*

The *NextEra* tribunal acknowledged that the DCF is "frequently invoked" and "has been applied by tribunals". A critical element for its application is "finding an appropriate base for the forecast of future earnings".[270]

The tribunal rejected the approach proposed by the claimants that long-term earnings can be based on the Special Regime, since changes to the regulatory framework "might have occurred", and the legitimate expectation was only that there would not be "a substantial or fundamental" change to the regulatory framework.[271]

The case concerned CSP plants which operated for less than 1 year.[272] This limited period of generating profits was insufficient to enable the DCF analysis to be applied, because there was "no obvious starting point for the "but for"

263 Ibid [508].
264 Ibid [511].
265 Ibid [512].
266 Ibid [529].
267 Ibid [532].
268 Cube v. Spain, ICSID Case No. ARB/15/20, Award (15.07.2019) [21].
269 Ibid [22]–[23].
270 Ibid [643].
271 Ibid [645]–[646].
272 NextEra v. Spain, *supra* note 55 [643].

analysis".[273] The tribunal applied the asset-based method, relying on the RRR "on that value".[274]

The parties agreed that the project's WACC was an appropriate basis to calculate the RRR, but disagreed on whether it should be supplemented by a premium.[275] The tribunal found that a premium was appropriate (noting that Spain's authorities themselves had tried to attract investors by promising returns equivalent to WACC, increased by a premium).[276] The tribunal observed that there is "no consistent practice of fixing the premium at 300bps in European jurisdictions that provide for a premium when calculating a return on investment in regulated sectors".[277] It declined to adopt the 300 basis points argued for by the claimants, and applied 200 basis points.[278] It then "left open the precise quantification of damages" and invited the claimants to recalculate their damages within 10 days of receiving the decision, which materialized as requested.[279]

The valuation date was originally proposed as 30.06.2014, but then amended to 30.06.2016 as the responded did not object.[280]

The tribunal took into account the value of the claimants' sunk costs.[281] Disputed elements, such as third-party financing costs, intercompany costs and investments in related companies were included as elements of these sunk costs.[282] The impact of the claimants' debt restructuring was not included in the calculation of damages, as the tribunal was not in a position to assess whether the options chosen by the claimants constituted the best arrangement for its restructuring.[283]

2.2.11 9REN

2.2.11.1 *Methodology and Calculations*

The *9REN* tribunal also considered the DCF to be appropriate.[284] It noted that even the respondent's expert had affirmed that "PV Plants have fixed operating

273 Ibid [647].
274 Ibid [648]–[650].
275 Ibid [662].
276 Ibid [662]–[663].
277 Ibid [664].
278 Ibid [666].
279 Ibid [680], [682], NextEra v. Spain, ICSID Case No. ARB/14/11, Award (31.05.2019) [16]–[17].
280 NextEra v. Spain, *supra* note 55 [652].
281 Ibid [655].
282 Ibid [661].
283 Ibid [668].
284 9REN v. Spain, *supra* note 56 [391].

costs and a relatively stable level of electricity generation", which contradicted the respondent's own position that there is a "high dependency of the cash flows on external, volatile and unpredictable elements".[285] It rejected the respondent's arguments that the claimant was entitled to a "reasonable return" or a "reasonable profit" only.[286]

The valuation date was established as 30.06.2014.[287] The DCF was used to calculate the actual value of the investments on this date in the actual scenario (understood as "the real world result after absorbing the impact of the disputed measures") and the but-for scenario (understood as "the theoretical universe where no such regulatory changes had been made").[288]

The tribunal noted that assessing compensation "is not a simple exercise in arithmetic" and that complex issues involved in this process "justify a margin of appreciation" for the tribunal.[289] It added that "while the DCF method presents a picture of mathematical precision", its output is dependent upon inputs which are "judgmental and subjective".[290] Thus, valuation typically involves "some degree of estimation and the weighing of competing (but equally legitimate) facts, valuation methods and opinions. The element of imprecision reinforces the inevitability of a certain amount of approximation when assessing damages".[291] Despite such hurdles, the tribunal considered itself bound to "arrive at an award based on the materials the parties have chosen to put before it".[292]

In doing so, the tribunal decided on several issues that were disputed by the parties' experts. For example, it assumed that the operational lifetime of the PV plants was 30 years (as opposed to 35 years), it applied no limit on the number of operating hours that were eligible for the FIT (as opposed to 1,250 operating hours) and it lowered the illiquidity discount (3.4% as opposed to somewhere between 18-26%, as had been argued for by the respondent).[293]

The tribunal agreed with the respondent's expert that "investment in a regulated industry is not a risk free proposition" and noted that a proper valuation should take into account the risk that Spain could lawfully make adjustments

285 Ibid [391].
286 Ibid [389], [407].
287 Ibid [406].
288 Ibid [397].
289 Ibid [405]. Similarly in [411] on the margin of appreciation.
290 Ibid [408].
291 Ibid.
292 Ibid [410].
293 Ibid [412].

to its regulatory regime without this amounting to a violation of the ECT.[294] It considered that "a prudent and well-informed investor would have been alive to the risk that Spain might reduce the FIT tariff and be held (despite the ECT) to be within its rights under international law to do so without compensation", which was assessed on the date of valuation.[295] One arbitrator disagreed on this issue.[296]

Finally, the tribunal observed that a "precise calculation on the basis of the materials" before it was impossible, as there were "too many contingencies and contingencies within contingencies". Nevertheless, it felt obliged to "work as best it can with the tools provided to it by the Parties".[297] It used its discretion to reduce by 20% the quantum asserted by the claimant, to reflect its decisions on a number of issues to be fed into the DCF.[298]

2.2.12 SolEs

2.2.12.1 *Methodology and Calculations*

In *SolEs*, the tribunal observed that calculating compensation "necessarily involves the use of certain assumptions and estimations", regardless of which valuation methodology is used. It added that neither the ECT nor international law "mandates the use of any particular methodology for determining damages".[299] It then decided that the DCF is "well-suited" to this case, as it provides a "sound basis" to compare the present value of the disputed investment with and without the Disputed Measures. It added that the "DCF method is widely used" and has been applied in other Spanish saga arbitrations.[300]

The valuation date was established as June 2014.[301] The tribunal observed that a "long period of historical performance of an investment can lend confidence to predictions about how it would have performed in the future". In this case, the plants had been operating since August 2010 and February 2011, but this was considered sufficient to apply the DCF. In addition to the plants' historical performance, the tribunal also considered contemporaneous forecasts prepared by the claimant before the dispute had arisen.[302]

294 Ibid [395].
295 Ibid [412].
296 Ibid [395].
297 Ibid [415].
298 Ibid [416].
299 SolEs v. Spain, *supra* note 60 [487].
300 Ibid [488].
301 Ibid [527].
302 Ibid [528].

The tribunal considered it irrelevant that the claimant was a brownfield, as opposed to a greenfield, investor.[303] Even though this distinction might be potentially relevant for calculations "premised on the calculation of project returns", it is not relevant to the DCF methodology, which focuses on "the net present value of future cash flows".[304]

The experts appointed by the parties were divided on the impact of the Disputed Measures. The claimant's experts claimed that they had led to a significant reduction of the net present value, whereas Spain's experts argued that the value of the investment had actually increased.[305] This discrepancy was explained by the use of different discount rates applied to future cash flows streams in the respective DCF analyses, "constructed by amalgamating various elements", such as systemic risk, regulatory risk, inflation and illiquidity discount.[306]

The tribunal sided with the DCF calculations presented by the claimant's experts, which provided a "sound basis" to determine the appropriate reduction to be made to the fair market value of the claimant's investment, after adjustments to reflect the decision that the tribunal lacked jurisdiction over the IVPEE and that the first set of measures did not violate the ECT.[307]

The tribunal agreed with the claimant's experts that there was a higher regulatory risk in the actual scenario, since the uncertainty existed regarding the methodology to be used in future adjustments under the New Regime.[308] Similarly, as regards the illiquidity discount, the tribunal considered that it would be higher in the actual scenario, as it would be more difficult to sell the investment under the New Regime.[309]

One arbitrator concurred with the tribunal's conclusions, but regretted that the evidence before the tribunal required it to choose between the claimant's valuation, which assumed a 25-year duration of the unmodified Special Regime, and the respondent's valuation, which the tribunal rejected as it would mean that the value of the investment had increased due to the treaty violation.[310] That arbitrator noted that "it was inevitable that Spain would not have let the tariff deficit continue to grow for 25 years and instead would have acted in some manner to address it". Therefore, he "would have welcomed

303 Ibid [526].
304 Ibid [526].
305 Ibid [529].
306 Ibid [530].
307 Ibid [537]–[538].
308 Ibid [532].
309 Ibid [533]–[534].
310 Ibid [544].

evidence" which would have allowed the tribunal to accept the claimant's general approach to liability and quantum, but without also accepting the premise that the Special Regime would remain "stable for 25 years". This would have allowed the tribunal to base its calculation of damages on the difference between this adjusted but-for scenario (with a shorter time horizon) and the actual scenario.[311] The tribunal was unable to perform such "complicated calculations on its own motion", particularly as the respondent "has not supplied the necessary information".[312]

2.2.12.2 *Tax Gross-Up*

As regards the tax gross-up, the claimant requested that the compensation level should include an amount to reflect the tax liability it would incur on the compensation awarded in the home state.[313] The tribunal commenced by observing that the legal memorandum prepared by a law firm on this issue had not been signed.[314] It then noted that it was not possible to identify a single "prior award that grosses-up an investor for taxes on an award that are due to its home State".[315]

The tribunal was rather skeptical and observed that "there is reason to question the general proposition that a respondent State that is found liable for an FET violation should be required to compensate a claimant for increased taxes that claimant will owe its home State".[316] It then escaped the need to decide this issue by noting that, even assuming that such losses are compensable, the evidence must be "well-substantiated".[317] The tribunal decided that it had "an incomplete picture" of the tax consequences for the claimant, as insufficient evidence had been provided to support the claim for a tax gross-up.[318]

2.2.13 InfraRed

2.2.13.1 *Methodology and Calculations*

The DCF was applied also in *InfraRed*.[319] The tribunal considered it "axiomatic that no model or methodology for assessing damages can determine with absolute precision the loss" suffered, given the numerous uncertainties and

311 Ibid [545].
312 Ibid [546].
313 Ibid [547].
314 Ibid [548]. Tribunal did not allow for a late submission of a signed copy, having identified no exceptional circumstances allowing for it.
315 Ibid [549].
316 Ibid [550].
317 Ibid [550].
318 Ibid [553].
319 InfraRed v. Spain, *supra* note 64 [521], [532].

variables inherent in projecting revenues, costs and risk over time.[320] A chosen method must be "reasonable in the light of all the circumstances", and when choosing between various available methods, "their respective merits are to be assessed on a balance of probabilities".[321]

The DCF was appropriate in this case, as the disputed CSP plants "derive the largest portion of their revenues from a regulated remuneration regime, the values of which are well-documented and easily accessible".[322] In this context, the disputed CSP plants, which were registered in RAIPRE and became operational in 2012,[323] were considered to have "a sufficiently long track record".[324] This was so even though the valuation date was set as June 2014.[325]

The tribunal decided not to apply the regulatory asset base as the valuation method, as had been proposed by the respondent. It considered this method to be "ill-adapted to the economic reality of this case". This was because the effects of the Disputed Measures were not primarily related to the plants' underlying assets but, rather, to the income stream accruing to the plants and, as a corollary, on the free cash flows available to the claimants.[326] "Equally ill-adapted" was reliance on the RRR, without regard to the actual remuneration that had been lost due to the Disputed Measures.[327]

2.2.13.2 *Joint Experts' Report*

The tribunal instructed the parties' experts to prepare a "joint and interactive quantum model", which they did.[328] This was a reaction to "wide-ranging disagreement" of the parties' experts on many of the variables used in their respective models. The joint model allowed the tribunal to: (i) identify the issues in contention between the experts, (ii) assess the impact on the damages calculation of the tribunal's decision in respect of each of the changes to the Special Regime (by "toggling", between "no breach/no liability/no damages" and "breach/liability/damages", i.e. switching "on" or "off" each element of the Disputed Measures, given that the violation of the FET was found to exist only in relation to three elements) and (iii) assess the impact on the damages calculation of a decision in respect of each of the disputed assumptions relied

320 Ibid [533].
321 Ibid.
322 Ibid [535].
323 Ibid [57].
324 Ibid [535].
325 Ibid [576].
326 Ibid [542].
327 Ibid [543].
328 Ibid [169].

upon by the experts (by "toggling" between the parties' respective positions on these factors).[329]

The tribunal concluded that the operational life of the CSP plants was 25 years.[330] The claimants had not discharged the burden of proof that these plants could operate for longer without significant additional investment.[331]

With respect to the regulatory risk (and the corollary illiquidity risk), the tribunal considered that it was greater in the actual scenario than in the but-for scenario. Even though the Disputed Measures reduced the tariff deficit, they introduced greater uncertainty into Spain's energy market and the dismantlement of the Special Regime "caused significant turmoil in that industry and market".[332] The tribunal noted that Spain's regulatory risk rating decreased from A+ in 2011 to BBB- in 2014 (on the date of valuation).[333] It concluded that the New Regime not only provided for lesser remuneration when compared to the Special Regime, but it is also created the risk of ongoing fluctuations, as it was subject to revision every 3 to 6 years.[334]

One arbitrator took a different position. He considered that the credit rating downgrade of the Spanish tariff deficit was not caused by increased regulatory risk triggered by the Disputed Measures but, rather, by a fear that these measures would be insufficient to end the tariff deficit. He stressed that this was "far from being a secondary issue", since this approach would result in a significant reduction of the amount of compensation awarded.[335]

The tribunal looked at the sunk costs as a "reality check" of the amount of compensation calculated based on the DCF.[336]

2.2.13.3 *Tax Gross-Up*

The claimants argued that the tax gross-up is necessary to give full effect to the principle of full reparation.[337] The tribunal did not decide on that issue and

329 Ibid [517], [519].

330 Ibid [573].

331 Ibid [566]–[567].

332 Ibid [579].

333 Ibid [580]–[583].

334 Ibid [584].

335 Ibid [fn 782]. The amount of compensation would be reduced from approx. 26.4 million Euro to 4.5 million Euro.

336 Ibid [600]. The sunk costs were of approx. 31 million Euro, compares to the DCF calculations of 28.2 million Euro.

337 Ibid [596].

simply noted that the claimants had not adduced "any" evidence to support this claim, and therefore failed to discharge the burden of proof.[338]

2.2.14 OperaFund

2.2.14.1 *Methodology and Calculations*

In *OperaFund*, the DCF was also applied. The tribunal rejected the argument that the DCF method is "excessively speculative". On the contrary, the DCF was viewed as "generally recognized and used as the most appropriate technique to calculate damages arising from breaches of in international law affecting investments in going concerns".[339]

The disputed plants began operations after 01.06.2007.[340] This gave them a sufficient operational track record of profitability in order for the DCF method to be applied.[341]

The valuation date was set as June 2014, when the final picture of the extent of damage suffered became known. The tribunal observed that the claimants are entitled to damages "valued as of the date of injury or as of the date of the Tribunal's award, whichever is higher". The tribunal also clarified that its calculations include the retroactive effect of the Disputed Measures.[342]

The tribunal decided that the expected lifetime of the PV plants was 35 years.[343] It disagreed with the respondent's experts' approach to the discount rates to be applied in the DCF. It rejected the view that the Disputed Measures made the actual scenario safer than the but-for scenario, which was argued to be associated with high regulatory risk and therefore requiring large discounts to be applied.[344]

The tribunal adopted the claimants' experts' valuation as the starting point, from which it deducted the amount corresponding to the IVPEE impact (which was outside its jurisdiction).[345]

---

338 Ibid [597]–[598].

339 OperaFund v. Spain, *supra* note 65 [621].

340 Ibid [441]. One of the plants commenced operations on 26.07.2007 – [161], but the award is unclear about the exact dates on which each of the disputed plants commenced operations.

341 Ibid.

342 Ibid [683].

343 Ibid [684]. The tribunal based this decision on the text of RD 661/2007 (which provided for fixed FITs for the first 25 years and a lower remuneration thereafter), EC study on PV plants and one of the plants' lease agreements (concluded for 25 years with two 5-year extensions).

344 Ibid [685]. Although the tribunal does not use the term "regulatory risk", it is understood that it refers to this term, as it was relied upon by the parties.

345 Ibid [687]–[688]. As a result, the tribunal awarded 29.3 million – albeit in USD, not Euro, which seems to be an error corrected by rectification of the award (which remains unpublished).

2.2.14.2 *Tax Gross-Up*

The tribunal found the claim regarding tax gross-up to compensate for tax liability in the claimants' home states to be too speculative, as no proof of the existence of such taxes had been offered.[346] It acknowledged, however, that tax gross-up is not prohibited under Art. 21 of the ECT. It saw "a need to clarify" that the principle of full reparation requires Spain to pay the entire amount of damages and to refrain from charging or deducting taxes in connection with that amount. As a "precaution", the tribunal expressly provided that the compensation "is made net of all taxes and/or withholdings by Spain, and Spain is ordered to indemnify Claimants for any tax liability or withholding that may be imposed in Spain".[347]

2.2.15 BayWa

2.2.15.1 *Methodology and Calculations*

In *BayWa*, the tribunal decided that the ECT had been violated only by the retroactive application of the New Regime, which meant that none of the primary claims on quantum were accepted.[348] As discussed in Chapter 4, the tribunal decided that the claimants' legitimate expectations to the RRR had not been violated by the New Regime.[349]

The expert reports filed by the parties did not allow the tribunal to quantify the level of compensation due. The tribunal instructed the parties to agree on the compensation level, assuming a 25-year regulatory life for the Wind energy plants.[350] In the absence of agreement, each party could request that the tribunal decide on the "outstanding issues", which would be preceded by a "prompt briefing schedule".[351] This eventually materialized, as the parties failed to reach an agreement.[352]

The valuation date was established as 13.07.2013.[353] This was because the detailed parameters, even though regulated later, would come into effect on the date that RDL 9/2013 was adopted.[354]

346 Ibid [704].

347 Ibid [705], [746.4]. Whilst the tax gross-up claim concerned taxes payable in the home states: Malta and Switzerland, this reservation concerned the host state: Spain.

348 BayWa v. Spain, *supra* note 67 [612], [615].

349 Ibid [515].

350 Ibid [616].

351 Ibid [617].

352 BayWa v. Spain, ICSID Case No. ARB/15/16, Award (25.01.2021) [6].

353 Ibid [20], [63].

354 Ibid [41].

The but-for scenario was that the New Regime had entered into force, but without considering the amounts previously earned in excess of the RRR, as in the actual scenario.[355] The compensation was based on the disputed Wind energy plants' "standard", as opposed to actual, net asset value, i.e. one calculated in accordance with the methodology of the New Regime, but without taking into account their retroactive effect.[356] This was calculated using the DCF, i.e. based on future cash flow and discounted to the present.[357] The tribunal took into account *ex post* data, i.e. events which took place after the valuation date, to eliminate the risk of over or under-compensation.[358] From the standard net asset value, the tribunal subtracted estimated returns from selling electricity and included applicable taxes, the claimants' shareholding and the fact that the claimants were compensated ahead of time.[359]

2.2.15.2 *Tax Gross-Up*

The tribunal considered that the tax gross-up claim was admissible.[360] It noted, however, that no precedent existed of an award for tax gross-up in respect of taxation to be paid in a third state (not being a party to the proceedings).[361] The tribunal avoided answering the issue of whether such a claim could be upheld "in principle" on the merits, because it had not been "substantiated" by the claimants.[362]

2.2.16 Stadtwerke

In *Stadtwerke*, the tribunal did not analyze the compensation issue because the claims were dismissed on their merits.

2.2.17 RWE

2.2.17.1 *Methodology and Calculations*

In *RWE*, the tribunal saw no basis for accepting the experts' opinions presented by the parties, which calculated the fair market value of the investment assuming a violation of the FET in a broader scope than had actually been found to

355 Ibid [19].
356 Ibid [26], [28], [39].
357 Ibid [51].
358 Ibid [51]–[52].
359 Ibid [27], [54].
360 BayWa v. Spain, *supra* note 67 [618].
361 Ibid [621].
362 Ibid [626].

exist by the tribunal (see Chapter 4).[363] A violation was found to have taken place only insofar as the IRR of each of the disputed plants fell below the benchmark level of the RRR.[364]

The tribunal ordered the parties to agree on the compensation level, failing which it would decide the issue based on further submissions.[365] The but-for scenario did not equate to maintaining the Special Regime perpetually but, rather, to any replacement through an equivalent of the New Regime ensuring that the RRR principle was respected, i.e. without the New Regime's disproportionate impact.[366] Therefore, the compensation amounted to the difference between the actual profits of the selected plants under the Disputed Measures (those which fell below the threshold of 7.398% IRR pre-tax) and the level which was deemed reasonable by the respondent, i.e. the 7.398% IRR pre-tax.[367]

2.2.17.2 *Joint Experts' Report*

The parties' experts prepared a joint report.[368] Notably, the parties disagreed as to the *res judicata* effect of the tribunal's findings in the previous decision. The claimants objected to some of those findings, merely in order to avoid the allegation, at the annulment stage, that they had waived the right to object.[369] In response to the allegations, the tribunal considered its decisions on disproportionality as part of the liability analysis, not quantum. There is no "general principle that an assessment of proportionality must await the detailed consideration of damages that forms part of a quantum phase".[370] Thus, the tribunal did not re-open the discussion on its finding regarding the retroactivity of the New Regime. It dismissed the claimants' attempt to inflate the amount

363 RWE v. Spain, *supra* note 12 [730].

364 Ibid [587].

365 Ibid [745].

366 Ibid [734], [742].

367 Ibid [735], [742].

368 RWE v. Spain, ICSID Case No. ARB/14/34, Award (18.12.2020) [12].

369 Ibid [83]. The tribunal noted that the case law suggests that intermediary decisions should be treated as *res judicata* and not open to reconsideration. This is not limited solely to decisions on jurisdiction and applicable law. Some ICSID tribunals apply a more nuanced approach, differentiating between decisions (intended to "be final" and bind the parties) and awards (having *res judicata* effect). But even within this approach, decisions can be revisited only in exceptional circumstances which were not present in this case – [86]–[91].

370 Ibid [84].

of compensation by arguing that 10 plants affected by the retroactivity were "merely illustrative".[371]

2.2.17.3 *Tax Gross-Up*

The tribunal in this case was also unconvinced that the award would be subject to taxation. The claimants had not provided "any legal authority supporting the case for a tax gross-up".[372] Moreover, the tribunal dismissed the request that damages are paid to the second claimant only – a Spanish entity – together with an order that Spain hold that entity harmless from any tax related to the award. First, the tribunal did not consider the tax gross-up as a problem "that calls for a solution". Second, this would not be a "practicable solution", because the tribunal would not be able to verify whether Spain had complied with the order or not, since it would be *functus officio* after issuing the award.[373]

2.2.18 Watkins

2.2.18.1 *Methodology and Calculations*

In *Watkins*, the tribunal applied the DCF. It considered the DCF as being widely applied in the RE sector, which operates based on a "simple business model with predictable income and costs".[374]

The tribunal established the valuation date as 20.06.2014.[375] The claimants acquired the disputed Wind energy plants 3 years earlier, and they were already operational at that time.[376] This was "a sufficient amount of time to generate sufficiently reliable information on which to calculate future cash flows" in the DCF.[377] The tribunal dismissed claims for lost historical cash flows, prior to the valuation date.[378]

Whilst it was undisputed that the claimants bear the burden of proof, the standard of proof was disputed by the parties.[379] The tribunal decided that (i)

---

371 Ibid [96]. The tribunal also considered it irrelevant that there was no direct repayment but, rather, the deduction of payments owed to the plants for the sale of electricity – [99].

372 Ibid [125].

373 Ibid [126].

374 Watkins v. Spain, *supra* note 73 [689].

375 Ibid [680]. The tribunal considered it impossible to ascertain the extent of the New Regime's impact on the claimants' investment prior to that date.

376 Ibid [134], [139].

377 Ibid [689].

378 Ibid [688]. Nevertheless, in its request for rectification, the respondent argued that the tribunal erred in its calculation of damages by failing to account of harm caused prior to the valuation date. The request was dismissed. See: Watkins v. Spain, ICSID Case No. ARB/15/44, Decision on Spain's Request for Rectification of the Award (13.07.2020) [44], [52].

379 Watkins v. Spain, *supra* note 73 [682].

"sufficient certainty" is required to establish the existence of damage, but that the standard of a "reasonable basis" suffices as regards the amount of loss.[380]

In applying the DCF, the tribunal broadly followed the model given by the claimants' experts, analyzing a number of corrections to the inputs, as proposed by the respondent's experts.[381] First, it considered it irrelevant for the actual scenario that the claimants sold their investment in 2016 for a higher price than it was acquired in 2011.[382] This was because the sale occurred after the valuation date and "in different economic conditions".[383] Second, it reduced to 25 years the estimated operational life of the Wind energy plants.[384] Third, the tribunal considered that the Disputed Measures had increased, rather than decreased, the regulatory risk.[385]

In its request for rectification, the respondent argued that the tribunal had erred in its calculation of damages, by failing to exclude the impact of the IVPEE.[386] This argument was dismissed.[387] The tribunal considered this to be a novel argument, not being presented in the pleadings, rather than a simple mathematical operation that can be rectified.[388] It was also contrary to the respondent's argument presented during the arbitration, namely that the IVPEE had temporary effect, with no continued impact after the New Regime was implemented.[389]

2.2.18.2 *Tax Gross-Up*

The tribunal rejected the claim for a tax gross-up, reasoning that the claimants had failed to discharge their evidentiary burden to show that a future obligation to pay tax would arise in the home state on any compensation awarded by the tribunal.[390] The claimants had failed to present a crucial piece of evidence, namely a tax ruling from the competent home state authorities.[391] The claimants relied on two judgments from the host state's court, but these seemed

380 Ibid [685].
381 Ibid [694].
382 Ibid [140], [697]. The claimants sold the investment in 2016 for 133 million Euro, compared to the purchase price of 91 million Euro in 2011.
383 Ibid [698].
384 Ibid [708].
385 Ibid [741]. A few other corrections were deemed to be of little impact and were not accepted – [743].
386 Watkins v. Spain, Rectification ..., *supra* note 378 [45].
387 Ibid [65].
388 Ibid [56], [60], [61].
389 Ibid [59].
390 Watkins v. Spain, *supra* note 73 [758].
391 Ibid [757].

irrelevant to the tribunal. They concerned taxes applicable to a contract to acquire shares and to transfer shares, as opposed to compensation related to the possession of shares, which seemed to be covered by a tax exemption.[392]

2.2.19 PV Investors

2.2.19.1 *Methodology and Calculations*

In *PV Investors*, the tribunal also applied the DCF.[393] It noted that the DCF "is an accepted valuation method in both financial theory and in the practice, including by arbitral tribunals". While its use may not always be justified, in particular when the valued business is not a "going concern" and lacks a clear record of profitability, it was justified in the circumstances of the case. First, the investments were operational since at least 2008. This provides a reliable and sufficient record of past financial performance for the use of the DCF method. Second, there was "no major uncertainty regarding the plants' future cash flows" because the Disputed Measures continue to provide the claimants with the RRR for the entire regulatory life of their plants.[394]

2.2.19.2 *Joint Experts' Report*

After consulting with the parties, the tribunal requested that the parties' experts agree a joint model on calculating damages.[395] It was intended to calculate the difference between (i) the RRR pursuant to Art. 30(4) LSE over the regulatory lifetime of a plant and (ii) the RRR to be achieved under the New Regime for the same period.[396] The experts prepared a model which included a "control panel" comprising of various parameters, with variables on inputs on which the experts disagreed.[397]

The tribunal had to decide the appropriate level of FITs to be used in a but-for scenario. The claimants' experts suggested the use of an alternative tariff, representing a revenue stream that provides an efficient plant with the assumed rate of return in the but-for scenario.[398] The tribunal dismissed Spain's criticism, noting that either this approach is to be followed, or Spain must accept that the claimants could have expected fixed FITs under the Special Regime

392 Ibid [754]–[756].
393 The PV Investors v. Spain, *supra* note 76 [691].
394 Ibid.
395 Ibid [653], [654].
396 Ibid [655].
397 Ibid [657], [658], [666], [667].
398 Ibid [689].

over the regulatory lifetime of a plant (an assumption which was dismissed when considering liability, as an element of the primary claim).[399]

Thus, in the joint model, the experts were instructed to use the methodology used by the claimants' experts in their DCF calculations.[400] The respondent's experts' criticism of the discount rate and the regulatory risk were raised too late to be considered.[401] The tribunal then continued to analyze specific parameters used in the model.

The IRR in the but-for scenario was set at the level of 7% after tax. The tribunal rejected the alternative proposal of 8% IRR after tax.[402] Most of the contemporary documents showed the respondent's "intent" to guarantee "approximately" or "around" 7%, depending on the capacity and type of a plant.[403] This is also in line with the rate of return granted in other EU member states.[404] The relevant IRR for the tribunal was a holding IRR, i.e. the IRR that an investor would receive throughout the entire regulatory life of a plant. This was envisaged in the regulations, and this is why an exit IRR, i.e. one at a moment of a sale of a plant, was irrelevant.[405] With respect to the costs base in the efficiency benchmark input of calculations of the RRR, the tribunal agreed to base it on a "standard or marginal plant" rather than actual greenfield investment costs.[406] This was in line with the RD 661/2007, which was based on the same basis.[407] The tribunal re-categorized the claimant's investments based on their size.[408]

The tribunal set the valuation date as 30.06.2014.[409] It preferred an *ex ante* valuation rather than an *ex post* valuation, on the date of the award. It noted that an *ex post* valuation may be sometimes preferred as being more in line

399 Ibid [690].
400 Ibid [697].
401 Ibid [696].
402 Ibid [709].
403 Ibid [708].
404 Ibid [710].
405 Ibid [713]–[714].
406 Ibid [748].
407 Ibid [749]–[754].
408 Ibid [758]. The tribunal decided that it should take into account the "tax shield" available due to tax savings arising from interest paid on loans when calculating the reasonable return after tax, according to which the claimants expected to pay "little or no taxes" on the revenues under the Special Regime. The tribunal noted that it need not systematically follow the methodology of the RD 661/2007 and did not decide whether the tax shield was available under the Special Regime. Since the claimants expected to benefit from the tax shield, they "cannot do better in litigation than in real life" – [790], [791], [798].
409 Ibid [723].

with the principle that reparation should stand *in lieu* of restitution. However, *ex ante* valuations are more appropriate when the consequences of subsequent developments are unrelated to the disputed measures and the higher amount resulting from an *ex post* valuation cannot "be deemed to derive from the measures".[410] That was the case at hand, as the main factors that occurred after the Disputed Measures were unrelated to them – i.e. interest rates (and the periodic revision of the returns linked to those interest rates).[411]

As part of the damages analysis, the tribunal also noted that efficient installations could outperform the RRR target under the Special Regime. The clawback provisions in the New Regime were considered as retroactive. The tribunal had "no hesitation to find that it is correct not to take past profits into account when calculating an investor's remuneration going forward".[412] Therefore, the claimants' past profits were not included in the RRR calculations in the but-for scenario.[413] This concerned only the profits considered as "excessive" under the New Regime.[414] This was needed to reflect the fact that the disputed plants started operations in 2008 and recovered 5⁄30 of the initial investment costs prior to the adoption of the New Regime.[415]

It was undisputed that the calculations of the RRR within the meaning of Art. 30(4) LSE should only include greenfield costs and should exclude brownfield costs.[416]

Based on the parameters above, the model prepared by the experts led the tribunal to conclude that the Disputed Measures meant that 10 of the 19 claimants saw their IRR fall below 7%, which violated the FET and required compensation.[417]

2.2.19.3 *Tax Gross-Up*

The tribunal confirmed that the decision on the tax gross-up claim was within its jurisdiction.[418] It nonetheless dismissed the claim. First, it considered it too speculative, despite the tax law memoranda presented by the claimants. It noted that various available options are subject to determination by the

---

410 Ibid [721].
411 Ibid [722].
412 Ibid [813].
413 Ibid [812].
414 Ibid [815].
415 Ibid [816].
416 Ibid [819]–[820]. Thus, the "developer premiums" were excluded from the calculations – [822].
417 Ibid [847].
418 Ibid [860].

competent tax authorities.[419] Second, the claim failed to meet the requirement of causation of the loss. Tax liability under home state law is not a consequential loss arising from the Disputed Measures of the host state.[420] Third, the tribunal was unable to identify a single investor-state arbitral award which had upheld a similar claim.[421]

2.2.20 Hydro

2.2.20.1 *Methodology and Calculations*

For the *Hydro* tribunal, the "real question" to determine was whether the remuneration for the facilities going forward and without the retroactive effect of the New Regime constitutes the RRR.[422] This approach was closely related to its decision on liability, which left open the question as to whether there was a violation of the FET (see Chapter 4), depending on whether the RRR threshold was observed under the New Regime.[423]

In answering this question, the tribunal was unable to follow the approach adopted by the *RREEF* tribunal, because the parties approached the question of compensation differently, without determining the IRR for each individual plant.[424] The tribunal considered the DCF model proposed by the claimants' experts to be incorrect.[425] The respondent's experts calculated IRR on an incorrect basis, because they took into account past remuneration when calculating future subsidies (in accordance with the claw-back provision of the New Regime, which was found to be in violation of the FET).[426] Moreover, they aggregated individual IRR's, whereas each plant should have been considered individually.[427]

Thus, the tribunal set out certain principles of damages to be observed when calculating compensation.[428]

419 Ibid [862].
420 Ibid [863].
421 Ibid [864].
422 Hydro v. Spain, *supra* note 81 [697], [717].
423 Ibid [685].
424 Ibid [699].
425 Ibid [717]. The incorrectness of the DCF was not about the method itself, but because it relied on a comparison of the actual scenario with the but-for scenario, understood as one in which the Special Regime remained in place. This should not be understood as a dismissal of the methodology itself.
426 Ibid [718].
427 Ibid [721]–[724].
428 Ibid [726].

First, the tribunal addressed what was considered as a RRR. It was not willing to simply accept the target of 7.398% pre-tax set out in the New Regime. In its view, taxes are costs which affect the claimants' return, so the RRR must be considered on a post-tax basis.[429]

Second, the arbitrators followed the reasoning of the tribunal in *RREEF* that the RRR could be calculated by taking the post-tax WACC, calculated at 5.86%, plus 1%.[430] However, unlike in the *RREEF* case, the tribunal was unable "to state categorically what constitutes a reasonable post-tax rate of return for small-hydro assets save to express the expectation that it is likely to be somewhere in the region of 5.5% to 7%".[431] The tribunal felt that the record proved that it could take the Spanish 10-year bonds as a risk-free rate (4.398%) and determine that June 2013 was the appropriate date for the WACC calculation, but it lacked sufficient information to determine the other relevant factors, such as market risk premium, the applicable beta, the debt/equity ratio and the cost of debt in 2014.[432]

Third, the IRR of the individual plants should be post-tax, to enable it to be compared with the RRR.[433] It should be an operational IRR, i.e. for operating the plants until the end of their useful life, with no assumed exit sale.[434] The actual lifetime of plants was relevant, understood as the end date of the relevant concessions, as opposed to the 25-year period established under the New Regime.[435]

The tribunal then invited the parties to agree on a post-tax RRR, calculated by using the WACC in June 2013 and post-tax IRRs for each individual plant.[436] In the absence of any agreement on this, the tribunal intended to set a timetable for submissions on the outstanding issues.[437]

2.2.20.2 *Joint Experts' Report*

The experts prepared a joint memorandum and model.[438] It allowed the tribunal to choose between different inputs for "areas of disagreement" between the

429 Ibid [727]–[731].
430 Ibid [732]–[740].
431 Ibid [746].
432 Ibid [741]–[743].
433 Ibid [747].
434 Ibid [752].
435 Ibid [753]–[754].
436 Ibid [762], [767]. However, in the *dispositif*, the tribunal established 60 days to report on that – [770.5]
437 Ibid [768].
438 Hydro v. Spain, ICSID Case No. ARB/15/42, Award (05.08.2020) [13].

experts.[439] The experts agreed, however, that the disputed Hydro energy plants fell short of the post-tax RRR and that compensation was due.[440] This led the tribunal to award compensation.[441]

2.2.21 Cavalum

2.2.21.1 *Methodology and Calculations*

In *Cavalum*, given its findings on liability (see Chapter 4), the tribunal saw it necessary to calculate the difference between the present value of the actual returns on disputed investments and the returns that would have been obtained under the RRR hypothesis.[442] Thus, in this case too, the tribunal blended its analysis of the merits with its analysis of liability. The "overall effect" of its findings was that, by enacting the New Regime, "to the extent (if any) the return on its investments in the plants falls short of a reasonable return by reference to the cost of money in the capital markets", legitimate expectations had been frustrated and therefore the FET had been violated.[443]

The tribunal considered that its task was to assess what would have happened if the New Regime had not been adopted. It concluded that the respondent would have adopted other measures to deal with the tariff deficit. For the purposes of calculating damages, the tribunal assumed that such alternative measures would have been enacted to give effect to the RRR.[444] Thus, this was the relevant but-for scenario, as opposed to the situation that would have existed if RD 661/2007 had remained in place.[445] Therefore, the tribunal's task was to determine the difference (if any) between the actual post-tax IRR for each of the plants in the actual scenario and the IRR post-tax in the but-for scenario.[446]

However, the decision was deferred. The tribunal considered it necessary to allow the parties to file further submissions. This was because its decision on liability considered that the parties and their experts "have not been able

439 Ibid [25], [120].
440 Ibid [26].
441 Ibid [123]–[124], [162].
442 Cavalum v. Spain, *supra* note 83 [655].
443 Ibid [656], [666].
444 Ibid [660].
445 Ibid [661].
446 Ibid [672]. The tribunal referred to the RRR, not the IRR, in the but-for scenario. It can be understood that the RRR was to be determined by reference to the IRR, in the same manner as in the actual scenario.

to engage fully".[447] If there was a breach of the FET, the claimant would also receive compensation for "wasted expenditure" for projects which had been abandoned due to the Disputed Measures.[448]

The tribunal clarified that the IRR should be calculated for each individual plant as a post-tax sum, as opposed to the pre-tax rate of 7.398% established by the New Regime.[449] The relevant date was 30.06.2014.[450] The operational lifetime of the PV facilities was considered to be 30 years.[451] The but-for scenario was to assume no retroactive application, unlike the New Regime.[452] The tribunal agreed with the *RREEF* tribunal that a WACC calculation was required.[453] Nevertheless, it considered that it had insufficient data to determine the WACC at this stage, so it deferred it for a later stage.[454]

2.2.21.2 *Joint Experts' Report*

The tribunal asked the parties to confirm that they agreed for their experts to prepare a joint memorandum, whilst reserving the right for the tribunal itself to appoint a quantum expert.[455] Publicly available information reveals that such a memorandum was prepared.[456]

2.3 *Lessons Learned*

The Spanish saga cases confirm that there is no golden rule regarding a single, generally applicable methodology to be used when calculating compensation for treaty breaches. In the words of the *Antin* tribunal, "there are no right or wrong valuation methods, but different methods that are appropriate depending on the specific circumstances of the case".[457] The *SolEs* tribunal correctly noted that neither the ECT nor international law "mandates the use of any particular methodology for determining damages".[458]

---

447 Ibid [667]–[668]. The choice to defer the decision on compensation (and therefore on liability) is closely related to the fact that the claimant did not present an alternative claim based on the RRR, and therefore the parties were not fully engaged in calculations based on the but-for scenario which was based on the RRR.

448 Ibid [699].

449 Ibid [676], [680]–[681].

450 Ibid [684].

451 Ibid [686].

452 Ibid [685].

453 Ibid [687].

454 Ibid [696]–[697].

455 Ibid [701]–[705].

456 https://icsid.worldbank.org/cases/case-database/case-detail?CaseNo=ARB/15/34.

457 Fn 194.

458 Fn 299.

They also confirm, in the words of the *Eiser* tribunal, that whichever methodology is applied, compensation typically "cannot be determined with mechanical precision".[459] The tribunal in *Masdar* rejected the test of "confidence approaching absolute certainty".[460] The *9REN* tribunal recognized that calculating compensation "is not a simple exercise in arithmetic"[461] and that the "element of imprecision reinforces the inevitability of a certain amount of approximation when assessing damages".[462] The *InfraRed* tribunal underlined that "no model or methodology for assessing damages can determine with absolute precision the loss" suffered.[463]

The arbitrators must feel comfortable that the chosen methodology is not speculative.[464] Reluctance to arrive at a speculative outcome is the key driver behind the decision as to which valuation methodology will be applied in a particular case.

2.3.1 First Lesson Learned – DCF Is the Most Common Valuation Method Applied in Disputes concerning the RE Sector. The Highly Regulated Nature of the RE Sector Enables the DCF to Be Applied to Assess Compensation Even regarding Investments Which Have a Shorter Operating Track Record Than Would Be Required in Other Sectors

Generally, as identified in Chapter 4, some of the tribunals decided that Spain had violated the FET because of revolutionary changes made to its regulatory framework, whereas other tribunals found the infringement to be more limited in scope, namely the extent to which the disputed RE plants had failed to receive the RRR as defined by the New Regime.

As regards the first group, which concluded that a "full" FET violation had occurred, the tribunals almost unanimously calculated compensation by applying the DCF.

The applicability of the DCF comes as no surprise when disputes relate to "going concerns", i.e. RE plants which had been producing energy for at least several years prior to the valuation date. *Novenergia* serves as an example, where the disputed PV plants had a track record of 8 years of relevant cash flow.[465] Similarly the *OperaFund* case concerned PV plants with a track record

459 Fn 157.
460 Fn 176.
461 Fn 289.
462 Fn 291.
463 Fn 320.
464 See for example: Novenergia v. Spain, *supra* note 21 [820].
465 Fn 164.

of 7 years.[466] In this context, DCF is perceived as "generally recognized and used as the most appropriate technique to calculate damages arising from breaches of in international law affecting investments in going concerns".[467]

The tribunals in the analyzed cases went further. They also applied the DCF to disputes concerning the valuation of RE plants with a shorter operating history. In the *Foresight* case, a track record of 4 years was viewed as relatively short, but sufficient to apply the DCF method.[468] A similar track record of almost 4 years was sufficient in *SolEs*.[469] The *Watkins* tribunal applied DCF to Wind energy plants that had operated for at least 3 years.[470] In *Eiser*, the tribunal remained silent on the CSP plants' track record of under 2.5 years.[471] The *Masdar* case concerned CSP plants which started supplying electricity to the grid just over 1 year before the notice of dispute was filed, and 2.5 years before the valuation date established by the tribunal.[472] The *InfraRed* tribunal also concerned CSP plants with a track record of 2 years prior to the valuation date.[473] However, the *NextEra* tribunal considered a period of under 1 year of generating profit to be insufficient for it to apply the DCF.[474]

The tribunals found this approach to be justified because of the nature of the RE sector. Three features of investments in this sector had special relevance.

First, one must remember about the costs structure of RE investments, as discussed in Chapter 2. Around 90% of the total installed costs are upfront capital costs (CAPEX), incurred when the relevant facility is constructed. Thus, predictions of future operating costs (OPEX) and their fluctuations have less impact in the DCF model than in many other sectors. This was explicitly confirmed by the *Masdar* tribunal, which relied on the fact that "costs incurred are relatively predictable in the renewable energy sector".[475]

Second, the tribunals emphasized that producing electricity is a "simple business model". In the *Masdar* tribunal's words, the RE plants "rely on a relatively simple business model – limited only to generating electricity, pursuant to generally stable parameters".[476] Similarly, the *Antin* tribunal underlined the

466 Fn 340.
467 Fn 339.
468 Fn 211.
469 Fn 302.
470 Fn 376–377.
471 Fn 159.
472 Fn 181–182.
473 Fn 323–324.
474 Fn 272–273.
475 Fn 184.
476 Ibid.

"relatively simple business, producing electricity, whose demand and long-run value can be analysed and modelled in detail, based on readily available data".[477] The *Watkins* tribunal described it as "simple business model with predictable income and costs".[478]

Third, the highly regulated nature of the RE sector allows cash flows for RE plants to be easily predicted, i.e. income from the sale of energy produced (relevant commodity price) and a guaranteed demand for it. The *Novenergia* tribunal explained that the DCF model is appropriate for valuations in regulated sectors, since they are less vulnerable to market fluctuations or changes when compared to non-regulated sectors.[479] The *Cube* tribunal underlined that the "operating history, even if relatively short, in a highly-regulated industry" enables estimations of cash flows based on regulatory formulas which apply for many years.[480]

Some tribunals explicitly endorsed the view that the regulated nature of this sector of the economy substitutes, or at least lessens the reliance on, the historical details that would otherwise be required about the operating history of an RE plant. The *Masdar* award suggested that, in highly regulated sectors such as the RE sector, future income can be calculated with reasonable certainty even in relation to projects with short operating periods. The regulated nature of the sector fulfils the precondition that RE plants are "going concerns" for the purposes of DCF calculations. Also the *Cube* tribunal underlined that the DCF method is appropriate in a "highly-regulated industry", even if the disputed investment has a short operating history. The *InfraRed* tribunal considered that 2 years is "a sufficiently long track record" because the CSP plants "derive the largest portion of their revenues from a regulated remuneration regime, the values of which are well-documented and easily accessible".[481]

Therefore, the regulatory framework proved to be not only the main factor in having created legitimate expectations, and of course the principal reason for such expectations having been frustrated (see Chapter 4), but also an important factor in justifying the application of a particular valuation method – the DCF model.

Once the applicability of the DCF had been established, the tribunals devoted much of their attention to the inputs which were fed into the calculations. Each single input can potentially have a significant impact on the

477 Fn 197.
478 Fn 374.
479 Fn 165.
480 Fn 252.
481 Fn 322–324.

results of the calculations and the final compensation awarded. This is clearly visible in the *InfraRed* case. The DCF calculations resulted in 28.2 million Euro compensation being awarded, but this would have been reduced to approx. 4.5 million Euro if the tribunal had decided differently on the causes of Spain's worsening credit rankings.[482] In the *Masdar* tribunal's words, "the DCF method does not necessarily yield inflated valuations, but rather requires a careful analysis of the reasonableness of the factual assumptions and estimates used for such a calculation".[483]

The relevant inputs in the Spanish saga cases concerned numerous factors, such as the regulatory risk, operational lifetime of the RE plants and illiquidity discount.

As regards regulatory risk, the *9REN* tribunal explained that the highly regulated nature of the RE sector entails a risk of regulatory changes which must be a factor fed into the DCF valuation model. Consequently, this lowers the outcome of any DCF calculations.[484] Other tribunals applied a discount rate to reflect the regulatory risk but without reference to its relationship with the highly regulated nature of the RE sector.[485]

This reveals a paradox related to the regulatory nature of the RE sector. On the one hand, it enabled the DCF model to be applied *per se*, curing the absence of a sufficient track record of the disputed investments. On the other hand, it became one of the inputs fed into the DCF model, which clearly lowered the results of such calculations.

Analyzing the DCF inputs reveals that, once the claimants discharged the burden of proof by showing that sufficient data existed for the DCF calculation to be used, the respondent could have presented evidence to challenge the assumptions of the DCF models. As the *9REN* tribunal recognized, the inputs are, at least to some degree, "judgmental and subjective".[486]

As regards regulatory risk, Spain was unsuccessful in arguing that introduction of the New Regime reduced regulatory risk in the future. The tribunals were unconvinced by the argument that a regulatory change which violated the ECT should be viewed as reducing the risk of regulatory changes in the future.[487] This conclusion was linked to certain features of the New Regime, such as the lack of any transparent explanation regarding its underlying

482 Fn 335.
483 Fn 186.
484 Fn 295.
485 Fn 256, 262, 308.
486 Fn 290.
487 Fn 219, 265, 344, 385.

assumptions, and the insecurity caused by periodic reviews which had no clearly defined borders.[488]

As regards the evidentiary burden, Spain was often successful in challenging the claimants' assumptions regarding the operational lifetime of the RE plants. However, one arbitrator in the *SolEs* case made it clear that Spain could have better presented the question of valuation, which could have reduced the amount of compensation awarded. The tribunal rejected Spain's contention that its treaty violation could have increased the investment's value.[489] Alternative calculations presented by the respondent's experts could have convinced the tribunal to award a lower figure.

The tribunals underlined that, as noted in the *Masdar* case, they "enjoy a wide margin of discretion" when determining compensation.[490] This was not just a theoretical observation. The *9REN* tribunal made use of "a margin of appreciation",[491] and reduced the amounts claimed by 20%, to reflect its decision on several factors which were to be reflected in the DCF.[492] The *Cube* tribunal applied a "revenue haircut" of 40%, to reflect additional discounts that needed to be reflected given the long operating lives of the Hydro energy plants.[493]

Notably, the tribunals were able to effectively implement their position on liability (i.e. that the ECT does not completely preclude the possibility of any changes being made to the regulatory framework, but only precludes revolutionary changes) when valuing compensation. This was done by factoring the regulatory risk into the DCF models (as discussed earlier) or, alternatively, by explicitly using their inherent discretion.

The tribunals also recognized that other valuation methods can serve as "reality checks" which can verify whether the outcome of a DCF valuation has produced realistic results. This was explicitly confirmed in *Eiser*,[494] *Foresight*,[495] *RREEF*,[496] *NextEra*[497] and *InfraRed*.[498]

488 Fn 308.
489 Fn 305–307.
490 Fn 173.
491 Fn 289.
492 Fn 298.
493 Fn 266.
494 Fn 158.
495 Fn 221.
496 Fn 230.
497 Fn 281.
498 Fn 336.

The *Cube* and *SolEs* tribunals emphasized that the ECT does not only protect greenfield investments, but also covers brownfield investments.[499] This was a relevant factor which, in the view of those tribunals, was left unaddressed in the RRR theory. As explained by the *Cube* tribunal, the RRR could have been achieved by greenfield investors who sold their investments prior to the ECT violations, but it provided no protection to those who had acquired the operating plants.[500] The fact that the *PV Investors* tribunal adopted a different approach is explained by the fact that it applied the RRR theory.[501] Accordingly, no contradiction exists between these two approaches.

The above considerations on compensation also remain relevant for the group of cases in which the tribunals found that the ECT had only been violated insofar as the disputed RE plants failed to receive the RRR defined in the New Regime – namely the *RREEF*, *BayWa*, *PV Investors*, *Hydro* and *Cavalum* cases.

In these cases, the tribunals also analyzed the actual scenario by using the future cash flow method. The difference was the but-for scenario, which was contrasted with the actual scenario to determine the difference which should be compensated by the arbitral award. Here, the but-for scenario was set at the RRR level. The tribunals determined the RRR level as being the WACC plus an additional premium.[502]

Accordingly, it seems that these tribunals also applied the DCF, or at least a variation thereof (based on future cash flow, but not necessarily with discounts aiming to calculate its present value). The *PV Investors* tribunal explicitly acknowledged that it applied the DCF. The *BayWa* tribunal did not refer to the DCF, but it seems that its calculation of the "standard" net asset value was calculated using DCF (or at least a variation thereof).[503] The *RREEF*, *Hydro* and *Cavalum* tribunals remained silent and did not specifically identify the methodology they applied.

All of the above demonstrates that the DCF is the most common valuation method applied in the disputes concerning the RE sector. The highly regulated nature of this sector enables non-speculative results to be achieved with a sufficient degree of certainty regarding projections of future cash flows and profitability. Whereas there is no one-size-fits-it-all approach regarding the choice

499 Fn 257, 303.

500 Fn 257.

501 Fn 416.

502 No consensus existed as to the appropriate level of premium above the WACC. For example, the *RREEF* tribunal applied a 1% premium, whereas the *NextEra* tribunal preferred 2%.

503 Fn 359.

of methodology to calculate compensation for treaty breaches in general, in disputes concerning the RE sector there is a visible trend towards preferring a forward-looking (income based) method. The highly regulated nature of the RE sector enables the DCF to be applied to assess compensation even as regards investments which have a shorter operating track record than would be required in other sectors. Moreover, arbitration provides flexibility regarding the procedure to be used, which allows tribunals to request calculations prepared jointly by the parties' appointed experts.

2.3.2 Second Lesson Learned – Arbitration Provides Flexibility regarding the Procedure to Be Used, Which Allows Tribunals to Request Calculations to Be Prepared Jointly by the Parties' Appointed Experts

The Spanish saga cases also confirm the flexibility of arbitration in terms of conducting proceedings. The tribunals in *RREEF*,[504] *Cube*,[505] *InfraRed*,[506] *RWE*,[507] *PV Investors*[508] and *Cavalum*[509] requested that the parties' experts work together and present a report of their joint efforts. Although this never resulted in the experts agreeing on an exact amount of compensation to be awarded, the experts did reach a consensus on certain issues relevant to the calculations. On other issues, where they were unable to reach a consensus, they prepared joint models which allowed the tribunals to toggle between final determinations made by the tribunals on the disputed issues. This produced an outcome which experts for both parties were able to sign-off on, as they had jointly prepared the model which produced that outcome.

This is demonstrated in *InfraRed*. The tribunal adopted this flexible approach when deciding which factors should be included in the DCF calculations. It instructed the parties' experts to prepare a "joint and interactive quantum model", which they did. The tribunal then decided all of the disputed factors and determined which inputs should feature in the interactive model, which then calculated the amount of compensation.[510]

504 Fn 245.
505 Fn 269.
506 Fn 328
507 Fn 368.
508 Fn 397.
509 Fn 456.
510 Fn 328–329.

2.3.3 Third Lesson Learned – Claimants May Request a Tax Gross-Up, but They Face a High Evidentiary Threshold to Prove That a Specific Tax Will Apply and That It Is More Burdensome Than the Tax Which Would Have Applied (in the But-for Scenario) to Profits Which Would Have Been Obtained If the Treaty Had Not Been Violated

Moreover, in many cases the claimants requested a tax gross-up, seeking to neutralize any possible tax burden which may exist in their home states in connection with the compensation award ordered by the tribunals.

Most of the tribunals had no doubt that a tax gross-up was theoretically available. Only the RREEF tribunal explicitly denied the possibility of awarding a tax gross-up, noting that compensation should be subject to the same taxation as the lost profits it sought to compensate.[511]

Nevertheless, no tribunal actually awarded a tax gross-up. The *Eiser*,[512] *Antin*,[513] RREEF,[514] *SolEs*,[515] *InfraRed*,[516] *OperaFund*,[517] *BayWa*,[518] *Watkins*,[519] and PV *Investors*[520] tribunals felt that none of the claimants had discharged the burden of proof to demonstrate that taxation would apply to the awarded compensation. The RWE tribunal did not view this issue as a problem "that calls for a solution".[521]

It can be concluded that the Spanish saga cases align with general investor-state arbitral case law where, to quote the *SolEs* tribunal, there is not a single arbitral award "that grosses-up an investor for taxes on an award that are due to its home State".[522]

One tribunal, in *OperaFund*, as a "precaution" stipulated that the compensation "is made net of all taxes and/or withholdings by Spain, and Spain is ordered to indemnify Claimants for any tax liability or withholding that may be imposed in Spain".[523] This approach seems to address the tax gross-up

511 Fn 246.
512 Fn 161.
513 Fn 203.
514 Fn 247.
515 Fn 317–318.
516 Fn 338.
517 Fn 346.
518 Fn 362.
519 Fn 390.
520 Fn 419.
521 Fn 373.
522 Fn 315.
523 Fn 347.

concern in a limited manner. It is limited to the taxes payable in the host state, whilst leaving unanswered the impact of taxes payable in the home state(s).

Consequently, another lesson can be learned in this context. The CIL principle of full reparation enables claimants to request a tax gross-up, to mitigate any negative outcomes if the amounts awarded as compensation are taxed. Although the legal framework theoretically allows tax gross-up claims, a high standard of proof seems to exist. It requires a claimant to provide evidence to establish that a specific tax will apply and that it is more burdensome that the tax which would have applied (in the but-for scenario) to profits which would have been obtained if the treaty had not been violated.

CHAPTER 6

Conclusions

The significance of renewable energy cannot be undervalued. This is true even if one adopts a purely economic perspective. In 2021 alone, worldwide investments in new renewable energy power plants were valued at approximately USD 371 billion.[1]

This is not the only context which proves the relevance of renewable energy. Its continued growth is an important element in the fight against climate change. The 2015 Paris Agreement, which implements the United Nations Framework Convention on Climate Change ("UNFCCC")[2] and supplements the Kyoto Protocol,[3] recognizes that renewable energy:

> aims to strengthen the global response to the threat of climate change, in the context of sustainable development and efforts to eradicate poverty, including by: (a) Holding the increase in the global average temperature to well below 2°C above pre-industrial levels and pursuing efforts to limit the temperature increase to 1.5°C above pre-industrial levels, recognizing that this would significantly reduce the risks and impacts of climate change.[4]

To meet this aim, the contracting parties:

> aim to reach global peaking of greenhouse gas emissions as soon as possible, recognizing that peaking will take longer for developing country Parties, and to undertake rapid reductions thereafter in accordance with best available science, so as to achieve a balance between anthropogenic emissions by sources and removals by sinks of greenhouse gases in the

1 International Energy Agency, World Energy Investment 2021 (IEA Publications 2021), available at: https://iea.blob.core.windows.net/assets/5e6b3821-bb8f-4df4-a88b-e891cd8251e3/WorldEnergyInvestment2021.pdf, p. 7: "Renewables dominate investment in new power generation and are expected to account for 70% of 2021's total of USD 530 billion spent on all new generation capacity".

2 United Nations Framework Convention on Climate Change, done in New York (09.05.1992).

3 Kyoto Protocol to the United Nations Framework Convention on Climate Change, done in Kyoto (11.12.1997).

4 The Paris Agreement, adopted on 12.12.2015 at the twenty-first session of the Conference of the Parties to the United Nations Framework Convention on Climate Change.

> second half of this century, on the basis of equity, and in the context of sustainable development and efforts to eradicate poverty.[5]

Renewable energy is indispensable to meeting these goals. It is an important element in the process of moving away from fossil fuels and achieving the long-term objective of carbon neutrality, as well as related reductions in CO_2 emissions.[6] This process is a fact, even if its end goals are far from being achieved. By way of example, the EU announced its European Green Deal initiative and declared its intention to become a carbon-neutral continent by 2050.[7] This is supported by legal tools such as the Just Transition Fund.[8] It is a global trend, not limited solely to the European context. Worldwide, 51 states have pledged a net-zero emissions target.[9] For example, China has announced that it "will strive to peak carbon dioxide emissions before 2030 and achieve carbon neutrality before 2060".[10]

Developing renewable energy is also relevant for sustainable development, which is an important factor for Sustainable Development Goals no. 7, 12 and

5 Ibid, Art. 4.

6 See for example: UNEP, Emissions Gap Report 2019 (United Nations 2019), p. XXII: "Renewables and energy efficiency, in combination with electrification of end uses,are key to a successful energy transition and to driving down energy-related CO2 emissions".

7 European Commission, The European Green Deal. Communication from the Commission to the European Parliament, the European Council, the Council, the European Economic and Social Committee and the Committee of the Regions, COM (2019) 640 final (11.12.2019), pp. 2, 4, 6.

8 Regulation (EU) 2021/1056 of the European Parliament and of the Council of 24 June 2021 establishing the Just Transition Fund (OJ L 231, 30.06.2021, pp. 1–20).

9 UNEP, The Heat Is On. A world of climate promises not yet delivered. Emissions Gap Report 2021 (United Nations 2021), available at: https://wedocs.unep.org/bitstream/handle/20.500.11822/36990/EGR21.pdf, p. XX.

10 Xi Jinping, Bolstering Confidence and Jointly Overcoming Difficulties To Build a Better World, statement given by the President of China at the general debate of the UN General Assembly's 76th session on 21.09.2021, available at: https://estatements.unmeetings.org/estatements/10.0010/20210921/AT2JoAvm71nq/KaLk3d9ECB53_en.pdf, p. 4. The stated goals were reflected in China's 14th Five-Year Plan for 2021–2025. See: Outline of the People's Republic of China 14th Five-Year Plan for National Economic and Social Development and Long-Range Objectives for 2035 (unofficial translation of the Center for Security and Emerging Technology), available at: https://cset.georgetown.edu/wp-content/uploads/t0284_14th_Five_Year_Plan_EN.pdf, p. 94, China Energy Transition Status Report 2021. Sino-German Energy Transition Project (2021), p. 12.

13.[11] In particular, Sustainable Development Goal no 7.2. seeks to "increase substantially the share of renewable energy in the global energy mix" by 2030.[12]

In this context, it is unsurprising that states have introduced subsidies and other support schemes to encourage investments in renewable energy.

Foreign investments are an important element of the renewable energy sector and its development. Even if they are not strictly necessary, in the sense that the sector can grow even without them, they certainly facilitate and accelerate such growth.

Investments in renewable energy projects are, by their very nature, long-term and capital-intensive upfront, having high CAPEX levels which are recouped over a long period. For this reason, the stability of legislation is extremely important from the investors' perspective.[13] Despite the undoubted importance of the stability for renewable energy sector, recent years have witnessed examples of states drastically changing their domestic regulations in this sector. Such reforms have resulted in numerous arbitral proceedings being commenced by foreign investors, based mainly on the Energy Charter Treaty ("ECT").

This book analyzes the "Spanish saga cases", a group of cases concerning foreign investments in the renewable energy sector, which concern the same respondent (Spain) and the same disputed measures – reforms to the regulatory framework applicable to investments in this sector.

Spain is the model example of the challenges currently faced by international investment law in the renewable energy sector. Based on publicly available information, Spain has faced at least 49 investor – state arbitrations triggered by its changes to renewable energy regulations.[14] These cases

---

11 Sustainable Development Goal no. 7: "Ensure access to affordable, reliable, sustainable and modern energy for all". Sustainable Development Goal no. 12: "Ensure sustainable consumption and production patterns". Sustainable Development Goal no. 13: "Take urgent action to combat climate change and its impacts". See: UN General Assembly Resolution No. 70/1 (25.09.2015), Transforming our world: the 2030 Agenda for Sustainable Development (UN A/RES/70/1), p. 14.

12 Ibid, p. 19.

13 Emma Johnson, Lucy McKenzie, Matthew Saunders, International Arbitration of Renewable Energy Disputes (Globe Law and Business 2021), p. 17. This is also one of the reasons why investments in the renewable energy sector are often funded by banks, financial institutions and other third parties.

14 Based on publicly available information as of 15.04.2022 (https://www.energychartertreaty.org/cases/list-of-cases/). The actual number may be higher, due to the confidentiality of potential cases based on treaties other than the ECT. According to Viñuales:

> between 1972 and 2020, at least 178 foreign investment claims with environmental components were filed. [...] Approximately 80% (143) of these disputes have been

will invariably impact on the development of investor-state arbitration case law concerning renewable energy. There is a number of lessons we can learn from them.

Given this project's time-limits, the analysis offered here covers 21 arbitral awards handed down in connection with the Spanish saga. Those awards were, in chronological order, as follows: *Charanne, Isolux, Eiser, Novenergia, Masdar, Antin, Foresight, RREEF, Cube, NextEra, 9REN, SolEs, InfraRed, OperaFund, BayWa, Stadtwerke, RWE, Watkins, PV Investors, Hydro* and *Cavalum*.[15] It would be an impossible task to constantly update the analysis so as to reflect the latest published award or annulment decision. Some proceedings were triggered as late as in 2022.[16] Any attempt to include an analysis of each of these awards and annulment decisions would delay the publication of this book for many years.

The Spanish saga cases confirm that the ECT plays an important role in protecting investments in renewable energy. All of the analyzed cases concerned investments in this sector and sought protection under the ECT, rather than under any other legal instruments.[17]

> brought after 2008, and over half of them (76) concern the energy transition, mostly (61) modern renewable energy projects (solar, wind and geothermal)

– Jorge E. Viñuales, Geopolitics of the Energy Transformation, Revue Européenne du Droit (Governing Globalization), 2 (2020), pp. 148–155, available at: https://geopolitique.eu/en/articles/geopolitics-of-the-energy-transformation/. As such, the Spanish saga cases represent approximately 80% of all investor-state arbitrations in the renewable energy sector.

15 The chronological nature of this list is based on the date of an award (final or partial) on liability, regardless of the date of any partial awards on jurisdiction and/or damages (if bifurcated).

16 WOC v. Spain, ICSID Case No. ARB/22/12, registered on 05.04.2022.

17 As already noted in 2014, in the context of a potential clash between environmental concerns and investment protection:

> investors operating in the energy sector have the capability to either foster environmental goals through pursuit of non-conventional energy sources, transfer of clean technology and import of international best practices, or to augment environmental harm by incentivising lax regulation and forcing a "race to the bottom"

– Makane Moïse Mbengue, Deepak Raju, Energy, Environment and Foreign Investment, in: Eric De Brabandere, Tarcisio Gazzini (eds.), Foreign Investment in the Energy Sector. Balancing Private and Public Interests (Brill 2014), p. 172. On p. 191 they add, for example, that substantive standards of protection included in the ECT and BITs:

> are capable of being invoked by investors pursuing clean and renewable energy with a view to forcing governments to remove disincentives to such energy and to call for higher environmental standards or to demand uniform and augmented enforcement of environmental norms.

This is the situation despite negotiations being ongoing to modernize the ECT. Whilst the treaty itself is "technology neutral",[18] since 2013 the number of claims concerning the renewable energy sector outnumbers claims concerning fossil fuels investments.[19] Thus, even in its current wording, the ECT protects investments in the renewable energy sector. This comes as no surprise in the light of the ECT's preamble.[20]

This permits the conclusion that the ECT is an important legal tool to protect investments that are crucial from the perspective of sustainable development concerns and the fight against climate change. The novelty of the Spanish saga cases (and other recent cases concerning renewable energy) is that the disputed measures "work against the protection of the environment, while in the past challenged measures were environmentally friendly".[21]

As such, the ECT protects renewable energy investments which, by their very nature support the process of moving away from fossil fuels, achieving the long-term objective of carbon neutrality and securing reductions in CO_2 emissions.[22] The Spanish saga cases did not involve a clash between the investors'

18 In the words of the Secretary-General of the ECT: "The ECT is technology neutral: it covers all sorts of energy from biomass all the way to uranium and thorium" – Urban Rusnák, Comment: Quo Vadis Energy Charter Treaty?, Energy Charter Secretariat News (12.04.2021), available at: https://www.energycharter.org/media/news/article/comment-quo-vadis-energy-charter-treaty/.

19 https://www.energychartertreaty.org/fileadmin/DocumentsMedia/Statistics/All_statistics_-_1_December_2021_Rev.pdf.

20 "[…] Recalling the United Nations Framework Convention on Climate Change, the Convention on Long-Range Transboundary Air Pollution and its protocols, and other international environmental agreements with energy-related aspects; and recognising the increasingly urgent need for measures to protect the environment, including the decommissioning of energy installations and waste disposal, and for internationally-agreed objectives and criteria for these purposes […]".

21 Fernando Dias Simões, Charanne and Construction Investments v. Spain: Legitimate Expectations and Investments in Renewable Energy, Review of European, Comparative & International Environmental Law, 26:2 (2017), p. 175.

22 See for example: UNEP, *supra* note 6, p. XXII: "Renewables and energy efficiency, in combination with electrification of end uses,are key to a successful energy transition and to driving down energy-related CO_2 emissions". In opposition to that conclusion, there are voices of concern, according to which the ECT may be contrary to sustainable development and the transition to clean energy. However, they relate to the fact that the ECT grants the same level of protection to investments in fossil fuels – see for example key finding no 11: "The ECT is a powerful tool in the hands of big oil, gas, and coal companies to discourage governments from transitioning to clean energy" – Pia Eberhardt, Cecilia Olivet, Lavinia Steinfort, One Treaty to Rule Them All. The Ever-Expanding Energy Charter Treaty and the Power It Gives Corporations to Halt the Energy Transition (Corporate Europe Observatory and Transnational Institute 2018), available at: https://www.tni.org/files/publication-downloads/one_treaty_to_ruled_them_all.pdf, p. 8. These concerns are reflected in the ongoing negotiations to modernize the ECT – see

protection and the state's right to pursue its agenda to fight climate change and ensure sustainable development. Rather, the conflict existed between the interests of investors and a state seeking to recalibrate its public spending and overturn a budget deficit.

The following five research questions are answered in this book.

Research Question 1: Which facts led to the unprecedented number of investor-state arbitrations filed against Spain, an EU member state?

Chapter 2 answers this question by describing the factual background of the Spanish saga cases. It confirms the uniqueness of those cases, which arises due to the fact that the disputed measures are almost identical in all of the publicly known cases. The Chapter provides a balanced description. On the one hand, the description is sufficiently detailed to enable the reader to understand the analysis which follows in the next Chapters. On the other hand, it does not become bogged down with unnecessary details. It does not aim to describe every nuanced fact in each case.

In short and in very general terms, this book analyses the story of an EU member state which had to incentivize investments in its renewable energy sector to meet its international obligations stemming from EU law and in line with the UNCCC and the Kyoto Protocol. Although the reader's natural assumption may be that Spain should focus on solar energy, wind and hydro power plants were also relevant to Spain's renewable energy strategy. Pre-2007 regulations were not sufficiently attractive to meet these goals. In 2007, Spain introduced RD 661/2007 (the "Special Regime"). The Special Regime offered attractive investment conditions and was successful in encouraging investments, at a higher speed than anticipated. This unexpected success led to a recalibration of the Special Regime insofar as it applied to PV installations, which was done by RD 1578/2008. The latter offered revised, but still attractive, incentives. The Special Regime guaranteed *inter alia* that any future revisions of the regulatory framework would not affect any renewable power plants that had already been accepted into the Spanish system. This was the principal feature leading to the Spanish saga disputes.

Shortly after, Spain's economy suffered the effects of the global financial crisis. This led, among other things, to a serious fall in the demand for electricity. In turn, this caused or contributed to the accumulation of a tariff deficit (the various tribunals assessed the evidence differently and arrived at diverging

for example: new definition of "Energy Materials and Products" excluding fossil fuels – EU additional submission to its text proposal for the modernisation of the Energy Charter Treaty, p. 2. In consequence, the role of the ECT in protecting the investments in the renewable energy sector is unaffected by these concerns.

conclusions as to when this accumulation began). The tariff deficit became a political topic, which caused a significant shift in Spain's policy shortly after elections were held in late 2011. The new government adopted the first in a series of new laws and regulations in early 2012. This process culminated in 2014, when Spain quashed the old regulatory framework and replaced it with a wholly new one.

There are, of course, differences between the cases. These are particularly visible with respect to two issues. First, the type of renewable energy plant at the heart of each dispute. This is connected with differences in the intensity of reforms to the regulatory framework prior to 2014. Second, the date on which a particular investment was made. The differences in timing affected the moment at which the tribunals considered whether legitimate expectations had arisen.

Notwithstanding some undeniable factual differences between the cases, these are trivial in the light of the overall context. Accordingly, the Spanish saga cases can be considered to be a "laboratory" for lawyers and academics. In the same circumstances (i.e., the same factual background) one can compare the observations, analyses and legal reasoning found in multiple cases. As such, they can be compared to a laboratory, understood as a space "providing opportunity for experimentation, observation, or practice in a field of study"[23] and "where scientific experiments, analyses, and research are carried out".[24]

Research Question 2: Can the arbitral awards rendered against Spain have an impact on proceedings commenced against other states (both EU Member States and non-members) in the future?

The analysis confirms the hypothesis presented in the Introduction, that this should be answered in the affirmative. Whilst it is true that no rule of precedent (or doctrine of *stare decisis*) exists in investor-state arbitrations,[25] the persuasive views of tribunals certainly can impact on subsequent cases.[26]

Based on a detailed analysis of each of the Spanish saga cases, the analysis zooms out from the finer details of each arbitration to reach a general plane

---

23 Definition from Merriam Webster dictionary, available at: https://www.merriam-webster.com/dictionary/laboratory.

24 Definition from Collins dictionary, available at: https://www.collinsdictionary.com/dictionary/english/laboratory.

25 See for example: AES v. Argentina, ICSID Case No. ARB/02/17, Decision on Jurisdiction (26.04.2005) [23.d)], [30]–[32]. Christoph H. Schreuer, Loretta Malintoppi, August Reinisch, Anthony Sinclair, The ICSID Convention. A Commentary (Cambridge University Press 2009), p. 1101.

26 In the words of the *de Nul* tribunal, "it is not bound by earlier decisions, but will certainly carefully consider such decisions whenever appropriate" – de Nul v. Egypt, ICSID Case No. ARB/04/13, Decision on Jurisdiction (16.06.2006) [64].

of international investment law (or a "helicopter view") so as to enable several general conclusions to be made. The book treats these as "lessons learned" for the future and for investment arbitrations in general, rather than being limited to the facts which occurred in Spain or the provisions of the ECT.

The specific nature of the lessons learned are included in each of the Chapters and separately for each stage of the arbitral proceedings (jurisdiction in Chapter 3, liability in Chapter 4 and remedies in Chapter 5). Below is a general summary of the lessons learned.

On jurisdiction, the following lessons are learned:

1. As regards the intra-EU objection:
   a. The Spanish saga cases were an important contribution to the factual matrix which led to the 2021 *Komstroy* judgment.
   b. The tensions between EU law and protection under the ECT are far from being resolved in a final manner, and the main points of the debate have evolved over time.
   c. The differences between ICSID and non-ICSID arbitrations have become more important than ever before.
   d. The nature of the intra-EU objection can be classified as *rationae personae*.
2. As regards tax carve-out objection:
   a. Arbitral tribunals not only can, but must, commence their analysis by looking beyond the "label" of a tax, to decide whether a disputed measure fulfils customary international law's prerequisites.
   b. Tax carve-out clauses do not apply to *mala fide* measures.

On liability, the following lessons are learned:

1. As regards the Fair and Equitable Treatment ("FET"):
   a. Regulatory frameworks can create legitimate expectations that are protected by international investment treaties.
   b. The content of domestic law is crucial to determine the scope of legitimate expectations based on a regulatory framework.
   c. Legal due diligence is essential to ensuring the existence of legitimate expectations to regulatory stability in highly regulated sectors.
   d. The sovereign right to regulate has its limits, which is related to the rule of law.
   e. The FET involves a balancing exercise.
   f. Contractual obligations can be game-changers.
2. As regards indirect expropriation:
   a. The impact of the state's measures on attributes of ownership and/or control are relevant factors in assessing whether a substantial deprivation occurred, and continued ownership and/or control of

investments elevates the threshold to be met by the economic impact of the disputed measures.

b. General regulatory measures can result in indirect expropriation.

3. As regards the umbrella clause contained in Art. 10(1) ECT ("Umbrella Clause"):

a. General legislation, directed at a broad class of addressees, falls outside the scope of the Umbrella Clause.

b. The Umbrella Clause may apply provided that a power purchase agreement is concluded between the investor and an agency whose actions are attributable to the state.

On remedies, the following lessons are learned:

1. As regards restitution:

a. Restitution may be awarded in investor-state arbitrations, although it is inappropriate in cases concerning violations of investment treaties caused by regulatory changes, given the disproportionate impact on a sovereign state's legislative autonomy.

b. If restitution is awarded, Art. 26(8) ECT requires to enable the respondent to "pay monetary damages in lieu of" restitution. It is recommended that, even outside the ECT context, similar reservations are made in the operative parts of arbitral awards in order to respect state sovereignty.

2. As regards compensation:

a. Discounted Cash Flow ("DCF") is the most common valuation method applied in the disputes concerning the renewable energy sector. The highly regulated nature of the renewable energy sector enables the DCF to be applied to assess compensation even regarding investments which have a shorter operating track record than would be required in other sectors.

b. Arbitration provides flexibility regarding the procedure to be used, which allows tribunals to request calculations to be prepared jointly by the parties' appointed experts.

c. Claimants may request a tax gross-up, but they face a high evidentiary threshold to prove that a specific tax will apply and that it is more burdensome than the tax which would have applied (in the but-for scenario) to profits which would have been obtained if the treaty had not been violated.

Research Question 3: Which legal grounds in international law serve, or may potentially serve, as the basis for investors' claims in the renewable energy sector?

Chapter 4 answers this question, focusing on the merits of the Spanish saga cases. It confirms that all of the standards of protection present in Arts. 10(1) and 13 ECT may potentially serve as bases for investors' claims in the renewable energy sector. The most significant bases are analyzed, meaning those which were at the heart of the most cases: the FET, expropriation and the Umbrella Clause. This Chapter also confirms that, in the modern reality, direct expropriation claims are marginal and limited to extreme situations.[27]

It also confirms that the lessons learned, summarized in the answer to Research Question 2, are of general applicability, rather than being limited to the ECT. Similar standards of protection as those envisaged in Arts. 10(1) and 13 ECT can be found in numerous bilateral investment treaties ("BITS") around the globe. This confirms the relevance of the analysis, since at least 2.646 BITS were in force around the world at the end of 2020.[28]

Research Question 4: Are the apparently mutually exclusive arbitral awards issued against Spain really contradictory, or can the different outcomes be explained by differences in the facts or the applicable law of those cases?

The answer to this question stems from the analysis contained in Chapter 4. It confirms the hypothesis that the Spanish saga cases are not, in fact, contradictory.

First, not a single tribunal concluded that expropriation had occurred or that the Umbrella Clause had been violated. Regarding these standards, the analyzed case law is uniform.

Second, as regards the FET, all but 3 tribunals found that it had been infringed. The *Charanne* case was launched early and was limited to initial measures undertaken by Spain. It did not deal with the measures that Spain adopted in 2014, revoking the old regulatory framework and introducing a new one. The *Isolux* case concerned investments made in late 2012, when several regulatory changes had already taken place. This led the tribunal to decide that the regulatory framework was no longer capable of generating legitimate expectations that it will not be modified, and further changes were inevitable. The third case to reject the FET claim was *Stadtwerke*, which is in fact consistent with other cases that recognized the existence of a legitimate expectation to receive a reasonable rate of return ("RRR"). The tribunal recognized the existence of such legitimate expectations, but concluded that the disputed investment continued to generate profits in line with these legitimate expectations even after the disputed measures were adopted.

27 As is correctly noted in the literature, states which decided to directly expropriate foreign property were mainly driven by an ideology based on the "rectification of historical injustice", which has become less relevant nowadays – Peter D. Cameron, Reflections on Sovereignty Over Natural Resources and the Enforcement of Stabilization Clauses, Yearbook on International Investment Law and Policy (2011–2012), p. 316.

28 UNCTAD, World Investment Report 2021. Investing in Sustainable Recovery (United Nations 2021), p. 122.

A discrepancy exists in the legal reasoning adopted in two groups of cases: those in which tribunals concluded that a "full" violation of the FET had occurred and those in which the tribunals found that the FET had been violated only insofar as the new regime failed to meet the RRR threshold.

The discrepancy is real and has significant practical consequences, as it affects the amount of compensation awarded. However, the reasons behind the discrepancy are identifiable. First, at least some degree of inconsistency can be explained by the existence of small, but significant, differences in the facts regarding the type and time of the investment at the heart of each dispute, as well as the ability to prove that specific assurances had been given to a particular investor (and how such assurances impacted on the scope of legitimate expectations). Second (and more importantly, because it applies uniformly to all of the cases), the diverging conclusions occurred due to the tribunals' interpretation of Spanish domestic law, including the hierarchy of domestic legal acts and the relationship between Royal Decrees and Acts of Parliament. Different interpretations of the domestic law led to diverging conclusions regarding the scope of legitimate expectations which enjoy protection under by international law.

Regardless of which position is assessed as "correct", the RRR concept is clearly context-specific and should not be deemed to apply to cases concerning other states.

Importantly for the future, regardless of their approach to the RRR issue, each of the tribunals confirmed that legitimate expectations can arise (and actually arose in the Spanish saga cases) from the regulatory framework of the respondent state.

Research Question 5: What relevance does EU law have on treaty-based arbitrations based on the ECT?

This question became especially relevant after the Court of Justice of the European Union ("CJEU") issued judgment in the *Achmea* case on 06.03.2018 ("*Achmea* judgment"),[29] but discussion regarding the intra-EU scope of arbitrations could be found in arbitral tribunals' considerations even before this date.

The analysis in Chapter 3 reveals that the intra-EU aspect essentially concerns the jurisdiction of arbitral tribunals. It shows the limited impact of the *Achmea* judgment on arbitral cases which were pending on 06.03.2018, as well

29 Judgment of the Court (Grand Chamber) of 06.03.2018, Slovakia v. Achmea, Case No. C-284/16 (ECLI:EU:C:2018:158).

as on cases commenced subsequently. Not a single tribunal in the Spanish saga declined jurisdiction due to the intra-EU nature of the dispute.[30]

The tribunals did not consider themselves to be bound by the *Achmea* judgment. More importantly, they were unimpressed by the CJEU's reasons justifying the judgment. Two approaches can be distinguished. One group of tribunals openly criticized the CJEU's reasoning in the *Achmea* judgment and explained why it was, in their view, incorrect. Other tribunals refrained from openly criticizing the judgment and instead adopted a more "diplomatic" approach, simply noting that the *Achmea* judgment is confined to a particular BIT and that it silent on the issue of multilateral treaties such as the ECT, to which the EU is itself a contracting party.

The approach of the arbitral tribunals does not resolve the intra-EU jurisdictional issue in a determinative manner. Even though the tribunals consistently decided that they had jurisdiction to decide in intra-EU ECT-based arbitrations, the issue is likely to be re-opened at enforcement and setting aside proceedings conducted before the common courts. This is a negative consequence, since it prolongs the duration of the full-scope proceedings and increases their costs.

In the light of the above, and of a similar attitude adopted by numerous other tribunals outside the Spanish saga cases, which have dismissed the intra-EU objections in treaty-based arbitration, the *Komstroy* judgment issued by the CJEU in 2021 appears to be a direct reaction to the negativity displayed by many arbitral tribunals.[31] That judgment appears to have been issued mainly to "correct" this line of arbitral tribunals' case law, unwelcomed by the CJEU and the European Commission.

As can be noticed from the answer to the second research question, much can be learned from the Spanish saga cases. An obvious implication is that the lessons learned will be useful for parties to treaty-based arbitrations commenced in the future, as well as for arbitrators (or other adjudicators, if permanent investment courts materialize in the future). Given the expanding

30 An important development occurred when this book was already in the production process, with a groundbreaking decision of the first tribunal to ever uphold the intra-EU jurisdictional objection – Green Power v. Spain, SCC Case No. V 2016/135, Award (16.06.2022). Keeping in mind the time constraints and the analysis here, which focuses on the first 21 Spanish saga cases, this cannot be dealt with in more detail in the first edition of this book.

31 Judgment of the Court (Grand Chamber) of 02.09.2021, Moldova v. Komstroy, Case No. C-741/19 (ECLI:EU:C:2021:655).

number of investments in the renewable energy sector, it is "very likely that the number of renewable energy arbitrations will significantly rise in the future".[32]

However, this is not the only context in which the analysis contained in this book may prove to be useful. The lessons learned may potentially become relevant earlier, before a dispute arises. It has been noted that "implementing an energy transition has also proven to be a difficult learning exercise for States".[33] The answers provided in reply to this research question can be a tool for policymakers and inform their understanding of the differences between non-compensable regulatory changes and reforms which are within the sovereign powers of a state but which, if introduced, will require the state to pay compensation to those adversely affected by such reforms. In other words, the analysis offered here can contribute to states' representatives making informed decisions, fully aware of where the "red line" is located, which states can cross but only if they are willing to accept consequences at the level of international law.

The lessons learned from the Spanish saga are useful for the renewable energy sector as a whole.[34] They apply to all types of technologies, including solar (photovoltaic – "PV" and concentrated solar power – "CSP"), wind (on-shore and off-shore), hydro and other renewable energy sources, such as geothermal or biomass. Moreover, these lessons are not confined to arbitrations involving an EU member state. On the contrary, they apply to similar factual situations, regardless of where in the world they occur.

Recent decreases in the costs of solar and wind energy production do not undermine the future relevance of the Spanish saga cases. Indeed, technologies which were considered as "an expensive niche" in 2010 are now capable

---

32 Marie-Provence Brue, Shaparak Saleh, Paris Arbitration Week Recap: Renewable Energies and Arbitration, Kluwer Arbitration Blog (16.04.2022), available at: http://arbitrationblog.kluwerarbitration.com/2022/04/16/paris-arbitration-week-recap-renewable-energies-and-arbitration/.

33 Nikos Lavranos, Cees Verburg, Renewable Energy Investment Disputes: Recent Developments and Implications for Prospective Energy Market Reforms, European Energy Law Report, 12 (2018), p. 93.

34 They may impact on the development of international investment law in general, not only as regards renewable energy or even the energy sector as a whole. Schill came to the correct conclusion that energy international investment law is part of "a building block" of international investment law, not a separate regime – Stephan W. Schill, Foreign Investment in the Energy Sector: Lessons for International Investment Law, in: Eric De Brabandere, Tarcisio Gazzini (eds.), Foreign Investment in the Energy Sector. Balancing Private and Public Interests (Brill 2014), p. 268.

of competing with fossil fuels on an arm's-length basis.[35] In just 10 years, significant cost decreases for newly commissioned projects occurred in the global-weighted average production cost of utility scale PV electricity (-85%), CSP electricity(-68%), onshore wind electricity (-56%) and off-shore wind electricity (-48%).[36] It appears that such technologies no longer require state support in order to be economically viable.[37] Renewable energy is currently considered as "the cheapest source of new power generation in most parts of the world".[38]

---

35 The decade 2010 to 2020 represents a remarkable period of cost reduction for solar and wind power technologies. The combination of targeted policy support and industry drive has seen renewable electricity from solar and wind power go from an expensive niche, to head-to-head competition with fossil fuels for new capacity. In the process, it has become clear that renewables will become the backbone of the electricity system and help decarbonise electricity generation, with costs lower than a business-as-usual future

– International Renewable Energy Agency, Renewable Power Generations Costs in 2020 (International Renewable Energy Agency 2021), available at: https://www.irena.org/-/media/Files/IRENA/Agency/Publication/2021/Jun/IRENA_Power_Generation_Costs_2020.pdf, p. 14. Similarly: World Meteorological Organization, United In Science 2020: A Multi-Organization High-Level Compilation of the Latest Climate Science Information (World Meteorological Organization 2020), available at: https://library.wmo.int/doc_num.php?explnum_id=10361, p. 19:

> Renewables are by now the cheapest source of new power generation in most parts of the world, with the global weighted average purchase or auction price for new solar power photovoltaic systems and onshore wind turbines now competitive with the marginal operating cost of existing coal plants by 2020.

See also: International Energy Agency, World Energy Outlook 2020 (IEA Publications 2020), available at: https://iea.blob.core.windows.net/assets/a72d8abf-de08-4385-8711-b8a062d6124a/WEO2020.pdf, p. 18: "With sharp cost reductions over the past decade, solar PV is consistently cheaper than new coal- or gas- fired power plants in most countries, and solar projects now offer some of the lowest cost electricity ever seen".

36 Renewable Power ..., ibid, p. 14.

37 Ibid, p. 16:

> As costs for solar PV and onshore wind have fallen, new renewable capacity is not only increasingly cheaper than new fossil fuel fired capacity, but increasingly undercuts the operating costs alone of existing coal fired power plants. Indeed, in Europe in 2021, coal-fired power plant operating costs are well above the costs of new solar PV and onshore wind (including the cost of CO_2 prices).

See also for example:

> [...] up to a few years ago, renewables were more costly than their alternatives, prompting States to provide support in the form of feed-in-tariffs, which were the main drive in the industry. This has changed fundamentally, and renewables are now becoming competitive in many jurisdictions without the need for State subsidies

– Brue, Saleh, *supra* note 32.

38 United In Science, *supra* note 35, p. 19, Johnson, McKenzie, Saunders, *supra* note 13, p. 8.

Nonetheless, at least three reasons explain why the Spanish saga experience regarding state support mechanisms is expected to remain relevant in the future. First, this fall in costs has not been replicated with respect to hydro, geothermal and biomass renewable energy. Moreover, COVID-19 pandemic and war in Ukraine are expected to have a negative impact on the supply side of the market, causing likely increase in prices. Second, notwithstanding such cost decreases, states will continue to support renewable energy projects in various ways, at least when it comes to accessing the national energy grid.[39] A new wave of incentivization is expected to become stronger in Europe, with the EU expected to undertake efforts to stop being net buyer of energy after the Russian invasion on Ukraine. Third, and most importantly, the book aims to distill from the Spanish saga lessons for the future. History repeats itself. The fall in energy demand is a good example. As noted in Chapter 2, Spain's accumulation of the tariff deficit was caused or accelerated by the fall in energy demand following the 2008 financial crisis. 12 years later, the COVID-19 pandemic caused a global decrease in energy demand, reaching 20% decrease in some jurisdictions.[40]

In addition, it is reasonable to assume that other technologies which are currently – or will be in future years – regarded as an "expensive niche", will be incentivized by states as part of their efforts to achieve long-term sustainable development goals and decarbonization.[41] Only by combining private innovation and public support will such new technologies transform into ones that are economically viable.[42] A "renewable hydrogen" is a good example, and

39 See for example: Johnson, McKenzie, Saunders, *supra* note 13, p. 67: "it is to be expected that many governments will continue to introduce support regimes to encourage foreign direct investment in renewables as part of climate change mitigation efforts".

40 In 2020, global energy demand fell by approximately 5% (World Energy Outlook 2020, *supra* note 35, p. 17). However, the pandemic had a stronger impact on some economies when compared with others, causing even a 20% fall in energy demand in some places – International Renewable Energy Agency, Post-COVID Recovery: An Agenda for Resilience, Development and Equality (International Renewable Energy Agency 2020), available at: https://www.irena.org/-/media/Files/IRENA/Agency/Publication/2020/Jun/IRENA_Post-COVID_Recovery_2020.pdf, p. 30: In several countries under lockdown, electricity demand has declined by 20% or more, given that higher residential usage is substantially outweighed by cuts in commercial and industrial demand.

41 See for example: United In Science, *supra* note 35, p. 19:

> Is it then possible to bridge the emissions gap? The short answer is yes, but time is running out. The Emissions Gap Reports have provided a detailed assessment of sectoral mitigation options in 2030, which shows that the economic and technical mitigation potential is sufficient to get on track to well below 2 °C and to 1.5 °C. A substantial part of the short-term potential can be realized through scaling up and replicating existing, well-proven policies that simultaneously contribute to other Sustainable Development Goals.

42 International Energy Agency identified "a boost to clean energy innovation" as one of four solutions to meet the emission cuts goals, noting that:

definitely not the only one.[43] A "new wave of incentivisation of renewable energy projects" has already been noted in the renewable energy industry.[44] As new technologies appear, old patterns in states' policies may be expected to return.

After all, there is nothing new under the sun.

> all the technologies needed to achieve deep emissions cuts to 2030 are available. But almost half of the emissions reductions achieved in the NZE [Net Zero Emissions – author's note] in 2050 come from technologies that today are at the demonstration or prototype stage

– International Energy Agency, World Energy Outlook 2021 (IEA Publications 2021), available at: https://iea.blob.core.windows.net/assets/4ed140c1-c3f3-4fd9-acae-789a4e14a23c/WorldEnergyOutlook2021.pdf, p. 18.

43 European Commission, A hydrogen strategy for a climate-neutral Europe. Communication from the Commission to the European Parliament, the European Council, the Council, the European Economic and Social Committee and the Committee of the Regions, COM(2020) 301 final (08.07.2020). On p. 2 it recognizes, among others, that:

> Investment in hydrogen will foster sustainable growth and jobs, which will be critical in the context of recovery from the COVID-19 crisis. [...] However, today renewable and low-carbon hydrogen are not yet cost competitive compared to fossil-based hydrogen. To harness all the opportunities associated with hydrogen, the European Union needs a strategic approach.

44 Brue, Saleh, *supra* note 32. This comes as no surprise if one is aware that capital flows are essential to ensuring growth in renewable energy production, since "most transition-related energy investment will need to be carried out by private developers, consumers and financiers responding to market signals and policies set by governments" – World Energy Outlook 2021, *supra* note 42, p. 18. As noted by Taylor, the energy sector is subsidized by states and will remain so, even if to a lesser degree. However, a rebalancing is expected, i.e. reducing subsidies for fossil fuels and increasing subsidies for renewable energies. See: Michael Taylor, Energy Subsidies: Evolution in the Global Energy Transformation to 2050 (International Renewable Energy Agency 2020), available at: https://www.irena.org/-/media/Files/IRENA/Agency/Publication/2020/Apr/IRENA_Energy_subsidies_2020.pdf, p. 7:

> The world's total, direct energy sector subsidies – including those to fossil fuels, renewables and nuclear power – are estimated to have been at least USD 634 billion in 2017. [...] IRENA's roadmap for more sustainable energy development sees a rebalancing of energy subsidies away from environmentally harmful ones to fossil fuels and towards support for renewables and energy efficiency by 2050.

Bibliography

Books and Reports

Alvarez, José E., The Boundaries of Investment Arbitration. The Use of Trade and European Human Rights Law in Investor-State Disputes (JurisNet 2018)

Balcerzak, Filip, Investor – State Arbitration and Human Rights (Brill 2017)

Bonnitcha, Jonathan, Substantive Protection under Investment Treaties: a Legal and Economic Analysis (Cambridge University Press 2014)

Born, Gary B., International Arbitration: Law and Practice (Kluwer Law International 2021)

Born, Gary B., International Commercial Arbitration (Kluwer Law International 2021)

Cameron, Peter D., International Energy Investment Law: The Pursuit of Stability (Oxford University Press 2010)

De Brabandere, Eric, Investment Treaty Arbitration as Public International Law (Cambridge University Press 2014)

Dolzer, Rudolf, Kriebaum, Ursula, Schreuer, Christoph, Principles of International Investment Law (Oxford University Press 2022)

Dugan, Christopher R., Wallace, Don Jr., Rubins, Noah, Sabahi, Borzu, Investor-State Arbitration (Oxford University Press 2019)

Eberhardt, Pia, Olivet, Cecilia, Steinfort, Lavinia, One Treaty to Rule Them All. The Ever-Expanding Energy Charter Treaty and the Power It Gives Corporations to Halt the Energy Transition (Corporate Europe Observatory and Transnational Institute 2018)

Gaillard, Emmanuel, Savage, John (eds.), Fouchard, Gaillard, Goldman On International Commercial Arbitration (Kluwer Law International 1999)

Ghouri, Ahmad, Interaction and Conflict of Treaties in Investment Arbitration (Kluwer Law International 2015)

Global Commission on the Geopolitics of Energy Transformation, A New World: The Geopolitics of the Energy Transformation (International Renewable Energy Agency 2019)

Henckels, Caroline, Proportionality and Deference in Investor-State Arbitration. Balancing Investment Protection and Regulatory Autonomy (Cambridge University Press 2015)

Hobér, Kaj, The Energy Charter Treaty. A Commentary (Oxford University Press 2020)

International Energy Agency, World Energy Investment 2021 (IEA Publications 2021)

International Energy Agency, World Energy Outlook 2020 (IEA Publications 2020)

International Energy Agency, World Energy Outlook 2021 (IEA Publications 2021)

International Renewable Energy Agency, Hydrogen from Renewable Power: Technology Outlook for the Energy Transition (International Renewable Energy Agency 2018)

International Renewable Energy Agency, Post-COVID Recovery: An Agenda for Resilience, Development and Equality (International Renewable Energy Agency 2020)

International Renewable Energy Agency, Renewable Power Generations Costs in 2020 (International Renewable Energy Agency 2021)

Johnson, Emma, McKenzie, Lucy, Saunders, Matthew, International Arbitration of Renewable Energy Disputes (Globe Law and Business 2021)

Kinsella, N. Stephan, Rubins, Noah D., International Investment, Political Risk, and Dispute Resolution: A Practitioner's Guide (Oceana Publications 2005)

Kläger, Roland, Fair and Equitable Treatment in International Investment Agreements (Oxford University Press 2011)

Kopar, Rahmi, Stability and Legitimate Expectations in International Energy Investments (Hart 2021)

Landmann, Niclas, Legitimate Expectations and Fair-and-Equitable-Treatment under the Energy Charter Treaty. A Comparative Analysis of the Renewable Energy Cases (Nomos 2022)

Newcombe, Andrew, Paradell, Lluís, Law and Practice of Investment Treaties: Standards of Treatment (Kluwer Law International 2009)

Özgür, Uğur Erman, Taxation of Foreign Investments under International Law: Article 21 of the Energy Charter Treaty (Energy Charter Secretariat 2015)

Palombino, Fulvio Maria, Fair and Equitable Treatment and the Fabric of General Principles (Springer 2018)

Reinisch, August, Schreuer, Christoph, International Protection of Investments. The Substantive Standards (Cambridge University Press 2020)

Resar, Alexander W., Cheng, Tai-Heng, Investor State Arbitration in a Changing World Order (Brill 2021)

Ripinsky, Sergey, Williams, Kevin, Damages in International Investment Law (British Institute of International and Comparative Law 2008)

Salacuse, Jeswald W., The Law of Investment Treaties (Oxford University Press 2021)

Schreuer, Christoph, Malintoppi, Loretta, Reinisch, August, Sinclair, Anthony, The ICSID Convention. A Commentary (Cambridge University Press 2009)

Sornarajah, Muthucumaraswamy, Resistance and Change in the International Law on Foreign Investment (Cambridge University Press 2015)

Taylor, Michael, Energy Subsidies: Evolution in the Global Energy Transformation to 2050 (International Renewable Energy Agency 2020)

Titi, Aikaterini, The Right to Regulate in International Investment Law (Nomos/Hart 2014)

UNCTAD, Fair and Equitable Treatment. UNCTAD Series on Issues in International Investment Agreements II (United Nations 2012)

UNCTAD, Investment Policy Framework for Sustainable Development (United Nations 2015)

UNCTAD, Taking of Property. UNCTAD Series on Issues in International Investment Agreements (United Nations 2000)

UNCTAD, World Investment Report 2021. Investing in Sustainable Recovery (United Nations 2021)

UNDP, Delivering Sustainable Energy in a Changing Climate. Strategy Note on Sustainable Energy 2017–2021 (United Nations 2016)

UNEP, Emissions Gap Report 2019 (United Nations 2019)

UNEP, The Heat Is On. A World of Climate Promises Not Yet Delivered. Emissions Gap Report 2021 (United Nations 2021)

Vadi, Valentina, Proportionality, Reasonableness and Standards of Review in International Investment Law and Arbitration (Edward Elgar 2018)

Vandevelde, Kenneth J., Bilateral Investment Treaties: History, Policy, and Interpretation (Oxford University Press 2010)

Vandevelde, Kenneth J., The First Bilateral Investment Treaties: U.S. Postwar Friendship, Commerce, and Navigation Treaties (Oxford University Press 2017)

World Meteorological Organization, United In Science 2020: A Multi-Organization High-Level Compilation of the Latest Climate Science Information (World Meteorological Organization 2020)

Yourow, Howard Charles, The Margin of Appreciation Doctrine in the Dynamics of European Human Rights Jurisprudence (Brill 1996)

Articles and Book Chapters

Anderle, Marek, Leontiev, Andrej, Here Comes Doomsday … Or Does It? – Implications of Achmea on Intra-EU Investment Arbitration in Light of Recent Case Law, European Investment Law and Arbitration Review, 6:1 (2022)

Arato, Julian, The Margin of Appreciation in International Investment Law, Virginia Journal of International Law, 54:3 (2014)

Argyropoulou, Venetia, Vattenfall in the Aftermath of Achmea: Between a Rock and a Hard Place?, European Investment Law and Arbitration Review, 4:1 (2019)

Arif, Sahra, The Future of Intra-EU Investment Arbitration: Intra-EU Investment Arbitration under the ECT Post Achmea, European Investment Law and Arbitration Review, 4:1 (2019)

Beharry, Christina L., Prejudgment Interest Rates in International Investment Arbitration, Journal of International Dispute Settlement, 8:1 (2016)

Bellantuono, Giuseppe, The Misguided Quest for Regulatory Stability in the Renewable Energy Sector, Journal of World Energy Law & Business, 10:4 (2017)

Bermann, George A., ECT and European Union Law, in: Scherer, Maxi (ed.), International Arbitration in the Energy Sector (Oxford University Press 2018)

Bernasconi-Osterwalder, Nathalie, Brauch, Martin Dietrich, Redesigning the Energy Charter Treaty to Advance the Low-Carbon Transition, Transnational Dispute Management, 1 (2019)

Biggs, Jack, The Scope of Investors' Legitimate Expectations under the FET Standard in the European Renewable Energy Cases, ICSID Review – Foreign Investment Law Journal, 36:1 (2021)

Bilanova, Anna, Kudrna, Jaroslav, The End of Investment Arbitration as We Know It, European Investment Law and Arbitration Review, 3:1 (2018)

Bjorklund, Andrea K., Waiver and the Exhaustion of Local Remedies Rule in NAFTA Jurisprudence, in: Weiler, Todd (ed.), NAFTA Investment Law and Arbitration: Past Issues, Current Practice, Future Prospects (Transnational Publishers 2004)

Bobek, Michal, The Court of Justice of the European Union, in: Arnull, Anthony, Chalmers, Damian (eds.), The Oxford Handbook of European Union Law (Oxford University Press 2015)

Boddicker, Joseph M., Whose Dictionary Controls?: Recent Challenges to the Term "Investment" in ICSID Arbitration, American University Law Review, 25:5 (2010)

Boltenko, Olga, The Umbrella Revolution: State Contracts and Umbrella Clauses in Contemporary Investment Law, in: Chaisse, Julien, Choukroune, Leïla, Jusoh, Sufian (eds.), Handbook of International Investment Law and Policy (Springer 2021)

Bonafé, Ernesto, Mete, Gökçe, Escalated Interactions between EU Energy Law and the Energy Charter Treaty, Journal of World Energy Law & Business, 9:3 (2016)

Bonafé, Ernesto, Georgiou, Natasha A., The New International Energy Charter and the Rule of Law in the Global Energy Architecture, European Energy Law Report, 11 (2017)

Brue, Marie-Provence, Saleh, Shaparak, Paris Arbitration Week Recap: Renewable Energies and Arbitration, Kluwer Arbitration Blog (16.04.2022)

Bungenberg, Marc, The Multilateral Investment Court – Royal Road Or Dead End for the EU Legal Order, International Business Law Journal, 5 (2019)

Burgstaller, Markus, Zarowna, Agnieszka, The Growing Importance of Investment Arbitration in Relation to Tax Measures in the Energy and Natural Resources Sectors, Turkish Commercial Law Review, 4:1 (2018)

Caetano, Xavier Junior Ely, Costa Morosini, Fabio, El Estándar de Trato Justo y Equitativo, in: Álvarez Zárate, José Manuel, Żenkiewicz, Maciej (eds.), El Derecho Internacional de las Inversiones. Desarrollo Actual de Normas y Principios (Universidad Externado de Colombia 2021)

Calamita, N. Jansen, The Principle of Proportionality and the Problem of Indeterminacy in International Investment Treaties, Yearbook on International Investment Law & Policy (2013–2014)

Cameron, Peter D., Stabilization and the Impact of Changing Patterns of Energy Investment, Journal of World Energy Law & Business, 10:5 (2017)

Cameron, Peter D., Reflections on Sovereignty Over Natural Resources and the Enforcement of Stabilization Clauses, Yearbook on International Investment Law and Policy (2011–2012)

Campbell, Christopher, House of Cards: the Relevance of Legitimate Expectations under Fair and Equitable Treatment Provisions in Investment Treaty Law, Journal of International Arbitration, 30:4 (2013)

Coe, Jack J. Jr., The Mandate of Chapter 11 Tribunals – Jurisdiction and Related Questions, in: Weiler, Todd (ed.), NAFTA Investment Law an Arbitration: Current Practice, Future Prospects (Transnational Publishers 2004)

Colaiuta, Virginie, When Does a Violation of the Domestic Law of the Host State Amount to a Violation of a Public International Law Principle in Determining Protection of Investors' Claims?, in: Coop, Graham (ed.), Energy Dispute Resolution: Investment Protection, Transit and the Energy Charter Treaty (JurisNet 2011)

Coop, Graham, Seif, Isabella, ECT and States' Right to Regulate, in: Scherer, Maxi (ed.), International Arbitration in the Energy Sector (Oxford University Press 2018)

Crawford, James, Treaty and Contract in Investment Arbitration, Arbitration International, 24 (2008)

Crawford, James R., State Responsibility, in: Wolfrum, Rüdiger (ed.), Max Planck Encyclopedia of Public International Law (online access)

Crawford, Jamieson, Assessing the CJEU's Decisions in Achmea and Opinion 1/17 in Light of the Proposed Multilateral Investment Court – Winner of the Essay Competition 2020, European Investment Law and Arbitration Review, 5:1 (2021)

Dalhuisen, Jan H., Guzman, Andrew T., Expropriatory and Non-Expropriatory Takings Under International Investment Law, UC Berkeley Public Law Research Paper No. 2137107 (2013)

Dias Simões, Fernando, Charanne and Construction Investments v. Spain: Legitimate Expectations and Investments in Renewable Energy, Review of European, Comparative & International Environmental Law, 26:2 (2017)

Dimitrov, Ivaylo, Legitimate Expectations in the Absence of Specific Commitment According to the Findings in Blusun v. Italy: Is there Inconsistency Among the Tribunals in the Solar Energy Cases?, Kluwer Arbitration Blog (18.08.2017)

Dolzer, Rudolf, Fair and Equitable Treatment: Today's Contours, Santa Clara Journal of International Law, 12:1 (2014)

Draguiev, Deyan, Investment Treaty Arbitration in the Renewable Energy Sector: Overview of Arbitral Case Law on Legitimate Expectations in the Light of Policy, Transnational Dispute Management, 7 (2018)

Draguiev, Deyan, 2018 In Review: The Achmea Decision and Its Reverberations in the World of Arbitration, Kluwer Arbitration Blog (16.01.2019)

Dromgool, Thomas, Ybarra-Enguix, Daniel, The Fair and Equitable Treatment Standard and the Revocation of Feed in Tariffs – Foreign Renewable Energy Investments in Crisis-Struck Spain, in: Mauerhofer, Voler (ed.), Legal Aspects of Sustainable Development (Springer 2016)

Faccio, Sondra, The Assessment of the FET Standard between Legitimate Expectations and Economic Impact in the Italian Solar Energy Investment Case Law, Questions of International Law (Zoom-In), 71 (2020)

Fouchard, Clement, Thieffry, Vanessa, CJEU Ruling in Moldova v. Komstroy: the End of Intra-EU Investment Arbitration Under the Energy Charter Treaty (and a Restrictive Interpretation of the Notion of Protected Investment), Kluwer Arbitration Blog (07.09.2021)

García-Castrillón, Carmen Otero, Spain and Investment Arbitration: the Renewable Energy Explosion, Investor-State Arbitration Series Paper no. 17, Centre for International Governance (2016)

Gáspár-Szilágyi, Szilárd, Usynin, Maxim, The Uneasy Relationship between Intra-EU Investment Tribunals and the Court of Justice's Achmea Judgment, European Investment Law and Arbitration Review, 4:1 (2019)

Gazzini, Tarcisio, Energy Charter Treaty: Achievements, Challenges and Perspectives, in: De Brabandere, Eric, Gazzini, Tarcisio (eds.), Foreign Investment in the Energy Sector. Balancing Private and Public Interests (Brill 2014)

Gordon, Brady, A Sceptical Analysis of the Enforcement of ISDS Awards in the EU Following the Decision of the CJEU on CETA, European Investment Law and Arbitration Review, 5:1 (2021)

Gotanda, John Y., Compound Interest in International Disputes, Law and Policy in International Business, 34:2 (2003)

Grierson-Weiler, Todd J., Laird, Ian A., Standards of Treatment, in: Muchlinski, Peter, Ortino, Federico, Schreuer, Christoph (eds.), The Oxford Handbook of International Investment Law (Oxford University Press 2008)

Grigera Naón, Horacio A., Should International Commercial Arbitrators Declare a Law Unconstitutional, in: Caron, David D., Schill, Stephan W., Cohen Smutny, Abby, Triantafilou, Epaminontas E. (eds.), Practising Virtue: Inside International Arbitration (Oxford University Press 2015)

Gritón Salias, María Cristina, Do Umbrella Clauses Apply to Unilateral Undertakings?, in: Binder, Christina, Kriebaum, Ursula, Reinisch, August, Wittich, Stephan (eds.), International Investment Law for the 21st Century: Essays in Honour of Christoph Schreuer (Oxford University Press 2009)

Halonen, Laura, Containing the Scope of the Umbrella Clause, in: Grierson Weiler, Todd J. (ed.), Investment Treaty Arbitration and International Law (JurisNet 2008)

Hirsch, Moshe, Between Fair and Equitable Treatment and Stabilization Clause: Stable Legal Environment and Regulatory Change in International Investment Law, Journal of World Investment & Trade, 12:6 (2011)

Hobér, Kaj, Overview of Energy Charter Treaty Cases, in: Scherer, Maxi (ed.), International Arbitration in the Energy Sector (Oxford University Press 2015)

Horvath, Gunther J., The Duty of the Tribunal to Render an Enforceable Award, Journal of International Arbitration, 18:2 (2001)

Karl, Joachim, FDI in the Energy Sector: Recent Trends and Policy Issues, in: De Brabandere, Eric, Gazzini, Tarcisio (eds.), Foreign Investment in the Energy Sector. Balancing Private and Public Interests (Brill 2014)

Kingsbury, Benedict, Schill, Stephan W., Public Law Concepts to Balance Investors' Rights with State Regulatory Actions in the Public Interest – the Concept of Proportionality, in: Schill, Stephan W. (ed.), International Investment Law and Comparative Public Law (Oxford University Press 2010)

Kingsbury, Benedict, Schill, Stephan W., Investor-State Arbitration as a Governance: Fair and Equitable Treatment, Proportionality and the Emerging Global Administrative Law, in: van den Berg, Albert Jan (ed.), 50 years of the New York Convention (Wolters Kluwer 2009)

Konoplyanik, Andrey A., Multiple Investment Regimes for Russian Subsoil Resources: Work in Progress or Utopia?, in: De Brabandere, Eric, Gazzini, Tarcisio (eds.), Foreign Investment in the Energy Sector. Balancing Private and Public Interests (Brill 2014)

Lamy, Pascal, Foreword, in: Selivanova, Yulia (ed.), Regulation of Energy in International Trade Law. WTO, NAFTA and Energy Charter (Wolters Kluwer 2011)

Laryea, Emmanuel T., Legitimate Expectations in Investment Treaty Law: Concept and Scope of Application, in: Chaisse, Julien, Choukroune, Leïla, Jusoh, Sufian (eds.), Handbook of International Investment Law and Policy (Springer 2021)

Lavranos, Nikos, Regime Interaction in Investment Arbitration: EU Law; From Peaceful Co-Existence to Permanent Conflict, Kluwer Arbitration Blog (13.01.2022)

Lavranos, Nikos, The World after the Termination of Intra-EU BIT s, European Investment Law and Arbitration Review, 5:1 (2021)

Lavranos, Nikos, Verburg, Cees, Renewable Energy Investment Disputes: Recent Developments and Implications for Prospective Energy Market Reforms, European Energy Law Report, 12 (2018)

Levashova, Yulia, Fair and Equitable Treatment and Investor's Due Diligence Under International Investment Law, Netherlands International Law Review, 67:2 (2020)

Levine, Matthew A. J., Emerging Practice on Investor Diligence: Jurisdiction, Admissibility, and Merits, in: Chaisse, Julien, Choukroune, Leïla, Jusoh, Sufian (eds.), Handbook of International Investment Law and Policy (Springer 2021)

Lew, Julian, The Law Applicable to the Form and Substance of the Arbitration Clause, in: van den Berg, Albert Jan (ed.), Improving the Efficiency of Arbitration Agreements and Awards: 40 Years of Application of the New York Convention (Kluwer Law International 1999)

Liebkind, Anina, Norburg, Fredrik, Dittmer Hvarfner, Ossian, The ECT, Achmea and Intra-EU Arbitration – Swedish Court Requests Preliminary Ruling from the CJEU, European Investment Law and Arbitration Review, 6:1 (2022)

López Escarcena, Sebastián, La Expropriación Condicionada en los Tratados de Inversión, in: Álvarez Zárate, José Manuel, Żenkiewicz, Maciej (eds.), El Derecho Internacional de las Inversiones. Desarrollo Actual de Normas y Principios (Universidad Externado de Colombia 2021)

Malinvaud, Carole, Non-pecuniary Remedies in Investment Treaty and Commercial Arbitration, in: van den Berg, Albert Jan (ed.), 50 Years of the New York Convention (Kluwer Law International 2009)

Marboe, Irmgard, Assessing Compensation and Damages in Expropriation versus Non-expropriation Cases, in: Beharry, Christina L. (ed.), Contemporary and Emerging Issues on the Law of Damages and Valuation in International Investment Arbitration (Brill 2018)

Maynard, Simon, Legitimate Expectations and the Interpretation of the Legal Stability Obligation, European Investment Law and Arbitration Review, 1:1 (2016)

Mbengue, Makane Moïse, Raju, Deepak, Energy, Environment and Foreign Investment, in: De Brabandere, Eric, Gazzini, Tarcisio (eds.), Foreign Investment in the Energy Sector. Balancing Private and Public Interests (Brill 2014)

McLachlan, Campbell, Investment Treaty Arbitration: The Legal Framework, in: van den Berg, Albert Jan (ed.), 50 Years of the New York Convention (Wolters Kluwer 2009)

Meltzer, Joshua P., Investment, in: Lester, Simon, Mercurio, Bryan (eds.), Bilateral and Regional Trade Agreements. Commentary and Analysis (Cambridge University Press 2015)

Mernier, André, Introductory Remarks, in: Coop, Graham (ed.), Energy Dispute Resolution: Investment Protection, Transit and the Energy Charter Treaty (JurisNet 2011)

Miles, Craig S., Where's My Umbrella? An "Ordinary Meaning" Approach to Answering Three Key Questions That Have Emerged from the "Umbrella Clause" Debate, in: Grierson Weiler, Todd J. (ed.), Investment Treaty Arbitration and International Law (JurisNet 2008)

Muchlinski, Peter, Caveat Investor – The Relevance of the Conduct of the Investor under the Fair and Equitable Treatment Standard, International and Comparative Law Quarterly, 55:3 (2006)

Negret, Auriane, Opinion of Advocate General Saugmandsgaard Øe in Anie and Others v. Italy – End of the Road for intra-EU ECT Arbitration?, European Investment Law and Arbitration Review, 6:1 (2022)

Noilhac, Amélie, Renewable Energy Investment Cases Against Spain and the Quest for Regulatory Consistency, Questions of International Law (Zoom-In), 71 (2020)

Odermatt, Jed, Is EU Law International? Case C-741/19 Republic of Moldova v Komstroy LLC and the Autonomy of the EU Legal Order, European Papers – A Journal on Law and Integration, 6:3 (2021)

Ortino, Federico, Investment Treaties, Sustainable Development and Reasonableness Review: A Case Against Strict Proportionality Balancing, Leiden Journal of International Law, 30:1 (2017)

Ottinger, Richard L., Mathews, Lily, Czachor, Nadia Elizabeth, Renewable Energy in National Legislation: Challenges and Opportunities, in: Zillman, Don, Redgwell, Catherine, Omorogbe, Yinka, Barrera-Hernández, Lila K. (eds.), Beyond The Carbon Economy: Energy Law in Transition (Oxford University Press 2008)

Pang Hui, Helen, The Role of Investor-State Arbitration in Promoting Climate Change Mitigation: from "Shield" to "Sword" through Renewable Energy Disputes?, Academy of European Law, European Society of International Law Paper, AEL 2022/05 (2022)

Paulsson, Jan, Arbitration Without Privity, ICSID Review – Foreign Investment Law Journal, 10:2 (1995)

Platte, Martin, An Arbitrator's Duty to Render Enforceable Awards, Journal of International Arbitration, 20:3 (2003)

Polanco, Rodrigo, Manrique de Lara Seminario, Jorge Luis, Cláusulas Paraguas, in: Álvarez Zárate, José Manuel, Żenkiewicz, Maciej (eds.), El Derecho Internacional de las Inversiones. Desarrollo Actual de Normas y Principios (Universidad Externado de Colombia 2021)

Power, Richard, Novenergia v. Kingdom of Spain, the ECT and the ECJ: Where to Now for Intra-EU ECT Claims?, Kluwer Arbitration Blog (20.03.2018)

Reuter, Alexander, Retroactive Reduction of Support for Renewable Energy and Investment Treaty Protection from the Perspective of Shareholders and Lenders, Transnational Dispute Management, 3 (2015)

Reynoso, Isabella, Spain's Renewable Energy Saga: Lessons for International Investment Law and Sustainable Sevelopment, Investment Treaty News (27.06.2019)

Rivkin, David W., Lamb, Sophie J., Leslie, Nicola K., The Future of Investor-State Dispute Settlement in the Energy Sector: Engaging with Climate Change, Human Rights and the Rule of Law, Journal of World Energy Law & Business, 8:2 (2015)

Rowe, Samantha J., Goh, Nelson, Resolving Perceived Norm Conflict through Principles of Treaty Interpretation. The January 2019 EU Member States' Declarations, European Investment Law and Arbitration Review, 5:1 (2021)

Rubins, Noah, Sinha, Vasuda, Roberts, Baxter, Approaches to Valuation in Investment Treaty Arbitration, in: Beharry, Christina L. (ed.), Contemporary and Emerging Issues on the Law of Damages and Valuation in International Investment Arbitration (Brill 2018)

Rusche, Tim Maxian, How to Enforce the Achmea Judgment – Tools for EU Member States before, during and after Investment Arbitration Proceedings Brought by an Investor from Another EU Member State, European Investment Law and Arbitration Review, 6:1 (2022)

Rush, Garrett, Sequeira, Kiran, Shopp, Matthew, Valuation Techniques for Early-Stage Businesses in Investor-State Arbitration, in: Beharry, Christina L. (ed.), Contemporary and Emerging Issues on the Law of Damages and Valuation in International Investment Arbitration (Brill 2018)

Rusnák, Urban, Comment: Quo Vadis Energy Charter Treaty?, Energy Charter Secretariat News (12.04.2021)

Sandberg, David, Rosell Svensson, Jacob, Achmea and the Implications for Challenge Proceedings before National Courts, European Investment Law and Arbitration Review, 5:1 (2021)

Scherer, Maxi, Introduction, in: Scherer, Maxi (ed.), International Arbitration in the Energy Sector (Oxford University Press 2018)

Scheu, Julian, Nikolov, Petyo, AG Szpunar's Opinion in Case C-741/19: Preparing the End of Intra-EU Investment Arbitration Under the Energy Charter Treaty?, Kluwer Arbitration Blog (25.05.2021)

Schill, Stephan W., Fair and Equitable Treatment under Investment Treaties as an Embodiment of the Rule of Law, Institute for International Law and Justice, IILJ Working Paper 2006/6

Schill, Stephan W., International Investment Law and the Rule of Law, Amsterdam Law School Legal Studies Research Paper No. 2017-18, Amsterdam Center for International Law No. 2017-15

Schill, Stephan W., Foreign Investment in the Energy Sector: Lessons for International Investment Law, in: De Brabandere, Eric, Gazzini, Tarcisio (eds.), Foreign Investment in the Energy Sector. Balancing Private and Public Interests (Brill 2014)

Schreuer, Christoph, Evolution of Investment Law in Treaty Making and Arbitral Practice, in: Hobbe, Stephan, Scheu, Julian (eds.), Evolution, Evaluation and Future Developments in International Investment Law. Proceedings of the 10 Year Anniversary Conference of the International Investment Law Centre Cologne (Nomos 2021)

Schreuer, Christoph, Fair and Equitable Treatment (FET): Interactions with Other Standards, in: Coop, Graham, Ribeiro, Clarisse (eds.), Investment Protection and the Energy Charter Treaty (JurisNet 2008)

Schreuer, Christoph, Kriebaum, Ursula, At What Time Must Legitimate Expectations Exist?, in: Werner, Jacques, Arif Hyder, Ali (eds.), A Liber Amicorum: Thomas Walde – Law Beyond Conventional Thoughts (Cameron May 2009)

Schreuer, Christoph, Non-Pecuniary Remedies in ICSID Arbitration, Arbitration International, 20:4 (2004)

Schumacher, Kai F., Klönne, Henner, Discounted Cash Flow Method, in: Beharry, Christina L. (ed.), Contemporary and Emerging Issues on the Law of Damages and Valuation in International Investment Arbitration (Brill 2018)

Selivanova, Yulia, The Energy Charter and the International Energy Governance, in: Selivanova, Yulia (ed.), Regulation of Energy in International Trade Law. WTO, NAFTA and Energy Charter (Wolters Kluwer 2011)

Selivanova, Yulia, Changes in Renewables Support Policy and Investment Protection under the Energy Charter Treaty: Analysis of Jurisprudence and Outlook for the Current Arbitration Cases, ICSID Review – Foreign Investment Law Journal, 33:2 (2018)

Shan, Wenhua, Zhang, Sheng, The Treaty of Lisbon: Half Way toward a Common Investment Policy, European Journal of International Law, 21:4 (2010)

Sinclair, Anthony C., The Origins of the Umbrella Clause in the International Law of Investment Protection, Arbitration International, 20:4 (2004)

Snodgrass, Elizabeth, Protecting Investors' Legitimate Expectations: Recognizing and Delimiting a General Principle, ICSID Review – Foreign Investment Law Journal, 21:1 (2006)

Soloch, Bartosz, International Investment Law: A Self-Proclaimed Ally in Commission's Rule of Law Endeavors, in: Chaisse, Julien, Choukroune, Leïla, Jusoh, Sufian (eds.), Handbook of International Investment Law and Policy (Springer 2021)

Sornarajah, Muthucumaraswamy, Developing Countries in the Investment Treaty System: A Law for Need or a Law for Greed?, in: Schill, Stephan W., Tams, Christian J., Hofmann, Rainer (eds.), International Investment Law and Development. Bridging the Gap (Edward Elgar 2015)

Söderlund, Christer, The Future of the Energy Charter Treaty in the context of the Lisbon Treaty, in: Coop, Graham (ed.), Energy Dispute Resolution: Investment Protection, Transit and the Energy Charter Treaty (JurisNet 2011)

Stern, Brigitte, 2019 Freshfields Lecture: Investment Arbitration and State Sovereignty, ICSID Review – Foreign Investment Law Journal, 35:3 (2020)

Stompfe, Philipp, The Higher Regional Court of Frankfurt am Main Is the First European Court to Declare the Achmea Case a Landmark Decision with Significance for All Intra-EU BITs, European Investment Law and Arbitration Review, 6:1 (2022)

Sukma Dwi, Andrina, Green Technology Disputes in Stockholm (2019), available at: https://sccarbitrationinstitute.se/sites/default/files/2022-11/green-technology-disputes-in-stockholm.pdf

Tanzi, Attila, International Law and Foreign Investment in Hydroelectric Industry: A Multidimensional Analysis, in: De Brabandere, Eric, Gazzini, Tarcisio (eds.), Foreign Investment in the Energy Sector. Balancing Private and Public Interests (Brill 2014)

Tietje, Christian, Ruff, Darius, Schmitt, Mathea, Final Countdown in EU Investment Protection Law: Does the ECJ's Komstroy Ruling also Apply in intra-EU ICSID Proceedings?, Beiträge zum Transnationalen Wirtschaftsrecht (2022)

Uchkunova, Inna, Temnikov, Oleg, A Procrustean Bed: Pre- and Post-award Interest in ICSID Arbitration, ICSID Review – Foreign Investment Law Journal, 29:3 (2014)

Vadi, Valentina, Foreign Investment in the Energy Sector and Public Health, in: De Brabandere, Eric, Gazzini, Tarcisio (eds.), Foreign Investment in the Energy Sector. Balancing Private and Public Interests (Brill 2014)

Vandevelde, Kenneth J., The Liberal Vision of the International Law on Foreign Investment, in: Lim, C. L. (ed.), Alternative Visions of the International Law on Foreign Investment. Essays in Honour of Muthucumaraswamy Sornarajah (Cambridge University Press 2016)

Vandevelde, Kenneth J., A Unified Theory of Fair and Equitable Treatment, New York University Journal of International Law & Politics, 43:1 (2010)

Vandevelde, Kenneth J., Rebalancing Through Exceptions, Lewis & Clark Law Review, 17:2 (2013)

Vedder, Hans, Rønne, Anita, Roggenkamp, Martha, del Guayo, Iñigo, EU Energy Law, in: Roggenkamp, Martha M., Redgwell, Catherine, Rønne, Anita, del Guayo, Iñigo (eds.), Energy Law in Europe: National, EU, and International Regulation (Oxford University Press 2016)

Viñuales, Jorge E., Geopolitics of the Energy Transformation, Revue Européenne du Droit (Governing Globalization), 2 (2020)

Viñuales, Jorge E., Investor Diligence in Investment Arbitration: Sources and Arguments, ICSID Review – Foreign Investment Law Journal, 32:2 (2017)

Vis-Dunbar, Damon, EU Member States Reject the Call to Terminate Intra-EU Bilateral Investment Treaties, Investment Treaty News (10.02.2009)

Waelde, Thomas W., Kolo, Abba, Environmental Regulation, Investment Protection and Regulatory Taking in International Law, International and Comparative Law Quarterly, 50:4 (2001)

Waelde, Thomas W., Ndi, George, Stabilizing International Investment Commitments: International Law Versus Contract Interpretation, Texas International Law Journal, 31:2 (1996)

Wälde, Thomas W., Sabahi, Borzu, Compensation, Damages and Valuation, in: Muchlinski, Peter, Ortino, Federico, Schreuer, Christoph (eds.), The Oxford Handbook of International Investment Law (Oxford University Press 2008)

Żenkiewicz, Maciej, Interferencia y Privación a la Propiedad y los Derechos, in: Álvarez Zárate, José Manuel, Żenkiewicz, Maciej (eds.), El Derecho Internacional de las Inversiones. Desarrollo Actual de Normas y Principios (Universidad Externado de Colombia 2021)

Živković, Velimir, Fair and Equitable Treatment Between the International and National Rule of Law, Journal of World Investment & Trade, 20:4 (2019)

Arbitral Documents (Awards, Decisions, Opinions, etc.)

Abaclat v. Argentina, ICSID Case No. ARB/07/5, Decision on Jurisdiction and Admissibility (04.08.2011)
Achmea v. Slovakia, PCA Case No. 2008-13, Award on Jurisdiction, Arbitrability and Suspension (26.10.2010)
Achmea v. Slovakia, PCA Case No. 2008-13, Final Award (07.12.2012)
Adamakopoulos v. Greece, ICSID Case No. ARB/15/49, Statement of Dissent of Professor Marcelo Kohen (03.02.2020)
Adamakopoulos v. Greece, ICSID Case No. ARB/15/49, Decision on Jurisdiction (07.02.2020)
ADC v. Hungary, ICSID Case No. ARB/03/16, Award (02.10.2006)
Addiko v. Croatia, ICSID Case No. ARB/17/37, Decision on Croatia's Jurisdictional Objection Related to the Alleged Incompatibility of the BIT with the EU Acquis (12.06.2020)
AES v. Argentina, ICSID Case No. ARB/02/17, Decision on Jurisdiction (26.04.2005)
AES v. Hungary, ICSID Case No. ARB/07/22, Award (23.09.2010)
Al-Bahloul v. Tajikistan, SCC Case No. V 064/2008, Partial Award on Jurisdiction and Liability (02.09.2009)
Al-Bahloul v. Tajikistan, SCC Case No. V 064/2008, Final Award (08.06.2010)
Alpha Projektholding v. Ukraine, ICSID Case No. ARB/07/16, Award (8.11.2010)
AMF v. Czech Republic, PCA Case No. 2017-15, Final Award (11.05.2020)
Amoco v. Iran, Case No. 56, Partial Award (Award No. 310-56-3) (14.07.1987)
Anglia Auto v. Czech Republic, SCC Case No. V 2014/181, Final Award (10.03.2017)
Antaris v. Czech Republic, PCA Case No. 2014-01, Award (02.05.2018)
Antin v. Spain, ICSID Case No. ARB/13/31, Award (15.06.2018)
Antin v. Spain, ICSID Case No. ARB/13/31, Decision on Annulment (30.07.2021)
Archer Daniels v. Mexico, ICSID Case No. ARB(AF)/04/05, Award (21.11.2007)
Arif v. Moldova, ICSID Case No. ARB/11/23, Award (08.04.2013)
ATA v. Jordan, ICSID Case No. ARB/08/2, Award (18.05.2010)
Azurix v. Argentina, ICSID Case No. ARB/01/12, Award (14.07.2006)
Bayindir v. Pakistan, ICSID Case No. ARB/03/29, Award (27.08.2009)
BayWa v. Spain, ICSID Case No. ARB/15/16, Decision on Jurisdiction, Liability and Directions on Quantum (02.12.2019)
BayWa v. Spain, ICSID Case No. ARB/15/16, Dissenting Opinion (02.12.2019)
BayWa v. Spain, ICSID Case No. ARB/15/16, Award (25.01.2021)
Bear Creek v. Peru, ICSID Case No. ARB/14/21, Award (30.11.2017)
Belenergia v. Italy, ICSID Case No. ARB/15/40, Award (06.08.2019)
BG v. Argentina, UNCITRAL, Final Award (24.12.2007)
Binder v. Czech Republic, UNCITRAL, Award on Jurisdiction (06.06.2007)
BIVAC v. Paraguay, ICSID Case No. ARB/07/9, Decision of the Tribunal on Objections to Jurisdiction (29.05.2009)

Biwater v. Tanzania, ICSID Case No. ARB/05/22, Award (24.07.2008)
Blusun v. Italy, ICSID Case No. ARB/14/3, Award (27.12.2016)
Burlington v. Ecuador, ICSID Case No. ARB/08/5, Dissenting Opinion of Arbitrator Orrego Vicuña (08.11.2012)
Burlington v. Ecuador, ICSID Case No. ARB/08/5, Decision on Liability (14.12.2012)
Busta v. Czech Republic, SCC Case No. V 2015/014, Final Award (10.03.2017)
Caratube v. Kazakhstan, ICSID Case No. ARB/13/13, Award (27.09.2017)
Cargill v. Mexico, ICSID Case No. ARB(AF)/05/2, Award (18.09.2009)
Cavalum v. Spain, ICSID Case No. ARB/15/34, Decision on Jurisdiction, Liability and Directions on Quantum (31.08.2020)
Cavalum v. Spain, ICSID Case No. ARB/15/34, Dissenting Opinion of David R. Haigh Q.C. (31.08.2020)
CC/Devas v. India, PCA Case No. 2013-09, Award on Jurisdiction and Merits (25.07.2016)
CEF v. Italy, SCC Case No. V 2015/158, Award (16.01.2019)
Charanne v. Spain, SCC Case No. V 062/2012, Dissenting Opinion of Prof. Guido Santiago Tawil (21.12.2015)
Charanne v. Spain, SCC Case No. V 062/2012, Award (21.01.2016)
Chemtura v. Canada, UNCITRAL, Award (02.08.2010)
CME v. Czech Republic, UNCITRAL, Partial Award (13.01.2001)
CMS v. Argentina, ICSID Case No. ARB/01/8, Award (12.05.2005)
CMS v. Argentina, ICSID Case No. ARB/01/8, Decision on Annulment (25.09.2007)
Compañía de Aguas v. Argentina, ICSID Case No. ARB/97/3, Award (20.08.2007)
ConocoPhillips v. Venezuela, ICSID Case No. ARB/07/30, Decision on Jurisdiction and the Merits (03.09.2013)
Continental Casualty v. Argentina, ICSID Case No. ARB/03/9, Award (05.09.2008)
Copper Mesa v. Ecuador, PCA Case No. 2012-2, Award (15.03.2016)
Crystallex v. Venezuela, ICSID Case No. ARB(AF)11/2, Award (04.04.2016)
Cube v. Spain, ICSID Case No. ARB/15/20, Decision on Jurisdiction, Liability and Partial Decision on Quantum (19.02.2019)
Cube v. Spain, ICSID Case No. ARB/15/20, Separate and Partial Dissenting Opinion (19.02.2019)
Cube v. Spain, ICSID Case No. ARB/15/20, Award (15.07.2019)
Cube v. Spain, ICSID Case No. ARB/15/20, Decision on the Continuation of the Provisional Stay of Enforcement of the Award (17.04.2020)
Cube v. Spain, ICSID Case No. ARB/15/20, Decision on Annulment (28.03.2022)
Dan Cake v. Hungary, ICSID Case No. ARB/12/9, Decision on Jurisdiction and Liability (24.08.2015)
de Nul v. Egypt, ICSID Case No. ARB/04/13, Decision on Jurisdiction (16.06.2006)
Duke Energy v. Ecuador, ICSID Case No. ARB/04/19, Award (18.08.2008)
Eastern Sugar v. Czech Republic, SCC Case No. 088/2004, Partial Award (27.03.2007)

EDF v. Argentina, ICSID Case No. ARB/03/23, Award (11.06.2012)
EDF v. Romania, ICSID Case No. ARB/05/13, Award (08.10.2009)
Eiser v. Spain, ICSID Case No. ARB/13/36, Award (04.05.2017)
Eiser v. Spain, ICSID Case No. ARB/13/36, Decision on the Kingdom of Spain's Application for Annulment (11.06.2020)
El Paso v. Argentina, ICSID Case No. ARB/03/15, Award (31.10.2011)
Electrabel v. Hungary, ICSID Case No. ARB/07/19, Decision on Jurisdiction, Applicable Law and Liability (30.11.2012)
Electrabel v. Hungary, ICSID Case No. ARB/07/19, Award (25.11.2015)
EnCana v. Ecuador, LCIA Case No. UN3481, Award (03.02.2006)
Energoalliance v. Moldova, UNCITRAL, Arbitral Award (23.10.2013)
Enron v. Argentina, ICSID Case No. ARB/01/3, Decision on Jurisdiction (14.01.2004)
Enron v. Argentina, ICSID Case No. ARB/01/3, Award (22.05.2007)
Eskosol v. Italy, ICSID Case No. ARB/15/50, Decision on Italy's Request for Immediate Termination and Italy's Jurisdictional Objection Based on Inapplicability of the Energy Charter Treaty to Intra-EU Disputes (07.05.2019)
Eskosol v. Italy, ICSID Case No. ARB/15/50, Award (04.09.2020)
ESPF v. Italy, ICSID Case No ARB/16/5, Award (14.09.2020)
EURAM v. Slovakia, UNCITRAL, Award on Jurisdiction (22.10.2012)
Eureko v. Poland, Ad Hoc, Partial Award (19.08.2005)
Feldman v. Mexico, ICSID Case No. ARB(AF)/99/1, Award (16.12.2002)
Festorino v. Poland, SCC Case No. V 2018/098, Award (30.06.2021)
Flemingo v. Poland, UNCITRAL, Award (12.08.2016)
Foresight v. Spain, SCC Case No. V 2015/150, Partial Dissenting Opinion (30.10.2018)
Foresight v. Spain, SCC Case No. V 2015/150, Final Award (14.11.2018)
Frontier v. Czech Republic, UNCITRAL, Final Award (12.11.2010)
Fynerdale v. Czech Republic, PCA Case No. 2018-18, Award (29.04.2021)
Garanti v. Turkmenistan, ICSID Case No. ARB/11/20, Award (19.12.2016)
Gavrilovic v. Croatia, ICSID Case No. ARB/12/39, Award (25.08.2018)
Gemplus v. Mexico ICSID Case No. ARB(AF)/04/3, Award (16.06.2010)
Generation v. Ukraine, ICSID Case No. ARB/00/9, Award (16.09.2003)
Glamis Gold v. US, UNCITRAL, Award (08.06.2009)
Gold Reserve v. Venezuela, ICSID Case No. ARB(AF)/09/1, Award (22.09.2014)
Gosling v. Mauritius, ICSID Case No. ARB/16/32, Award (18.02.2020)
GPF v. Poland, SCC Case No. V 2014/168, Award (29.04.2020)
Grand River v. US, UNCITRAL, Award (12.01.2011)
Green Power v. Spain, SCC Case No. V 2016/135, Award (16.06.2022)
Greentech v. Italy, SCC Case No. V 2015/095, Final Award (23.12.2018)
Hamester v. Ghana, ICSID Case No. ARB/07/24, Award (18.06.2010)
Horthel v. Poland, PCA Case No. 2014-31, Final Award (16.02.2017)

Hulley v. Russia, UNCITRAL, PCA Case No. 2005-03/AA226, Final Award (18.07.2014)
Hydro v. Spain, ICSID Case No. ARB/15/42, Decision on Jurisdiction, Liability and Directions on Quantum (09.03.2020)
Hydro v. Spain, ICSID Case No. ARB/15/42, Award (05.08.2020)
I.C.W. v. Czech Republic, PCA Case No. 2014-22, Award (15.05.2019)
ICS v. Argentina, PCA Case No. 2015-12, Award on Jurisdiction (08.07.2019)
Impregilo v. Argentina, ICSID Case No. ARB/07/17, Award (21.06.2011)
InfraRed v. Spain, ICSID Case No. ARB/14/12, Award (02.08.2019)
InfraRed v. Spain, ICSID Case No. ARB/14/12, Decision on Claimant's Objection under ICSID Rule 41(5) to Respondent's Application for Revision (08.03.2021)
Invesmart v. Czech Republic, UNCITRAL, Award (26.06.2009)
Isolux v. Spain, SCC Case No. V 2013/153, Dissenting Opinion of Prof. Guido Santiago Tawil (06.07.2016)
Isolux v. Spain, SCC Case No. V 2013/153, Award (12.07.2016)
Joy Machinery v. Egypt, ICSID Case No. ARB/03/11, Award on Jurisdiction (06.08.2004)
Khan v. Mongolia, PCA Case No. 2011-09, Decision on Jurisdiction (25.07.2012)
Khan v. Mongolia, PCA Case No. 2011-09, Award on the Merits (02.03.2015)
Lemire v. Ukraine, ICSID Case No. ARB/06/18, Decision on Jurisdiction and Liability (14.01.2010)
Levy v. Peru, ICSID Case No. ARB/10/17, Award (26.02.2014)
LG&E v. Argentina, ICSID Case No. ARB/02/1, Decision on Liability (3.10.2006)
LG&E v. Argentina, ICSID Case No. ARB/02/1, Award (25.07.2007)
Liman v. Kazakhstan, ICSID Case No. ARB/07/14, Excerpts of the Award (22.06.2010)
Magyar Farming v. Hungary, ICSID Case No. ARB/17/27, Award (13.11.2019)
Mamidoil v. Albania, ICSID Case No. ARB/11/24, Award (30.03.2015)
Manchester v. Poland, UNCITRAL, Award (07.12.2018)
Marfin v. Cyprus, ICSID Case No. ARB/13/27, Award (26.07.2018)
Masdar v. Spain, ICSID Case No. ARB/14/1, Award (16.05.2018)
Masdar v. Spain, ICSID Case No. ARB/14/1, Annulment Proceeding – Procedural Order No. 3, Decision on the Kingdom of Spain's Request for a Continuation of the Stay of Enforcement of the Award (20.05.2020)
Merrill & Ring v. Canada, ICSID Case No. UNCT/07/1, Award (31.03.2010)
Metalclad v. Mexico, ICSID Case No. ARB(AF)/97/1, Award (30.08.2000)
Metalpar v. Argentina, ICSID Case No. ARB/03/5, Award on the Merits (06.06.2008)
Methanex v. US, UNCITRAL, Final Award (03.08.2005)
Micula v. Romania, ICSID Case No. ARB/05/20, Decision on Jurisdiction and Admissibility (24.09.2008)
Micula v. Romania, ICSID Case No. ARB/05/20, Award (11.12.2013)
MTD v. Chile, ICSID Case No. ARB/01/7, Award (25.05.2004)
Murphy v. Ecuador, PCA Case No. 2012-16, Partial Final Award (06.05.2016)

Muszynianka v. Slovakia, PCA Case No. 2017-08, Award (07.10.2020)
National Grid v. Argentina, UNCITRAL, Award (3.11.2008)
NextEra v. Spain, ICSID Case No. ARB/14/11, Decision on Jurisdiction, Liability and Quantum Principles (12.03.2019)
NextEra v. Spain, ICSID Casc No. ARB/14/11, Award (31.05.2019)
NextEra v. Spain, ICSID Case No. ARB/14/11, Decision on Stay of Enforcement of the Award (06.04.2020)
NextEra v. Spain, ICSID Case No. ARB/14/11, Decision on Annulment (18.03.2022)
Nissan v. India, PCA Case No. 2017-37, Decision on Jurisdiction (29.04.2019)
Noble Energy v. Ecuador, ICSID Case No. ARB/05/12, Decision on Jurisdiction (05.03.2008)
Noble Ventures v. Romania, ICSID Case No. ARB/01/11, Award (12.10.2005)
Novenergia v. Spain, SCC Case No. 2015/063, Final Arbitral Award (15.02.2018)
Nykomb v. Latvia, SCC Case No. 118/2001, Arbitral Award (16.12.2003)
Occidental v. Ecuador, UNCITRAL, LCIA Case No. UN 3467, Final Award (01.07.2004)
Occidental v. Ecuador, ICSID Case No. ARB/06/11, Award (05.10.2012)
OKO v. Estonia, ICSID Case No. ARB/04/6, Award (19.11.2007)
Olin v. Libya, ICC Case No. 20355/MCP, Final Award (25.05.2018)
Oostergetel v. Slovakia, UNCITRAL, Decision on Jurisdiction (30.04.2010)
OperaFund v. Spain, ICSID Case No. ARB/15/36, Dissent on Liability and Quantum (13.08.2019)
OperaFund v. Spain, ICSID Case No. ARB/15/36, Award (06.09.2019)
OperaFund v. Spain, ICSID Case No. ARB/15/36, Decision on the Request for the Continuation of the Stay of Enforcement of the Award (16.11.2020)
Oxus Gold v. Uzbekistan, UNCITRAL, Award (17.12.2015)
Pan American v. Argentina, ICSID Case No. ARB/03/13, Decision on Preliminary Objections (27.07.2006)
Parkerings v. Lithuania, ICSID Case No. ARB/05/8, Award (11.09.2007)
Perenco v. Ecuador, ICSID Case No. ARB/08/6, Decision on Remaining Issues of Jurisdiction and Liability (12.09.2014)
Philip Morris v. Uruguay, ICSID Case No. ARB/10/7, Award (08.07.2016)
Philip Morris v. Uruguay, ICSID Case No. ARB/10/7, Concurring and Dissenting Opinion (08.07.2016)
Phoenix v. Czech Republic, ICSID Case No. ARB/06/5, Award (15.04.2009)
Plama v. Bulgaria, ICSID Case No. ARB/03/24, Award (27.08.2008)
PL Holdings v. Poland, SCC Case No. V 2014/163, Partial Award (28.06.2017)
PL Holdings v. Poland, SCC Case No. V 2014/163, Final Award (28.08.2017)
PSEG v. Turkey, ICSID Case No. ARB/02/5, Award (19.01.2007)
Quiborax v. Bolivia, ICSID Case No. ARB/06/2, Award (16.09.2015)
Renta 4 v. Russia, SCC No. 24/2007, Award (20.07.2012)

Rockhopper v. Italy, ICSID Case No. ARB/17/14, Decision on the Intra-EU Jurisdictional Objection (29.06.2019)

RosInvestCo v. Russia, SCC Case No. V 079/2005, Final Award (12.09.2010)

RREEF v. Spain, ICSID Case No. ARB/13/30, Decision on Jurisdiction (06.06.2016)

RREEF v. Spain, ICSID Case No. ARB/13/30, Decision on Responsibility and on the Principles of Quantum (30.11.2018)

RREEF v. Spain, ICSID Case No. ARB/13/30, Partially Dissenting Opinion of Professor Robert Volterra to the Decision on Responsibility and the Principles of Quantum (30.11.2018)

RREEF v. Spain, ICSID Case No. ARB/13/30, Award (11.12.2019)

Rumeli v. Kazakhstan, ICSID Case No. ARB/05/16, Award (29.07.2008)

Rusoro v. Venezuela, ICSID Case No. ARB(AF)/12/5, Award (22.08.2016)

RWE v. Spain, ICSID Case No. ARB/14/34, Separate Opinion of Mr. Judd L. Kessler (01.12.2020)

RWE v. Spain, ICSID Case No. ARB/14/34, Decision on Jurisdiction, Liability, and Certain Issues of Quantum (30.12.2019)

RWE v. Spain, ICSID Case No. ARB/14/34, Award (18.12.2020)

S.D. Myers v. Canada, UNCITRAL, Partial Award (13.11.2000)

Saint-Gobain v. Venezuela, ICSID Case No. ARB/12/13, Decision on Liability and the Principles of Quantum (30.12.2016)

Saluka v. Czech Republic, UNCITRAL, Partial Award (17.03.2006)

Santa Elena v. Costa Rica, ICSID Case No. ARB/96/1, Final Award (17.02.2000)

Sempra v. Argentina, ICSID Case No. ARB/02/16, Award (28.09.2007)

SGS v. Pakistan, ICSID Case No. ARB/01/13, Decision on Objections to Jurisdiction (06.08.2003)

SGS v. Paraguay, ICSID Case No. ARB/07/29, Decision on Jurisdiction (12.02.2010)

SGS v. Paraguay, ICSID Case No. ARB/07/29, Award (10.02.2012)

SGS v. Philippines, ICSID Case No. ARB/02/6, Decision of the Tribunal on Objections to Jurisdiction (29.01.2004)

Siemens v. Argentina, ICSID Case No. ARB/02/8, Award (06.02.2007)

Silver Ridge v. Italy, ICSID Case No. ARB/15/37, Dissenting Opinion of Judge O. Thomas Johnson (24.02.2021)

Silver Ridge v. Italy, ICSID Case No. ARB/15/37, Award (26.02.2021)

SolEs v. Spain, ICSID Case No. ARB/15/38, Award (31.07.2019)

SolEs v. Spain, ICSID Case No. ARB/15/38, Decision on the Continuation of the Stay of Enforcement of the Award (26.08.2020)

SolEs v. Spain, ICSID Case No. ARB/15/38, Decision on Annulment (16.03.2022)

South American Silver v. Bolivia, PCA Case No. 2013-5, Award (22.11.2018)

Spyridon v. Romania, ICSID Case No. ARB/06/1, Award (07.12.2011)

Stadtwerke v. Spain, ICSID Case No. ARB/15/1, Dissenting Opinion (20.11.2019)

Stadtwerke v. Spain, ICSID Case No. ARB/15/1, Award (02.12.2019)

Stati v. Kazakhstan, SCC Case No. V 116/2010, Award (19.12.2013)
Strabag v. Libya, ICSID Case No. ARB(AF)/15/1, Award (29.06.2020)
Suez v. Argentina, ICSID Case No. ARB/03/19, Decision on Liability (30.07.2010)
Suez v. Argentina, ICSID Case No. ARB/03/19, Separate Opinion of Arbitrator Pedro Nikken (30.07.2010)
Sun Reserve v. Italy, SCC Case No. V 2016/32, Award (25.03.2020)
Supervision v. Costa Rica, ICSID Case No. ARB/12/4, Final Award (18.01.2017)
Tallinn v. Estonia, ICSID Case No. ARB/14/24, Award (21.06.2019)
Talsud v. Mexico, ICSID Case No. ARB(AF)/04/3, Award (16.06.2010)
Tecmed v. Mexico, ICSID Case No. ARB (AF)/00/2, Award (29.05.2003)
TECO v. Guatemala, ICSID Case No. ARB/10/23, Award (19.12.2013)
Teinver v. Argentina, ICSID Case No. ARB/09/1, Award (21.07.2017)
Telenor v. Hungary, ICSID Case No. ARB/04/15, Award (13.09.2006)
Tethyan v. Pakistan, ICSID Case No. ARB/12/1, Decision on Jurisdiction and Liability (10.11.2017)
The PV Investors v. Spain, PCA Case No. 2012-14, Concurring and Dissenting Opinion of Judge Charles N. Brower (10.10.2014)
The PV Investors v. Spain, PCA Case No. 2012-14, Preliminary Award on Jurisdiction (13.10.2014)
The PV Investors v. Spain, PCA Case No. 2012-14, Concurring and Dissenting Opinion of Charles N. Brower (28.02.2020)
The PV Investors v. Spain, PCA Case No. 2012-14, Final Award (28.02.2020)
Thunderbird v. Mexico, UNCITRAL, Separate Opinion (01.12.2005)
Tokios Tokeles v. Ukraine, ICSID Case No. ARB/02/18, Award (26.07.2007)
Total v. Argentina, ICSID Case No. ARB/04/01, Decision on Liability (27.12.2010)
Toto v. Lebanon, ICSID Case No. ARB/07/12, Award (07.06.2012)
Tradex v. Albania, ICSID Case No. ARB/94/2, Award (29.04.1999)
Tza Yap Shum v. Peru, ICSID Case No. ARB/07/6, Award (07.07.2011)
UAB E energija v. Latvia, ICSID Case No. ARB/12/33, Award (22.12.2017)
Ulysseas v. Ecuador, UNCITRAL, Final Award (12.06.2012)
Unglaube v. Costa Rica, ICSID Case No. ARB/08/1 and ICSID Case No. ARB/09/20 (consolidated cases), Award (16.05.2012)
Unión Fenosa v. Egypt, ICSID Case No. ARB/14/4, Award (31.08.2018)
United Utilities v. Estonia, ICSID Case No. ARB/14/24, Award (21.06.2019)
UP and C.D v. Hungary, ICSID Case No. ARB/13/35, Award (09.10.2018)
Vattenfall v. Germany, ICSID Case No. ARB/12/12, Decision on the Achmea Issue (31.08.2018)
Vestey v. Venezuela, ICSID Case No. ARB/06/4, Award (15.04.2016)
Veteran v. Russia, UNCITRAL, PCA Case No. 2005-05/AA228, Final Award (18.07.2014)
Vivendi v. Argentina, ICSID Case No. ARB/97/3, Award (20.08.2007)
Voltaic v. Czech Republic, PCA Case No. 2014-20, Award (15.05.2019)

Von Pezold v. Zimbabwe, ICSID Case No. ARB/10/15, Award (28.08.2015)
WA v. Czech Republic, PCA Case No. 2014-19, Award (15.05.2019)
Waste Management v. Mexico, ICSID Case No. ARB(AF)/00/3, Award (30.04.2004)
Watkins v. Spain, ICSID Case No. ARB/15/44, Dissent on Liability and Quantum (09.01.2020)
Watkins v. Spain, ICSID Case No. ARB/15/44, Award (21.01.2020)
Watkins v. Spain, ICSID Case No. ARB/15/44, Decision on Spain's Request for Rectification of the Award (13.07.2020)
White Industries v. India, UNCITRAL, Final Award (30.11.2011)
Wirtgen v. Czech Republic, PCA Case No. 2014-03, Dissenting Opinion of Arbitrator Gary Born (11.10.2017)
Wirtgen v. Czech Republic, PCA Case No. 2014-03, Final Award (11.10.2017)
WNC v. Czech Republic, PCA Case No. 2014-34, Award (22.02.2017)
Yukos v. Russia, UNCITRAL, PCA Case No. 2005-04/AA227, Final Award (18.07.2014)
9REN v. Spain, ICSID Case No. ARB/15/15, Award (31.05.2019)

Judgments and Opinions of the International Court of Justice and the Permanent Court of International Justice

Case Concerning the Factory at Chorzów (Germany v. Poland) (Jurisdiction), Judgment (26.07.1927)
Case Concerning the Factory at Chorzów (Germany v. Poland) (Merits), Judgment (13.09.1928)
Case Concerning the Gabčíkovo-Nagymaros Project (Hungary v. Slovakia), Judgment (15.09.1997)
Case Concerning the Arrest Warrant of 11 April 2000 (Democratic Republic of the Congo v. Belgium), Judgment (14.02.2002)
Case Concerning Avena and Other Mexican Nationals (Mexico v. US), Judgment (31.03.2004)
Legal Consequences of the Construction of a Wall in the Occupied Palestinian Territories, Advisory Opinion (09.07.2004)

Judgments and Opinions of the Court of Justice of the European Union and Its Predecessor

Judgment of the Court (15.07.1964), Costa v. E.N.E.L., Case No. 6–64, ECLI:EU:C:1964:66
Judgment of the Court (Fifth Chamber) (11.06.1987), Pretore di Salò, Case No. 14/86, ECLI:EU:C:1987:275

Judgment of the Court (17.10.1989), Danfoss, Case No. 109/88, ECLI:EU:C:1989:383
Judgment of the Court (27.04.1994), Almelo, Case No. C-393/92, ECLI:EU:C:1994:171
Judgment of the Court (17.09.1997), Dorsch Consult, Case No. C-54/96, ECLI:EU:C:1997:413
Judgment of the Court (Grand Chamber) (27.02.2018), Western Sahara, Case No. C-266/16, ECLI:EU:C:2018
Judgment of the Court (Grand Chamber) (06.03.2018), Slovakia v. Achmea, Case No. C-284/16, ECLI:EU:C:2018:158
Judgment of the General Court (Second Chamber, Extended Composition) (18.06.2019), European Food, Micula and others, Cases No. T624/15, T694/15 and T704/15, ECLI:EU:T:2019:423
Judgment of the Court (Grand Chamber) (02.09.2021), Moldova v. Komstroy, Case No. C-741/19, ECLI:EU:C:2021:655
Judgment of the Court (Grand Chamber) (26.10.2021), Poland v. PL Holdings, Case No. C-109/20, ECLI:EU:C:2021:875
Judgment of the Court (Grand Chamber) (25.01.2022), European Food, Micula and others, Case No. C-638/19 P, ECLI:EU:C:2022:50
Opinion 1/91 of the Court (14.12.1991), ECLI:EU:C:1991:490
Opinion 1/09 of the Court (Full Court) (08.03.2011), ECLI:EU:C:2011:123
Opinion 2/13 of the Court (Full Court) (18.12.2014), ECLI:EU:C:2014:2454
Opinion 1/17 of the Court (Full Court) (30.04.2019), ECLI:EU:C:2019:341
Opinion 1/20 of the Court (Fourth Chamber) (16.06.2022), ECLI:EU:C:2022:485

International Treaties

Agreement for the Termination of Bilateral Investment Treaties between the Member States of the European Union
BIT Argentina–US
BIT Canada–Ecuador
BIT France–Colombia
BIT Germany–Greece
BIT Germany–Portugal
BIT India–Latvia
BIT Jordan–Turkey
BIT Netherlands–Paraguay
BIT Pakistan–Turkey
BIT Switzerland–Pakistan
BIT Switzerland–Philippines
Canada – EU Comprehensive Economic and Trade Agreement

Convention on the Settlement of Investment Disputes between States and Nationals of Other States
Energy Charter Treaty
European Convention on Human Rights (Convention for the Protection of Human Rights and Fundamental Freedoms)
Kyoto Protocol to the United Nations Framework Convention on Climate Change
North American Free Trade Agreement
Paris Agreement
Svalbard Treaty (Treaty Concerning Spitsbergen)
Treaty of Lisbon amending the Treaty on European Union and the Treaty establishing the European Community
Treaty on European Union
Treaty on the Functioning of the European Union
United Nations Convention on the Law of the Sea
United Nations Framework Convention on Climate Change
United States-Mexico-Canada Agreement
Vienna Convention on the Law of Treaties

Spanish Legislation

Civil Code (1889), BOE-A-1889-4763, *«Gaceta de Madrid» núm. 206, de 25/07/1889, Real Decreto de 24 de julio de 1889 por el que se publica el Código Civil* (RD on publication of the Civil Code)

Constitution (1978), BOE-A-1978-31229, *«BOE» núm. 311, de 29 de diciembre de 1978, páginas 29313 a 29424, Constitución Española* (Spanish Constitution)

Law 54/1997 (LSE), BOE-A-1997-25340, *«BOE» núm. 285, de 28 de noviembre de 1997, páginas 35097 a 35126, Ley del Sector Eléctrico* (on the Electric Sector)

RD 2818/1998, BOE-A-1998-30041, *«BOE» núm. 312, de 30 de diciembre de 1998, páginas 44077 a 44089, Real Decreto 2818/1998, de 23 de diciembre, sobre producción de energía eléctrica por instalaciones abastecidas por recursos o fuentes de energía renovables, residuos y cogeneración* (on electricity production installations supplied by renewable energy, waste incineration or combined heat and electric resources or sources)

RD 436/2004, BOE-A-2004-5562, *«BOE» núm. 75, de 27 de marzo de 2004, páginas 13217 a 13238, Real Decreto 436/2004, de 12 de marzo, por el que se establece la metodología para la actualización y sistematización del régimen jurídico y económico de la actividad de producción de energía eléctrica en régimen especial* (establishing the methodology for the updating and systematization of the legal and economic regime for electric power production in the special regime)

RD 661/2007, BOE-A-2007-10556, *«BOE» núm. 126, de 26 de mayo de 2007, páginas 22846 a 22886, Real Decreto 661/2007, de 25 de mayo, por el que se regula la actividad de producción de energía eléctrica en régimen especial* (regulating the activity of electricity production under the special regime)

Resolution of 27.09.2007, BOE-A-2007-17108, *«BOE» núm. 234, de 29 de septiembre de 2007, páginas 39745 a 39745, Resolución de 27 de septiembre de 2007, de lu Secretaría General de Energía, por la que se establece el plazo de mantenimiento de la tarifa regulada para la tecnología fotovoltaica, en virtud de lo establecido en el artículo 22 del Real Decreto 661/2007, de 25 de mayo* (of the General Secretariat of Energy, which establishes the period of maintenance of the regulated rate for photovoltaic technology, by virtue of the provisions of article 22 of Royal Decree 661/2007, of 25 of May)

RD 1578/2008, BOE-A-2008-15595, *«BOE» núm. 234, de 27 de septiembre de 2008, páginas 39117 a 39125, Real Decreto 1578/2008, de 26 de septiembre, de retribución de la actividad de producción de energía eléctrica mediante tecnología solar fotovoltaica para instalaciones posteriores a la fecha límite de mantenimiento de la retribución del Real Decreto 661/2007, de 25 de mayo, para dicha tecnología* (on the remuneration for the electric energy production activity using photovoltaic solar technology for installations after the deadline for maintenance of the remuneration of Royal Decree 661/2007, of May 25, for said technology)

RDL 6/2009, BOE-A-2009-7581, *«BOE» núm. 111, de 23 de mayo de 2009, páginas 39404 a 39419, Real Decreto-ley 6/2009, de 30 de abril, por el que se adoptan determinadas medidas en el sector energético y se aprueba el bono social* (which adopts certain measures in the energy sector and enacts the discount tariff)

RD 1565/2010, BOE-A-2010-17976, *«BOE» núm. 283, de 23 de noviembre de 2010, páginas 97428 a 97446, Real Decreto 1565/2010, de 19 de noviembre, por el que se regulan y modifican determinados aspectos relativos a la actividad de producción de energía eléctrica en régimen especial* (regulating and modifying specific aspects related to energy production in the special regime)

RD 1614/2010, BOE-A-2010-18915, *«BOE» núm. 298, de 8 de diciembre de 2010, páginas 101853 a 101859, Real Decreto 1614/2010, de 7 de diciembre, por el que se regulan y modifican determinados aspectos relativos a la actividad de producción de energía eléctrica a partir de tecnologías solar termoeléctrica y eólica* (regulating and modifying certain issues related to the production of energy from CSP and wind sources)

RDL 14/2010, BOE-A-2010-19757, *«BOE» núm. 312, de 24 de diciembre de 2010, páginas 106386 a 106394, Real Decreto-ley 14/2010, de 23 de diciembre, por el que se establecen medidas urgentes para la corrección del déficit tarifario del sector eléctrico* (establishing urgent measures for the correction of the tariff deficit of the electric sector)

RDL 1/2012, BOE-A-2012-1310, *«BOE» núm. 24, de 28 de enero de 2012, páginas 8068 a 8072, Real Decreto-ley 1/2012, de 27 de enero, por el que se procede a la suspensión de los procedimientos de preasignación de retribución y a la supresión de los incentivos económicos para nuevas instalaciones de producción de energía eléctrica a partir de cogeneración, fuentes de energía renovables y residuos* (proceeding to the suspension of the remuneration pre-assignment procedures and the elimination of the economic incentives for new electric energy production plans using cogeneration, renewable energy sources, and waste)

Law 15/2012, BOE-A-2012-15649, *«BOE» núm. 312, de 28 de diciembre de 2012, páginas 88081 a 88096, Ley 15/2012, de 27 de diciembre, de medidas fiscales para la sostenibilidad energética* (on tax measures for energy sustainability)

RDL 2/2013, BOE-A-2013-1117, *«BOE» núm. 29, de 2 de febrero de 2013, páginas 9072 a 9077, Real Decreto- Ley 2/2013, de 1 de febrero, de medidas urgentes en el sistema eléctrico y en el sector financiero* (concerning urgent measures in the electric system and financial sector)

RDL 9/2013, BOE-A-2013-7705, *«BOE» núm. 167, de 13 de julio de 2013, páginas 52106 a 52147, Real Decreto-Ley 9/2013, de 12 de julio, por el que se adoptan medidas urgentes para garantizar la estabilidad financiera del sistema eléctrico* (adopting urgent measures to ensure the financial stability of the electric system)

Law 24/2013 (New LSE), BOE-A-2013-13645, *«BOE» núm. 310, de 27 de diciembre de 2013, páginas 105198 a 105294, Ley 24/2013, de 26 de diciembre, del Sector Eléctrico* (on Energy Sector)

RD 413/2014, BOE-A-2014-6123, *«BOE» núm. 140, de 10 de junio de 2014, páginas 43876 a 43978, Real Decreto 413/2014, de 6 de junio, por el que se regula la actividad de producción de energía eléctrica a partir de fuentes de energía renovables, cogeneración y residuos* (on the regulation of the electric energy production activity from renewable energy, cogeneration and waste)

Order IET/1045/2014, BOE-A-2014-6495, *«BOE» núm. 150, de 20 de junio de 2014, páginas 46430 a 48190, Orden IET/1045/2014, de 16 de junio, por la que se aprueban los parámetros retributivos de las instalaciones tipo aplicables a determinadas instalaciones de producción de energía eléctrica a partir de fuentes de energía renovables, cogeneración y residuos* (approving the remuneration parameters for model facilities, applicable to certain facilities of electric energy production using renewable energy resources, cogeneration, and waste)

Order IET/1882/2014, BOE-A-2014-10475, *«BOE» núm. 251, de 16 de octubre de 2014, páginas 83700 a 83707, Orden IET/1882/2014, de 14 de octubre, por la que se establece la metodología para el cálculo de la energía eléctrica imputable a la utilización de combustibles en las instalaciones solares termoeléctricas* (establishing methodology for calculating the electricity produced by solar installations attributable to the use of fossil fuels)

RDL 17/2019, BOE-A-2019-16862, *«BOE» núm. 282, de 23 de noviembre de 2019, páginas 129281 a 129288, Real Decreto-ley 17/2019, de 22 de noviembre, por el que se adoptan medidas urgentes para la necesaria adaptación de parámetros retributivos que afectan al sistema eléctrico y por el que se da respuesta al proceso de cese de actividad de centrales térmicas de generación* (which adopts urgent measures for the necessary adaptation of remuneration parameters that affect the electricity system and which responds to the process of cessation of activity of thermal generation plants)

Spanish Courts' Judgments

Supreme Court, Judgment of 15.12.2005, STS 7633/2005, 73/2004
Supreme Court, Judgment of 25.10.2006, STS 6317/2006, 11/2005
Supreme Court, Judgment of 20.03.2007, STS 1653/2007, 12/2005
Supreme Court, Judgment of 09.10.2007, STS 6315/2007, 13/2006
Supreme Court, Judgment of 09.12.2009, STS 7629/2009, 149/2007
Supreme Court, Judgment of 03.12.2009, STS 7961/2009, 151/2007
Supreme Court, Judgment of 12.04.2012, STS 2320/2012, 40/2011
Supreme Court, Judgment of 12.04.2012, STS 2577/2012, 59/2011
Supreme Court, Judgment of 19.06.2012, STS 4253/2012, 62/2011
Supreme Court, Judgment of 24.09.2012, STS 6280/2012, 60/2011
Supreme Court, Judgment of 25.09.2012, STS 5894/2012, 71/2011
Supreme Court, Judgment of 16.03.2015, STS 966/2015, 118/2013
Supreme Court, Judgment of 17.03.2015, STS 1114/2015, 115/2013
Supreme Court, Judgment of 17.03.2015, STS 1115/2015, 127/2013
Supreme Court, Judgment of 11.05.2016, STS 2059/2016, 833/2014
Supreme Court, Judgment of 01.06.2016, STS 2430/2016, 649/2014
Supreme Court, Judgment of 20.06.2016, STS 2859/2016, 485/2014
Supreme Court, Judgment of 12.07.2016, STS 3421/2016, 456/2014
Supreme Court, Judgment of 22.07.2016, STS 3796/2016, 500/2014
Supreme Court, Judgment of 18.05.2017, STS 1971/2017, 4953/2017
Constitutional Court, Judgment of 06.11.2014, Case No. 183/2014
Constitutional Court, Judgment of 19.02.2015, Case No. 28/2015
Constitutional Court, Judgment of 17.12.2015, Case No. 270/2015
Constitutional Court, Judgment of 04.02.2016, Case No. 29/2016
Constitutional Court, Judgment of 18.02.2016, Case No. 30/2016
Constitutional Court, Judgment of 17.03.2016, Case No. 61/2016

Other Sources

Bohmer, Lisa, Masdar v. Spain case is discontinued (IA Reporter, 01.12.2020, available at: https://www.iareporter.com/articles/masdar-v-spain-case-is-discontinued/)

Bohmer, Lisa, RREEF and Stadtwerke are said to renounce their arbitration claims against Spain (IA Reporter, 22.10.2020, available at: https://www.iareporter.com/articles/rreef-and-stadtwerke-are-said-to-renounce-their-arbitration-claims-against-spain/)

China Energy Transition Status Report 2021. Sino-German Energy Transition Project (2021)

CIMVal Standards and Guidelines (Standards and Guidelines for Valuation of Mineral Properties issued by the Special Committee of the Canadian Institute of Mining, Metallurgy and Petroleum on Valuation of Mineral Properties) (2003)

CIMVal Code for the Valuation of Mineral Properties (2019)

Commission asks Member States to terminate their intra-EU bilateral investment treaties (18.06.2015), available at: https://ec.europa.eu/commission/presscorner/detail/en/IP_15_5198

Commission provides guidance on protection of cross-border EU investments – Questions and Answers (19.07.2018), available at: https://ec.europa.eu/commission/presscorner/detail/fi/MEMO_18_4529

Commission Regulation (EU) No 838/2010 of 23 September 2010 on laying down guidelines relating to the inter-transmission system operator compensation mechanism and a common regulatory approach to transmission charging (OJ L 250, 24.09.2010, p. 5–11)

Communication from the Commission to the Council and the European Parliament, An Energy Policy for Europe, COM(2007) 1 final (10.01.2007)

Communication from the Commission to the Council and the European Parliament, Renewable Energy Road Map Renewable energies in the 21st century: building a more sustainable future, Brussels, COM(2006) 848 final (10.01.2007)

Communication from the Commission to the European Parliament and the Council, Protection of intra-EU investment, COM(2018) 547 (19.07.2018)

Declaration of the Representatives of the Governments of the Member States on the Legal Consequences of the Judgment of the Court of Justice in *Achmea* and on Investment Protection in the European Union, issued by 22 EU Member States: Austria, Belgium, Bulgaria, Croatia, Cyprus, Czech Republic, Denmark, Estonia, France, Germany, Greece, Ireland, Italy, Latvia, Lithuania, Netherlands, Poland, Portugal, Romania, Slovakia, Spain, and United Kingdom (15.01.2019)

Declaration of the Representative of the Government of Hungary on the Legal Consequences of the Judgment of the Court of Justice in Achmea and on Investment Protection in the European Union (16.01.2019)

Declaration of the Representatives of the Governments of the Member States on the Enforcement of the Judgment of the Court of Justice in *Achmea* and on Investment Protection in the European Union, issued by: Finland, Luxembourg, Malta, Slovenia and Sweden (16.01.2019)

Directive 2001/77/EC of the European Parliament and of the Council of 27 September 2001 on the promotion of electricity produced from renewable energy sources in the internal electricity market (OJ L 283, 27.10.2001, p. 33–40)

Directive 2009/28/EC of the European Parliament and of the Council of 23 April 2009 on the promotion of the use of energy from renewable sources and amending and subsequently repealing Directives 2001/77/EC and 2003/30/EC (OJ L 140, 05.06.2009, p. 16–62)

Draft articles on Responsibility of States for Internationally Wrongful Acts, with commentaries (ILC Articles), text adopted by the International Law Commission at its fifty-third session, in 2001, and submitted to the General Assembly as a part of the Commission's report covering the work of that session (A/56/10) (2001), Yearbook of the International Law Commission, II:2 (2001)

EU text proposal for the modernisation of the Energy Charter Treaty

European Commission, A hydrogen strategy for a climate-neutral Europe. Communication from the Commission to the European Parliament, the European Council, the Council, the European Economic and Social Committee and the Committee of the Regions, COM(2020) 301 final (08.07.2020)

European Commission, Energy Charter Treaty: Progress continues in modernisation negotiations, News Archive (05.10.2021)

European Commission, The European Green Deal. Communication from the Commission to the European Parliament, the European Council, the Council, the European Economic and Social Committee and the Committee of the Regions, COM (2019) 640 final (11.12.2019)

European Commission Decision (30.03.2015), Case No. C(2015) 2112, State Aid SA.38517 (2014/C) (ex 2014/NN) – Romania

European Commission Decision (28.11.2016), Case No. C(2016) 7827, State Aid SA.40171 (2015/NN) – Czech Republic

European Commission Decision (10.11.2017), Case No. C(2017) 7384, State Aid SA.40348 (2015/NN) – Spain

European Commission Decision (19.07.2019), Case No. C(2021) 450/02, State Aid SA.54155 (2021/NN) – Spain

ICC Arbitration Rules (2021)

ICSID Arbitration Rules

ICSID Schedule of Fees and 2005 ICSID Memorandum on the Fees and Expenses

Judgment of the English High Court of Justice, GPF v. Poland, Case No. CL-2017-000174 (02.03.2018)

Judgment of the German Federal Court of Justice, Case No. I ZB 16/21 (17.11.2021)

Judgment of the German Higher Regional Court in Frankfurt, Case No. 26 SchH 2/20 (11.02.2021)

Judgment of the Swiss Federal Tribunal, Case No. 4A_187/2020 (23.02.2021)

LCIA Arbitration Rules (2020)

Opinion of Advocate General Wathelet delivered on 19.09.2017, Slovakia v. Achmea, Case No. C-284/16, ECLI:EU:C:2017:699

Order of the German Federal Court of Justice, Case No. I ZB 2/15 (31.10.2018)

Outline of the People's Republic of China 14th Five-Year Plan for National Economic and Social Development and Long-Range Objectives for 2035 (unofficial translation of the Center for Security and Emerging Technology), available at: https://cset.georgetown.edu/wp-content/uploads/t0284_14th_Five_Year_Plan_EN.pdf

Polish Code for the Valuation of Mineral Assets (2008)

Possible reform of investor-State dispute settlement (ISDS). Submission from the European Union and its Member States (A/CN.9/WG.III/WP.159/Add.1)

Regulation (EU) 2021/1056 of the European Parliament and of the Council of 24 June 2021 establishing the Just Transition Fund (OJ L 231, 30.06.2021, pp. 1–20)

Rio Declaration on Environment and Development, UN A/CONF.151/26 (1992)

Rosenthal, Elisabeth, Solar Industry Learns Lessons in Spanish Sun, The New York Times (03.08.2010)

SCC Arbitration Rules (2017)

Schedule of Costs to the 2017 Arbitration Rules of the Arbitration Institute of the Stockholm Chamber of Commerce

Statement submitted by the European Communities to the Secretariat of the Energy Charter pursuant to Article 26(3)(b)(ii) of the Energy Charter Treaty made on 17.11.1997 (OJ L 69/115 09.03.1998)

Statement submitted to the Energy Charter Treaty (ECT) Secretariat pursuant to Article 26(3)(b)(ii) ECT replacing the statement made on 17.11.1997 on behalf of the European Communities (OJ L 115/1, 02.05.2019)

Statute of the Court of Justice of the European Union

UN General Assembly Resolution No. 70/1 (25.09.2015), Transforming our world: the 2030 Agenda for Sustainable Development (UN A/RES/70/1)

US District Court for the District of Columbia, Case No. 17-cv-02332 (APM), Memorandum Opinion and Order (20.11.2020)

UNCITRAL Arbitration Rules

Xi Jinping, Bolstering Confidence and Jointly Overcoming Difficulties To Build a Better World, statement given by the President of China at the General Debate of the UN General Assembly's 76th session on 21.09.2021, available at: https://estatements.unmeetings.org/estatements/10.0010/20210921/AT2JoAvm71nq/KaLk3d9ECB53_en.pdf

Index

www.ingramcontent.com/pod-product-compliance
Lightning Source LLC
LaVergne TN
LVHW010622300926
849162LV00001B/36